World Scientific Proceedings Series on
Computer Engineering and Information Science 6

Methods for Decision Making in an Uncertain Environment

Proceedings of the XVII SIGEF Congress

World Scientific Proceedings Series on Computer Engineering and Information Science

---

Vol. 1: Computational Intelligence in Decision and Control
edited by Da Ruan, Javier Montero, Jie Lu, Luis Martínez, Pierre D'hondt and Etienne E. Kerre

Vol. 2: Intelligent Decision Making Systems
edited by Koen Vanhoof, Da Ruan, Tianrui Li and Geert Wets

Vol. 3 Computational Intelligence in Business and Economics
edited by Anna M. Gil-Lafuente and José M. Merigó

Vol. 4 Computational Intelligence: Foundations and Applications
edited by Da Ruan, Tianrui Li, Yang Xu, Guoqing Chen and Etienne E. Kerre

Vol. 5 Quantitative Logic and Soft Computing
edited by Guojun Wang, Bin Zhao and Yongming Li

Vol. 6 Methods for Decision Making in an Uncertain Environment
edited by Jaime Gil-Aluja and Antonio Terceño

World Scientific Proceedings Series on
Computer Engineering and Information Science 6

Methods for Decision Making in an Uncertain Environment

Proceedings of the XVII SIGEF Congress

Reus, Spain 6 – 8 June 2012

editors

Jaime Gil-Aluja

Royal Academy of Economic and Financial Sciences, Spain

Antonio Terceño

Department of Business, Universitat Rovira I Virgili, Spain

World Scientific

NEW JERSEY • LONDON • SINGAPORE • BEIJING • SHANGHAI • HONG KONG • TAIPEI • CHENNAI

Published by

World Scientific Publishing Co. Pte. Ltd.
5 Toh Tuck Link, Singapore 596224
USA office: 27 Warren Street, Suite 401-402, Hackensack, NJ 07601
UK office: 57 Shelton Street, Covent Garden, London WC2H 9HE

British Library Cataloguing-in-Publication Data
A catalogue record for this book is available from the British Library.

World Scientific Proceedings Series on Computer Engineering and Information Science — Vol. 6
METHODS FOR DECISION MAKING IN AN UNCERTAIN ENVIRONMENT
Proceedings of the XVII SIGEF Congress

ISBN-13 978-981-4415-76-7
ISBN-10 981-4415-76-6

Printed in Singapore by B & Jo Enterprise Pte Ltd

PREFACE

The most prominent feature of late twentieth century and the beginning of this century is given by the profound changes taking place in social, economic and corporate environments. The problems that these new situations arise are increasingly complex and changing, and traditional models based on determinism and stochastic models, are not sufficient to deal with this reality, so changeable that has become uncertain. The appearance of the first applications of multivalent logics and the theory of fuzzy subsets to economics and business problems has suggested the need to group all those people, businesses and institutions, wishing to contribute to the development and promotion of new techniques emerging from these achievements that current science into the hands of academics, economists, managers and executives.
To achieve this goal was born almost twenty years, the Association for Fuzzy-Set Management and Economy (SIGEF), whose creation we have driven the research, study and treatment of all problems associated with the economy in general and administration companies in particular. SIGEF addresses this task in an open and inclusive so that the exchange of knowledge, progress, or views can be enriching for all. SIGEF therefore been proposed as main objectives: to promote research and development of new modeling for the treatment of uncertainty in Economics and Business Economics; promote training of postgraduates by organizing courses, meetings, conferences, etc.., foster mutual understanding between the University and the Company, promoting the interest of society in the use of new techniques for the treatment of uncertainty in the different areas of Economics and Business Administration and disseminate research , developments and innovations of its members.
To achieve these objectives, among other activities, SIGEF publishes the scientific journal *Fuzzy Economic Review* and regularly organizes international conferences. Additionally, SIGEF created the Kaufmann Gold Medal award to recognize outstanding scholars who dedicated their careers to developing new methodologies for the treatment of economics and business problems o in uncertain environments. Past Kaufmann Medal laureates are: Dr. Hans Jürgen Zimmermann, Dr. Madan M. Gupta, Dr. George J. Klir, Dr. Jaime Gil-Aluja, Dr. Lotfi A. Zadeh and Dr. Janusz Kacprzyk.

The conference aims to provide a forum for academics and professionals working in the field of economics, finance, management and organization. During the working sessions, participants can exchange ideas and experiences on the progress of research, methodologies, techniques, applications and projects

based on fuzzy logic, neural systems, genetic algorithms, theory of uncertainty, complexity theory and soft computing. Previous congresses have been held in: Reus, Santiago de Compostela, Lugo and Leon (Spain), Buenos Aires and Bahia Blanca (Argentina), Santiago (Cuba), Lausanne (Switzerland), Morelia (Mexico), Naples and Reggio Calabria- Messina (Italy), Chania (Greece), Mérida (Vanezuela), Hammamet (Tunisia) and Poiana Brasov (Romania).
This publication contains a selection of the best papers presented at the XVII Congress of the Association for Fuzzy-Set Management and Economy (SIGEF) which is held under the motto: Methods for decision making in an Uncertain Environment. The congress was held in Reus (Catalonia, Spain) and organized by the Faculty of Economics and Business and the Department of Business Management at Universitat Rovira i Virgili from 6 to 8 June 2012.

The main goal of the conference is to stimulate scientific exchange, promoting international cooperation between academia and business, and disseminate the results of international research through the publication of the presented papers. The major topics developed in the congress are: Business and Management Intelligence, Chaos Theory, Data Mining, Decision Making Systems, Evolutionary Modeling, Fuzzy Games Theory, Fuzzy Logic and Expert Systems in Management, Fuzzy Multicriteria Methods, Knowledge Management Methods, Linguistic Information, artificial Intelligence, Modeling of Economic Processes in Uncertainty, Neural Networks, Neuro-Fuzzy Models, Rough Set Analysis and Soft Computing.

The book is organized as follows. First, there are the papers that corresponds to the first and second plenary sessions taught by professors Dr. Jaime Gil-Aluja, president of the Royal Academy of Economics and Finance, Dr. Christer Carlsson, president of IFSA. Then the selected works are organized according to their theme in the following sections: Theoretical Foundations, Finance, Economics and Politics, Management, Neural Networks, Knowledge Management and Innovations. The aim of this publication is to present the advances developed by the community of scholars and practitioners involved in SIGEF. It is also an example of the quality of inputs to get the Economics and Business Administration increasingly used new tools to better allocation and management of scarce resources, the main objective of economists. Finally, we would like to thank all the authors and reviewers that participated by presenting and reviewing the scientific papers.

Reus June 6, 2012

Dr. Jaime Gil-Aluja
Dr. Antonio Terceño

SCIENTIFIC COMMITTEE

Special thanks to the members of the Scientific Committee for their support in the organization of the XVII SIGEF Congress

General Co-Chairs

Jaime Gil Aluja (Royal Academy of Economic and Financial Sciences, Spain)
Antonio Terceño (University Rovira i Virgili, Spain)

Scientific Committee

M. Glòria Barberà Mariné (University Rovira i Virgili, Spain)
Ildar Batyrshing (Mexican Petroleum Institute, Mexico)
José Manuel Brotons (University Miguel Hernández, Spain)
Christer Carlsson (Åbo Akademi University, Finland)
María Teresa Casparri (University of Buenos Aires, Argentina)
Oscar Castillo (Tijuana Institute of Technology, Mexico)
Sergio de los Cobos (University Autónoma Metropolitana, Mexico)
M. Ángeles Fernández (University Jaume I, Spain)
Emma Fernández Loureiro (University of Buenos Aires, Argentina)
Joan Carles Ferrer (University of Girona, Spain)
Pablo Sebastián García (University of Buenos Aires, Argentina)
Vasile Georgescu (University of Craiova, Romania)
Anna M. Gil Lafuente (University of Barcelona, Spain)
Fernando Gomide (University of Campinas, Brazil)
Federico Gonzalez Santoyo (University Michoacana, Mexico)
Peijun Guo (Yokohama National University, Japan)
Madan M. Gupta (University of Saskatchewan, Canada)
Emmanuel Haven (University of Leicester, United Kingdom)
Kaoru Hirota (Tokyo Institute of Technology, Japan)
Luca Iandoli (University of Naples Federico II, Italy)
Mariano Jiménez (University of País Vasco, Spain)
Janusz Kacprzyk (Polish Academy of Sciences, Poland)
George Klir (Binghamton University, USA)
Viktor V. Krasnoproshin (Bielorrusian State University, Bielorrusia)
Son Kuswadi (Indonesian Society for Soft Computing, Indonesia)
Luisa L. Lazzari (University of Buenos Aires, Argentina)
Vicente Liern (University of Valencia, Spain)

ORGANIZING COMMITTEE

Special thanks to the members of the Scientific Committee for their support during the preparation of the XVII SIGEF Congress

Co-Chairs of the Organizing Committee

Aurelio Fernández Bariviera (University Rovira i Virgili, Spain)
M. Teresa Sorrosal Forradellas (University Rovira i Virgili, Spain)

Organizing Commitee

Xavier Càmara Turull (University Rovira i Virgili, Spain)
M. José Garbajosa Cabello (University Rovira i Virgili, Spain)
M. Belén Guercio (University Rovira i Virgili, Spain)
Lisana B. Martínez (University Rovira i Virgili, Spain)
Cristina Tomás Monterde (University Rovira i Virgili, Spain)

The XVII SIGEF Congress is supported by

CONTENTS

PART 6: KNOWLEDGE MANAGEMENT AND INNOVATION

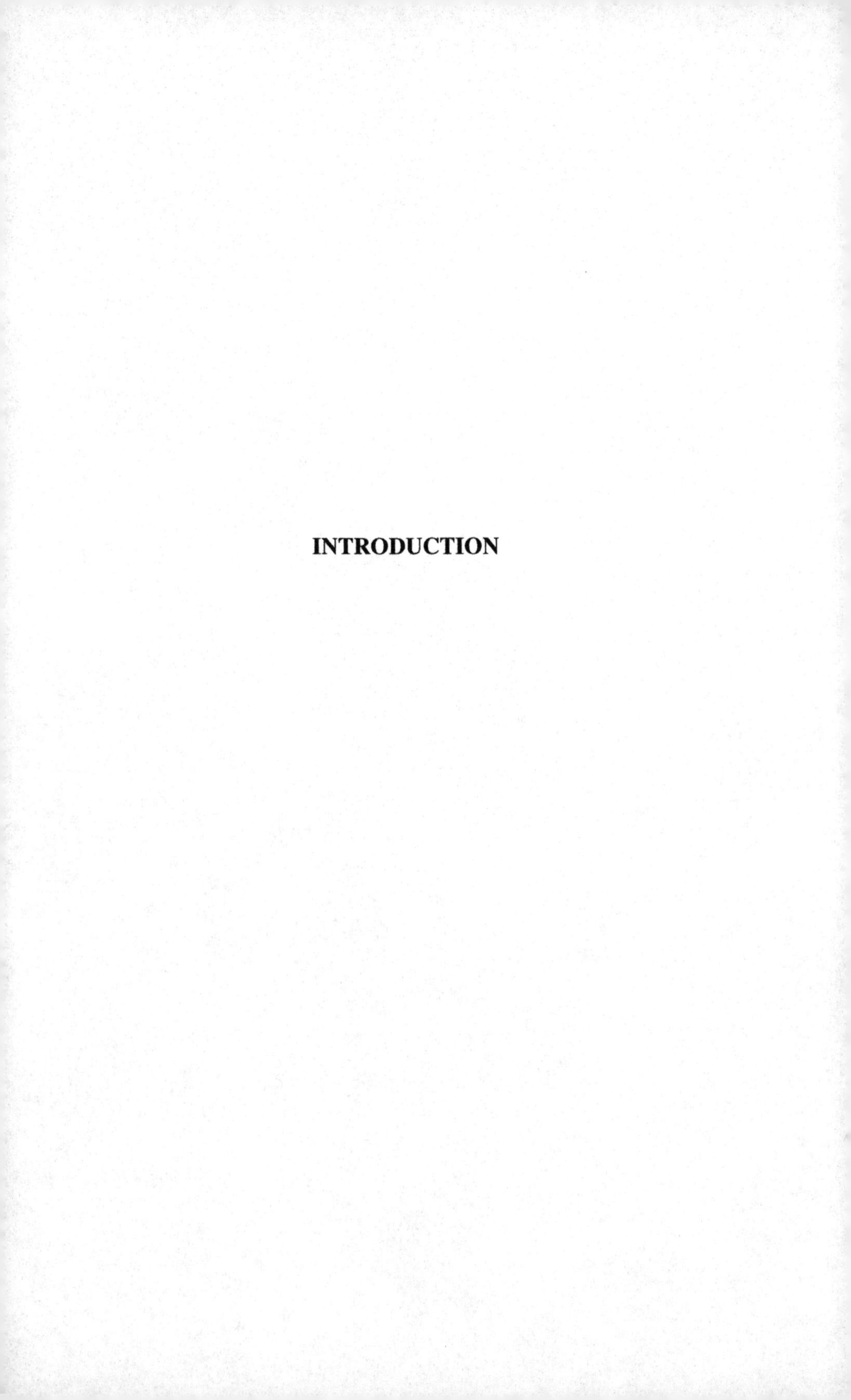

INTRODUCTION

THE SPANISH SCHOOL OF FUZZY ECONOMICS

JAIME GIL ALUJA

Real Academia de Ciencias Económicas y Financieras, Via Laietana, 32
Barcelona,Spain

The beginnings of the now flourishing "Spanish School of Economics Fuzzy" must fit into the rigors of the Spanish postwar period, a time when this country was trying to find their place in the international scientific community after two decades of autarky and isolationism. In this context, my teaching began in October 1959 having just finalized my degree studies and at the same time initiating the courses and works required for my doctorate.

Those who lived and survived that dark era will recall the difficulties experienced by undergraduates when they wished to open their intellectual horizon to scientific activity taking place outside our practically closed frontiers. The dream of every young researcher was not the American universities. For a middle class family the Mecca was much closer (although still outside the possibilities of most) and that was France.

I was one of the more fortunate, thanks to a rare conjugation of circumstances that were almost unforeseeable. I had the opportunity to attend, in Grenoble, a course on "*Methods of Operations Research*" before it reached the public eye, given by Professor Arnold Kaufmann and written in conjunction with Robert Faure: "Invitation à la Recherche Opérationnelle", published by Dunod in 1961.

The permanent contacts from then onwards with my teacher and friend Kaufmann were of an inestimable value. And not only from an intellectual, speculative or theoretical point of view but, also, with regards to the possibilities of using the theoretical or technical elements in order to arrive at solutions to problems that were constantly being brought to light by reality. These problems I found in my capacity as Senior Manager of the "*Sociedad* de *Automóviles* de *Turismo*, S.A. (SEAT), a job which I found was difficult to combine with my teaching and research activity.

A few years later it was precisely this teaching and research vocation which led to my abandoning of the business field in order to concentrate all my efforts in the sphere of research. However, there remained from this period a concern that would continuously appear, whenever we drew up a new model or the work of a researcher arrived in our hands: What possibilities existed for using these schemes for arriving at a solution to the economic and social problems which were becoming more and more immersed in a context of complexity and uncertainty?

We were not particularly very convinced of the efficiency of these formal elements, impeccable in their formality, but, in my opinion, rather remote from the questions raised on a daily basis, from the routine of businesses and institutions. I had passed on this concern to Arnold Kaufmann a number of times with so much insistence that he considered this as "*my obsession*".

On one particular day, the date of which I cannot specify, but it would have been in the interval [1968-1970], I received a call from Professor Kaufmann advising me textually: "*I have mailed you a work from Professor Lotfi A. Zadeh which I believe could be the solution to your problems*". A few days later I received a photocopy of the article, "Fuzzy Sets", a copy which I keep very safe, and the reading of this would totally change the direction of my modest works, at the same time giving a new sense to my teaching and research tasks carried out up to that time.

At that time practically a dream we set as our first ideal objective that our city should be the centre around which our studies, research and teaching of the *Economic and Management Systems* within the sphere of uncertainty, supported on *Fuzzy Sets* would revolve. In the meantime, Arnold Kaufmann was putting the finishing touches to what would be the first book known to us on *Fuzzy Logic* written by a single author: "*Introduction à la théorie des sous-ensembles flous*", Published by Masson in 1973, which would be followed by a further three volumes under the same title (1973-1978), translated into Spanish, English and Russian. A few years later, in 1980, Professor Enric Trillas had his work: "Conjuntos borrosos" [Fuzzy Sets] published by Vicens.

We felt that this overall objective could be attained, to a high degree, if we acted in three directions: in teaching, in research and in the organisation, systematization, and coordination of the human groups that were interested in this new conception of economic and business studies. On this hopeful horizon, we had the great fortune of getting the enthusiastic cooperation of young professors from the Universities of Barcelona, Rovira i Virgili and Gerona, the latter two headed by the very much missed Professor Carlos Cassú and Professor Joan Carlos Ferrer in Gerona and by Professors Antonio Terceño and Gloria Barberà in Reus-Tarragona.

We commenced the teaching crusade by organising seminars at universities and other institutions: the first given by Professor Kaufmann at the University of Barcelona, Fundación Abad Oliba, at the headquarters of the U.B. in Reus (which would later become the Faculty of Economy and Business of the Rovira i Virgili University, to later move on to seminars at which the teaching was shared by Professor Kaufmann and myself, at the same time extending the teaching territorially to other communities: Andalucía, Galicia, the Basque Country, Extremadura, Valencia, Castilla-León.. Little by little research groups were formed, the presence of which at national and international congresses becomes ever more notorious.

But our objective was far more ambitious: to make sure that in the teaching plans of the Universities subjects were taught with explicit "Fuzzy" contents. This became a reality at the University of Barcelona, Faculty of Economic and Business Sciences, under the following titles: "Operational Research (methods and models in uncertainty)"; "Operational Techniques for Management in Uncertainty"; "Investment in Uncertainty"; Financial Direction II (financial analysis in uncertainty)" and "Business Creativity".

The teaching of these subjects gave rise, sometime later, to the drawing up of Doctoral Theses which warranted, always, the highest consideration by the respective tribunals that judged them. We will mention as an example: "Financial Management in Uncertainty. From singular expertise to the R+expertons" (Ana Mª Gil Lafuente 1992); "Commercial management: the taking of decisions in a sphere of uncertainty" (Jordi Bachs Ferrer 1993); "Determination of the uncertainty that is inherent to commercial operations with Latin America based on the theory of fuzzy sub-sets" (Ricardo Onses 1994); "Instruments for the Analysis of Financial Operations with uncertain data" (Antonio Terceño 1995); "Numerical and non-numerical marketing in uncertainty" (Jaime Gil Lafuente 1996); "Expectations of agricultural businessmen on the price of raw materials as a basis for a model of optimization by means of the technique of Fuzzy Sets in programming" (Vicente Sanjosé Mitjans 1997); "Adaptation of travel agencies to a digital sphere by means of implementing the theory of affinities" (Jordi Oller Nogués 2000); "Multivalent logic in the management of businesses with high risk products" (Mari Carmen Sanahuja Pi 2004). All these doctoral theses form a part of those that were directed by me during my latter years of activity at the University of Barcelona.

Later, other professors have taken up the baton. The last thesis presented in this field at the University of Barcelona, was titled: "Modelos para análisis de atributos contemplados por los clientes en una estrategia de Marketing Relacional" (Carolina Luis, December 15th 2011) and was directed by Professor Ana Mª Gil Lafuente, obtaining the maximum classification of First Class Honours "Cum Laude".

The quality, dedication and enthusiasm of the research professors who have taken over allow us to visualise a splendid future for this "new" conception of economic and management studies, based on the inspired idea of "Fuzzy Sets" of Lotfi Zadeh.

Teaching can nearly always be found on the threshold of research. And if at the beginning works in the field of economy and management always carried the name of A, Kaufmann, followed by that of J. Gil-Aluja, little by little valuable works have appeared, nearly always due to the pen of young university professors.

From a global point of view, scientific contributions have been concentrated on the incorporation to economic research of new elements based on Fuzzy

Logic, all of which are capable of treating complex economic phenomena. For this, a conceptual and methodological redefinition was made of the very foundations on which the instruments that were normally used for the treatment of economic realities in a context characterised by a very high degree of uncertainty were founded and from here on, a harmonious set of models and algorithms were developed.

The works of Lotfi Zadeh allowed for delving into the very roots of the structure of economic thinking. The incapacity of the "principle of the excluded third" for basing valid reasoning for the study of complex economic phenomena much later led us to draw up the "principle of gradual simultaneity", presented at the 1996 SIGEF Congress in Buenos Aires. This principle constituted the starting out point for the development of new logical operators which has allowed the development of important elements for the treatment of the components of subjectivity inherent to economic and management problems. The models and algorithms that were drawn up are providing important results in the treatment of the real problems of current society, where decisions are faced with new highly complex challenges.

Our first works saw the light of day, on the one hand by means of participating in Congresses, both Spanish and international, defending, on occasions not without a certain difficulty, positions that started out from the findings of Lotfi Zadeh: How difficult it still is to jog the minds of those who hold the "truth" of inherited science!

Little by little university companions joined forces, attracted by the possibilities of the new schemes faced by the speedy and unforeseeable changes in economic systems, people who also belonged to the most diverse schools of economy. Faced with the growing demand for giving courses and seminars, our trips to teaching and research centres on the five continents multiplied. Jointly or individually with A. Kaufmann, we travelled to 52 different countries, attempting to plant in them the seeds for carrying out new works. Just a few pieces of data are irrefutable proof of the success attained by the works of Lotfi Zadeh when they were used in the field of economy,: I have participated on the Editorial and Scientific Board of 19 economic and management reviews and have formed a part of 111 Scientific and Organisation Committees for Congresses, presiding over 49 of the same.

It would be rather extensive to list the more than 200 works published in scientific reviews and congress and conference proceedings, but we would like to dedicate a paragraph to the writing and publication of our works in book form.

The first book on management was published in Spanish in 1986 under the title of "Introducción a la teoria de los subconjuntos borrosos a la gestión de la empresa" [Introduction to the theory of fuzzy sub-sets to business management], with the signature of A. Kaufmann and J.Gil-Aluja. Following this book and under the signature of both authors there were 7 other books, the last of which:

"Grafos neuronales para la economía y gestión de la empresa", (1995) [Neural graphs for economy and business management], saw the light of day a year after the death of Professor Kaufmann. In the latter years of his life we had incorporated into our working team two brilliant and young professors: Antonio Terceño from the Rovira i Virgili University who joined us in the writing of the book "Matemática para la economía y gestión de empresas", (1994) [Mathematics for economy and business management] and Ana Mª Gil-Lafuente with whom we wrote the well known work "La creatividad en la gestión de empresas" (1994) [Creativity in business management] with later translations into several languages. With this our intention was to ensure our continuity, and this has been the case.

One of the fields of study which has attained the most popularity in latter years is the economic-financial management of sport. In this field of study, I published a book in fuzzy code: "Algoritmos para la excelencia. Claves para el éxito en la gestión deportiva" (2002), [Algorithms for excellence. Keys to success in sports management] which has signified for the author the fact of being considered as one of the most important specialists in the world on the economy of sport (see University of Strasbourg).

The untimely death of Kaufmann required certain changes in our working teams, as well as a restructuring of the numerous tutorships of other teams. For me personally it meant carrying on alone with the tasks that for so many years we had carried out together. I have published five books, now with a greater economic content: "La gestión interactiva de los recursos humanos en la incertidumbre" (1996) [The interactive management of human resources in uncertainty]; "Invertir en la incertidumbre (1997), [Investment in uncertainty]; "Elementos para una teoría de la decision en la incertidumbre" (1999), [Elements for a theory of decision in uncertainty]; and "Introducción a la teoría de la incertidumbre en la gestión de empresas" (2002), [Introduction to a theory of uncertainty in business management], the first three with a version in English published by Kluwer A.P. and the latter by Springer. Finally, a work published in Spanish: "Algoritmos para el tratamiento de fenómenos económicos complejos. Bases, desarrollos y aplicaciones (2007), [Algorithms for the treatment of complex economic phenomena. Bases, development and applications], was written in conjunction with Ana Mª Gil Lafuente and is currently being published by Springer under the title of "Towards an Advanced Modelling of Complex Economic Phenomena".

Throughout so many years of work, academic and university communities have wanted to recognize the work done in the sphere of economy and management by following the path left by Lotfi Zadeh. Thus we have been honoured with 24 "Honoris Causa" Doctorates by universities on four continents and the doors have been opened for us at 11 Scientific Academies. For one of these, the Real Academia de Ciencias Económicas y Financieras of Spain I was elected President, office which I have held since 2002.

With the work published as a book in 1986 we systematically incorporated the Fuzzy Sets of Lotfi Zadeh to the analysis and treatment of management problems. From this research activity new theories have arisen and the generalisation of many other existing ones has taken place. In this regard we should mention the theory of forgotten effects, the theory of affinities and the theory of expertons. On the other hand, the creation and development of the concept of the neural graph constitutes a further step for "explaining" the multiple connections of economic and management relations, which we consider as important.

- The theory of forgotten effects came about starting out from an idea of Ramón Llull (1235-1315) and allows for the establishment of the set of relations of causality of second and higher degrees, which the human mind, in its current state, is not capable of carrying out and which on the other hand is quite possible by means of logical operators. In a first approximation we used the max-min convolution.
- The theory of affinities constitutes a generalisation of the relations of similarity, which can be formalised by means of rectangular matrices and presented by means of lattice structures.
- The theory of expertons, mentioned by Kaufmann in one of his works, means a profound change in the treatment of problems of aggregation, given the fact that, by means of its development, it is possible to maintain all the information which is available initially right up to the end of the process, at the same time that non-linear operations are being carried out with the added information.

Over the latter years we have dedicated our efforts to bringing to light that it is ever more difficult to base economic knowledge on the "geometric conception", with its mechanism and irreversibility. Thanks to the flexibility and adaptability of Fuzzy Sets we were able to incorporate into management studies the Darwinian idea with its components of asymmetry and irreversibility. The difference carried out by Ilya Prigogine between a structure of balance and a dissipative structure with its generating activity of entropy allowed us to envisage new possibilities for developing elements that were capable of better understanding the complexity of economic relations. Up until now the results have been encouraging as is shown in the last book, in which two possible lines of Fuzzyfying pre-topological and topological spaces with the object of making them suitable for the construction of algorithms capable of treating economic situations with a very high degree of uncertainty was presented.

Geographic, but also ideological dispersion in an academic sense of all, people and groups, who became incorporated into our lines of Fuzzy teaching and research required the construction of organisational structures, if what was desired was to successfully channel and give opportunities to researchers who desired the commencement of a promising scientific trajectory.

After multiple steps were taken and carefully considering the possibilities of the time, we took the decision to establish as the centre and headquarters of our activities the City of Reus, where the Faculty of Economic and Business Sciences of the Rovira i Virgili University is located. The legal coverage of our scientific organisation would be provided by two institutions: an association which took the name of SIGEF (International Society for Fuzzy Management and Economy) which would organise a yearly meeting under the format of a congress and would publish a review, and a foundation (FEGI) (Foundation for the Study of Management in Uncertainty), the principal objective of which would be to obtain financial means in order to subsidise the needs of SIGEF, and at the same time would periodically grant an award in order to honour researchers within the sphere of Fuzzy Economy and Management. The presidency of this foundation would be held by the Mayor of the City of Reus. In April 1994, the association and foundation were set up and in the same city where they have their headquarters, Reus, on the 16-18 of November 1994 the 1st International Congress on Fuzzy Management and Economy took place.

This congress has been followed every year without interruption by congresses in different European and American cities. In 2012 the International Congress of SIGEF will once again carry out all of its activities in the place of its headquarters, in Reus.

Likewise, in 1994 The Fuzzy Economic Review was created to include scientific works, which at quarterly intervals today carries on the task of making known all those works that are considered of quality from among those who use elements of Fuzzy Logic to provide solutions to the problems that concern those responsible for economy and management at all times, both in the micro and the macro-economic world.

The FEGI foundation on the other hand, continues its task of encouraging and feeding the activities of the association. And this independently of the ups and downs of municipal policies, which mean changes in the presidency, as a consequence of the election results for the designation of the government of local entities.

In 1994, on the occasion of the sudden death of Professor Arnold Kaufmann the FEGI foundation unanimously agreed to institute the Kaufmann Award in order to recompense those scientists who stood out due to their research in the sphere of the study of economic or management systems with the use of Fuzzy

Logic. The design of the medal was entrusted to the great sculptor Josep Mª Subirachs, author of the façade of the Passion of the temple of the Sagrada Familia by Gaudi (born in Reus). Subirachs accepted the task and designed and created the Kaufmann Medal, cast in gold.

Since then illustrious researchers who have worked in the sphere of economy and creating methods, models or algorithms that were useable in this field, making highly interesting scientific and/or technical contributions have been awarded the prize. Among others the following have been honoured: H.J. Zimmermann, M.M. Gupta, J. Klir and J. Kacprzyk. In 2004, we had the honour of granting the Kaufmann Medal to Lotfi Zadeh. This year, 2012, on the occasion of the SIGEF Congress this prize will once again be awarded to a personality, at this time not designated as we are awaiting the meeting of the Jury.

It is now nearly half a century since Lotfi Zadeh published his fundamental work "Fuzzy Sets". The message contained therein continues to be alive, and, what perhaps is most important, it continues to be useful for awaking sleeping consciences, and to illuminate new paths towards a better knowledge of physical, biological and social phenomena. For those, like us, who have dedicated 56 years of our life in attempting to understand, explain and adequately treat economic and management realities, the work of Lotfi Zadeh has meant an impulse, which we would hope to be permanent.

These have so far been the beginnings and the first steps of "The Spanish School of Economics Fuzzy", demanding, but fruitful. We expect nothing less of those to come, because now we are more and better. And the proof is the quality of the research which I am proud to present here.

They are the evidence that all the effort has paid off and that the witness of fuzzy logic, science and knowledge is in the best hands to achieve a better world, a fairer, freer and more united.

PART 1: THEORETICAL FOUNDATIONS

SPECIFIC MAX. TRAVELING SALESMAN PROBLEMS[†]

RAUL O. DICHIARA

Depto. de Economía (UNS), IIESS (UNS-CONICET),12 de Octubre 1198, Piso 3º

Bahía Blanca, B-8000 CTX, Buenos Aires, Argentina

BLANCA I. NIEL

Depto. de Matemática, Universidad Nacional del Sur, Av. L. N. Alem 1253

Bahía Blanca, B-8000, Buenos Aires, Argentina

We single out every longest path of $n-1$ order that solves each of the $\frac{n}{2}$ Longest Euclidean Hamiltonian Path Problems (Max. Traveling Salesman Path Problems) on the even n-th roots of the unity, by means of a geometric and arithmetic procedure. This identification is done regardless of planar rotations and orientation. In addition, the uniqueness of the Euclidean Hamiltonian cycle that resolves the Maximum Traveling Salesman.

[†] This work was supported by Grants 24-E/073 ("Redes logísticas en el sistema del transporte de cereales: Área de influencia del Puerto de Bahía Blanca") and 24-E/074 ("Estrategias de organización y trayectorias productivas de Pymes Regionales. Desempeño en los mercados internos y de exportación"). General Science and Technology Secretary, UNS.

1. Introduction

Let us consider the network $N(K_n(\sqrt[n]{1}), D)$, where $K_n(\sqrt[n]{1})$ is the complete graph with vertices on the n-th roots of the unity and $D = (d_{ij})$ is the $n \times n$ matrix of the Euclidean distances between nodes. Herein, we deal with the Longest cyclic and non-cyclic Euclidean Hamiltonian Paths. The search for the Euclidean Hamiltonian optimum involves tough computational tasks, since the network with its K_n graph architecture has $(n-1)!/2$ Hamiltonian cycles [1,3,8] . Even for a moderate number of nodes n, checking all such cycles would be ludicrous. Thus, there are other approaches known as approximation techniques [7]. We have applied the simplest strategies called the nearest and farthest neighbour techniques [2,5]. These algorithmic explorations attain the shortest cycles in $N(K_n(\sqrt[n]{1}), D)$ networks and the longest cycles in $N(K_{n=2p+1}(\sqrt[n]{1}), D)$ networks. These optimal Hamiltonian cycles have the perfect form, i.e. the regular n-gons and the maximum-density star polygons $\{n/p\}$, respectively [4,9]. On the contrary, the cycle rendered up by the furthest neighbour exploration is far from the longest cycle in $N(K_{n=2p+2}(\sqrt[n]{1}), D)$ networks [7]. The furthest neighbour cycle inspired us with the construction of the representative configurations that resolve the $n/2$ different Longest non-cyclic Euclidean Hamiltonian Path Problems in these networks [12]. In this disclosure, we have posed a procedure to determine the Euclidean Hamiltonian cycles of order n, if they exist, under the pre-assignment of n inter node Euclidean directed segments. The proposed methodology arises from the intrinsic geometry and the inherent arithmetic of the vertex locus [11, 10, 6]. It allows us to single out every Hamiltonian path that resolves the $n/2$ different Longest non-cyclic Euclidean Hamiltonian Path Problems in $N(K_{n=2p+2}(\sqrt[n]{1}), D)$ networks. Regardless of planar rotations and orientation, the uniqueness of the Hamiltonian cycle that resolves the maximum travelling salesman problem in $N(K_{n=2p+2}(\sqrt[n]{1}), D)$ networks is shown.

After the formulation of the Longest Euclidean Hamiltonian Path Problems that we deal with, Section 2 deploys our proposed methodology. Section 3 confirms a representative path of every Longest Euclidean Hamiltonian Path Problems by direct application of the posed methodology. Section 4 accords how to hamper redundancy in the enumeration of the optimum Hamiltonian cycles by the definition of a congruence. Section 5 singles out the optimum Hamiltonian paths and Section 6 encloses the spectrum of the pathways that resolve any of the $n/2$ different Longest non-cyclic Euclidean Hamiltonian Path Problems in $N(K_{n=2p+2}(\sqrt[n]{1}),D)$ networks. Section 7, Conclusion, sets forth our geometric insight to capture these solutions.

2. The proposed methodology

Let $V_0,\cdots,V_{n-1}$ be the points of the set $e^{i\pi}\sqrt[n]{1}$ and let them be clockwise enumerated by the set of integers modulo n, Z_n, from the vertex $V_0=(-1,0)$. For each k in $0\le k\le \lfloor n/2\rfloor$ and each $j\in Z_n$, let $L^-_{k,j}$ denote the segment that joins V_j with V_{j+k}, while $L^+_{k,j}$ denotes the one that joins V_j to $V_{j+(n-k)}=V_{j-k}$. From now onwards, L^-_k and L^+_k denote to $L^-_{k,0}$ and $L^+_{k,0}$, respectively. Let $l_{\max}$ be the diameter, it joins the vertex V_j with its opposite $V_{j+n/2}$, only if n is even. Furthermore, $L^-_{\lfloor n/2\rfloor}$ = $L^-_{n/2}$ = $L^+_{n/2}$ = $l_{\max}$. In addition, $l^-_{q_{\max}}$ and $l^+_{q_{\max}}$ respectively designate, the quasi-diameters $L^-_{\lfloor n/2\rfloor-1}$ and $L^+_{\lfloor n/2\rfloor-1}$ if n is even, while $L^-_{\lfloor n/2\rfloor}$ and $L^+_{\lfloor n/2\rfloor}$ if n odd (see Figure 1).

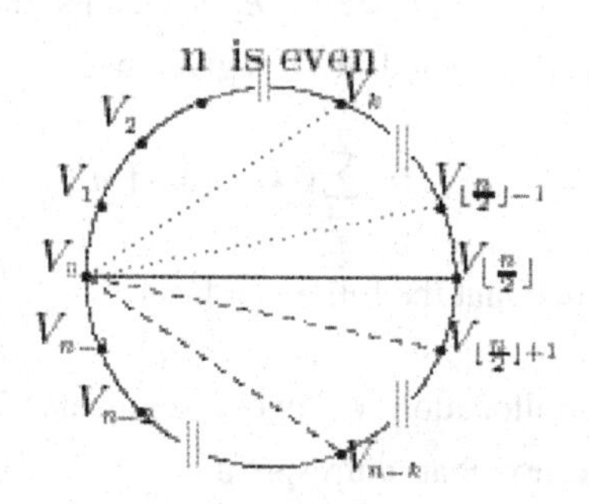

Figure 1

2.1. *Intrinsic Geometry and Inherent Arithmetic*

If P_n symbolizes a regular n-gon inscribed in the unitary circle and with vertices in $V_0,\cdots,V_{n-1}$, P_n can be considered as the polygonal of sides $L^-_{1,0}$, $L^-_{1,1}$, $\cdots$, $L^-_{1,n-1}$ [9]. For example, from the vector interpretation of the segments $L^{\pm}_{k,j}$, it is interesting to note that $L^+_{1,j} = -L^-_{1,j-1}$. Moreover, $L^-_{k,j}$ can be interpreted as the resultant of the polygonal of k sides of P_n, that joins clockwise V_j to V_{j+k}, while $L^+_{k,j}$ is the resultant of the polygonal of $n-k$ sides that joins clockwise V_j to $V_{j-k} \equiv V_{j+(n-k)}$. The segments $L^-_{k,j}$ and $L^+_{k,j}$ are the respective chords (or resultants) of the polygonal $sn+k$ and $rn+n-k$ consecutive sides of P_n, whichever are the integers s and r. Therefore, it is natural to associate $L^-_{k,j}$ with the integer $e(L^-_{k,j}) = k$, and likewise $L^+_{k,j}$ with the integer $e(L^+_{k,j}) = n-k \equiv -k$ (mod n).

Definition 2.1 For any integer n, L is a L_k segment if for any k, $0 \le k \le \lfloor n/2 \rfloor$, and for any $j \in Z_n$, L is equal to $L^-_{k,j}$ or $L = L^+_{k,j}$.

Definition 2.2 If L is an L_k segment, the integer associated to L, noted as $e(L)$, is given by:

$$e(L) = k \text{ if } L = L^-_{k,j} \text{ or } e(L) = n-k \equiv -k \text{ if } L = L^+_{k,j}$$

If $S: L_1, L_2, \ldots, L_j$ is a sequence of L_k segments, the integer associated to the path determined by S, denoted $e(S)$ is given by:

$$e(S) = \sum_{i=1}^{j} e(L_i) \pmod{n}$$

It should be taken into account the following facts:

1. The consecutive collocation of two L_k segments from any vertex V_i determines the vertex that corresponds to collocate, from V_i and in clockwise, as many sides of P_n as correspond to the sum of the integers associated to each one of the two L_k segments. In other words, the resultant of a polygonal built by two L_k segments, is other L_k segment and its associated integer is the sum (mod n) of the integers associated to the components of the polygonal.

2. The L_k segment L is $L = L^{-}_{e(L),j}$ by considering any fixed value of j, when $0 \le e(L) \le \lfloor n/2 \rfloor$. However, if $\lfloor n/2 \rfloor \le e(L) \le n$, the L segment is $L = L^{+}_{n-e(L),j} = L^{+}_{-e(L),j}$.

The concept of the associated integer $e(L_k)$ and its addition modulo n, deploy the following geometric correlate over the set of vertices $\{V_0 = (-1,0), \cdots, V_{n-1}\}$: For each i, $0 \le i \le n-1$, the geometric place that corresponds to the vertex V_i coincides with the place that corresponds to V_{i+sn}, for each integer s. Since the segments $L^{-}_{k,0}$ and $L^{+}_{k,0}$ respectively connect the vertices V_0 to V_k and V_0 to $V_{-k} \equiv V_{n-k}$, it is clear that for any integer k between 0 and $\lfloor n/2 \rfloor$, the vertices V_k and V_{-k} are symmetric with respect to the horizontal axis. This correlation prompts Lemma 2.1.

Lemma 2.1 Two vertices V_i, V_j are symmetric vertices with respect to the horizontal axis if and only if $i + j \equiv 0 \pmod{n}$.

Proof Let V_i and V_j be symmetric vertices with respect to the horizontal axis. That is, $V_i \equiv V_{-j} \Leftrightarrow V_j \equiv V_{-i}$. Therefore, $i = -j + sn \Leftrightarrow j = -i + rn$ $\Leftrightarrow i + j \equiv 0 \pmod{n}$.

Given a sequence of L_k segments, henceforward the polygonal that they determine is in a one-to-one relationship with the sum of each one of these directed sides that belong to the sequence.

Since $e(L^{\pm}_{k,i}) = e(L^{\pm}_{k,j})$, whichever i and j are, without loss of generality in the sequences of L_k segments, the second sub indices of these directed sides are rooted out.

2.2. *Fundamental Statements: Lemma 2.2 and Theorem 2.1*

Definition 2.3 Let $S_m : a_1, a_2, \ldots, a_m$ be a finite sequence. A proper subsequence of S_m is every subsequence S_{jr} such that: $S_{jr} : a_j, a_{j+1}, \ldots, a_{j+r-1}, a_{j+r}$ for $1 \le j \le m$ and $r \ge 0$ with $j + r < m$ if $j = 1$, and $j + r \le m$ if $j > 1$.

Based on the previous analysis, the following Lemma 2.2 and Theorem 2.1 ensue:

Lemma 2.2 *The pathway determined by a sequence S of L_k segments starts and ends at the same vertex V_j if and only if $e(S) \equiv 0$.*

Theorem 2.1 *A sequence S of n L_k segments determines a Euclidean Hamiltonian cycle of order n if and only if any proper subsequence has associated integer neither n nor a multiple of n and $e(S) \equiv 0$.*

Proof Let $S: L_{k_1}, L_{k_2}, \ldots, L_{k_{m-1}}, L_{k_m}$ be a Euclidean Hamiltonian cycle of order n, then any proper subsequence S' determines a Euclidean Hamiltonian path and $e(S') \not\equiv 0$. Reciprocally, if any proper subsequence S' of S is such that $e(S') \not\equiv 0$, the trajectory associated with $L_{k_2}, \ldots, L_{k_{m-1}}, L_{k_m}$ is a Euclidean Hamiltonian path that joints the n vertices $V_{i,0}, \ldots, V_{i,n-1}$. The presumption that L_{k_1} does not link the final with the initial vertices of the trajectory associated to $L_{k_2}, \ldots, L_{k_m}$ implies the existence of a proper subsequence that determines a cycle. It is a contradiction. Hence, $e(S) \equiv 0$.

3. Representative strategies of the max. traveling salesman path problems

The ensuing sequences Γ_k' and Γ_k, defined in (1) at page 8 and (2) at page 9 respectively, and composited of the directed segments L_k^-, $l_{q_{max}}^-$, $l_{q_{max}}^+$, and l_{max} play a remarkable role in the resolution of the $n/2$ different Longest Euclidean Hamiltonian Path Problems in $N(K_{n=2p+2}(\sqrt[n]{1}), D)$ networks. Precisely, Γ_k', $1 \leq k \leq \lfloor n/2 \rfloor - 1$ with the L_k^- as putative rooted out side, are representative paths of every Longest Euclidean Hamiltonian Path Problem (Refer to [12]).

Note 3.1 In $N(K_{n=2p+2}(\sqrt[n]{1}), D)$ networks C_H^m stands for a Euclidean Hamiltonian cycle of order m less than or equal to n in $N(K_{n=2p+2}(\sqrt[n]{1}), D)$ networks. In addition, P_H^m stands for a Euclidean Hamiltonian path of order m less than or equal to $n-1$. Let $\longleftrightarrow$ symbolize the rooted up of terms in a sequence of L_k segments.

Note 3.2 $L_{k_1} + L_{k_2} + \ldots + L_{k_{m-1}} + L_{k_m}$ stands for the pathway determined by the sequence $L_{k_1}, L_{k_2}, \ldots, L_{k_{m-1}}, L_{k_m}$. If $S: L_{k_1}, L_{k_2}, \ldots, L_{k_{m-1}}, L_{k_m}$ is a sequence of L_k segments, $\Lambda(S) = \Lambda(L_{k_1} + L_{k_2} + \ldots + L_{k_{m-1}} + L_{k_m})$ stands for the associated Euclidean length to S.

Lemma 3.1 *The following sequences of* L_k *segments determine Euclidean Hamiltonian cycles, i.e.* C_H^m, *in* $N(K_{n=2p+2}(\sqrt[n]{1}), D)$ *networks:*

1. C_H^2 : *a)* $l_{q_{max}}^- + l_{q_{max}}^+$; *b)* $l_{max} + l_{max}$; *c)* $l_{q_{max}}^+ + l_{q_{max}}^-$

2. C_H^{2i+2}: *d)* $\underbrace{l_{q_{max}}^-}_{i} + l_{max} + \underbrace{l_{q_{max}}^+}_{i} + l_{max}$, $1 \le i \le n/2-2$

3. C_H^{2i+2}: *e)* $\underbrace{l_{q_{max}}^+}_{j} + l_{max} + \underbrace{l_{q_{max}}^-}_{i} + l_{max} + \underbrace{l_{q_{max}}^+}_{i-j}$, $0 \le j \le i$, $1 \le i \le n/2-1$

4. C_H^{2i+2}: *f)* $\underbrace{l_{q_{max}}^-}_{j} + l_{max} + \underbrace{l_{q_{max}}^+}_{i} + l_{max} + \underbrace{l_{q_{max}}^-}_{i-j}$, $0 \le j \le i$, $1 \le i \le n/2-1$

Proof From direct application of Theorem 2.1 and the assumed arithmetic

Theorem 3.1 *Let* $N(K_{n=2p+2}(\sqrt[n]{1}), D)$ *the networks with their* $n = 2p+2$ *nodes,* $V_0, \cdots, V_{n-1}$, *corresponding to the* n*-th roots of the unity clockwise ordered from* $V_0 = (-1, 0)$. *Each trajectory* Γ_k', *with initial point* V_k, $1 \le k \le n/2-1$, *determined by the next sequence of segments*

$$\Gamma_k' : \overleftrightarrow{L_k^-} ; \underbrace{l_{q_{max}}^-}_{k-1}, l_{max}, \underbrace{l_{q_{max}}^+}_{k}, \underbrace{l_{max}, l^+_{q_{max}}}_{n/2-k-1}, l_{max}, \quad (1)$$

is a P_H^{n-1} *in* $N(K_{n=2p+2}(\sqrt[n]{1}), D)$ *networks, with final point at* V_0.

Proof From direct application of Theorem 2.1 and Lemma 3.1

Since $e(l_{q_{max}}^-) = n/2-1$, $e(l_{max}) = n/2$ and $e(l_{q_{max}}^+) = n/2+1$, it follows that the associated integers to every proper subsequence of Γ_k' are:

1. $h(n/2-1) = h(n/2) - h \not\equiv 0$ for $1 \le h \le k-1 < n/2-1$

2. $h(n/2-1) + n/2 \not\equiv 0$ for $1 \le h \le k-1 < n/2-1$

3. $h(n/2-1) + n/2 + i(n/2+1) = (h+i+1)(n/2) + (i-h) \not\equiv 0$ for $0 \le h \le k-1$; $1 \le i \le k$

4. $n/2 + i(n/2+1) \not\equiv 0$ for $1 \le i \le k$

5. $h(n/2-1) + n/2 + k(n/2+1) + n/2 = (h+k)(n/2) + n + (k-h) \not\equiv 0$ for $0 \le h \le k-1 < k$

6. $h(n/2-1) + n/2 + k(n/2+1) + j(n+1) = (h+k+1)(n/2) + jn + (k-h-j) \not\equiv 0$ for $\begin{cases} 0 \le h \le k-1 \\ 1 \le j \le n/2-k-1 \end{cases}$

7. $h(n/2-1)\ n/2 + k(n/2+1) + j(n+1) + n/2 = (h+k+2)(n/2) + jn + (k-h-j) \not\equiv 0$ for $\begin{cases} 0 \le h \le k-1 \\ 1 \le j \le n/2-k-1 \end{cases}$.

This item computes $e(\Gamma_k^{'}) = n(n/2) - k \not\equiv 0$ for $h = k-1$; $j = n/2-k-1$

8. $i(n/2+1) + j(n+1) = i(n/2) + jn + (i+j) \not\equiv 0$ for $0 \le i \le k$; $1 \le j \le n/2-k-1$

9. $i(n/2+1) + j(n+1) + n/2 \not\equiv 0$ for $0 \le i \le k$; $1 \le j \le n/2-k-1$.

Hence, the associated integer to every proper subsequence of $\Gamma_k^{'}$, including $e(\Gamma_k^{'})$, is non-congruent with 0 (mod n). Then, by Theorem 2.1 $\Gamma_k^{'}$ is a Euclidean Hamiltonian path of order $n-1$ for each $1 \le k \le n/2-1$. (An alternative proof has been posed in Appendix)

Corollary 3.1 *Let Γ_k stand for the pathway determined by the sequence of segments that comes from the anchoring of the initial side L_k^{-} to $\Gamma_k^{'}$ (see sequence (1)),* $1 \le k \le n/2-1$. *For each k, the trajectory Γ_k built by the sequence (2) is a Euclidean Hamiltonian cycle of order n in $N(K_{n=2p+2}(\sqrt[n]{1}), D)$ networks with initial and final ending points at V_0.*

$$\Gamma_k : L_k^-, \underbrace{l_{q_{max}}^-}_{k-1}, l_{max}, \underbrace{l_{q_{max}}^+}_{k}, \underbrace{l_{max}, l^+_{q_{max}}}_{n/2-k-1}, l_{max}, \quad (2)$$

Proof It is straightforward from the proof of Theorem 2.1 and Theorem 3.1 and that $e(\Gamma_k^{'}) = -k$ and $e(L_k^-) = k$. (For other approach, see Appendix B, in [12]).

4. Congruent cyclic strategies with Γ_k

Let K_k, $1 \le k \le n/2-1$, be the set of all Euclidean Hamiltonian directed cycles in $N(K_{n=2p+2}(\sqrt[n]{1}), D)$ networks, built by one L_k^- (or L_k^+) side, $(n/2-k+1)$ diameters l_{max}, $(n/2+k-2)$ quasi-diameters $l^{\pm}_{q_{max}}$ with $k-1$ $l^-_{q_{max}}$ (or $k-1$ $l^+_{q_{max}}$) sides. The cyclic path Γ_k, built by the sequence (2), is a trajectory in K_k and for each k all the pathways in K_k have the same length, $\Lambda(\Gamma_k)$. It is interesting to know how many and what are the K_k paths like. Once this goal is overtaken, the resolution of the $n/2$ different Longest Euclidean Hamiltonian Path Problems in $N(K_{n=2p+2}(\sqrt[n]{1}), D)$ networks is overcome, because Theorem 3.1.4 in [12] shows that $\Lambda(\Gamma_k^{'})$ with $1 \le k \le n/2-1$ is the longest travelled length of any Euclidean Hamiltonian path with initial and final ends at V_k and V_0, respectively.

Definition 4.1 Given T, $T^{'} \in \mathrm{K}_k$, T is congruent with $T^{'}$ (notation: $T \sim T^{'}$), if $T = T^{'}$, or if $T^{'}$ is obtained from the directed Euclidean Hamiltonian cycle T by an inversion of the orientation, or if $T^{'}$ is obtained by a rotation of T, or if $T^{'}$ is obtained by a rotation and an inversion of the orientation of the cycle T.

Lemma 4.1 *Given a sequence of* L_k *segments in* K_k, $1 \le k \le n/2-1$ *whose last element has* j *as the associated integer, once this last side is relocated in the initial end, the renewal sequence has the trajectory of the original one, but clockwise rotated* j *vertices.*

Proof Let the sequence be L_{k_1}, L_{k_2}, ..., L_{k_n} without loss of generality, it can consider the trajectory built from the initial vertex V_0 with the starter side L_{k_1}

followed by the segment L_{k_2} pinned at $V_{(0+e(L_{k_1}))}$ and so on with the $n-2$ remainder sides in the order established by the previous sequence.

If the segment L_{k_n} with associated integer j is relocated in the first place, the initial and final vertices of the segment L_{k_1} change to V_{0+j} and $V_{(j+e(L_{k_1}))}$, respectively in the renewal sequence. After the rearrangement side-by-side of the ordered remainder segments $L_{k_2},\ldots,$ $L_{k_{n-1}}$, the issuing trajectory corresponds to the original one, but clockwise rotated j vertices.

Lemma 4.2 *For n even and* $1\leq k\leq n/2-1$, *the corresponding trajectories to the following sequences are the* $n-1$ *planar rotations associated to sequence (2), that is to* Γ_k :

$$1.\quad \Gamma_k:\ L_k^-,\ \underbrace{l_{q_{\max}}^-}_{k-1},\ l_{\max},\ \underbrace{l_{q_{\max}}^+}_{k},\ \underbrace{l_{\max}, l^+_{q_{\max}}}_{n/2-k-1},\ l_{\max}, \tag{2}$$

$$2.\quad l_{\max},\ L_k^-,\ \underbrace{l_{q_{\max}}^-}_{k-1},\ l_{\max},\ \underbrace{l_{q_{\max}}^+}_{k},\ \underbrace{l_{\max}, l^+_{q_{\max}}}_{n/2-k-1},$$

....

$$(n\text{-}k)\quad \underbrace{l_{q_{\max}}^+}_{k},\ \text{-}\underbrace{l_{\max}, l^+_{q_{\max}}}_{n/2-k-1},\ l_{\max},\ L_k^-,\ \underbrace{l_{q_{\max}}^-}_{k-1},\ l_{\max},$$

....

$$(n)\quad \underbrace{l_{q_{\max}}^-}_{k-1},\ l_{\max},\ \underbrace{l_{q_{\max}}^+}_{k},\ \underbrace{l_{\max}, l^+_{q_{\max}}}_{n/2-k-1},\ l_{\max},\ L_k^-$$

Proof It results after $n-1$ successive applications of the Lemma 4.1 to the sequence (2), Γ_k.

Since any L_k segment verify that $L_k^{\pm}+L_k^{\mp}\equiv 0 \Leftrightarrow L_k^{\mp}+L_k^{\pm}\in C_H^2$ and $L_k^{\pm}$ $=-L_k^{\mp}$. If $L_k^{\pm}$ links the vertex V_{i0} to the vertex V_{i1} follows that $L_k^{\mp}$ connects V_{i1} to V_{i0}.

Lemma 4.3 *Given a sequence* S *of* m $L_k^{\pm}$ *segments,* $S:\ L^{\pm}_{k_1},\ L^{\pm}_{k_2},\ \ldots,$ $L^{\pm}_{k_{m-1}},\ L^{\pm}_{k_m}$ *the renewal sequence* $-S:\ L^{\mp}_{k_m},\ L^{\mp}_{k_{m-1}},\ \ldots,\ L^{\mp}_{k_2},\ L^{\mp}_{k_1}$ *determines the opposite orientated pathway of* S.

Proof If $L^{\pm}{}_{k_1}$ links the vertex V_{i0} to the vertex V_{i1}, $L^{\pm}{}_{k_2}$ links the vertex V_{i1} to the vertex V_{i2} and so on until $L^{\pm}_{k_m}$ which links the vertex V_{im-1} to the vertex V_{im}, then $L^{\mp}_{k_m}$ which links the vertex V_{im} to the vertex V_{im-1}, $L^{\mp}_{k_{m-1}}$ links the vertex V_{im-1} to the vertex V_{im-2} and so on to $L^{\mp}{}_{k_1}$ which connects V_{i1} to V_{i0}.

5. Max. traveling salesman paths singled out in $\mathrm{K}_k/\sim$

For $k \neq n/2-1$ any planar rotation or inversion of orientation of Γ_k implies the disappearance of L_k^- at the first place in the sequence or its inversion of sign. Consequently, a thorough examination of the non-congruent trajectories with Γ_k imposes to consider neither cyclic re-locations of the elements of the sequence nor changes of all the signs of its directed segments. Therefore, in the present aim only the re-orderings that maintain L_k^- at the first place of the sequence should be considered.

Lemma 5.1 *Let $T \in \mathrm{K}_k$ so that $T \nsim \Gamma_k$. Then, T exists, $T' \in \mathrm{K}_k$, with L_k^- as its first term and $T \sim T'$. In other words, in order to determine all the trajectories in K_k that are non-congruent cycles with Γ_k, it is enough to determine the pathways that both start with L_k^- and are non-congruent cycles with Γ_k.*

Proof Let $T \in \mathrm{K}_k$ and $T \nsim \Gamma_k$. If L_k^- is the first side of T, the proof is done. If T does not start with L_k^-, then T: L_{s_1}, ..., $L_{s_{j-1}}$, L_k^-, $L_{s_{j+1}}$, ..., L_{s_n}. Let T': L_k^-, $L_{s_{j+1}}$, ..., L_{s_n}, L_{s_1}, ..., $L_{s_{j-1}}$. Then T' is a planar rotation of T i.e. $T' \sim T$ and hence $T \nsim \Gamma_k$.

Definition 5.1 S: L_{k_1}, L_{k_2}, ..., $L_{k_{m-1}}$, L_{k_m} and S': L'_{k_1}, L'_{k_2}, ..., $L'_{k_{m-1}}$, L'_{k_m} are called opposites if L_{k_1}, L_{k_2}, ..., $L_{k_{m-1}}$, L_{k_m} $=$ L'_{k_m}, $L'_{k_{m-1}}$, ..., L'_{k_2}, L'_{k_1}.

Definition 5.2 Let S: L_{k_2}, L_{k_3},..., $L_{k_{n-1}}$, L_{k_n} so that its completed sequence L_k^-; S $=$ L_k^-, L_{k_2}, L_{k_3},..., $L_{k_{n-1}}$, L_{k_n} $\in$ K_k. Then, the sequences T_S: L_k^-, L_{k_2}, L_{k_3},..., $L_{k_{n-1}}$, L_{k_n} and T_S^*: L_k^-, L_{k_n}, $L_{k_{n-1}}$, ..., L_{k_3} are called associated sequences with S.

Lemma 5.2 *Let S and S' so that their completed sequences* $\in$ K_k. *Then, S and S' have the same pair of associated sequences, if and only if S and S' are opposites.*

Proof S *and* S' are opposites $\Leftrightarrow$ $T_S = T_S^*$ and $T_S^* = T_S$.

Lemma 5.3 *Let* T: L_k^-, L_{k_2}, L_{k_3},..., $L_{k_{n-1}}$, L_{k_n} $\in$ K_k. *Then,* T': L_k^-, L_{k_n}, $L_{k_{n-1}}$, ..., L_{k_3} $\in$ K_k.

Proof $T \in K_k \Leftrightarrow S: L_{k_2}, L_{k_3},..., L_{k_{n-1}}, L_{k_n} \in P_H^{n-1} \Rightarrow S': L_{k_n}$, $L_{k_{n-1}}$, ..., L_{k_3} $\in$ P_H^{n-1}. In addition, $e(S') = e(S) = -k$. Therefore, T': L_k^-, $S' \in K_k$.

Lemma 5.4 *Let* $k \neq n/2-1$ *and* $T \in K_k$ *so that* T: L_k^-, L_{k_2}, L_{k_3},..., $L_{k_{n-1}}$, L_{k_n} *and* T' : L_k^-, L_{k_n}, $L_{k_{n-1}}$, ..., L_{k_3}. *Then* $T \sim T'$ *if and only if* S: L_{k_2}, L_{k_3},..., $L_{k_{n-1}}$, L_{k_n} *is a palindrome.*

Proof $k \neq n/2-1 \Rightarrow L_k^- \neq L_{k_i}$, $2 \leq i \leq n$. Let $T \sim T'$. If $T = T'$ then S is a palindrome. Let $T \neq T'$. Since both trajectories have the same initial segment L_k^- follows that $T \neq T' \Rightarrow S: L_{k_2}, L_{k_3},..., L_{k_{n-1}}, L_{k_n} \neq S': L_{k_n}, L_{k_{n-1}}, ..., L_{k_3}$, i.e. S is not a palindrome.

Corollary 5.1 *For* $1 \leq k \leq n/2-2$, *if* $S: L_{k_2}, L_{k_3},..., L_{k_{n-1}}, L_{k_n}$ *is not a palindrome, and* $L_k^-, S \in K_k$ *then* $L_k^-, L_{k_2}, L_{k_3},..., L_{k_{n-1}}, L_{k_n} \nsim L_k^-, L_{k_n}, L_{k_{n-1}}, ..., L_{k_3}$.

Let (3) be the pre-established directed sides:

$$\underbrace{l_{q_{\max}}^-}_{k-1} \quad \underbrace{l_{q_{\max}}^+}_{n/2-1} \quad \underbrace{l_{\max}}_{n/2-k-1} \tag{3}$$

Lemma 5.5 *Let* $\$$ *be* $l_{\max}$; $\overbrace{l_{q_{\max}}^-}^{u}$; $l_{\max}$; $\overbrace{l_{q_{\max}}^+}^{y}$; $l_{\max}$, $u \geq 0$, $y \geq 0$. *Then* $\$$ *is an inadmissible subsequence of any* P_H^{n-1} *of the assignment (3) for* $1 \leq k \leq n/2-2$.

Proof If $u = 0$ and/or $y = 0$, they bring forth one or two elementary cycles $l_{\max}$; $l_{\max}$, (item b) Lemma 3.1). If $u \geq 1$, $y \geq 1$ and $u \geq y$, they give birth to the following cycle C_H^{2y+2}, (item d) Lemma 3.1):

$l^-_{q_{max}} + l^+_{q_{max}}\ l_{max}\ ;\ \overbrace{l^-_{q_{max}}}^{u-y}\ ;\ \overbrace{l^-_{q_{max}}}^{y}\ ;\ l_{max}\ ;\ \overbrace{l^+_{q_{max}}}^{y}$. If $u \geq 1$, $y \geq 1$ and $u \geq y$, they beget the following cycle C_H^{2u+2} , (item e) with $j = 0$ Lemma 3.1):

$$l_{max}\ ;\ \overbrace{l^-_{q_{max}}}^{u}\ ;\ l_{max}\ ;\ \overbrace{l^+_{q_{max}}}^{u}\ ;\ \overbrace{l^+_{q_{max}}}^{y-u}\ ;\ l_{max}\ .$$

Theorem 5.1 *The $k-1$ directed sides $l^-_{q_{max}}$ pre-established in (3) should be implanted at the left and/or right hand side(s) of any admissible P_H^{n-1} sequence built with the assignment of the directed segments given by (3). Consequently, regardless of planar rotations, the k ensuing sequences (4) are all the admissible P_H^{n-1} paths for each k, $1 \leq k \leq n/2-2$ built with (3) in $N(K_{n=2p+2}(\sqrt[n]{1}), D)$ networks.*

$$\underbrace{l^-_{q_{max}}}_{i}\ ;\ l_{max}\ ;\ \underbrace{l^+_{q_{max}}}_{i+1}\ ;\ \underbrace{l_{max}, l^+{}_{q_{max}}}_{n/2-k-1}\ ;\ \underbrace{l^+_{q_{max}}}_{k-i-1}\ ;\ l_{max}\ ;\ \underbrace{l^-_{q_{max}}}_{k-i-1} \qquad 0 \leq i \leq k-1. \qquad (4)$$

Proof Lemma 5.5 and Lemma 3.1 show that the $k-1$ sides $l^-_{q_{max}}$ pre-established in (3) should be implanted at the left- and/or right-hand side(s) of any admissible P_H^{n-1} sequence built with the assignment of directed segments given by (3).

$$\ell)\qquad \underbrace{l^-_{q_{max}}}_{i}\ ;\ l_{max}\ ;\ \underbrace{l^+_{q_{max}}}_{j}\ ;\ l_{max}\ ;\ \llcorner\ldots\lrcorner\ ; \qquad 0 \leq i < j \quad \therefore \quad j \geq i+1 \qquad (5)$$

$$r)\qquad \llcorner\ldots\lrcorner\ ;\ l_{max}\ ;\ \underbrace{l^+_{q_{max}}}_{j'}\ ;\ l_{max}\ ;\ \underbrace{l^-_{q_{max}}}_{i'}\ ; \qquad j' > i' \geq 0 \quad \therefore \quad j' \geq i'+1$$

Specifically, Lemma 5.5 states that ℓ) is a sequence where no sides l_{max} or $l^+_{q_{max}}$ can be appended to its left end. Moreover, Lemma 5.5 states that r) is a sequence where no sides l_{max} or $l^+_{q_{max}}$ can be appended to its right end. Otherwise, they give birth to Hamiltonian cycles that appear in Lemma 3.1. Hence, every admissible sequence in P_H^{n-1} built with the segments in (3) should maintain the following form:

$$\underbrace{l^-_{q_{max}}}_{i}\ ;\ l_{max}\ ;\ \underbrace{l^+_{q_{max}}}_{j}\ ;\ l_{max}\ ;\ \llcorner\ldots\lrcorner\ ;\ \underbrace{l^+_{q_{max}}}_{j'}\ ;\ l_{max}\ ;\ \underbrace{l^-_{q_{max}}}_{i'}\ ;$$

$$i' + j' = k-1, \quad i < j,\ i' < j' \qquad (6)$$

The remnants of the $l_{\max}$ sides to be implanted in (6) are equal to $n/2-k-2$. Meanwhile, there are $n/2-1-j-j'$ directed segments $l^{\cdot}_{q\max}$ that should be inserted in (6). Since $j+j' \geq k+1$ it results that $n/2-1-j-j' \leq n/2-k-2$. If $n/2-1-j-j' < n/2-k-2$, there is at least one $l_{\max}$ more than the $l^{\cdot}_{q\max}$ sides. Therefore, their implants in (6) bring about at least an elementary cycle, $l_{\max}; l_{\max}$. However, if $n/2-1-j-j' = n/2-k-2$ there are this amount of $l^{+}_{q\max}$ and $l_{\max}$ and $j+j' = k-1$. Their insertions in (6) as couples $\underbrace{l^{+}{}_{q\max}, l_{\max}}_{n/2-k-2}$ beget the following Euclidean Hamiltonian path:

$$\underbrace{l^{-}_{q\max}}_{i}; l_{\max}; \underbrace{l^{+}_{q\max}}_{j}; l_{\max}; \llcorner \underbrace{l^{+}{}_{q\max}, l_{\max}}_{n/2-k-2} \lrcorner; \underbrace{l^{+}_{q\max}}_{j'}; l_{\max}; \underbrace{l^{-}_{q\max}}_{i'};$$

$$i'+i = k-1, \; i<j, i'<j'$$

From $i<j$, $i'<j'$, $i'+i = k-1$ and $j+j' = k+1$, it results $j=i+1$, $i' = k-1-i$ and $j' = k-i$.
Their respective substitutions in the previous sequence, together with the identification of the proper subsequence $l_{\max}; \llcorner \underbrace{l^{+}{}_{q\max}, l_{\max}}_{n/2-k-2} \lrcorner; l^{+}_{q\max}; \underbrace{l^{+}_{q\max}}_{k-i-1};$

as $\underbrace{l_{\max}, l^{+}{}_{q\max}}_{n/2-k-1}; \underbrace{l^{+}_{q\max}}_{k-i-1}$, give birth the k sequences (4) with $0 \leq i \leq k-1$.

Theorem 5.2 *In $N(K_{n=2p+2}(\sqrt[n]{1}), D)$ networks, the quotient set $\mathrm{K}_k/\!\sim$ has k classes of equivalence with $2n$ paths each one for $1 \leq k < n/2-1$, and a unique class if with n pathways.*

Proof By Theorem 5.1, for each k, $1 \leq k < n/2-1$, there are exactly k sequences, built with the $n-1$ pre-established segments (3), in P^{n-1}_{H}:

$$\Gamma'_{k,i}: \underbrace{l^{-}_{q\max}}_{i-1}; l_{\max}; \underbrace{l^{+}_{q\max}}_{i}; \underbrace{l_{\max}, l^{+}{}_{q\max}}_{n/2-k-1}; \underbrace{l^{+}_{q\max}}_{k-i}; l_{\max}; \underbrace{l^{-}_{q\max}}_{k-i} \in P^{n-1}_{H} \qquad 1 \leq i \leq k \quad (7)$$

Furthermore, $e(\Gamma'_{k,i}) = -k$, $1 \leq i \leq k$, then

$$\Gamma_{k,i}: L^{-}_{k}; \Gamma'_{k,i} = L^{-}_{k}; \underbrace{l^{-}_{q\max}}_{i-1}; l_{\max}; \underbrace{l^{+}_{q\max}}_{i}; \underbrace{l_{\max}, l^{+}{}_{q\max}}_{n/2-k-1}; \underbrace{l^{+}_{q\max}}_{k-i}; l_{\max}; \underbrace{l^{-}_{q\max}}_{k-i} \in \mathrm{K}_k$$

$$1 \leq i \leq k$$

and $\Gamma_{k,i} \neq \Gamma_{k,j}$ if $i \neq j$.

If $k = 2p$ the sequences $\Gamma'_{k,i}$ are opposite by pairs (Definition 5.1), i.e. $\Gamma'_{k,i}$ with $\Gamma'_{k,k+1-i}$, $1 \le i \le k/2$ and none of them is a palindrome. Then, by Lemma 5.3 and Corollary 5.1, the associated sequences $T_{\Gamma'_{k,i}}$, $T^*_{\Gamma'_{k,i}} \in K_k$ and $T_{\Gamma'_{k,i}} \ne T^*_{\Gamma'_{k,i}}$, $1 \le i \le k$. Otherwise, the pairs of associated sequences corresponding to $\Gamma'_{k,i}$ and $\Gamma'_{k,k+1-i}$ are the same (Lemma 5.2). Then, in order to obtain all non congruent vis-à-vis cycles in K_k, from each pair of opposite sequences one should be discarded. The selection of $\Gamma'_{k,1}$, ..., $\Gamma'_{k,k/2}$ brings forth the corresponding k associated sequences that are vis-à-vis non congruent:

$$\Gamma_k \sim \Gamma_{k,k} = T^*_{\Gamma'_{k,1}} : L_k^-; \underbrace{l^-_{q_{\max}}}_{k-1}; l_{\max}; \underbrace{l^+_{q_{\max}}}_{k}; \underbrace{l_{\max}, l^+_{q_{\max}}}_{n/2-k-1}; l_{\max}$$

$$T_{\Gamma'_{k,1}} : L_k^-; l_{\max}; \underbrace{l^+_{q_{\max}}, l_{\max}}_{n/2-k-1}; \underbrace{l^+_{q_{\max}}}_{k}; l_{\max}; \underbrace{l^-_{q_{\max}}}_{k-1}$$

....

$$T^*_{\Gamma'_{k,k/2}} : L_k^-; \underbrace{l^-_{q_{\max}}}_{k/2}; l_{\max}; \underbrace{l^+_{q_{\max}}}_{k/2+1}; \underbrace{l_{\max}, l^+_{q_{\max}}}_{n/2-k-1}; \underbrace{l^+_{q_{\max}}}_{k/2-1}; l_{\max}; \underbrace{l^-_{q_{\max}}}_{k-1}$$

$$T_{\Gamma'_{k,i}} : L_k^-; \underbrace{l^-_{q_{\max}}}_{k/2-1}; l_{\max}; \underbrace{l^+_{q_{\max}}}_{k/2}; \underbrace{l_{\max}, l^+_{q_{\max}}}_{n/2-k-1}; \underbrace{l^+_{q_{\max}}}_{k/2}; l_{\max}; \underbrace{l^-_{q_{\max}}}_{k/2}$$

Hence, K_k has k classes of equivalence. In addition, the procedures in Lemma 4.2 and Lemma 4.3 allow us to confirm that each class has $2n$ congruent trajectories.

Meanwhile, if k is odd, $k = 2p+1 \ge 3$, the previous arguments show that the unique sequences in P_H^{n-1} built by the assignment (3) are the k sequences $\Gamma'_{k,i}$, (7). However, in this case $\Gamma'_{k,(k+1)/2}$ is a palindrome and the $k-1$ remnant are opposite by pairs. Specifically, $\Gamma'_{k,1}$ with $\Gamma'_{k,k}$, $\Gamma'_{k,2}$ with $\Gamma'_{k,k-1}$ and so on until $\Gamma'_{k,(k-1)/2}$ with $\Gamma'_{k,(k+3)/2}$. In the same way as in the k even case, $\Gamma'_{k,(k+3)/2}$, ..., $\Gamma'_{k,k-1}$ and $\Gamma'_{k,k}$ are discarded. Every one of the $(k-1)/2$ remaining sequences admit two associated sequences (cycles) $T^*_{\Gamma'_{k,i}}$, $T_{\Gamma'_{k,i}}$, $1 \le i \le (k-1)/2$. Since $\Gamma'_{k,(k+1)/2}$ is a palindrome, it verifies $T^*_{\Gamma'_{k,(k+1)/2}} = T_{\Gamma'_{k,(k+1)/2}}$. Consequently, the following k cyclic sequences $T^*_{\Gamma'_{k,1}} = \Gamma_{k,k} \sim \Gamma_k, T_{\Gamma'_{k,1}}, \ldots, T^*_{\Gamma'_{k,(k-1)/2}}$, $T_{\Gamma'_{k,(k-1)/2}}$ and $T^*_{\Gamma'_{k,(k+1)/2}} = T_{\Gamma'_{k,(k-1)/2}}$ are vis-`a-vis non-congruent.

Finally, if $k = n/2-1$, Lemma 5.4 is not applicable since $L_k^- = l_{q_{\max}}^-$. Theorem 3.1 and its Corollary 3.1 state $\Gamma'_{n/2-1}: \overleftrightarrow{l_{q_{\max}}^-} ; \underbrace{l_{q_{\max}}^-}_{n/2-2} ; l_{\max} ; \underbrace{l_{q_{\max}}^+}_{n/2-1} ; l_{\max}$ and $\Gamma_{n/2-1}: l_{q_{\max}}^- ; \Gamma'_{n/2-1}$. Specifically, $\Gamma_{n/2-1}$ and its reversed orientation are respectively obtained in Lemma 3.1 by the substitution of $j = i = n/2-1$ in the items f) and e). In general, the n rotations -Lemma 3.1 item f) $i = n/2-1$, $0 \leq j \leq n/2-1$ and item e) $i = n/2-1$, $0 \leq j \leq n/2-1$- bring forth the n feasible reorders of the $n/2-1$ sides $l_{q_{\max}}^-$, two $l_{\max}$ and $n/2-1$ sides. Moreover, the n changes of orientations are included amongst these n reorders. In conclusion, if $k = n/2-1$, the quotient set $K_k/\sim$ has a unique class with n elements.

Corollary 5.2 *The Maximum TSP in $N(K_{n=2p+2}(\sqrt[n]{1}),D)$ networks, i.e. $\Lambda(\Gamma_{n/2-1})$* [2], *regardless of planar rotations, is unique.*

Proof It is straightforward from the previous Theorem 5.2 and Theorems 3.1.3 and 3.1.5 in [12]

6. The outcome of maximum overall-length statements

In [12] Theorems 3.1.4 and 3.1.5 state that, in $N(K_{n=2p+2}(\sqrt[n]{1}),D)$ networks, the traversed length of the trajectory Γ'_k, $\Lambda(\Gamma'_k)$, $1 \leq k < n/2-1$, is the Maximum of the non-cyclic Euclidean Hamiltonian Path Problem of order $n-1$, with initial and final ends at V_k and V_0... and the maxima of the Euclidean Hamiltonian Cyclic Problems of order $n = 2p+2$, correspond to $\Lambda(\Gamma_{n/2-1})$.

From Theorem 2.2 in § 2.2 and Theorem 5.2 in § 5 it follows:

Corollary 6.1 *For every k, $1 \leq k < n/2-2$, the sequences $\overleftrightarrow{L_k^-}$, $\Gamma'_{k,i}$, $1 \leq i \leq k$ are Hamiltonian paths, that respectively start and end at the vertices V_k and V_0 in $N(K_{n=2p+2}(\sqrt[n]{1}),D)$ networks. Since $\Lambda(\Gamma'_k) = \Lambda(\Gamma'_{k,i}) = \Lambda(\overleftrightarrow{L_k^-}, \Gamma'_{k,i})$ for every $1 \leq i \leq k$, the sequences $\overleftrightarrow{L_k^-}, \Gamma'_{k,i}$ are the whole spectrum of the Longest Hamiltonian Paths of any of the $\overleftrightarrow{L_k^-}$, $1 \leq k < n/2-2$ different Longest Euclidean Hamiltonian Path Problems in $N(K_{n=2p+2}(\sqrt[n]{1}),D)$ networks.*

Proof For every k, $1 \leq k < n/2-2$, this statement is straightforward from equation (7), the proof of Theorem 2.2 and Theorem 5.2 .

$\Gamma_{n/2-1}$ and its $n-1$ congruent cycles (Refer to Lemma 3.1 and Theorem 5.2) accomplish $\Lambda(\Gamma_{n/2-1})$. Specifically, they resolve the Longest Euclidean Hamiltonian Cyclic problem in $N(K_{n=2p+2}(\sqrt[n]{1}),D)$ networks [12]. Furthermore, the Longest Euclidean Hamiltonian Paths that solve $\Lambda(\Gamma'_{n/2-1})$ and $\Lambda(\Gamma_{n/2-1})$-$\Lambda(l_{\max})$ are determined from the longest cycles in $N(K_{n=2p+2}(\sqrt[n]{1}),D)$ networks. Optimum Pathway Principle [‡] allows us to establish that every longest C_H^n contains longest P_H^{n-1}s with specific initial and final vertices in $N(K_{n=2p+2}(\sqrt[n]{1}),D)$ networks (see Theorem 6.1 and Theorem 6.2).

Theorem 6.1 *In* $N(K_{n=2p+2}(\sqrt[n]{1}),D)$ *networks there are* $n/2-1$ *Longest Euclidean Hamiltonian Paths* $\overleftrightarrow{l^-_{q_{\max}}}\,;\,\underbrace{l^-_{q_{\max}}}_{j-1} + l_{\max} + \underbrace{l^+_{q_{\max}}}_{n/2-1} + l_{\max} + \underbrace{l^-_{q_{\max}}}_{n/2-j-1}$ *with* $1 \leq j < n/2-1$ *that start at* $V_{n/2-1}$ *and end at* $V_0 = (-1,0)$ *with overall travelled length* $\Lambda(\Gamma'_{n/2-1})$.

Proof From Optimum Pathway Principle and Lemma 3.1 item f) with $i = n/2-1$ and $1 \leq j < n/2-1$ after the putative rooted out of their first $l^-_{q_{\max}}$ side.

Theorem 6.2 In $N(K_{n=2p+2}(\sqrt[n]{1}),D)$ networks there are two Longest Euclidean Hamiltonian Paths $\overleftrightarrow{l_{\max}}\,;+\underbrace{l^-_{q_{\max}}}_{n/2-1} + l_{\max} + \underbrace{l^+_{q_{\max}}}_{n/2-1}$ and $\overleftrightarrow{l_{\max}}\,;\,\underbrace{l^+_{q_{\max}}}_{n/2-1} + l_{\max} + \underbrace{l^-_{q_{\max}}}_{n/2-1} + l_{\max}$ that start at $V_{n/2} = (1,0)$ and end at $V_0 = (-1,0)$ with overall travelled length $\Lambda(\Gamma_{n/2-1})$- $\Lambda(l_{\max})$.

Proof From Optimum Pathway Principle and Lemma 3.1 items e) and f) with $j = 0$, $i = n/2-1$ and after the putative rooted out of their respective first $l_{\max}$ side.

---

‡ Any part of an extremal that yields a minimum (a maximum) is an extremal that yields a minimum (a maximum)

5. Conclusion

This paper is an offspring from the Hamiltonian maximum overall traveled length $\Lambda(\Gamma_k^{'})$ and $\Lambda(\Gamma_{n/2-1})$ theorems demonstrated in [12]. All the Euclidean Hamiltonian pathways that resolve the $n/2$ different maximum traveled Hamiltonian paths of order $n-1$ in $N(K_{n=2p+2}(\sqrt[n]{1}), D)$ networks are singled out. As a by-product of the geometric methodology and regardless of rotations and change of the orientation, the uniqueness, of the Euclidean Hamiltonian cycle that attains the Maximum Traveling Salesman Problem in $N(K_{n=2p+2}(\sqrt[n]{1}), D)$ networks is shown. The approach is a step forward on the intrinsic geometry and inherent arithmetic of the vertex locus in order to capture the spectra of these optimum Hamiltonian in $N(K_{n=2p+2}(\sqrt[n]{1}), D)$ networks. Furthermore, at this point, we point out that our geometric and arithmetic procedure allows us to single out every Hamiltonian path that resolves the $\lfloor n/2 \rfloor$ different Longest non-cyclic Euclidean Hamiltonian Paths in $N(K_{n=2p+1}(\sqrt[n]{1}), D)$ networks [10].

APPENDIX

Alternative process to construct $\Gamma_k^{'}$, for $1 \le k \le \lfloor n/2 \rfloor - 2$ from $\Gamma_{n/2-1}^{'}$. From the proposed methodology, we unravel a representative sequence of any of the Longest Euclidean Hamiltonian Path of order $n-1$ in $N(K_{n=2p+2}(\sqrt[n]{1}), D)$ networks built by a putative L_k^{-} with $1 \le k \le \lfloor n/2 \rfloor - 1$, $k-1$ directed sides $l_{q_{\max}}^{-}$, $n/2-1$ directed segments $l_{q_{\max}}^{+}$ and $(n/2-k+1)$ diameters.

Theorem 2.1 and Lemma 3.1 state that the reiteration of the next process of the lift-offs of $l_{q_{\max}}^{-}$ and $l_{q_{\max}}^{+}$ starting at --; $\overleftrightarrow{l_{q_{\max}}^{-}}$; $\underbrace{l_{q_{\max}}^{-}}_{n/2-3}$; $l_{\max}$; $\overleftrightarrow{l_{q_{\max}}^{+}}$; $\underbrace{l_{q_{\max}}^{+}}_{n/2-2}$; $l_{\max}$, which is the lift-offs in $\Gamma_{n/2-1}^{'}$ symbolized by $\overleftrightarrow{\Gamma_{n/2-1}^{'}}$. The lifting action is followed by the implant of $l_{\max}$ and the relocation of $l_{q_{\max}}^{+}$. These actions bring forth step-by-step the sequences $\Gamma_k^{'}$ from $k = n/2-2$ to $k = 1$, as Euclidean Hamiltonian paths of order $n-1$ in $N(K_{n=2p+2}(\sqrt[n]{1}), D)$ networks.

The following steps should be taken:

- [I)] Let $i = 1$,
- [II)]

$$\{--\}\ \underbrace{l^-_{q_{\max}}}_{n/2-2-i};l_{\max};\ \underbrace{l^+_{q_{\max}}}_{n/2-i-1};\ l_{\max};\ \underbrace{l^+{}_{q_{\max}},l_{\max}}_{i-1},\{--\}\in P_H^{n-3},\ \overleftrightarrow{\Gamma'_{n/2-i=k+1}}\quad 1\le i<n/2-2$$

$$\{--\}\ \underbrace{l^-_{q_{\max}}}_{n/2-2-i};l_{\max};\ \underbrace{l^+_{q_{\max}}}_{n/2-i-1};\ l_{\max};\ \underbrace{l^+{}_{q_{\max}},l_{\max}}_{i},\{--\}\in P_H^{n-1}\ ,\ \Gamma'_{n/2-1-i=k}\quad 1\le i<n/2-2$$

- [III)] Let $i = i+1$, if $i \le n/2-2$ go to II)
  otherwise stop.

References

[1] T. Andreescu and F. Zuming. *A Path to Combinatorics for Undergraduates. Counting Strategies.* Boston, Ed. Birkhauser (2004).

[2] D. Applegate, R.E. Bixby, V. Chavatal and W. J. Cook. *Traveling Salesman Problem: A Computational Study.* Princenton, Princeton University Press (2006).

[3] F. Buckley and F. Harary. *Distance in Graphs.* Redwood City, Addison-Wesley (1990).

[4] H.S.M. Coxeter. *Introduction to Geometry.* New York, John Wiley & Sons, Inc. (1961).

[5] R.O. Dichiara and B.I. Niel. “Networking and Logistic Strategies Enacting Assembling Synergism”. *MS'10 International Conference.* Barcelona (Spain). World Scientific Proceedings Series on Computer Engineering and Information Science 3, p. 313 - 322 (2010).

[6] R.O. Dichiara, B.I. Niel and A. Claverie. “Min. and Max. Traveling Salesman Problems in Bilayered Networks”. *Proceedings of the XV SIGEF Congress*, Universidad de Santiago de Compostela, Lugo, (Spain), October 29-30, 2009, p. 1-20 (2009).

[7] S.P. Fekete, H. Meijer, A. Rohe and W. Tietze. “Solving a Hard Problem to Approximate an Easy One: Heuristics for Maximum Matchings and Maximum

Traveling Salesman Problems". *Journal of Experimental Algorithms.* Vol. 7, No. 11 (2002).

[8] A. Kaufmann and J.G. Aluja Grafos *neuronales para la economía y la gestión de empresas.* Madrid, Pirámide (1995).

[9] A. A. Kirillov "On Regular Polygons, Euler's Function, and Fermat Numbers". Kvant Selecta: Algebra and Analysis. I , p. 87-98, American Mathematical Society, Providence R. I., Serge Tabachnikov (1999).

[10] B.I. Niel, W.A. Reartes and N.B. Brignole "Every Longest Hamiltonian Path in Odd N-gons". *SIAM Conference on Discrete Mathematics.* Austin, Texas, June 14-17 (2010).

[11] B.I. Niel "On a General Method for Finding the Longest Traveling Salesman Paths in Specific Networks" *Proceedings of the XIV SIGEF Congress.* Poaina Brasov, Romania, University of Craiova. Supported by the University of Brasov, November 1-3, pg. 490-503 (2007).

[12] B.I. Niel "Geometry of the Euclidean Hamiltonian Subptimal and Optimal Paths in the $N(K_{n=2p+2}(\sqrt[n]{1}), D)$ Networks. *Proceedings of the VIII Dr. Antonio A. R. Monteiro, Congress of Mathematics,* May 2005, Bahía Blanca, Argentina., p. 67 – 84. Mathematics Department, Universidad Nacional del Sur (2005). Available at http://inmabb.criba.edu.ar/cm/actas/pdf_09niel.pdf.

SOLVING FUZZY MATHEMATICAL PROGRAMMING: A PARAMETRIC APPROACH

RICARDO COELHO SILVA
Institute of Science and Technology, Federal University of São Paulo,
State rua Talim, 330, Vila Nair, 12231-280, São José dos Campos, SP, Brazil.

CARLOS CRUZ CORONA, JOSÉ LUIS VERDEGAY
Dept. Computer Sciences and Artificial Intelligence, University of Granada
Granada, E-18071, Spain

Convex optimization has applications in a wide range of real-world applications, whose data often cannot be formulate precisely. Hence it makes perfect sense to apply fuzzy set theory as a way to mathematically describe this vagueness. In this work we consider the portfolio selection problems, which can be classified as convex programming problems, under uncertain environment. Besides we present a novel fuzzy set based method that solves a class of convex programming problems with vagueness. This proposed method is applied in two portfolio selection numerical examples by using Latibex data of some Brazilian securities.

1. Introduction

The convex programming represents a special class of mathematical programming in which the objective is a convex function or there are various convex functions over a convex feasible set. There are several classes of problems that are naturally expressed as convex problems. Examples of such problems can be found in game theory, engineering modeling, design and control, problems involving economies of scale, facility allocation and location problems, problems in microeconomics among others. Several applications and test problems for quadratic programming can be found in (Floudas et al, 1999; Hock and Schittkowski, 1981; and Schittkowski, 1987). Nowadays we can use highly efficient and robust algorithms and software for convex programming that are important tools for solving problems in diverse fields. However in many real practical applications one lacks of exact knowledge (Klir, 1987), and only approximate, vague and imprecise values are known. Experience shows that the best way of modeling these kinds of problems is using Soft Computing methodologies (Verdegay et al, 2008).

Soft Computing, and Fuzzy Logic in particular, has shown great potential for modeling systems which are non-linear, complex, ill- defined and not well understood. In the fuzzy environment, as it happens in the case of linear programming problems, a variety of fuzzy convex programming problems can be defined: Convex programming problems with a fuzzy objective, i.e., with fuzzy numbers defining the costs of the objective function, convex programming problems with a fuzzy goal, i.e., with some fuzzy value to be attained in the objective, convex programming problems with fuzzy numbers defining the coefficients of the technological matrix and, finally, with a fuzzy constraint set, i.e., with a feasible set defined by fuzzy constraints.

Thus, fuzzy convex programming is applied in a wide range of disciplines, such as risk investment analysis, first introduced by (Markowitz, 1991). It is an important research field in the modern finance. However, vagueness, approximate values and lack of precision are very frequent in that context, and that convex programming problems have shown to be extremely useful to solve a variety of portfolio models. In the following we will present a general solution approach for fuzzy convex programming problems that, if needed, can be easily particularized to solve more specific portfolio models (Carlsson *et al.*, 2002; León et al, 2002; and Tanaka *et al.*, 2000). In any case, it is important to emphasize that the aim of this work is not to solve portfolio models. It was considered only for the sake of illustrating the proposed fuzzy approach, which in fact is the main goal of this contribution.

The paper is organized as follows: Section 2 introduces the proposed method to solve fuzzy convex multi-objective programming problems. The approach uses two parts: the first one transforms the problem to be optimized into a parametric convex multi-objective programming problem while in the second part the parametric problem is solved for a satisfaction level given by means of classical optimization techniques. To illustrate the approach Section 3 offers a general portfolio selection problem formulated as a fuzzy convex multi-objective programming. Section 4 presents numerical simulations and an analysis of the results obtained. Finally in Section 5 some conclusions are pointed out.

2. Fuzzy Linear Programming

Tanaka (1974) defined the concept of fuzzy mathematical programming applying the theory of fuzzy sets to decision problems based on the concept of (Bellman and Zadeh, 1970) for decision making under fuzzy conditions. Negoita and Sularia (1976) used fuzzy logic to solve the problem of turning a system of linear inequalities without a solution into one with a solution by observing some tolerances given at free terms. They showed that the problem of determination of a maximizing decision can be reduced to a mathematical programming problem. Also, Zimmermann (1976, 1978) developed an approach for a symmetric model of fuzzy linear programming where the fuzzy objective and resource constraints were transformed into crisp ones by using tolerance description. In this way, a unique exact optimal solution with highest membership degree can be achieved via the simplex method for crisp linear programming. This type of fuzzy mathematical programming is called flexible programming (Inuiguchi and Ramik, 2000) because the fuzzy goals and constraints represent the flexibility of the target values of objective functions and the elasticity of constraints. An interesting paper where many of these methods were overviewed is by (Zimmermann, 1985).

While flexible programming deals with right-hand side uncertainties, there are another types of fuzzy mathematical programming with fuzzy parameters and where the fuzzy coefficients can be regarded as possibility distributions on coefficients values is called possibilistic programming. Dubois and Prade (1980) defined the linear fuzzy constraints where coefficients were fuzzy numbers for the first time, extending the classical linear constraints with tolerance constraints or approximate (in)equality constraints. Later other authors proposed treatments of linear programming problems with fuzzy coefficients as (Tanaka and Asai, 1984; and Tanaka *et al.*, 1984), (Orlovski, 1984) and (Ramik and Rimanek, 1985). Dubois and Prade developed several remarkable approaches (Dubois, 1987; Dubois and Prade, 1983 and 1988) to such kind of problems based on the possibility theory (Zadeh, 1978) into mathematical programming problems with fuzzy coefficients.

There are several interesting classifications of fuzzy mathematical programming such as: the first was made by Zimmermann into symmetrical when the relationship between constraints and objective functions are fully symmetrical, i.e. there is no longer a difference between the former and the latter, and nonsymmetrical models when the objective function is a crisp set and the constraint is a fuzzy set (Zimmermann, 1985 and 1987; Zimmermann and Zysno, 1985). Yee (1988) made a classification into four categories: precise objective and fuzzy constraints, fuzzy objectives and precise constraints, a fuzzy objective and fuzzy constraints, robust programming considered as one of the possibilistic mathematical problems. Luhandjula (1989) used three categories: flexible programming with symmetrical and nonsymmetrical methods as Zimmermann did, mathematical programming problems with fuzzy parameters grouped into problems with deterministic objective function and problems with a fuzzy objective function, and stochastic programming that involves the parameters with fuzzy and stochastic natures. Inuiguchi *et al.* (1994) consider that two major different kinds of uncertainties, ambiguity and vagueness exist in the real life. They classify into three categories: fuzzy mathematical programming with vagueness, fuzzy mathematical programming with ambiguity, and fuzzy mathematical programming with vagueness and ambiguity. While ambiguity is associated with one-to-many relations, that is, situations in which the choice between two or more alternatives is left unspecified, vagueness is associated with the difficulty of making sharp or precise distinctions in the world; that is, some domain of interest is vague if it cannot be delimited by sharp boundaries.

Lai and Hwang (1992) also used a problem-oriented classification distinguishing fuzzy linear programming and possibilistic linear programming as follows:

- Fuzzy linear programming in five problems based on possible combinations of the fuzziness of matrix coefficients (A), independent term (b), costs (c) and/or relations of the objective function (z), and also an expert decision making support system which integrates all possible last combinations;
- Possibilistic linear programming in four problems based on possible combinations of the imprecision of matrix coefficients (A), independent term (b), costs (c) and/or relations of the objective function (z). Also, the problems in which some coefficients have preference-based membership functions and others have possibilistic distribution are included here.

The area of fuzzy mathematical programming, as indicated by (Lai and Hwang, 1992; Shinidis, 2004), has been productive and applied to many disciplines, leave out transportation, production planning, water supply planning and resource management, forest management, bank management, portfolio selection, pattern classification, and others when using such as.

In many actual problems cannot be adequately represented as a linear program because of the nature of the nonlinearity of the objective function and/or the nonlinearity of any of the constraints. Among these nonlinear systems are those known as quadratic programming problems that will be explained in the next section.

3. Fuzzy Quadratic Programming

Quadratic programming represents a special class of nonlinear programming in which the objective function is quadratic and the constraints are linear. Thus, quadratic programming problems can be formalized in the following form:

Let x belongs to R^n space, a symmetric $n \times n$ matrix Q, and an $n \times 1$ vector c. Then,
Minimize (with respect to x)

$$\min \quad c^t x + \tfrac{1}{2} x^t Q x \qquad (1)$$

Subject to one or more constraints of the form:

$$Ax \leq b \text{ (inequality constraint); } Ex = d \text{ (equality constraint)} \qquad (2)$$

where the notation $Ax \leq b$ means that every entry of the vector Ax is less than or equal to the corresponding entry of the vector b.

Several methods are available in the literature (Wolfe, 1959; and Beale, 1959) for solving such problems. An interesting web page about quadratic programming is (Gould and Toint). Quadratic programming can be viewed as a generalization of the linear programming problems with a quadratic objective function, and as it happens in the case of the real world linear problems their parameters are seldom known exactly and have to be estimated by the decision maker. Therefore the application of the fuzzy logic is a way to describe this vagueness mathematically. Uncertainties can be found in the relation, constants, decision variables or in all parameters of the problem and a variety of fuzzy quadratic programming problems can be defined:

- Quadratic programming problems with a fuzzy objective, i.e. with fuzzy numbers defining the costs of the objective function;
- Quadratic programming problems with a fuzzy goal, i.e. with some fuzzy value to be attained in the objective;
- Quadratic programming problems with fuzzy numbers defining the coefficients of the technological matrix; and
- with a fuzzy constraint set, i.e. with a feasible set defined by fuzzy constraints.

Several authors have applied Soft Computing methodologies to quadratic programming. Thus, Tang and Wang (1997) proposed an interactive approach for a type of model of quadratic programming problems with different types of membership functions in accordance with the different types of fuzzy objective and fuzzy resource constraints in production problems. The authors introduced the concept of fuzzy optimal solution which is a neighbor domain including the optimal solution such that the satisfaction degree of every solution in the neighbor domain is acceptable, namely it is an 'optimal' solution under fuzzy environment. Then, a Genetic Algorithm with mutation along the weighted gradient direction is used to find a family of solutions with acceptable membership degree but also the solutions preferred by decision maker under different criteria can be achieved by means of the human-computer interaction.

Giove (2006) proposed an iterative algorithm for fuzzy non linear programming problems and under the hypothesis that a solution exists for a corresponding crisp sub-problem. Based on some natural hypotheses on the membership functions, on the target and on the constraints, the convergence of the algorithm is assured in a finite number of steps modifying the admissible region in such a way as to increase at each step the global performance. The algorithm is applied to a simple instance of two-dimensional quadratic problem with linear constraints, showing good numerical performances.

Xu *et al.* (2005) investigated the decision-making problem with a finite set of alternatives, in which the decision information takes the form of a fuzzy preference relation and a priority vector is obtained. They developed a practical approach to obtain the priority vector by a simple formula, which is derived from a quadratic programming model. They utilized the consistency ratio to check the consistency of fuzzy preference relation. If the fuzzy preference relation is of unacceptable consistency, then it is can be returned to the decision maker to reconsider structuring a new fuzzy preference relation until the fuzzy preference relation with acceptable consistency is obtained. The priority approach is illustrated by two numerical examples.

One the problem most used to show the application and efficiency of the quadratic mathematical programming methods is the portfolio selection problem. The classical portfolio selection problem was formulated by (Markowitz, 1952) as a quadratic programming problem, based on time series of the return rate. The mean-variance approach decides the best investing rate to each investment, which minimizes the risk or the variance of the profits to affirm the least rate of the expected return, which a decision maker expects.

This classical mean–variance model is a well-established method, which provides good results. However, it is also well known that the sample average is not always the best option for describing a data set. Fuzzy methodology allows to incorporate uncertainty into databases and also to incorporate subjective characteristics into the models, which are basic aspects for establishing different estimations of risk and expected return. Thus, the imperfect knowledge of the returns on the assets and the uncertainty involved in the behavior of financial markets may also be introduced by means of fuzzy quantities and/or fuzzy constraints.

Watada (1997) presented the fuzzy portfolio selection problem introducing vague and uncertain goals for the expected return rate and risk. Tanaka *et al.* (2000) used possibility distributions to model uncertainty in the returns of securities associated with possibility grades offered by portfolio experts, reflecting the degree of similarity between the future state of stock markets and the state of previous periods. The average vector and covariance matrix in Markowitz's model were replaced with the weighted average vector and covariance matrix by the expert judgment. Comparing a fuzzy probability method and a possibility method, the simulation results shown that the possibility model was more suitable than the fuzzy probability one in real investment problems.

Inuiguchi and Ramik (2000), also used possibilistic fuzzy mathematical programming approaches in the setting of an optimal portfolio selection problem showing the advantages in the tractability of the reduced problem over the stochastic programming approaches.

Liern *et al.* (2002) proposed a specialization of a fuzzy method to repair infeasibility in linearly constrained problems usually provoked by the conflict between the desired return and the diversification requirements proposed by the investor. They take into account the special structure of the constraints in the linear and quadratic programming models for the portfolio selection problem, in such a way that the diversification and the expected return conditions are considered as soft constraints, while the remaining are hard constraints. Investor opinion is used in the end stage to select a portfolio in the framework of trade-off analysis.

Ammar and Khalifa (2003) investigated the fuzzy portfolio optimization problem as a convex quadratic programming approach. The concept of fuzzy optimal solution was developed in this work where these fuzzy solutions were characterized by fuzzy numbers.

Recently, Vercher *et al.* (2007) presented two fuzzy portfolio selection models where the objective is to minimize the downside risk constrained by a given expected return. They assumed that the rates of returns on securities are approximated as LR-fuzzy numbers of the same shape, and that the expected return and risk are evaluated by interval-valued means. The relationship between those mean-interval definitions for a given fuzzy portfolio is established by using suitable ordering relations. Finally, the portfolio selection problem is formulated as a linear program when the returns on the assets are of trapezoidal form.

4. Parametric Convex Programming Approaches

There are several approaches that solve fuzzy mathematical programming problems, see (Bector and Chandra, 2005; Lai and Hwang, 1992), which use some defuzzification index, represent the fuzzy coefficients by intervals or transform this fuzzy problem into a parametric mathematical programming problem. The main goal is to transform this imprecise problem into a classical problem and using classical techniques to solve the equivalent problem. In this work, we will focus on the parametric approach in order to transform fuzzy problems into many classical problems with a parameter representing the satisfaction level, which belongs to the interval [0,1]. Another way would be defining a new parameter as a new decision variable and to find out the optimal satisfaction level. However, due to space limitations we will not consider this approach. The parametric approaches are divided into two parts: transforming a fuzzy problem into a classical parametric problem; a mathematical formulation of the classical parametric problem that is equivalent to the original fuzzy problem.

4.1. *Convex programming problems with fuzzy relations*

A quadratic programming problem with fuzzy relations can be formulated on the following way:

$$\begin{aligned} \min \quad & c^t x + \tfrac{1}{2} x^t Q x \\ \text{s.t.} \quad & Ax \leq^f x \\ & x \geq 0 \end{aligned} \tag{3}$$

where the vagueness is represented for membership functions defined by decision maker.

As in (Cruz et al, 2011, Silva et al, 2007; Silva et al, 2010), the constraints of a quadratic problem are defined with fuzzy nature, that is, some violations in the accomplishment of such restrictions are permitted. Therefore if we denote each constraint $\sum_{j \in J} a_{ij} x_j$, by $(Ax)_i$, the problem can be addressed as follows:

$$\begin{aligned} \min \quad & c^t x + \tfrac{1}{2} x^t Q x \\ \text{s.t.} \quad & (Ax)_i \leq^f b_i,\ i \in I \\ & x_j \geq 0,\ j \in J \end{aligned} \tag{4}$$

where $I = \{1,2,\ldots m\}$ that determines the set of constraints, $J = \{1,2,\ldots n\}$ that represents the decision space and the membership functions

$$\mu_i : \Re^n \rightarrow (0,1],\ i \in I$$

on the fuzzy constraints are given by the decision maker. It is clear that each membership function will give the membership (satisfaction) degree such that any $x \in R^n$ accomplishes the corresponding fuzzy constraint upon which it is defined. This degree is equal to 1 when the constraint is perfectly accomplished (no violation), and decreases to zero for greater violations. For non-admissible violations the accomplishment degree will equal zero in all cases. In the linear case (and formally also in the non linear one), these membership functions can be formulated as follows

$$\mu_i(x(1-\alpha)) = \begin{cases} 1 & (Ax)_i \le b_i \\ 1 - \dfrac{(Ax)_i - b_i}{d_i} & b_i \le (Ax)_i \le b_i + d_i \\ 0 & (Ax)_i \ge b_i + d_i \end{cases}$$

In order to solve this problem in a two-phase method, first let us define for each fuzzy constraint, $i \in I$

$$X_i = \{x \in \Re^n \mid (Ax)_i \le^f b_i, x \ge 0\}$$

If $X = \bigcap X_i$ then the former fuzzy quadratic problem can be addressed in a compact form as

$$\min \ \{c'x + \tfrac{1}{2}x'Qx \mid x \in X\}$$

It is clear that for any $\alpha \in (0,1]$, an α-cut of the fuzzy constraint set will be the classical set

$$X(\alpha) = \{x \in \Re^n \mid \mu_X(x) \ge \alpha\}$$

where for any $x \in R^n$,

$$\mu_X(x) = \inf \mu_i(x(1-\alpha)), i \in I$$

Hence an α-cut of the i-th constraint will be denoted by $X(\alpha)$. Therefore, if for any $\alpha \in (0,1]$,

$$S(\alpha) = \{x \in \Re^n \mid c^t x + \tfrac{1}{2}x^t Qx = \min c^t y + \tfrac{1}{2}y^t Qy,\ y \in X(\alpha)\}$$

the fuzzy solution to the problem will therefore be the fuzzy set defined by the following membership function:

$$S(\alpha) = \begin{cases} \sup\{\alpha : x \in S(\alpha)\} & x \in \bigcup_{\alpha} S(a) \\ 0 & \text{otherwise.} \end{cases}$$

Provided that for any $\alpha \in (0,1]$,

$$X(\alpha) = \bigcap_{i \in I} \{x \in \Re^n \mid (Ax)_i \le r_i(\alpha),\ x \ge 0\}$$

with $r_i(\alpha) = b_i + d_i(1-\alpha)$. The operative solution to the former problem can be found, α-cut by α-cut, by means of the following auxiliary parametric quadratic programming model,

$$\begin{aligned} \min \quad & c^t x + \tfrac{1}{2} x^t Q x \\ \text{s.t.} \quad & (Ax)_i \le b_i + d_i(1-\alpha), i \in I \\ & x_j \ge 0,\ j \in J, \alpha \in (0,1]. \end{aligned} \qquad (5)$$

Thus, the fuzzy quadratic programming problem is parameterized at the end of the first phase.

In the second phase the parametric quadratic programming problem is solved for each of the different α values using conventional quadratic programming techniques. We must find solutions to Problem (5) for each α that satisfies Karush-Kuhn-Tucker's necessary and sufficient optimality conditions.

The obtained results for each α value generate a set of solutions and then the Representation Theorem can be used to integrate all these specific α-solutions. It is then demonstrated that the outlined solution to the parametric method is a valid solution to the fuzzy quadratic problem.

Proposition: If (x^*, α) is the optimal solution to Problem (5) then $x^*(\alpha)$ is a unique solution for each value of $\alpha \in (0,1]$ of the set of optimal solutions to Problem (4).

Proof

- If we suppose that $x^*(\alpha)$ is not unique, then there exists another $x^0(\alpha) \in X(\alpha)$ to the same α. Since at least one constraint of Problem (5) is active, then $x^*(\alpha) = (A^t A)^{-1} A^t (b + d(1-\alpha))$ and $x^0(\alpha) = (A^t A)^{-1} A^t (b + d(1-\alpha))$ to the same α. Thus, $x^0(\alpha) = x^*(\alpha)$ is a contradiction.

Suppose $x^*(\alpha_1)=x^*(\alpha_2)$ with $\alpha_1 \neq \alpha_2$. Then,

$$(A^tA)^{-1}A^t(b+d(1-\alpha_1))=(A^tA)^{-1}A^t(b+d(1-\alpha_2))$$
$$A^t(b+d(1-\alpha_1))=A^t(b+d(1-\alpha_2))$$
$$A^t(b+d(1-\alpha_1)-b-d(1-\alpha_2))=0$$
$$A^td(\alpha_2-\alpha_1)=0$$

and as $d \neq 0$, then $\alpha_1=\alpha_2$ is a contradiction.

4.2. *Convex programming problems with fuzzy costs*

A multi-objective approach that solves a fuzzy linear programming problem with imprecise costs in the objective functions is presented in (Verdegay et al, 1987 and 1990). This approach can be extended to solve nonlinear programming problems with one or several objectives. In (Jiménez, 2006), another multi-objective approach is developed that solves nonlinear programming problems with only one objective with imprecise coefficients in the objective function and in the set of constraints. But it can be extended to solve fuzzy multi-objective problems too.

In this work, multi-objective programming problems with fuzzy costs in the objective functions are formulated in the following way:

$$\begin{array}{ll} \min & [f_1(\tilde{c}_1;x), f_2(\tilde{c}_2;x),\ldots,f_m(\tilde{c}_m;x)] \\ s.t. & x \in \Omega \end{array} \tag{6}$$

where x is an n vector of real numbers, the cost vector is formed by fuzzy numbers with p_i components, $i = \{1, 2, \ldots, m\}$. The fuzzy numbers are characterized by the membership functions that are defined by the decision maker. The membership functions are defined as:

$$\mu_j(y)=\begin{cases} 0 & \text{if } c_j^U < y \text{ or } y < c_j^L \\ L_j(y) & \text{if } c_j^L \le y \le c_j^1 \\ R_j(y) & \text{if } c_j^2 \le y \le c_j^U \end{cases} \qquad j \in J \tag{7}$$

where L(·) and R(·) are strictly increasing and decreasing continuous functions, respectively, $L_j(c_j^1) = R_j(c_j^2)$, $j \in J$.

The problem considered in (Verdegay *et al.*, 1987) presents trapezoidal membership functions to describe the fuzzy numbers. In this work, we consider it as defined in (7).

Thus, according to the parametric transformations shown above, a fuzzy solution to a fuzzy problem can be obtained from a parametric solution of a equivalent parametric multi-objective programming problem which is formulated as:

$$\begin{array}{ll} & [f_1(c^1{}_1;x), f_1(c_1^2;x), \ldots, f_1(c_1^{2^{p_1}};x), \\ \min & f_2(c^1{}_2;x), f_1(c_2^2;x), \ldots, f_1(c_2^{2^{p_2}};x), \ldots, \\ & f_m(c^1{}_m;x), f_m(c_m^2;x), \ldots, f_m(c_m^{2^{p_m}};x)] \\ s.t. & x \in \Omega, c^k \in E(1-\alpha), \alpha \in [0,1], \\ & k = 1,2,\ldots,2^{p_j} \end{array} \tag{8}$$

where E(1 – α), for each α Є [0, 1], is the set of vectors in R_j^p, such that p_j informs the amount of fuzzy numbers that represent the imprecise costs in each objective function, for j Є {1,2,...,m}.

Each (1 – α)-cut level element of this set is in the lower bound, L^{-1} (1 – α), or in the upper bound, R^{-1} (1 – α), i.e., and k = 1,2,..., 2_j^p,

$$c^k = (c_1^k, c_2^k, \ldots, c_m^k) \in E(1-\alpha)$$

where c^k is equal to L^{-1} (1 – α), or R^{-1} (1 – α), for all j = 1,...,m.

It is clear that a parametric optimal solution to (4) is part of the fuzzy optimal solution to (2). This approach was developed to the convex case with one only objective, as described in (Silva et al, 2009), and here is extended to the convex case with several objectives. The parametric optimal solutions can be obtained by using any optimization method to solve classical multi-objective programming problems.

5. Portfolio Selection Problem

In order to illustrate the above described parametric method to solve fuzzy convex programming problems, we are going to focus on general portfolio problems. It is important to emphasize that, at the present time, we do not try to improve other solution methods for this kind of important problems, but only to show how our solution approach per- forms. In (Markowitz, 1987), a description of a classical portfolio selection problem is given that was formulated by Markowitz as a convex programming problem.

Markowitz's model combines probability and optimization techniques to model the behavior of investment under uncertainty. The investors are assumed to strike a balance between minimizing the risk and maximizing the return of their investment. The risk is characterized by the variance, and the return is quantified by the mean, of a portfolio of assets. The two objectives of an investor are thus to minimize the variance of a portfolio and to maximize the expected value of return.

Markowitz model for portfolio selection can be formulated mathematically in two ways: minimizing risk when a level of return is given and maximizing return when a level of risk is given. Hence, assume that there are n securities denoted by S_j ($j = 1, \ldots, n$), the former problem is formulated on the following way:

$$\begin{array}{ll} \min & x'\Sigma x \\ \text{s.t.} & E(R)x \geq^f \rho \\ & 1x = 1 \\ & x \geq 0 \end{array} \qquad (9)$$

where x is an n vector that represents the percentage of money invested in asset, i.e., the proportion of total investment funds devoted to each security; E(R) is the average vector of returns over m periods because R = $[r_{ij}]$ is an $m \times n$ matrix that represents the random variables of the returns of asset varying in m discrete times; ρ is a parameter representing the minimal rate of return required by an investor; and Σ is the covariance matrix of returns over m periods.

On the other hand, the latter problem is formulated as:

$$\begin{array}{ll} \min & x'\Sigma x \\ \text{s.t.} & E(R)x \geq \rho + d(1-\alpha) \\ & 1x = 1 \\ & x \geq 0 \end{array} \qquad (10)$$

where γ is the maximum risk level the investor would bear. The expected return rate, ρ, and the maximum risk level, γ, are decision maker's values that represent an expert's knowledge. These two formulations of portfolio selection problems can be mixed and formulated as a bi-objective convex programming problem. Moreover, uncertainty and multiple objectives are the important factors in decision making. From a practical viewpoint, it is usually difficult to determine exactly the coefficients in mathematical programming problems due to various kinds of uncertainties. However, it is sometimes possible to estimate the perturbations of coefficients by intervals, fuzzy numbers or possibilistic distributions. The portfolio problem is a typical decision making problem under uncertainty which has received considerable attention in the literature recently. This problem addresses the dilemma that each investor faces the conflicting objectives of high profit versus low risk. In this work, the uncertainties in the objective functions are represented by fuzzy costs and the fuzzy bi-objective portfolio selection problem can be formulated in the following way:

$$\begin{aligned} \min \quad & x'\Sigma x \\ \max \quad & E(R)x \\ \text{s.t.} \quad & 1x = 1 \\ & x \geq 0 \end{aligned} \tag{11}$$

There are many formulations to describe a portfolio selection problem that are more realistic than one was presented in this work. One of them is to put another objective function called "Value at Risk", as described in (Jorion, 2006). It is defined as a threshold value, which is a given probability level of the worse loss on the portfolio over the given time horizon. However, we choose this convex formulation to show the efficiency of our approach, and we will extend it to apply in other formulations in the next step.

6. Numerical Examples

In this section, two portfolio selection problems with fuzzy costs are analyzed. In subsection 6.1 we will show the used data to formulate the fuzzy portfolio problems. Then in subsection 6.2 the computational results and a comparative analysis of the classic and parametric approaches responses will be presented.

The tests were all performed on a PC with 2.26GHZ Intel Core 2 Duo processor, 4GB RAM running Ubuntu 9.10 operational system. All the problems presented in this work were resolved using NSGA-II evolutionary algorithm [5] which was implemented in MATLAB 7.8.0 program. The evolutionary algorithm parameters are 100 generations and 100 individuals in the population, while the crossover and mutation index are 0.6 and 0.3, respectively.

6.1. *Formulation of the Numerical Examples*

In order to show the performance of our method, we used the set of historical data shown in Table I took by Latibex that is an international market for a Latin American securities and it is regulated by the Spanish Securities

Market Law. It was chosen five Brazilian securities and the columns 2-6 represent Eletrobras, Cemig, Copel, Vale Rio and Petrobras securities data, respectively. The returns on the five securities, during the period of January 2004 up to January 2010, are presented in Table I.

Table 1. Fuzzy portfolio selection problem

Periods	#1 Eletrobras	#2 Cemig	#3 Copel	#4 Vale Rio	#5 Petrobras
Jan/2004	-0.0391	0.0288	-0.0106	0.0485	0.1365
Apr/2004	-0.0475	-0.0450	-0.1662	-0.0715	0.0087
Jul/2004	-0.2438	-0.0707	-0.1415	-0.2084	-0.1833
Oct/2004	0.5294	0.4058	0.1273	-0.4863	0.3933
Jan/2005	-0.2338	-0.0662	-0.0100	0.0239	-0.0673
Apr/2005	0.0241	0.1815	0.2617	0.2240	0.1708
Jul/2005	-0.0039	0.2344	0.1809	0.0352	0.2716
Oct/2005	0.4665	0.2533	0.3604	0.4286	0.2936
Jan/2006	0.0376	0.1208	0.1258	0.0533	0.1313
Apr/2006	0.2264	0.1066	0.2044	0.1149	0.1670
Jul/2006	-0.1762	-0.1320	-0.0989	-0.1127	-0.0807
Oct/2006	0.0960	-0.0723	0.2398	-0.0940	-0.0752
Jan/2007	-0.0105	0.2027	-0.0109	0.3385	0.2525
Apr/2007	-0.0177	-0.0115	-0.0088	0.2958	-0.0530
Jul/2007	0.2608	-0.5770	0.4326	0.1798	0.2147
Oct/2007	-0.0305	-0.0536	-0.1409	0.3884	0.1540
Jan/2008	-0.1396	-0.1496	-0.0824	-0.0607	0.4277
Apr/2008	0.1291	-0.0214	0.1293	-0.0011	-0.1385
Jul/2008	0.0121	0.2413	0.1119	-0.0768	0.2647
Oct/2008	-0.1210	-0.0881	-0.2327	-0.3434	-0.3127
Jan/2009	-0.0933	-0.2625	-0.1783	-0.2142	-0.3571
Apr/2009	0.0502	0.1212	0.0037	-0.0177	0.1848
Jul/2009	0.1386	-0.1574	0.2634	0.2629	0.2561
Oct/2009	0.0189	0.0698	0.2183	0.2900	0.1267
Jan/2010	0.3666	0.2303	0.2760	0.2690	0.1206

This example will consider performance of portfolios with respect to "return" and "risk". This assumes that a euro of realized or unrealized capital gains is exactly equivalent to one euro of dividends, no better and no worse. This assumption is appropriate for certain investors, for example, some types of tax-free institutions. Other ways of handling capital gains and dividends, which are appropriate for other investors, can be viewed in (Markowitz, 1987).

6.2. *Results and Analysis*

The problems described in this work were solved by using the equivalent parametric multi-objective problem as presented in Section 4. The data from Latibex shown in Table 1 was used on two ways: (i) the order relations of the set of constraints are imprecise; (ii) only linear objective function that maximizes the return has imprecise costs.

Table 2. Results of the first phase of the portfolio selection problem

Satisfaction	Decision variables					Solutions
0.0	0.2195	0.4872	0.0035	0.2897	0.0000	0.0213
0.1	0.2045	0.5180	0.0000	0.2775	0.0000	0.0217
0.2	0.1800	0.5523	0.0000	0.2677	0.0000	0.0223
0.3	0.1555	0.5866	0.0000	0.2579	0.0000	0.0229
0.4	0.1310	0.6208	0.0000	0.2481	0.0000	0.0237
0.5	0.1065	0.6551	0.0000	0.2384	0.0000	0.0246
0.6	0.0820	0.6894	0.0000	0.2286	0.0000	0.0256
0.7	0.0575	0.7237	0.0000	0.2188	0.0000	0.0267
0.8	0.0330	0.7580	0.0000	0.2090	0.0000	0.0279
0.9	0.0085	0.7923	0.0000	0.1993	0.0000	0.0292
1.0	0.0000	0.8252	0.0000	0.1748	0.0000	0.0306

This example will consider performances of portfolios with respect to "return" thus defined. This assumes that a dollar of realized or unrealized capital gains is exactly equivalent to a dollar of dividends, no better and no worse. This assumption is appropriate for certain investors, for example, some types of tax-free institutions. Other ways of handling capital gains and dividends, which are appropriate for other investors.

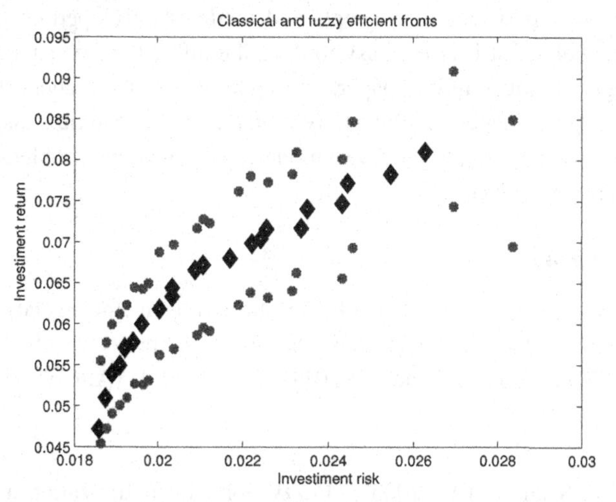

Figure 1. The classical efficient solutions are represented by black diamonds while fuzzy efficient solutions are in the belt dormed by gray points

7. Conclusions

Convex Programming problems are very important in a variety of both theoretical and practical areas. When real-world applications are considered, the vagueness appears in a natural way, and hence it makes perfect sense to think in Fuzzy Convex Programming problems. In contrast to what happens with Fuzzy Linear Programming problems, unfortunately until now no solution method has been found for this important class of problems. In this context this paper has presented two operative and novel methods for solving Convex Programming problems with fuzzy order relations or fuzzy costs. These methods are carried out by performing two phases that finally provide the user with a fuzzy solution. The methods have been validated by solving a portfolio selection problem. The obtained solutions allow the authors to follow along this research line trying to solve real problems in practice, in such a way that oriented Decision Support Systems involving Fuzzy Convex Programming problems can be built.

This paper shows also a general view about fuzzy linear mathematical programming. Afterwards, Fuzzy quadratic mathematical programming is reviewed, and some known methods that were developed to solve quadratic problems with uncertainties in the relationships and coefficients are described.

The methods have been illustrated by solving example problems. This study is only a first approach to the fuzzy quadratic mathematical programming. It tries to give a state-of-art survey of concepts and methods developed concerning to this emergent field. But it is not easy to describe all of the fuzzy mathematical programming techniques in one paper. We apologize to the readers if we have omitted any relevant papers. If this study motivates to researchers and decision makers to use and investigate the fuzzy modeling to quadratic problems then the aim of the paper will be completed.

Acknowledgements

The authors would like to thank the support from the agency FAPESP (project number 2010/51069-2) and the Spanish projects TIC-02970-JA, TIN2008-06872-C04-04/TIN and TIN2011-27696-C02-01 (ASCETAS)

References

1. Ammar E, Khalifa HA. (2003). "Fuzzy portfolio optimization a quadratic programming approach". *Chaos, Solitons and Fractals*.18:1045-1054.

2. Beale E. (1959). "On quadratic programming". *Naval Research Logistics Quarterly*. 6:227-244.

3. Bector CR, Chandra S. (2005). "Fuzzy mathematical programming and fuzzy matrix games". *Studies in Fuzziness and Soft Computing*. Springer, Berlin, 169.

4. Bellman R.E., Zadeh L.A. (1970). "Decision-making in a fuzzy environment". *Management Science, Application Series*; 17(4): B141-B164.

5. Carlsson, C., Fullér, R., and Majlender, P. (2002) "A possibilistic approach to selecting portfolio with highest utility score," *Fuzzy Sets and Systems*, 131:13-21.

6. Cruz, C. Silva, RC and Verdegay, JL. (2011). "Extending and relating different approaches for solving fuzzy quadratic problems". *Fuzzy Optimization and Decision Making*. Volume 10, Number 3, 193-210.

7. Delgado, M., Verdegay, JL., and Vila, M. (1987). "Imprecise costs in mathematical programming problems". *Control and Cybernetics*. 16:2, 113-121.

8. Delgado, M., Verdegay, JL., and Vila, M. (1990). "Relating different approaches to solve linear programming problems with imprecise costs". *Fuzzy Sets and Systems*. Volume 37, 33-42.

9. Dubois D. (1987). "Linear programming with fuzzy data". In, *Analysis of fuzzy information: Applications in engineering.and science*, CRC Press, Boca Raton, FL; 3: 241-263.

10. Dubois D, Prade H. (1980). "Systems of linear fuzzy constraints". *Fuzzy Sets and Syst*. 3: 37-48.

11. Dubois D, Prade H. (1983). "Ranking fuzzy numbers in the setting of possibility theory". *Inform Sci.* 30:183-224.
12. Dubois D, Prade H. (1988). *Possibility theory: An approach to computerized processing of uncertainty.* Plenum Press, New York.
13. Floudas CA, Pardalos P, Adjiman C, *et al.* (1999). *Handbook of test problems in local and global optimization, Nonconvex Optimization and its Applications.* Kluwer Academic Publishers, Dordrecht; 33.
14. Giove S. (2006). "An iterative algorithm for fuzzy quadratic programming problems". In, *Lecture Notes in Artificial Intelligence*, Springer-Verlag Berlin Heidelberg; 2955: 133-139.
15. Gould N, Toint P. A quadratic programming page. Available at: www.numerical.rl.ac.uk/qp/qp.html.
16. Hock W, Schittkowski K. (1981). "Test examples for nonlinear programming codes". In, *Lecture Notes in Economics and Mathematical Systems.* Springer-Verlag; 187.
17. Inuiguchi M, Sakawa M, Kume Y. (1994). "The usefulness of possibilistic programming in production planning problems". *Int J Prod Economics.* 33:45-52.
18. Inuiguchi M, Ramik J. (2000). "Possibilistic linear programming: A brief review of fuzzy mathematical programming and a comparison with stochastic programming in portfolio selection problem". *Fuzzy Sets and Syst.* 111(1):3-28.
19. Jiménez, F., Cadenas, J., Sánches, G., Gómez-Skarmeta, A, and Verdegay, J.L. (2006). "Multi-objective evolutionary computation and fuzzy optimization". *International Journal of Approximate Reasoning.*43(1):59-75.
20. Jorion, P. *Value Risk: The New Benchmark for Managing Financial Risk*, 3rd ed., McGraw Hill, 2006.
21. Klir G (1987). "Where do we stand on measures of uncertainty, ambiguity, fuzziness, and the like". *Fuzzy Sets and Systems.* 24:141-160.
22. Lai YJ, Hwang CL (1992). "Fuzzy mathematical programming : Methods and applications". In, *Lecture Notes in Economics and Mathematical Systems.* volume 394. Springer, Berlin.
23. Leon T, Liern V, Vercher E. (2002). "Viability of infeasible portfolio selection problems: A fuzzy approach". *Eur J Oper Res.*139:178-189.
24. Luhandjula MK. (1989). "Fuzzy optimization: An appraisal". *Fuzzy Sets Syst.* 30(3):257-282.
25. Markowitz H. (1952). Portfolio selection. J Finance; 7(1):77-91
26. Markowitz H. (1991). *Portfolio Selection: Efficient Diversification of Investiments.* 2nd ed. Massachussetts, USA: Blackwell Publisher.
27. Negoita C, Sularia M. (1976). "On fuzzy mathematical programming and tolerances in planning". *Econ Comput Econ Cybern Stud Res.* 1:3-15.
28. Orlovsky S. (1984). "Multiobjective programming problems with fuzzy parameters". *Control Cybernet.*13(3):175-183.
29. Ramik J, Rimanek J. (1985). "Inequality relation between fuzzy numbers and its use in fuzzy optimization". *Fuzzy Sets and Systems.* 16:123-138.

30. Schittkowski K. (1987). "More test examples for nonlinear programming codes". In, *Lecture Notes in Economics and Mathematical Systems*. Spring-Verlag; 282.

31. Silva RC, Cruz, C., Yamakami A. (2009). "A parametric to solve quadratic programming problems with fuzzy costs". *Proceedings of IFSA/EUSFLAT 2009*, Lisbon, Portugal; 1-6.

32. Silva RC, Verdegay JL, Yamakami A. (2007). "Two-phase method to solve fuzzy quadratic programming problems". *Proceedings of FUZZ-IEEE 2007 IEEE International Conference Fuzzy Systems*, London, UK; 1-6.

33. Silva, RC., Cruz, C., Verdegay, JL. and Yamakami, A. (2010). "A Survey of Fuzzy Convex Programming Models". *Fuzzy Optimization, Studies in Fuzziness and Soft Computing*, Volume 254/2010, 127-143

34. Tanaka H, Okuda T, Asai K (1974)."On fuzzy-mathematical programming". *J Cybernetics*.1(4):37-46.

35. Tanaka H, Asai K. (1984). "Fuzzy linear programming problems with fuzzy numbers". *Fuzzy Sets and Syst* 1984;13: 1-10.

36. Tanaka H, Ichihashi H, Asai K. (1984). "A formulation of fuzzy linear programming problem based on comparison of fuzzy numbers". *Control Cybernet.* 13:185-194.

37. Tanaka H, Guo P, Täurksen B. (2000). "Portfolio selection based on fuzzy probabilities and possibity distributions". *Fuzzy Sets and Syst.* 111:387-397.

38. Tang J, Wang D. (1997). "An interactive approach based on a genetic algorithm for a type of quadratic programming problems with fuzzy objective and resources". *Comp and Oper Res.* 24(5):413-422.

39. Sahinidis N. (2004). "Optimization under uncertainty: State-of-the-art and opportunities". *Computers and Chemical Engineering*. 28(6-7):971-983.

40. Vercher E, Bermúdez JD, Segura JV. (2007). "Fuzzy portfolio optimization under downside risk measures". *Fuzzy Sets Syst.* 158(7):769-782.

41. Verdegay JL, Yager RR, Bonissone PP (2008). "On heuristics as a fundamental constituent of soft computing". *Fuzzy Sets and Sys.* 159(7):846-855.

42. Watada J. (1997). "Fuzzy portfolio selection and its applications to decision making". *Tatra Mountains Mathematics Publication*. 13: 219-248.

43. Wolfe P. (1959)." The simplex method for quadratic programming". *Econometrica*. 27:382-398.

44. Xu Z, Da Q, Chen Q. (2005). "Priority approach based on quadratic programming model to fuzzy preference relation". *J Southeast Univ (English Edition)*. 21(1):108-110.

45. Yee L. (1989). *Spatial Analysis and Planning under Imprecision Studies in Regional Science*. North Holland, Amsterdam, 17.

46. Zadeh, LA. (1978). "Fuzzy sets as a basis for a theory of possibility". *Fuzzy Sets and Systems*. 1:3-28.

47. Zimmermann HJ. (1976). "Description and optimization of fuzzy system". *Int J General Systems*. 2: 209-215.

48. Zimmermann HJ. (1978). "Fuzzy programming and linear programming with several objective functions". *Fuzzy Sets and Systems*.1:45-55.
49. Zimmermann HJ. (1985). "Applications of fuzzy sets theory to mathematical programming". *Information Sciences*. 36:29-58.
50. Zimmermann HJ, Zysno P. (1985). "Quantifying vagueness in decision models". *Eur J Oper Res*. 22:148-158.
51. Zimmermann HJ. (1987). *Fuzzy sets, decision making, and expert systems*. Springer.

STUDY OF FUZZY MODEL WITH CONSTANT DEVELOPMENT

XAVIER BERTRAN, NARCÍS CLARA, DOLORS COROMINAS
Departament d'Empresa, Departament d'Informàtica i Matemàtica Aplicada, Universitat de Girona, Campus Montilivi s/n
Girona, 17071, Spain

In this work we propose a fuzzy approach to the logistic equation that permits to deal with uncertainty. This fuzzy proposal is based on the extension principle and shows a different behavior of the equilibrium points with regard to the crisp model.

1. Introduction

Thomas Robert Malthus modelized the growth of the populations supposing that the species are closed to any exterior influence, and, in consequence, all the changes that take place depend on the births and to the deaths. In this situation, population growth rate x(t) is

$$\frac{dx(t)}{dt} = kx(t) \tag{1}$$

This equation has only one equilibrium point at $x = 0$ and the population tends to infinity if $k > 0$ (0 is unstable) or vanishes if $k < 0$ (0 is stable). This point of view implies an exponential growth of the population.

The logistic equation

$$\frac{dx(t)}{dt} = rx(t)\left(1 - \frac{x(t)}{k}\right) \tag{2}$$

Solves the question of the existence of a positive equilibrium point because $x = k$ is an asymptotically stable point and the size of the population tends to k.

We are going to focus our attention to a variation of the previous model on the case that the population is commercial exploited and, therefore, we must consider predator to see the effect on the growth. Under this hypothesis, if we call $h(x(t))$ the development, this one supposes, logically, a decrease of the population absolute growth rate, therefore, the equation will be

$$\frac{dx(t)}{dt} = rx(t)\left(1 - \frac{x(t)}{k}\right) - h(x(t)) \tag{3}$$

The form that adopts the additional function depends on the form in which the development is realized. There are different strategies of development. In this work we are going to analyze the case in which the development is constant. The differential equation for modeling the population growth taking into account this aspect is

$$\frac{dx(t)}{dt} = f(x) = rx(t)\left(1 - \frac{x(t)}{k}\right) - h \tag{4}$$

Equation (4) have 0, 1 or 2 equilibrium points depending on the form of $f(x)$ Figures 1, 2 and 3 shows the different behavior of function $f(x)$. In case 1, there do not exist equilibrium points but from the analysis of the flow we can concludes that, independently of the initial conditions, the population tends to become extinct. In the case 2, exists one equilibrium point unstable and in the case 3 exist two equilibrium points, one is stable and the other one unstable.

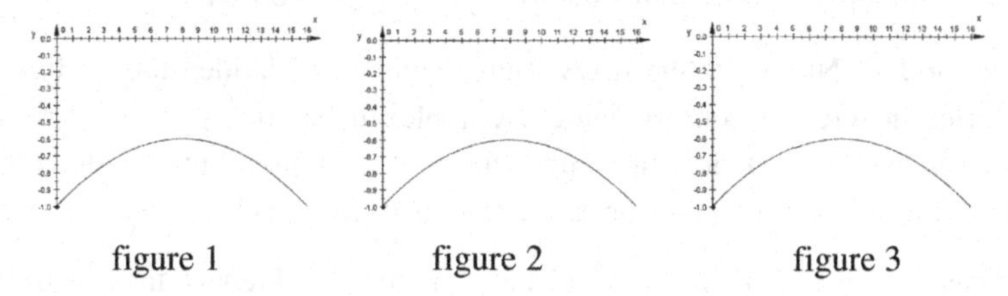

figure 1 figure 2 figure 3

In this work we centre the attention on the previous model (4) under uncertainty.

2. Fuzzy analysis based on the extension principle

Environmental and economical systems are usually subject to uncertainty which affects the mathematical structure of them. References dealing with theoretical or applied [14] fuzzy differential equations show a great number of subjects of interest and points of view. J.J. Buckley, P. Diamond y J.J. Nieto deal with first order differential equations ([3, 6, 7, 11, 12]), Buckley y D.N. Georgiou with high order differential equations ([4, 9]), X. Bertran y N. Clara deal with fuzzy allee effect ([7]) and for more applied focus related to this work we cite ([2, 8, 10, 13, 15]).

In our context we must considerer that the population is given by a fuzzy real number $\tilde{x}(t)$ for every t with membership function $\mu_{\tilde{x}(t)}(s)$ satisfying

- Normality: $\exists s_0 \in \Re \,/\, \mu_{\tilde{x}(t)}(s_0) = 1$
- $\mu_{\tilde{x}(t)}(s)$ is convex
- $\mu_{\tilde{x}(t)}(s)$ is upper-continuous
- The support of $\mu_{\tilde{x}(t)}(s)$ is a compact set

Let $f : \Re \to \Re$ be a real function. Given a fuzzy number $\tilde{x} \subseteq \Re$, then the fuzzy extension $\tilde{f}$ of f , following the Zadeh's extension principle [16] is defined as

$$\tilde{f}(\tilde{x})(s') = \begin{cases} \sup\limits_{s \in f^{-1}(s')} \{\tilde{x}(s)\} & si \;\; f^{-1}(s') \neq 0 \\ 0 & si \;\; f^{-1}(s') = 0 \end{cases} \tag{5}$$

and the level sets (or α-levels with $\alpha \in [0,1]$) of the fuzzy number $\tilde{f}(\tilde{x}(t)) = \tilde{y}(t)$ take the known form $\tilde{y}(\alpha,t) = \left[\underline{y}(\alpha,t), \overline{y}(\alpha,t)\right]$ where

$$\underline{y}(\alpha,t) = min\left\{f(s) / s \in \left[\underline{x}(\alpha,t), \overline{x}(\alpha,t)\right]\right\} \qquad (6)$$

$$\overline{y}(\alpha,t) = max\left\{f(s) / s \in \left[\underline{x}(\alpha,t), \overline{x}(\alpha,t)\right]\right\}$$

In order to simplify the notation we note $\underline{x}(\alpha,t) = x_1$ and $\overline{x}(\alpha,t) = x_2$.

The author J. J. Nieto, for the fuzzy logistic equation, divided the study of the trajectories in three regions showing a complex behavior. As general rule the trajectories leave one region and enter into another region, but can also tend to infinite. This behavior depends on the initial conditions [11].

In our case, the real function $f(x)$ of the equation (4) attains a maximum at $\frac{k}{2}$ (we note $f\left(\frac{k}{2}\right) = q$).

Applying de Zadeh's extension principle given by (5) three cases arises depending on x_1 and x_2 belong to the zones $Z_1 = \left[0, \frac{k}{2}\right)$, $Z_2 = \left[\frac{k}{2}, \infty\right)$. This zones lead to the study of three regions

$$R_1 = \left\{(x_1, x_2) \in \Re^2 / x_1 \in Z_1 \wedge x_2 \in Z_1\right\}$$

$$R_2 = \left\{(x_1, x_2) \in \Re^2 / x_1 \in Z_1 \wedge x_2 \in Z_2\right\}$$

$$R_3 = \left\{(x_1, x_2) \in \Re^2 / x_1 \in Z_2 \wedge x_2 \in Z_2\right\}$$

The fuzzy first order differential equation is transformed to a bidimensional system of differential equations which variables are x_1 and x_2. In the next section we analyze the trajectories of this system.

3. Solution of the fuzzy equation

From the definition of the system it is clear that the solutions depen on which región the initial condition belongs. When it is posible we get the solutions, if not, we obtain the trajectories and explain their behaviour. We considerer as initial conditions $x_1(t_0)=x_{10}$ and $x_2(t_0)=x_{20}$.

3.1. *Case1: Equation (4) don't have any equilibrium point.*

In this case $h>\frac{kr}{4}$.

3.1.1 Solution of $\tilde{x}'=\tilde{f}(\tilde{x})$ in region R_1

In this case $f(x_1)<f(x_2)$, so

$$[x'_1,x'_2]=[f(x_1),f(x_2)]\Rightarrow\begin{cases}x'_1=rx_1\left(1-\frac{x_1}{k}\right)-h\\x'_2=rx_2\left(1-\frac{x_2}{k}\right)-h\end{cases}$$

Wich is an uncoupled system of differential equations. Solving it

$$\frac{-k}{r}\frac{2}{\sqrt{4hk-rk^2}}arctan\frac{2\left(x_i-\frac{k}{2}\right)}{\sqrt{4hk-rk^2}}=t+C_i \qquad i=1,2$$

Imposing the initial conditions for $i=1,2$

$$C_i=\frac{-k}{r}\frac{2}{\sqrt{4hk-rk^2}}arctan\frac{2\left(x_{i0}-\frac{k}{2}\right)}{\sqrt{4hk-rk^2}}-t_0 \qquad i=1,2$$

3.1.2 Solution of $\tilde{x}'=\tilde{f}(\tilde{x})$ in region R_2

$$[x'_1,x'_2]=[min\{f(x_1),f(x_2)\},q]$$

We need to distinguish two cases.

Case A: $f(x_1)\leq f(x_2)$

$$\begin{cases} x'_1 = rx_1\left(1-\frac{x_1}{k}\right)-h \\ x'_2 = q \end{cases}$$

Which is an uncoupled system of differential equations. Solving it

$$\begin{cases} \frac{-k}{r}\frac{2}{\sqrt{4hk-rk^2}}\arctan\frac{2\left(x_1-\frac{k}{2}\right)}{\sqrt{4hk-rk^2}} = t + C_1 \\ x_2 = qt + C_2 \end{cases}$$

Imposing the initial conditions

$$C_1 = \frac{-k}{r}\frac{2}{\sqrt{4hk-rk^2}}\arctan\frac{2\left(x_{10}-\frac{k}{2}\right)}{\sqrt{4hk-rk^2}} - t_0$$

$$C_2 = x_{10} - qt_0$$

Case B: $f(x_1) > f(x_2)$

$$\begin{cases} x'_1 = rx_2\left(1-\frac{x_2}{k}\right)-h \\ x'_2 = q \end{cases}$$

Solving the trajectories we get

$$C + x_1 = \left(\frac{-r}{k}\frac{x_2^3}{3} + r\frac{x_2^2}{2} - hx_2\right)\frac{1}{q}$$

Applying the initial conditions we obtain

$$C = \left(\frac{-r}{k}\frac{x_{20}^3}{3} + r\frac{x_{20}^2}{2} - hx_{20}\right)\frac{1}{q} - x_{10}$$

3.1.3 *Solution of* $\tilde{x}' = \tilde{f}(\tilde{x})$ *in region* R_3

In this case $f(x_1) > f(x_2)$ so

$$[x'_1, x'_2] = [f(x_2), f(x_1)] \Rightarrow \begin{cases} x'_1 = rx_2\left(1 - \dfrac{x_2}{k}\right) - h \\ x'_2 = rx_1\left(1 - \dfrac{x_1}{k}\right) - h \end{cases}$$

We get a non linear system of differential equations. Dividing both equations and integrating we obtain the implicit solution of the trajectories:

$$\frac{-r}{k}\frac{x_1^3}{3} + r\frac{x_1^2}{2} - hx_1 = \frac{-r}{k}\frac{x_2^3}{3} + r\frac{x_2^2}{2} - hx_2 + C$$

We obtain the value of C imposing the initial conditions

$$C = \frac{r}{k}\left(\frac{x_{20}^3}{3} - \frac{x_{10}^3}{3}\right) + r\left(\frac{x_{10}^2}{2} - \frac{x_{20}^2}{2}\right) + h(x_{20} - x_{10})$$

In this first case, we notice that in any of three situations, the population tends to become extinct.

3.2. *Case2: Equation (4) have one equilibrium point*

In this case $h = \dfrac{kr}{4}$ and the equilibrium point is $\dfrac{k}{2}$.

3.2.1 *Solution of* $\tilde{x}' = \tilde{f}(\tilde{x})$ *in region* R_1

$$[x'_1, x'_2] = [f(x_1), f(x_2)] \Rightarrow \begin{cases} x'_1 = \dfrac{-r}{k}\left(x_1 - \dfrac{k}{2}\right)^2 \\ x'_2 = \dfrac{-r}{k}\left(x_2 - \dfrac{k}{2}\right)^2 \end{cases}$$

Which is an uncoupled system of differential equations. Solving it

$$x_i = \frac{1}{\frac{r}{k}t - C_i} + \frac{k}{2} \qquad i = 1,2$$

Imposing the initial conditions for $i = 1,2$

$$C_i = \frac{r}{k}t_0 - \frac{1}{x_{i0} - \frac{k}{2}} \qquad i = 1,2$$

Analyzing the behavior of the trajectories in this region, we observe that all of them go out of the region and, therefore the population tends to become extinct.

3.2.2 *Solution of $\tilde{x}' = \tilde{f}(\tilde{x})$ in region R_2*

$$[x'_1, x'_2] = [min\{f(x_1), f(x_2)\}, 0]$$

We need to distinguish two cases.

Case A: $f(x_1) \leq f(x_2)$

$$\begin{cases} x'_1 = \frac{-r}{k}\left(x_1 - \frac{k}{2}\right)^2 \\ x'_2 = 0 \end{cases}$$

Solving and applying initial conditions

$$\begin{cases} x_1 = \frac{1}{\frac{r}{k}t - C_1} + \frac{k}{2} \\ x_2 = x_{20} \end{cases} \quad \text{where} \quad C_1 = \frac{r}{k}t_0 - \frac{1}{x_{10} - \frac{k}{2}}$$

Notice that, in this case, the trajectories tend to the line $x_1 = 0$.

Case B: $f(x_1) > f(x_2)$

$$\begin{cases} x'_1 = \frac{-r}{k}\left(x_2 - \frac{k}{2}\right)^2 \\ x'_2 = 0 \end{cases}$$

Solving and applying the initial conditions we obtain the following trajectory

$x_1 = x_{10} + \frac{r}{k}\left(x_{20} - \frac{k}{2}\right)^2 (t_0 - t)$. As in the *case A (3.2.2)* the trajectories tend to the line $x_1 = 0$.

3.2.3 *Solution of $\tilde{x}' = \tilde{f}(\tilde{x})$ in region R_3*

$$[x'_1, x'_2] = [f(x_2), f(x_1)] \Rightarrow \begin{cases} x'_1 = \dfrac{-r}{k}\left(x_2 - \dfrac{k}{2}\right)^2 \\ x'_2 = \dfrac{-r}{k}\left(x_1 - \dfrac{k}{2}\right)^2 \end{cases}$$

Solving and applying the initial conditions

$$\left(x_1 - \frac{k}{2}\right)^3 = \left(x_2 - \frac{k}{2}\right)^3 + C \quad \text{where} \quad C = \left(x_{10} - \frac{k}{2}\right)^3 - \left(x_{20} - \frac{k}{2}\right)^3$$

Analyzing the behavior of the trajectories in this region, we observe that the trajectories tend to the line $x_1 = \frac{k}{2}$.

3.3. *Case3: Equation (4) have two equilibrium points*

In this case $h < \frac{kr}{4}$ and we note b and c the two equilibrium points with $0 < b < c$.

3.3.1 *Solution of $\tilde{x}' = \tilde{f}(\tilde{x})$ in region R_1*

$$[x'_1, x'_2] = [f(x_1), f(x_2)] \Rightarrow \begin{cases} x'_1 = \dfrac{-r}{k}(x_1 - b)(x_1 - c) \\ x'_2 = \dfrac{-r}{k}(x_2 - b)(x_2 - c) \end{cases}$$

Solving the uncoupled system we obtain

$$\frac{x_i - b}{x_i - c} = C_i e^{\frac{r(c-b)t}{k}} \qquad i = 1,2$$

Applying the initial conditions for $i = 1,2$

$$C_i = \frac{x_{i0} - b}{x_{i0} - c} e^{\frac{-r(c-b)t_0}{k}} \qquad i = 1,2$$

There are different possibilities for the behaviour of the trajectories that we summarize as follows

- Behaviour starting at Region R_1

  – If $x_{10} < x_{20} < b$ then the trajectories tend to the line $x_1 = 0$.
  – If $x_{10} = x_{20} < b$ then the trajectories tend to the point $(0,0)$.

  – If $x_{10} = x_{20} > b$ then the trajectories tend to the point $\left(\frac{k}{2}, \frac{k}{2}\right)$.

  – If $x_{10} = 0$ y $x_{20} < b$ then the trajectories leave the region.

  – If $x_{10} = 0$ y $x_{20} > b$ then the trajectories leave the region.
  – If $x_{10} < b$ y $x_{20} = b$ then the trajectories tend to the point $(0, b)$.
  – If $x_{10} < b$ y $x_{20} > b$ then the trajectories leave the region.
  – If $x_{10} > b$ y $x_{20} > b$ then the trajectories leave the region.

  – If $x_{10} = b$ y $x_{20} > b$ then the trajectories tend to the point $\left(b, \frac{k}{2}\right)$.

3.3.2 *Solution of* $\tilde{x}' = \tilde{f}(\tilde{x})$ *in region* R_2

$$[x'_1, x'_2] = [min\{f(x_1), f(x_2)\}, 0]$$

We need to distinguish two cases.

Case A: $f(x_1) \le f(x_2)$

$$\begin{cases} x_1' = \dfrac{-r}{k}(x_1 - b)(x_1 - c) \\ x_2' = q \end{cases}$$

Solving and applying initial conditions

$$x_2 = ln\left(\frac{(x_{10} - c)(x_1 - b)}{(x_{10} - b)(x_1 - c)}\right)^{\frac{qk}{r(c-b)}} + x_{20}$$

- Behavior starting at region R_2 *(Case A)*

– If $x_{10} < b$ then the trajectories tend to the line $x_1 = 0$.

– If $x_{10} > b$ then the trajectories tend to the line $x_1 = \dfrac{k}{2}$.

Case B: $f(x_1) > f(x_2)$

$$\begin{cases} x_1' = \dfrac{-r}{k}(x_2 - b)(x_2 - c) \\ x_2' = q \end{cases}$$

Calculating the trajectories we get

$$\frac{x_2^3}{3} - (c+b)\frac{x_2^2}{2} + bcx_2 = \frac{-kq}{r}x_1 + C$$

Applying the initial conditions

$$C = \frac{x_{20}^3}{3} - (c+b)\frac{x_{20}^2}{2} + bcx_{20} + \frac{kq}{r}x_{10}$$

- Behavior starting at region R_2 *(Case B)*

  – If $x_{20} < c$ then the trajectories tend to the line $x_2 = c$.

  – If $x_{20} > c$ then the trajectories tend to the line $x_1 = 0$.

3.3.3 *Solution of* $\tilde{x}' = \tilde{f}(\tilde{x})$ *in region* R_3

$$[x'_1, x'_2] = [f(x_2), f(x_1)] \Rightarrow \begin{cases} x'_1 = \dfrac{-r}{k}(x_2 - b)(x_2 - c) \\ x'_2 = \dfrac{-r}{k}(x_1 - b)(x_1 - c) \end{cases}$$

Solving and applying the initial conditions we get

$$\frac{x_1^3}{3} - (c+b)\frac{x_1^2}{2} + bcx_1 = \frac{x_2^3}{3} - (c+b)\frac{x_2^2}{2} + bcx_2 + C$$

where

$$C = \frac{x_{10}^3}{3} - \frac{x_{20}^3}{3} + (c+b)\left(\frac{x_{20}^2}{2} - \frac{x_{10}^2}{2}\right) + bc(x_{10} - x_{20})$$

- Behavior starting at region R_3
  - If $x_{10} < x_{20} < c$ then the trajectories tend to the line $x_2 = c$.
  - If $x_{10} = x_{20}$ then the trajectories tend to the point (c, c).
  - If $x_{10} = c$ then the trajectories keep on the region.
  - If $x_{10} < c$ and $x_{20} = c$ then the trajectories keep on the region.
  - If $x_{10} < c$ and $x_{20} > c$ then the trajectories keep on the region.
  - If $x_{10} > c$ and $x_{20} > c$ then the trajectories tend to the line $x_1 = c$.

4. Conclusion

The study of the logistic equation under uncertainty from the pint of view of the fuzzy extension principle shows that fuzziness changes the behavior of the set of solutions.

References

1. Aguirre, P.; González-Olivares, E.; Sáez, E. , "Three limit cycles in a Leslie-Gower predator-prey model with additive Allee effect",. SIAM J. Appl. Math., 69 (5), p.1244-1262. (2009).
2. Barros, L.C.; Bassanezi, R.C.; Tonelli, P.A. , "Fuzzy modelling in population Dynamics", Ecological Modelling, 128, p. 27-33. (2000).
3. Buckley, J.J.; Feuring, T., "Fuzzy differential equations", Fuzzy sets and systems, 110, p. 43-54. (2000).
4. Buckley, J.J.; Feuring, T., "Fuzzy initial value problema for N th-order linear differential equations", Fuzzy sets and systems, 121, p. 247-255. (2001).
5. Bertran, X.; Clara, N., "A fuzzy differential approach to strong allee effect based on the fuzzy extension principle", ICS'10 Proceedings of the 14th WSEAS international conference on Systems, 1, p.111-117. (2010).
6. Deeba, E.Y.; Dekorvin, A., "On a fuzzy logistic difference equation", Differential Equations Dynamical Systems, 4, p. 149-156. (1996).
7. Diamond, P., "Brief note on the variation of constants formula for fuzzy differential equations", Fuzzy sets and Systems, 129, p. 65-71. (2002).
8. Diamond, P.; Kloeden, P., "Metric spaces of fuzzy sets. Theory and applications", World Scientific Publishing Co. (1994).
9. Giorgiou, D.N.; Nieto, J.J.; Rodríguez López, R., "Initial value problems for higher-order fuzzy differential equations", Nonlinear analysis, 63, p. 587-600. (2005).
10. Lande, R.; Engen, S.; Saether, B.E., "Optimal harvesting, econòmic discounting and extinction risk in fluctuating populations", Nature, 372, p. 88-90. (1994).
11. Nieto, J.J.; Rodríguez López, R., "Analysis of a differential model with uncertainty", Int. J. Dynamical Systems and Differential Equations, 1(3), p. 164-177. (2008).
12. Nieto, J.J.; Rodríguez López, R.; Franco, L., "Linear first order fuzzy differential equations, Internat",J. Uncertain, Knowliedge-Based Systems, 14(6), p. 687-709. (2006).
13. Poggiale, J.C., "From behavioural to population level: growth and competition", Math. Comput. Model, 27, p. 41-49. (1998).
14. Ratiu, I.G.; Carstea, C.; Doru Plesea, L.P.; Boscoianu, M., "Fuzzy model economics", Proceedings of the 9th WSEAS International conference on simulation, modelling and optimization, p. 51-56. (2009).
15. Sutherland, w.j., "The importance of behavioural studies in conservation biology",Anim. Behav., 56, p. 801-809. (1998).
16. Zadeh, L.A., "Fuzzy sets", Information and Control, 8, p. 338-353. (1965).

PART 2: FINANCE

A DECISION SUPPORT SYSTEM FOR SCORING DISTRESSED DEBTS AND PLANNING THEIR COLLECTION

GIANLUCA MURGIA

Department of Information Engineering, University of Siena, Via Roma 56 Siena, 53100, Italy

SIMONE SBRILLI

Department of Business Engineering, "Tor Vergata" University of Rome, Viale del Politecnico 1, Rome, 00133, Italy

The current financial and economic crisis has strengthened the importance of correctly scoring and managing distressed debts. In scientific literature, the scoring of distressed debts has been handled using different methods, while the interest in managing those debts is limited to the choice of the best collection activity.

We develop a Decision Support System which scores the recovery rate of each distressed debt, starting only from a limited set of debt's features, and calculates the debts' daily planning and their assignment to the collection agency operator. Our DSS, which integrates artificial neural network, Analytic Hierarchy Process, integer programming, and hidden Markov model, is already under experimentation. Now, we have validated the scoring of the recovery rate of the packages of debts, comparing our results with those obtained by a collection agency, and we achieved a classification performance very similar to other methods presented in literature. Besides, we compared also our scoring system with logistic regression, Bayesian classifier, and regression tree, supporting the primacy of artificial neural network on these methods, in accordance with the conclusions of previous literature.

1. INTRODUCTION

The current financial and economic crisis is growing the number of customers who have difficulties to respect their debt repayment plan. For example, in Italy, from 2010 to 2011 the amount of consumers' distressed debts to banks is increased of more than 46% [3].

In this context, companies affected by customers' debts are increasingly outsourcing these debts' recovery to third party collectors, which specialize in recovering debts, using several tools, such as phone calls, letters and visits. The recourse to outsourcing of debt collection differs from one sector to another, in accordance with the specific regulation and the best practices of each sector; for example, financial companies tend to internalize debt collection activities, while utilities companies tend to outsource them. In Italy, the 39% of the debts managed by collection agencies comes from financial service, while the 50%

comes from utilities; beyond these sectorial differences, the total value of debts outsourced to these agencies is doubled from 2007 to 2010 [26].

Generally, a company decides to outsource the collection of a debt only after some months, when its efforts to directly recover it fail. A company can sell the package of distressed debts to a debt buyer or can assign the collection to an agency, asking for the achievement of a certain minimum target return on their debts and providing strong incentives to surpass it. In both cases, it's important to make a correct *a priori* estimate of the return rate on the collection of each package of debts. This estimate is necessary for correctly negotiating the clauses of the contract (*e.g.* the minimum target return, the fee, *etc.*) between the creditor and the collection agency, but it could also support the collection agency in the planning and control of its activities and resources.

No wonder the problem of the correct estimate of the recovery rate of a package of debts has attracted the attention of many authors, who propose different methods to score these debts [12].

In particular, some authors [4; 14] present approaches similar to credit scoring systems, which are originally used to measure the credit rating through the observation of some peculiar features at the time of the request of a new loan. So, the application of credit scoring systems on debt collection is based only on the current status of the debt, whose recovery rate is summarized through a score calculated thanks to artificial neural networks, multivariate statistical techniques, or some hybrid methods.

Alternatively, other authors [10; 12] have recourse to behavior scoring systems, which takes into consideration also the evolution of the relations between the creditor and the debtor, after the first credit loan. In debt collection, these methods have been applied starting from the historical data of the debtor's payment status [12], or from the data of the collection process that involves the collection agency and the debtor [10]. The techniques used for behavior scoring systems are very similar to those used for credit scoring, even if the former are dynamically applied so to have an updated score of the debt.

The development of these scoring methods makes possible to reduce the intrinsic unpredictability of the return rate of the debt collection activities, which depends on several factor, such as the macroeconomic situation, some demographic and socio-economic characteristics of the debtor, the nature and the clauses of the contract between the creditor and the debtor, the amount and the timeline of the debt, and, last but not least, the ability of the collection agency operators.

Unfortunately, the principal scoring methods presented in literature are specifically designed to financial services, where the credit loan is often secured by some collaterals and, in Italy, is strictly protected by the law, which prescribes the forced registration of the bad debtors in the Central Risk Register. Besides, some of these methods are based on historical data of the relations between the creditor and the debtor, but these data are not always available to collection companies [19].

In this paper, we propose a scoring method for customers' debts which come from a utilities sector, specifically from a phone provider. These debts are outsourced to a collection agency, ECR spa, which has at disposal a very limited set of data, detailed in Section 2, about the characteristics of the debtors, of the contract between the phone company and the debtors, and of the debts. Our scoring method, that fall into credit scoring systems, calculates the expected rate of return of a given package of debts and is based on Artificial Neural Networks (ANN) techniques, with the integration of a classifier and a regressor. The Section 3 illustrates the structure of this ANN scoring, while the next Section highlights its results both in comparison with the literature, and with some alternative scoring techniques, such as cluster analysis, Bayesian classifier, regression tree, and logistic regression.

In literature, credit scoring system are used for calculating the expected rate of return of a given package of debts and, sometimes, to address the planning of debt collection activities. McAllister and Eng [18] suggest that credit scoring system could support the planning of debtors' contacts through the detection of the debts that require a debt collection effort, avoiding to contact the debtors that are not recoverable and those that pay autonomously. Differently, other authors [10; 27] propose some more interesting uses of the results of credit scoring systems, which could support the planning of collection activities thanks to the prioritization of the debts characterized by specific features.

Our ANN scoring not only calculates the expected rate of return of a given package of debts, but it gives also the input for a more comprehensive Decision Support System (DSS) which could assist collection agencies in the planning of their activities. Until now, the most advanced DSSs presented in literature for supporting debt collection are based on rule-based decision, obtained through the application of artificial intelligence [1; 7]. These DSSs suggest the best action so to maximize the recovery probability of each debt, sometimes taking into consideration also the cost of each action. Makuch *et al.* [16] and De Almeida *et al.* [8] evaluate also the impact of these action on the resource planning, but their solutions pertain to tactical level and do not consider the operative one.

Our DSS does not consider the problem of the choice of the best action, because the collection agency under analysis has recourse essentially to phone calls. So, our focus is in the support to collection agency in estimating the return rate of each package of debt, but also in debts' daily planning and in assigning them to the collection agency operators, in accordance with their skill level. As shown in Figure 1, our DSS is composed, besides the ANN scoring described above, by three other components, which are detailed in Section 5:

- a scoring for human resources, based on Analytic Hierarchy Process (AHP HR scoring), which calculates the skill level of each operator of the collection agency;
- a scoring for debts, based on Hidden Markov Models (HMM scoring), which considers the data of the collection process that involves the collection agency and the debtor. In particular, HMM scoring updates the recovery probability of each debt in processing, in accordance with the calls and their results made by the collection agency;
- an optimizer, based on integer programming, that calculates the best daily planning of the debts and the best assignment to the collection agency operator, in order to maximize the daily expected amount of recovered capital. This optimizer prioritizes a new debt in accordance with its *a priori* recovery probability calculated by the ANN scoring, while the prioritization of the debts in processing is based on the recovery probabilities calculated by the HMM scoring. In case of incorrect phone contacts, the recovery probability of the related debts decays. The assignment of the debts to the

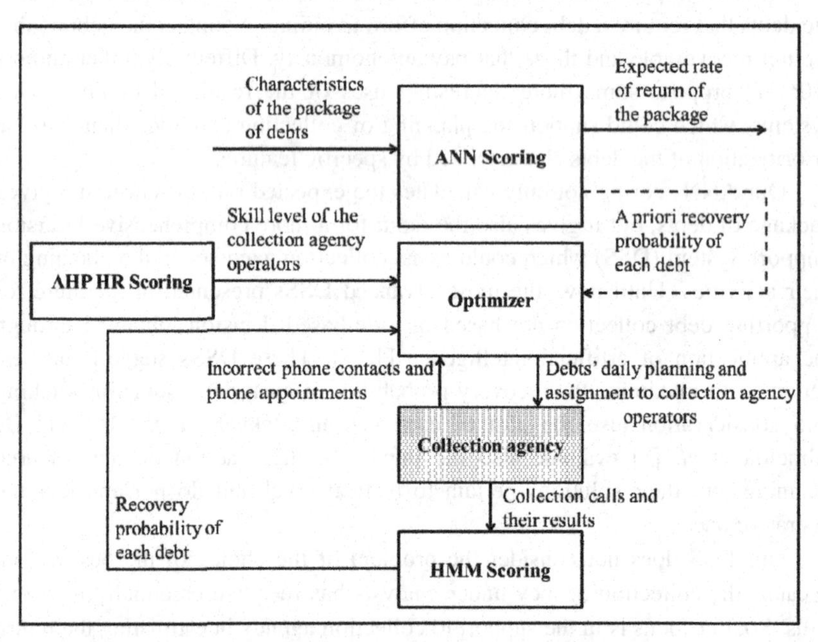

Figure 1. General framework of the Decision Support System.

operators is based on the results of the AHP HR scoring, but considering also the phone appointments arranged by each operator. The optimizer's output is the daily planning for each operator that the collection agency could use for the development of the actual call planning.

Except for the ANN scoring, the other components of our DSS are already under experimentation. So, in this paper we can present only their structure and some first results, even if the experiment in progress will make possible to calibrate and validate our DSS.

The application of our DSS might give some insights for the solution of the planning problem of debt collection calls, so to maximize the recovery rate obtained by the collection agency and reverse the negative trend registered in Italy, where the rate of return on debt collection activities decreased of 5% from 2007 to 2010 [26].

2. CASE STUDY AND DATASET

As remarked in the previous Section, the data used in this paper comes from utilities sector, specifically from a phone provider, which has outsourced the collection of its debts to a collection agency. This agency has at disposal only a very limited set of data about the outsourced distressed debts. In particular, the collection agency knows:

- the debtors' residence, in particular their Italian region of residence;
- some information about the contract between the phone provider and the debtor, such as the contract type (business/consumer), its duration, and the reason for contract termination (*i.e.* if the contract has been terminated by the debtor or by the phone provider);
- some information about the distressed debts, such as their seniority (*i.e.* the number of days from the expiration of the first unpaid bill), the number of bills not paid by the debtor, the presence of termination costs (due to the application of a law called "decreto Bersani"), and the debts amount, also split into those due to unpaid bills before the contract termination, and those due to unpaid bills after the contract termination.

Other than these data, the collection agency has at disposal also some data of the collection process activated with the debtor, such as the starting and the final day of the debt assignment to the collection agency, the number and total amount of the cancellations granted to the debtors.

Instead, the collection agency does not know the historical data of the debtors, nor if he has just been contacted from another collection agency in the past.

In this paper we analyze five packages of distressed debts, which are described in Table 1. These packages are essentially composed of debts related to consumer contracts, while the distribution between the contracts terminated by the provider versus those terminated by the debtor varies from a package to another. Every package has a different temporal window, *i.e.* the days from the starting to the final date of the recovery process, and the collection agency obtained a different global performance, from almost 6% to less than 29%, in its collection activities.

Table 1. Main features of the packages of debts under analysis.

	Number of debts	Consumer contract	Business contract	Contracts terminated by debtor	Contracts terminated by provider	Temporal window	Performance
Set 1	3,308	75.9%	24.1%	47.6%	52.4%	479	14.48%
Set 2	6,433	76.7%	23.3%	6.4%	93.6%	370	28.68%
Set 3	5,855	83.9%	16.1%	76.9%	23.1%	317	10.98%
Set 4	4,635	93.0%	7.0%	65.0%	35.0%	211	15.41%
Set 5	3,676	89.3%	10.7%	50.5%	49.5%	170	5.98%

3. ANN SCORING

Artificial intelligence techniques such as artificial neural networks, Bayesian classifiers and cluster analysis are widely used in debt recovery literature, as well as statistical methods like Markov decision process, logistic regression and rule-based systems. These methods are used in various applications, especially related to financial sector, such as bankruptcy prediction, credit card scoring, recovery rate estimation and collection strategies [14; 28; 13; 24; 12; 11].

This paper is based on some debts owned by a phone provider that, basically, are harder to analyze because of the lack of some very important information about the debtors, such as their current financial situation and their historical data. The only available information, as described in Section 2, is related to some features of the debtors, of their contracts with the creditor and of the debts. In this case, the variance of the dataset cannot be fully explained by the observed variables, so the use of artificial intelligence techniques seems to be even more appropriated. Our ANN scoring module aims to find the global expected return rate for a new package of debts by summing the global expected return rate of each debt. The values of these return rates are obtained by using two artificial neural networks (ANN).

The former, called "classifier" assigns a certain debt to one of these two classes:

- Class 1, $\omega 1$: the set of the debts that are recoverable;
- Class 0, $\omega 0$: the set of the debts that are very hard to recover.

The latter, called "regressor", estimates the return rate of the debts assigned to the Class 1 by the classifier.

The choice of using two distinct neural networks in series (Figure 2) is due to the nature of the debts under analysis. In fact, our ANN scoring has been applied to debts that are very hard to recover, as shown by the performance obtained by the collection agency (Table 1). There are a lot of debts whose recovery rate is very low or null, so we decide to filter out these debts and focus on the most promising ones.

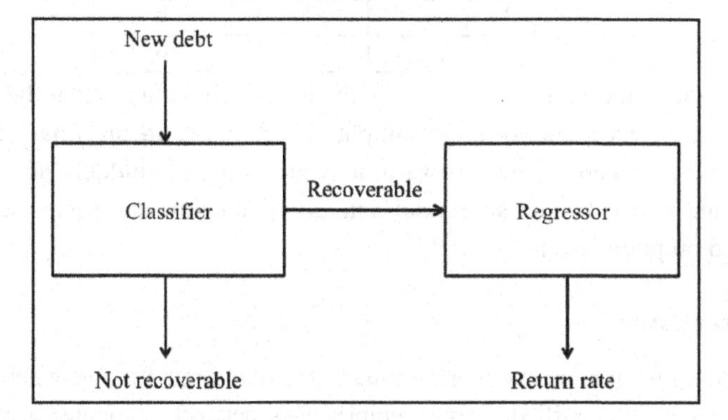

Figure 2. The ANN structure.

Indeed, the classifier has been trained using all the available debts, while the regressor has been trained only with recovered debt so to have a more precise tool for evaluating the factors that lead to recovery.

After the training, every new package of debts is processed as follow: for each new debt classified as recoverable by the classifier (Class 1), the regressor estimates its return rate, *i.e.* the amount of money that the collection agency might recover. The total return rate of the package can be calculated simply by summing the return rate of each debt classified as recoverable.

3.1. The classifier

The first artificial neural network classifies a new debt as recoverable or not. This network has been trained using a large database of labeled and closed debts.

Classic Multi-Layer Perceptron (MLP) has been used as network architecture and the learning algorithm is the well-known back-propagation:

given a set of example $\tau = \{(x, y)\}$, where x is the input pattern and y is the associated target, the Lippmann and Richard theorem [15] assures that if

$$y = \begin{cases} 1 \text{ if } x \in \omega_1 \\ 0 \text{ if } x \in \omega_0 \end{cases}$$

the output of the network is the estimate of $P(\omega_1 | x)$, *i.e.* the probability that the debt associated to the input x is recoverable.

Then, a new debt is associated to ω_1 if its probability is greater than a selected threshold. The results of the training have been shown and evaluated using the subsequent confusion matrix:

		Target	
		ω_1	ω_0
Predicted	ω_1	a	b
	ω_0	c	d

where the scalar values a, b, c, d are the number of patterns that the network assigns to the corresponding target-output combination. In the final model we trained and validated a feed-forward network with 50 hidden neurons and learning rate $\eta = 0.1$. The sigmoidal activation function has been used in the hidden and output neurons.

3.2. The regressor

The second artificial neural network estimates the return rate for a new debt that the classifier has been classified as recoverable. This network computes a regression over a set of debts for which the collection agency recovered at least 1€.

Given a set of pairs $\tau = \{(x, y)\}$ where x is the debt and y the recovered capital, the regressor calculates the regression: $y = \varphi(x)$. Even for this artificial neural network, we choose a simple MLP architecture with the same features of the previous one, in term of number of hidden layers and number of neurons. Even in this case the learning has been accomplished by using back-propagation. The two architectures differ for the output layer activation function: for the classifier we choose a sigmoidal activation function, while for the regressor we choose a linear one. Also the learning rate used in the learning process is different ($\eta = 0.01$) .

4. ANN RESULTS

We tested our ANN scoring with a training set composed by over 20.000 closed debts, of which 35% has been recovered and 65% has been not recovered. In order to get a uniform distribution of the input pattern value, we used the normalization technique of the variables proposed by Trentin [25]. The results of the training of our ANN scoring on these debts are shown in Table 2.

Table 2. Training results of ANN scoring with a classification threshold equal to 0.5.

		Per cent
Real ω_1 debts correctly classified on total ω_1 debts classified	a/(a+b)	58.6%
Real ω_0 debts correctly classified on total ω_0 debts classified	d/(d+c)	76.7%
Real ω_1 debts correctly classified on total real ω_1 debts	a/(a+c)	44.0%
Real ω_0 debts correctly classified on total real ω_0 debts	d/(d+b)	85.6%
Total debts correctly classified	(a+d)/(a+b+c+d)	72.4%

The ANN scoring classifies correctly the 72.4% of the input patterns. Anyway there is a relevant difference in the classification score for the single classes: while input patterns belonging to Class 0 are classified correctly in 85.6% of cases, the classifier achieves a low performance (44%) in classifying patterns belonging to Class 1. With this configuration, using a classification threshold that maximizes the global percentage of debts correctly classified, a certain debt classified as recoverable will be really recoverable in 58.6% of cases.

4.1. *ANN scoring versus other learning techniques*

In order to better evaluate the performance of our ANN scoring, we applied other learning techniques on the same training set. In particular, we took into consideration the subsequent learning techniques:

- Regression tree [6];
- Logistic regression, which could considered as a particular form of neural network without hidden layer and with only one output neuron characterized by a sigmoidal activation function;
- Bayesian classifier, where the conditional probability $P(\omega_1 | x)$ is obtained by using the Bayes theorem:

$$P(\omega_1 | x) = \frac{P(x | \omega_1)P(\omega_1)}{P(x)} \tag{1}$$

$P(x | \omega_1)$ is computed using the class distribution, a mixture Gaussian estimated distribution using samples belonging to Class 1. A debt is classified as belonging to ω_1 if

$$P(\omega_1 | x) > P(\omega_0 | x) \tag{2}$$

- Cluster analysis integrated with an artificial neural network. Following the approach suggested by Kajdanowicz and Kazienko [14] and Zurada and

Lonial [28], the input space has been partitioned into clusters by using the K-means algorithm. Then, a particular ANN has been trained for each cluster. In presence of a new debt, the algorithm firstly finds the nearest centroid in the input space. Then the corresponding ANN is used to classify the debt as recoverable or not. We test this learning procedure for several values of the number of clusters.

The performance of our ANN scoring could be compared with that obtained by these learning techniques (Table 3).

Table 3. Benchmarking of the performance of the learning techniques under analysis.

Learning technique	Performance
ANN	72.1%
Regression Tree	64.3%
Logistic Regression	58.4%
Bayesian classifier	68.7%
Cluster analysis + ANN	72.4%

In general, the performance of our ANN scoring seems to be superior to those obtained by the other learning techniques, In particular, the regression tree showed the best classification performance over the learning set, 92%, but the performance over the validation set was not so good; in fact, the learning algorithm focuses too much on the learning set (over fitting phenomenon). The results of this benchmarking could be more clearly understood if compared to those presented in another research [28], which analyzes debt collection in a different sector. The unique difference with the results of this latter research is due to the performance of logistic regression that in our experiment is very low, because the data exhibit high overlap between the classes, so a simple hyper plan is not sufficient to adequately separate the patterns. In fact, in our benchmarking, the Bayesian classifier performs better than logistic regression because it doesn't search a separation criterion on the input space, but uses the class probability distribution separately. The presence of an overlap between classes is shown even by the results obtained by several ANNs, after a cluster analysis on the input space: this approach does not provide a significant improvement in the classification performance. We choose our ANN scoring because it obtains a very similar performance to the integration of cluster analysis and ANN, but with a lower computational cost.

Kajdanowicz & Kazienko [14] apply artificial neural networks to debt scoring, obtaining better performance than our ANN scoring, but they consider a multi-period recovery process; besides, it's not clear which variables have been used by the authors in their classification.

4.2. ANN results with different thresholds

Our ANN scoring aims to achieve a good forecast of the return rate of each package of debts but it is also a component of a DSS, detailed in Section 5, that supports the planning of the collection process. In particular, the ANN scoring gives an *a priori* recovery probability of each debt, so the removal of some debts, that are very unlikely to be recovered, guarantees a resource allocation more focused on the promising debts. Exactly, our ANN scoring has to reach these two objectives:

- correctly classify the maximum number of recoverable debts, *i.e.* the maximization of $a/(a+c)$;
- classify a debt as not recoverable only when it is really not recoverable, i. e. the maximization of $d/(c+d)$.

Both these objectives could be reached by using a lower classification threshold, as shown in Table 4.

Table 4. Classification performance for the validation set using a lower threshold.

		Per cent
Real ω_1 debts correctly classified on total ω_1 debts classified	a/(a+b)	47.4%
Real ω_0 debts correctly classified on total ω_0 debts classified	d/(c+d)	**86.9%**
Real ω_1 debts correctly classified on total real ω_1 debts	a/(a+c)	**80.7%**
Real ω_0 debts correctly classified on total real ω_0 debts	d/(d+b)	58.8%
Total debts correctly classified	(a+d)/(a+b+c+d)	65.7%

By lowering this threshold, the debts classified as hard to recover by the ANN scoring are really hard with a good confidence. At the same time, most of the recoverable debts will be classified correctly.

By the way, focusing on maximizing the correct classification of recoverable debts implies that, in a multivariate space with a high overlap between classes, the global classification performance decreases. Another consequence is the increase of the number of unrecoverable debts that are classified as recoverable; so, the regressor will process a lot of practices very hard to recover and the total return of the package of debts will be overestimated.

4.3. *Regressor results*

The regressor has been trained using back-propagation and the learning result has been analyzed through a scatterplot which indicates the target value (x-axis) versus the output given by the network (y-axis). The results of the learning phase show that the regressor fits quite well the data, even if it tends to overestimate the output in case of debts with high return rate. The Pearson correlation between observed and simulated data is 0.875.

4.4. *ANN scoring test*

In order to evaluate the global performance, a package of closed debts - not used in the learning phase - has been processed by the ANN scoring. This test set is composed by 4,800 closed debts; the real recovery rate of this set was 14.41%. The estimated recovery rate is calculated using two different classification thresholds in the classifier: 0.5 and 0.25, the same value used for maximizing the true positive rate, as explained in Section 4.2. The results of the test are, respectively, 5% and 15.64%.

Using a low threshold (0.25), our DSS tends to overestimate the number of recoverable debts. The global simulated performance is similar to the real value. Even working with a set of features that cannot explain the whole variance of the data, our ANN scoring filters away the debts that are very hard to recover and reaches a good performance in the estimate of the global return rate.

4.5. *The input variable relevance*

In order to improve its debt collection activities, a collection agency should be very interested in knowing which variables have a greater impact on debt recoverability. Anyway ANNs could be considered as "black box", where the real influence of the input variables does not appear clearly. Nevertheless, there are some methods in literature, applied in other fields, that could provide a rank of the input values, in accordance to their impact. In this paper, we used a simple "connection weights" method [20]: a high value of the variables with a high score contributes to a higher value of ANN output. In our case a high connection weights value means that a high value in input makes more likely that the debt belongs to the recoverable debts class. We implement the classifier providing, among the input variables, one variable for each Italian region so to rank them in accordance with their attitude to paying distressed debts. The results are shown in Table 5, where the Bold rows indicate the Italian regions.

The most important factor in debt recovery process seems to be the contract duration: if a debtor has been a customer of the phone provider for long time, so he'll be more willing to pay. On the other hand, this analysis reveals that the

Table 5. Ranking of the input variables.

Variable	Score
Contract duration	6.337
Reason for contract termination	5.765
Marche	4.691
Sardegna	4.402
Starting date of debt assignment	2.474
Veneto	2.428
Final date of debt assignment	2.061
Presence of termination costs	1.566
Molise	1.269
Total amount of cancellations	1.261
Numbers of cancellations	1.132
Valle d'Aosta	0.779
Friuli-Venezia Giulia	0.572
Emilia-Romagna	-0.242
Calabria	-0.261
Consumer/Business contract	-0.658
Trentino-Alto Adige	-0.830
Puglia	-1.023
Umbria	-1.080
Toscana	-1.120
Liguria	-1.158
Piemonte	-1.438
Presence of bills after the contract termination	-1.441
Lombardia	-1.797
Basilicata	-1.828
Lazio	-1.830
Debt seniority	-2.599
Campania	-3.202
Amount of bills after the contract termination	-3.477
Number of unpaid bills	-3.583
Sicilia	-3.861
Abruzzo	-4.069
Amount of bills before the contract termination	-4.521
Total debt amount	-6.602

collection process is very hard in case of debtors that have a high total amount to pay, a lot of unpaid bills and a high debt seniority.

Considering only the impact of the regional residence, it is interesting to compare the results of our analysis with the ranking provided by UNIREC [26] about the regional recovery rate. Table 6 shows the ranking of the recovery difficulty, according to UNIREC and our analysis.

These two rankings points in evidence the low recovery rate of some Italian regions, especially in the South of Italy. The similarity of these two rankings is witnessed by the level of the non-parametric Spearman correlation coefficient (0.52), with a significance level equal to 0.025. So, starting from a limited set of input variables, our ANN scoring detects the differences among the regional recovery rates, obtaining results that are very close to the real ones.

Table 6. Ranking of regional debt recovery difficulty.

	UNIREC	ANN
Sicilia	1	2
Campania	2	3
Lombardia	3	6
Lazio	4	4
Puglia	5	11
Piemonte	6	7
Toscana	7	9
Emilia-Romagna	8	14
Veneto	9	18
Calabria	10	13
Sardegna	11	19
Liguria	12	8
Abruzzo	13	1
Marche	14	20
Umbria	15	10
Friuli-Venezia Giulia	16	15
Basilicata	17	5
Trentino - Alto Adige	18	12
Molise	19	17
Valle d'Aosta	20	16

5. OPTIMIZING DEBT COLLECTION: INFORMATION FROM THE OUTCOMES

Credit scoring is one of the most analyzed topics in literature about debt collection. The scoring mechanism described above does not totally responds to the goals of a collection agency that aims to be efficient: assigning a credit scoring value for every single debt is only the beginning. In fact the call center is the core of the collection process: every day it provides new information about the debtors and the recovery strategy. Relatively few works have studied the task of optimizing the daily operations in a call center environment [16; 9].

Some authors also investigate the use of artificial intelligence such neural networks [10], or decision rule engine [7]. Instead, in this work we use an operation research approach already proposed by De Almeida et al. [8] that use dynamic programming to determine what collection actions should be taken. In this paper, we propose a mathematical programming approach to determine the operative problem of daily calls planning for the operators. This optimization is done using some key parameters about the operators' skills and debts' state. The next Sections show how the AHP module and a hidden Markov model based architecture could provide these scores and how the optimizer combines them, in order to obtain the daily calls list and the optimal matching operator-debt.

5.1. AHP module

For any team of operators that works on a given set of debts, the team leaders use the Analytic Hierarchy Process [22] technique to create a rank for the operators. The main idea of this method is to make all the pairwise comparisons between the operators considering their skill in a certain set of criteria. The highlighted criteria, provided by team leaders' suggestions, are:

- Problem solving: the skill of solving complex and unplanned situations.
- Determination: the strength in facing even the most complicated debts.
- Product knowledge: the level of knowledge on the debts' features and on the legal aspects.
- Speed: the skill on facing several calls in a workday.

Team leaders interview have been used so to get the AHP scores by using the Saaty scale. The team leaders even decide which is the correct scoring of the criteria. In this case, we obtained that the rank of the criteria is: "Problem solving", "Determination", "Speed" and "Product knowledge".

Given a set of n operators the AHP module provides the skills value $s_j \in [0,\dots,1], j = 1 \dots n$.

The final operators' score obtained with this method are quite statics: the AHP skill scoring should be considered as referred to the current time (*e.g.* a new operator with no experience can't have the same skill of a more experienced colleague). For this reason, the evaluation has to be repeated every week or at the team leader's request.

5.2. Hidden Markov Model for probability estimation

For each debtor $i\ (i = 1 \ldots n)$ contacted by the call center we compute every day a score d_i that identifies the probability that at the next call the debtor will grant the payment. The idea is that this parameter changes as a function of the calls outcomes: if a debtor refuses to pay for more than five calls, it is more likely that he'll never pay. On the other hand, if a debtor tells that he'll pay as soon as possible, it's fair to consider that the recover probability is high. According to this idea, the sequence of the calls outcomes could be used to estimate the probability that the debtor will grant the payment at the next call. In the collection agency where this model has been tested each call is marked with a code that identifies the outcome of the deal: these marks tells if the debtor refuses to pay, if he grants the payment, if there is a negotiation in progress and so on. The sequence of these marks has been used by a learning mechanism to estimate the desired probability.

The Hidden Markov Models are widely used in sequence recognition application such voice recognition and bioinformatics applications [21]. In economics, there are some application in financial time series analysis [17], but there is not any known application in a debt collection context. In our case, we assume that the call center calls change the debtor's state and that these state changes are the results of an hidden process that we can only observe through a correlated observed process, *i.e.* the sequence of marks. Any observable mark has a certain emission probability in each state: we can estimate these values, as well as transition probabilities of the state model, using a large database that collects all the marks of the calls. Then, given a set of possible events (calls marks) $Y = \{y_1, y_2, \ldots, y_n\}$, the basic idea is to calculate the probability that, given a sequence of known mark, the next mark will be a Promise to Pay (PP):

$$P(Y_{t+1} = PP | Y_t = y_t, Y_{t-1} = y_{t-1}, \ldots, Y_0 = y_0) \quad (3)$$

This probability is computed indirectly: given a sequence of emitted marks, we compute the most likely state sequence by using the well-known Viterbi algorithm. The last state of this sequence is the current debtor's state: if all the model parameters are known, it's easy to compute the conditional probability:

$$d_i = P(Y_t = PP|X_t = X_l(i)) = \sum_{j \in \delta^+(X_l(i))} a_{X_l(i)j}\, e_j(PP) \tag{4}$$

Where:

- $X_l(i)$ is the last state of the most likely state sequence generated by Viterbi algorithm on the debt i ;
- $\delta^+(X_l(i))$ is the set of the adjacent states of $X_l(i)$;
- $a_{X_l(i)j}$ is the transition probability from the state $X_l(i)$ to the state j ;
- $e_j(PP)$ is the emission probability of the "promise to pay" mark (PP).

In this way we obtain m different probabilities, one for each state. So, the sequence analysis is reduced to a state estimate problem. The basic concept is that debtors who show similar behaviors are stochastically linked to the marks that indicate the outcomes of calls.

One of the most important factors in building a hidden Markov model is the state topology: the learning algorithm for parameter estimation [5] finds the maximum likelihood estimate for a set of parameters for a given model structure. So, the results depend strictly on the model topology: in other application, *e.g.* the problems of biological sequence analysis, the model structure is given by physical consideration about the nature of the considered system. Furthermore, the Baum-Welch algorithm finds a local maximum in the parameter space, starting from an initial point. So, even the choice of the initial parameter values impacts on the final goodness of the solution.

In this case we don't have any a priori knowledge about the nature of the hidden process and the initial parameter values, and a wide and fully connected model topology was unable to find good results. The basic idea for building the model topology is that there are some debtors classes that generates similar sequences *i.e.* the sequences clusters exist. The global model is then a HMM mixture with a single HMM for each cluster [23].

The available call outcomes database provides the data for estimate the parameters for this model. Once the model is fixed, the HMM module computes the Promise to pay probability d_i for any debtor called by the call center.

5.3. The optimizer

The last block of our DSS provides the optimal daily planning for the call center with the correct assignment operator-debt. This block is mainly composed by two sub blocks: the first is *the planner* that uses the information given by the HMM module, the ANN scoring and the call center and provides the list of the debtors that the operators must contact in the next day. The second sub-block is *the assigner* that computes the correct operator-debt matching.

5.3.1. The planner

The planner has the task to choose which debts should be processed in the next day. This is computed by ordering the debts by the value $\alpha_i t_i$ where:

- t_i is the total amount of debt i ;
- α_i is a parameter that prioritizes the debt i .

The value of the last parameter depends on the debt state:

- Processing debts. For the debtors already contacted by the call center, α_i is the Promise to Pay computed by HMM module;
- Open debts: for the debtors not called yet, α_i is equal to the value $p_0(i)$ given by the classifier showed in Section 3.1;
- Contact research: if the contacts given by the client are incorrect, an operator could try a research through the Internet so to retrieve information. If the operator can't find useful contacts the probability α_i decreases. This is modeled by an empirical probability density function that assigns a certain probability value as a function of the number of research activity: be R_i the number of completed research;

$$[(a_{\downarrow}i = r)_{\downarrow}i(k) = P(recover \mid R_{\downarrow}i = k) = p_{\downarrow}0(i) \cdot P(conctact \mid R \downarrow i = k)] \quad (8)$$

with $P(conctact \mid R_i = k)$ distributed as shown in Table 7

The planner takes into account even the phone appointment planned by the operators for a certain date. These calls are assigned for the scheduled day to the correct operators. The maximum number of calls assignable to each operator is decremented by the number of phone appointments already planned.

Table 7. The empirical probability density function for incorrect phone contacts.

k	1	2	3	4	5	6	7	8
Prob.	0.25	0.5	0.14	0.05	0.02	0.02	0.01	0.01

Summarizing, the planner rankes the debt by the value $\alpha_i t_i$ where:

$$\alpha_i = \begin{cases} d_i & \text{if } i \text{ was already processed (HMM)} \\ p_0(i) & \text{if } i \text{ is open debt} \\ r_i(k) & \text{if } i \text{ is a research debt} \end{cases}$$

And takes the first $N - A$ debts, where N is the maximum number of call that the call center can process in a day and A is the number of phone appointments planned in the next day by the operators.

5.3.2. The allocator

The allocator solves an optimization model that aims to maximize the expected daily global recovered capital. Given a set of *n* debts that have to be processed and a set of *m* available operators, we define:

$$X_{ij} = \begin{cases} 1 \text{ if the debt } i \text{ is assigned to operator } j \\ 0 \text{ otherwise} \end{cases}$$

The objective function is the expected recovered capital:

$$min_{X_{ij}} \sum_{i=1}^{n} \sum_{j=1}^{m} t_i p_{ij} X_{ij} \tag{9}$$

Where:

- t_i is the total amount of the debt i ;
- p_{ij} is the probability that the debt i is recovered by operator j .

The optimization is subjected to two kinds of constraints:

- Each practice $\mathbf{i}$ must be processed at least by one operator:

$$\sum_{j=1}^{m} X_{ij} \leq 1 \forall i = 1 \dots n \tag{10}$$

- Each operator for a single day can't process more than $\mathbf{M_j}$ debts:

$$\sum_{i=1}^{n} X_{ij} \leq M_j \forall j = 1 \dots m \tag{11}$$

The value of M_j is obtained by decreasing the maximum number of daily calls made by an operator by the number of planned phone appointments for that day.

The presented model has a very simple structure. The crucial information is the estimate of the parameters p_{ij} . These probabilities could be interpreted as the union of two distinct factors:

$$p_{\downarrow}ij = P(\text{"debt" } i \text{ "is easy to recover } \cup \text{operator" } j \text{ "is able to recover"})$$

By assuming that the debtor's predisposition and the operator's skill are independent:

$$p_{ij} = \alpha_i \cdot s_j \tag{12}$$

In this model, we assume that the parameter α_i could be an estimate of the recover probability of debt i . At the same time, the operator's score provided by the AHP module s_j is considered as a Bayesian subjective probability value.

6. CONCLUSIONS

While the ANN scoring has been tested and validated on real data, the optimizer has been not already validated, because its experimentation is still in process.

The idea is to use our DSS in a test team with few operators in a real collection agency. The test should last almost three months in order to get significant data to prove the effectiveness of these methods. Besides, we are investigating the use of some more complex architectures of hidden state models in order to improve the debtors' behavior model.

References

1. N. Abe, P. Melville, C. Pendus, C. K. Reddy, D. L. Jensen, V. P. Thomas, J. J. Bennett, J. F. Anderson, B. R. Cooley, M. Kowalczyk, M. Domick and T. Gardinier, *Proc. 16th ACM SIGKDD on Knowledge discovery and data mining*, 75 (2010).
2. A. F. Atiya,. *IEEE trans. neur. net.*, **12**, 929 (2001).
3. Banca d'Italia (2012). *Moneta e banche - supplementi al bollettino statistico, indicatori monetari e finanziari*, Year XXII - January 11.
4. A. Banerjee, *Vikalpa*, **6**, 7 (2001).
5. L. E. Baum, *Inequalities*, **3**, 1 (1972).
6. L. Breimann, J. H. Freidmann, R. Olsen and J. Stone, *Classification and regression tree*, Wadsworth International Group (1984).
7. A. G. Chin and H. Kotak, *Int. j. inform. manage.*, **6**, 81 (2006).
8. A. T. De Almeida Filho, C. Mues and L. C. Thomas, *Prod. oper. manag.*, **19**, 698 (2010).
9. M. Del Vecchio, J. Shu, A. Mistretta, H. Rolando and H. Tuck, *Systems and information engineering design symposium*, 168 (2006).
10. E. F. Georgopoulos and S. M. Giannaropoulos, *19th IEEE int. conf. on tools with artificial intelligence*. 405 (2007).
11. X. Guo, R. A. Jarrow and H. Lin, *Rev. derivatives res.*, **11**, 171 (2009).
12. S. H. Ha, *Inform. sciences*, **180**, 3703 (2010).
13. Z. Huang, H. Chen, C. J. Hsu, W-H. Chen and S. Wu, *Decis. support syst.*, **37**, 543 (2004).
14. T. Kajdanowicz and P. Kazienko, *Proc. 14th Iberoamerican conference on pattern recognition CIARP 2009*, 337 (2009).
15. R. Lippman and M. Richards, *Neural comput.*, **3**, 461 (1991).
16. W. M. Makuch, J. L. Dodge, J. G. Ecker, D. C. Granfors and G. J. Hahn, *Interfaces*, **22**, 90 (1992).
17. R. Mamon and R. J. Elliott, *Hidden Markov Models in Finance*, Springer, (2010).
18. P. Mcallister and D. Eig, "Score-based collection strategies" in E. Mays (ed.) *Handbook of Credit Scoring*, 303, Fitzroy Deaborn Publisher (2001).
19. A. Moore, "Consumer debt recovery models incorporating economic and operational effects", *Doctoral Thesis*, University of Southampton, (2011).
20. J. Olden, M. Joy, and R. Death, *Ecol. Modelling*, **178**, 389 (2004).
21. L. T. Rabiner, *Proc. IEEE*, **77**, 257 (1989).

22. T. L. Saaty, *Interfaces*, **24**, 19 (1994).
23. P. Smyth, *Adv. Neural Inf. Process. Syst.*, **9**, 648 (1997).
24. L. C. Thomas, *Int. J. Forecasting*, **16**, 149 (2000).
25. E. Trentin, *Proc. 16th int. conf. on artificial neural networks*, 410 (2006).
26. UNIREC (2001). *Primo rapporto annuale sui servizi per la tutela del credito*. May 20, Roma.
27. S. Zeng, P. Melville, C. A. Lang, I. Boier-Martin and C. Murphy, *Proc. 14th ACM SIGKDD on knowledge discovery and data mining*, 1043 (2008).
28. J. Zurada and S. Lonial, *J. Appl. Bus. Res.*, **21**, 37 (2005).

AN ASSESSMENT OF ABNORMAL RETURNS IN SOCIALLY RESPONSIBLE FIRMS USING FUZZY JENSEN´S ALPHA VALUES

KLENDER AIMER CORTEZ ALEJANDRO

Universidad Autónoma de Nuevo León, Manuel L. Barragán s/n y Pedro de Alba, San Nicolás Nuevo León, México, Tel: (0052) 81 13404430, Fax: (0052) 81 83767025, Email: klender.corteza@uanl.mx

MARTHA DEL PILAR RODRÍGUEZ GARCÍA

Universidad Autónoma de Nuevo León, Manuel L. Barragán s/n y Pedro de Alba, San Nicolás Nuevo León, México, Tel: (0052) 81 13404430, Fax: (0052) 81 83767025, Email: marthadelpilar2000@yahoo.com

MARÍA TERESA SORROSAL -FORRADELLAS

Universidad Rovira i Virgili, Av. de la Universidad 1 - 43204 REUS – España, Tel: (0034) 977759833, Fax: (0034) 977 75 98 10, Email: mariateresa.sorrosal@urv.cat

This study analyzes the differences in financial performance between sustainable firms and non-sustainable firms through the use of a fuzzy Jensen's alpha to measure abnormal returns. The sample consisted of 28 of the 35 firms from various sectors that composed the Mexican Price and Quotation Index (IPC) from 2008 to 2011. We compared two different methodologies to measure the Jensen's alpha values, namely, ordinary least squares and Fuzzy Regression. Our results demonstrate that sustainable firms have greater possibilities of obtaining abnormal returns and evince less uncertainty than non-sustainable firms. Finally, we mention the Corporate Social Responsibility (CSR) trends in the Mexican capital market to emphasize the importance of the disclosure of non-financial issues as part of the process of generating long-term sustainability profits.

Keywords: Sustainability Index, Jensen´s Alpha, Fuzzy Regression, Mexico.
JEL: C58, G32, M14.

1. Introduction

As Corporate Social Responsibility (CSR) has become more important in our society, many companies have decided to use social and ethics manuals to disclose their social activities to project a positive corporate image to the society and industry in which they function. Currently, CSR is accompanied by many external and internal factors, including the attitude and participation of company employees and the corporate social programs instituted by the government that promote the creation of new, responsible businesses.

As mentioned by Maak[1] and Jamali[2], lingering skepticism towards CSR persists in the field of financial research. For example, Maak[1] argued that skepticism existed towards CSR but not towards related concepts, such as business ethics, corporate social performance, or stakeholder theory. This skepticism may be because many scholars, particularly in Europe, perceive CSR as a concept that is narrow, blurred, or overly ''American.'' In addition, Jamali[2] noted that the proliferation of different conceptualizations of CSR has generated confusion.

However, there are findings indicating that positive impacts in economic, social and environmental issues result when companies consider social practices in their objectives. The implementation and practice of CSR principles are key indicators for measuring society and stakeholder expectations, as mentioned by Asif et al. (2011). Several different efforts have been made to demonstrate whether CSR practices have a positive impact on financial performance.[3-5] Clarkson *et al.* (2008) and Clarkson *et al.*[6] found that firms with better environmental performance are more forthcoming about their social practices through discretionary disclosure channels (social practices). In the Mexican economy, studies have demonstrated a positive association between financial performance and the implementation of CSR practices.[7]

In this paper, we analyze the abnormal returns of companies listed on the Mexican Stock Exchange Index from 2008 to 2011, comparing sustainable firms with non-sustainable firms. We used two methodologies in this analysis: 1) ordinary least squares (OLS) and 2) Fuzzy Regression. The article is divided into seven sections. First, we review the CSR concept. In Section 2, we provide a snapshot of the theoretical evidence linking socially responsible investments and financial performance. Next, the methodology and theory of abnormal returns are discussed. Thereafter, in Sections 4 and 5, we present the methodology of Fuzzy Regression and our estimation model. Finally, the results and conclusions are analyzed.

2. Corporate social responsibility

The idea of CSR has changed in various ways throughout history. Carroll[8] analyzed the evolution of CSR and argued that the CSR concept has passed through several distinct stages of development. During the 1930s, Barnard[9] and several other researchers conducted studies that focused upon the functions of executives, with significant attention to those executives' social responsibilities.

In the 1950s, Bowen[10] wrote a book addressing the doctrine of social responsibility and his work formed the foundations for modern discussions of this topic. In fact, Carroll[8] named him "The Father of CSR". Other important works from this period include the writings of Selekman[11] and Eells[12].

The 1960s marked a significant growth in attempts to formalize the meaning of the CSR concept, through studies such as that of McGuire[13]. Subsequently, Heald[14] provided an interesting and provocative discussion of the theory and practice of CSR during the first half of the twentieth century; however, he did not provide a definition of CSR. The 1970s featured a growing interest in Corporate Social Performance (CSP) as well as CSR. According to Carroll[15], the company is the basic unit of society and its main goal is to be financially responsible.

In the 1980s, CSR research focused upon the acceptance of the notion of CSP as a theory. For instance, Cochran and Wood[16] presented the evolution of the CSR model across three dimensions: responsibility, responsiveness and social issues. CSR research during the 1990s was characterized by studies of topics such as CSP, stakeholder theory, business ethics theory and corporate citizenship.

Recently, the literature has focused on the impacts of economic, environmental, social and ethical behaviors on the use of CSR. Clarkson *et al.*[6] showed that companies with social disclosures tended to have better environmental performance. Barnea and Rubin[17] demonstrated that CEOs in controversial industry sectors are immoral managers that use CSR as a means of enhancing their own private reputation-building benefits as social citizens at the cost of shareholder wealth.

Cai *et al.*[18] indicated that the CSR concept has indeed been defined in various ways, ranging from the narrow economic perspective of increasing shareholder wealth[19] to broader economic, legal, ethical and discretionary aspects of responsibility[15]. The variety of definitions regarding CSR has made this concept vague.

Jamali[20] noted that the CSR notion has not generated significant interest in developing countries due to their disorganized civil societies and the lack of CSR promotion by the governments of those nations. This situation mainly arises from the fact that the institutions, standards and systems that form the foundations of CSR in Europe and the US are comparatively weak in developing nations[21].

Mexico has been conducting efforts to incorporate CSR practices into the strategies of its companies, although progress in this regard has not been as rapid or efficient as the CSR development observed in Europe and the US There are two initiatives in Mexico that attempt to measure CSR performance. The first of these initiatives is the Mexican Center for Philanthropy (CEMEFI). This institution was created by six participant firms focused upon corporate philanthropy. CEMEFI annually recognizes the firms that perform best on assessments of the following four criteria: business ethics, community outreach, standard of living within the firm and environmental awareness and conservation.

Recently, another initiative was created based upon the new Mexican sustainability index. This index is comprised of the most liquid shares on the Mexican Stock Exchange (BMV)[a]. Companies eligible for inclusion are assessed according to their performance and the impact of their responses to emerging environmental, social and governance (ESG) issues. These topics include climate change, human rights, policies and systems to counter bribery. The BMV selected two autonomous institutions, EIRIS (Empowering Responsible Investments)[b] and Anahuac University, as its lead partners in developing the methodology and assessment framework behind the new sustainability index. Both of these institutions also undertake research on behalf of the BMV to evaluate the ESG performance of Mexican companies and determine which firms meet the sustainability requirements for listing on the index[22].

3. Sustainability and financial performance

Ziegler and Schroder[23] defined "Social Responsibility Investments" (SRIs) as an investment strategy characterized by the practice of choosing stocks via environmental and social screening methods. Sauer[24] stated that socially responsible investors set their investment criteria in accordance with their personal value systems and beliefs. SRI also involves one or more of the following selection and monitoring practices: negative screening of companies or sectors; positive investment in sustainable industries; analysis of companies for their environmental, social or governance performance; investing in the most sustainable companies within all sectors; and the engagement of companies regarding environmental, social or governance issues[25].

SRI assets have experienced strong growth around the world, as mentioned in Ziegler and Schroder[23]; for example, a 1200% growth in SRI assets occurred between 1995 and 2005 in the US This growth has led to SRI assets comprising

[a] The BMV abbreviation derives from the Spanish name of the stock exchange (Bolsa Mexicana de Valores).

[b] The partner of EIRIS in Mexico is Ecovalores.

approximately 10% of the total US management assets and over 10% of European funds.

The financial performance of sustainable firms has been studied through two variables: sustainability indices and sustainability investment funds. The main difference between these two variables is that funds involve costs[c]. However, investigations into this performance have not produced a consensus conclusion, as certain studies [3, 7, 26-30] found superior financial performance from investments into CSR issues and projects, whereas other analyses concluded that CSR-related investments exhibit lower financial performance than traditional funds [31-34]. Moreover, several studies, such as Sauer (1997), Goldreyer *et al.*[35], Bauer *et al.*[36] and Schroder[37], have concluded that no statistically significant difference exists between the returns of ethically screened investments and unscreened assets.

Graves and Waddock[30] demonstrated that institutional investors prefer to promote CSR practices, choosing to invest in socially responsible organizations even if they are not socially responsible themselves. In particular, investors that are actually committed to the CSR issue invest in the Dow Jones Sustainability Index (DSI), whereas certain others invest in this index simply to improve their reputations. Griffin and Mahon[29] explored the social and financial performance of six firms in the petrochemical industry between 1990 and 1992 and discovered that their quantifiable metrics indicated a positive relationship between the KLD and Fortune indices. Margolis and Walsh[27] found 122 studies published between 1971 and 2001 and used these investigations to empirically examine the positive relationship between corporate social responsibility and financial performance screening. Derwall *et al.*[3] ranked equities using an eco-efficiency rating. By developing different portfolios of high-ranked and low-ranked equities, these authors found that SRI screening produces a highly significant increase in asset performance.

Petersen and Vredenburg[26] investigated the oil sector in Canada, revealing evidence of economic value added by CSR practices and showing that investment efforts in CSR projects are recognized and rewarded in capital markets by a higher economic profitability. In addition, Lee and Faff[28] found that European and American investors bet upon the success of CSR firms. In the Mexican case, Almeida *et al.*[7] showed that Mexican firms evinced a large, positive relationship between social responsibility and financial performance, as evaluated by the ROE, ROA, earnings per share (UPA) and price over book value (P/VL) variables.

[c] These expenses include the costs for fund operations, fund timing activities and skillful fund managers.

However, negative results of CSR evaluations exist, as Mueller[32], Hamilton *et al.*[34], Statman[31] and Lima *et al.*[33] demonstrated that socially responsible mutual funds have lower performance than conventional mutual funds. Mueller[32] examined the risk-adjusted returns of 10 socially responsible investments from 1984 to 1988, finding that socially responsible mutual funds earned an average of 1.03% less in annual returns than comparable, unrestricted investments. Hamilton *et al.*[34] used estimates of Jensen´s alpha to examine the risk-adjusted performance of all of the socially responsible mutual funds listed in the Lipper Analytical databank as of December 1990 and discovered that socially responsible mutual funds tend to exhibit similar or lesser performance relative to comparable unrestricted mutual funds on a risk-adjusted basis. Statman[31] reported that the Domini Social Index, an index of socially responsible stocks, performed as well as the S&P 500 index over the 1990-1998 time period. Finally, Lima *et al.*[33] found an inverse relationship between CSR and financial performance for 78 Brazilian firms from 2001 to 2006, conjecturing that this relationship was caused by the role of traditional cultural beliefs in producing a lack of motivation for investment into responsible firms.

As mentioned above, studies also exist that found no significant difference between the performance of socially responsible firm indices and the returns of unrestricted indices. For instance, Sauer[24] compared the DSI with two unrestricted indices and concluded that the application of social responsibility screens does not necessarily produce an adverse impact on investment performance. The empirical evidence presented in his paper clearly indicates that investors can choose socially responsible investments that are consistent with their value system and beliefs without being forced into financial sacrifices. Goldreyer *et al.*[35] considered an extended sample of ethical funds, including equity, bond and balanced funds, using Jensen´s alpha estimates, Sharpe ratios and Treynor ratios and concluded that social screening does not affect the investment performance of ethical mutual funds in any systematic way. Bauer *et al.*[36] used an international database containing 103 German, UK and US ethical mutual funds and found no significant statistically difference in performance between ethical and conventional mutual fund returns after controlling for common factors, such as size, book-to-market and momentum. Schroder[37] analyzed 29 SRI stock indices and found that these indices lead to neither a significant outperformance nor an underperformance compared with their benchmark indices.

4. Abnormal returns

The concept of portfolio "performance" incorporates at least two distinct dimensions[38]: 1) The ability of the portfolio manager to increase returns on the portfolio through the successful prediction of future security prices and 2) the ability of the portfolio manager to minimize the amount of "insurable risk" borne by the holders of the portfolio.

The Jensen´s alpha of a portfolio is derived from a direct application of the theoretical results of the Capital Asset Pricing Model (CAPM) established independently by Sharpe[39], Lintner[40] and Treynor[41]. This model is based on the following assumptions: (1) all investors are averse to risk and seek to maximize the expected utility of their terminal wealth over a single holding period; (2) all investors have identical decision horizons and homogeneous expectations regarding investment opportunities; (3) all investors are able to choose among portfolios solely based on expected returns and variance of returns; and (4) all transaction costs and taxes are zero; and (5) all assets are infinitely divisible.

Jensen[38] created the first model to test the performance of mutual funds and thereby examine whether any portfolio will earn more than the "normal" premium expected given its level of risk, i.e., whether any portfolio will "beat the market". The metric measuring abnormal earnings was therefore named Jensen´s alpha. Jensen[38] used a sample of annual returns from a portfolio of 115 funds from 1945-1964. These returns were then subjected to separate OLS time series regressions of the form:

$$R_{jt} - R_{ft} = a_j + B_j\left(R_{mt} - R_{ft}\right) + u_t \quad (1)$$

where R_{jt} is the return on portfolio j at the time t, R_{ft} is the return on a risk-free proxy (an one-year government bond), R_{mt} is the return on a market portfolio proxy, u_t is an error term and a_j and B_j are parameters to be estimated. In particular, a_j defines whether a fund outperforms or underperforms the market index. A positive and significant a_j for a given fund would suggest that the fund is able to earn significant abnormal returns in excess of the market required return given that fund's level of risk.

Jensen[38] mentioned that the ability of a portfolio manager to correctly forecast security prices will produce a positive a_j. Jensen´s alpha is the average incremental rate of return for the portfolio per unit of time that is due solely to the manager's ability to forecast future security prices. Jensen's alpha is expected to be zero for a policy that involves buying and holding a naïve, random selection of investments. Thus, if the manager is not doing as well as a buy-and-hold policy of random selections, Jensen's alpha will be negative. At first glance, it might appear difficult to do worse than a random selection policy, but such results can very well occur if too many expenses are generated by unsuccessful forecasting attempts.

5. Fuzzy Regression model

In the literature, various studies, such as those of De Andres and Terceño[42], Terceño *et al.*[43] and De los Cobos-Silva *et al.*[44], apply Fuzzy Regression to finance issues. Fuzzy Regression models, similarly to other regression techniques, seek to determine functional relationships between a dependent variable Y (also called the response variable) and one or more independent (explanatory) variables, $X=(X_0,X_1,...,X_n)$, for which $X_0=1$ if the parameters are estimated using confidence intervals (CIs). A CI is represented either by its minimum (a_1) and maximum (a_2) values as $A=[a_1,a_2]$ or through its center (a_C) and radius (a_R) as follows:

$$a_C=\frac{a_2+a_1}{2} \qquad a_R=\frac{a_2-a_1}{2} \tag{2}$$

For a particular phenomenon, Tanaka and Ishibuchi[45] assumed that the observer has a sample represented as $(Y_1,X_1),...,(Y_n,X_n)$, subject to the following conditions:

1. Y_j is a real interval $[Y_j^1,Y_j^2]$ corresponding to the *j*-th value of the dependent variable, where *j*=1, 2,…, *n* and it can be assumed that Y_j is given by a fuzzy interval determined by its center and its radius as:

$$Y_j=\langle Y_{jC},Y_{jR}\rangle \tag{3}$$

$$Y_{jC}=\frac{Y_j^2+Y_j^1}{2} \qquad Y_{jR}=\frac{Y_j^2-Y_j^1}{2}$$

   If Y_j is known with complete accuracy, then $Y_{jR}=0$.

2. Furthermore, X_j is the vector observed for the *j*-th observation of the independent variables, with *j*=1, 2,…,*n*. Thus, X_j is a *m*-dimensional variable and $X_j=(X_{0j},X_{1j},X_{2j},...,X_{mj})$ where $X_{0j}=1\ \forall\ j$ and X_{ij} is the value of the *j*-th observation of the sample for the *i*-th variable. In any event, we assume that certain observations are treated as "crisp data".

We further assume that the relationship between the dependent variable Y can be given by a confidence interval and that the independent variable

$X=(X_0,X_1,X_2,...,X_m)$, which is a vector with certain components, is linearly related such that the following relationship holds:

$$Y=A_0+A_1X_1+A_2X_2+...+A_mX_m \tag{4}$$

where A_i, i=0, 1, …, m, are confidence intervals of the form: $A_i=\langle A_{iC},A_{iR}\rangle$, with $i=0, 1, ..., m$.

The ultimate goal of this process is to determine centers and radii for these confidence intervals such that A_i is consistent with the available observations.

Thus, if we refer to $\hat{Y}_j=\langle \hat{Y}_{jC},\hat{Y}_{jR}\rangle$ as the confidence interval for the estimated value for the j-th independent variable Y_j, after finding the parameters $A_0,A_1,A_2,...,A_m$, this estimate can be obtained via the following sum: $\hat{Y}_j=A_0+A_1X_{1j}+A_2X_{2j}+...+A_mX_{mj}$, where j=0, 1, …, n. We can express the $\tilde{Y}_j$ estimates using their centers and radius, which will be functions of the centers and radius of the parameters A_i, for i=0, 1, …, m:

$$\langle \hat{Y}_{jC},\hat{Y}_{jR}\rangle=\sum_{i=0}^{m}\langle a_{iC},a_{iR}\rangle X_{ij}=\langle \sum_{i=0}^{m}a_{iC}X_{ij},\sum_{i=0}^{m}a_{iR}|X_{ij}|\rangle, j=1,2,...,n \tag{5}$$

The goodness of fit is the inverse of the uncertainty (amplitude) of estimates of the observations. Thus, the amplitude of $\hat{Y}_j$ is the radius of the CI, which is calculated in the following manner:

$$\hat{Y}_{jR}=\sum_{i=0}^{m}a_{iR}|X_{i,j}|=a_{0R}+a_{1R}|X_{1j}|+...+a_{mR}|X_{mj}| \tag{6}$$

Therefore, z, the total of all uncertainty estimates within the sample, is the sum of the radii of the estimates:

$$z=\sum_{j=1}^{n}\hat{Y}_{jR}=\sum_{j=1}^{n}\sum_{i=0}^{m}a_{iR}|X_{ij}| \tag{7}$$

The final goal is to minimize the total uncertainty of the estimates. The parameters A_i should ensure not only that the uncertainty $\hat{Y}_j$ is as small as possible but also that Y_j is as consistent as possible with the observations of the dependent variable that are intended to approximate Y_j. To estimate the parameters A_i, three models can be considered:

1) Tanaka and Ishibuchi[45] postulated that the observation must be included in the estimate, i.e., $Y_j\subseteq\hat{Y}_j$, in accordance with the following conditions:

$$Y_{jC}-Y_{jR}\geq\hat{Y}_{jC}-\hat{Y}_{jR} \text{ and } Y_{jC}+Y_{jR}\leq\hat{Y}_{jC}+\hat{Y}_{jR} \tag{8}$$

The parameters are estimated by solving the following linear programming problem:

$$Min\ z = \sum_{j=1}^{n} \hat{Y}_{jR} = \sum_{j=1}^{n} \sum_{i=0}^{m} a_{iR} \left| X_{ij} \right| \tag{9}$$

subject to:

$$Y_{jC} - Y_{jR} \geq \hat{Y}_{jC} - \hat{Y}_{jR} = \sum_{i=0}^{m} a_{iC} X_{ij} - \sum_{i=0}^{m} a_{iR} \left| X_{ij} \right|, \quad j = 1,2,...,n$$

$$Y_{jC} + Y_{jR} \leq \hat{Y}_{jC} + \hat{Y}_{jR} = \sum_{i=0}^{m} a_{iC} X_{ij} + \sum_{i=0}^{m} a_{iR} \left| X_{ij} \right|, \quad j = 1,2,...,n$$

$$a_{iR} \geq 0, \qquad i=0,1,\ldots,m$$

2) Sakawa and Yano[46] believed that the observations must be "equal" to their estimates, i.e., that $Y_j = \hat{Y}_j$ in accordance with the following conditions:

$$Y_{jC} + Y_{jR} \geq \hat{Y}_{jC} - \hat{Y}_{jR} \text{ and } Y_{jC} - Y_{jR} \leq \hat{Y}_{jC} + \hat{Y}_{jR} \tag{10}$$

The parameters are estimated by solving the following linear programming problem:

$$Min\ z = \sum_{j=1}^{n} \hat{Y}_{jR} = \sum_{j=1}^{n} \sum_{i=0}^{m} a_{iR} \left| X_{ij} \right| \tag{11}$$

subject to:

$$Y_{jC} + Y_{jR} \geq \hat{Y}_{jC} - \hat{Y}_{jR} = \sum_{i=0}^{m} a_{iC} X_{ij} - \sum_{i=0}^{m} a_{iR} \left| X_{ij} \right|, \quad j = 1,2,...,n$$

$$Y_{jC} - Y_{jR} \leq \hat{Y}_{jC} + \hat{Y}_{jR} = \sum_{i=0}^{m} a_{iC} X_{ij} + \sum_{i=0}^{m} a_{iR} \left| X_{ij} \right|, \quad j = 1,2,...,n$$

$$a_{iR} \geq 0, \qquad i=0,1,\ldots,m$$

3) Fuzzy Regression with crisp values can be used. In this case, crisp values are considered to be those for which the extremes of a confidence interval are identical. If the central values are considered to be the crisp values with the radius set to zero, then the parameters are estimated by solving the following linear programming problem:

$$Min\ z = \sum_{j=1}^{n} \hat{Y}_{jR} = \sum_{j=1}^{n} \sum_{i=0}^{m} a_{iR} \left| X_{ij} \right| \tag{12}$$

subject to:

$$Y_{jC} \geq \hat{Y}_{jC} - \hat{Y}_{jR} = \sum_{i=0}^{m} a_{iC} X_{ij} - \sum_{i=0}^{m} a_{iR} \left| X_{ij} \right|, \quad j = 1,2,...,n$$

$$Y_{jC} \leq \hat{Y}_{jC} + \hat{Y}_{jR} = \sum_{i=0}^{m} a_{iC} X_{ij} + \sum_{i=0}^{m} a_{iR} \left| X_{ij} \right|, \quad j = 1,2,...,n$$

$$a_{iR} \geq 0, \qquad i=0,1,\ldots,m$$

6. Model estimation

To estimate the abnormal returns and the performance differences between the firms that engage in CSR practices and those companies that do not utilize

CSR, we used the BMV database. The sample consists of firms that were included in the Prices and Quotations Index (IPC)[d] from 2008 to 2011.

Because we obtained complete information for 28 of the 35 companies that compose the IPC as of the end of December 2011, we considered these 28 firms to be our sample. From the total sample, only 19 of the 28 firms are included in the Mexican sustainability index (IPCS); thus, these 19 constitute the sustainable firms of the sample, whereas the remaining 9 are considered to be non-sustainable firms.

For the purposes of this study, we considered the monthly values of the minimum and maximum prices for each firm and the IPC as a whole, obtaining our data from Infosel[47]. For the free risk variable, we also used the maximum and minimum annual interest rates from each month that were reported by Banxico[48].

To estimate and compare the Jensen´s alpha between the sustainable and non-sustainable firms, two types of annual returns were calculated. In these calculations, the interval $P_t^{\min}, P_t^{\max}$ corresponds to the *t*-th value of the minimum and maximum prices (or index), respectively, for *t=1, 2,..., n*, where *n* is the number of observations in the analyzed period:

a) Fuzzy returns: These returns are calculated from the extreme values of the prices (or index) as follows:

$$R_t^{\min} = \begin{cases} \dfrac{P_t^{\min} - P_{t-1}^{\max}}{P_{t-1}^{\max}} & \text{if } \left(P_t^{\min} - P_{t-1}^{\max}\right) \geq 0 \\ Min\left[\dfrac{P_t^{\min} - P_{t-1}^{\max}}{P_{t-1}^{\max}}, \dfrac{P_t^{\min} - P_{t-1}^{\max}}{P_{t-1}^{\min}}, \dfrac{P_t^{\max} - P_{t-1}^{\min}}{P_{t-1}^{\min}}, \dfrac{P_t^{\max} - P_{t-1}^{\min}}{P_{t-1}^{\max}}\right] & \text{if } \left(P_t^{\min} - P_{t-1}^{\max}\right) < 0 \end{cases} \tag{13}$$

$$R_t^{\max} = \begin{cases} \dfrac{P_t^{\max} - P_{t-1}^{\min}}{P_{t-1}^{\min}} & \text{if } \left(P_t^{\max} - P_{t-1}^{\min}\right) \geq 0 \\ Max\left[\dfrac{P_t^{\min} - P_{t-1}^{\max}}{P_{t-1}^{\max}}, \dfrac{P_t^{\min} - P_{t-1}^{\max}}{P_{t-1}^{\min}}, \dfrac{P_t^{\max} - P_{t-1}^{\min}}{P_{t-1}^{\min}}, \dfrac{P_t^{\max} - P_{t-1}^{\min}}{P_{t-1}^{\max}}\right] & \text{if } \left(P_t^{\max} - P_{t-1}^{\min}\right) < 0 \end{cases} \tag{14}$$

In accordance with equation (3), the central value (R_t^C) and the radius (R_t^r) are calculated as:

$$R_t^C = \frac{R_j^{\max} + R_j^{\min}}{2}, \qquad R_t^R = \frac{R_j^{\max} - R_j^{\min}}{2} \tag{15}$$

---

[d] The abbreviation IPC is derived from this index's Spanish name (Indice de Precios y Cotizaciones). The IPC is the main indicator of BMV performance, expressing the stock market yield based upon the price variations of a balanced, weighted and representative subgroup of stocks selected from all firms listed in the stock market as a whole.

Thus, the fuzzy returns are expressed as:

$$R_t = \langle R_t^C, R_t^r \rangle = [R_t^{\min}, R_t^{\max}] \quad t = 1,2,\ldots,n \tag{16}$$

b) Crisp returns: These returns are expressed as a confidence interval in which the extremes are identical. We considered the central value to be the crisp returns, i.e., we set the radius (R_t^r) from equation (16) equal to zero.

The Fuzzy Regression was estimated using the three models discussed in equations (9), (11) and (12). Table 1 shows the z/n values calculated from these three models. In this case, we can conclude that the lowest uncertainty is obtained when using the model proposed by Sakawa and Yano[46].

Table 1. Model Selection (z/n Values)

Ticker Mexican Capital Market	Sector	Uncertainty (Average, %)		
		Crisp Returns	Tanaka & Ishibuchi	Sakawa & Yano
AC*	Basic consumer products	43.28	60.88	27.63
ALFA*	Industrial	61.00	115.41	28.18
ALSEA	No basic consumer products	47.96	76.96	25.18
AMX*	Telecommunications	20.08	37.41	9.73
ARA	Industrial	34.79	68.39	15.97
ASUR*	Industrial	21.54	47.36	5.49
AXTEL	Telecommunications	85.80	105.44	66.15
AZTECA*	Telecommunications	39.10	58.71	21.74
BIMBO*	Basic consumer products	25.36	46.62	6.72
CEMEX*	Material	31.59	64.15	5.66
COMERCI*	Basic consumer products	685.85	1384.42	60.60
ELEKTRA	No basic consumer products	89.47	119.62	70.96
GAP	Industrial	36.45	54.75	18.86
GEO*	Industrial	50.96	85.91	24.07
GFNORTE*	Financial services	27.72	64.02	4.03
GMEXICO*	Material	48.68	96.73	20.75
GMODELO*	Basic consumer products	25.86	44.49	15.66
GRUMA	Basic consumer products	76.93	147.43	45.10
HOMEX*	Industrial	37.48	68.90	19.60
ICA*	Industrial	58.46	85.88	42.12
KIMBER*	Basic consumer products	23.30	40.99	9.20
LIVERPOL	No basic consumer products	31.97	39.09	30.57
MEXCHEM*	Material	95.87	137.58	64.87
PEÑOLES*	Material	89.86	135.37	56.46
SORIANA	Basic consumer products	19.44	39.11	6.09
TLEVISA	Telecommunications	19.44	31.12	8.53
URBI*	Industrial	23.01	50.24	8.59
WALMEX*	Basic consumer products	24.96	40.24	12.86
	Mean	**67.01**	**119.54**	**26.12**

*Firms in the Sustainability Index

Once we have selected the best model for our analyses, our next step was to estimate Jensen´s alpha values using the model proposed by Sakawa and Yano[46] and compare the results with the estimates obtained using the OLS method. Table 2 indicates the Jensen´s alpha values estimated by both methodologies. The fuzzy Jensen's alpha value of firm X is denoted as follows:

$$\langle a_C, a_R \rangle = [a^{min}, a^{max}] \quad (17)$$

where the subscripts C and R represent the center and radius alphas, respectively, whereas the superscripts *min* and *max* denote the minimum and maximum alphas, respectively.

Table 2. Jensen´s alpha estimates

Ticker Symbol on the Mexican Capital Market	OLS		Fuzzy Regression (Sakawa & Yano)				Abnormal Returns Possibility
	Jensen´s Alpha (α)	*p-value*	α_C	α_R	α^{min}	α^{max}	
AC*	10.71	0.00	18.64	25.58	-6.95	44.22	86%
ALFA*	35.39	0.00	14.54	22.63	-8.09	37.17	82%
ALSEA	-3.87	0.35	-11.18	25.18	-36.36	13.99	28%
AMX*	-3.38	0.03	1.44	9.73	-8.29	11.17	57%
ARA	-20.58	0.00	-33.05	6.74	-39.79	-26.32	0%
ASUR*	1.82	0.30	2.07	5.49	-3.42	7.56	69%
AXTEL	-19.78	0.00	14.78	66.15	-51.37	80.93	61%
AZTECA*	0.78	0.76	2.51	21.74	-19.23	24.25	56%
BIMBO*	10.09	0.00	2.34	2.15	0.19	4.49	100%
CEMEX*	-28.82	0.00	-37.75	2.75	-40.50	-35.00	0%
COMERCI*	61.71	0.26	-15.06	60.60	-75.65	45.54	38%
ELEKTRA	47.14	0.00	56.74	70.96	-14.23	127.70	90%
GAP	-3.80	0.09	-8.61	18.86	-27.48	10.25	27%
GEO*	-10.38	0.03	-30.17	17.04	-47.21	-13.14	0%
GFNORTE*	4.03	0.14	-3.70	0.41	-4.11	-3.29	0%
GMEXICO*	32.51	0.00	15.10	3.72	11.38	18.81	100%
GMODELO*	3.53	0.08	0.40	15.66	-15.26	16.06	51%
GRUMA	11.49	0.01	-11.29	32.90	-44.20	21.61	33%
HOMEX*	-18.54	0.00	-30.25	19.60	-49.85	-10.64	0%
ICA*	-15.45	0.00	-0.35	42.12	-42.46	41.77	50%
KIMBER*	6.47	0.00	5.05	9.20	-4.15	14.24	77%
LIVERPOL	9.19	0.00	13.53	30.57	-17.04	44.11	72%
MEXCHEM*	52.19	0.00	50.68	64.87	-14.19	115.54	89%
PEÑOLES*	43.59	0.00	58.83	56.46	2.37	115.30	100%
SORIANA	-3.32	0.02	-9.51	6.09	-15.59	-3.42	0%
TLEVISA	-6.49	0.00	-12.31	8.53	-20.84	-3.78	0%
URBI*	-14.27	0.00	-27.98	5.13	-33.11	-22.85	0%
WALMEX*	8.40	0.00	-5.93	10.19	-16.11	4.26	21%
Mean	**6.80**		**0.70**	**23.61**	**-22.91**	**24.31**	**51%**

*Firms in the Sustainability Index

Jensen´s rule states that a positive and significant alpha for a given financial asset would suggest that it is able to earn significant abnormal returns in excess of risk-adjusted market expectations. Using a 95% confidence level, the OLS results suggest that eleven firms fulfill this requirement, 73% of which are sustainable firms. However, these results do not indicate the magnitude of the possibility that a firm will provide abnormal returns.

In fact, only three firms have a 100% possibility of outperforming the market, according to the Sakawa and Yano[46] model and all three of these companies are sustainable firms. To calculate the abnormal returns possibility of a firm X, $Poss^{AR}(X)$, we propose the following metric:

$$Poss^{AR}(X) = \begin{cases} 1 & \textit{if} \quad a^{\min}, a^{\max} > 0 \\ \dfrac{a^{\max}}{\left|a^{\min}\right| + a^{\max}} & \textit{if} \quad a^{\min} < 0,\ a^{\max} > 0 \\ 0 & \textit{otherwise} \end{cases} \tag{17}$$

When we consider the percentage of occasions for which the estimates are equal to the real interval (%Hits), there are notable differences between the OLS results and the Fuzzy Regression results. The fuzzy alphas always hit the real interval, as this constraint is incorporated into the model, as we mentioned in equation (10) above. However, this is not the case with OLS estimates, as is shown in Table 3, even if we consider the 95% confidence interval estimated by OLS.

Table 3. Estimate performance vs. real intervals

OLS		2008	2009	2010	2011	2008-
Estimated Jensen´s	%Hits	48%	63%	70%	47%	57%
Alpha	%Failures	52%	37%	30%	53%	43%
95% Confidence	%Hits	57%	68%	86%	69%	70%
Interval	%Failures	43%	32%	14%	31%	30%

7. Results

As we previously mentioned, CSR research is growing rapidly, raising the question of whether CSR practices positively impact the financial performance of firms. To address this issue, we applied the Fuzzy Regression model proposed by Sakawa and Yano[46] to the Mexican capital market. We also analyzed the relationship between uncertainty and abnormal returns.

The results depicted in Table 4 indicate that sustainable firms (SFs) have greater possibilities of obtaining abnormal returns than non-sustainable firms (NSFs). For instance, 16% of the SFs have a 100% possibility of producing abnormal returns, compared with 0% of NSFs and one out of every three NSFs (33%) has no possibility (0%) of beating the market, whereas this probability is only found for approximately one out of every four (26%) of the SFs. The principle of risk/returns does not apply to these results because the z/n value, i.e., the uncertainty, is greater in the NSFs than the SFs, although the former category of firms has a lesser possibility of obtaining abnormal returns.

When conducting a sector analysis, we found that SFs in the materials sector have greater possibilities of obtaining abnormal or excess returns than other firms and all of the firms sampled in this sector are SFs. The uncertainty of the estimates is also greater in the firms of the materials sector than for other SFs. In contrast, financial services and telecommunications companies have lower possibilities of beating the market.

Table 4. Sector analysis of abnormal returns vs. uncertainty

	IPC Sector	IPC Firms	Abnormal Returns Possibility						Uncertainty (Average) Sakawa & Yano	
			0%	>0%	>25%	>50%	>75%	100%	z/n (%)	Sector Rank
Sustainable – Fuzzy Alpha's Jensen	**Total**	**19**	**26%**	**74%**	**68%**	**58%**	**37%**	**16%**	**23.4**	-
	Basic consumer products	6	0%	100%	83%	67%	50%	17%	22.1	2
	Financial services	1	100%	0%	0%	0%	0%	0%	4.0	5
	Industrial	6	50%	50%	50%	33%	17%	0%	21.3	3
	Material	4	25%	75%	75%	75%	75%	50%	36.9	1
	No basic consumer products	0	-	-	-	-	-	-	-	-
	Telecommunications	2	0%	100%	100%	100%	0%	0%	15.7	4
Not Sustainable – Fuzzy Alpha's Jensen	**Total**	**9**	**33%**	**67%**	**67%**	**33%**	**11%**	**0%**	**31.9**	-
	Basic consumer products	2	50%	50%	50%	0%	0%	0%	25.6	3
	Financial services	0	-	-	-	-	-	-	-	-
	Industrial	2	50%	50%	50%	0%	0%	0%	17.4	4
	Material	0	-	-	-	-	-	-	-	-
	No basic consumer products	3	0%	100%	100%	67%	33%	0%	42.2	1
	Telecommunications	2	50%	50%	50%	50%	0%	0%	37.3	2
Overall Sample – Fuzzy Alpha's Jensen	**Total**	**28**	**29%**	**71%**	**68%**	**50%**	**29%**	**11%**	26.1	-
	Basic consumer products	8	13%	88%	75%	50%	38%	13%	23.0	4
	Financial services	1	100%	0%	0%	0%	0%	0%	4.0	6
	Industrial	8	50%	50%	50%	25%	13%	0%	20.4	5
	Material	4	25%	75%	75%	75%	75%	50%	36.9	2
	No basic consumer products	3	0%	100%	100%	67%	33%	0%	42.2	1
	Telecommunications	4	25%	75%	75%	75%	0%	0%	26.5	3

8. Conclusions

Social Responsibility Investments have experienced a strong growth around the world from 1995 to the present. Companies from emerging markets that wish to enter the world financial markets must now report their social, environmental and corporate governance issues if they wish to gain in reputation and competitiveness. Mexican firms could begin to accomplish this process by fulfilling the IPCS standards, thereby obtaining more visibility, demonstrating transparency and indicating their commitment to their stakeholders. However, many question whether these practices can produce profitable firms.

Three conclusions can be drawn from this paper. First, we briefly reviewed the different investigations that probed the relationship between social indices and financial performance and explained that no consensus exists from the results of these studies. However, our results in this study indicate that SFs demonstrate greater possibilities of obtaining abnormal returns than NSFs. This conclusion is in accordance with the findings of Graves and Waddock[30], Griffin and Mahon[29], Margolis and Walsh[27], Derwall *et al.*[3], Petersen and Vredenbur[26], Lee and Faff[28] and Almeida *et al.*[7].

Second, on a macro level, the uncertainty found in the sample was greater for the NSFs than the SFs. These results indicate that more positive expectations exist for companies that are responsible than for firms that are not. This conclusion offers one important incentive for firms to have more transparent reporting mechanisms, which will promote social mechanisms for reporting growth.

Third, the OLS alpha estimates are less reliable than the Fuzzy Regression, especially for uncertain periods, such as the timespan studied in this paper. The years with greatest uncertainty were 2008 and 2011, when Mexico faced international financial crises that affected its capital market; in particular, 2008 was characterized by the US crisis, whereas the economy in 2011 was shocked by the Greece crisis. The years 2008 and 2011 were the occasions when the OLS estimates had their lowest accuracy. Fuzzy logic offers a means to deal with the uncertainties inherent in a wide variety of tasks, especially when the uncertainty is not the result of randomness but the result of unknown factors and relationships that are difficult to explain[49].

Finally, the trends and challenges of social investment are worth mentioning. First, there should be a new role for capital markets, as the function of such markets should be not only to focus on providing capital funds for companies but also to encourage firms to adopt a positive corporate image. For example, EIRIS[50] argued that sustainability indices, such as the BM&FBOVESPA ISE Index, the Dow Jones Sustainability Index and the JSE

SRI Index, greatly contributed to the improvement of the environmental, social and corporate governmental performance of companies and that these indices implicitly help raise the international profile of responsible investment practices. Second, the institutions that promote CSR in Mexico are very weak[21] and EIRIS[50] found that stocks of world exchanges demonstrate poor environmental, social and governmental performance. Thus, it is a challenge not only for the Mexican IPCS but also for the world sustainability indices to maintain a clear listing of rules that promote CSR practices.

Acknowledgments
This article was written as part of a research project titled "Impact of Social Responsibility in Risk and Performance Business: Latin America Case" (IDCA9113, UANL-CA-280), which was financed by the Mexican Ministry of Education. Part of this study was also sponsored by the Universidad Autónoma de Nuevo León (PAICYT, GCS043-10).

REFERENCES

1. T. Maak. *Journal of Business Ethics* **82**, (2008).
2. D. Jamali. *Journal of Business Ethics* **82**, (2008).
3. J. Derwall, N. Guenster, R. Bauer and K. Koedijk. *Financial Analysts Journal* **61**, (2005).
4. M. Orlitzky, F. Schmidt and S. Rynes. *Organization Studies* **24**, (2003).
5. J. Peloza. *Journal of Management* **35**, (2009).
6. P. Clarkson, M. Overell and L. Chapple. *Abacus* **47**, (2011).
7. M. Almeida, G.M. Rodríguez, K. Cortez and J. Abreu-Quintero. *Contaduría y Administración* **57**, (2011).
8. A. Carroll. *Business and Society* **38**, (1999).
9. C. Barnard, *The functions of the executive*. Harvard University Press: Cambridge (1938).
10. H. Bowen, *Social responsibilities of businessman*. Harper and Row: New York (1953).
11. B. Selekman, *A moral philosophy for business*. Mc Graw-Hill: New York (1959).
12. R. Eells, *Corporate giving in a free society*. New York (1956).
13. J. Mcguire, *Business and society*. Mc Graw-Hill: New York (1963).
14. M. Heald, *The social responsibilities of business: Company and community 1900-1960*. Case Western Reserve University Press: Cleveland, OH (1970).
15. A. Carroll. *The Academy of Management Review* **4**, (1979).
16. P. Cochran and R. Wood. *Academy of Management Journal* **27**, (1984).
17. A. Barnea and A. Rubin. *Journal of Business Ethics* **97**, (2010).
18. Y. Cai, H. Jo and C. Pan. *Journal of Business Ethics* **1-14**, (2011).
19. M. Friedman. *New York Times Magazine* **13 September**, (1970).

20. D. Jamali. *Bus Soc Rev* **112**, (2007).
21. M. Kemp, *Corporate Social Responsibility in Indonesia: Quixotic Dream or Confident expectation? Program Paper 6*. United Nations Research Institute for Social Development: Geneva (2001).
22. Eiris. **http://www.eiris.org/files/press%20releases/Mexsustindex.pdf**, (2011).
23. A. Ziegler and M. Schroder. *Ecological Economics* **69**, (2009).
24. D. Sauer. *Review of Financial Economics* **6**, (1997).
25. A. Bilbao-Terol, M. Arenas-Parra and V. Cañal-Fernández. *Information Sciences* **189**, (2012).
26. H. Petersen and H. Vredenburg. *Journal of Business Ethics* **90**, (2009).
27. J. Margolis and J. Walsh, *Social Enterprise Series 19 --Misery Loves Companies: Whither Social Initiatives by Business?* Harvard Business School Working Paper Series 01-058: (2001).
28. D. Lee and R. Faff. *The Financial Review* **44**, (2009).
29. J. Griffin and J. Mahon. *Business and Society* **36**, (1997).
30. S. Graves and S. Waddock. *Academy of Management Journal* **37**, (1994).
31. M. Statman. *Financial Analysts Journal* **56**, (2000).
32. S. Mueller. *Sociological Analysis* **52**, (1991).
33. V. Lima, F. De-Souza and F. Vasconcellos. *Social Responsibility Journal* **7**, (2011).
34. Hamilton, H. Jo and M. Statman. *Financial Analysts Journal* **49**, (1993).
35. E. Goldreyer, P. Ahmed and J. Diltz. *Managerial Finance* **25**, (1999).
36. R. Bauer, K. Koedijk and R. Otten. *Journal of Banking & Finance* **29**, (2005).
37. M. Schroder. *Journal of Business Finance & Accounting* **34**, (2007).
38. M. Jensen. *Journal of Finance* **23**, (1968).
39. Sharpe and Wf. *Journal of Finance* **19**, (1964).
40. Lintner. *Journal of Finance* **20**, (1965).
41. J. Treynor, *Toward a Theory of Market Value of Risky Assets*. Unpublished manuscript: ((Undated)).
42. J. De-Andrés-Sánchez and A. Terceño-Gómez. *Fuzzy Sets and Systems* **139**, (2003).
43. A. Terceño, G. Barberà, H. Vigier and Y. Laumann. *Cuadernos del CIMBAGE* **13**, (2011).
44. S. De-Los-Cobos-Silva, J. Goddard-Close and M. Gutierrez-Andrade. *Revista de Matemática Teoría y Aplicaciones* **18**, (2011).
45. H. Tanaka and H. Ishibuchi, A possibilistic regression analysis based on linear programming. In *Fuzzy Regression Analysis*, Kacprzyk, J.; Fedrizzi, M., Eds. Physica-Verlag: Heidelberg (1992) pp 47–60.
46. M. Sakawa and H. Ya, Fuzzy regression and its applications. In *Fuzzy Regression Analysis*, Kacprzyk, J.; Fedrizzi, M., Eds. Physica-Verlag: Heidelberg (1992) pp 91–101.
47. Infosel. **http://mx.plus.invertia.com**, (2012).
48. Banxico. **http://www.banxico.org.mx/estadisticas/statistics.html**, (2012).

49. S. Liu and C. Lindholm. *International Journal of Intelligent Systems in Accounting, Finance & Management* **14**, (2007).
50. Eiris, *Sustainable Stock Exchanges: improving ESG standards among listed companies.* http://wwweirisorg/files/press%research%20publications/sustainabilityStockspdf: (2010).

RETURN AND RISK: THE SPANISH PUBLIC DEBT MARKET

JOSE M. BROTONS

Department of Economic and Financial Studies. Miguel Hernández University. Avda. Ferrocarril s/n.Elche, 03202,Alicante. jm.brotons@umh.es. 34- 96 665 89 67

ANTONIO TERCEÑO

Department of Business Administration. Rovira i Virgili University. Avda. de la Universidad, nº 1. Reus, 43204, Tarragona. atg@fcee.urv.es. 34-977 75 98 32

M. GLORIA BARBERÁ-MARINÉ

Department of Business Administration. Rovira i Virgili University. Avda. de la Universidad, nº 1. Reus, 43204, Tarragona. gloria.barbera@urv.cat. 34-977759832

Immunization is the main method to assure a certain yield in a future date departing from an initial portfolio. Although the objective of passive strategies is to design a portfolio that will achieve the performance of a predetermined benchmark, active bond management strategies rely on expectations of interest rate movements or changes in yield-spread relationships. However, the variation of the duration increases the risk of a portfolio, that`s why the decision maker will have to chose the combination of expected return (mid-point of the fuzzy number) and risk (width of the fuzzy number) which provides the higher utility. Finally, the construction of a fuzzy return risk map will allow the DM to know the over risk and the over return as regards immunization strategy for each duration and for each risk aversion of the DM. The construction of a risk return map presents the results in an appropriate way. This methodology will help the DM to choose the best duration for the interest rate forecast.

1. Introduction

In 1952, Markowitz proposed the mean-variance methodology for the portfolio selection problem proposed in which the investor is averse to risk. On the other hand, Redington (1952) suggests a parallel treatment to the assets and liabilities in actuarial valuation. This topic has been broadly dealt with in financial literature. In Van Der Meer and Smink (1993) an extensive revision of these techniques is considered. It divides them in static methods (cash flow payment, gap analysis, segmentation and cash floor matching) and dynamic ones (passive, such as immunization or active, such as contingent immunization).

However, some authors, like Gerber (1995), point out that the use of stochastic models is not suitable for the prediction of long term interest rates.

They consider it is much more realistic the use of discount rates based on fuzzy numbers (FN), since only data available is the one facilitated by experts. In our opinion, the use of FN presents important advantages: as bond prices oscillate between a maximum and a minimum price we consider much more appropriate to consider the price, and thus, the corresponding internal rate return (IRR), as fuzzy magnitudes. Taking this into account, we can use all the information that the market provides. Terceño et al. (2007), Brotons and Terceño (2010) and Brotons (2010) apply immunization strategy in a fuzzy environment. However, our goal is to design active bond management in a fuzzy environment, in order to anticipate changes in interest rates. From a starting immunized portfolio, the DM will have to decide whether to increase the expectation return (modifying portfolio duration), increasing the risk as well, or not.

One reasonable function that is commonly employed by financial theorists (Bodie, 1996) assigns a risky portfolio P with risky rate of return r_p, an expected rate of return $E(r_p)$ and a variance of the rate of return σ^2 the utility score $U(P)=R(r_p)-0.005.A.\sigma^2(r_p)$ where A is an index of the DM's risk aversion. Carlsson et al. (2002), in a fuzzy environment, uses E(.) as a measure of return and $\sigma^2(.)$ as a measure of risk.

In practical applications, the use of utility theory has proved to be problematic (Carlsson et al., 2002), which should be more serious than having axiomatic problems, that's why we deal with fuzzy interest and we propose the use of possibility theory. In literature, in the works of fuzzy utility (Sengupta, 1998; Bouyssou, 1997; Banerjee, 1995; De Wilde, 2004; Chen and Klein, 1997) fuzzy parameters are assumed to be known membership functions. However, it is actually not always easy for a DM to specify the membership function or probability distribution in an inexact environment (Carlsson et al, 2002). At least in some of the cases, the use of interval coefficients may serve the purpose better.

Consequently, the main goal of the present work is to design active management strategies in a fuzzy environment, starting from the Sengupta's methodology and proposing a new way to evaluate the risk and the return of a portfolio. So the main purpose of this paper is to design a new index to choose between risk and return, in which the investor can choose the level of risk that want to assume, specially, he will have to weigh the possibility that one alternative of the expectation return has a part that beat a second one in front that this second one has a part that beat the first one.

The structure of the paper is as follows, section 2 is devoted to describing the preliminary fuzzy concepts used in the paper. In section 3, we introduce the concept of bond portfolio duration that we extend to the fuzzy environment. Then, in section 4 we present a new way to choose between different strategies in which there is different levels of risk and return, and finally, in section 5, we illustrate our approach with an application to the Spanish Public Debt Market.

2. Preliminary concepts and fuzzy introduction

Or main objective is to compare the risk and the return of portfolios in a fuzzy environment. Sometimes is very difficult to construct the fuzzy membership of a magnitude like the duration, or the final yield of an immunized portfolio, so we will study the relationship between these interval-valued expectations by using properly ordered relations.

The interval $A=[a_L,a_R]$ may be alternatively represented by $A=<m(A),hw(A)>$ where $m(A)$ is the midpoint of A, and $hw(A)$ the half-width of A. According to this, Ishibuchi and Tanaka (1990), let A and B be two closed intervals on the real line, then $A\leq_{LR} B$ if and only if $a_R\leq b_R$, and $A\leq_{mw} B$ if and only if $m(A)\leq m(B)$ and $hw(A)\geq hw(B)$.

An alternative ordering mean-valued intervals is introduced by Sengupta and Pal (2000). Let A and B be two closed intervals such that $m(A)\leq m(B)$. Denote by $\prec$ an order relation, in such a way that we say A is inferior to B, $A\prec B$, in terms of the value of the acceptability index

$$A\prec(A,B)=\frac{m(B)-m(A)}{hw(B)+hw(A)},\ \text{where } hw(B)+hw(A)\neq 0 \tag{1}$$

$A\prec(A,B)$ may be considered as the grade of acceptability of the first interval to be inferior to the second interval, and interpreted further on the basis of comparative position of mean of interval B with respect to those of interval A as follows:

$$A\prec(A,B)=\begin{cases} 0 & \text{if } m(A)>m(B) \\ 0<(A,B)<1 & \text{if } m(A)=m(B) \text{ and } a_R>b_L \\ \geq 1 & \text{if } m(A)<m(B) \text{ and } a_R\leq b_L \end{cases} \tag{2}$$

The DM will accept "A is inferior to B" if $A\prec(A,B)>1$ and he will not accepted if it is equal to zero. Between zero and one the premise will be accepted in a degree of satisfaction.

Sengupta and Pal (2000) improve the comparison between two fuzzy numbers, in a financial context, considering that is better more money than less money and less uncertainty than more uncertainty. If more money is associated with more uncertainty, a DM undergoes a trade-off between the two, and finally, for a pessimistic DM is more important to have less uncertainty than more money.

According to these authors, if a portfolio presents less uncertainty (width) and more mean, it is preferred to others with more uncertainty and less mean. The problem is portfolios that presents more mean and more uncertainty. The degree of this relation is measured by the membership function:

$$\mu_{B'}(x)=\begin{cases} 1 & \textit{if } \mathrm{m(X)} \geq \mathrm{m(B)} \\ \max\left\{0, \dfrac{m(X)-(b_L+w(X))}{m(B)-(b_L+w(X))}\right\} & \textit{if } \mathrm{m(B)} \geq \mathrm{m(X)} \geq \mathrm{b_L} + \mathrm{w(X)} \\ 0 & \textit{otherwise} \end{cases} \quad (3)$$

Where $w(.)$ is the width of the interval. We can interpret different values of $\mu_{B'}$ as follows i) $\mu_{B'}=1$ • B is rejected; ii) $\mu_{B'}=0$, B is accepted, and iii) $\mu_{B'}\in[0,1]$ this indicates different degrees of rejection of B. In order to introduce the degree of pessimism, Sengupta and Pal use the index $\pi_B=(\mu_{B'})^p$, $\mu_{B'}\in[0,1]$, where p is the (non-fuzzy) level of pessimism parameter . Sengupta and Pal (2000) propose the values of p: ½, 2, 1 for a pessimistic, moderate and optimistic DMs respectively.

3. Bond and portfolio's duration

Let us assume that at time t_0 we have a portfolio. For an Investor Planning Horizon (IHP) of $T-t_0$ years, and assuming that the DM has n bonds[1] with maturities t_1-t_0 ... t_n-t_0, the proportion of the investment in each kind of bond has to fulfil the set of equations $\sum_{s=1}^{n} x_s=1$; $\sum_{s=1}^{n} x_s(t_s-t_0)=T-t_0$. The DM will have to buy b_s type s, $s=1...n$. The cost of the portfolio at t_0 is P_0^F (the prices of the bonds are crisp numbers, P_0^s, and the interest rate is a crisp number, a particular realization of the unknown fuzzy number), being $P_0^F=\sum_{s=1}^{n} b_s P_0^s$ and the value at the investor planning horizon (IPH) $P_{IPH}^F(i)=\sum_{s=1}^{n} b_s P_0^s(1+i)^{T-t_0}$.

According to the dynamic immunization theorem (Khang, 1983), if there is a variation in the interest rates from i to $\tilde{i}_s=(i_s,l_s,r_s)$ with probability p_s, $s=1,...,n$, the value of the portfolio at the IPH moment will be at least

[1] We assume zero coupon bonds just for simplicity, because duration is equal to maturity.

$P_{IPH}^{F}(i)$. The value of the portfolio is $\tilde{P}_{IPH}^{F}=\left(P_{IPH_C}^{F},l_{P_{IPH}}^{F},r_{P_{IPH}}^{F}\right)$[2]. Note that if there is no change in interest rates the accumulated portfolio value remains at V. However, if interest rates either increase or decrease, the portfolio value increases (due to bond convexity), without any change in the portfolio composition. Now, we define the portfolio return as,

$$\tilde{h}_{IPH}=\left(h_{IPH_C},l_{h_{IPH}},r_{h_{IPH}}\right)=\left(\begin{array}{l}\left(\dfrac{P_{IPH_C}^{F}}{P_0^{F}}\right)^{\frac{1}{T-t_0}}-1,\left(\dfrac{P_{IPH_C}^{F}}{P_0^{F}}\right)^{\frac{1}{T-t_0}}-\left(\dfrac{P_{IPH_C}^{F}+r_{P_{IPH}}^{F}}{P_0^{F}}\right)^{\frac{1}{T-t_0}},\\ \left(\dfrac{P_{IPH_C}^{F}-l_{P_{IPH}}^{F}}{P_0^{F}}\right)^{\frac{1}{T-t_0}}-\left(\dfrac{P_{IPH_C}^{F}}{P_0^{F}}\right)^{\frac{1}{T-t_0}}\end{array}\right) \tag{4}$$

Consequently, the midpoint of the portfolio return is $m\left(\tilde{h}_{IPH}\right)=h_{IPH_C}+\frac{1}{2}\left(r_{h_{IPH}}-l_{h_{IPH}}\right)$ and the width $w\left(\tilde{h}_{IPH}\right)=l_{h_{IPH}}+r_{h_{IPH}}$. However, the width for an immunized portfolio is nearly zero.

Assuming, without loss of generality, that the DM expects a reduction in the interest rate, the duration must be increased if the return is to be higher, but the risk will be greater. For a duration equal to D^*, with $D^*>D$, the proportion of the assets must be $\left(x_1^*,\ldots,x_n^*\right)$, and the number of each kind of bonds that a DM needs to buy is $\left(b_1^*,\ldots,b_n^*\right)=\left(P_0^F x_1^*/P_0^1,\ldots,P_0^F x_n^*/P_0^n\right)$. Hence, the value of the portfolio at the IPH is $\tilde{P}_{IPH,D^*,\tilde{i}}^{F}=\left(P_{IPH_C}^{F}\left(D^*,\tilde{i}^*\right),l_{P_{IPH}}^{F}\left(D^*,\tilde{i}^*\right),r_{P_{IPH}}^{F}\left(D^*,\tilde{i}^*\right)\right)$, a function of D^* and $\tilde{i}^*=\sum_{s=1}^{n}p_s\left(i_s,l_s,r_s\right)$.

The return for the new interest rate $\tilde{i}^*=\sum_{s=1}^{n}p_s\left(i_s,l_s,r_s\right)=\left(i_C^*,l_i^*,r_i^*\right)$ is:

[2] Interest rate is a fuzzy number; however, bonds are bought at a particular price that involves a particular crisp interest rate. That is why we consider a crisp interest if there is no change, and a fuzzy interest rate for any unknown change.

$$\tilde{h}_{IPH,D^*}(\tilde{i})=\left(\begin{array}{l}\left(\frac{P^F_{IPH_c}(D^*)}{P^F_0}\right)^{\frac{1}{T-t_0}}-1,\left(\frac{P^F_{IPH_c}(D^*)}{P^F_0}\right)^{\frac{1}{T-t_0}}-\left(\frac{P^F_{IPH_c}(D^*)+r^F_{P_{IPH}}(D^*)}{P^F_0}\right)^{\frac{1}{T-t_0}},\\ \left(\frac{P^F_{IPH_c}(D^*)-l^F_{P_{IPH}}(D^*)}{P^F_0}\right)^{\frac{1}{T-t_0}}-\left(\frac{P^F_{IPH_c}(D^*)}{P^F_0}\right)^{\frac{1}{T-t_0}}\end{array}\right) \tag{5}$$

The midpoint of the portfolio return,

$$m\left(\tilde{h}_{IPH}\left(D^*\right)\right)=h_{IPH_c}\left(D^*\right)+\frac{1}{2}\left(r_{h_{IPH}}\left(D^*\right)-l_{h_{IPH}}\left(D^*\right)\right) \tag{6}$$

and the width,

$$w\left(\tilde{h}_{IPH}\left(D^*\right)\right)=l_{h_{IPH}}\left(D^*\right)+r_{h_{IPH}}\left(D^*\right) \tag{7}$$

However, our goal is to compare these results with those of an immunized portfolio. The over return $m^*\left(\tilde{h}_{IPH}\left(D^*\right)\right)$ is defined as:

$$\begin{aligned} m^*\left(\tilde{h}_{IPH}\left(D^*\right)\right)&=m\left(\tilde{h}_{IPH}\left(D^*\right)\right)-m\left(\tilde{h}_{IPH}\right)=\\ &=h_{IPH_c}\left(D^*\right)+\frac{1}{2}\left(r_{h_{IPH}}\left(D^*\right)-l_{h_{IPH}}\left(D^*\right)\right)-h_{IPH_c}-\frac{1}{2}\left(r_{h_{IPH}}-l_{h_{IPH}}\right)\end{aligned} \tag{8}$$

and the over risk is:

$$w^*\left(\tilde{h}_{IPH}\left(D^*\right)\right)=w\left(\tilde{h}_{IPH}\left(D^*\right)\right)-w\left(\tilde{h}_{IPH}\right)=l_{h_{IPH}}\left(D^*\right)+r_{h_{IPH}}\left(D^*\right)-l_{h_{IPH}}-r_{h_{IPH}} \tag{9}$$

We can construct the fuzzy risk return map taking for each duration, the over risk corresponding to each over return. It is possible to check that the over risk increases in the same way that the over return increases. So, we will have one relation over risk – over return for each duration.

4. The choice between active and passive bond management

Once the fuzzy risk map has been constructed, the DM will have to choose one alternative: immunization, o active bond management, and in the second case, he will have to select the duration that provides the best combination between risk and return. For this purpose, in the crisp environment, utility functions have been widely studied (see for example Bell, 1995). For an approximation to the possibilistic risk premium associated with a fuzzy number, see Carlsson et al. (2002), Karimi et al. (2007) and Georgescu (2009).

In bond management, the DM must consider some cases in which it is not clear to choose between risk and return. Considering two fuzzy intervals like $A=[a_L,a_R]$ and $B=[b_L,b_R]$, it is clear that if $b_L > a_R$, B is always preferred to A, and on the contrary, if $a_L < b_R$ A is preferred over B. But there are some situations in which some DM are interested not only in the mean difference, but in the whole interval:

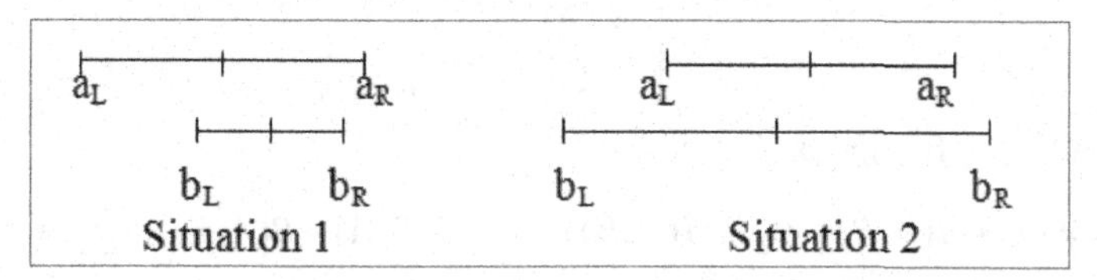

Figure 1. Comparing fuzzy intervals.

In Figure 1, Situation 1, following Sengupta and Pal, B is the best choice, but there are some points in which A is preferred to B: the segment $a_R - b_R$. A similar interpretation is used for the second situation. In order to solve this situation, we propose a new index to evaluate FN in general that allows us to choose between risk and interest. Obviously, this index is just for situations in which there is an overlap between two fuzzy numbers. We must consider i) Difference in means, ii) Difference in risk, that is, the difference in widths, iii) The part of fuzzy number A beats B and iv) The part of the B fuzzy number that beats A.

All these considerations must be weighted according to the DM risk aversion.

i) Difference in means (md):

$$md(A,B)=\begin{cases} 1 & a_L > b_R \\ \dfrac{m(A)-m(B)}{hw(a)+hw(B)} & a_L \le a_R \text{ and } a_R \ge b_L \\ -1 & a_R < b_L \end{cases} \tag{10}$$

ii) Difference in width (wd), which takes values between -1 and 1:

$$wd(A,B)=\frac{w(A)-w(B)}{w(A)+w(B)} \tag{11}$$

iii) A beats B

$$B(B,A)=\begin{cases} 0 & a_R < b_R \\ \dfrac{a_R - b_R}{w(A)} & a_L < b_R < a_R \\ 1 & a_L > b_R \end{cases} \tag{12}$$

iv) B beats A

$$B(A,B)=\begin{cases} 0 & b_R < a_R \\ \dfrac{b_R - a_R}{w(B)} & b_L < a_R < b_R \\ 1 & b_L > a_R \end{cases} \tag{13}$$

Finally, the full index $I(A,B)$ is:

$$I(A,B)=\omega_1 \cdot md(A,B)+\omega_2 \cdot wd(A,B)+\omega_3 \cdot \left(B(B,A)+B(A,B)\right),\ \sum_s \omega_s = 1 \tag{14}$$

As $B(B,A)$ and $B(A,B)$ cannot be positives at the same time, we weight them with the same coefficient.

The DM can considers only the relation between risk and return, taking in consideration only the two first components, or he can consider the fact that a part of the FN be higher than the other. In that way, a very aggressive DM will prefer the alternative that provides the option that has the possibility to beat the other, although it was very little. Others DM do not consider this possibility and they prefer to value only the mean difference, and if they are very similar, they take the option with less width.

Example 1. Being the FNs $(a_L,a_R)=(3,9)$, $(b_L,b_R)=(5,7.5)$. In this case, we have m_A=6.0, m_B=6.25, w_A=6.0 and w_B=2.5. Consider that the DM has very little aversion to risk, and he considers the most important thing to get the alternative that provides the maximum return, although its possibility is very little. So he assigns the followings weights: ω_1=0.25, ω_2=0.25 and ω_3=0.5.

According to Sengupta and Pal, the FN $(b_L,b_R)=(5,7.5)$ is preferred because its mean is higher and its width is smaller, but considering the full index, we get $md(A,B)=-0.02$, $md(A,B)=-0.41$, $B(B,A)=0.25$ and $B(A,B)=0$, so $I(A,B)=0.02$. As a result, the DM will have to choose the first alternative $(a_L,a_R)=(3,9)$.

The return of the portfolio at t is not a triangular fuzzy number, and sometimes it is very difficult to define it, especially for the construction of fuzzy utility functions. For this purpose, the application of the Ful Index has been proposed, so the midpoint and the half-width of the interval-valued expectations return at IPH have been taken as the return and the risk of the portfolio. The DM will have to assign weightings the mean difference, the width difference and to the possibility that some values of one interval are higher than all of the values of the other interval.

The starting point for the utility function definition is an immunized portfolio, the duration of which is equal to that of the IPH, which has a guaranteed return and will increase if there is any variation in interest rate. The initial value of the initial width of the interval used as the return risk is near zero. If the DM wants to increase the portfolio return, he will have to vary the portfolio duration and, consequently, the risk will increase, because the initial risk is almost zero due to the immunization. Only a duration that enhances the portfolio return will be chosen, because any variation will increase the risk. Our main objective is to compare the result of passive and active bond management.

According to active bond management, for an expected increase (decrease) in the interest rate, the DM will have to reduce (increase) the portfolio duration. Nevertheless, this rule presents some problems, as for example, what should a DM do if he expects the interest rates to change from i_0 to $\tilde{i}_s = \left(i_{s_C}, l_{i_s}, r_{i_s}\right)$ with probability p_s for $s = 1,\ldots,n$ and $\sum_{s=1}^{n} p_s = 1$. And, how much will he have to decrease (increase) the portfolio duration to maximize the DM utility?

Denoting the return at the IPH, $m\left(\tilde{h}_{IPH}(D)\right)$, with $m(D)$ and the risk, $w\left(\tilde{h}_{IPH}(D)\right)$, with $w(D)$, in active bond management, if there is an increase in risk (width of the possible interval) and decrease in the return (central point of the interval): $m\left(D^*\right) < m(D)$ and $w\left(D^*\right) > w(D)$. Active management is rejected; but if there is increase in risk and return, the DM must choose between risk and return. For this purpose, we are going to use the full index, that combines differences in mean and width, and the possibility that one alternative beat the other in some part of the interval.

5. Spanish public debt market

We shall illustrate the proposed methodology with an application to the Spanish Public Debt Market. For this purpose we choose the interest rates on the secondary market for government securities, in particular we take medium term government bonds with maturities from one to two years. This information has been taken from the web page of the Spanish Central Bank (www.bde.es).

The evolution of the interest rate for the last five years can be followed in Figure 2. It is possible to check that in the summer of 2008 starts a decline in the return of the public debt, similar to other markets like the Euribor or the Spanish AIAF, but at the beginning of the 2010, the stress in the European public debt markets started, and as a result, this index, like other similar, has risen shapely.

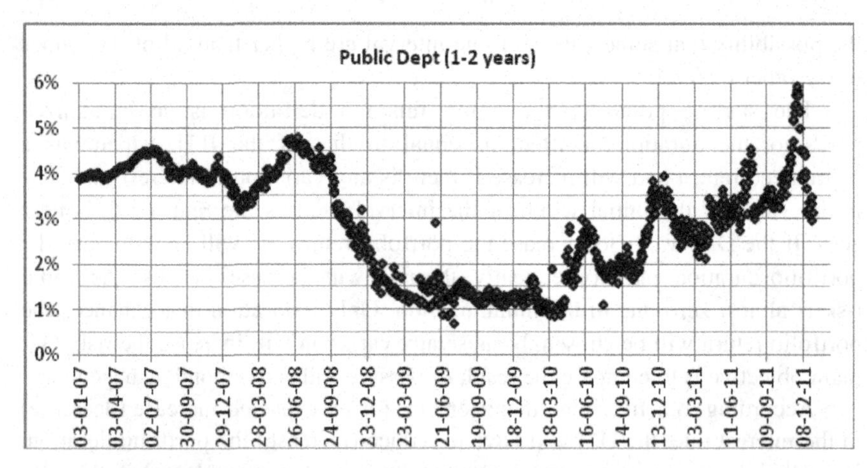

Figure 2. Index of the Spanish Public Debt for maturities from one to two years.

We are going to consider the period from January 2008 to December 2011, an IPH of 10 months, and two zero coupon bonds with maturities 4 and 14 months. The Interest rates of the Spanish Public Debt for maturities from one to two years will be used as the market interest rate at each day of the considered period.

Only two situations will be assumed, the first one that we will consider the pessimistic one with a probability 0,30 (obviously, the optimistic one with a probability 0,7) with an interest rate of 95% of the one considered as the market interest, with left and right hand of 90% and 100% of it respectively. On the other hand, for the optimistic assumption we will consider as central point 105% of the market interest, with left and right hand of 100% and 110% of it respectively.

Figure 3 shows the difference between predicted interest rate for the following period and the real interest, being the red square points the upper limit of the error and triangle green points the lower limit of it, both of them in the left axis. We overlap the rates of interest of the Spanish Public Debt for maturities from one to two years that correspond to the right axis. As our prediction for the following year is just a function of the current year, the error increases during 2010 and especially in 2011.

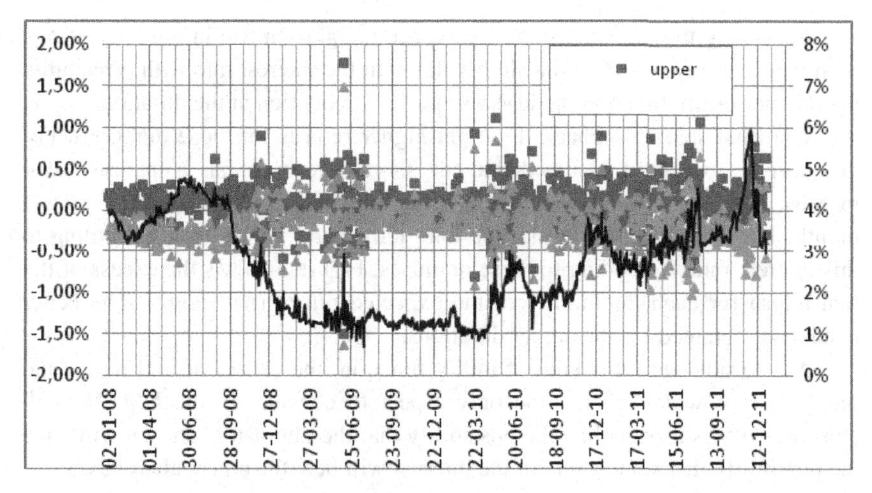

Figure 3. Interest forecast y real Public Debt Interest.

The utility function at the beginning of the process when the interest rate is 3.879% has been obtained for the previous assumption of the interest rate forecast and using the following weighting coefficients: $\omega_1 = 0.5$, $\omega_2 = 0.3$ and $\omega_3 = 0.2$. Figure 4 shows the utility for each duration. According to this preferences, it is clear that the DM prefers to reduce the duration, but the utility shown does not increase a lot when the duration is reduced from 9 to 4 months. In this case is evident that the DM will have to analyse periodically the situation in order to improve his utility after each change in the interest rate, and mainly, when the forecast of it changes a lot.

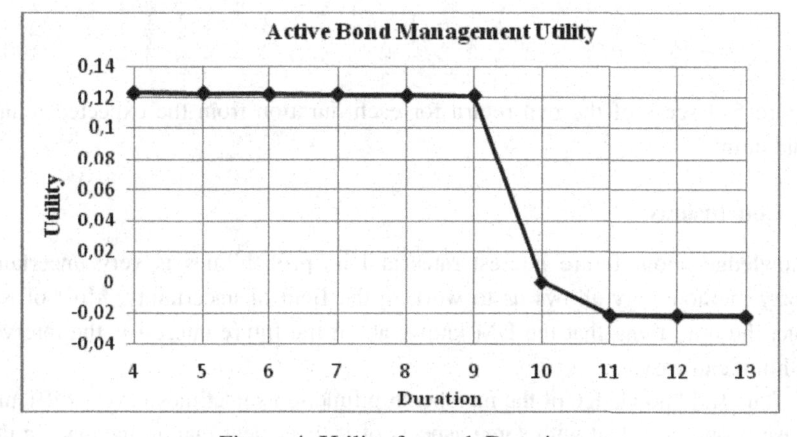

Figure 4. Utility for each Duration

According to our forecast, as we expect a slightly a rise in the interest rate with a probability of 0,3, and a slighty down in the interest rate with probability 0,7, for our utility function the DM will prefer a reduction in the duration.

The final step is to check if we get higher returns for those durations. For this purpose, we have assumed that the short time bone has a maturity of 4 months, and we reinvest it at the interest rate of the public dept existing 4 months later. On the other hand, the long term bond will be sold according to this interest rate. According to these premises, Figure 5 shows the excess of the real return for each duration from the expected return (mid point). The better results are obtained for the higher durations.

As a result, with this kind of utility function, the excess of mid return and the excess of width are not the only aspect to consider in the DM. He will considers others aspects like the possibility that the alternative chosen will have the possibility that some value of the interval will beat the others alternatives.

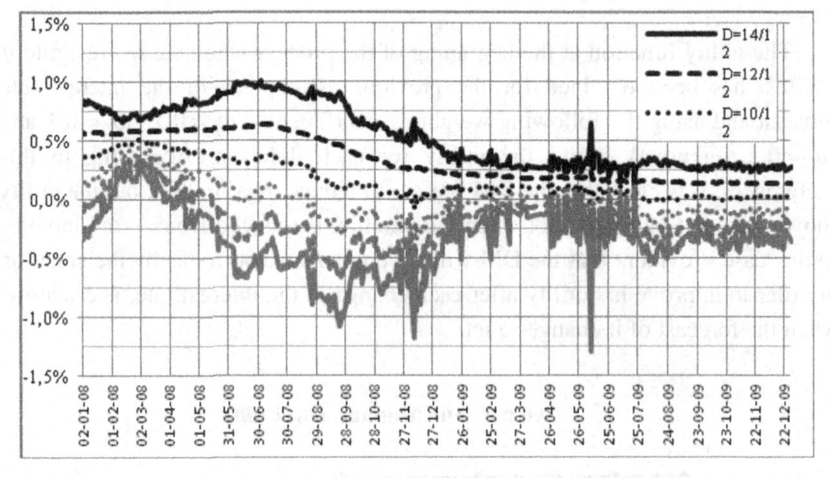

Figure 5. Excess of the real return for each duration from the expected return (mid point).

6. Conclusions

Knowledge about future interest rates and its probabilities is very uncertain. Fuzzy methodology allows us to work in the field of uncertainty. Most of the time, the only thing that the DM knows about the future interest is the interval within it can vary.

The full knowledge of the membership function sometimes is very difficult, so we propose to deal with some aspects of it. It is clear that an increase in the duration for a falling forecast of the interest rate will increase the return, but it will increase the risk, as well, that we measure for the width of the interval.

Some DMs will consider positively others aspects like the possibility that an alternative presents the possibility of some higher values, even thought it has the possibility of lower values.

Finally, the application to the Spanish Public Dept market (for short periods) shows the utility function at the beginning of the period, and the result of each decision in yields terms.

Further researches will introduce fuzzy random variables in order to improve the development of the fuzzy utility membership function. In this case, the DM will have to anticipate the future interest rate and the probability of each scenario, but the forecast will be able to have fuzzy interest.

7. References

BANERJEE, A. (1995). "Fuzzy choice functions, revealed preference and rationality". *Fuzzy Sets Systems,* Vol. 70 (1), 31–43.

BELL, D.E. (1995). *Risk, Return, and Utility.* Management Science, Vol. 41 (1), 23-30

BODIE, Z.; KANE, A.; MARCUS, A.J. (1996). *Investments.* Times Mirror Higher Education Group. Boston, Irwin

BOUYSSOU, D. (1997). "Acyclic fuzzy preferences and the Orlovsky choice function: a note". *Fuzzy Sets Systems,* Vol. 89, 107–111.

BROTONS, J.M. (2010). "Bond Management: An Application to the European Market". *Communications in Computer and Information Science*, Vol. 81, 316-323.

BROTONS, J.M.; TERCEÑO, A. (2010). "Risk premium in the Spanish Market: an empirical study". *Journal of Economic Computation and Economic Cybernetics Studies and Research,* Vol. 1/2010, 81-100.

CARLSSON,CH.; FULLER, R.; MAJLENDER, P. (2002). "A possibilistic approach to selecting portfolios with highest utility score". *Fuzzy Sets and Systems,* Vol. 131 (1), 13-21

CHEN, C.B.; KLEIN, C.M. (1997). "A simple approach to rankin a group of aggregated fuzzy utilities". *IEEE Transactions on systems, man, and cybernetics, part B: Cibernetics,* Vol 27, 26-35.

DE WILDE, P. (2004). "Fuzzy Utility and Equilibria". *IEEE Transactions on systems, man, and cybernetics, part B: Cibernetics,* Vol. 34 (4), 1774 – 1785.

GEORGESCU, I. (2009). "Possibilistic. Risk aversion". Fuzzy Sets Systems, Vol. 160, 2608-2619.

GERBER, H.U. (1995). *Life Insurance Mathematics.* Heidelberg. Springer.

ISHIBUCHI, H.; TANAKA, H. (1990). "Multiobjective programming in optimization of the interval objective function". *European Journal of Operational Research*, Vol. 48, 219-225.

KARIMI, I. HÜLLERMEIER, E. (2007). "Risk Assessment system of natural hazards: A new approach based on fuzzy probability". *Fuzzy Sets Systems*, Vol. 158, 987-999.

KHANG, C. (1983). "A dynamic global immunization strategy in the world of multiple interest rate changes: A dynamic immunization and minmax theorem". Journal *of Finance and Quantitative Analisis*, Vol. 18, 355-363.

MARKOWITZ, H. (1952). "Portfolio selection". *Journal of Finance*, Vol. 7, 77-91

REDINGTON, F.M. (1952). "Review of the Principles of Life Office Valuations". *Journal of the Institute of Actuaries* 78 (350, part 3), 286–340

SENGUPTA, A.; PAL, T.K. (2000). "Theory and Metodology on comparing interval numbers". *European Journal of Operational Research*, Vol. 127(2), 28-43.

SENGUPTA, K. (1998). "Fuzzy preference and Orlovsky choice procedure," *Fuzzy Sets Systems*, Vol. 93 (2), 231–234.

Spanish Central Bank, (www.bde.es).

TERCEÑO A.; BROTONS, J.M.; FERNANDEZ, A. (2007). "Immunization strategy in a fuzzy environment". *Fuzzy Economic Review*, Vol. XII (2), 95-116

VAN DER MEER, R.; M. SMINK (1993). "Strategies and Techniques for Asset-Liability Management: An Over-view". *The Geneva Papers on Risk and Insurance,* Vol. 18(67), 144–57.

TIME ANALYSIS OF RESPONSIBILITY IN FINANCE

DAVID CEBALLOS

Department of Economic, Financial and Actuarial Mathematics,
University of Barcelona, Av. Diagonal 690
Barcelona, 08034, Spain

In Finance, responsibility can be studied according to the temporality of the effect: past, present and future. These differences can be analyzed through the Greek concept of time: Chronos (god of duration and sequential time), Kairos (god of opportunity and moment time) and Aeon (god of eternity and long-term time).

0. Introduction

Responsibility is the legal, moral or other debt or obligation to repair or to satisfy an effect, which is the consequence of an action, fault or legal cause. In Finance the common use of this term refers to the process of managing money and other assets in a manner that is considered productive and in the best interests of an individual or family. However, responsibility also has another meaning, which is the maximum monetary amount that your insurance covers you if you produce a negative effect in the development of your work.

In this paper we use the first definition in keeping with the ethical and sustainable aspects commonly associated with works like "Documents of Corporate Social Responsibility", "Principles for Responsible Investment" or "Journal of Business Ethics". These ethical and sustainable aspects are studied in opposition to the general rule of the shareholder wealth maximization objective: reasonable earnings as against the possibility of big earnings, where the difference is the risk of dangerous or disastrous consequences for the manager, the investor, the institution or society in general.

The analysis of responsibility is extensive in the literature and in business: social and corporate responsibilities are scientific fields enjoying a current expansion in the financial literature; reputation and ethical codes are highlighted elements in financial firms; the recent financial crisis has opened up social and institutional discussions about the responsibility of financial consequences, and so on. In this respect, Hawley (1991) studied the ethical dimension of applying the maximization objective in Finance, Gill (2008) explored different orientations towards ethical and social responsibility in corporate core values, and Jin et al. (2012) studied the implication of the recent financial meltdown for financial professionals. Another example of the interest devoted to this subject is the creation in 2011 of the Center for Responsibility in Finance at the University of Zurich. The aims of the institution are to promote education on responsibility in finance and in management and to develop measures and tools for the assessment and promotion of individual ethical competences, among others.

However, another opportunity for the study of responsibility in Finance lies in the temporality of financial effects: past, present and future. These effects have different natures: the past is chronological with temporal regularities, the present is marked by attention to the immediately best options and opportunities, and the future introduces an uncertainty as to long-term effects and their duration. These differences can be analyzed using different concepts of time, in particular the concepts represented by the Greek gods of time: Chronos, Kairos and Aeon, who are the gods of duration, moment and eternity, respectively.

A chronological vision of past responsibilities supposes a quantification of the risk of their effects according to regular mathematical and statistical models.

An opportune or momentary vision of present responsibilities supposes an analysis of the risk of their effects according to the process of decision and intention.

A long-term vision of future responsibilities supposes an analysis of the risks of their effects without identifying their origin or their end, given that it can be difficult to associate an action or responsible cause with each negative effect.

These visions help us to understand the implications of responsibility in Finance and the different risks that may be involved. For an analysis of these visions, the paper is divided into four sections. The first section discusses responsibility in Finance. The second focuses on time analysis in Finance. The different representations of time in ancient Greece are treated in the third section and, finally, the last section addresses the time analysis of responsibility in Finance.

1. Responsibility in Finance

In this paper we use the definition of responsibility as the process of managing money and other assets in a manner that is considered productive and in the best interests of a financial agent and society. Based on this definition, three dimensions of responsibility in Finance can be distinguished:

- First, you have to respect the rules and be diligent in financial decisions.

- Second, you have to be able to pay for the negative effects of a wrong financial decision or of an unfavorable context.
- Third, you have to be aware of the risks and consequences of your financial decisions.

This three-part definition implies that being financially responsible refers to understanding and applying financial concepts in order to take management decisions that address the allocation of funds, accurate reporting and management of risk.

Moreover, you can add the ethical and sustainable aspects of social acceptance and the stability of financial operations.

Additionally, the financial principle of the positive relation between earnings and risk – in other words "the greater the risk, the more you can make" – is a fundamental variable when analyzing responsibility in Finance because a big loss or a bad outcome is not proof of irresponsibility. Similarly, a positive outcome does not signify a responsible action because diligent risk and its ethical or sustainable aspects are relative to the social and market relationship between earnings and risk.

Rendtorff (2009) divided the responsibility of a financial corporation or manager into four categories according to a pyramid of importance. The first responsibility is economic (i.e., paying for negative effects). The next is legal (i.e., respecting rules). The third is the ethical. It concerns values, social justice and sustainability, while the top of the pyramid features philanthropic responsibility and the search for social benefits and the global interest.

Finally, markets and corporations introduce two possible perspectives into the analysis of responsibility: the individual and the institutional. Individual responsibility is related to the management of risk and of decisions, while institutional responsibility is related to the role in the system and the time dependence of values.

All these dimensions, aspects, categories or perspectives show the complexity of the concept of responsibility in Finance. Time is also present in the analysis of responsibility in Finance because financial operations are temporal relations and responsibility supposes a time separation between action and effect.

The introduction of time into the analysis of responsibility in Finance and its attendant complexity can provide a way to structure the analysis of responsibility.

2. Time in Finance

Guitton (1970) distinguished financial time from economic time. The former fluctuates more and is typical of speculation and investment dynamics, while the latter is associated with consumption decisions, which are more stable. However, financial time is not only a specific and differential rhythm with unexpected changes. Rodríguez (1994) also considers moment and duration important in its definition.

Time is essential in defining any financial phenomenon. If we examine the influence of time and its mathematical applications in Financial Analysis, the variable is clearly of great significance in the theoretical responses to the main financial problem. And yet, the nature and role of time in Finance are far from clear, despite the fact that the mainstream defends a definition of time in terms of physical measurement.

Capital (monetary quantities), the interest rate and time (moments and periods) are the three variables that describe a financial phenomenon (Rodriguez, 1994). Time is useful to localize the different payments exchanged in a financial operation; measure the duration of exchanges (short-term, long-term, gap between costs and benefits and so on), and define the regular or chaotic dynamics of the payment stream or flow.

Moreover, the form of time in Finance is treated differently according to the division of past, present and future in relation to the moment of valuation. The comparison of financial capital or financial quantities is possible if they are homogeneous in the moment of valuation, and in this sense it is necessary to move monetary quantities in time from past to present (capitalization) or from future to present (actualization).

The differing nature of the forms and relative positions of time in Finance plays an important role in understanding the configuration and risks of a financial operation because the description, valuation and interpretation of the operation must incorporate time.

3. Greek gods of time

In primitive societies, time was not understood as a physical coordinate. It was explained as powerful and mysterious forces that dominated events. Time could be good or bad, favorable or hostile[*].

---

[*] Franz (1978) and Adam (2004) have studied the conception of time in early civilization and its subsequent evolution.

In primitive cultures, a cyclical idea of time was implicit in beliefs, pictures and calendars. However, in Greek culture one can observe some characteristics of a linear idea of time, above all in lyric and tragedy, where death, desperation and felicity substitute for eternity and a cyclical evolution in the narration of stories.

In Greek mythology, time existed in relation to the problems of change and motion, without a clear distinction drawn between these concepts[†]. This mythology conceptualized time through a divine trilogy: Aeon, Chronos and Kairos[‡]:

- Aeon is the god of absolute and perfect time, who represents eternity, duration without beginning or end, the simultaneity of all times. Frequently, it is represented by cyclical motion.
- Chronos is the god of time as an empirical dimension, that is to say, its measure. This time is mobile, limited and imperfect. In the words of Plato, it is "a moving image of eternity". Chronos is a successive presence or image of the mirror of Aeon. It personifies order in succession, harmony in finite durations. It is the time that is measurable, the common time of humans.
- Kairos is the favorable moment, the non-regular opportunity. It is the fair point or the equilibrium value for right decisions. It was similar to the time of human activity in the terminology of Jaques (1984). It was a technical time for action and decision dependent on context and on the intelligence needed to take profit, according to the interpretation of Plato in *The Republic*, II, 370b and 374c. Kairos captures the risk of action and the ultimate success.

This triad shows three wills at work in the temporal analysis of an event or situation: timeless analysis (Aeon), relational study (Chronos) and the use of the moment (Kairos).

4. Time analysis of responsibility in Finance

The Greeks' divine triad of time offers an interesting approach to the analysis of responsibility in Finance because time and risks are related in this area. A financial obligation has a temporal component and a risk component. The former component arises from the different moments at the beginning of the operation, the payment flow and the execution of obligations. The latter component arises from the fact that a financial obligation is hypothetical, because it can have a

---

[†] Aristotle in *Physics* IV, II, 220b commented that time is measured by motion, but also that motion is measured by time. Plato in *Timaeus* compared time with cyclical motion.

[‡] Campillo (1991).

random occurrence or because the monetary quantity and moment that define it are not the necessary to its execution.

Responsibility can be interpreted as the risk for the demand of a financial obligation. This risk is included in the category of "operational risk" in the terminology of Basel II: fraud, legal risk, damages in financial or commercial relations, fragile model or operation, long-term uncertainty. These situations or effects entail a financial responsibility.

The Greek triad supposes a temporal analysis according to the temporality of the event. The common division of temporality is among the past, present and future, and each of these three Greek gods adds a useful interpretation to the vision of responsibility according to the time effect.

According to this time effect, the different nature of implicit or explicit obligations can be distinguished as follows:

- Obligations for past actions or effects, like fraud or damages, which a causal or explicit relation.
- Obligations based on public and market confidence in the diligence and quality of actions. This covers the efficiency and profit of an opportunity.
- Implicit obligations embodied in social demands and the functioning of the system, implying a permanent or long-term responsibility.

Therefore, responsibility in Finance can be studied according to the temporality of the effect in the past, present and future, thanks to this interpretation of the Greek gods.

In summary, financial responsibility has three components with ethical and sustainable aspects and two perspectives:

- The three components are: respect for rules and diligence, credit to pay for negative effects (monetary support), and the management of risk, including ethical and sustainable aspects.
- The two perspectives are: individual (interest in the management of risk), social (ethics and sustainability) and institutional (interest in the system).

If responsibility is studied according to the two perspectives, the time analysis is different for each perspective. The individual perspective refers to financial agents (e.g., the individual, investor, firm) and the institutional perspective is more closely related to the market, regulator and policy.

For financial agents, the temporality of their obligations or responsibility has a different conception of how debt is due. Commonly, past obligations have to be proved by means of a temporal relation between a cause and a negative effect. This conception is applied to respecting rules, securing credit to pay for negative effects and managing risks as well as ethical and sustainable aspects. It requires proof of any damage caused by the non-fulfillment of the components of responsibility. The chronological order relation above concerns the interpretation of time added by Chronos, while present decisions in Finance consider the market's earnings to risk relation and examine the confidence and profit in an opportunity, which captures the view of temporality represented by Kairos. Lastly, the future, in general, has a long-term, non-linear relation with the present, and this is represented by Aeon. However, respect for rules and diligence is not an issue in this timeless model. In the future, taking profit from opportunities is also a value for respecting rules and diligence. The obligation to be able to pay for the negative effects of a wrong financial decision in the future is not a timeless conception either. For the future, as for the past, a credit obligation is demanded as a logical proof of its possibility.

From an institutional perspective, the future is always timeless because an institution's responsibility lies in the permanent sustainability of the system or a respect for the maintenance of agreements. Respect for rules and diligence is a maxim for institutional agents, and its interpretation does not vary according to fluctuating temporality. For past credit and risk obligations and present credit obligations, a causal or logical relation is demanded to explain these responsibilities. Finally, confidence and opportunities form the basis of the other options, because past and present ethics and present risks are well described according to the time of an activity.

The table below shows a summary of the time analysis of responsibility in Finance:

Table 1. Summary of time analysis of responsibility by components.

Responsibility / Time	Individual				Institutional			
	Respect	Credit	Risk	Ethics	Respect	Credit	Risk	Ethics
Past	**Chronos**	**Chronos**	**Chronos**	**Chronos**	**Aeon**	**Chronos**	**Chronos**	**Kairos**
Present	**Kairos**	**Kairos**	**Kairos**	**Kairos**	**Aeon**	**Chronos**	**Kairos**	**Kairos**
Future	**Kairos**	**Chronos**	**Aeon**	**Aeon**	**Aeon**	**Aeon**	**Aeon**	**Aeon**

5. Conclusions

This paper has explored the composition of financial responsibility and the possibility of time analysis, distinguishing three components of financial responsibility and three natures of time.

The time analysis of responsibility in Finance shows the right interpretation of time in the justification of responsibility.

In general, responsibility for past facts supposes a chronological conceptualization. A time relation must be proved between a cause and an effect.

Kairos is the Greek god of the favorable moment and success in a decision taken. As such, it is a relevant variable in the analysis of present responsibilities.

Finally, responsibility for the future, for the long-term, is conceptualized most of the time as a timeless analysis, because there is a permanent component to the obligation.

Structuring an analysis of responsibility according to temporality can offer different strategies to avoid or to detect financial responsibilities because time analysis pays heed to this conspicuous characteristic of the obligation. For example, responsibility for a deficient management of future risks has to be demanded based on a permanent or timeless obligation, because a chronological or a momentaneous analysis will be insufficient to be able to interpret the long-term responsibility.

6. References

1. B. Adam, Time. (2004)
2. A. Campillo, *La otra Historia* **3**, 33-70. (1991).
3. M.L. Franz, Time: Rhythm and Repose. (1978)
4. H. Guitton, A la recherché du temps économique. (1970)
5. D.D. Hawley, J. Bus Ethics **10**, 711-721. (1991)
6. K.G. Jin, R. Drozdenko and S. DeLoughy, *J. Bus Ethics* **106**, 1-10. (2012)
7. J.D. Rendtorff, Responsibility, Ethics and Legitimacy of Corporations. (2009)
8. A. Rodriguez, matemática de la financiación. (1994)

ONLINE CHANGE-POINT DETECTION IN FINANCIAL TIME SERIES: CHALLENGES AND EXPERIMENTAL EVIDENCE WITH FREQUENTIST AND BAYESIAN SETUPS

VASILE GEORGESCU

Department of Statistics and Informatics, University of Craiova, 13 A.I.Cuza, 200585, Craiova, Romania

Change point detection is the identification of abrupt changes in the generative parameters of sequential data. In application areas such as finance, online rather than offline detection of change points in time series is mostly required, due to their use in predictive tasks, possibly embedded in automatic trading systems. However, the complex structure of the data generation processes makes this a challenging endeavor. Two radically different approaches are addressed here to experimentally test the effectiveness of change point detection algorithms designed for the online use, when applying to highly noisy and time-varying financial processes: a frequentist approach based on Singular Spectrum Analyses and an adaptive sequential Bayesian approach. Both the price series and return series are considered.

1. Challenges of Change-Point Detection in Financial Time Series

Change point detection attempts to reduce the impact of nonstationarity, or changes in the generative parameters, by recognizing regime change events and adapting the predictive model appropriately. At a change point, the statistics that explained the previous data are not appropriate to explain later data. This fundamental statistical change could take on many forms.

For instance, a change point can be thought of as a change in the parameter(s) of the sampling distribution. This could be exemplified by a shift in the mean or in the variance of data sampled (say) from a Gaussian distribution. A shift in the mean would seem like a natural choice to describe the weather patterns, where abrupt changes alternate with long periods of relative stationarity. By contrast, financial data patterns are typically characterized by a shift in variance. Volatility, a concept directly related to that of variance, is a key issue in financial time series analysis. Many financial time series exhibit a time-varying conditional variance, which means that they suffer from *heteroscedasticity* (the amplitude of fluctuations is expected to be larger for some time period than the others).

More dramatically, a time series could switch from being sampled from a specific distribution to being sampled from a different one. This case of a deep instability in the data generation process is one of the most challenging. Such turbulent periods may be caused by financial and economic crises. Benoît Mandelbrot first observed that stock price variations follow complex dynamics where periods characterized by near random walk movements are occasionally disrupted by large movements (i.e. crashes). Such turbulent events are much more common than would be predicted in a normal distribution. The current opinion is that the nature of market movements is generally much better explained using nonlinear dynamics and concepts of chaos theory.

Change-point detection methods have been designed for different purposes. Some of them were conceived to analyze time series structure in a non-sequential (off-line) manner. In many practical situations, however, change-point detection problems are typically sequential (on-line) problems. From this viewpoint, there are two concerns for the practical application of change point models in financial area.

An earlier concern of change point models was to come to a greater understanding of the data retrospectively. A retrospective analysis of the stock market, for instance, may attempt to tell us where fundamental changes in the past occurred.

However, a more exciting and effective concern is to make online predictions, which is the ultimate goal of the investor looking to profit from a stock market model.

Whenever noisy data is a major concern, scientists depend on statistical inference to pursue structural complexity of stochastic processes. Frequentist and Bayesian approaches are two traditional, but distinct, directions of research. Now, they compete on the field of change point detection, too.

Frequentist approaches to change point detection have yielded online filtering and prediction techniques earlier than Bayesian approaches, which have been mostly offline and retrospective until some relatively recent work ([1], [11]).

The main concern in this paper is to experimentally test the effectiveness of two of the most representative change point detection methods (one for each of the theoretical directions: frequentist and Bayesian), when applying to financial time series. Both of them have specifically been designed for online use.

2. Change Point Detection in Financial Time Series: A Frequentist Sequential Approach Using Singular Spectrum Analysis

2.1. *An Overview of Singular Spectrum Analysis*

Singular Spectrum Analysis (SSA) is a nonparametric method for time series structure recognition and identification. It tries to overcome the problems of finite sample length and noisiness of sampled time series not by fitting an assumed model to the available series, but by using a data-adaptive basis set.

The SSA algorithm has two basic stages: decomposition and reconstruction.

The decomposition stage is carried out in two steps:

(D1) The *Embedding* step maps the original one-dimensional time series $\{x_1, x_2, \ldots, x_N\}$ to a sequence of $K = N - M + 1$ lagged vectors of dimension M (where M is called *window length*):

$$X_i = (x_i, \ldots, x_{i+M-1})', \quad i = 1, \ldots, K, \quad 1 < M < N. \tag{1}$$

This lagged vectors form the columns of the *trajectory matrix* X, which is actually a Hankel matrix (i.e., it has equal elements on the diagonals $i + j - 1$=const.): $X = [X_1 : X_2 : \ldots : X_K]$.

(D2) The SVD step is the *singular value decomposition* of the trajectory matrix. Let $R = 1/N \cdot X \cdot X'$ be an $M \times M$ matrix, called *lag-covariance matrix.* Denote by $\lambda_1, \ldots, \lambda_M$ the eigenvalues of R taken in the decreasing order of magnitude $(\lambda_1 \geq \ldots \geq \lambda_M \geq 0)$ and by $U_1, \ldots, U_M$ the orthonormal system of the eigenvectors of the matrix R corresponding to these eigenvalues. Let $d = \max\{ i$, such that $\lambda_i > 0 \}$. If we denote $V_i = X'U_i / \sqrt{\lambda_i}$ ($i = 1, \ldots, d$), then the SVD of the trajectory matrix X can be written as $X = X_1 + \ldots + X_d$, where $X_i = \sqrt{\lambda_i}\, U_i \otimes V_i'$ and $\otimes$ is the outer product. The matrices X_i are elementary matrices (have rank one).

The reconstruction stage is also carried out in two steps:

(R1) The *grouping* step consists of partitioning the set of indices $\{1, \ldots, d\}$ into m disjoint subsets $I_1, \ldots, I_m$. The case of practical interest for our application is that of a dichotomic partitioning: split the set of indices into two groups, $\{1, \ldots, d\} = I + \bar{I}$, where $I = \{i_1, \ldots, i_\ell\}$ and $\bar{I} = \{1, \ldots, d\} \setminus I$, and sum the matrices X_i within each group:

$$X = X_I + X_{\bar{I}} \tag{2}$$

where $X_I = \Sigma_{i \in I} X_i$ and $X_{\bar{I}} = \Sigma_{i \in \bar{I}} X_i$.

The choice of the ℓ most contributing eigenvalues λ_i, $i \in I$, and thus of the corresponding ℓ eigenvectors is an appropriate way to control and reduce the distance between the M-dimensional vectors that form the columns of trajectory matrix and the ℓ-dimensional hyperplane determined by the ℓ eigenvectors. For example, we can choose the index set I such that $\Sigma_{j=1}^{\ell} \lambda_j / \Sigma_{j=1}^{d} \lambda_j > 0.95$ corresponding to the set of eigenvalues whose contribution exceed 95%.

(R2) The last step transforms each matrix of the grouped decomposition (2) into a new series of length N, by *diagonal averaging*. It consists of averaging over the diagonals $i+j-1$=const. ($i=1,\dots,M$, $j=1,\dots,K$) of the matrices X_I and $X_{\bar{I}}$. Applying then twice the one-to-one correspondence between the series of length N and the Henkel matrices of size $M \times K$ (with $K=N-M+1$), we obtain the SSA decomposition of the original series $\{x_t\}$ into a sum of two series: $x_t = z_t + \varepsilon_t$, $t=1,\dots,N$ .In this context, the series z_t (obtained from the diagonal averaging of X_I) can often be associated with signal and the residual series ε_t with noise.

2.2. *The SSA based change-point detection algorithm*

A frequentist, non-parametric algorithm for multiple change-point detection in time series based on sequential application of the Singular Spectrum Analysis was developed in [6]. The idea behind the algorithm is to apply SSA to a windowed portion of the signal in order to pick up its structure through an ℓ-dimensional subspace spanned by the eigenvectors of the lag-covariance matrix, computed in a sequence of moving time intervals [n+1; n+m] of a given length m, where n = 0, 1, ... is the iteration number. If at a certain time moment τ the mechanism generating the time series x_t has changed then an increase in the distance between the ℓ-dimensional hyperplane and the M-lagged vectors ($x_{\tau+1},\dots,x_{\tau+M}$) of trajectory matrix is to be expected. This increase will indicate the change. However, if the generating mechanism does not change further along the signal, then the corresponding lagged vectors will stay close to this hyperplane.

Due to its sequential nature, this algorithm can be embedded into a predictive framework. If the time series $\{x_t\}_{t=1}^{N}$ is continued for $t > N$ and there is no change in the mechanism generating x_t then the vectors X_j for $j \geq K$ should lie close to the ℓ-dimensional subspace (the corresponding distances should stay reasonably small). However, if at a certain time moment $N + \tau$ the mechanism generating x_t, $t \geq N+\tau$, has changed then an increase in the distance between the ℓ-dimensional hyperplane and vectors X_j, for $j \geq K+\tau$, is to be expected.

Let $\{x_1, x_2, \dots, x_N\}$ be a time series, where N is large enough. Two parameters have to be chosen: the window width m ($m < N$), and the lag parameter M ($M \leq m/2$). Define also $K = m - M + 1$.

For each $n = 0, 1, ..., N-m$, a three-stage procedure is executed:

Stage 1. Perform the SSA algorithm for the time interval $[n + 1, n + m]$.

1. Construct the trajectory matrix $X^{(n)}$ (here called *base matrix*), whose columns are the vectors $X_j^{(n)}$:

$$X^{(n)} = \left(x_{n+i+j-1}\right)_{i=1:M;\, j=1:K} = \begin{pmatrix} x_{n+1} & x_{n+2} & \cdots & x_{n+K} \\ x_{n+2} & x_{n+3} & \cdots & x_{n+K+1} \\ \vdots & \vdots & \vdots & \vdots \\ x_{n+M} & x_{n+M+1} & \cdots & x_{n+m} \end{pmatrix} \quad (3)$$

$X_j^{(n)} = (x_{n+j}, \ldots, x_{nM+j-1})'$, $j = -n+1, -n+2, \ldots, N-n-M+1$.

2. Perform the SDV of the lag-covariance matrix $R_n = 1/K \cdot X^{(n)}\left(X^{(n)}\right)'$. This gives us a collection of M eigenvectors.

3. Select a particular group I of $\ell < M$ of these eigenvectors; this determines an ℓ-dimensional subspace $S_{n,\ell}$ in the M-dimensional space of vectors $X_j^{(n)}$. Denote the ℓ eigenvectors that determine the subspace $S_{n,\ell}$ by $U_{i_1}, \ldots, U_{i_\ell}$.

Stage 2. Construction of the test matrix.

Denote $Q = q - p$ (thus $q = p + Q$) and construct the following $M \times Q$ trajectory matrix (called *test matrix*):

$$X_{test}^{(n)} = \left(x_{n+p+i+j-1}\right)_{i=1:M;\, j=1:Q} = \begin{pmatrix} x_{n+p+1} & x_{n+p+2} & \cdots & x_{n+q} \\ x_{n+p+2} & x_{n+p+3} & \cdots & x_{n+q+1} \\ \vdots & \vdots & \vdots & \vdots \\ x_{n+p+M} & x_{n+p+M+1} & \cdots & x_{n+q+M-1} \end{pmatrix} \quad (4)$$

The part of sample $x_{n+1}, \ldots, x_{n+m}$ that is used to construct the (base) trajectory matrix $X^{(n)}$ will be called 'base sample', and another part, $x_{n+p+1}, \ldots, x_{n+q+M-1}$, which is used to construct the vectors $X_j^{(n)}$ $(j = p+1, \ldots, q)$ and thus to compute the sum of squared distances $\mathcal{D}_{n,I,p,q}$ will be called "test sample".

Stage 3. Computation of the detection statistics

The detection statistics are:

- $\mathcal{D}_{n,I,p,q}$, the sum of squares of the (Euclidean) distances between the vectors $X_j^{(n)}$ $(j = p+1, \ldots, q)$ and the ℓ-dimensional subspace $S_{n,\ell}$. Since the eigenvectors are orthogonal, the square of the Euclidean distance between an M−vector ZY = $X_j^{(n)}$ and the subspace $S_{n,\ell}$ spanned by the ℓ eigenvectors P_1, ..., P_ℓ, is just $\|Z\|^2 - \|P'Z\|^2 = Z'Z - Z'PP'Z$, where $\|\cdot\|$ is the Euclidean norm and P is the M× ℓ-matrix with columns P_1, ..., P_ℓ. Therefore

$$\mathcal{D}_{n,I,p,q} = \sum_{j=p+1}^{q} \left(X_j^{(n)}\right)' X_j^{(n)} - \left(X_j^{(n)}\right)' P P' X_j^{(n)} \tag{5}$$

- The normalized sum of squared distances

$$\mathcal{D}_{n,\ell,p,q} / \mu_{n,\ell,p,q} \geq h \tag{6}$$

- $S_n = \mathcal{D}_{n,I,p,q} / v_n$. Here v_j is an estimate of the sum of squared distances $\mathcal{D}_{n,I,p,q}$ at the time intervals $[\,j+1,\ j+r\,]$ where the hypothesis of no change can be accepted. Actually, $v_n = 1/(n-m/2) \cdot \sum_{i=0}^{n-m/2-1} \mathcal{D}_{n,I,p,q}$ or $v_n = \mathcal{D}_{r,I,0,K}$ can be two alternative choices for v_n, where r is the largest value of $r \leq n$ so that the hypothesis of no change is accepted.
- The CUSUM-type statistic:

$$W_1 = S_1,\ W_{n+1} = \max(0, a),\ n > 1 \tag{7}$$

where $a = W_n + S_{n+1} - S_n - k$ and $k = 1/\left(s \cdot \sqrt{MQ}\right)$, which correspond to the "s·σ-rule" ($s = 3$ is suggested).

Large values of $\mathcal{D}_{n,I,p,q}$, S_n and V_n indicate a change in the structure of the time series.

The decision rule in the algorithm, denoted by $A(M, m, \ell, p, q, h)$, is to announce that a change in the mechanism generating x_t occurs at a certain point τ, if for a certain n

$$\mathcal{D}_{n,I,p,q} / v_n \geq h \tag{8}$$

where h is a fixed threshold. Then we would expect than the vectors $X_j = X_{j-n}^{(n)}$ with $j > \tau$ lie further away from the ℓ-dimensional subspace $S_{n,I}$ than the vectors X_j with $j \leq \tau$. This means that the sequence $D(n) = \mathcal{D}_{n,I,p,q}$, considered as a function of n, is expected to start growing somewhere around

$\hat{n}$, such that $\hat{n}+q+M-1=\tau$. The value $\hat{n}=\tau-q-M+1$ is the first value of n such that the test sample $x_{n+p+1},\ldots,x_{n+q+M-1}$ contain the change point.

The CUSUM-type statistic can also be used to make a decision rule. The first point with non-zero value of W_n before this statistic has reached a high value should be considered as an estimate of the change point. The algorithm announces the structural change if for some n we observe $W_n > h$, with some threshold h.

2.3. *Applying the SSA based change point detection algorithm to financial time series*

Two datasets are presented to the SSA based change point detection algorithm:

1. Bucharest Stock Exchange BET index (see Fig. 1);
2. The Daily returns, calculated from the BET index (see Fig. 5).

BET (Bucharest Exchange Trading) is the reference index for the Bucharest Stock Exchange (BSE) market. It is a free float weighted capitalization index of the 10 most liquid stocks listed on the BSE regulated market.

The results are shown in the figures below.

Figure 1 displays the daily values of the Bucharest Stock Exchange BET index that have been selected to be included in analysis.

Figure 1. Bucharest Stock Exchange BET index.

The most contributing eigenvalues (sorted in decreasing order) are shown in Figure 2. The dominant eigenvalue is λ_1, whose contribution in the sum of eigenvalues is 99.668%.

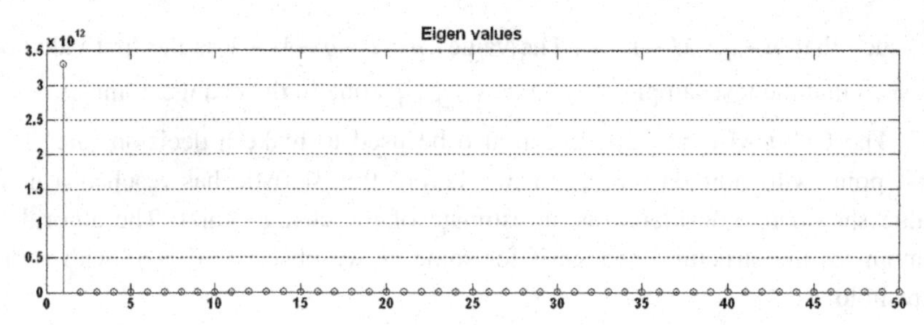

Figure 2. Eigenvalues: 99.668% from the sum of eigenvalues is represented by λ_1.

Figure 3 shows the SSA-based time series reconstruction and the associated residuals.

The results of applying the SSA based change-point detection algorithm to the Bucharest Stock Exchange BET index are shown in Figure 4

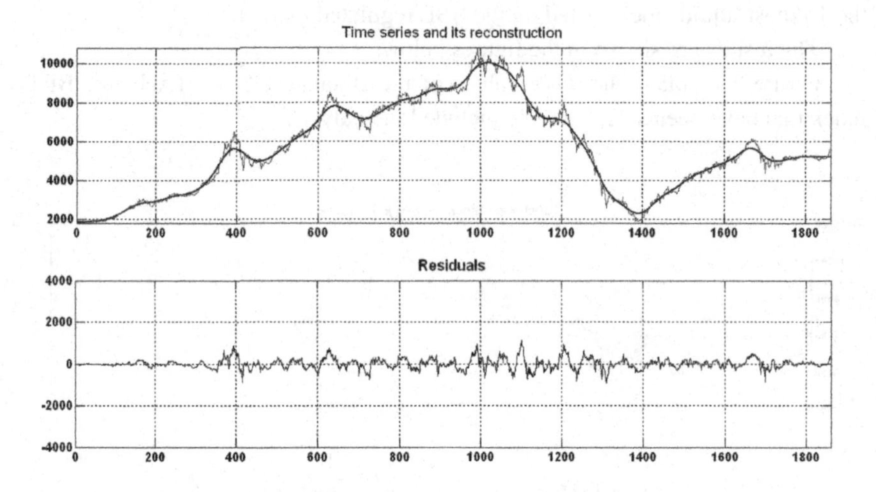

Figure 3. Reconstruction and residuals of Bucharest Stock Exchange BET index.

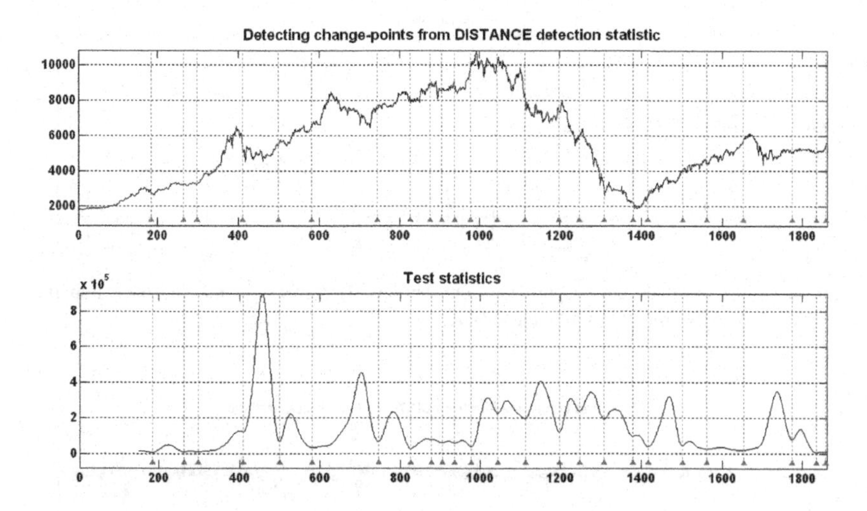

Figure 4. Detecting change points from Distance detection statistic. The location of change points is in the local minima of test statistic function.

Figures 5 to 7 show the results of applying the SSA based change point detection algorithm to the daily returns, calculated from the BET index.

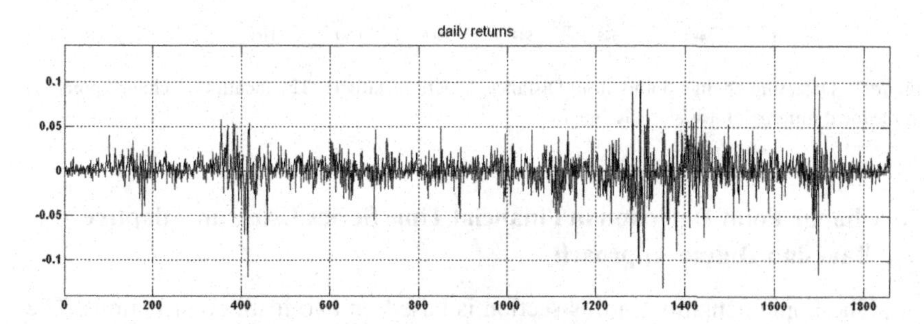

Figure 5. The Daily returns, calculated from the BET index.

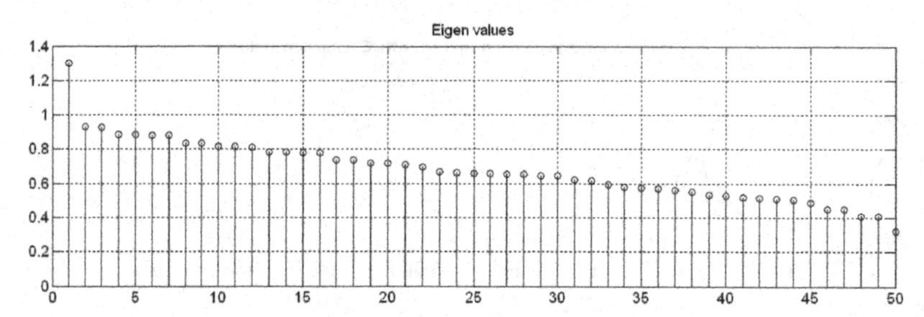

Figure 6. All eigenvalues have significant contributions. However, λ_1 has the most important contribution: 3.856% from the sum of eigenvalues.

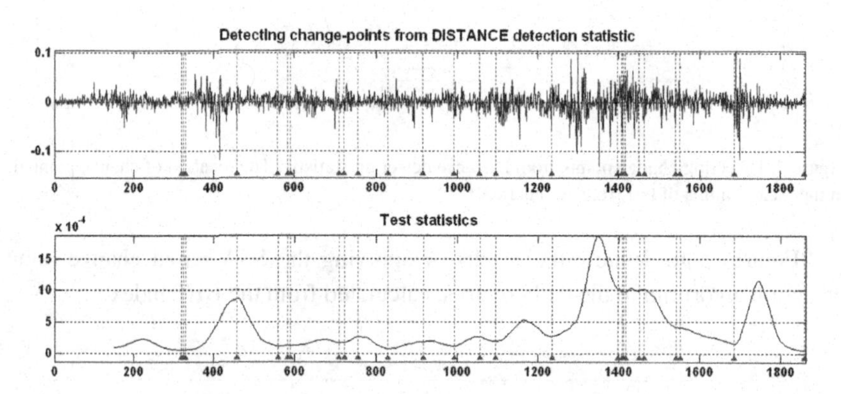

Figure 7. Detecting change points from Distance detection statistic. The location of change points is in the local minima of test statistic function.

3. Change Point Detection in Financial Time Series Using an Adaptive Bayesian Online Approach

The implementation in this section is based on two main contributions. The initial contribution refers to the basic Bayesian Online Change Point Detection (BOCPD) algorithm, which was recently introduced by Adams and MacKay ([1]); similar work has been done by Fearnhead and Liu ([4]). However, some important refinements to this basic algorithm have been proposed by Turner, Saatci and Rasmussen ([11]), that significantly improved both the performance and applicability area.

3.1. *The basic Bayesian Online Change Point Detection (BOCPD) algorithm*

3.1.1. *Specification of the model*

Real-world time series are often nonstationary with respect to the parameters of some underlying prediction model (UPM). Furthermore, it is often desirable to adapt the UPM to incoming regime changes as soon as possible, necessitating sequential inference about change point locations. Central to the online predictor is the time since the last change point, namely the run length. One can perform exact online inference about the run length at every time step, given an underlying predictive model (UPM) and a hazard function. Given all the observations up to time t, x_1, ..., $x_t \in X$, the UPM is used to compute $P(x_t \mid x_{(t-\tau):(t-1)}, \theta_m)$ for any $\tau \in [1, \ldots, (t-1)]$, at time t. The UPM can be thought of as a simpler base model whose parameters change at every change point; for instance, the UPM could be iid Gaussian with a different mean and variance within each regime. The hazard function $H(r \mid \theta_h)$ describes how likely we believe a change point is given an observed run length r. Notice that through $H(r \mid \theta_h)$ we can specify, a priori, arbitrary duration distributions for parameter regimes. The standard BOCPD algorithm also treats its hyper-parameters, $\theta = \{\theta_h, \theta_m\}$, as fixed and known. It is clear empirically that the performance of the algorithm is highly sensitive to hyper-parameter settings.

In the BOCPD algorithm, uncertainty about the last change point location is updated sequentially. In other words, BOCPD calculates the posterior run length at time t, i.e. $P(r_t \mid x_{1:t})$, sequentially. This posterior can be used to make online predictions robust to underlying regime changes, through marginalization of the run length variable:

$$P(x_{t+1} \mid x_{1:t}) = \sum_{r_t} P(x_{t+1} \mid r_t, x_{1:t}) \cdot P(r_t \mid x_{1:t}) = \sum_{r_t} P(x_{t+1} \mid x_t^{(r)}) \cdot P(r_t \mid x_{1:t}) \tag{9}$$

where $x_t^{(r)}$ refers to the last r_t observations of x, and $P(x_{t+1} \mid x_t^{(r)})$ is computed using the UPM.

The run length posterior can be found by normalizing the joint likelihood:

$$P(r_t \mid x_{1:t}) = \frac{P(r_t, x_{1:t})}{P(x_{1:t})} = \frac{P(r_t, x_{1:t})}{\sum_{r_t} P(r_t, x_{1:t})} \tag{10}$$

The joint likelihood can updated online using a recursive message passing scheme

$$\gamma_t = P(r_t \mid x_{1:t}) = \sum_{r_{t-1}} P(r_t, r_{t-1}, x_{1:t}) = \sum_{r_{t-1}} P(r_t, x_t \mid r_{t-1}, x_{1:t-1}) \cdot P(r_{t-1}, x_{1:t-1})$$
$$= \sum_{r_{t-1}} \underbrace{P(r_t, r_{t-1})}_{hazard} \cdot \underbrace{P(x_t \mid r_{t-1}, x_t^{(r)})}_{likelihood\ (UPM)} \cdot \underbrace{P(r_{t-1}, x_{1:t-1})}_{\gamma_{t-1}} \tag{11}$$

This defines a forward message passing scheme to recursively calculate γ_t from γ_{t-1}. The conditional can be restated in terms of messages as $P(r_{t-1}, x_{1:t-1}) \propto \gamma_t$. All the distributions mentioned so far are implicitly conditioned on the set of hyper-parameters θ.

3.1.2. *Specification of distributions and hyper-parameters*

BOCPD requires a set of fixed hyper-parameters which allow the user to fully specify the hazard function for change points and the prior distribution over the parameters of the UPM.

A simple example would be to use a constant hazard function $H(r \mid \theta_h)$, meaning $P(r_t = 0 \mid r_{t-1}, \theta_h)$ is independent of r_{t-1} and is constant, giving rise, a priori, to geometric inter-arrival times for change points. A constant hazard implies the presence of a change point at time t is determined independently of how long it has been since the last change point. The geometric inter-arrival distribution is the discrete time analog of the exponential distribution, which is often used to model arrival processes where events are unrelated to one another.

The UPM can be set to the predictive distribution obtained when placing a Normal-Inverse-Gamma prior on iid Gaussian observations (i.e., a Student-*t* predictive): $x_t \sim N(\mu, \sigma^2)$, $\mu \sim N(\mu_0, \sigma^2/\kappa)$, $\sigma^{-2} \sim Gamma\,(\alpha, \beta)$.

In this example, the model hyperparameters are: $\theta_m = \{\mu_0, \kappa, \alpha, \beta\}$.

3.2. *The refined BOCPD model: learning the hyper-parameters*

Learning the Hyper-parameters is the most important refinement proposed by Turner, Saatci and Rasmussen In practice, finding the "right" hyper-parameters can be quite difficult. Therefore BOCPD can be extended by introducing hyper-parameter learning, without sacrificing the online nature of the algorithm. Hyper-parameter learning is performed by optimizing the marginal likelihood of the BOCPD model, a closed-form quantity which can be computed sequentially.

It is possible to evaluate the (log) marginal likelihood of the BOCPD model at time *T*, as it can be decomposed into the one-step-ahead predictive likelihoods:

$$\log P\left(x_{1:T} \mid \theta\right) = \sum_{t=1}^{T} \log P\left(x_t \mid x_{1:T-1}, \theta\right) \tag{12}$$

Hence, we can compute the derivatives of the log marginal likelihood using the derivatives of the one-step-ahead predictive likelihoods. These derivatives can be found in the same recursive manner as the predictive likelihoods. Using the derivatives of the UPM, $\partial/\partial\theta_m\, P\left(x_t \mid r_{t-1}, x_t^{(r)}, \theta_m\right)$, and those of the hazard function, $\partial/\partial\theta_h\, P\left(r_t \mid r_{t-1}, \theta_h\right)$, the derivatives of the one-step ahead predictors can be propagated forward using the chain rule, as shown in Alg. (1). The derivatives with respect to the hyper-parameters can be plugged into a conjugate gradient optimizer to perform hyper-parameter learning.

3.3. *Applying the refined BOCPD model to financial time series*

The same datasets are presented to the refined BOCPD algorithm:

1. Bucharest Stock Exchange BET index;
2. The Daily returns, calculated from the BET index.

The results are shown in the figures below.

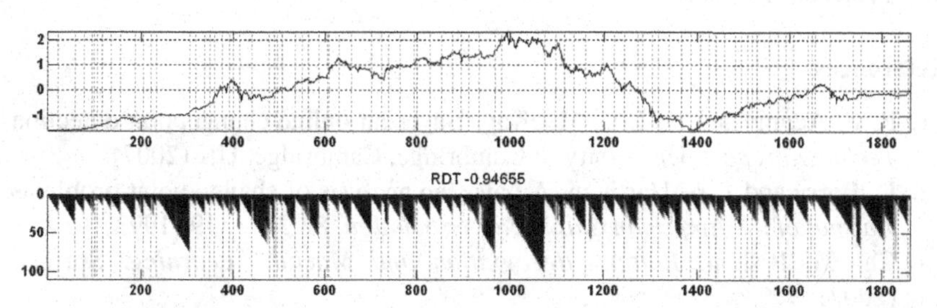

Figure 8. Top plot shows daily BET index values. The bottom plot shows the posterior probability of the current run length $P(r_t \mid x_{1:t})$ at each time scale, using a logarithmic color scale. Darker pixels indicate higher probability.

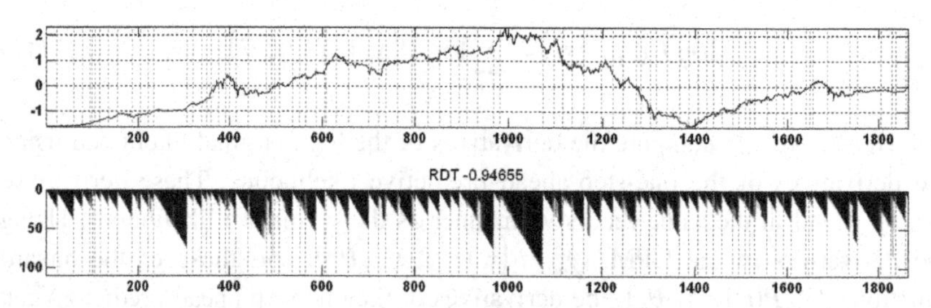

Figure 9. Top plot shows daily returns , calculated from the BET index. The bottom plot shows the posterior probability of the current run length $P(r_t \mid x_{1:t})$ at each time scale, using a logarithmic color scale. Darker pixels indicate higher probability.

4. Conclusion

A frequentist approach based on Singular Spectrum Analyses and an adaptive sequential Bayesian approach have been addressed in this paper to experimentally test the effectiveness of change point detection algorithms designed for the online use. Their goal is to recognize and further to predict regime change events in highly noisy and time-varying financial processes. The two methods were applied to price series and return series taken from Bucharest Stock Exchange market.

References

1. R. P. Adams and D. J. C. MacKay, Bayesian online changepoint detection. *Technical report*, University of Cambridge, Cambridge, UK (2007).
2. D. Barry and J. A. Hartigan, A bayesian analysis of change point problems. *Journal of the American Statistical Association*, 88:309–319 (1993).
3. Ch. M. Bishop, *Pattern Recognition and Machine Learning,* Springer (2007).
4. P. Fearnhead and Z. Liu, Online inference for multiple changepoint problems, *Journal of the Royal Statistical Society*, 69:589–605 (2007).
5. N. Goljadina, V. Nekrutkin, A. Zhigljavky, Analysis of Time Series Structure: SSA and related techniques, London: Chapman and Holl (2001).
6. V. Moskvina, *Applications of the singular-spectrum analysis for change point detection in time series*, Ph.D. thesis, School of Mathematics, Cardiff University, Cardiff (2001).
7. V. Moskvina, Distribution of random quadratic forms arising in singular-spectrum analysis, *Mathematical Communications*, 5, 161-171 (2000).
8. E. S. Page, A test for a change in a parameter occurring at an unknown point. *Biometrika*, 523–527:42 (1955).

9. Judea Pearl, Reverend Bayes on inference engines: A distributed hierarchical approach, in *AAAI*, pages 133—136, Pittsburgh, PA, USA, August (1982).
10. C. E. Rasmussen and C. K. I. Williams, *Gaussian Processes for Machine Learning* the MIT Press (2006).
11. Ryan Turner, Yunus Saatci, and Carl Edward Rasmussen, Adaptive sequential Bayesian change point detection, in Zaid Harchaoui, editor, *Temporal Segmentation Workshop at NIPS 2009*, Whistler, BC, Canada, December (2009).

APPLICATION OF A FUZZY MODEL OF ECONOMIC-FINANCIAL DIAGNOSIS TO SMES

ANTONIO TERCEÑO

Faculty of Business and Economic, Universitat Rovira i Virgili, Avinguda Universitat, 1 (43204) Reus, Spain. antonio.terceno@urv.net

HERNÁN VIGIER

Economic Department, Universidad Nacional del Sur- Universidad Provincial del Sudoeste– CIC, 12 de Octubre 1198 7º Piso (8000) Bahía Blanca, Argentina. hvigier@uns.edu.ar

VALERIA SCHERGER

Economic Department, Universidad Nacional del Sur, 12 de Octubre 1198 7º Piso (8000) Bahía Blanca, Argentina. valeria.scherger@uns.edu.ar

The aim of the following paper is to make a diagnosis of firms using the theory developed by Vigier and Terceño [1], an overall approach for analyzing the causes and symptoms of the future economic-financial situations of firms. The methodological postulates of the model are adapted and applied to a group of SMEs in the construction sector for a particular timeline, using the tools and methods of fuzzy logic. By working with multiple qualitative variables and modeling the expert's knowledge, this methodology overcomes many of the traditional models' restrictions regarding the treatment of subjectivity and uncertainty. This research shows the results of the estimates of the matrix of economic–financial knowledge, as well as the treatment of causes, taking as a reference the first theoretical approach presented in Terceño *et al.* [2].

Keywords: Economic-financial diagnosis; Symptoms and causes; Fuzzy relations.

1. Introduction

There is a great deal of literature on the early detection of firms' problems. Since the 1950s most theoretical and empirical models have tried to explain the performance of businesses as a function of the evolution of their financial statements. Within this framework are the traditional ratio model, which uses indicators to make an economic-financial diagnosis; the econometric models of discrimination analysis to predict firm failure (Altman [3]; Beaver [4]; *etc.*); the models of conditional likelihood analysis Logit and Probit (Olshon [5]; *etc.*);

and the models of firm survival (Wilcox [6]; Santomero and Vinso [7]; *etc.*). These models generally evaluate bankruptcy or the failure of entrepreneurs, and use quantitative indicators to estimate the future evolution of firms, distinguishing between healthy and unhealthy businesses.*

This paper aims to make an empirical application of the model developed by Vigier and Terceño [1] to firms in the construction sector. This model uses an overall approach and fuzzy relations to diagnose the causes and symptoms, which can be used to determine a group of relations and to predict future problems at firms. The tools and methodology of fuzzy logic relations overcome many of the restrictions of the traditional models in terms of subjectivity and uncertainty by working with multiple qualitative variables and modeling the expert's knowledge.

On the basis of the Vigier and Terceño model [1], and the analytical theory of the Balanced Scorecard by Kaplan and Norton [8], [9] and [10], the diagnosis model is applied to small and medium firms in the construction sector. In Terceño *et al.* [2] it was first suggested that the businesses diagnosis theory be integrated into the Balanced Scorecard. This integration involved developing an analytical and conceptual framework to identify a group of disease-generating causes and make a contribution to the theory of causes as an element of businesses' diagnosis.†

The model constructs the incidence matrixes of symptoms and causes, which define the degrees of incidence of various diseases present in firms. This research shows the results of estimating the matrix of economic-financial knowledge and analyzes its ability to predict and diagnose.

2. The Diagnosis Model

The suggested model, Vigier *et al.* [1], estimates a matrix of symptoms and a matrix of causes, of both endogenous and exogenous origin, that can lead to the matrix of economic-financial knowledge (R). This is then used to make forecasts about the level of incidence of each cause defined in the model.

$$R = Q^{-1} \alpha P, \text{ being, } Q^{-1} = [q_{hi}]^{-1} = [q_{ih}] \quad (1)$$

* Furthermore, some of the models add qualitative variables as an effort to improve the estimated results (Edminster [17]; Keasey *et. al* [17], *etc.).*

† Very few authors have studied the causes. Among those who have, we should mention Argenti [12], Gabás Trigo [13], Gil- Aluja [14], Gil- Lafuente [15], *etc*., who point out some of the causes that should be analyzed when diagnosing firms. Despite the fact that these models improve the explanatory power of the traditional models by including qualitative and quantitative features, they do not manage to schematize the overall process of detecting causes.

That is,

$$R = Q^{-1} \alpha P = [\, q_{ih}] \,\alpha\, [\, p_{hj}] = [r_{ij}] \quad (2)$$

where,

$$q_{ih} \,\alpha\, p_{hj} = \begin{cases} 1 & \text{si } q_{ih} \leq p_{hj} \\ p_{hj} & \text{si } q_{ih} > p_{hj} \end{cases}$$

R = Matrix of economic-financial knowledge
Q^{-1} = Transposition matrix of the firms' symptoms
P = Matrix of the firms' causes

The construction of the matrix of economic-financial knowledge (R) is determined by a group of symptoms $S = \{ S_i \}$, where i=1,2,….,n., of causes $C = \{ C_j \}$, where j= 1,2,, p., of periods $T = \{T_k\}$, where k=1,2,3,…,t., and of firms in which is possible to identify symptoms and causes $E=\{E_h\}$, where h=1,2,3,…,m.

The group of symptoms (S) is built from ratios taken from previous papers on solvency prediction (Ratios Theory, models for predicting a firm's failure, *etc.*) and which differentiate a firm's health. Once the cardinal matrix of symptoms has been obtained (S), the membership matrix of each symptom is determined (Q).

As far as causes are concerned, we suggest constructing a group of subjectively measured causes (C_j^s where j=1,2,……s); and a group of objectively measured causes (C_j^o where j=s+1,s+2,……p). The membership matrix of objective causes is obtained by the same mechanism used for building the membership matrix of symptoms. In the case of the subjective causes, the expert's opinion is formalized by any of the three methods suggested in the model (Linguistic Labels, Confidence Intervals and Simple Evaluation) so that the membership matrix of objective and subjective causes can be determined.

Considering the local nature of the diagnosis, the model suggests not only that the group of selected firms should be from a particular region and production area (E) but also that it should be made up of healthy and unhealthy firms so that the differences in the indicators between both groups can be easily spotted. Finally, the years or periods of time (T) over which the estimation is made must be defined.

As mentioned above, each element of the matrix R of economic-financial knowledge is obtained by the operation between the transposition of the membership matrix of symptoms and the membership matrix of causes which satisfies the minimum relation ($R = Q^{-1} \alpha P$). As the model evokes the determination of the possible causes and diseases of the firm based upon the estimates of R, each r_{ij} shows the level of incidence between the symptom S_i (q_{hi}) and the cause C_j (p_{hj}).

This model enables the possible diseases that a firm can have to be predicted by analyzing the relation between the vector that shows the levels of membership of the symptoms and the matrix of economic-financial knowledge. The matrix R is used to make predictions about the health of firms. Meaningful levels of incidence between symptoms and causes need to be determined if a degree of occurrence is to be assigned to a specific disease. Hence, the likelihood of different diseases can be determined and, on the basis of the diagnosis, measures can be taken to correct the situation.

Fuzzy tools are used in the estimation to help overcome the main weaknesses: the selection of the dependent variable, the selection of the sample, the choice of the explanatory variables, and the treatment and inclusion of the sorting errors that subsist in the models mentioned. Several authors have identified these factors as weaknesses (Jones [18]; Zavgren [19]; Zmijewski [20]; Mora Enguidanos [21]; among others) since most models have a high predictive power when evaluated with the same sample that that was used to construct them, but this power is considerably lower when a different sample is used for the validation. Another important issue is that it is necessary to model the knowledge of the expert who has a major role in defining the relations between the elements of the model.

As mentioned by these authors, it is difficult to find an integral solution using a classical solution method because of the considerable number of variables and parameters used in the diagnosis, which is evaluated on the basis of the qualitative variables or the experts' opinions. All this information adds elements of subjectivity and uncertainty to the process of the economic-financial diagnosis, and so the traditional methodologies have severe limitations. This opens up the possibility of using tools and methods of fuzzy mathematics, which can work with qualitative variables and model the expert's knowledge.

As mentioned above, the initial weakness of the diagnosis model is that the causes that are a part of the model are not explicitly defined. However, the authors that developed the BSC model conceive an analytical framework that systematizes a group of causes that result from the identification of a firm's problems.

3.The detection of causes using the Balanced Scorecard Model

The Balanced Scorecard (BSC) model was initially conceived by Kaplan and Norton as a mechanism to complement traditional financial accounting measures, which give a partial and incomplete vision of business performance [8]. The model transcended financial indicators by adding measures of internal efficiency, customer performance and firm growth and learning, so that the firm's strategy could be designed and management indicators included in the company's key areas. According to the authors, the Balanced Scorecard can lead to better decisions because it adds ratios of future performance to the financial indicators.

Kaplan and Norton define the BSC as a management tool that tries to explain a firm's performance. It also provides benefits because it explains the reasons for the organization's success. The concept underlying the BSC reflects the administrators' attempt to strike a balance between short- and long-term objectives, between financial and non-financial indicators, and between internal and external perspectives.

From the management point of view, the BSC is defined as a model that translates the firm's mission and strategy into objectives and indicators from four perspectives: finance, customers, the internal business process, and learning and growth.

To conceptualize the detection of causes, the cause-effect relationship proposed by Kaplan and Norton in the generation of the "Balanced Scorecard" is taken as a reference [8], [9], [10] and [11]. The scorecard monitors the performance of firms as a function of the causal relations between management indicators and the firms' objectives. These causal relations, expressed through strategic maps, help to join the strategic objectives of each perspective of the company (finance, customers, the internal business process, and learning and growth) into a single strategy that binds the whole causal chain.

The integration of the fuzzy diagnosis model and the Balanced Scorecard, as mentioned in Terceño *et al.* [2], formalizes and generalizes the aspects stated in the theory of management control to the universe of firms, and supplements the developments and theoretical contributions with the formalization of the fuzzy tools and methods. Thus, the construction of a list of causes, based on the perspectives suggested by Kaplan and Norton, enables the analyst to identify the critical factors that create diseases in a firm and which can damage its performance.

As a function of the causal logic suggested by Kaplan and Norton, each of the perspectives is related to different causes that can give rise to difficulties in firms. This creates a cycle, which by its very nature, is negative; for example, the cause "lack in the perspective of learning and growth" creates the disease "operational and commercial inconvenience" which is revealed through weak or insufficient economic-financial indicators. Figure 1 presents a strategic map with some key factors for a firm's evolution.

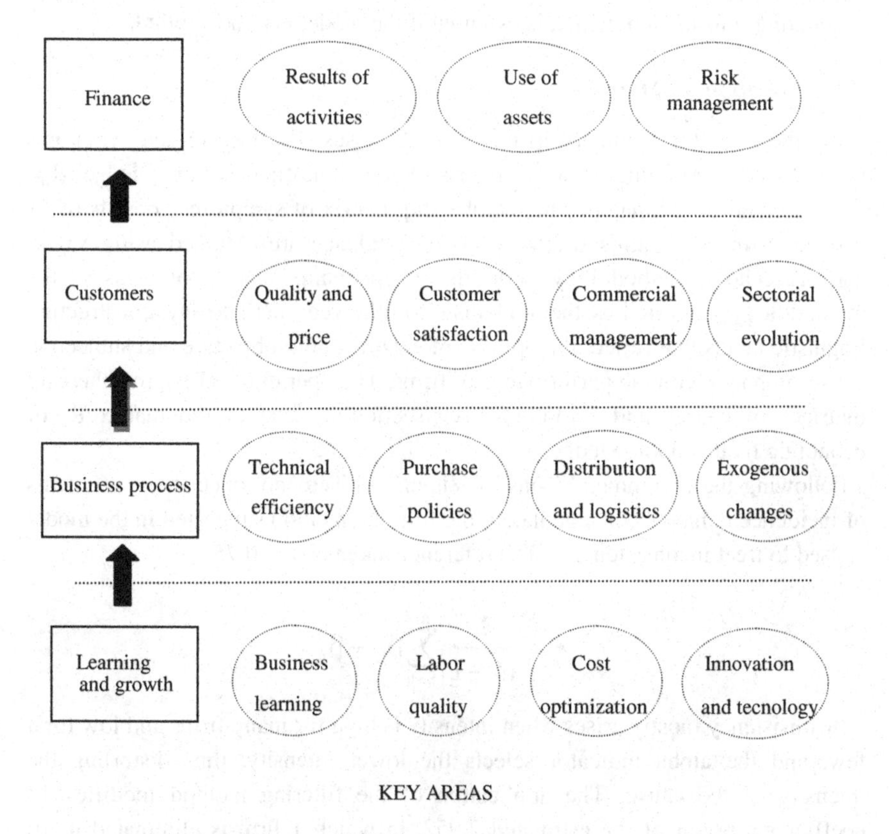

Figure 1: Areas to control
Source: Terceño *et al.* [2]

Once these key areas have been identified, the causes that can affect performance in the key areas must be classified according to the four perspectives mentioned. These causes can generate unwanted results that have an impact on the economic financial ratios of the firms.

4. Application of the model

This section shows the results of applying the model of business diagnosis, described by Vigier and Terceño [1]. The analysis consists of interviews with experts and the analysis of the financial statements of approximately 15% of the companies registered in construction and building materials.[‡] One of the most important restrictions on the selection of the firms is the availability of accounting information, which is essential if the model is to be applied.

1.1 Estimation of Matrix r_{ij}

From the data, the membership matrices of causes (P_{hj}=15x72) and symptoms (Q_{ih}=15x41) were built so that the matrix of economic-financial knowledge (R_{ij}= 41x72) could be estimated. The membership matrix of symptoms consists of 41 economic-financial ratios whose levels of incidence are obtained using Vigier and Terceño's methodology. For the membership matrix of causes, the methodology suggested by the model is also followed: that's to say, constructing linguistic labels that reflect the opinion of experts about objective and subjective causes impacting on the performance of firms. The operations of the membership matrices of causes and symptoms (see section 2) lead to the matrix R_{ij} of economic financial knowledge.

Following the recommendations of Vigier and Terceño, once the coefficients of incidence r_{ij} have been calculated, the filtering method suggested in the model is used to treat inconsistencies. The reference taken is $\phi^*= 0.75$

$$\phi = \frac{1}{m-1} . \sum_{h=1}^{m} \beta_h - \beta_h^*$$

Inconsistency mostly arises when intensity is high for many firms and low for a few, and the alpha indicator selects the lower intensity, thus distorting the intensity of the cause. The application of the filtering method modifies 18 coefficients r_{ij} out of the estimated 2,952, in which 1 firm is eliminated in 16 cases and 3 firms in 2 cases. This method substantially improves the degree of incidence of the r_{ij}.

‡ We analyze 15 firms out of a total of 98 registered in the activities of construction and building materials in the cities of Bahía Blanca and Punta Alta (Argentina).

4.2 Grouping the causes

One of the advantages of the fuzzy methodology is that it makes it possible to work with a large number of variables. In this case, once the incidence coefficients have been estimated, the 72 causes of the final R_{ij} matrix are grouped (using the filtering method) taking as reference the causal relations mentioned in section 3 in the framework of the BSC theory (figure 2). The Vigier and Terceño model does not make an in-depth study of the analysis and treatment of the causes. Hence, the grouping and analysis of causes represents a breakthrough in theory.

The causes are clustered in minimum, maximum and mean incidence rates, and three R_{ij} matrixes are calculated with 14 causes for minimum, maximum and mean incidence values (R_{ij}=41x14).

Learning and Growth				Internal Business			Clients				Finance		
Business Learning	Innovation and Technology	Labor Quality	Cost Optimization	Technical Efficiency	Purchase Policies	Exogenous Changes	Commercial Management	Customer Satisfaction	Quality and Prices	Sectorial Evolution	Use of assets	Risk management	Results of activity

Figure 2: Clusters of causes

4.3 Approximate solutions

The results generated by the diagnosis model are analysed using Brignole *et al.* proposal [22] of approximate solutions, which reveals the extent to which the estimated results satisfy the original problem. This methodology is suggested by Vigier and Terceño for evaluating the prediction power of the R_{ij} matrix.

This application uses [22] to analyze the degree of fit of the cluster of causes. This supposes the estimate of a goodness measure of the approximate solution (P’), which is expressed in terms of an equality index when, in the composition to get the matrix R, it is used the approximate solution (P’) instead of the original matrix (P).

Brignole *et al.* [22] refer to this index as a goodness measure of P and P’, which can also be referred to as the Hamming distance;

$$[P = P'] = 1 - \frac{1}{n} \sum_{x \in X} \left| \mu_P(x) - \mu_P(x) \right|$$

This element is important to determine the degree of fit of the set of causes and the prediction capacity of the matrix of economic-financial knowledge. Following the suggested methodology, we operate the matrix of symptoms with the 3 matrixes R_{ij} (in minimum, maximum and mean levels of causes) to get a new estimated matrix of causes in minimum, maximum and mean rates of incidence ($P'_{h'} = Q_{h'} \circ R$; being $P'_{h'j} = \max(\min(q_{h'i}, r_{ij}))$).

Moreover, to contrast the results of the R_{ij} matrix through the approximate solutions, we have grouped the original matrix of causes (P_{hj}=15x72) according to the three levels of incidence, for obtaining 3 matrixes of membership of causes: in maximum, minimum and mean rates of incidence (P'_{hj}=15x14).

Once we have the original matrix (P_{hj}) and the estimated (P'_{hj}) matrix of causes, we apply the postulates of approximate solutions to the three forms of grouping to determine the degree of fit of the estimation. This needs to be done to determinate the degree of fit of the grouping of the causes and the prediction capacity of the matrix of economic-financial knowledge. This analysis concludes that the best fit is obtained with minimum rates, which reflect a higher goodness measure, with a degree of fit of 89% (see table 1).

Table 1: Degree of fit

Firm	Mean	Max	Min
1	0.77	0.65	0.90
2	0.92	0.86	0.94
3	0.83	0.74	0.93
4	0.83	0.74	0.94
5	0.82	0.83	0.89
6	0.83	0.81	0.85
7	0.82	0.78	0.85
8	0.83	0.81	0.86
9	0.79	0.66	0.92
10	0.79	0.78	0.85
11	0.77	0.61	0.93
12	0.73	0.69	0.85
13	0.78	0.72	0.87
14	0.76	0.69	0.85
15	0.82	0.77	0.88
Mean	0.81	0.74	0.89

4.4 Matrix aggregation

Once the operation and filter procedures described above have finished for each period T_k of the timeline T, we aggregate the matrices $R_k=[\ r_{ij}\ ]_k$ for the three periods. It should be pointed out that the methodology of aggregation is linked directly to the fact that some trends distort the temporal validity of the results. As mentioned in Vigier and Terceño [1] if r_{ij} is increasing, the use of a mean aggregation procedure would underestimate the real relation. On the other hand, if the component is decreasing over time, the generalized average will overestimate the relation.

Therefore, the behavior of each r_{ij} is evaluated in an attempt to determine the aggregation operator that best suits the trend of the component, as pointed out in the model. The tendency is analyzed with the function of the indicator of the tendency level ξ.

$$\xi = \frac{\sum_{k=2}^{t}\left([ri_j]_k - [r_{ij}]_{k-1}\right)}{\sum_{k=2}^{t}\left|[r_{ij}]_k - [r_{ij}]_{k-1}\right|}$$

For the case analyzed, an increasing trend is observed in 289 r_{ij}, and the aggregation is carried out by means of the $r_{ij}= (r_{ij})_{k-1}\ o\ (\ r_{ij}\ )_k = \text{Max}\ (\text{Min}\ ((r_{ij}\ )_k\ ,(r_{ij}\ )_{k-1}))$. In the remaining 2,663 r_{ij} no such trend is observed. In the cases in which there is no trend, the aggregation is done through the generalized average $rij= h_{\varphi}(r_{ij\ 1}, r_{ij\ 2},\ldots,r_{ij\ k},\ldots,r_{ij\ t}) = [1/t\ .\ \Sigma\ (r_{ij\ k})^{\varphi}]^{1/\varphi}$.

The same aggregation procedure was followed for the membership matrix of symptoms, and the trend in most coefficients was increasing. A total of 549 out of the 615 incidence indicators of symptoms were aggregated using the technique recommended for increasing trend cases.

4.5 Verification

Finally, the goodness of fit of the model is verified using the aggregated matrixes and the approximate solutions method. Using the methodology described in section 4.3 it is confirmed that the best fit is attained when the minimum incidence rates of the causes are grouped together, which reflects a higher goodness index with a degree of fit of 89% (see table 2). In this case, it is estimated using the goodness measure between the three versions of the aggregate R_{ij} matrix (maximum, minimum and mean values of the groupings of the causes) and the aggregate matrix of symptoms. Appendix shows the aggregate matrix of economic-financial knowledge (R_{ij}) for minimum incidence rates of causes. This matrix shows the degree of incidence of the symptoms on the causes present in the firms.

Table 2: Degree of fit considering several periods

Firm	Mean	Max	Min
1	0.75	0.61	0.90
2	0.90	0.81	0.95
3	0.81	0.68	0.93
4	0.81	0.71	0.94
5	0.79	0.75	0.89
6	0.81	0.74	0.86
7	0.80	0.74	0.86
8	0.80	0.73	0.86
9	0.78	0.62	0.92
10	0.76	0.70	0.85
11	0.75	0.58	0.94
12	0.71	0.62	0.86
13	0.76	0.67	0.88
14	0.73	0.66	0.85
15	0.79	0.72	0.88
Mean	0.78	0.69	0.89

The goodness measure of the model, of 89% through the grouping of causes in their minimum rates of incidence, is also confirmed when we doing the test between the aggregate matrix of knowledge and the matrix of incidence of symptoms of the last analyzed period.[§]

4.6 Forecast

One of the main results of the Vigier and Terceño [1] diagnosis model is that it makes it possible to forecast a firms' health: that is to say, it can detect the diseases a firm is going to suffer from.

The simulation developed for the sampled firms, through $B_{h'} = A_{h'}$ or $\Re = [b_{h'j}]$—where $B_{h'}$, expresses the possible causes (or diseases) that are the root of

[§] In this test the equality or degree of fit index of the model is 0.78 when the mean rates of incidence are used, 0.69 when the rates are maximum and 0.98 when they are minimum.

all the firm's problems; A_h the incidence level of each symptom S_i in the firm E_h, and $\mathfrak{R}$ the economic-financial knowledge matrix—detects that some of the causes affect all the firms in this sector similarly. The information is listed in table 3.

It should be pointed out that in the Learning and Growth cluster, the diseases related to innovation and technology and cost optimization are not important problems for these firms but those related to business learning and labor quality are. The factors related to business learning are the firm's age, type of organization, manager's education, frequency of management changes, the centralization of decision making, the participation of partners in the organization, management information, mistakes and delays involved in the decision making, the computerization of the firm, information fluidity, the type of internal communication, stakeholders' restrictions and the adaptability to change. In 8 out of the 15 firms analyzed business learning is a cause of concern for the company, with a b_h= 0.53. Labor quality (b_h=0.60 and 0.61) takes into account the importance of the work force's educational level, the difficulty of getting qualified labor, the degree of unionization and the frequency of employee training.

The most important factors in the Internal Process cluster are technical efficiency and purchase policies with a b_h higher than 0.50. In five firms there are issues with purchase policies (suppliers' choice, problems with deliveries, stock policies and suppliers' mean time of payment) with a b_h= 0.71. In the case of technical efficiency (oversizing, work accidents, absenteeism, productivity, use facilities, lead times, unnecessary costs, excess capacity, cost level compared to other companies in the sector) 8 out of the 15 firms have a value of 0.57.

In the Clients cluster, the quality and prices factor (quality level, price level, advertising and promotions) is the most relevant (b_h= 0.57 and 0.59).

In the Finance cluster, the use of assets (budget control, cash flow frequency, financial planning, search for short and long term funding, capital contribution frequency and taking financial decisions) is the most important with b_h=0.60 for most firms.

Tabla 3 Estimated matrix of diseases

	Learning and Growth			Internal Business					Clients			Finance		
	1	2	3	4	5	6	7	8	9	10	11	12	13	14
Firms	Business Learning	Innovation and Technology	Labor Quality	Cost Optimization	Technical Efficiency	Purchase Policies	Exogenous Changes	Commercial Management	Client Satisfaction	Quality and Prices	Sectorial Evolution	Use of assets	Risk management	Results of activity
1	0.53	0.16	0.61	0.20	0.57	0.62	0.20	0.43	0.37	0.59	0.31	0.60	0.50	0.57
2	0.50	0.16	0.60	0.20	0.57	0.62	0.20	0.43	0.31	0.57	0.33	0.60	0.50	0.57
3	0.50	0.16	0.61	0.20	0.43	0.57	0.20	0.43	0.28	0.57	0.33	0.53	0.50	0.57
4	0.53	0.16	0.60	0.20	0.57	0.62	0.20	0.43	0.33	0.57	0.33	0.60	0.50	0.57
5	0.50	0.16	0.60	0.20	0.57	0.62	0.20	0.43	0.37	0.59	0.33	0.60	0.50	0.57
6	0.53	0.16	0.60	0.20	0.57	0.62	0.20	0.43	0.37	0.57	0.33	0.60	0.50	0.57
7	0.53	0.16	0.61	0.20	0.57	0.62	0.20	0.43	0.31	0.57	0.33	0.60	0.50	0.57
8	0.50	0.16	0.60	0.20	0.57	0.62	0.20	0.43	0.37	0.59	0.33	0.60	0.50	0.57
9	0.53	0.16	0.61	0.20	0.47	0.71	0.20	0.40	0.37	0.59	0.31	0.60	0.50	0.57
10	0.50	0.16	0.60	0.20	0.57	0.71	0.20	0.43	0.37	0.57	0.33	0.60	0.50	0.57
11	0.53	0.16	0.60	0.20	0.43	0.67	0.20	0.43	0.37	0.57	0.33	0.60	0.50	0.57
12	0.50	0.16	0.61	0.20	0.43	0.71	0.20	0.38	0.37	0.59	0.31	0.60	0.50	0.57
13	0.53	0.16	0.61	0.20	0.53	0.71	0.20	0.43	0.37	0.59	0.31	0.60	0.50	0.57
14	0.53	0.16	0.61	0.20	0.43	0.60	0.20	0.43	0.31	0.57	0.33	0.60	0.50	0.57
15	0.50	0.16	0.61	0.20	0.43	0.71	0.20	0.40	0.37	0.59	0.33	0.60	0.50	0.57

5. Conclusions

The most important feature of this proposal is the application of Vigier and Terceño's integral model of economic-financial diagnosis [1] to small and medium firms in a specific sector. A fuzzy methodology is used, which helps overcome the fact that other models have some limitations with regard to the addition of qualitative aspects. The design of causes detection suggested by some of these authors, through the BSC, allows us to introduce objective and subjective elements which influence the firms' performance. The simulation of the model, demonstrates that the best diagnosis is obtained when the causes are grouped in minimum incidence rates, with a goodness measure of 89%. These results are confirmed both for the last estimated period and for the aggregate matrix.

This application has also shown that the model can make forecasts about the health of firms by simulating the work carried out by an expert. Correspondingly, the results show that the firms studied have problems in the four clusters proposed by the BSC. The most important diseases, which have high incidence rates in some firms, are purchase policies, labor quality, price and product quality, use of assets and results of activities. The features related to cost optimization, innovation and technology, and exogenous changes, on the other hand, have the least impact.

Our aim is to continue working on the coefficients and analysis of incidence rates and to test the model with firms from outside the initial sample so that the model's capacity to diagnose and predict diseases can be evaluated further.

References

1. H. Vigier and A. Terceño, "A model for the prediction of diseases of firms by means of fuzzy relations". Fuzzy Sets and System. Vol 159. No. 17. September (2008).
2. A. Terceño, H. Vigier, G. Barberá and V. Scherger, "Hacia una integración de la Teoría del Diagnóstico Fuzzy y del Balanced Scorecard". XV SIGEF Conference Economic and Financial Crisis. New Challenges and Perspectives", Lugo, Spain, 29-30. ISBN: 978-84-613-5575-4, pp 364-379 (2009).
3. E. Altman, "Financial ratios, Discriminant Analysis and the Prediction of Corporate Bankruptcy". Journal of Finance. Vol XXIII, No. 4. September. pp. 589-609 (1968).
4. W. Beaver, "Financial ratios as Predictors of Failures", in Empirical Research in Accounting, selected studies (1967).
5. J. Olshon, "Financial Ratios and the Probabilistic Prediction of Bankruptcy". Journal of Accounting Research. Vol 18 No. 1 Spring, pp.109-131 (1980).
6. J. Wilcox, "The Gambler´s Ruin Approach to Business Risk". Sloan Management Review, Fall, pp.33-46 (1976).
7. A. Santomero and J. Vinso, "Estimating the Probability of Failure for Firms in the Banking System". Journal of Banking and Finance. September, pp.185-205 (1977).

8. R. Kaplan, and D. Norton, "The Balanced Scorecard: measures that drivers performances". Harvard Business Review, vol 70, N° 1, Fall, pp 71-79 (1992).
9. R. Kaplan, and D. Norton, Using the Balanced Scorecard as a strategic management system" Harvard Business Review, vol 74, N° 1, pp 75-85 (1996a).
10. R. Kaplan and D. Norton, "Linking the Balanced Scorecard to Strategy", California Management, vol 39, 1, Fall (1996b).
11. R. Kaplan and D. Norton, "Having problem with your strategy. Then map it". Harvard Business Review (September–October), pp 167–176 (2000).
12. J. Argenti, "Corporate Collapse: The Causes and Symptoms". John Wiley and Sons, New York (1976)
13. F. Gabás Trigo, "Predicción de la Insolvencia Empresarial". In Predicción de la Insolvencia Empresarial, Antonio Calvo-Flores Segura y Domingo García Pérez de Lema. Asociación Española de Contabilidad y Administración de Empresas (AECA). Madrid. pp.11-32 (1997).
14. J. Gil Aluja, "Ensayo sobre un Modelo de Diagnóstico Económico - Financiero" Actas de las V Jornadas Hispano-Lusas de Gestión Científica, Vigo, September 1990, pp 26-29 (1990).
15. J. Gil Lafuente, "El Control de las Actividades de Marketing" - III Congreso de SIGEF, Vol. III, Buenos Aires, paper 244., pp. 1-21 (1996).
16. R. Edmister, "An Empirical Test of Financial Ratio Analysis for Small Business Failure Prediction". Journal of Finance and Quantitative Analysis. Marzo..pp. 1477-1493 (1972).
17. K. Keasey and R. Watson, "Non Financial Sympstons and The Prediction of Small Company Failure: A test of Argenti ´s Hypothesses". Journal of Bussiness & Accounting. Autumn, pp.335-354 (1987).
18. F. L. Jones, "Current Techniques in Bankruptcy Prediction". Journal of Accounting Literature, Vol 6, pp 131-164 (1987).
19. C. Zavgren, "The prediction of Corporate Failure: The State of Art", Journal of Accounting Literature, Vol.2, pp.1-37 (1983).
20. M. Zmijewski, "Methodological Issues Related to the Estimation of Financial Distress Prediction Models". Journal of Accounting Research, pp. 59-86 (1984)
21. A. Mora Enguidanos, "Limitaciones Metodológicas de los Trabajos Empíricos sobre la Predicción del Fracaso Empresarial". Revista Española de Financiación y Contabilidad. Vol. XXII. No. 80, pp. 709-732 (1984).
22. D. Brignole and H. Vigier, "El Diagnóstico en la Empresa ". III Congreso de SIGEF, Vol. I, Buenos Aires, paper 2.4. pp. 1-17 (1996).

Appendix

Aggregate matrix of diagnosis (Rij: minimum incidence rates)

	Learning and Growth				Internal Business			Clients				Finance		
Symptoms	Business Learning	Innov- Technol.	Labor Quality	Cost Optimizat.	Technical Efficiency	Purchase Policies	Exog. Changes	Commerc. Managem.	Customer Satisfact.	Quality - Prices	Sectorial Evolution	Use of assets	Risk Manag.	Results of activity
1	0.14	0.12	0.14	0.17	0.07	0.20	0.20	0.13	0.20	0.29	0.13	0.11	0.14	0.17
2	0.14	0.12	0.14	0.17	0.07	0.20	0.20	0.13	0.20	0.38	0.13	0.11	0.14	0.17
3	0.14	0.12	0.14	0.17	0.07	0.20	0.20	0.13	0.20	0.29	0.13	0.00	0.14	0.17
4	0.14	0.12	0.14	0.17	0.07	0.20	0.20	0.13	0.20	0.29	0.13	0.11	0.14	0.17
5	0.14	0.12	0.14	0.17	0.00	0.20	0.20	0.13	0.20	0.29	0.13	0.11	0.14	0.17
6	0.14	0.12	0.14	0.17	0.07	0.20	0.20	0.13	0.20	0.43	0.13	0.00	0.14	0.20
7	0.14	0.12	0.14	0.17	0.07	0.20	0.20	0.13	0.20	0.29	0.13	0.11	0.14	0.17
8	0.14	0.12	0.14	0.17	0.07	0.20	0.20	0.13	0.20	0.29	0.13	0.00	0.14	0.17
9	0.14	0.12	0.14	0.17	0.07	0.20	0.20	0.13	0.20	0.29	0.13	0.00	0.14	0.20
10	0.14	0.12	0.14	0.17	0.00	0.20	0.20	0.13	0.20	0.29	0.13	0.11	0.14	0.17
11	0.14	0.12	0.14	0.17	0.07	0.20	0.20	0.13	0.20	0.29	0.13	0.11	0.14	0.24
12	0.14	0.12	0.14	0.17	0.07	0.20	0.20	0.13	0.20	0.29	0.13	0.00	0.14	0.17
13	0.14	0.12	0.14	0.17	0.07	0.20	0.20	0.13	0.20	0.29	0.13	0.11	0.14	0.17
14	0.14	0.12	0.14	0.17	0.00	0.20	0.20	0.13	0.20	0.29	0.13	0.11	0.14	0.17
15	0.14	0.12	0.14	0.17	0.04	0.20	0.20	0.13	0.20	0.29	0.13	0.00	0.14	0.17
16	0.14	0.12	0.14	0.17	0.07	0.20	0.20	0.13	0.20	0.29	0.13	0.11	0.14	0.17
17	0.14	0.12	0.14	0.17	0.07	0.13	0.20	0.13	0.20	0.29	0.13	0.11	0.14	0.17
18	0.14	0.12	0.14	0.17	0.07	0.13	0.20	0.13	0.20	0.29	0.13	0.11	0.14	0.17
19	0.14	0.12	0.14	0.17	0.07	0.20	0.20	0.13	0.20	0.29	0.13	0.00	0.14	0.17
20	0.14	0.12	0.14	0.17	0.07	0.20	0.20	0.13	0.20	0.29	0.13	0.11	0.14	0.20
21	0.14	0.12	0.14	0.17	0.07	0.20	0.20	0.13	0.20	0.29	0.13	0.11	0.14	0.17
22	0.14	0.13	0.14	0.17	0.07	0.20	0.20	0.13	0.20	0.29	0.13	0.11	0.14	0.17
23	0.14	0.13	0.14	0.17	0.07	0.20	0.20	0.13	0.20	0.29	0.13	0.11	0.14	0.17
24	0.14	0.12	0.14	0.17	0.07	0.20	0.20	0.13	0.20	0.29	0.13	0.11	0.14	0.17
25	0.14	0.13	0.14	0.17	0.07	0.27	0.20	0.13	0.20	0.29	0.13	0.11	0.14	0.17
26	0.14	0.13	0.14	0.17	0.07	0.27	0.20	0.13	0.20	0.29	0.13	0.11	0.14	0.20
27	0.14	0.12	0.14	0.17	0.07	0.20	0.20	0.13	0.20	0.29	0.13	0.11	0.14	0.17
28	0.14	0.13	0.14	0.17	0.04	0.20	0.20	0.13	0.20	0.29	0.13	0.11	0.14	0.17

29	0.14	0.12	0.14	0.17	0.07	0.20	0.20	0.13	0.20	0.29	0.13	0.11	0.14	0.17
30	0.14	0.12	0.14	0.17	0.04	0.20	0.20	0.13	0.20	0.29	0.13	0.11	0.14	0.17
31	0.14	0.12	0.14	0.17	0.04	0.20	0.20	0.13	0.20	0.29	0.13	0.11	0.14	0.17
32	0.14	0.12	0.14	0.17	0.07	0.20	0.20	0.13	0.20	0.29	0.13	0.11	0.14	0.17
33	0.14	0.12	0.14	0.17	0.04	0.20	0.20	0.13	0.20	0.29	0.13	0.11	0.14	0.17
34	0.14	0.12	0.14	0.17	0.04	0.20	0.20	0.13	0.20	0.29	0.13	0.11	0.14	0.17
35	0.14	0.12	0.14	0.17	0.04	0.20	0.20	0.13	0.20	0.29	0.13	0.11	0.14	0.17
36	0.14	0.12	0.14	0.17	0.07	0.20	0.20	0.13	0.20	0.29	0.13	0.11	0.14	0.20
37	0.14	0.12	0.14	0.17	0.07	0.20	0.20	0.13	0.20	0.29	0.13	0.11	0.14	0.17
38	0.14	0.12	0.14	0.17	0.07	0.20	0.20	0.13	0.20	0.29	0.13	0.11	0.14	0.17
39	0.14	0.12	0.14	0.17	0.07	0.20	0.20	0.13	0.20	0.29	0.13	0.11	0.14	0.17
40	0.14	0.12	0.14	0.17	0.07	0.20	0.20	0.13	0.20	0.29	0.13	0.00	0.14	0.17
41	0.14	0.12	0.14	0.17	0.07	0.20	0.20	0.13	0.20	0.29	0.13	0.11	0.14	0.17

PART 3: ECONOMICS AND POLITICS

THE EUROZONE CRISIS AND THE "ARGENTINEAN" SOLUTION: FUZZY SIMILARITY AND DEFAULT RISK

JORGE PAZZI[†]

Departamento de Economía, Universidad Nacional del Sur, 12 de Octubre y San Juan Bahía Blanca, Buenos Aires 8000, Argentina

FERNANDO TOHMÉ

IIESS UNS-CONICET, 12 de Octubre y San Juan Bahía Blanca, Buenos Aires 8000, Argentina

We present a comparison between the situation of the most troubled countries in the Eurozone and 2001 Argentina, evaluated in terms of a fuzzy similarity relation. This allows us to assess the possibility that the former economies will end up following the path of Argentina.

1. Introduction

The events that followed the 2008 financial crisis have shown that countries believed to be shielded against financial turmoil were much frailer than thought. In the last year numerous voices raised the analogy between the situation in the most challenged countries of the Eurozone and Argentina in 2001. As it is well known, the convertibility of the Argentinean peso allowed the banks to carry dollar-nominated accounts, making their balance sheets susceptible to financial fragility at rapid exchange rate changes. While the latter were forbidden by law, the current account deficits and the increasing difficulties to pay back external obligations ended up forcing a default of the debt and a sharp and disordered devaluation of the currency, which at the beginning seemed a source of endless mishaps but ended up (together with a rapid improvement of the international prices of Argentinean exports) creating the conditions for a fast rebound of the Argentinean economy.

It is no wonder than a chorus of experts in various fields has started to recommend Greece (and eventually other EU members) to follow the Argentinean path. These arguments, based on rough analogies, deserve a deeper

[†] Work partially supported by grant PGI 24/Z22 of the Universidad Nacional del Sur.

analysis, part of which we intend to carry out in this paper. While the purely macroeconomic scenario has been analyzed once and again in the macroeconomic literature (as well as by pundits and politicians), we focus here on an implicit counterfactual exercise. To wit: are really the troubled euro-economies and 2001 Argentina so similar? And, if so, to what extent should be expect them to default on their debt and abandon the euro, as seen in the perspective of the 2001 devaluation of the peso? The answers to these questions require the formulation of an appropriate notion of *similarity* among economies and the exploration of means to infer future events out from analogies.

The approach to be followed in this paper consists in applying Zadeh's (1971) notion of fuzzy similarity to the comparison of the economic status of different nations. We will see that 2001 Argentina and currently troubled Eurozone countries belong to a common (fuzzy) equivalence class. From this we will draw the degree of possibility to be assigned to a devaluation and change of currency in the light of the events in Argentina a decade ago.

The plan of the paper is as follows. In section 2 we will provide a conventional account of the current economic situation in some European countries and 2001 Argentina. In section 3 we will discuss the epistemological justification for counterfactual analyses and the conditions under which they can be run. In section 4 we introduce a version of fuzzy similarity and its application to the evaluation of future consequences in similar situations. In section 5 we apply it to the comparison of the aforementioned economies and draw conclusions for the Eurozone. Finally, section 6 concludes.

2. "Crisatvia" and Argentina

The pervasiveness of systemic risk and fragility in some Eurozone economies forces a comparison with the crises in emergent countries at the end of the 1990s and particularly with the end of the convertibility regime in Argentina. In order to present a streamlined argument, assume that we take a generic European country currently in dire straits. To avoid entering into national specifics let us talk of a generic country named *Crisatvia*. To make the comparison with Argentina more focused, we will concentrate on the role and perspectives of the banking sector and the public debt.

In 2001, Argentina's banking sector was heavily "dollarized", but its lender of last resort, the nation's central bank, was unable to ensure enough liquidity to face a run. Worse yet, neither the central bank nor the government itself could borrow in international markets to get additional foreign money.

Nowadays the Eurozone banks are entirely "eurized" but unlike the Argentinean case, their potential lender of last resort, the European Central Bank is able to provide unlimited liquidity to back them. Still, it is unclear whether the ECB will always be willing to fulfill this function.

It must be noted that in both cases the debt is nominated in foreign currency. But unlike in Europe, in Argentina as in other emergent markets, it was impossible to borrow in domestic money, generating a mismatch between the nomination of debts and credits taken and lent by the banks, making them financially fragile.*

So, if the ECB does not play the role of lender of last resort, Crisatvia will be left out of the Euro while its debt will remain nominated in foreign money, namely in €. This is very much like Argentina and its US$ nominated debt after the abrupt end of the convertibility of the national currency (AR$) with the American dollar.

In fact, many analogies can be established between 2001 Argentina and Crisatvia, summarized in the following items (Frenkel, 2010):

Argentina in 2001

The financial sector exhibited these characteristics:

- Need of external financing: the country ran a deficit in the Current Account and had to make large capital payments.
- Unfeasibility of adjusting the balance of payments: the economy was in recession and austerity measures were taken, but still foreign borrowing was the main source of resources.
- Sustainability in time: since the amount of the debt depended on the interest rate determined by an increasing risk Premium, it kept growing in time.

The consequence of this was:

- Default: foreign lenders stopped providing loans, which on top of an acute recession induced a lack of liquidity in US$. In December 2001 this situation forced a default on the national debt.
- Devaluation: the value of national assets fell, due to the depletion of the reserves, forcing a fall of the exchange rate.

---

* This is known in the literature as the *original sin* (see Eichengreen and Hausmann, 2005 and the references therein).

Crisatvia 2012

The financial sector exhibited these characteristics:

- Need of external financing: the country runs a fiscal deficit and has to make large interest and capital payments.
- Unfeasibility of deeper fiscal adjustments: the political situation restricts severely the possibility of further cuts in fiscal expenditures.
- Sustainability in time: it may not obtain the euros needed to reach a recovery phase.

The risks the country may incur:

- Default: for the lack of enough euros.
- Loss of the Euro as national currency: to facilitate a devaluation of the currency.

In both cases the assessment of the sustainability of the national debt requires conjecturing the reaction of the entire market (very much like Keynes' Beauty Contest) leading to multiple equilibria, with either low or high risk premiums. Therefore, the country may default on its debt as a result of a self-fulfilling prophecy: if most of the lenders think that a default will ensue, the risk premium will be high, making the debt unsustainable and leading to a default on the debt (Pazzi and Tohmé, 2005).

As discussed above, the danger of default can be averted if the country has a **lender of last resort**. Argentina lacked one (able to provide all the US$ needed), while for Crisatvia the European Central bank could act as such.[†] But this depends on many factors, some of them of political nature, but if the ECB leaves Crisatvia on its own, it will increase the risk for other Eurozone countries as well. If the ECB abandons Crisatvia, the country might be forced to default and return to its former currency, devaluated with respect to euro, but keeping its defaulted debt nominated in the European money. If, instead, the ECB acts in behalf of the country, the default might be averted. But in this case the Crisatvian economy will be in recession, albeit honoring its debt without increasing it, a politically challenging scenario.

In either case, to make a claim about the future perspectives of the Crisatvian economy involves a counterfactual claim. We would like to make this claim using empirical information (instead of theoretical). But this means to look

[†] Even if the statutes of the ECB do not allow acting as such, it could change them to facilitate the provision of liquidity in case of need.

at "similar" cases. This is where the comparison with Argentina becomes relevant.

3. Counterfactual reasoning

The methodology of analysis to be pursued here follows the prescription given by Helmer and Rescher (1959) in their analysis of the epistemology of inexact sciences, in particular, in the discussion on the nature of the so-called "historical laws". Their point of view is that research in history can be deemed as scientific only if it intends to determine the validity of claims about historical events. These claims must be propositions concerning the actions of one or more human groups subject to certain constraints. If the claims are shown to be true, they can be seen as representing historical laws.

Nevertheless, the scope of the term "law" must somehow be restricted in order to keep it different from the meaning in physical sciences. The "confirmation" of claims is clearly less applicable than in those sciences, and the presence of counterexamples does not always imply the non-validity of historical claims. In consequence, Helmer and Rescher redefine the class of propositions that can be candidates to represent historical laws. Firstly, they have to be *vague* enough to not be falsified trivially by counterexamples. Secondly, they have to be *legaliform*, that is, they must be able to be used as explanations (and therefore not be mere descriptions of facts) and must have counterfactual power. They must, therefore, be able to explain events to which they do not make direct reference, that is, they should have the following form:

If system S reaches value s, event x* will happen*

To confirm a statement of this form the counterfactual method is required. That is, to check its validity in a context "close" to the real one, in which s^* is accompanied by x^*. The degree of arbitrariness – reflected in the notion of "closeness" used above– is higher than in more exact disciplines, requiring *expertise* to fix the degree of precision required in establishing the validity of a statement. The statement is true if, in the possible case that is closer to the true one, the validity of the antecedent goes together with the validity of the consequent.

This notion is due to Robert Stalnaker (1968) and David Lewis (1973). It is completed with a notion of *closeness* among cases. It is quite difficult to say that "everything is identically true". In practice, the method consists of finding a context that minimizes the differences with the one under analysis.

4. Fuzzy similarity

To assess the prospects of the Crisatvian economy, making a counterfactual claim on the possibility of defaulting on its debt and dropping the euro as national currency, we need a "close" case. Our candidate is, of course, Argentina 2001. But to ground this claim we need to formalize the notion of closeness to be used. Since it involves the qualitative idea of *similarity*, we appeal to its formalization due to Zadeh (1971).

Let us consider a class of elements $\boldsymbol{S}$ understood as "situations". Similarity of situations can be understood in terms of a binary relation $\Phi \subseteq \boldsymbol{S} \times \boldsymbol{S}$. But since this is a crisp set, in which membership is either true or false, making it too precise for our needs, we will appeal to fuzzy similarity, in which membership is up to a degree.

We consider the fuzzy similarity in $\boldsymbol{S} \times \boldsymbol{S}$ to be given by the following membership function:

$$\mu_\Phi: \boldsymbol{S} \times \boldsymbol{S} \rightarrow [0,1]$$

To be a similarity relation, μ_Φ has to fulfill the following properties (Dubois and Prade, 1980):

- ***Reflexivity***: for every $s \in \boldsymbol{S}$, $\mu_\Phi(s,s) = 1$.
- ***Symmetry***: for every pair of elements $s,t \in \boldsymbol{S}$, $\mu_\Phi(s,t) = \mu_\Phi(t,s)$.
- ***Max-min Transitivity***: for every triple $s,t,u \in \boldsymbol{S}$, $\mu_\Phi(s,u) \geq \mathrm{Min}(\mu_\Phi(s,t), \mu_\Phi(t,u))$, where $\mathrm{Min}(A,B)$ is A if $B \geq A$, and B otherwise.

Of interest for our purposes is the class of corresponding α-cuts of μ_Φ. It is a trivial consequence of the properties of a fuzzy similarity relation that:

- μ_Φ is a similarity if and only if $\mu_\Phi^\alpha = \{(s,t): \mu_\Phi(s,t) \geq \alpha\}$ is an equivalence relation in $\boldsymbol{S}$ for every $\alpha \in (0, 1]$.

Two situations s and t will be deemed *equivalent* if and only if $\mu_\Phi(s,t) = 1$. Or equivalently, if $(s,t) \in \mu_\Phi^1$.

A relevant question is how to derive $\mu_\Phi(s,t)$ from the individual assessments of s and t. Our proposal consists in considering a finite family of criteria $\mathbf{C} = \{c_1, \ldots c_n\}$, in which each criterion c_i is such that $c_i: \boldsymbol{S} \rightarrow [0,1]$, i.e. it is a fuzzy membership function indicating the degree in which a situation satisfies the criterion. Then, according to the i-th criterion, the similarity between two situations s and t is given by $\mu_i(s,t) = \mathrm{Min}(c_i(s), c_i(t))$, i.e. the degree of similarity between s and t should be as strong as the lowest degree in which the criterion is satisfied.

In turn, the similarity between two situations s and t, evaluated according the whole family of criteria **C** cannot exceed the lowest degree of similarity according to the criteria. That is:[‡]

$$\mu\Phi(s,t) = \text{Min}\ (\mu 1(s,t),\ldots, \mu n(s,t)) \qquad (1)$$

Consider now a class of consequences that may ensue in situations of $\boldsymbol{S}$, denoted $\boldsymbol{K}$. The degree in which a situation $s \in \boldsymbol{S}$ may yield a consequence $k \in \boldsymbol{K}$ will be captured by a fuzzy membership function ρ: $\boldsymbol{S} \times \boldsymbol{K} \rightarrow [0,1]$.

The goal of our counterfactual assessment is to use the following conditional statement, for any pair of situations s and t, and a consequence k (where $\wedge$ is a logical "and" while   is a logical implication):

$$\text{Similar(s,t)} \wedge \text{Consequence(s,k)} \quad \text{Consequence(t,k)} \qquad (2)$$

In our counterfactual exercise we assume that s had already consequence k, while t has yet to yield a consequence. So the degree of verisimilitude of the claim that t will have consequence k can be represented by $\rho(t,k)$, while $\rho(s,k)=1$ since we know that s had k as a consequence. We have then:

Proposition 1: $\rho(t,k) \geq \mu_\Phi(s,t)$.

Proof: *Trivial. In an implication the consequent has at least the degree of validity of the antecedent, so* $\rho(t,k) \geq Min(\mu_\Phi(s,t), \rho(s,k))$. *But since* $\rho(s,k)=1$, $Min(\mu_\Phi(s,t), \rho(s,k)) = \mu_\Phi(s,t)$.

On the other hand, if we fix a degree in which we believe (2), say $\beta<1$, we have:

Proposition 2: $\rho(t,k) = \mu_\Phi(s,t)$ *if* $\mu_\Phi(s,t) \geq \beta$ *and* $\beta > \rho(t,k) \geq \mu_\Phi(s,t)$, *otherwise.*

Proof: *this follows from Proposition 1 and the characterization of modus ponens in Dubois and Prade (1980, pp. 167).*

5. Figures/Illustrations

To apply the results of the previous section we have to construct the similarity relation. As an intermediate step we will consider some intermediate (between *false* and *true*) *linguistic variables* (Haack, 1978; Hajek, 1998): *low* (l), *medium-low* (m-l), *medium* (m), *medium-high* (m-h) and *high* (h) indicating the degree to which the situation fulfills the criteria. Then, we will consider a degree in which Crisatvia 2012 and Argentina 2001 satisfy the following criteria:

[‡] Notice that other ways of characterizing $\mu_\Phi(s,t)$can be defined. For instance by using weights on the criteria, lending more importance to the degree in which the more relevant criteria are satisfied.

Highly Indebted, *Unable to Make Large Adjustments*, *Un-sustainability of the Debt* and *Has no Lender of Last Resort*.

The following table summarizes our assessment:

Table 1. Similarity criteria.

	Argentina	Crisatvia
Highly Indebted	h	h
Unable to Make Large Adjustments	h	h
Un-sustainability of the Debt	h	m-h
Has no Lender of Last Resort	h	m

If we translate the linguistic variables into numerical values, say low (0.1), medium-low (0.3), medium (0.5), medium-high (0.7) and high (0.9), we can obtain, using (∗):

$$\mu_\Phi(\text{Argentina,Crisatvia}) = \text{Min}(0.9, 0.9, 0.7, 0.5) = 0.5$$

On the other hand, we have that while ρ(Argentina, Default) = 1 (corresponding to the linguistic variable *true*), the value of ρ(Crisatvia, Default) can be determined according to Proposition 2, once a level of belief in the validity of (∗∗) is established a priori. For the sake of the argument assume that $\beta = 0.7$ (indicating a medium-high belief). Then, we would have:

$$\rho(\text{Crisatvia, Default}) \in [0.5, 0.7)$$

This result is obtained when we lend a medium-high degree to the belief in the claim that if two countries are similar, if one experienced a consequence the other will experience it too. This, added to a medium degree in the belief in the similarity of Argentina and Crisatvia, leads to a constrained degree of belief (between medium and medium-high) in the possibility of a default in Crisatvia.

6. Conclusions

In summary, we obtained two interesting qualitative assessments. The first one is that far from being similar, currently troubled Eurozone countries have only a half-way resemblance with Argentina in 2001. The main reason is that while the latter lacked a lender of last resort, the European Central Bank (plus other relevant international organizations) could still act as such for the Eurozone countries.

This fact has in turn another consequence: it reduces the degree in which a default can be expected in the Eurozone. The coverage provided by the lender of last resort makes a default less than certain.[§]

In summary, this exercise indicates that the perspectives in the Eurozone are less bleak than they were ten years ago in Argentina. Nevertheless, we have to caution that the exercise makes too many simplifying assumptions, not going deep into very relevant details, which we plan to explore as further work.

Acknowledgments

We thank Dr. Marcelo Auday for interesting discussions and CONICET for additional financial support for this research (PIP 2009-2011).

References

1. Eichengreen, B. and Hausmann, R. (2005). *Other people's money: debt denomination and financial instability in emerging market economies.* Chicago, Chicago University Press
2. Dubois, D. and Prade, H.(1980). *Fuzzy sets and systems.* New York, Academic Press.
3. Frenkel, R. (2010). "El riesgo país en la zona del euro y en las economías de mercado emergentes". Available at http://www.itf.org.ar/lectura_detalle.asp?id=53
4. Haack, S. (1978). *Philosophy of logics.* Cambridge (UK), Cambridge University Press.
5. Hájek, P. (1998). *Metamathematics of fuzzy logic.* Amsterdam, Kluwer.
6. Helmer, O. and Rescher, N. (1959). "On the epistemology of the inexact sciences". *Management Science*, Vol. 6, No. 1, p. 25-52.
7. Lewis, D. (1973). *Counterfactuals.* Oxford, Blackwell.
8. Pazzi, J.and Tohmé, F. (2005). "A fuzzy characterization of uncertainty in financial crises". *Fuzzy Economic Review*, Vol. X, No. 2, p. 61-70.
9. Stalnaker, R. (1968). "A theory of conditionals", in: Rescher, N. (ed.). *Studies in logical theory*, p. 98-112. Oxford, Blackwell.
10. Zadeh, L. (1971). "Similarity relations and fuzzy orderings". *Information Sciences*, Vol. 3, No. 2, p. 177-200.
11. Zadeh, L. (1975). "Fuzzy logic and approximate reasoning". *Synthese*, Vol. 30, No. 3-4, p. 407-428.

[§] In March of 2012 a heavy restructuring of the Greek debt was carried out, which some pundits called a "default". In fact, it was a voluntary debt swap

A DISCRETE PARTICLE SWARM OPTIMIZATION ALGORITHM FOR DESIGNING ELECTORAL ZONES

ERIC A. RINCÓN-GARCÍA

Systems Departament, Autonomous Metropolitan Univesity-Azcapotzalco, Av. San Pablo 180, Col. Reynosa Tamauluipas, México D.F. 02200

MIGUEL A. GUTIÉRREZ-ANDRADE

Deparment of Electrical Engineering, Autonomous Metropolitan Univesit-Iztapalapa, Av. San Rafael Atlixco 186, Col. Vicentina, Del. Iztapalapa, D.F., 09340, México

SERGIO G. DE-LOS-COBOS-SILVA

Deparment of Electrical Engineering, Autonomous Metropolitan Univesit-Iztapalapa, Av. San Rafael Atlixco 186, Col. Vicentina, Del. Iztapalapa, D.F., 09340, México

PEDRO LARA-VELÁZQUEZ

Systems Departament, Autonomous Metropolitan Univesity-Azcapotzalco, Av. San Pablo 180, Col. Reynosa Tamauluipas, D.F., 02200, México

ROMAN A. MORA-GUTIÉRREZ

Systems Engineering Department, National Autonomous University of Mexico, Av. Universidad 3000, C.U., D.F., 04510, México

ANTONIN S. PONSICH

Systems Departament, Autonomous Metropolitan Univesity-Azcapotzalco, Av. San Pablo 180, Col. Reynosa Tamauluipas, D.F., 02200, México

Redistricting is the redrawing of the boundaries of legislative districts for electoral purposes in such a way that the federal and state requirements, such as contiguity, population equality and compactness, are fulfilled. The resulting optimization problem involves the former requirement as a hard constraint while the latter two are considered as conflicting objectives. In this paper, the performances of two classical algorithms, simulated annealing (SA) and a discrete particle swarm optimization (DPSO), are compared for the solution of a practical real example in Mexico. Numerical experiments highlighted that the DPSO algorithm outperforms SA, providing a better set of efficient solutions and, thus, leading to higher quality zones.

1. Introduction

The zone design problem arises from the need of aggregating small geographical units (GU's) into regions, in such a way that one or several objectives are optimized and some constraints are satisfied. The GU's can be cities, postal code regions, blocks or geographic areas, specially designed for the studied problem. The constraints can include, for example, the construction of connected zones, with the same amount of population, clients, mass media, public services, etc. The zone design is applied in diverse problems like school districting [4], police district [3], service and maintenance zones [13] and land use [12].

The design of electoral districts is a commonly tackled case among zone design problems, due to its influence in the results of electoral processes and to its computational complexity, which has been shown to be NP-Hard [1, 5]. In this framework, the GU's are grouped into a predetermined number of zones or districts, and democracy must be guaranteed through the implementation of restrictions that are imposed by law [6]. There are actually different principles to control the construction of electoral districts, which guarantee fair and competitive elections. In particular, some generally proposed criteria are population equality, to ensure the "one man one vote" principle; compactness, to avoid any unfair manipulation of the border or shape of electoral zones for political purposes, and contiguity, to prevent the design of fragmented districts. These restrictions are regarded as essential in any democratic electoral process.

This study particularly focuses on the design of electoral zones in Mexico. For the electoral process in 2006 the Federal Electoral Institute of Mexico (IFE) used a Simulated Annealing (SA) based technique to solve this highly combinatorial problem. However, we consider that it is possible to improve the solutions obtained with this heuristic, especially considering the current availability of advanced, diversified optimization heuristic methods.

In order to improve state-of-the-art solutions, we introduce in this work a discrete particle swarm optimization (DPSO) algorithm to solve the problem of electoral district design with multiple objectives. Although this stochastic optimization technique has proved to achieve good performance for a variety of problems see [2] and [9], it was initially designed for the continuous optimization framework. Thus, an adaptation of the initial algorithm, inspired by path relinking techniques, is proposed here for handling the discrete variables involved in the redistricting problem. Note that the multi-objective feature of the problem is addressed through the strategy based on a weighted linear aggregation function, similar to that adopted by IFE. The resulting algorithm is then tested on the Mexican states of Chiapas and Mexico and its performance levels are then compared with those of a classical Simulated Annealing (SA) algorithm, working with the same weighted function aggregating the tackled objectives. The obtained results show that the DPSO algorithm produces better zoning plans, achieving better quality and diversification of the Pareto front than SA does. The remainder of this paper is organized as follows. In section 2, the objective functions of the redistricting problem model are cast in mathematical terms. Then, a brief overview of the inner working mode of SA is provided in section 3. The classical PSO algorithm is presented in section 4 while its discrete version (DPSO) is described in section 5. The above mentioned real world problem and computational results are detailed in section 6. Section 7 concludes the paper and discusses some future work.

2. Objective Function

As mentioned previously, population equality and compactness are important principles that should be promoted in the design of electoral districts. For this reason, the objective functions should guide the search towards regular shaped districts with approximately the same amount of population. To measure population equality, we apply the definition of the Federal Electoral Institute of Mexico used in Mexico's redistricting process in 2006:

$$C_1(P) = \sum_{s \in S} \left(\frac{100 P_E}{d(P_N/300)} \right)^2 \left(\frac{P_S}{P_E} - \frac{1}{n} \right)^2 \tag{1}$$

Where $P = \{Z_1, Z_2, \ldots, Z_n\}$ is a districting plan. Each district Z_s is defined through a set of binary variables x_{is} such that $x_{is} = 1$ if the GU i belongs to district s and $x_{is} = 0$ otherwise, for all $s \in S$. P_N is the population of Mexico, P_E is the population of the considered state, P_s is the electoral population of the district, d is the maximum percentage of deviation allowed for the entity, n is the number of electoral districts that must be generated in the entity and $S = \{1, 2, 3, \ldots, n\}$ is the set of electoral districts that must be generated in the entity. The number of electoral districts that must be generated in Mexico is 300.

Thus, the lower the cost C_1, the better the population equality of a solution. Indeed, the perfect population equality is achieved when all districts have the same number of inhabitants, and in this case the measure assigns a value of zero to C_1. Regarding the assessment of district compactness, several measures have been proposed but none is able to achieve a perfect representation of this concept, as observed by Young [14]. Thus, we decided to use a metric that can be easily computed. After some experimentation, we opted for a compactness measure that compares the perimeter of each district with that of a square having the same area.

$$C_2(P) = \sum_{s \in S} \left(\frac{PC_s}{4(AC_s)^{1/2}} - 1 \right) \quad (2)$$

Where PC_s and AC_s are the perimeter and the area of the considered district s, respectively. Thus, districts with a good compactness will have a C_2 value close to 0. To handle the multi-objective nature of the problem, a weight aggregation function strategy was adopted here. Finally the objective function is:

$$\text{Minimize } f(P) = \alpha_1 C_1(P) + \alpha_2 C_2(P) \quad (3)$$

Where $P = \{Z_1, Z_2, \ldots, Z_n\}$, is a districting plan, Z_s is the set of GU's in district $s \in S$, $C_1(P)$ is the equality population cost for plan P, $C_2(P)$ is the compactness cost for plan P, α_1, α_2 are weighting factors that measure the relative importance of equality population and compactness in a districting plan.

Thus, the objective function seeks for a districting plan that has the best balance between population equality and compactness, a balance obviously biased by the weighting factors. In addition, the minimization is subjected to constraints that guarantee that:

R1. Each district is fully connected.

R2. The number of districts is equal to n.

R3. Each GU is assigned to exactly one district.

3. Simulated Annealing

Simulated annealing is a metaheuristic, which has become a popular tool because of its simplicity and good results in different problems and areas of optimization. SA was introduced by Kirkpatrick [8]. The name and inspiration come from the physical process of cooling molten materials down to the solid state. To end up with the best final product, the steel must be cooled slowly to a low energy, optimal state.

By analogy with this process, the SA algorithm starts with an initial solution and generates, in each iteration, a random neighbor solution. If this neighbor improves the current value of the objective function, i.e., reaches a lower energy state, it is accepted as the current solution. If the neighbor solution does not improve the objective's value, then it is accepted as the current solution according to a probability ρ based on the Metropolis criterion:

$$\rho = \exp\left(\frac{f(P_X) - f(P_Y)}{T}\right) \tag{4}$$

Where, $f(P_X)$ and $f(P_Y)$ represent the objective value of the current and neighbor solutions, respectively. T is a parameter called temperature, which is controlled through a cooling schedule that defines the temperature decrement and the (finite) number of iterations for each temperature value.

At large values of the temperature, virtually all proposed solutions are accepted and the algorithm can explore the search space, in order to avoid premature convergence. However, during the execution, the temperature and, as a consequence, the probability of deterioration of the objective function, gradually decrease. The algorithm then reduces to a classical local search process.

The main steps of the SA algorithm are given in Table 1.

Table 1. Algorithm for SA.

```
Begin
Generate an initial solution P_X.
Set initial temperature T_i.
Set final temperature T_f.
Set number of iterations Num
Set decreasing temperature rate as α ∈ (0,1).
Set T = T_i
while T > T_f do
   for i = 0 to Num
      Generate a neighbor solution P_Y
      if f(P_Y) < f(P_X).
         P_X ← P_Y
      else If random(0,1) < ρ
         P_X ← P_Y
   end for
   T=T*α
end while
```

4. Particle Swarm Optimization

Particle swarm optimization (PSO) is a population based metaheuristic, inspired by the social behavior of animals such as a flock of birds looking for a food source or a school of fish protecting themselves from a predator [7]. The PSO algorithm first randomly initializes a swarm of K particles, where each particle, $P_k = (x_{k1}, x_{k2}, \ldots, x_{kD})$, represents a candidate solution in a D-dimensional space. The movement of each particle is influenced by its own previous best position, *pbest*, and the previous best position reached by any particles of the swarm, *gbest*. Each particle has velocity, which directs the movement of the particle over the solution space. In each generation of the PSO algorithm, the velocity and the position of particles will be updated by the following equations:

$$V_k^{l+1} = wV_k^l + c_1 r_1 \left(pbest_k - P_k^l \right) + c_2 r_2 \left(gbest - P_k^l \right) \quad (5)$$

$$P_k^{l+1} = P_k^l + V_k^{l+1} \quad (6)$$

Where:
V_k^l, V_k^{l+1}, are velocity of particle k at iteration l and $l+1$.
w, is a inertia weight.
c_1, c_2, are acceleration factors.
r_1, r_2, are random numbers between 0 and 1.
$pbest_k$, is the best position of particle k.
$gbest$, is the best position in a population.
P_k^l, P_k^{l+1}, are the position of the particle k at iteration l and $l+1$.
The main steps of the DPSO algorithm are given in Table 2.

Table 2. Algorithm for PSO.

```
Begin
Initialize a population of K particles with random positions and
velocities.
Evaluate each particle according to the objective function, and update
individual a global best positions.
while Requirements are not met do
   For each particle update velocity and position using Eq. (5) and Eq.
   (6).
   Evaluate each particle according to the objective function.
   Update individual a global best positions.
   Memorize the best position found so far.
end while
```

5. Discrete Particle Swarm Optimization

The PSO algorithm was originally designed for continuous optimization problems, and cannot directly be used for discrete cases. However, several proposals for extending the PSO working mode to discrete search spaces exist in the specialized literature [10, 11]. In this work, in order to handle discrete decision variables, we propose some new modifications to the PSO algorithm based on the path relinking strategy. The originality of the resulting technique is that each district is considered as a variable, and not anymore the GU's. In our representation, a particle is defined as a solution $P = \{Z_1, Z_2, \ldots, Z_n\}$, where $Z_s = \{i : x_{is} = 1\}$ is a set of GU's. The initial population of K particles is generated randomly in such a way that each solution satisfies R1-R3.

According to the basic PSO algorithm, each particle adjusts its movement toward two positions, *pbest* and *gbest*, taking in account the velocity in the previous iteration. Inspired by this, we used an approach based on the path relinking technique, which simulates the movement towards *pbest* and *gbest*, to generate new solutions for the particles, and we included a random perturbation to simulate the velocity in the previous iteration. However, while using this strategy the particles reached poor quality solutions, so we decide to include a greedy selection process. In this case, each particle only accepts a new position when the objective function is improved. Thus, the current position is the *pbest* position for all particles, and the movement is towards only one solution, *gbest*.

Suppose that P_1 is the current position of a particle and P_2 is *gbest*. A GU x is randomly selected. Thus, there is a zone Z_i in P_1 and a zone Z_j in P_2 such that $x \in Z_i$ and $x \in Z_j$. We consider the following sets:

$$H_1 = \{x_{hi} : x_{hi} = 0, x_{hj} = 1\}$$
$$H_2 = \{x_{hj} : x_{hj} = 1, x_{hj} = 0\}$$

Then a percentage r of GU's in H_1 are inserted into Z_i. The same percentage of GU's in H_2 are extracted from Z_i, and inserted into any randomly chosen zone contiguous to Z_i. Here, r is a uniformly distributed real random number in the range [0,1]. Finally, a random GU is moved to an adjacent zone to produce a perturbation.

Note that these moves can produce an infeasible solution, so a repair process is applied to ensure that properties R1-R3 are preserved.

Thus, if the current position of an particle is P_k^i, our proposed DPSO algorithm produces a new position P_k^{i+1} through the insertion and extraction of GU's process explained above. If P_k^{i+1} has a better position than or equal to that of P_k^i, then P_k^{i+1} replaces P_k^i and becomes a new solution in the population.

The main steps of the DPSO algorithm are given in Table 3.

6. Computational Experiments

The SA and DPSO algorithms described in the previous sections were tested on the Mexican states of Chiapas and Mexico. Chiapas is a state with 3,920,892 inhabitants and 229 GU's, constructed by IFE (see figure 1) from which 12 districts must be created.

Table 3. Algorithm for dPSO.

```
Begin
Initialize a population of K feasible solutions.
Evaluate each particle according to the objective function, and update
individual a global best positions.
while Requirements are not met do
    For each particle produce a new position using the path relinking
    based approach towards gbest, and a random perturbation.
    Evaluate each particle according to the objective function and apply
    a greedy selection process.
    Update individual a global best positions.
    Memorize the best position found so far.
end while
```

While the state of Mexico has 13,096,686 inhabitants and 836 GU's (see figure 2), from which 40 districts must be created. In agreement with the federal requirements stipulated in Mexico's 2006 elections, a maximum percentage of deviation (in terms of population in each district) $d = 15\%$ was considered while, according to the National Population Census carried out in 2000, the total population in Mexico has 97,483,412 inhabitants.

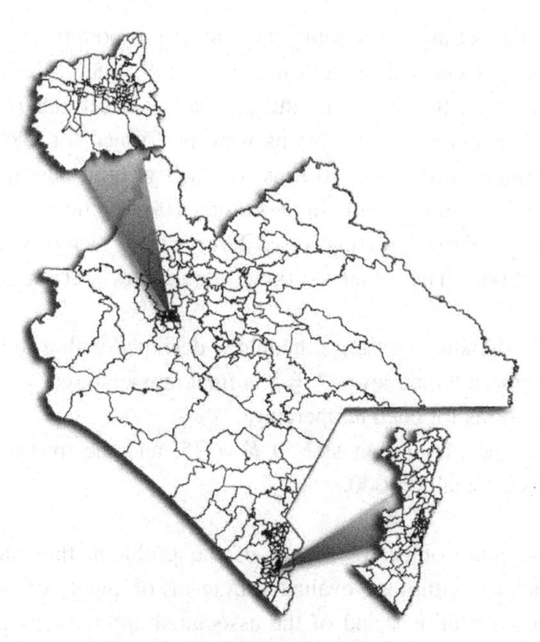

Figure 1. Geographic units of Chiapas.

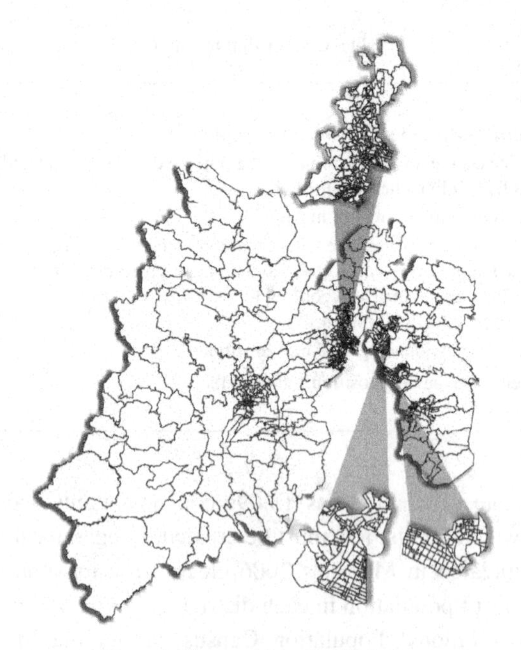

Figure 2. Geographic units of Mexico.

Regarding the settings of parameters common to both techniques, the set of weighting factors is defined as follows: α_1 = {0.9, 0.8, …, 0.1, 0.01}, while $\alpha_2 = 1 - \alpha_1$. In order to deal with the stochastic effect inherent to heuristic techniques, 100 independent executions were performed for each algorithm on the above-mentioned instances (10 runs for each weight pair α_1, α_2). Each run produces a single solution and the resulting 100 solutions are subsequently filtered through a Pareto sorting procedure, which identifies the final non-dominated solutions. The other working parameters were tuned after some experiments:

- For SA: the dynamic cooling schedule is designed with a reduction factor α = 0.99, an initial temperature $T_i = 5$, a final temperature $T_f = 0.001$ and Num = 1500 iterations for each temperature.
- For DPSO: the population size is $K = 75$, and the maximum number of generations is equal to 3000.

Due to the multi-objective nature of the problem, the numerical results obtained by each algorithm are evaluated in terms of quality of the produced set of non-dominated solutions, and of the associated approximation of the Pareto front. This quality of the Pareto front commonly includes the number of non-dominated solutions, but also convergence (the obtained solutions should lie close to the real front) and distribution (the obtained solutions should be evenly distributed over the front width) concepts, for which a variety of metrics were proposed, see for instance [15]. These metrics may be either unary (based on the non-dominated solutions produced by one algorithm) or binary (comparing the solution sets produced by two algorithms). It was demonstrated in [16] that a single metric cannot account for all the desirable features of the obtained Pareto front, so that the comparison of two algorithms should be carried out in terms of several metrics.

Therefore, the following criteria are used in this study to evaluate and compare the Pareto sets obtained by the two tackled methods: the number of non-dominated solutions in the set, the Efficient Set Spacing (ESS) and the set coverage metric. Obviously, the first criterion should be higher as possible, since the aim is to provide the decision-maker with a sufficient number of efficient, non-dominated solutions.

The unary ESS metric measures the dispersion of the solutions over the front width as the variance of distances between adjacent solutions. For a bi-objective problem such as ours, ESS is computed according to the following equation:

$$ESS = \sqrt{\frac{1}{e-1}\sum_{i=1}^{e}\left(\bar{d}-d_i\right)^2} \tag{7}$$

Where:

e, is the number of non-dominated solutions in the approximated front PF obtained by an algorithm A.

$\bar{d}$, is the average of all d_i.

$$d_i = \min_{P_j \in PF \setminus \{P_i\}} \left\{ \sqrt{\left(C_1(P_i)-C_1(P_j)\right)^2 + \left(C_2(P_i)-C_2(P_j)\right)^2} \right\} \text{ for all } 1 \le i \le e.$$

The lower the value of ESS, the better the evaluated approximated front in terms of distribution of the solutions.

Finally, the front coverage $C(A_1,A_2)$ is a binary metric that computes the ratio of efficient solutions produced by one algorithm A_2 dominated by or equal to at least one efficient solution produced by another competing algorithm A_1. Note that, commonly, $C(A_1,A_2) \neq C(A_2,A_1)$, so that both values must be computed. The expression of $C(A_1,A_2)$ is:

$$C(A_1,A_2)=\frac{\left|\{s_2 \in PF_2 : \exists s_1 \in PF_1, s_1 \succ s_2\}\right|}{|PF_2|} \tag{8}$$

Where PF_1 and PF_2 are the approximated Pareto sets obtained by algorithms A_1 and A_2 respectively, and $s_1 \succ s_2$ means that solution s_1 dominates solution s_2. If $C(A_1,A_2)$ is equal to 1, then all the efficient solutions produced by A_2 are dominated by efficient solutions produced by A_1. Note, moreover, that in addition to the above-mentioned metrics, a global approximated Pareto set can be defined as the combination of the Pareto sets provided by all the tested algorithms. The proportion in which each algorithm participates to this global set is also used to assess for the performance of each technique.

7. Results

The approximated Pareto fronts obtained with SA and DPSO for the states of Chiapas and Mexico are illustrated in figure 3 and 4 respectively (the vertical axe is for population deviation while the horizontal one is for compactness). It is clear, from the graphical observation of the Pareto sets, that DPSO provided the best results, in terms of convergence (most of the DPSO solutions are "under" those of the SA algorithm).

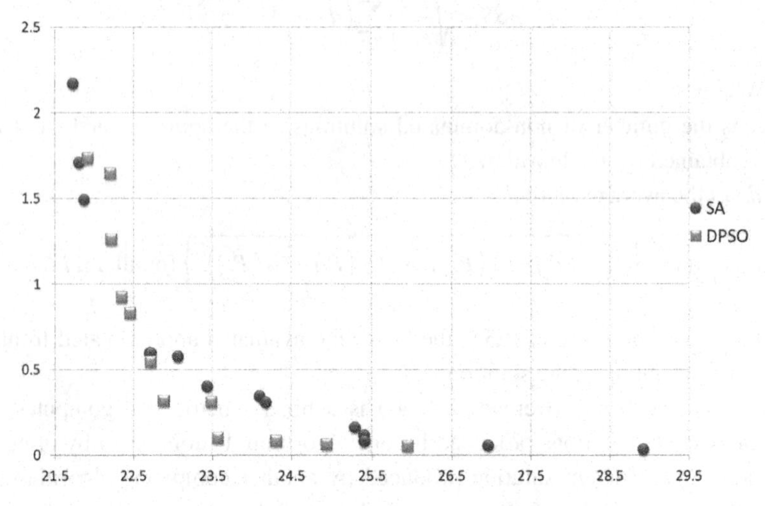

Figure 3. Obtained solutions for Chiapas.

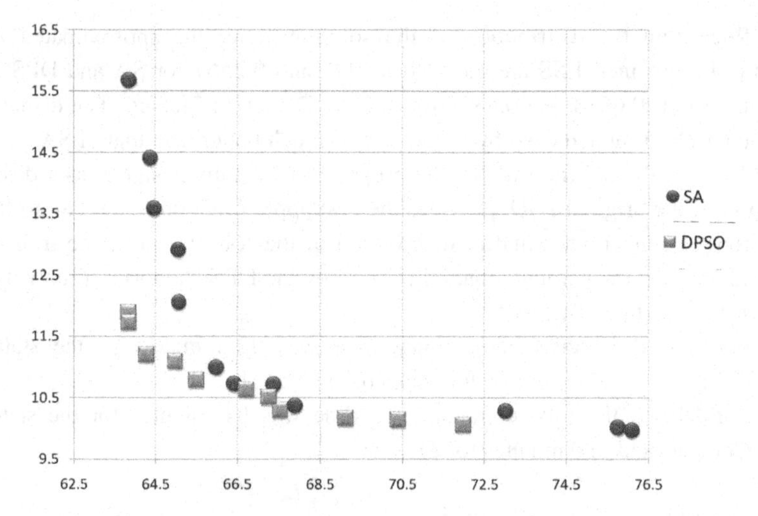

Figure 4. Obtained solutions for the state of Mexico.

This first trend is confirmed when observing the results for the above described performance metrics. Although SA found more non-dominated solutions than DPSO, the proportion in which they participate to the global approximated Pareto front, obtained by combining both techniques' fronts, is clearly in favor of DPSO.

- For Chiapas the global front has 15 non-dominated solutions and is composed of 10 DPSO solutions and 5 SA solutions (representing respectively 66.67% and 33.33% of the global Pareto solutions).
- For Mexico the global front has 14 non-dominated solutions and is composed of 11 DPSO solutions and 3 SA solutions (representing respectively 78.57% and 21.43% of the global Pareto solutions).

The set coverage metric provides a confirmation of these observations.

- For Chiapas, *C(DPSO;SA)* is equal to 0.7143, meaning that 71.43% of the non-dominated solutions produced by SA are dominated by at least one efficient solution obtained with DPSO. On the other hand, *C(SA;DPSO)* = 0.1667.
- For Mexico, *C(DPSO;SA)* is equal to 0.75, while *C(SA;DPSO)* = 0.0. Thus SA's efficient solutions do not dominate a single DPSO's efficient solution.

Thus, in terms of convergence to an ideal front, DPSO proves undoubtedly to obtain better solutions that its counterpart.

Regarding the distribution of the solutions over the approximated front width, the obtained ESS are equal to 0.5992 and 0.2557 for SA and DPSO, in Chiapas, and 0.6518 and 0.4831 for SA and DPSO, in Mexico. The dispersion of the Pareto front achieved by DPSO is thus much better than that of SA.

Thus, our conclusion is that the proposed algorithm, designed as a discrete version of the original PSO, provides the best approximation of the Pareto front, in terms of convergence and of distribution of the solutions over the front. We should add that the computational time used by the DPSO algorithm run is twice lower than the time used by SA:

- For SA, the total computational time was 92 minutes for the state of Chiapas, and 250 minutes for Mexico.
- For DPSO, the total computational time was 84 minutes for the state of Chiapas, and 230 minutes for Mexico.

8. Conclusions

We presented in this paper an original adaptation of the Particle Swarm Optimization algorithm, DPSO, for the solution of a NP-hard combinatorial bi-objective optimization problem: the electoral zone redistricting. This algorithm, as well as a classical Simulated Annealing (SA) procedure, were tested on a typical instance drawn from the Mexican electoral institute database. Their respective performances were evaluated in terms of convergence and dispersion of the resulting approximation of the Pareto front: the computational experiments proved that the proposed DPSO algorithm produces better quality efficient solutions than SA, within lower running times. However, some immediate perspectives for future work might be proposed in two directions. First, these preliminary results should be confirmed through the treatment of several other instances in order to provide more robust conclusions on the performance levels achieved by DPSO. The second path is motivated by the observation that DPSO fails to identify efficient solutions in the extreme, single-objective related, regions. An analysis of the reasons explaining this behavior and consistent improvements of our algorithm should thus be implemented. In addition, a further guideline might be the integration of more advanced techniques for handling the multi-objective nature of the considered problem.

References

1. Altman, M., *Rutgers Computer and Law Technology Journal, Vol. 23.* **Is automation the answer: The computational complexity of automated redistricting**, 81-141 (1997).

2. Boeringer D.W. and Werner D.H., *IEEE Trans. Antennas Propagat., Vol. 52, No. 3.* **Particle swarm optimization versus genetic algorithms for phased array synthesis**, 771-779 (2004).
3. D'Amico S. J., Wang, S. J., Batta, R., and Rump, C. M., *Computers & Operations Research, Vol. 29.* **A simulated annealing approach to police district design**, 667-684 (2002).
4. Ferland, J., *Operations Research, Vol. 38.* **Decision support system for the school districting problem**, 15-21 (1990).
5. Gilbert, K., D.D., H., and Rosenthal R., *Management Science, Vol. 31.* **A multiobjective discrete optimization model for land Allocation**, 1509-1522 (1985).
6. Gutiérrez-Andrade, M. A., and Rincón-García, E. A., *Lecture Notes in Computer Science, Vol. 584.* **Redistricting by square cells**, 669-679 (2009).
7. Kennedy J. and Eberhart R.C., *Proc IEEE Int. Conf. Neural Networks, vol. 4.* **Particle swarm optimization**, 1942-1948 (1995).
8. Kirkpatrick, S., Gellat, C., and Vecchi, M., *Science, Vol 220.***Optimization by simulated annealing**, 671-680 (2012).
9. Lima M. J. Q. and Barán B. C., *Revista Iberoamericana de Inteligencia Artificial, Vol. 10, No. 32.* **Optimización de enjambre de partículas aplicada al problema del cajero viajante bi-objetivo**, 67-76 (2006).
10. Premalatha K. and Natarajan A.M., *International Journal of Recent Trends in Engineering, Vol. 1, No. 1.* **Discrete PSO with GA Operators for Document Clustering**, 20-24 (2009).
11. Shayeghi H., Mahdavi M. and Bagheri A., *Energy Conversion and Management. Vol. 51.* **Discrete PSO algorithm based optimization of transmission lines loading in TNEP problem**, 112-121 (2010).
12. Shirabe, T., *Geographical Analysis, Vol. 37.* **A model of contiguity for spatial unit allocation**, 2-16 (2005).
13. Shortt, N. K., Moore, A., Coombes, M., and Wymer, C., *Social Science & Medicine, Vol. 60.* **Defining regions for locality health care planning: A multidimensional approach**, 2715-2727 (2005).
14. Young, P., *Legislative Studies Quarterly, Vol. 13.* **Measuring the compactness of legislative districts**, 105-115 (1988).
15. Zitzler, E., Deb, K., and Thiele L., *Evolutionary Computation, Vol. 8, No. 2.* **Comparison of multiobjective evolutionary algorithms: Empirical Results**, 173-195 (2000).
16. Zitzler, E., Laumanns, M., Thiele, L., Fonseca, C. M., and Grunert da Fonseca, V. *Proceedings of the Genetic and Evolutionary Computation Conference.* **Why quality assessment of multiobjective optimizers is difficult**, 666-674 (2002).

LOCATING ENTERPRISES USING A FUZZY LOGIC-BASED STRATEGY

GONZÁLEZ SANTOYO FEDERICO
Rincón de Barranquillas 555, Fracc. Arboledas,
C.P. 58000 Morelia, Michoacán, MEXICO

FLORES ROMERO BEATRIZ, FLORES ROMERO JUAN JOSÉ
Rincón de Barranquillas 555, Fracc. Arboledas,
C.P. 58000 Morelia, Michoacán, MEXICO

Abstract

Through the use of uncertainty theory, this paper presents extensions to the Center of Gravity Method and the Transport Method to the efficient determination of an enterprise location. The proposal recommends the exact location of an enterprise that guarantees for it to be more competitive in the global markets, using its location as a management strategy.

Keywords: enterprise, location, Center of Gravity Method, Transport Method.

1. Introduction

The determination of the site where an enterprise must be located is a strategic element for its development. This fact holds for companies that are public or private, that produce consumer goods, intermediate goods, or capital, that offer services, etc.

The location of a company (plant) is represented by the site (geographic location – A_i) where it will perform its production activities, or offer services, as well as its commercial transactions (González S.F. (1985)). The location must guarantee the highest level of financial profitability and a full social acceptance.

This is fundamental, since current organizations face great changes in their environmets. Castro García et al. (2010) indicate that the market is highly competitive, and globalization is a reality. This requires a high level of competence from all companies in the world, given that they are located in a global market. Therefore, it is of fundamental importance to operate the companies based on the existence of a long term Strategic Development Plan. A fundamental factor in the company development is the efficient location of the plant.

González S.F. (2000) considers that fostering the idea of operational planning, conveys the need to consider the current conditions of (A_i; i=1,2,…,n), as well as its environment conditions.

There exist many methods in the theory of enterprise location. In this work we present and apply theoretical extensions to the Center of Gravity Method (CGM) and the Transport Model (TM).

The rest of the paper is organized as follows: Section1 presents an introduction, Section 2 states the problem of Enterprise Location at the macro and micro levels, Section 4 presents the Transport Model, Section 5 presents a case analysis, and Section 6 presents the paper conclusions.

2. Enterprise location

In the problem of optimal location of a company, we seek to maximize the level of financial return. To this end, we use a strategic location for the company, at a given area of interest ($\mathbf{A_i}$). This area can be regarded as a first approximation, either locally, regionally, nationally, or internationally. We refine its location until we arrive to the optimal location.

Enterprise location is performed in a first stage at the macro-location level. This stage requires the definition of an area unit ($\mathbf{A_i}$). We proceed to a second stage to determine the exact place where the new company will be placed.

In this location strategy we need to consider factors such as: a) location of the potential consumers market, and b) location of the sources of raw materials and inputs.

Both factors (a and b) need to be located as close as possible at the macro-location level. These factors are closely related to production costs, which can be optimized so that the acquisition of raw materials, their processing, and transport of the final goods to the consumer markets is as inexpensive as possible.

The *basic costs* are represented by the minimal cost of the inputs and raw materials. That is the cost of the cheapest source at the local environment selected at the macro level to locate the company. The locational costs represent the additional expense due to the distance between the selected location and the cheapest source for raw materials and inputs, plus the transportation and commercialization costs.

Macrolocation. Represents a description of the area selected to locate the company. It is recommended to take into consideration the following factors:

- When there is only one consumer market and only one source of raw material, the problem reduces to deal with two alternatives and select the one with minimum cost that satisfies both factors.

- When the company uses raw materials of different sources and produces different goods, there is a tendency to seek for an intermediate point between these factors to locate the enterprise.

In the analysis at the macro level, it is necessary to take into consideration the following aspects: geographical, socioeconomic, cultural, infrastructure, institutional, and financial, among others.

Once the geographical location has been set as the reference framewors, we proceed to stablish a smaller land extension within the reference framework stablished in the first part of this process. González S. F. et al (2011) establish that descriptions at that stage must include the following elements:

- Territorial limits, boundaries, topography, climate, vegetation, population, services, education, characterization and specialization of labor, transportation and infrastructure, government policies in the area, etc.

Among the most common methods for this stage of analysis exist the techniques of apparent association, and the web method.

Microlocation. Once the location has been established at the macro level, we perform a detailed study of the different alternatives of places with the desired characteristics to place the enterprise. Microlocation defines the exact place where the plant will be located.

The analysis and selection is performed in three stages, where the following factors are considered:

Stage 1. This stage involves the determination of all minimum necessary factors the location land must fulfill. The minimum requirements are:

- Available area – the prospect land must fulfill the current needs and future foreseen expansions.

- Topography – the land must have a uniform topography with a slope no greater than 4%.

- Elevation – the land must be high enough as to prevent possible flooding in the process areas and raw material, inputs, and finished product storage areas.

- Roads – the land must be accessible through important ways.

- Utilities – the land must have continuous sufficient water and electricity supplies.

- Drainage – the land must have the facilities to treat and drain residual waters and wastes.

- Geography – it must be as close as possible to the most important urban centers in the region where the plant is to be located.

- Etc.

Stage 2. In this stage one study has to be performed per location prospect. All aspects in the previous stage must be considered in each study. At this point the following basic elements must be considered:

- Water supply with the required quality and continuous volume.
- Electrical energy supply.
- Ease of access (distance to the most important communication ways).
- Availability of qualified skilled labor.
- Land cost in the region.

Stage 3. The most used criteria in this stage are the following:

- Weigh assignment to each factor – location basic factor $\{FBL_i; i = 1, 2, \ldots, n\}$. A panel of experts is gathered, to assess the different available lands. This panel issues a recommendation about the best land to place the enterprise.
- Evaluation of the investment amount required for each land prospect. The land selection criterion must be oriented towards those of minimum investment that fulfills at a highest level the $\{FBL_i; i = 1, 2, \ldots, n\}$.

To determine the specific land where the enterprise will be located it is necessary the highest level of satisfaction and fulfillment of the set $\{FBL_i; i = 1, 2, \ldots, n\}$. To that end, the following elements are required:

- Raw materials, electrical energy, water, infrastructure, telecommunications, industrial parks, tax incentives, community acceptance studies, ecological and environmental studies, skilled labor, etc.

The size of the set {FBL_i; i = 1, 2, ..., n} depends on the type of enterprise ad the activities it performs. I.e., agricultural, fishing, mining, forestry, etc.

Acording to Weber (1929), the location theory considers the existence of two kinds of industries: those oriented to raw materials, and those oriented to final products. The former focus on concrete points, independently of where the main population centers are, while the latter tend to locate at points of greatest population concentration.

This proposal uses two methods to determine the optimal location of enterprises: the Center of Gravity Method and the Transport Model. Those two methods are presented in the following two sections.

3. Center of gravity method

According to Machuca D. J. (1994), this methos is frequently used to analyze transportation cost as a fundamental location factor. This factor takes into account the sources from where the enterprise receives raw materials. Under these considerations, the problem to solve is to find a central location that minimizes the total transportation cost. This approach assumes transportation costs are proportional to distance and volume or weight of the transported goods to or from the company.

Thus, the total transportation cost is:

$$CTT = \sum_{i=1}^{n} C_i V_i D_i$$

Where:

CTT = total transportation cost,
C_i = unitary transportation cost corresponding to point (i),
V_i = volume or weight of the transported materials from or to (i),
D_i = distance between point (i) and the proposed location.

The determination of the total transportation cost presumes the estimation of the amounts of material to transport to each point in a given period of time.

C_i V_i = weight or importance each point (i) has with respect to the prospect location under consideration.

The authors of this method considered to make an extension so that its applicability results more practical. The extension includes the following stages:

1. Definition of a macro area (A_i) of interest to locate the enterprise. This can be done at the local, regional, state, or country level.

2. Define a reference system (x,y) for 1.

3. Define the set $\{FBL_i; i = 1, 2, \ldots, n\}$.

4. Place 3 in 2.

5. Compute the coordinates of the center of gravity (CG) in 2.

6. Set up a radio of 500 m. around 5 (if the location determined in 5 in not prohibited). This will be the optimal location for the enterprise, otherwise.

7. Perform a physical visit to 6 in the marked radio, and select any available place that fulfills the company's requirements, and is adequate for locating the enterprise.

To compute the center of gravity we use:

$$C_x = \frac{\sum_{i=1}^{n} CF_i x_i}{\sum_{i=1}^{n} CF_i}$$

$$C_y = \frac{\sum_{i=1}^{n} CF_i y_i}{\sum_{i=1}^{n} CF_i}$$

where:
C_x = coordinate (x) of the (C.G),
C_y = coordinate (y) of the (C.G.)
CF_i = importance level (weight) of the FBL_i.
X_i = coordinate (x) of the FBL_i.
Y_i = coordinate (y) of the FBL_i.

An example of the application of the proposed method is shown in Figure 1.

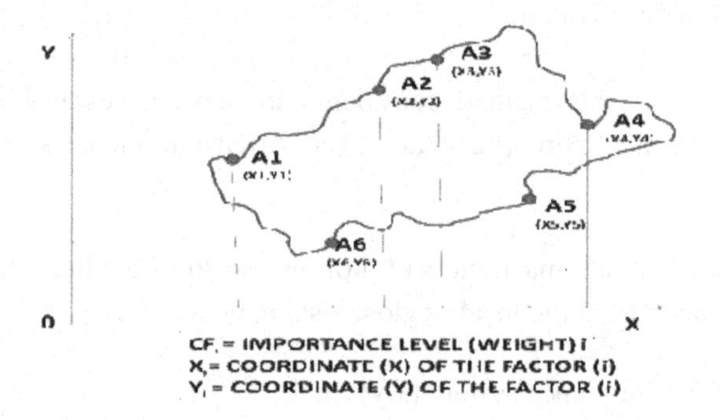

Fig. 1. Location of $\{FBL_i; i = 1, 2, \ldots, n\}$

The importance levels of (FBL_i) are determined using a set of experts. The coefficients depend on the level of importance it has in the production process the company develops. This process is related to the kind of enterprise to locate.

For instance, water is one of the factors with a highest level of importance in an industry producing plywood, since the water saturation of the wood chips makes the machining process easier. The chosen location for this kind of enterprise needs this kind of resource at the required levels for its operation in the planning horizon. Otherwise, its operation would be excessively costly. The same applies to the electrical energy supply.

4. The transport method

This method is based on minimizing costs associated to transportation of final products to different consumption centers, departing from the fact that the locations that provide possibilities for different plants are the best microlocation possibilities. From that set we seek to determine the best option, for the case where only one plant needs to be located.

According to González S. F et al (1985, 2000, 2011), Gil Lafuente J (2001), Gil Aluja J. (1990), Gil Lafuente A.M. (2001, 2004), and Prawda J. (1982), to extend the proposed method to deal with uncertainty, we need to:

1. Express the transport method in terms of costs under uncertainty.
2. Solve 1.
3. Express the solution of 2, able to select the best choice to locate the enterprise.

To solve the transport problem we can use any of the existing methods. The transport problem can be expressed as:

$$Min.\ Z = \sum_{i=1}^{m}\sum_{j=1}^{n} C_{ij}X_{ij}$$

s.t.

$$\sum_{i=1}^{m} X_{ij} = b_j; j = 1,2, \dots, n$$

$$\sum_{j=1}^{n} X_{ij} = a_i\ ; i = 1,2, \dots, m$$

$$\forall X_{ij} \geq o$$

This implies that $\sum_{i=1}^{m} a_i = \sum_{j=1}^{n} b_j$.

where:

C_{ij} = Per unit associated product transport cost from a source (i) to a destination (j).
X_{ij} = amount of product to transport from (i) to (j).
b_j = potential demand at market (j).
a_i = offer level at source (i).

The classical solution to this problem is shown in Figure 2.

Fig. 2. Transport Model

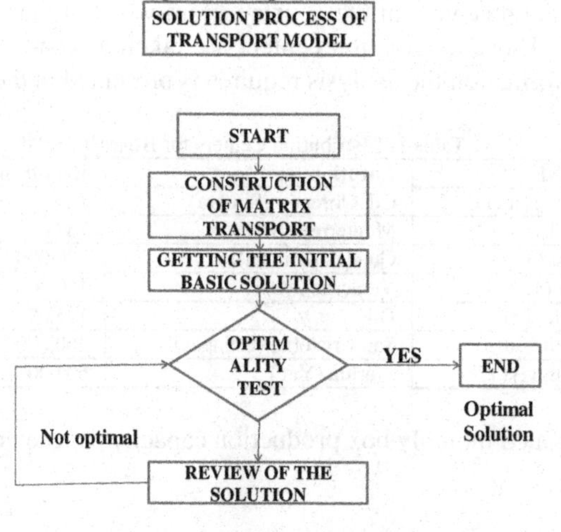

Source: González S.F. et al (2011).

To locate a plant, we use point 3 of the proposed method. Starting from the basic initial solution, optimal with respect to stage 2, depending on the case, the recommended methodology is:

- Determine the unitary cost for each column in all places here there is an assignment for $\mathbf{X}_{ij}$ from the solution of stage 2.

- Take the cost associate to each column where there are assignments in the solution table, according to the following equation:

$$Min\left\{\sum_{j=1}^{n} C_{ji}\ ; i = 1,2,\dots,m\right\}$$

At the cell where the smallest value for the sum of associated cost for the assignments is found, determine what cell contains the minimal cost and relate it to the origin. That point is defined as the best location option for the enterprise.

Verify the solution to satisfy the market to satisfy, as well as its volume. Based on that make a decision to select it or go to the next best choice that satisfies that condition.

5. Case analysis

This case is hypothetical, used to illustrate the applicability of the methods proposed in this paper. Consider Corporation W plans to distribute packing boxes to ship staples in the commercialization program for year 2012. The shipping box factory is intended to be located in Morelia, Michoacán (M), Monterrey, Nuevo León (MO), and Guadalajara, Jalisco (G). Corporation W has 7 distribution centers in the country, from which it plans to distribute along the country. Those distribution centers are taken as centroids of each regional unit. The information the analysis requires is presented in the following Tables.

Table 1. Distribution Centers for Boxes Type "β"

ZONE	Location (storage)	Requirements (MES)
Northeast (1)	Cd. Obregón (Sonora)	100,000
Northwest (2)	Monterrey (NL)	75,000
West (3)	Guadalajara (Jal)	200,000
East (4)	Veracruz (Ver)	100,000
Center (5)	D.F.	125,000
Southeast (6)	San Cristóbal (Chiapas)	200,000
Southwest (7)	Mérida (Yuc)	50,000

The estimated monthly box production capacity for each company is:

Table 2. Production Capacity for Boxes Type "β"

Company	Production Capacity (boxes)
Morelia (MO)	150,000
Guadalajara (G)	300,000
Monterrey (MO)	400,000

The railroad transportation cost in Mexican Pesos per box type "β", for each factory to the different distribution centers is expressed as triangular fuzzy numbers TFN as:

Table 3. Transportation Costs using TFN (p.u.)

Factory/ Zone	1	2	3	4	5	6	7
M	(5,8,10)	(5,6,7)	(3,4,5)	(2,3,4)	(1,2,3)	(2,4,5)	(3,5,6)
G	(3,6,7)	(3,5,8)	(4,7,8)	(3,4,5)	(2,3,4)	(2,5,7)	(4,6,7)
MO	1,3,5)	(1,2,3)	(3,4,6)	(5,7,9)	(3,4,6)	(4,6,7)	(5,7,9)

To illustrate the process, we will use a basic initial solution, obtained using he Minimum Cost Method. This solution is efficient and effective with respect to cost and the distribution system for the product provided for Corporation "W".

The representation of cost is computed using the mean value for each case. Table 4 shows the results for each case.

Table 4. Mean Transportation Cost (p.u.)

	1	2	3	4	5	6	7	
M	7.66	6	4	3	2	3.66	4.66	150
G	5.33	5.33	6.33	4	3	4.66	5.66	300
Mo	3.33	2	4.33	7	4.33	5.66	7	400
	100	75	200	100	125	200	50	

The solution to the classical transport problem is:

Table 5. Solution to the Transport Problem

	1	2	3	4	5	6	7	
M	7.66	6	4	3 (25)	2 (125)	3.66	4.66	150
G	5.33	5.33	6.33	4 (75)	3	4.66 (200)	5.66 (25)	300
Mo	3.33 (100)	2 (75)	4.33 (200)	7	4.33	5.66	7 (25)	400
	100	75	200	100	125	200	50	

To determine the best location, we use the second stage of the method. Computing $Min. \{C_{ji}\}$ we get:

Table 6. Enterprise Location

	1	2	3	4	5	6	7	
M	7.66	6	4	3 (25)	2 (125)	3.66	4.66	150
G	5.33	5.33	6.33	4 (75)	3	4.66 (200)	5.66 (25)	300
Mo	3.33 (100)	2 (75)	4.33 (200)	7	4.33	5.66	7 (25)	400
	100	75 (2)	200	100	125 (2)	200	50	

$Min.\{C_{ji}\}$, where there are assignments is expressed as:

$Min\ \{(3.33), (2), (4.33), (3,4), (2), (4.66), (5.66,7)\}$

$Min.\{C_{ji}\}$ = 2, which in this case is related to Morelia and Monterrey.

The optimal location has a direct relationship between installed capacity and potential demand. This is also related to the amount of available capital to invest in setting the enterprise. If there s no limit in this concept and the plans are to participate with the highest potential demand level, then the best place to locate the plant is Monterrey (MO). In case the plans are to participate in the market with a lower level of demand satisfaction, the place to locate the company is Morelia (M).

For the Centor of Gravity Method (CGM), once we know at the Macro-Micro level that the locaton is Monterrey, Nuevo Leon, supported by a set of experts, the importance levels or weighting of the set $\{FBL_i; i = 1, 2, \ldots, n\}$, and their locations in the reference systems are the following:

Table 7. $\{FBL_i; i = 1, 2, \ldots, n\}$

i	FBL	CF_i	Coordinates (x,y)
1	Raw material	0.3	(8,21), (4,3), (7,9), (12,18)
2	Inputs	0.06	(1,3), (18,21), (13,10), (9,8)
3	Electrical energy	0.2	(1,3), (12,9), (7,4), (16,15), (13,12)
4	Water	0.2	(1,4), (1,3), (16,14), (13,10),(9,8)
5	Resources ($)	0.01	(1,4), (9,8), (16,14), (13,12)
6	Market	0.02	(9,17), (14,12), (18,21),(17,32)
7	Labor	0.1	(7,18), (4,13), (9,16), (7,3)

For the analysis case we will use these factors, making evident that the importance and inclusion of other factors depends on the type of enterprise and the importance of those factors in the production process. The $\mathbf{CF_i}$ level is in the interval $0 < CF_i \leq 1$; 1 when all needs of each required $\{\mathbf{FBL_i}\}$ are fulfilled.

Using the Center of Gravity method, the resulting location is in the coordinates:

GG = {37.5, 45.44}

If there is no available plot at that location, the best choice is to perform a physical visit to the land in the indicated radius and select the location that is available and fulfills all requirements in $\mathbf{A_i}$.

Conclusions

The application of classical theory is efficient in this kind of analysis. Nevertheless, the extension proposed in this paper was possible by means of fuzzy logic and the use of experts. The study cases for enterprise location show better results in determining locations for new enterprises. This fact will make new companies more competitive in global markets, since they will operate at higher levels of efficiency and efficacy. Enterprise studies in this area must be supported by this kind of methodologies, since they are best suited for the analysis and precision of results in the recommendations they produce.

References

1. A.Kaufmann, J. Gil Aluja. *Las matemáticas del azar y de la incertidumbre (elementos básicos para su aplicación en economía).* Editorial Centro de Estudios Ramón Areces. España. (1990)
2. Bazaraa M. S, JArvis J., Sherali H. *Linear programming and network flows.* Wiley. USA. . (1977)
3. Castro García, González S.F., Pacheco D.C. *Lógica difusa aplicada como una herramienta adicional a los medios convencionales de localización: Caso localización de un negocio de servicios.* XVI Congress of the SIGEF-Economic and Financial Systems in Eemerging Economies . Morelia México. (2010)
4. Gil Lafuente J.. *Algoritmos para la excelencia (claves para el éxito en la gestión deportiva).* Milladoiro. España. (2002)
5. Gil Lafuente A.M.. *Nuevas estrategias para el análisis financiero en la empresa.* Ariel. España. (2001)
6. Gil Lafuente A.M. *El análisis de las inmovilizaciones en la incertidumbre.* Ariel. España. (2004)
7. González S.F, Flores R. B, Gil Lafuente A.M. *Procesos para la toma de decisiones en un entorno globalizado.* Editorial Universitaria Ramón Areces. España. (2011)
8. González S.F., Flores R. B. *Estrategias para la toma de decisiones empresariales (en un entorno de incertidumbre).* Editorial Académica Española. Alemania. (2011)
9. González S.F., et al, *La incertidumbre en la evaluación financiera de empresas.* FeGoSa-Ingeniería Administrativa, UMSNH. Morelia México. (2000).
10. González S.F. *Los proyectos en la industrialización forestal.*UMSNH. Morelia México. (1985).

11. Machuca D.J. *Dirección de operaciones: aspectos tácticos y operativos en la producción y en los servicios.*Mc. Graw Hill. Madrid. (1994)
12. Prauda J. *Métodos y modelos de investigación de operaciones. Vol.1.*Limusa. México. (1982)
13. Wayne L, Winston *Investigación de operaciones (aplicaciones y algoritmos).* Grupo Editorial Iberoamérica. México. (1991)
14. Weber A. *Theory of the location of industries.*University of Chicago. Chicago. (1929)

A MATHEMATICAL MODEL OF PRICE STABILIZATION IN CONTEXT OF UNCERTAINTY

JOAN BONET AMAT

JOAN CARLES FERRER COMALAT

ELVIRA CASSU SERRA

SALVADOR LINARES MUSTARÓS

Department of Business Administration, University of Girona, Campus de Montilivi s/n, 71017 Girona, Spain.

In this paper we propose a mathematical model in which product prices (P>0) experiment, over time t, a growth rate P'=dP/dt (P'>0) higher than is considered normal, P'e, which is the balanced growth. We also analyze the situation in a second phase, and believe there is a tendency to stabilization of the rate of change P' due to a series of economic measures. For the model to their greater likelihood, we assume that the parameters of the function that models the dynamic path of prices are uncertain and are expressed by fuzzy numbers, which we assume are in triangular form, or, as we have done in previous works, by the curve of Agnesi.

1. Model Approach

We start from a dynamic path of prices for a given asset over time P(t) where we assume that the rate of growth of prices will be higher than the equilibrium ($P'>P'_e$) and that the function P '= f (t) is decreasing (P" <0) since the rate of price change is assumed to diminish in different consecutive periods. Furthermore, we also set the condition that P' is increasingly and gently closer to P'_e, thereby simulating the growth rate P' through a mathematically concave curve (P'''>0), as we represent in Figure 1.

We will simulate the function P'=f(t) with the upper branch of the equilateral hyperbola limited in the first quadrant (t>0, P'>0). At first, we can write $P'=(a_0+a_1\cdot t)/(a_2+a_3\cdot t)$, but dividing all parameters by a_3, we get:

$$P' = \frac{a + b \cdot t}{c + t} \qquad a, b, c > 0 \qquad [1]$$

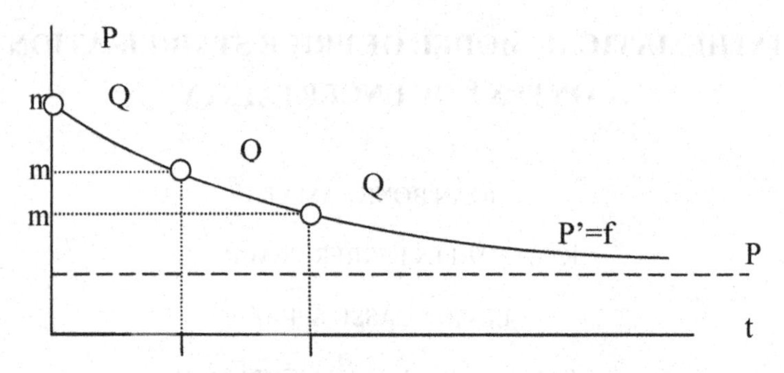

Figure 1. Modeling the growth rate of prices P'=f(t)

The positivity of these three parameters is justified by noting that in the first quadrant there is no vertical asymptote (c>0), yet horizontally (b>0) and all P' have to be positives (a>0). Moreover, since $P''=dP'/dt=(b\cdot c-a)/(c+t)^2$ and $P''<0$, it is verified that $a > b\cdot c$, or $a-b\cdot c > 0$. Calling q the first member of the inequality, we have:

$$q = a - b\cdot c \qquad q > 0 \tag{2}$$

We begin from the initial product price, which is a known value, P_0. Also, to determine the above parameters, in t=0 and in the next two periods, t=1 and t=2, we suppose that growth rates P'_0, P'_1 and P'_2, which will decrease, will likely be:

$$P'_0 = m_0 \quad , \quad P'_1 = m_1 \quad , \quad P'_2 = m_2 \qquad (m_0 > m_1 > m_2) \tag{3}$$

Naturally, these values will not be sharp but, to be a future forecast, will implicitly load uncertainty denoted by the percentages p_0, p_1 and p_2, which are expected to increase over time, and therefore $p_0 < p_1 < p_2$.

To simplify the notation, with m_0, m_1 and m_2 we will use the two first-order, Δ_1 and Δ_2, and the second-order, Δ_{12}. Assuming the above hypotheses that P' is decreasing and the result is concave, we get:

$$\Delta_1 = m_1 - m_0 < 0 \quad , \quad \Delta_2 = m_2 - m_1 < 0 \quad , \quad \Delta_{12} = \Delta_2 - \Delta_1 = m_2 - 2m_1 + m_0 > 0 \tag{4}$$

If we particularize [1] for the plane points $Q_0(0,m_0)$, $Q_1(1,m_1)$ y $Q_2(2,m_2)$, we will obtain the system $\{a-m_0\cdot c=0,\ a+b-m_1\cdot c=m_1,\ a+2b-m_2\cdot c=2m_2\}$, which, once solved, leads to the solution:

$$a = -\frac{2m_0 \cdot \Delta_2}{\Delta_{12}} \qquad b = \frac{m_0 \cdot \Delta_2 - m_2 \cdot \Delta_1}{\Delta_{12}} \qquad c = -\frac{2 \cdot \Delta_2}{\Delta_{12}} \tag{5}$$

Note that the concavity condition, $\Delta_{12}>0$, implies that $m_1<(m_0+m_2)/2$, which means the central term m_1 must be less than the arithmetic mean m_A of the ends m_0 and m_2, and therefore $m_1<m_A$. Since Δ_1 and Δ_2 are negative, clearly a and c are positive. Due b is also positive then $m_0\cdot\Delta_2>m_2\cdot\Delta_1$, which is $m_1<2m_0\cdot m_2/(m_0+m_2)$, or $m_1<2/[(1/m_0)+(1/m_2)]$.

Moreover, note that the second member of the previous inequality is simply the *harmonic mean* m_H of the ends, so we write $m_1<m_H(m_0,m_2)$. Since it is always the inequality $m_H<m_A$, the only condition to be met is:

$$m_1 < m_H(m_0,m_2) \qquad \text{where} \quad m_H(m_0,m_2) = \frac{2m_0 \cdot m_2}{m_0 + m_2} \qquad [6]$$

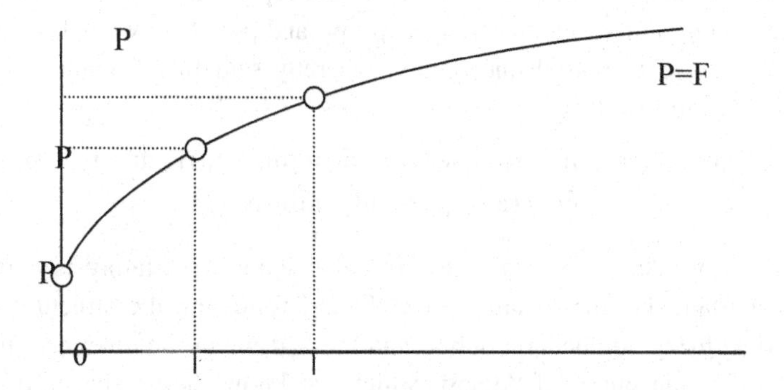

Figure 2. Representation of the dynamic path of price P = F(t)

Moreover, we obtain the price dynamic expression of P = F(t) across the integrating function of growth rate, P'=f(t), which is:

$$P = \int \frac{a + b \cdot t}{c + t} \cdot dt \qquad [7]$$

Solving the indefinite integral, using [2] and symbolized by C, the constant of integration, we obtain:

$$P = b\cdot t + q\cdot \ln(t+c) + C \qquad (q = a - b\cdot c)$$

Since for t=0 we know the price P_0, which turns out to be $P_0 = q\cdot\ln(c) + C$, where $C = P_0 - q\cdot\ln(c)$, and consequently the price dynamic expression is given by:

$$P = b \cdot t + q \cdot \ln\left(\frac{t}{c} + 1\right) + P_0 \qquad [8]$$

Note that because P>0 and also that P'>0 and P"<0, the price curve will be located in the first quadrant, and will be increasing and mathematically convex.

2. Approach under parameter uncertainty

While the initial price P_0 is a determined value, initial growth rates P'_0, are not accurately known and, of course, we not know the next two periods, P'_1 and P'_2. In the crisp case we expected them to be m_0, m_1 and m_2, but in this section we will consider the uncertainty and denote the respective growth rates through fuzzy numbers denoted by $\tilde{m}_0$, $\tilde{m}_1$, and $\tilde{m}_2$.

As we have done in previous works, we will represent these quantities using fuzzy percentages of variation (or error) p_0, p_1, and p_2, where we will assume $p_0 < p_1 < p_2$ due to increased uncertainty, whereby said fuzzy numbers will be represented as follows:

$$\tilde{m}_0 = (m_0 - p_0 \cdot r_0 \, , m_0 \, , m_0 + p_0 \cdot r_0) \qquad \tilde{m}_1 = (m_1 - p_1 \cdot r_1 \, , m_1 \, , m_1 + p_1 \cdot r_1)$$
$$\tilde{m}_2 = (m_2 - p_2 \cdot r_2 \, , m_2 \, , m_2 + p_2 \cdot r_2) \qquad [9]$$

We can consider, as we indicated in [9] that the uncertainty is expressed through a triangular fuzzy number (NBT), or, following the structure of the symmetrical fuzzy numbers of Dubois and Prade using as the reference function on both sides the curve of Agnesi, which we know, has a shape similar to graphical Gaussian models and has the expression $L(x)=R(x)=a/(b+c \cdot x^2)$.

In both cases, as we stated in [9], we take as central values and *radii of uncertainty* as the products of schools by the percentage of variation, ie, $r_0 = m_0 \cdot p_0$, $r_1 = m_1 \cdot p_1$ and $r_2 = m_2 \cdot p_2$. Given the expression [9], to facilitate the notation, we use the nomenclature of Dubois and Prade and express these fuzzy numbers as follows:

$$\tilde{m}_0 = (m_0, r_0)_{L\text{-}R} \quad , \quad \tilde{m}_1 = (m_1, r_1)_{L\text{-}R} \quad , \quad \tilde{m}_2 = (m_2, r_2)_{L\text{-}R} \qquad [10]$$

In fact, we will omit the subscript L-R, understanding that the fuzzy numbers are symmetric (L(x)=R(x)), and we use as areference function the linear function (thus generating a triangular fuzzy number) or the function of Agnesi (by which we generate a fuzzy number we call Agnesian).

Thus, by determining their *lower ends* ($m_{0i}=m_0-r_0$, $m_{1i}=m_1-r_1$, $m_{2i}=m_2-r_2$) and also their *upper ends* ($m_{0s}=m_0+r_0$, $m_{1s}=m_1+r_1$, $m_{2s}=m_2+r_2$), we represent them by the triplets:

$$\tilde{m}_0 = (m_{0i}, m_0, m_{0s}) \qquad \tilde{m}_1 = (m_{1i}, m_1, m_{1s}) \qquad \tilde{m}_2 = (m_{2i}, m_2, m_{2s}) \qquad [11]$$

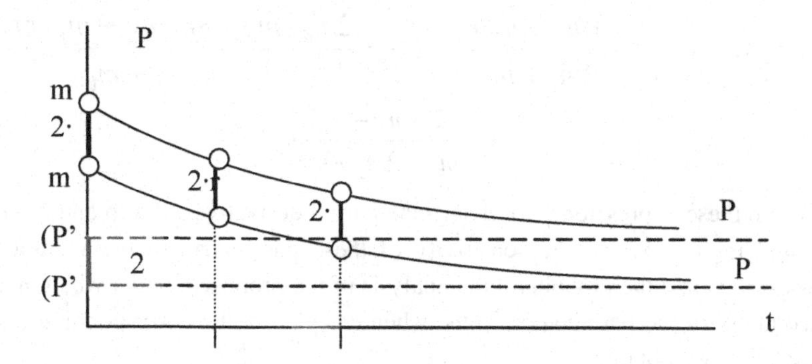

Figure 3. Representation of the fuzzy rate of price change

The condition imposed by the restriction [3] that the price-rate curve is downward, $m_0 > m_1 > m_2$, in the case of uncertainty results in the fact that $m_{0i} > m_{1s}$ and that $m_{1i} > m_{2s}$, that is $m_0\text{-}r_0 > m_1+r_1$ and $m_1\text{-}r_1 > m_2+r_2$. From this it follows, that if the initial percentage p_0 is known, the other two must be met:

$$p_1 < \frac{m_{0i}}{m_1} - 1 \qquad\qquad p_2 < \frac{m_{1i}}{m_2} - 1 \qquad [12]$$

Note further that the restriction stated in [6] $m_1 < m_H(m_0, m_2)$, due to the condition of concavity of the curve P' = f(t), will generalize to the fuzzy case with the condition $m_{1s} < m_H(m_{0i}, m_{2i})$, namely, $m_{1s} < [2m_{0i} \cdot m_{2i}/(m_{0i}+m_{2i})]$. This condition is equivalent to $m_{2i} > [(m_{0i} \cdot m_{1s}/m_2)/(2 \cdot m_{0i} - m_{1s})]$, so the percentage p_2 as well as [12] must meet the following condition:

$$p_2 < 1 - \frac{m_{0i} \cdot m_{1s}}{2 \cdot m_2 \cdot (m_{0i} - m_{1s})} \qquad [13]$$

3. Determination of the fuzzy parameters in the rate of price growth

After determining the fuzzy numbers $\tilde{m}_0$, $\tilde{m}_1$ and $\tilde{m}_2$ that express uncertain growth rates in different periods and that can be represented in the forms given in [9], [10] and [11], we will determine the fuzzy parameters $\tilde{a}$, $\tilde{b}$ and $\tilde{c}$ of the function P', which, as seen in [1] for the crisp case, is $P'=(a+b \cdot t)/(c+t)$. This will start from the relations given in [5], which when expressed only in terms of m_0, m_1 and m_2 give rise to:

$$a = -\frac{2m_0 \cdot (m_2 - m_1)}{m_2 - 2m_1 + m_0} \qquad b = \frac{2m_0 \cdot m_2 - m_0 \cdot m_1 - m_1 \cdot m_2}{m_2 - 2m_1 + m_0}$$

$$c = -\frac{2 \cdot (m_2 - m_1)}{m_2 - 2m_1 + m_0} \qquad [14]$$

From these expressions, we determine partial derivatives of a, b and c on m_0, m_1 and m_2 to analyze the sensitivity of these parameters to the variation in growth rate, and thereby obtain the analysis of the proposed model when there is uncertainty in the parameters. Thus, when calculating the corresponding partial derivatives we obtain:

$$\frac{\partial a}{\partial m_0} = -\frac{2 \cdot \Delta_2 \cdot (\Delta_{12} - m_0)}{(\Delta_{12})^2} \quad \frac{\partial a}{\partial m_1} = -\frac{2 \cdot m_0 \cdot (\Delta_1 + \Delta_2)}{(\Delta_{12})^2} \quad \frac{\partial a}{\partial m_2} = \frac{2 \cdot m_0 \cdot \Delta_1}{(\Delta_{12})^2}$$

$$\frac{\partial b}{\partial m_0} = \frac{2 \cdot \Delta_2^{\,2}}{(\Delta_{12})^2} \qquad \frac{\partial b}{\partial m_1} = -\frac{(\Delta_1 + \Delta_2)^2}{(\Delta_{12})^2} \qquad \frac{\partial b}{\partial m_2} = \frac{2 \cdot \Delta_1^{\,2}}{(\Delta_{12})^2}$$

$$\frac{\partial c}{\partial m_0} = \frac{2 \cdot \Delta_2}{(\Delta_{12})^2} \qquad \frac{\partial c}{\partial m_1} = -\frac{2 \cdot (\Delta_1 + \Delta_2)}{(\Delta_{12})^2} \qquad \frac{\partial c}{\partial m_2} = \frac{2 \cdot \Delta_1}{(\Delta_{12})^2} \qquad [15]$$

We will use the above expressions to obtain uncertain values of the parameters $\tilde{a}$, $\tilde{b}$ and $\tilde{c}$. Following the same nomenclature that we used to represent $\tilde{m}_0$, $\tilde{m}_1$ and $\tilde{m}_2$ in expression [10], we determine the center and radius of the fuzzy numbers $\tilde{a}$, $\tilde{b}$ and $\tilde{c}$ in two different ways.

Earlier form of the calculations applying the techniques of arithmetic of uncertainty. For this reason, to determine the approximate radius r_a of the first parameter, we look at the sign of the partial derivatives above, recalling that $\Delta_1<0$, $\Delta_2<0$, $\Delta_{12}>0$ and seeing also that $\Delta_{12}<m_0$, because $\Delta_{12}-m_0=m_2-2m_1<0$. We will have $\partial a/\partial m_0<0$, $\partial a/\partial m_1>0$ and $\partial a/\partial m_2<0$. Therefore, the parameter a decreases with m_0, increases with m_1 and decreases with m_2.

Thus, the lower end a_i of $\tilde{a}$ is deducted from [14] taking m_{0s}, m_{1i} and m_{2s}, while the upper end a_s will be found with the opposite ends, m_{0i}, m_{1s} and m_{2i}. An approximate value of radius r_a will be the end of the half of the sum a_i and a_s, that is to say, $r_a \approx (a_s - a_i)/2$. The same procedure is followed with the radius r_b and r_c of the fuzzy parameters $\tilde{a}$ and $\tilde{b}$.

Alternatively, we propose a second way to determine the center and radius using the positive differential operator that we have treated in more detail in previous works quoted in the references. In this particular case, to depend ã, $\tilde{b}$ and $\tilde{c}$ of three variables, we use the total differential of a function of several variables, $df(x,y,z)=(\partial f/\partial x)\cdot dx+(\partial f/\partial y)\cdot dy+(\partial f/\partial z)\cdot dz$. Now, since we work in fuzziness, to apply the principle of entropy increase in the fuzzy operations we take the absolute value of the partial differential. Furthermore, as justified in our previous works, the differential of the independent variables will be the radius. Consequently, the positive differential, $|df|^+$ will be obtained from the expression:

$$|df|^+ = \left|\frac{\partial f}{\partial x}\right| \cdot r_x + \left|\frac{\partial f}{\partial y}\right| \cdot r_y + \left|\frac{\partial f}{\partial z}\right| \cdot r_z \qquad [16]$$

Based on the positive differential we will obtain an approximation of the radius of the fuzzy numbers ã, $\tilde{b}$ and $\tilde{c}$, which in our case will be:

$$r_a \approx \left|\frac{\partial a}{\partial m_0}\right| \cdot r_0 + \left|\frac{\partial a}{\partial m_1}\right| \cdot r_1 + \left|\frac{\partial a}{\partial m_2}\right| \cdot r_2$$

$$r_b \approx \left|\frac{\partial b}{\partial m_0}\right| \cdot r_0 + \left|\frac{\partial b}{\partial m_1}\right| \cdot r_1 + \left|\frac{\partial b}{\partial m_2}\right| \cdot r_2$$

$$r_c \approx \left|\frac{\partial c}{\partial m_0}\right| \cdot r_0 + \left|\frac{\partial c}{\partial m_1}\right| \cdot r_1 + \left|\frac{\partial c}{\partial m_2}\right| \cdot r_2 \qquad [17]$$

Having identified the anterior radius, and using the percentage of variation $p_a= r_a/a$, $p_b= r_b/b$ and $p_c= r_c/c$, we can write fuzzy parameters ã, $\tilde{b}$ and $\tilde{c}$, in the forms $\tilde{a} = (a, r_a)$,
$\tilde{b} = (b, r_b)$ and $\tilde{c} = (c, r_c)$, or $\tilde{a} = (a - p_a\cdot r_a , a , a + p_a\cdot r_a)$, $\tilde{b} = (b - p_b\cdot r_b , b , b + p_b\cdot r_b)$ and $\tilde{c} = (c - p_c\cdot r_c , c , c + p_c\cdot r_c)$.

4. Determination of fuzzy curves of price and rate of price growth

Having identified the fuzzy parameters of the curves, we will determine the blurred expression of the curve representing the rate of price growth. We have transformed the role of price growth $P'=(a+b\cdot t)/(c+t)$ in another fuzzy $\tilde{P}'$ whose parameters are fuzzy numbers ã, $\tilde{b}$ and $\tilde{c}$. The center of $\tilde{P}'$ will naturally be the crisp value P', while the radius r' is found in two ways, as we did in the previous section.

First, if we apply the arithmetic of uncertainty, the lower end of the fuzzy growth $\tilde{P}'$ will be $P'_i=(a_i+b_i\cdot t)/(c_s+t)$, where $a_i=a-r_a$, $b_i=b-r_b$ and $c_s=c+r_c$. Moreover, the upper end is $P'_s=(a_s+b_s\cdot t)/(c_i+t)$, with $a_s=a+r_a$, $b_s=b+r_b$ and $c_i=c-r_c$. An approximation of the radius r' will be half of the sum of the extremes, namely $r'\approx(P'_s-P'_i)/2$.

Secondly, using the partial derivatives $\partial P'/\partial a=1/(c+t)$, $\partial P'/\partial b=t/(c+t)$ and $\partial P'/\partial c=-(a+b\cdot t)/(c+t)^2$, the positive differential will be $r'=|dP'|^+=|\partial P'/\partial a|\cdot da+|\partial P'/\partial b|\cdot db+|\partial P'/\partial c|\cdot dc$. Substituting, we obtain the radius r' expressed as a linear combination of r_a, r_b and r_c:

$$r'=\frac{1}{c+t}\cdot r_a+\frac{t}{c+t}\cdot r_b+\frac{a+b\cdot t}{(c+t)^2}\cdot r_c \qquad [18]$$

Note that for t=0, 1 and 2 these radii should be similar to those we have taken to start, r_0, r_1 and r_2. In fact, they would be somewhat higher due to increased uncertainty when performing operations with uncertain values.

Then we follow a similar process to obtain the blurred expression of the stock price from the clear expression [8], $P=b\cdot t+q\cdot \ln[(t/c)+1]+P_0$, where $q=a-b\cdot c$.

When we apply the uncertainty arithmetic, we must consider the partial derivatives to be $\partial P/\partial a=\ln[(t/c)+1]$, $\partial P/\partial b=t-c\cdot \ln[(t/c)+1]$ and $\partial P/\partial c=-b\cdot \ln[(t/c)+1]+[(a-b\cdot c)/(t+c)]$. In the first note that $\partial P/\partial a>0$, and thus P is increasing with a. In the second, generally $\ln(x+1)<x$ will be $\ln[(t/c)+1]<(t/c)$, or $c\cdot \ln[(t/c)+1]<t$, whereby $\partial P/\partial b>0$, and P is increasing with b. Finally, in the third it can be seen that $q=a-b\cdot c$ and $\ln[(t/c)+1]$ decreases with increasing c, whereby P is decreasing with c, that is to say $\partial P/\partial c<0$. Therefore, the lower and upper ends of the price function will be:

$$P_i=b_i\cdot t+(a_i-b_i\cdot c_s)\cdot \ln\left(\frac{t}{c_s}+1\right)+P_0$$

$$P_s=b_s\cdot t+(a_s-b_s\cdot c_i)\cdot \ln\left(\frac{t}{c_i}+1\right)+P_0 \qquad [19]$$

Since $r_b=(b_s-b_i)/2$, if we denote $q_i=a_i-b_i\cdot c_s$ and $q_s=a_s-b_s\cdot c_i$, it turns out that the uncertainty ratio of price $r=(P_s-P_i)/2$ is given by the expression:

$$r = r_b \cdot t + \frac{q_s}{2} \cdot \ln\left(\frac{t}{c_i} + 1\right) - \frac{q_i}{2} \cdot \ln\left(\frac{t}{c_s} + 1\right) \qquad [20]$$

Moreover, we can also determine the radius of price uncertainty using a positive differential. To do this, remember that we have calculated the radius of the price-rate curve [18] based on the positive differential, $r' = |dP'|^+ = |\partial P'/\partial a| \cdot r_a + |\partial P'/\partial b| \cdot r_b + |\partial P'/\partial c| \cdot r_c$. From this expression, to find the radius r of the price curve $P = \int P' \cdot dt$, we must integrate each of the summands of r'.

Denoting $k_a = \int |\partial P'/\partial a| \cdot dt$, $k_b = \int |\partial P'/\partial b| \cdot dt$ and $k_c = \int |\partial P'/\partial c| \cdot dt$, and using C for the constant of integration, the uncertainty radius of prices will be:

$$r = k_a \cdot r_a + k_b \cdot r_b + k_c \cdot r_c + C \qquad [21]$$

Making the respective integrations we will obtain the values of these coefficients:

$$k_a = \ln(c+t) \qquad k_b = t - c \cdot \ln(c+t) \qquad k_c = \frac{b \cdot c - a}{c+t} + b \cdot \ln(c+t) \qquad [22]$$

Since $q = a - b \cdot c$, if we denote $s = r_a + b \cdot r_c - c \cdot r_b$, we can write:

$$r = r_b \cdot t + s \cdot \ln(c+t) - [q \cdot r_c/(c+t)] + C$$

As the origin of price is known, P_0, there is no uncertainty and $r(0)=0$. This initial condition allows us to deduce the integration constant C, whose value is $C = (q \cdot r_c/c) - s \cdot \mathrm{Ln}(c)$. If we now substitute and operate, we obtain as an expression of the radius:

$$r = r_b \cdot t + \frac{q \cdot r_c \cdot t}{c \cdot (c+t)} + s \cdot \ln\left(\frac{t}{c} + 1\right) \qquad [23]$$

Then we see the similarity between the radius obtained by applying the uncertainty arithmetic and applying the method of positive differential, given in the respective expressions [20] and [23]. These expressions have the respective form $r_1 = r_b \cdot t + A$ y $r_2 = r_b \cdot t + B$, with the expressions A and B given by:

$$A = \frac{q_s}{2} \cdot \ln\left(\frac{t}{c_i} + 1\right) - \frac{q_i}{2} \cdot \ln\left(\frac{t}{c_s} + 1\right) \qquad B = \frac{q \cdot r_c \cdot t}{c \cdot (c+t)} + s \cdot \ln\left(\frac{t}{c} + 1\right) \qquad [24]$$

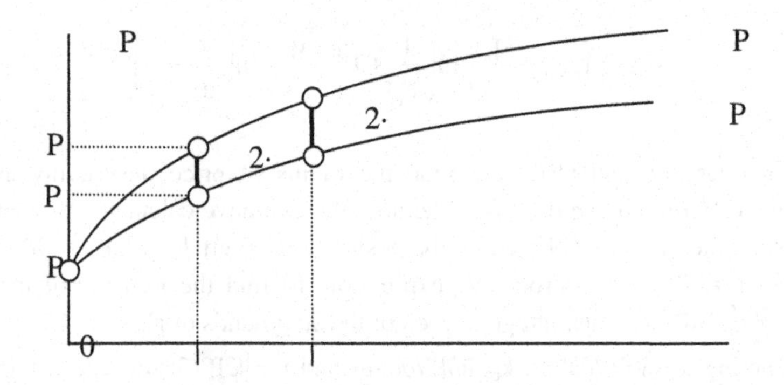

Figure 4. Fuzzy representation of the price curve

Recall also that we have used the following symbols:

$$q_s = a_s - b_s \cdot c_i \qquad q_i = a_i - b_i \cdot c_s \qquad q = a - b \cdot c \qquad s = r_a + b \cdot r_c - c \cdot r_b \qquad [25]$$

We will prove that $A \approx B$, with what will be $r_1 \approx r_2$. Let us first values of q_s and q_i is a function of q and s. We start from $q_s=(a+r_a)-(b+r_b)\cdot(c-r_c)$. Multiplying and neglecting the term $r_b \cdot r_c$, which is very small compared with the other summands, we have $q_s=q+s$. Similarly $q_i=q-i$. If r_c is replaced by r to simplify the notation, we have:

$$A=[(q+s)/2]\cdot \ln([t/(c-r)]+1) - [(q-s)/2]\cdot \ln([t/(c+r)]+1)$$

Grouping the terms we get A=M+N, where:

$$M=(q/2)\cdot(\ln[(t+c-r)/(c-r)]-\ln[(t+c+r)/(c+r)])$$
$$N=(s/2)\cdot(\ln[(t+c-r)/(c-r)]+\ln[(t+c+r)/(c+r)])$$

We will simplify M and N, using the properties of logarithms:

$$M=(q/2)\cdot \ln([(t+c-r)\cdot(c+r)]/[(t+c+r)\cdot(c-r)]) = (q/2)\cdot \ln([t\cdot(c+r)+c^2-r^2]/[t\cdot(c-r)+c^2-r^2])$$

Neglecting the terms r^2, as very small, we obtain:

$$M\approx(q/2)\cdot\ln([t\cdot(c+r)+c^2]/[t\cdot(c-r)+c^2]) = (q/2)\cdot\ln([(c^2+t\cdot c)+r\cdot t]/[(c^2+t\cdot c)-r\cdot t])$$

Multiplying and then dividing by $(c^2+t\cdot c)+r\cdot t$, gives:

$$M\approx(q/2)\cdot\ln((c^2+t\cdot c+r\cdot t)^2/[(c^2+t\cdot c)^2-(r^2\cdot t^2)])$$

Neglecting also the term $r^2\cdot t^2$, we obtain:

$$M\approx(q/2)\cdot\ln[(c^2+t\cdot c+r\cdot t)^2/(c^2+t\cdot c)^2] = (q/2)\cdot\ln([(c^2+t\cdot c+r\cdot t)/(c^2+t\cdot c)]^2) =$$

$$= q\cdot\ln[(c^2+t\cdot c+r\cdot t)/(c^2+t\cdot c)] = q\cdot\ln(1+[(r\cdot t)/(c^2+t\cdot c)])$$

Applying the Mac-Laurin formula to the natural logarithm $\ln(1+x)\approx(x/1)-(x^2/2)+(x^3/3)-(x^4/4)$ with which if $x\approx0$ we have the approximation $\text{Ln}(1+x)\approx x$, being now $x=r\cdot t/(c^2+t\cdot c)$, finally results in:

$$M \approx q\cdot\frac{r\cdot t}{c^2+t\cdot c} = \frac{q\cdot r_c\cdot t}{c\cdot(c+t)} \qquad [26]$$

Operating similarly on the N terminus we have successively:

$$N = \frac{s}{2}\cdot\ln\frac{t+c-r}{c-r} + \ln\frac{t+c+r}{c+r} = \frac{s}{2}\cdot\ln\frac{(t+c-r)\cdot(t+c+r)}{(c-r)\cdot(c+r)} =$$

$$= \frac{s}{2}\cdot\ln\frac{(t+c)^2-r^2}{c^2-r^2} \approx \frac{s}{2}\cdot\ln\left(\frac{t+c}{c}\right)^2 = s\cdot\ln\left(\frac{t}{c}+1\right) \qquad [27]$$

We note with all that $A=M+N\approx(q\cdot r_c\cdot t)/[c\cdot(c+t)]+ s\cdot\text{Ln}[(t/c)+1]=B$. Therefore, $A\approx B$, and we conclude that the two radii r_1 and r_2, obtained by applying the uncertainty arithmetic and the positive differential respectively, are similar, that is to say $r_1\approx r_2$.

5. Application of the model through a numerical example

Suppose the price of a product is P_0=654€ and that the price growth rate at the initial time is P'_0=9'3. Furthermore, as we considered in the model assumptions we assume that the price growth slows down, and that next month the growth rate will be $\tilde{P}'_1$=8'2±0'1% and two months from now $\tilde{P}'_2$=7'9±0'2%. We will have, therefore, m_0=9'3, m_1=8'2, m_2=7'9, p_0=0, p_1=0'001 and p_2=0'002. Note that decreasing condition [3] is satisfied $m_0>m_1>m_2$ and the harmonic mean $m_1<m_H(m_0,m_2)$ is satisfied since 8'2<8'543.

With the approach set out, we have the radii $r_0=0$, $r_1=0'0082$, $r_2=0'0158$, and the crisp value $m_0=9'3$ and fuzzy rates $\tilde{m}_1=(8'1918,\ 8'2,\ 8'2082)$ and $\tilde{m}_2=(7'8842,\ 7'9,\ 7'9158)$. See that all curves P'=f(t) are decreasing and concave, with the formulas [12] ($p_1<0'134146$, $p_2<0'036937$) and [13] ($p_2<0'07015$), thereby complying with all restrictions imposed on our model.

From the differences $\Delta_1= -1'1$, $\Delta_2= -0'3$ and $\Delta_{12}= 0'8$, we calculate crisp parameters a, b and c for the function that expresses the price growth rate with what we have in our case $P'=(6'975+7'375\cdot t)/(0'75+t)$, stabilizing the rate at value $P'_e=7'375$. As for the fuzzy case, with the Excel spreadsheet and applying in each case the uncertainty arithmetic, we obtain values $a_i=6'1687$, $a_s=7'8489$, $b_i=7'2868$, $b_s=7'4567$, $c_i=0'6633$ and $c_s=0'8440$, thus the radius of uncertainty will be $(r_a)_1=0'8401$, $(r_b)_1=0'0850$, $(r_c)_1=0'0903$. Moreover, if we calculate ratios by positive differential, using the partial derivatives $|\partial a/\partial m_0|=7'9688$, $|\partial a/\partial m_1|=40'6875$, etc. we obtain $(r_a)_2=0'8387$, $(r_b)_2=0'0849$, $(r_c)_2=0'0902$.

If finally we take the radius as the mean of anterior radii $r_a=0'8394$, $r_b=0'0849$ and $r_c=0'0903$, we will have the parameters for the fuzzy function, which expresses that the price growth rate will be $\tilde{a}=(6'1356,\ 6'975,\ 7'8144)$, $\tilde{b}=(7'2901,\ 7'375,\ 7'4599)$ and $\tilde{c}=(0'6597,\ 0'75,\ 0'8403)$.

Then, as forecasted by the model, we analyze the fuzzy rate P' and the price P corresponding product for the next period t=3. Applying the arithmetic of uncertainty, we deduce the lower rate $P'_i=7'2927$ and the upper rate $P'_s=8'2504$, so the radius will be $r'_1=0'4788$. Moreover, using the positive differential and [18] we obtain $r'_2=0'2667\cdot r_a+0'8\cdot r_b+2'0693\cdot r_c=0'4786$. Since the central value is $P'(3)=7'76$, if we take $r'=(r'_1+r'_2)/2$, the new growth rate will be given by the fuzzy number $\tilde{P}'(3)=(7'2813,\ 7'76,\ 8'2387)$.

We will then determine the price value for the period t=3. The central value [8] is approximately p(3)=678'45€, and to find the corresponding fuzzy number arithmetic using uncertainty arithmetic we will employ [19] with $q_i=0'0100$ and $q_s=2'8928$, with lower prices $P_i(3)=675'8854$ and upper prices $P_s(3)=681'3360$, and with the uncertainty radius $r_1=(P_s-P_i)/2=2'7253$. If we work with a positive differential we can use [23] with s=1'4414, obtaining the radius $r_2=2'7136$.

Finally, taking as radius $r=(r_1+r_2)/2=2'7195$ we deduce that, for the third month the price of the product is given by the fuzzy number $\tilde{P}(3)=(675'73,\ 678'45,\ 681'17)$.

6. Conclusions

1. It is plausible to treat the model of balanced growth of prices under uncertainty with the hypotheses considered but only under certain restrictions.

2. In the fuzzy set model, the trajectories of the price and the price growth rate are stable if the restrictions are verified in the percentage of variation given by formulas [12] and [13].
3. Subject to the conditions imposed, the price trajectory and the growth rate can be determined by considering that the respective parameters determining the fuzzy functions are represented by symmetrical fuzzy numbers, whose centers coincide with the values obtained with the crisp version of the model, and the radius of variation is determined from the percentage of variation considered. In the absence of uncertainty, the results obtained with the model coincide with those obtained by direct application of the crisp model.
4. The radius of variation was determined in the model proposed from two different methods. One of them applies the techniques of arithmetic operational uncertainty. The alternative method has been employed using the positive differential equation, as presented in the work of Ferrer, J.C., Bonet, J., Bonet, G. (2005a), indicated in the references.
5. Great similarity has been found between the results obtained using the methods, as long as the percentages of variation of the parameters are small, therefore making possible the approximations presented at the end of paragraph 4.

References

1. J. Bonet, J.C. Ferrer and G. Bonet "Los números borrosos agnesianos y su aplicación a la resolución de ecuaciones polinómicas fuzzy en la economía". *Proceedings of the XIII SIGEF Congress.* Hammamet (Tunisia), November 30-December 2. (2006).
2. J. Bonet, J.C. Ferrer, G. Bonet and S. Linares "Un nuevo criterio de decisión para la valoración de un proyecto de inversión con capitales borrosos." *Actas del XV Congreso de SIGEF.* Lugo (España), October 29-30. (2009).
3. J. Bonet, J.C. Ferrer and E. Cassú "Toma de decisiones en inversiones económicas fuzzy, usando la regresión lineal múltiple." *Actas del XVI Congreso de SIGEF.* Morelia (México), October 28-29. (2010).
4. J.C. Ferrer *Un estudi de la teoria dels subconjunts borrosos amb aplicacions a models econòmics i problemas empresarials.* Girona (Espanya). Universitat de Girona. (1998).
5. J.C. Ferrer, G. Bonet and J. Bonet "Introduction to the concept of agnesian fuzzy number with some economic applications" in Gil Aluja, J. Marino, D., Morabito, F. C. (eds) *Techniques and Methodologies for the Information and Knowledge Economy,* p. 80-92. Reggio Calabria (Italy). Falzea Editore. (2004).
6. J.C. Ferrer, J. Bonet and G. Bonet. "Actual value of a financial investment with uncertain capitals and interest rates, using fuzzy numbers." *Proceedings of the MS'05.* Rouen (France), July 6-8. (2005)

7. J.C. Ferrer, J. Bonet and G. Bonet "Applications of the agnesian fuzzy numbers to economic functions. Derivatives and elasticity." *Proceedings of the International Conference on Modelling and Simulation.* Marrakech (Morocco), November 22-24. (2005).
8. J. Gil Aluja "Towards a new concept of economic research". *Fuzzy Economic Review,* No. 0, p. 5-23. (1995).
9. J. GIL ALUJA (Ed.) *Handbook of management under uncertainty.* Dordrecht (The Netherlands). Kluwer Academic Publishers. (2001).
10. A. Kaufmann, J. Gil Aluja and A. Terceño *Matemática para la economía y la gestión de empresas. Aritmética de la incertidumbre.* Barcelona (España). Foro Científico. (1991).
11. A. Kaufmann and M.M. Gupta *Introduction to fuzzy arithmetic. Theory and applications.* USA. International Thomson Computer Press. (1991).
12. Y. M. Mansur *Fuzzy sets and Economics.* Vermont (USA). Edward Elgar Publishing. (1995).
13. H. J. Zimmermann, *Fuzzy set theory and its applications (3rd. ed.).* Dordrecht (The Netherlands). Kluwer Academic Publishers. (2000).

AN STOCHASTIC MODEL OF THE PRECAUTIONARY PRINCIPLE*

MARÍA TERESA CASPARRI
CMA, FCE, UBA, Argentina
Córdoba 2120 (CABA)
+54 11 437061390

JAVIER GARCÍA FRONTI
CMA, FCE, UBA, Argentina
Córdoba 2120 (CABA)
+54 11 437061390

This paper formalises the precautionary principle, quantifying the value of delaying a certain inversion which involves social risks. Thereby, an stochastic model of optimal stopping is proposed, which articulates risk techniques and benefit-cost analysis.

1. Introduction

The European programme "Converging Technologies for the European knowledge society" (CTEKS) emphasises the importance of a "knowledge" society guided by a precautionary principle (Echeverría, 2005, Klinke et al., 2006). While it exists a great amount of literature about the precautionary principle, it is hard to make it operational.

Following Scott Farrow (2004), this paper mathematically formalises the precautionary principle. This formalisation gives policymakers a tool to evaluate projects with social impacts. This model articulates risk techniques and benefit-cost analysis in uncertain contexts, in order to quantify the social value of "precaution".

Therefore, the proposal is to socially evaluate whether, implement a certain project immediately, or wait for new information. The challenge is to use a quantitative decision method that incorporates uncertainty and irreversibility into the government criteria of risk management. This paper shows that, when the uncertainty and irreversibility of the project are contemplated, a higher threshold of net benefits is required.

* This work is supported by the UBACYT grant 20020100100478. For comments, we thank Rocío Ferreiro.

To accomplish the proposed objective, this paper is structured in three sections. The first one develops an stochastic model to quantify the value of waiting. In the second part, it is proposed a governmental procedure to make decisions when a new project involves social risks. In the last section, it is discussed how the uncertainty of the probabilistic model and the experts´ subjective observations can be included in the government decision process.

2. The Model

Any commercial project involves irreversible social costs, and, probably, social benefits. Following (Farrow, 2004) proposal, the value of delaying an investment project is similar to an option to wait (Dixit and Pindyck, 1994).

The irreversible social cost (C) mentioned is determined by the specialists, while the social benefits (B) are modelled using a geometric Brownian motion:

$$dB(t) = \alpha B(t)dt + \sigma B(t)dz \qquad (2.1)$$

Formally, if the discount rate is ρ , Bellman´s recursive equation of the value of the option of waiting at the moment "t" is:

$$F(B(t)) = Max(B(t) - C \ , e^{-\rho dt}E(F(B(t + dt)))) \qquad (2.2)$$

Where $F(B(t))$, is the quantification of the precautionary principle from the government´s point of view.

The challenge is to construct a decision rule that helps the government to decide between allowing the project to start immediately or force the investor to wait for new information. The rule at moment "t", is: compare the project value as executed today , **[B(t) – C]** with the value of waiting:

$$e^{-\rho dt} E\left(F\left(B(t + dt)\right)\right).$$

Mathematically, the problem is an "optimum stopping time". The aim is to calculate the critical value of the social benefit (B^*) that divides the region where it is optimum to wait ($B < B^*$), from the one where it is convenient to start the project immediately.

So that the decision rule is established by:

Si $B < B^* \Rightarrow F_E(B(t)) = e^{-\rho dt}E(F_E(B(t + dt)))$

Si $B > B^*$ $F_D(B(t)) = B(t) - C \Rightarrow$

Si $B = B^* \Rightarrow F_E(B^*) = F_D(B^*)$ (Continuity of the function F)

$\frac{dF_E}{dV}(B^*) = \frac{dF_D}{dV}(B^*)$ (Continuity of the first derivative).

Likewise, the monotony condition for F_D y F_E and for B(t+dt) given B(t) is required to be fulfilled.

Therefore, in the region in which is optimum to wait it is given that:

$$F_E(B(t)) = e^{-\rho dt}E(F_E(B(t+dt)))$$

Multiplying both members by $e^{\rho dt}$,

$$e^{\rho dt}F_E(B(t)) = E(F_E(B(t+dt)))$$

Subtracting $F_E(B(t))$

$$(e^{\rho dt}-1)F_E(B(t)) = E(F_E(B(t+dt)) - F_E(B(t)))$$

Dividing by Δt

$$\frac{(e^{\rho dt}-1)}{\Delta t}F_E(B(t)) = \frac{E(F_E(B(t+dt)) - F_E(B(t)))}{\Delta t}$$

If $\Delta t \to 0$

$$\rho F_E(B) = \frac{E(dF_E(B))}{dt}$$

On the other side, as we know that B follows a geometric Brownian motion, we can write (using Ito´s lemma) the $dF_E(B)$ process in the following way:

$$dF_E(B) = \left(F'_E(B)\alpha B + \frac{1}{2}F''_E(B)\sigma^2B^2\right)dt + F'_E(B)\sigma B dz$$

And the expectation is:

$$E(dF_E(B)) = \left(F'_E(B)\alpha B + \frac{1}{2}F''_E(B)\sigma^2B^2\right)dt$$

So

$$\rho F_E(B) = \frac{E(dF_E(B))}{dt} = F'_E(B)\alpha V + \frac{1}{2}F''_E(B)\sigma^2B^2$$

This equation, clearly convert the original stochastic problem into an ordinary differential equation attached to the following restrictions:

$$\frac{1}{2}\sigma^2B^2F''_E(B) + \alpha BF'_E(B) - \rho F_E(B) = 0 \qquad (2.3)$$

s.a. $F_E(0) = 0$, $F_E(B^*) = B^* - C$, $F'_E(B^*) = 1$

It is proposed the solution form: $F_E(B) = C\,B^v$, so that the characteristic equation is:

$$\frac{1}{2}\sigma^2 v(v-1) + \alpha v - \rho = 0$$

Solving the quadratic equation:

$$v_1 = \frac{1}{2} - \frac{\alpha}{\sigma^2} + \sqrt{\left[\frac{\alpha}{\sigma^2} - \frac{1}{2}\right]^2 + \frac{2\rho}{\sigma^2}} > 1 \quad ;$$

$$v_2 = \frac{1}{2} - \frac{\alpha}{\sigma^2} - \sqrt{\left[\frac{\alpha}{\sigma^2} - \frac{1}{2}\right]^2 + \frac{2\rho}{\sigma^2}} < 0$$

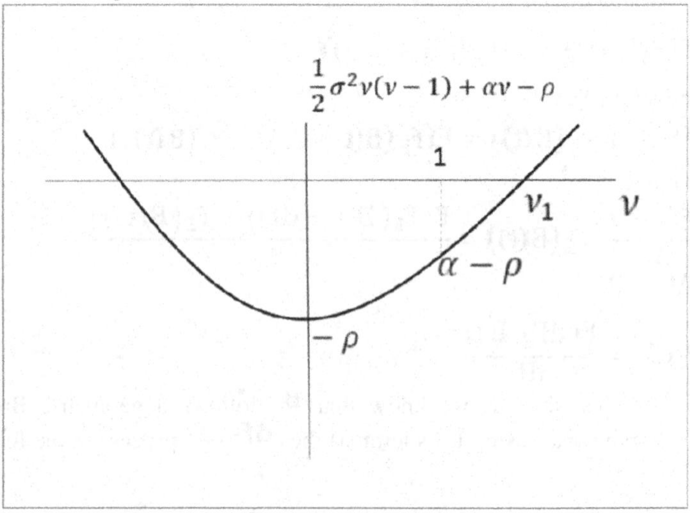

Figure 1. Quadratic solution. Source: (Dixit and Pindyck, 1994)

Summarising, the general form of the solution is $F_E(B) = D_1 \; B^{v_1} + D_2 \; B^{v_2}$. Now, the restriction $F_E(0) = 0$ establishes that the term with negative exponent cannot exist, so $D_2 = 0$.

Furthermore, the other restrictions establish that

$$B^* = \frac{v_1}{(v_1 - 1)} C \quad \text{and} \quad D_1 = \left(\frac{v_1 - 1}{C}\right)^{v_1 - 1} v_1^{-v_1}.$$

This implies that the option of waiting (if $B < B^*$) is given by:

$F_E(B) = D_1 B^{v_1}$

So greater volatility, lower v_1, and greater the critical threshold.

$$\frac{\partial v_1}{\partial \sigma} = 2\frac{\alpha}{\sigma^3} + \frac{1}{2}\left(\left[\frac{\alpha}{\sigma^2} - \frac{1}{2}\right]^2 + \frac{2\rho}{\sigma^2}\right)^{-\frac{1}{2}}\left(-4\frac{\alpha^2}{\sigma^5} + 2\frac{\alpha}{\sigma^3} - 2\frac{2\rho}{\sigma^3}\right) < 0 \Rightarrow \frac{v_1}{(v_1 - 1)} \uparrow \Rightarrow B^* \uparrow$$

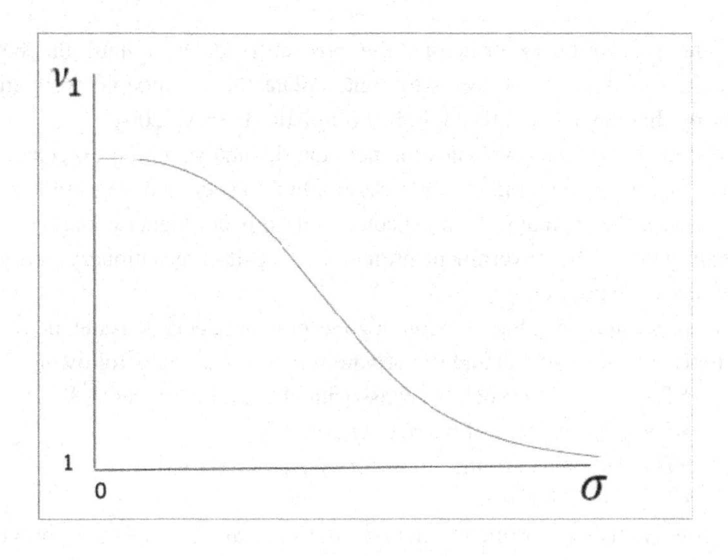

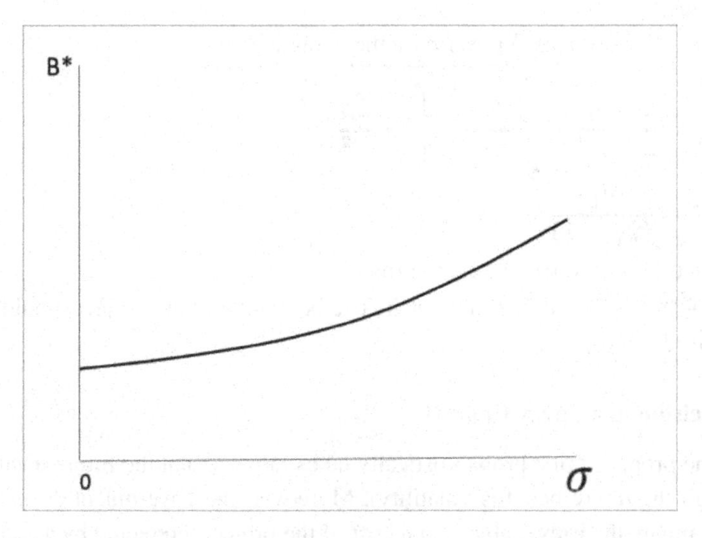

Figure 2. The root v_1 and the critical benefit (B*) according to the process volatility.

3. The Governmental Decision

The decision threshold presented in the previous section is more prudent than the traditional one (where it is only required that the present value of the net benefits should be equal to the irreversible social cost of the project) (B=C).

Using the precautionary principle, the project is delayed until the benefits exceed significantly the costs, as to contemplate the irreversible costs and the possibility that the net benefit might be optimistic (Farrow, 2004).

So, the government evaluates the net benefits analysing the expected social benefits, but also contemplating the risks implied to society due to innovation. If by the time of the evaluation, the expected benefit is not higher enough (than the irreversible cost), the government prefers to keep its precautionary option and not authorise the project.

The proposed procedure to get to a governmental decision is detailed below:

Firstly, the government and the private sector agree on the following values:

- The irreversible social cost associated with the project (C)
- The present value of the net benefit $B(0)$
- The parameters of the net benefit process (α y σ)
- The discount rate: ρ

Secondly, the government calculate the critical value (B^{*}) previously mentioned:

The calculation of v_1 based on the parameters:

$$v_1 = \frac{1}{2} - \frac{\alpha}{\sigma^2} + \sqrt{\left[\frac{\alpha}{\sigma^2} - \frac{1}{2}\right]^2 + \frac{2\rho}{\sigma^2}}$$

$$B^* = \frac{v_1}{(v_1 - 1)} C$$

So, the governmental decision rule is:

If $B(0) \leq B^*$, they should wait. The beginning of the project should not be authorised.

4. Decision in a Fuzzy Context

The proposed rule probabilistically takes into account the future uncertainty (through the future benefits volatility). Moreover, the government decision rule is to compare the irreversible social cost of the project (corrected by a factor that depends on the volatility), with the expected actual benefit (both certain values). This implies assuming that the future is the repetition of the past, without taking into account neither subjective aspects nor uncertainties in the probabilistic model.

A way to overcome this, is to incorporate the uncertainty of the future through fuzzy numbers (Dubois and Prade, 1978), so that the irreversible social cost and the expected value of the benefit can be modelled. Carlsson y Fullér

(2003) introduce a rule for real options in a fuzzy context, where the expected actual values and the costs are estimated through trapezoidal fuzzy numbers (Grzegorzewski and Mrówka, 2005, Grzegorzewski and Mrówka, 2007).

The needed decision rule should compare two fuzzy numbers to decide whether the inversion project is authorised or not. An available methodology to carry out this comparison is the concept of distance between fuzzy numbers (Cheng, 1998), revised in a recent paper by Asady(2011). In a recent work, Abbasbandy(2009) introduces diverse methodologies to make this comparison: D-distance, minimal distance, sign-distance, H-distance and Magnitude.

5. Conclusion

We live in a knowledge society where innovations are constantly motivated. While most of the time they are beneficial for society, they involve certain risks.

The present paper has developed an stochastic model that quantifies the value of waiting and proposes a government procedure for decision making. It also mathematically formalises the precautionary principle, articulating risk evaluation techniques and cost-benefit analysis in uncertain contexts. It is shown that, when the uncertainty and irreversibility of the project are contemplated, a higher threshold of net benefits is required.

References

1. S. Abbasbandy. *Ranking of fuzzy numbers, some recent and new formulas.* IFSA-EUSFLAT 2009, 642-646. (2009)
2. B. Asady. Revision of distance minimization method for ranking of fuzzy numbers. *Applied Mathematical Modelling*, **35**, 1306-1313. (2011)
3. C. Carlsson and R. Fullér. On optimal investment timing with fuzzy real options. *Fuzzy Sets and Systems*, **139,** 297–312. (2003)
4. C. H. Cheng. A new approach for ranking fuzzy numbers by distance method. *Fuzzy sets and systems*, **95**, 307-317. (1998)
5. A. K. Dixit and R. S. Pindyck. *Investment under uncertainty*, Princeton University Press Princeton, NJ. (1994)
6. D. Dubois and H. Prade. Operations on fuzzy numbers. *International Journal of Systems Science*, **9**, 613-626. (1978)
7. J. Echeverría. *Gobernanza de las nanotecnologías*. Documento de Ciencia, Tecnología y Sociedad, Instituto de Filosofía, CSIC. (2005)
8. S. Farrow. Using Risk Assessment, Benefit Cost Analysis, and Real Options to Implement a Precautionary Principle. *Risk Analysis*, **24**, 727-735. (2004)
9. P. Grzegorzewski and E. Mrówka. *Trapezoidal approximations of fuzzy numbers*. Fuzzy Sets and Systems, **153**, 115-135. (2005)

10. P. Grzegorzewski and E. Mrówka. Trapezoidal approximations of fuzzy numbers--revisited. *Fuzzy Sets and Systems*, **158**, 757-768. (2007)
11. A. Klinke, M. Dreyer, O. Renn, A. Stirling and P. Van Zwanenberg. Precautionary Risk Regulation in European Governance. *Journal of Risk Research*, **9**, 373-392. (2006)

PART 4: MANAGEMENT

AN ANALYSIS OF THE QUALITY COST IN A BUSINESS

JOSÉ M. BROTONS MARTÍNEZ,
MANUEL E. SANSALVADOR SELLES

Economic and Financial Department. Miguel Hernandez University. Avda. de la Universidad, s/n
Elche, 03202. Alicante. Tel: 034966658967. jm.brotons@umh.es.

Total Quality Cost can be classified into Quality Cost, originated from investments in prevention or evaluation, and Non Quality Cost, originated from some mistakes. The first ones can be quantified for the investment of the business, but the second ones are extremely difficult to quantify. That is why, in this paper we propose a methodology based in expert opinions, but through an indirect way, identifying the stage in which, according to Crosby's Maturity Grid, the business in question was. From this information, and from the investment effectively fulfilled, the main purpose is to get the Total Quality Cost. Finally, a fuzzy regression will help to forecast of the Quality Cost for the forthcoming years.

1. Introduction

An effective control over quality is required for surviving the present economic crisis, establishing indicators to base a strategy on and being able to quantify observed improvements. It is precisely here where the study of Quality Costs can play a fundamental role. While admitting the importance of implementing a system that provides information about the distinct components of Quality Costs, the benefits deriving from it will be diminished considerably if subsequently no detailed analysis is conducted of the information obtained.

This paper's main objective is the incorporation of the uncertainty and subjectivity involved in Quality Cost quantification to regression analysis techniques, a consequence of the existence of Hidden Quality Costs. Using a case study as research methodology, we will develop a proposal whose first aim is to make possible the acquisition, and then the analysis and prediction of reliable Quality Cost values.

First, proper treatment will be given to the implicit uncertainty in Quality Cost data using fuzzy logic, for which an original and easily applied method will be introduced. Data analysis will follow this using both linear and possibilistic regression. This will facilitate the comparison between both types and demonstrate the suitability of fuzzy regressions for analyzing Quality Costs.

The application of fuzzy set theory is a suitable approach in cases where uncertainty is due to incompleteness or imprecision. In this way, Zebda (1984) and Korvin, Strawser and Siegel (1995) have applied fuzzy logic in cost-benefit analysis researching deviations; Kaufmann (1984) did so in zero-based budgeting; Tanaka, Okuda and Asai (1976) employ this instrument to resolve capital budgeting problems; Chan and Yuan (1990) apply this methodology in their cost-volume-profit analysis to assist the accountant facing uncertainty and risk; Mansur (1995) uses this to assess opportunity costs, and there are even application precedents of fuzzy logic toward Quality Costs (Gutierrez and Carmona, 1995); Sansalvador, Cavero and Reig, 2004, 2008) although dealing with work centered on the quantification of specific elements of the cost and not their posterior analysis.

Before furthering the proposal made, there should be a brief go around the conceptual foundations of fuzzy mathematics where the techniques subsequently applied to it are based.

2. Fuzzy concepts

A fuzzy set of a set *X* is defined by a membership function $\mu(x)$ that takes for each value of x a membership value in the range $[0,1]$. A fuzzy set of R is called a fuzzy number if the membership function $\mu(x)$ is convex and normalized. A trapezoidal fuzzy number can be defined by its support and its kernel bounds $A=(K_A,R_A)=\left(\left[K_A^-,K_A^+\right],\left[S_A^-,S_A^+\right]\right)$, Where, support: $S_A=\left[S_A^-,S_A^+\right]$, Kernel: $K_A=\left[K_A^-,K_A^+\right]$. The α-cut of a trapezoidal fuzzy number (TrFN) is defined as $[A]_\alpha=\left[\left(A^-\right)_\alpha,\left(A^+\right)_\alpha\right]$, $\left(A^-\right)_\alpha=\inf\left\{x/\mu(x)\geq\alpha;x\geq S_A^-\right\}$, $\left(A^+\right)_\alpha=\inf\left\{x/\mu(x)\geq\alpha;x\geq S_A^+\right\}$ A Triangular Fuzzy Number, TFN, $\left(K_A,S_A^-,S_A^+\right)$ is a particular case of a trapezoidal fuzzy number, where $K_A^-=K_A^+=K_A$

Desfuzzificación. According to the fuzzy mean method, the crisp value A representative of the fuzzy number $\tilde{A}$, is obtained as average fuzzy mean of the values of the support of $\tilde{A}$, $x\in sop\left(\tilde{A}\right)$ for its membership function $\mu_{\tilde{A}}(x)$:

$$A = \frac{\int_{Sop(\tilde{A})} x \cdot \mu_{\tilde{A}}(x)dx}{\int_{Sop(\tilde{A})} \mu_{\tilde{A}}(x)dx} \tag{1}$$

Trapezoidal fuzzy regression. Let us consider a set of N observed data samples defined on an interval $D = [x_{\min}, x_{\max}]$. Let the jth simple be represented by the couple (x_j, Y_j), $j = 1 \ldots N$, where x_j are crisp and Y_j are the corresponding fuzzy output. The objective is to determine a predicted functional relationship

$$Y(x) = A_0 \oplus A_1.x \tag{2}$$

Defined on the domain D. The parameters A_0 and A_1 are triangular fuzzy coefficients. As a result, the output is fuzzy, as well. In order to identify the parameters A_0 and A_1, it must be imposed that all the observed data are included in the predicted ones for any α-cut. As the output of the model is a trapezoidal fuzzy number, two constraints must be taken into consideration in order to guarantee the total inclusion of the data in the predicted one for each level α:

$$[Y_j]_{\alpha=0} \subseteq [\hat{Y}_j]_{\alpha=0}, \text{ and } [Y_j]_{\alpha=1} \subseteq [\hat{Y}_j]_{\alpha=1} \tag{3}$$

The output model tendencies are not taken into account in the conventional method. In order to solve this problem, Bisserier et al.(2008) propose a modified model expression in which the model output can have any kind of spread variation for any sign of x by introducing a shift on the original model input.

$$Y(x) = A_0 \oplus A_1(x - shift) \tag{4}$$

When the model has an increasing radius, $shift = x_{\min}$ will be taken, and $shift = x_{\max}$ will be taken in the contrary, if the model has a decreasing radius. Denoting $w_j = x_j - shift$, the output of the fuzzy model is a trapezoidal interval given by:

$$\forall w \in D: \begin{cases} K_{\hat{Y}}^- = K_{A_0}^- + \left(M(K_{A_1}) - R(K_{A_1}).\Delta\right)w \\ K_{\hat{Y}}^+ = K_{A_0}^+ + \left(M(K_{A_1}) + R(K_{A_1}).\Delta\right)w \\ S_{\hat{Y}}^- = S_{A_0}^- + \left(M(S_{A_1}) - R(S_{A_1}).\Delta\right)w \\ S_{\hat{Y}}^+ = S_{A_0}^+ + \left(M(S_{A_1}) + R(S_{A_1}).\Delta\right)w \end{cases} \tag{5}$$

where $\Delta = sign(w_{\min} + w_{\max})$, and M() is the mid point and R() is the radius (for example, $M\left(K_{A_1}\right) = \left(K_{A_1}^- + K_{A_1}^+\right)/2$ and $R\left(K_{A_1}\right) = \left(K_{A_1}^- - K_{A_1}^+\right)/2$,

and the output spread is given by $R\left(\left[S_{\hat{Y}_j}\right]\right) = R([A_0]) + R([A_1])w_j$

The optimization program (Bisserier et al., 2008):

$$\min \quad (w_{\max} - w_{\min})\left(R\left(K_{A_0}\right) + R\left(S_{A_0}\right)\right) + \frac{1}{2}\left(w_{\max}^2 - w_{\min}^2\right)\left(R\left(K_{A_1}\right) + R\left(S_{A_1}\right)\right)\Delta \quad (6)$$

$$\text{For } \alpha = 1,\ K_{Y_j} \in \left[K_{\hat{Y}_j}^-, K_{\hat{Y}_j}^+\right] \Leftrightarrow \left|M\left(K_{\hat{Y}_j}\right) - K_{Y_j}\right| \leq R\left(K_{\hat{Y}_j}\right) \quad (7)$$

$$\text{For } \alpha = 0,\ \left[K_{Y_j} - R_{Y_j}, K_{Y_j} + R_{Y_j}\right] \subseteq \left[S_{Y_j}^-, S_{Y_j}^+\right] \Leftrightarrow \left|M\left(S_{\hat{Y}_j}\right) - K_{Y_j}\right| \leq R\left(S_{\hat{Y}_j}\right) - R_{Y_j} \quad (8)$$

The inclusion de the kernel into the support:

$$\left[K_{\hat{Y}_j}^-, K_{\hat{Y}_j}^+\right] \subseteq \left[S_{\hat{Y}_j}^-, S_{\hat{Y}_j}^+\right] \Leftrightarrow \left|M\left(S_{\hat{Y}_j}\right) - M\left(K_{\hat{Y}_j}\right)\right| \leq \left|R\left(S_{\hat{Y}_j}\right) - R\left(K_{\hat{Y}_j}\right)\right| \quad (9)$$

Where

$$M\left(K_{\hat{Y}_j}\right) = M\left(K_{A_0}\right) + M\left(K_{A_1}\right)w_j$$

$$R\left(K_{\hat{Y}_j}\right) = R\left(K_{A_0}\right) + R\left(K_{A_1}\right)w_j\Delta$$

$$M\left(S_{\hat{Y}_j}\right) = M\left(S_{A_0}\right) + M\left(S_{A_1}\right)w_j$$

$$R\left(S_{\hat{Y}_j}\right) = R\left(S_{A_0}\right) + R\left(S_{A_1}\right)w_j\Delta$$

3. Development of the proposed model

3.1. *Introduction to the cases studied*

In order to analyze the validity of our proposed, we asked for the collaboration of a Spanish footwear manufacturer that has implemented a quality cost system since 2004. The company is situated in the southeast of Spain, where is focused more than 65% of national production and almost two thirds of enterprises and workers in the footwear industry in the country.This footwear manufacturer, whose turnover during the study period oscillate between 9 million euro during 2004 tax year and the 5,5 million euro during 2009, can be considered an average sized company in the context of the characteristics of this sector in Spain.

Table 1 shows the results provided by the company about the Quality Cost calculated from the moment the company began quantifying it in 2004 until 2009. To compare figures from distinct periods, certain homogeneity in the values is required. Due to its simplicity, net sales are the comparison basis used most between businesses.

Table 1. Quality Costs (% of sales)

Year	Quality Costs (% sales)
2004	4.57
2005	4.89
2006	6.43
2007	7.32
2008	7.02
2009	5.50

3.2. *Acquisition of the fuzzy number capable of synthesizing the information about the quality costs*

The uncertainty and subjectivity inherent in the process of estimating various Quality Cost components advise treating them properly. In this regard, fuzzy logic is an especially appropriate tool, as it allows processing the information present, and not in specific terms, but instead by incorporating the existing ambiguity and uncertainty into the model. The problem facing us is on the one hand, seeking a simple and easy method for businesses themselves to implement, whose cost for obtaining the information is not burdensome. And on the other hand, we must be mindful that the degree of accuracy of the estimated values will depend upon data availability as well as the calculation processes utilized in each case, which logically will be different for each business.

Calculated Costs are defined as the Quality Costs initially quantified by businesses. For their part, Achievable Costs will be defined as the Quality Costs that may actually occur in the businesses because of the existence of the intangible component not considered in the first estimations made. It is precisely the acquisition of the Achievable Costs, and consequently the determination of the fuzzy number that best synthesizes the information about the Quality Cost, which is the objective of the methodology proposed in this section. This methodology can be followed in Terceño et al. (2009), and Brotons and Terceño (2010).

Studying Quality Cost behavior in organizations is an important reference in the figure of Crosby. This author, through his Quality Management Maturity Grid, analyzes the evolution of such costs in relation to the development of quality management by simply observing the attitude of the organization's human component about quality management (Crosby, 1979).

According to Crosby, businesses found at the first stage, Uncertainty, do not make any Quality Cost estimations. In the Awakening stage, they are only capable of quantifying one-sixth of the Quality Costs. As the business strengthens its quality functions and advances along the maturity grid stages, it perfects the Quality Cost quantification system, and so the values reported become ever nearer to those real (Crosby, 1979).

Five experts, including the person responsible for quality and its manager, were requested to assess the stage where the analyzed business found itself on Crosby's maturity grid. They were asked to consider the level the business belonged to each of Crosby's proposed stages, depending upon their degree of agreement or disagreement using a scale of six elements, 1 (totally disagree), 2 (strongly disagree), 3 (disagree), 4 (neutral), 5 (true) and 6 (very true). Specifically, those surveyed were asked to evaluate for six consecutive years (2004 to 2009) whether the business in question was found at the stage awakening (A_2), enlightenment (A_3), Wisdom (A_4) or Certainty (A_5).

The Grid's first stage (Uncertainty) was not considered because Quality Cost estimations are not made from there. The respondent's position for each proposition, which is uncertain, is considered a fuzzy subset, and the six possible values the respondent may take is what we will call referential. Thus, we can speak of a level of membership. In short, this attempts to overcome the problems of measuring the different alternatives for each situation.

Table 2. Survey results and acquisition of the business's membership function for each year at each of Crosby's Maturity Grid stages. A_2-A_5 represent the four stages considered, and numbers 1-6 are the linguistic labels considered; μ is the membership function.

2004	1	2	3	4	5	6	μ
A_2				2	2	1	0.76
A_3	1	3	1				0.20
A_4	5						0.00
A_5	5						0.00

2005	1	2	3	4	5	6	μ
A_2			1	3	1		0.60
A_3		1	3	1			0.40
A_4	5						0.00
A_5	5						0.00

2006	1	2	3	4	5	6	μ
A_2		2	3				0.32
A_3				1	3	1	0.80
A_4	2	3					0.12
A_5	5						0.00

2007	1	2	3	4	5	6	μ
A_2	3	2					0.08
A_3				1	2	2	0.84
A_4	1	4					0.16
A_5	5						0.00

2008	1	2	3	4	5	6	μ
A_2	3	2					0.08
A_3					2	3	0.92
A_4	1	3	1				0.20
A_5	5						0.00

2009	1	2	3	4	5	6	μ
A_2	3	2					0.08
A_3					3	2	0.88
A_4	1	3	1				0.20
A_5	5						0.00

Table 2 shows the results obtained by the survey and the membership function value for each of the four stages in question over the six-year study period. The membership function is obtained by multiplying the values assigned to each linguistic label (0.00, totally disagree, …, 1.00 very true) by the number of experts choosing that linguistic label, then dividing by the total number of experts who answered.

In accordance with Crosby, the business calculates some costs in each stage that are inferior to what it actually incurs. Table 3 shows the acquisition of what we call Crosby's Corrector Coefficient, obtained as a quotient between the Achievable Costs according to Crosby, and the Calculated Costs in each stage. In this manner, a business found in stage 2 (Awakening) will obtain the Achievable Costs by multiplying the Calculated Costs by 6; if it is found in the Enlightenment stage, the Achievable Costs will be obtained multiplying the Calculated Costs by 1.5, and like that successively.

Table 3. Obtaining Crosby's Corrector Coefficient for the distinct Maturity Grid stages.

STAGE	*(A) Calculated Costs according to Crosby (% sales)*	(B) Achievable Costs according to Crosby (% sales)	(C = B / A) Crosby's Corrector Coefficient
2. Awakening	3	18	6.00
3. Enlightenment	8	12	1.50
4. Wisdom	6.5	8	1.23
5. Certainty	2.5	2.5	1.00

However, just as Table 2 reflects, every year the experts assess the business's degree of membership in each Maturity Grid stage. Therefore, for example 2004, the business belongs to stage 2 (Awakening) with a degree of membership of 0.76 and to stage 3 (Enlightenment) with a degree of membership of 0.20. Table 4 shows the process for obtaining the weighting factor for 2004 that, by beginning with the business's initial Calculated Costs, will allow approximating the Achievable Costs depending upon their degree of membership in each stage of Crosby's Maturity Grid.

Table 4. Obtaining the weighting factor for 2004

STAGE	Crosby's Corrector Coefficient (C)	Membership function (D)	$E = C\frac{D}{\sum D}$
2. Awakening	6.0	0.76	4.75
3. Enlightenment	1.5	0.20	0.31
4. Wisdom	1.2	0.00	0.00
5. Certainty	1.0	0.00	0.00
		Total: 0.96	Weighting factor: 5.06

As Table 4 outlines, the weighting factor is obtained by multiplying Crosby's Corrector Coefficient by the quotient between the corresponding membership function and the sum of all membership functions for that business and year for all stages.

The Achievable Cost will be the result of the product of the business's Calculated Cost multiplied by the Weighting Factor for each year. The result for all years analyzed are shown in Table 5.

Table 5. Calculation of the Achievable and Average costs for the business analyzed between 2004 and 2009.

Year	Calculated Costs	Weighting Factor	Achievable Costs	Average Costs
2004	4.57	5.06	23.14	10.76
2005	4.89	4.20	20.54	10.11
2006	6.43	2.64	16.94	9.93
2007	7.32	1.79	13.13	9.26
2008	7.02	1.76	12.32	8.79
2009	5.50	1.76	9.70	6.90

Table 5 shows that every year, the Quality Costs reach a minimum in the values of the Calculated Costs column and a maximum in the Achievable Costs column. The business incurs the Calculated Costs as a minimum, with a 100% probability, but the existence of the so-called Hidden Quality Costs will make the business's Quality Costs oscillate between that value (4.57% of net sales for 2004) and the maximum value (the so-called Achievable Costs, which in 2004 were 23.14%).

The Calculated and Achievable costs could be considered fuzzy numbers whose membership function is maximum for the Calculated Cost (4.57 in 2004) and decreases in superior values until reaching a value of zero for the so-called Achievable Cost (23.14 in 2004). Therefore, in 2004, the Quality Costs were as a minimum 4.57% of sales, but the presence of Hidden Quality Costs can give it superior values, able to reach 23.14% of sales.

To summarize, all the information contained in the fuzzy number ([4.57, 23.14] in 2004) can be synthesized in a central value we call Average Cost. This is obtained by defuzzifying such number in accordance with Expression (1) from the fuzzy concepts section, and provides timely information far more exact about the Quality Cost than does the value initially calculated by the business. As a result, for 2004 a value of 10.76 is obtained, which is found between the lower (Calculated Costs) and the superior (Achievable costs) extremes, summarizing all the preceding information. The estimation for the remaining years can be observed in Figure 2.

3.3. *Regression Analysis: Quality Cost Prediction*

At this point, we propose making the Quality Cost prediction for 2010, starting with the information available for the 2004-2009 period. First, we will proceed to carry out linear regression with the data calculated by the business. However, we must be aware of the limitations in this type of analysis, as it only contemplates a portion of the information (a problem that is extendable to any other type of statistical regression).

We will proceed by conducting linear regression between the Quality Costs as quantified by the business and the time. This is the most common form of expressing the relationship between two variables. To do this, from the information available for 2004-2009, the following simple linear regression model is proposed:

$$Q_t = \alpha + \beta \cdot year_t + e_t \tag{10}$$

Q_t indicates the Quality Costs obtained by the business for year t, $year_t$ is the year being measured (2004 to 2009), α and β are the parameters being estimated, and e_t is the error committed. The result of this estimation is $\alpha = -677.975$ with $\beta = 0.341$, with a p-value for the independent term of 0.25; 0.248 is the coefficient of the year, and so it can be concluded that the coefficients are not significant. Moreover, the adjusted $R^2 = 0.142$ indicates that the linear relationship between the evolution of time and the Quality Costs is very weak, and so because of this, the model is not adequate to explain the evolution of Quality Costs.

In light of the results, we will propose the use of a possibilistic regression, introduced by Tanaka et al. (1982, 1989, 1991). Tanaka and Ishibuchi propose the use of quadratic membership functions to estimate the parameters, due to the problem that the spread of the output increases around a central point. In this way, Bisserier et al. (2010) propose a tendency problem solution introducing the shift term.

Consequently, Quality Costs are considered fuzzy numbers having a minimum in the Calculated Cost and a maximum in the Achievable Cost values, with a maximum presumption level in the Average Costs. In this regard, possibilistic regression with trapezoidal fuzzy coefficients 1) allows each year's estimation to not only be a concrete value, but moreover an interval and central point, values representative of the business's Quality Costs fuzzy number; 2) the use of trapezoidal fuzzy numbers (TrFN) ensures the inclusion of the observed costs (Calculated, Average and Achievable) in the predicted costs by the regression model for any significance level (Bisserier et al., 2010), 3) the type of model utilized adequately incorporates the trend evolution of the difference between Calculated and Achievable costs. This difference annually decreases accordingly as the business advances along Crosby's Maturity Grid, and therefore, improves the quality measurement systems.

Because of this, the following possibilistic regression model is proposed that is based on the use of trapezoidal fuzzy coefficients to estimate Quality Costs:

$$\tilde{Q}_t = \tilde{A}_0 + \tilde{A}_1 \cdot (Year_t - shift) \tag{11}$$

$\tilde{Q}_t$ is the TrFN representative of the Quality Costs, $Year_t$ is the year (2004 to 2009), and *shift* is the maximum or minimum of years that minimizes Besserier's objective function (in this case, the maximum value, 2009). As Figure 2 shows, the interval's amplitude between the Achievable and Calculated costs diminishes, by which the introduction of the shift term allows the amplitude of the estimation to do likewise. The coefficients $\tilde{A}_0 = \left[[6.90, 8.02], [5.50, 9.70]\right]$ and $\tilde{A}_1 = \left[[-0.77, -0.77], [-2.71, 0.19]\right]$ have been estimated in accordance with expressions (6) to (9). Applying the preceding coefficients allows obtaining the prediction for all the study's object years. Particularly, for 2004, the result obtained (Figure 1) is $\tilde{Q} = \left[[10.76, 11.87], [4.57, 23.25]\right]$, i.e., the Average Cost must be between the values of maximum possibility prediction in the regression (10.76 and 11.87). For their part, the business's Calculated Costs (4.57) must be superior to the minimum value obtained in the regression (lower extreme, 4.57), and the business's Achievable Costs (23.14) must be inferior to the maximum value obtained by the regression (superior extreme, 23.25).

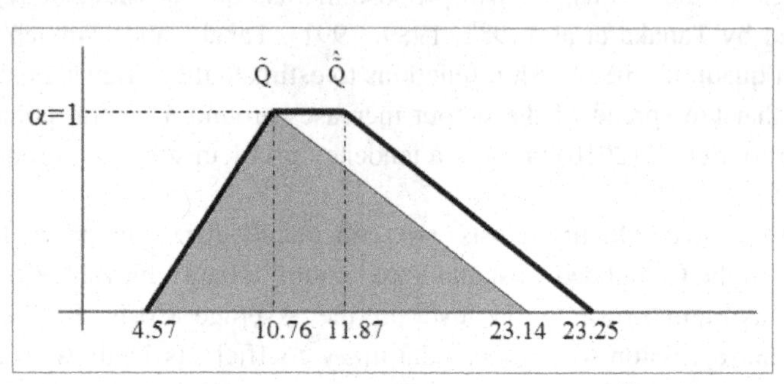

Figure 1. Observed ($\tilde{Q}$, gray area) and estimated costs ($\hat{\tilde{Q}}$) for 2004

Figure 1 shows the estimated cost by regression model $\hat{\tilde{Q}} = \left[[10.76, 11.87], [4.57, 23.25]\right]$ and the observed cost (gray area) $\tilde{Q} = \left[[10.76, 10.76], [4.57, 23.14]\right]$. The results for the remaining years (2004-2009) are shown in Figure 2.

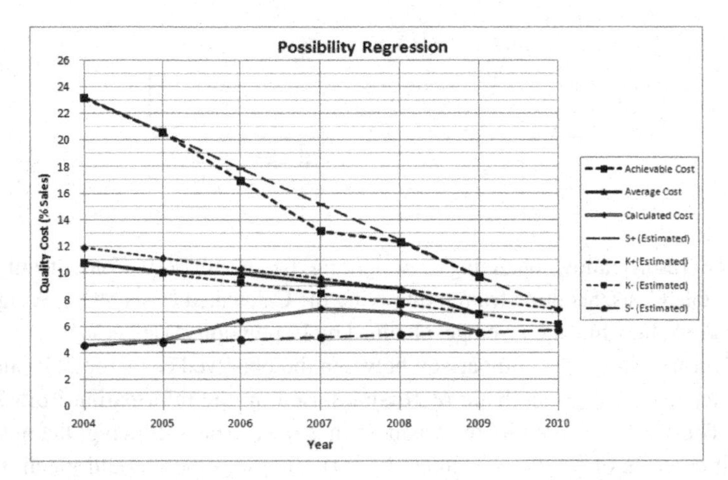

Figure 2. Evolution of the costs estimated by the possibilistic model from 2004 until 2010 and of the Observed Costs up to 2009.

Figure 2 shows, among other things, the evolution of the Calculated, Achievable and Average costs. The differential between the Calculated and Achievable costs diminishes over time, and therefore the shift term introduced in the prediction has been of great help. The latter is represented, on the one hand, by the exterior extremes [S-(Estimated), S+(Estimated)], which as shown, include the Calculated and Achievable costs at all times; on the other hand, the interior extremes [K-(Estimated), K+(Estimated)] include the Average Cost all years. The prediction for 2010 indicates that the Calculated Costs will be 5.69% of sales, with the Achievables as much as 7.24%. Moreover, the Average Costs must be between 6.13 and 7.24% of sales.

3.4. *Validation*

Starting from the business's Calculated Costs, in this section we intend to acquire the Achievable and Average costs in order to validate the prediction made in the preceding section. To do this, the experts were asked to assess the stage of Crosby's Maturity Grid the business was found to be in for 2010 in the same manner as they did for 2004-2009. The results and membership function for each stage, obtained in accordance with the linguistic labels explained previously, are shown in Table 6.

Table 6. Results 2010.

	2010						
	1	2	3	4	5	6	μ
A_2	4	1					0,04
A_3					3	2	0,88
A_4	1	2	2				0,24
A_5	5						0,00

The results allow obtaining a weighting factor of 1.60. Consequently, the Achievable Costs, resulting from multiplying the Calculated Costs by the Weighting Factor are 8.48, while the Average, obtained by Expression (1) are 6.36.

Figure 3 shows the comparison between the observed costs for 2010 and the estimated costs by possibilistic regression based on the information from 2004-2009. The costs observed by the business in 2010 are the following: the business quantifies costs of 5.30% (Calculated Cost), although these could reach 8.48% of sales (Achievable Cost). This latter result was obtained through the proper treatment of the opinions provided by the aforementioned experts.

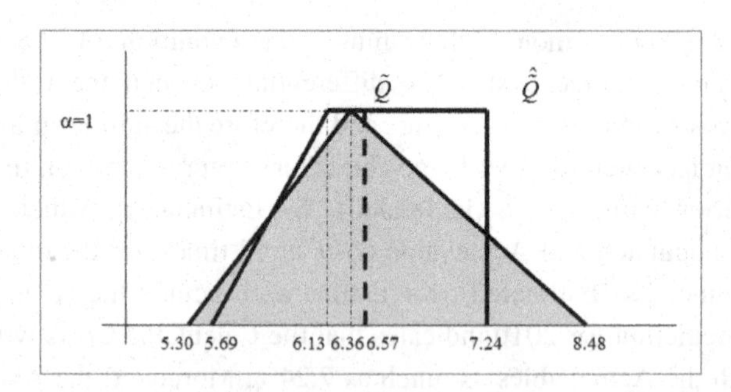

Figure 3. Comparison of the costs observed by the business (shaded portion) and the costs estimated by possibilistic regression ($\hat{\tilde{Q}}$) for 2010.

Possibilistic estimation by trapezoidal fuzzy numbers ensures, for the calculated period (2004-2009), the inclusion of all Calculated Costs by the business and the Achievables in the estimated exterior intervals, as well as all the Average Costs in the estimated interior intervals. For its part, the 2010 Quality Cost prediction offers an estimated central interval (6.13, 7.24) that includes the observed Average Cost (6.36) and an external interval (5.69, 7.24) that includes the Calculated Costs (5.30) and the Achievable Costs (8.48) in an important part, which shows this is an excellent estimation.

4. Conclusions

One of the main problems with Quality Cost estimation in businesses is the existence of certain elements that are called Hidden Quality Costs, whose quantification is at best uncertain and subjective. That is why, first, a unique tool has been developed, based on the position each business occupies on Crosby's famed Quality Management Maturity Grid, which allows transforming a business's calculated Quality Costs into fuzzy numbers. Just one of this work's most noteworthy contributions enables the introduction of fuzzy logic and the concept of possibility in Quality Cost quantification in a simple and affordable manner for any business.

These concepts come closer to natural reason in situations of uncertainty better than does the concept of probability, which is too rigid, in addition to offering a series of instruments that improve the transmission and interpretation of information, like for example fuzzy numbers. Possibilistic regression allows proper treatment of information. On the one hand, it provides an interval within which the costs initially quantified by the business (Calculated Costs), as well as those that can actually be achieved (Achievable Costs), must both be found. On the other hand, it supplies the interval within which the Average Costs are expected to be, a reduction in specific terms of all the preceding information being possible where appropriate. Therefore, the advantage of this methodology with respect to probabilistic estimation is evident. Lastly, given that uncertainty (measured as the difference between the Calculated and Achievable costs) is reduced over time as the business advances in its quality management and measurement, the proposed model, with the inclusion of the shift term, can adapt to this circumstance, reducing the amplitude of the estimated interval every year.

To end, it was thought suitable to proceed with the validation of the estimations made by the possibilistic model (the scarce significance of the simple linear regression model directly discourages its use). The comparison between the predictions made by the model for 2010 and the values observed that year, in accordance with the methodology introduced in the first part of this work, demonstrates the estimations' high reliability. Therefore, the estimation's central interval includes all Average Costs, and its external intervals also include the business's Calculated Costs as well as the Achievable Costs in a sufficiently high percentage; so from this, the validity of the possibilistic regression model emerges for analyzing both the evolution of Quality Costs over time as well as for making predictions of them for future periods.

5. References

1. BISSERIER, A. R. BOUKEZZOULA AND S. GALICHET (2010). "Linear Fuzzy Regression Using Trapezoidal Fuzzy Intervals". *Journal of Uncertain Systems,* Vol.4, No.1, p.59-72.

2. Brotons, JM, Terceño, A. (2010). “A Risk Premium In The Spanish Market: An Empirical Study”. *Economic Computation And Economic Cybernetics Studies And Research,* Vol: 44, No. 1, p. 81-99.
3. Crosby, P. (1979). *Quality is free: The Art of Making Quality Certain,* New York, Penguin Books.
4. Chan, Y.; Yuan, Y. (1990). “Dearling with fuzziness in Cost-Volume-Profit analysis”, *Accounting & Business Research, Vol.* 78, p. 83 – 95.
5. Gutierrez, I.; Carmona, S. (1995). “Ambiguity in Multicriteria Quality Decisions”. *International Journal of Production Economics*, September, p. 25- 38.
6. Kaufmann, A. (1984). “Fuzzy set Zero-Based Budgenting”. *TIMS/Studies in Management Sciences,* No 20, 489 – 494.
7. Korvin, A.; Strawer, J.; Siegel, P. (1995). “An application of control system to cost variance anlysis”, *Managerial Finance*, No. 21, p. 17 – 38.
8. Mansur, Y. (1995). *Fuzzy sets and economics: Applications of fuzzy mathematics to non-cooperative oligopoly,* London, Ed. Edward Elgar Publishing.
9. Sansalvador, M.; Cavero, J.; Reig, J. (2004). “Los costes intangibles de la calidad: propuesta metodológica de cuantificación”. *Revista Española de Financiación y Contabilidad,* No.122, 741-772.
10. Sansalvador, M.; Cavero, J.; Reig, J. (2008). “Development of a Quantification Proposal for hidden quality costs: applied to the construction sector”, *Journal of Construction Engineering and Managament,* Vol. 134, No. 10, 749 – 758.
11. Tanaka H. and Ishibuchi, H. (1991). “Identification of possibilistic linear systems by quadratic membership functions of fuzzy parameters”. *Fuzzy Sets and Systems,* Vol. 41, p. 145-160.
12. Tanaka, H.; Okuda, T.; Asai, K. (1976). “A foundation of fuzzy decision problems and its aplication to an investment problems”, *Kybernetes*, No. 5, 25 – 30.
13. Tanaka, H.Uejima, S. Asai, K. (1982). “Linear regression analysis with fuzzy model”, *IEEE, Systems, Trans. Systems Man Cybernet. SMC*-2: 903-907.
14. Tanaka,H.Hayashi, I. Watada, J. (1989). “Possibilistic linear regression analysis for fuzzy data”. *European Journal of Operational Research,* Vol. 40, p. 389-396.
15. Terceno-Gomez A, Brotons-Martinez JM, Trigueros-Pina, JA., (2009). “Assessment of water needs in Spain”. *Ingenieria Hidraulica En Mexico*, Vol. 24 No. 4, p.7-22.
16. Zebda, A. (1984). “The investigation of cost variances: a fuzzy sets theory approach”, *Decision Sciencies*, Vol. 15, p. 359 – 388

ENVIRONMENTAL PERFORMANCE MEASUREMENT IN AGRI-FOOD COMPANIES USING FUZZY INFERENCE SYSTEM

ELENA ESCRIG-OLMEDO*
MARÍA JESÚS MUÑOZ-TORRES
JUANA MARÍA RIVERA-LIRIO
MARÍA ÁNGELES FERNÁNDEZ-IZQUIERDO

Department of Finance and Accounting, Universiat Jaume I,
Campus del Riu Sec - Avda. Vicent Sos Baynat s/n, Castellón, 12071, Spain

Sustainability ratings agencies evaluate companies in economic, social, environmental and corporate governance terms. However, some of these scores are associated with problems of how positive and negative assessments are offset. This study contributes to research on the evaluation of the performance in organizations using Fuzzy Inference Systems. The proposed methodology will be applied to measure the environmental performance in agri-food companies. After determining the criteria to evaluate the environmental performance in agri-food companies, Fuzzy Inference Systems methodology is applied to a sample of European, North American, and Australasian agri-food companies.

1. Introduction

In the Brundtland Report [1] the concept of sustainable development is built on three basic pillars: economic prosperity, social equity and environmental protection. However, there is no single concept of sustainability and there is no commonly accepted method of measuring it [2, 3].

The Commission of the European Communities has started its consultation process on their future 2020 strategy. This new approach for the European Union [4] is based on *"a new sustainable social market economy, a smarter greener economy, where our prosperity will come from innovation and from using resources better, and where the key input will be knowledge."*

Currently, civil society and media request companies to consider the social and environmental impacts of their activities and to provide more information with respect to their actions [5]. In that sense, sustainability rating agencies

*Corresponding author: eescrig@cofin.uji.es, Phone number + 34 964 387 145 and Fax: +34 964 728 565.

study businesses and make evaluations in social, environmental and corporate governance terms – using their own research methodologies. However, the scoring modes employed by the rating agencies to evaluate the social and environmental performance are associated with problems of how positive and negative assessments are offset [6]: "*Work included under the term 'triple bottom line' involves keeping balanced scorecards in the areas analysed under the focus of sustainability, so that good results in some of the indicators or domains cannot hide the absence or inadequacy of policies or processes in other areas. In these sense, the offsetting effect is unwanted when high scores in one domain may have on very low scores in another domain because under our assumptions a firm is socially responsible when there is a balance between the analysed domains*".

For this reason, the first objective of this paper is to evaluate the performance in organizations by means of Fuzzy Inference System methodology, in order to correct one of the main weaknesses of methodologies based on scores aggregation -that is the possible offsetting of negative scores with good scores- and introduce the role of the investor and decision-maker in the assessment. The proposed method will be tested to measure the environmental performance in agri-food companies.

In the last years, quality and safety of raw and processed food production is becoming increasingly important both in terms of human health and competition [7]. Concerns about the environmental impact and social consequences of food production and consumption have grown as well, making people more interested in the way in which their food is produced [8]. Moreover, citizens have come to expect high levels of food safety, and the European institutions have adopted specific policies to ensure control over food production and to promote food quality [9]. On the other hand, reduction in environmental emissions, adoption of green technology, disposition of harmful wastes, products and practices are among the objectives of several organizations [10]. In order to obtain this, food standards are increasingly important in global markets [11].

In this context, the second objective of this research is to analyse the environmental sustainability in the agri-food industry in Europe, North America and Australasia through the generation of a sector rating.

This paper is structured as follows: the introduction is followed by a brief analysis of agri-food industry and its environmental implications. Subsequently, we analyse the main characteristics of the methodology used and explain the design of the study. After the presentation of the results obtained, the main conclusions are provided in the final section.

2. Theoretical background

2.1. *Agri-food industry and environment*

Following Global Industry Classification Standard (GICS) - that is an industry taxonomy developed by MSCI and Standard & Poor's- the food processing industry covers different subsectors quite different among then, such as food and staples retailing or food, beverage and tobacco.

Agri-food sector is highly dependent on natural resources and produces different impacts on the environment [12, 13, 14]. During the last years, this sector has been studied in detail by academic researchers due to the importance of the environmental impact of food production, processing and distribution and the food safety and quality aspect or animal welfare issues [13].

The OECD recently concluded that world population growth is expected to average 1.1% per annum to 2019. Based on commodities [a], analysed in OECD-FAO Agricultural Outlook 2010-2019 [15], China may grow significantly by 26% to 2019, when compared to the 2007-09 base period. While Australia is projected to grow some 17%, United Stated and Canada is projected in the 10-15% range over the same period. In contrast, in this period, net agricultural output in the European Union -27 will have grown less than 4%. Bearing in mind this, it is necessary a sustainable agri-food sector. In this sense, SustainAbility Organization defines a sustainable food system as "*one that is reliable, resilient and transparent, which produces food within ecological limits, empowers food producers, and ensures accessible, nutritious food for all*".

2.2. *Sustainability rating agencies*

Specialised rating agencies have appeared developing new rating typologies in response to changing attitudes towards responsible behaviour, and global stock markets have introduced indices to measure sustainability performance. These ratings study companies according to economic, social, environmental, and corporate governance indicators. In this context, environmental sustainability indices have proliferated quickly in recent years responding to the demands of society and financial markets. Some of the most important environmental sustainability indices in the global market are: MSCI ESG 'Environmental' Indices that reflect specific environmental themes, such as renewable energy or clean technology; FTSE4Good Environmental Leaders Europe 40 Index which

[a] The OECD perspective of multifunctionality is of an agriculture that jointly produces a range of commodity outputs (foods, fibres, energy crops etc.) and also a range of non-commodity outputs, including public goods, in particular environmental and social products and services.

is designed to identify European companies with leading environmental practices or FTSE CDP Carbon Strategy Index Series that aims to support investors in incorporating climate change risks into their investment strategy.

In general terms, the final overall rating is the result of adding the scores in each of the key domains or indicators but this overall rating has several limitations: first, higher scores for one domain may hide very low scores in another domain; second, the balance is not reflected between the various aspects of management necessary for a firm to be listed as socially responsible; and third, the varying assessments that different stakeholders may give to each criterion are not included.

2.3. *Fuzzy inference system*

The multi-dimensionality aspect of corporate social and environmental performance makes difficult the task of choosing the sustainable companies. In order to avoid an information loss problem the multi-criteria methods have been the most applied methodologies for the weighting and aggregation of multidimensional information. Several techniques has been applied to aggregate indicators in order to generate synthetic indicators: factor analysis, including a dynamic factor analysis extension [16]; P2-distance analysis [17, 18]; Data Envelopment Analysis [19]; meta-analysis program [20]; the Analytic Hierarchy Process [21, 22]; or Fuzzy Inference [23, 24].

Fuzzy logic theory is a large theory that includes fuzzy set theory, fuzzy measure, etc. It is a sort of non dichotomic logic which tries to quantify the uncertainty frequently related to phenomena. This quantification admits different degrees of truth whereas dichotomic logic only considers two possibilities: true or false. Based on fuzzy logic theory, it has been developed the Fuzzy Set Theory [25].

According to Zadeh [25] a fuzzy set is defined as a 'class' with a continuum of grades of membership. A fuzzy subset A of a universal set is defined by a membership function $fA(x)$ which associates each element into a real number in the interval (0, 1). The Fuzzy Inference System, known also as 'fuzzy-rule-based system', 'fuzzy expert system' or 'fuzzy model', is a popular methodology for implementing fuzzy logic [26]. The fuzzy-rule-base or Fuzzy Inference System consists of fuzzy "if–then" (also called "Antecedent–Consequence") rules which are generated based on the concept of the dominant rule of a data sample [27]. Jang [28] describes the five functional blocks that compose the fuzzy inference system:

1. database which defines the membership functions of the fuzzy sets;

2. rule base, containing fuzzy if–then rules;
3. decision-making unit or inference engine [26];
4. fuzzification interface and
5. defuzzification interface.

According Andriantiatsaholiniaina *et al.* [29], Muñoz *et al.* [30] and Rivera and Muñoz [24] fuzzy logic [25] is an appropriate methodology for assessing the concept of sustainability due to fuzzy logic is capable of representing uncertain data of complex concepts and polymorphs that are difficult to quantify; emulating skilled humans; and handling vague situations where traditional mathematics is ineffective.

3. Methodology

3.1. *Sample*

Data have been collected from ASSET4 Database to the year 2010. The final sample is composed of 54 European companies, 57 North American companies and 55 Australasian belonging to the agri-food industry (Table 1).

Table 1. Classification of the sample according to GICS (Global Industry Classification Standard)

<table>
<tr><td rowspan="7">Consumer Staples
166 companies</td><td rowspan="4">Food & Staples Retailing
41 companies</td><td rowspan="4">Food & Staples Retailing
41 companies</td><td>Drug Retail
6 companies</td><td>Owners and operators of primarily drug retail stores and pharmacies.</td></tr>
<tr><td>Food Distributors
6 companies</td><td>Distributors of food products to other companies and not directly to the consumer.</td></tr>
<tr><td>Food Retail
27companies</td><td>Owners and operators of primarily food retail stores.</td></tr>
<tr><td>Hypermarkets & Super Centers
2 companies</td><td>Owners and operators of hypermarkets and super centers selling food and a wide-range of consumer staple products. Excludes Food and Drug Retailers classified in the Food Retail and Drug Retail Sub-Industries, respectively.</td></tr>
<tr><td rowspan="3">Food, Beverage & Tobacco
125 companies</td><td rowspan="3">Beverages
35 companies</td><td>Brewers
12 companies</td><td>Producers of beer and malt liquors. Includes breweries not classified in the Restaurants Sub-Industry.</td></tr>
<tr><td>Distillers & Vintners
8 companies</td><td>Distillers, vintners and producers of alcoholic beverages not classified in the Brewers Sub-Industry.</td></tr>
<tr><td>Soft Drinks
15 companies</td><td>Producers of non-alcoholic beverages including mineral waters. Excludes producers of milk classified in the Packaged Foods Sub-Industry.</td></tr>
</table>

		Food Products *80 companies*	**Agricultural Products** *13 companies*	Producers of agricultural products. Includes crop growers, owners of plantations and companies that produce and process foods but do not package and market them. Excludes companies classified in the Forest Products Sub-Industry and those that package and market the food products classified in the Packaged Foods Sub-Industry.
			Packaged Foods & Meats *67 companies*	Producers of packaged foods including dairy products, fruit juices, meats, poultry, fish and pet foods.
		Tobacco *10 companies*	**Tobacco** *10 companies*	Manufacturers of cigarettes and other tobacco products.

Source: Own creation

3.2. ***Sustainability key indicators selection***

The first step in the methodology was the choice of the agri-food industry environmental indicators. The indicators were selected according to the information that ASSET4 declares to use in assessing environmental performance. ASSET4 provides environmental, social and governance (ESG) information of publicly available sources (e.g. annual reports, NGO websites or CSR reports).

In order to select the most relevant environmental indicators applicable to agri-food industry, Global Reporting Initiative Guidelines -GRI- 2006 [31] as well as specific tools and protocols of the agri-food sector, such as Sustainability Reporting Guidelines & Food Processing Sector Supplement -FPSS- 2011 [32] were matched with ASSET4 indicators (Table 2). The final number of indicators was reduced to 62.

Table 2. Environmental Indicators by agri-food industry

Code	Indicator name	GRI Guidelines	Accountability Rating
En_En_ER_D01_1	Emission Reduction/ Policy_1	GRI-EN18	SI
En_En_ER_D01_2	Emission Reduction/ Policy_2	Monitoring and Follow-up	SI
En_En_ER_D02_1	Emission Reduction/ Implementation_1	Policy	SI
En_En_ER_D02_2	Emission Reduction/ Implementation_2	GRI-EN18	GM
En_En_ER_D03	Emission Reduction/ Monitoring	Monitoring and Follow-up	GM
En_En_ER_D04	Emission Reduction/ Improvements	Goals and performance	SI

En_En_ER_O01	Emission Reduction/ Biodiversity Impact	GRI-EN12 GRI-EN14	E
En_En_ER_O02	Emission Reduction/ Biodiversity Controversies	Monitoring and Follow-up	E
En_En_ER_O03	Emission Reduction/ Greenhouse Gas Emissions	GRI-EN16 GRI-EN17 GRI-EN20	OP
En_En_ER_O05	Emission Reduction/ CO2 Reduction	GRI-EN18	GM
En_En_ER_O06	Emission Reduction/ F-Gases Emissions	Disclosure on Management approach	E
En_En_ER_O07	Emission Reduction/ Ozone-Depleting Substances Reduction	Disclosure on Management approach	E
En_En_ER_O08	Emission Reduction/ NOx and SOx Emissions Reduction	Disclosure on Management approach	E
En_En_ER_O09	Emission Reduction/ VOC or Particulate Matter Emissions Reduction	Disclosure on Management approach	E
En_En_ER_O10	Emission Reduction/ Waste	GRI-EN22	OP
En_En_ER_O11	Emission Reduction/ Waste Recycling Ratio	GRI-EN24 GRI-EN22	OP
En_En_ER_O12	Emission Reduction/ Hazardous Waste	GRI-EN24	OP
En_En_ER_O13	Emission Reduction/ Discharge into Water System	GRI-EN23 GRI-EN25	OP
En_En_ER_O14	Emission Reduction/ Waste Reduction	Disclosure on Management approach GRI-EN14	E
En_En_ER_O15	Emission Reduction/ Innovative Production	Disclosure on Management approach	E
En_En_ER_O16	Emission Reduction/ Environmental Partnerships	Disclosure on Management approach	E
En_En_ER_O17	Emission Reduction/ Environmental Management Systems	GRI-EN26	OP
En_En_ER_O18	Emission Reduction/ Environmental Restoration Initiatives	Disclosure on Management approach	E
En_En_ER_O19	Emission Reduction/ Transportation Impact Reduction	Disclosure on Management approach	E
En_En_ER_O20	Emission Reduction/ Spills and Pollution Controversies	Additional contextual information	E
En_En_ER_O21	Emission Reduction/ Spill Impact Reduction	Disclosure on Management approach	E
En_En_ER_O22	Emission Reduction/ Climate Change Risks and Opportunities	Training and awareness/ Additional contextual information	SI
En_En_ER_O23	Emission Reduction/ Environmental Compliance	GRI-EN28	OP
En_En_ER_O24	Emission Reduction/ Environmental Expenditures	GRI-EN30	E
En_En_PI_D01	Product Innovation/ Policy	GRI-EN26	SI

En_En_PI_D02	Product Innovation/ Implementation	Disclosure on Management approach	GM
En_En_PI_D03	Product Innovation/ Monitoring	Disclosure on Management approach	GM
En_En_PI_D04	Product Innovation/ Improvements	Goals and performance	SI
En_En_PI_O01	Product Innovation/ Environmental Products	GRI-EN26	E
En_En_PI_O07	Product Innovation/ Renewable/Clean Energy Products	GRI-EN6	GM
En_En_PI_O13	Product Innovation/ Eco-Design Products	GRI-EN26 GRI-EN27	E
En_En_PI_O15	Product Innovation/ Organic Products	Disclosure on Management approach	E
En_En_PI_O16	Product Innovation/ Product Impact Minimization	Training and awareness	E
En_En_PI_O17	Product Innovation/ GMO Free	Policy	SI
En_En_PI_O20	Product Innovation/ Environmental Labels and Awards	Additional contextual information	GM
En_En_PI_O21	Product Innovation/ Product Impact Controversies	Additional contextual information	E
En_En_RR_D01_1	Resource Reduction/ Policy	Policy	SI
En_En_RR_D01_2	Resource Reduction/ Policy	Monitoring and Follow-up	SI
En_En_RR_D02_1	Resource Reduction/ Implementation	Policy	SI
En_En_RR_D02_2	Resource Reduction/ Implementation	Disclosure on Management approach	GM
En_En_RR_D03	Resource Reduction/ Monitoring	Monitoring and Follow-up	GM
En_En_RR_D04_1	Resource Reduction/ Improvements	Goals and performance	SI
En_En_RR_D04_2	Resource Reduction/ Improvements	Monitoring and Follow-up	SI
En_En_RR_O01	Resource Reduction/ Materials	GRI-EN1	OP
En_En_RR_O02	Resource Reduction/ Materials Recycled and Reused Ratio	GRI-EN2	OP
En_En_RR_O03	Resource Reduction/ Toxic Chemicals	Disclosure on Management approach	E
En_En_RR_O04	Resource Reduction/ Energy Use	GRI-EN3 GRI-EN4	OP
En_En_RR_O06	Resource Reduction/ Renewable Energy Use	GRI-EN3 GRI-EN4	OP
En_En_RR_O07	Resource Reduction/ Green Buildings	Policy	GM
En_En_RR_O08_1	Resource Reduction/ Energy Efficiency Initiatives	GRI-EN6	E
En_En_RR_O08_2	Resource Reduction/ Energy Efficiency Initiatives	GRI-EN5 GRI-EN7	E
En_En_RR_O09	Resource Reduction/ Water Use	GRI-EN8	OP
En_En_RR_O10	Resource Reduction/ Water Recycling	GRI-EN10	E

En_En_RR_O11_1	Resource Reduction/ Environmental Supply Chain Management	Monitoring and Follow-up	GM
En_En_RR_O11_2	Resource Reduction/ Environmental Supply Chain Management	Monitoring and Follow-up	E
En_En_RR_O12	Resource Reduction/ Land Use	Disclosure on Management approach GRI-EN11	E
En_En_RR_O13	Resource Reduction/ Environmental Resource Impact Controversies	Additional contextual information	E

Source: Own creation

After that, the environmental indicators were classified in four domains (system inputs): strategic intent (SI), governance and management (GM), engagement (E), and operational performance (OP) according to the methodology of Accountability Rating (Table 3).

Table 3. Definition of the Accountability indicators

Domains	Definitions
Strategic intent (SI)	Accountability assesses whether an organisation seeks to address social, environmental, and economic issues in its core business strategy.
Governance and management (GM)	The implementation of corporate social responsibility strategies requires the formalization of management systems that define policies, procedures, or mechanisms for the measurement of economic, social, and environmental performances.
Engagement (E)	This domain takes into consideration aspects such as dialogue with stakeholders, the preparation and publication of information on sustainability, and the quality of the information in terms of whether it is subject to credible independent monitoring.
Operational performance (OP)	Accountability Rating assesses a firm's effectiveness in implementing its environmental strategies, management systems, and engagement mechanisms through this domain.

Source: Own creation based on Accountability Rating foundations (www.accountabilityrating.com)

Authors such as Schäfer *et al.* [33] and Eccles *et al.* [34] highlight the relevance of this rating and have studied its methodology for analysing sustainability in organisations.

3.3. *Fuzzy inference system*

The next step in the methodology was the rating design, which includes membership function design and fuzzy rules design (Table 4). Figure 1 shows the inputs and outputs of the system, as well as the definition of linguistic variables.

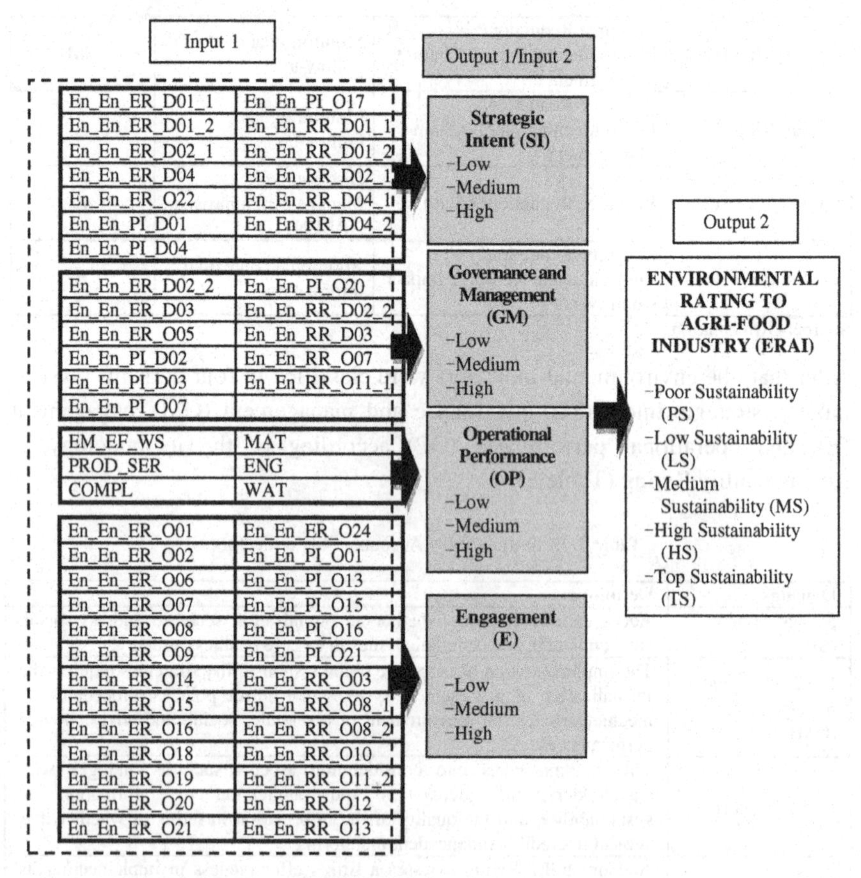

Figure 1. Environmental rating to agri-food industry. An Outline.

Given the disparity in measurement units employed by the core indicators, a process of normalization has been applied before their fuzzification. Thus, in keeping with Krajnc and Glavič [35], we distinguished between indicators whose increase has a positive impact on environment and those whose increase has a negative impact, where I^+N,ijt; the normalized indicator i (with positive impact) for a group of indicators *j* for time (year) *t* and I^-N,ijt; the normalized indicator *i* (with negative impact) for a group of indicators *j* for the same time (year) *t*.

$$I^-_{N,ijt} = 1 - \frac{I^-_{A,ijt} - I^-_{\min,jt}}{I^-_{\max,jt} - I^-_{\min,jt}} \quad I^+_{N,ijt} = \frac{I^+_{A,ijt} - I^+_{\min,jt}}{I^+_{\max,jt} - I^+_{\min,jt}} \qquad (1)$$

Furthermore, in order to simplify the process and according to the aspects that GRI [31] has identified as relevant, the environmental indicators classified in the operational performance domain were grouped to generate other global indicators (Table 4). Moreover, for computation of each aspect a penalization has been applied to those cases where the volume of not available information was relatively high (Operational Performance Availability indicator-OPA-).

Table 4. Operational performance indicators

GRI Aspect	Asset 4 Indicator	Number of rules
Emissions, Effluents and Waste (EM_EF_WS)	En_En_ER_O03	$3^6 = 729$
	En_En_ER_O10	
	En_En_ER_O11	
	En_En_ER_O12	
	En_En_ER_O13	
	OPA_EM_EF_WS	
Products & Services (PROD_SER)	En_En_ER_O17	$3^2 = 9$
	OPA_PROD_SER	
Compliance (COMPL)	En_En_ER_O23	$3^2 = 9$
	OPA_COMP	
Materials (MAT)	En_En_RR_O01	$3^3 = 27$
	En_En_RR_O02	
	OPA_MAT	
Energy (ENG)	En_En_RR_O04	$3^3 = 27$
	En_En_RR_O06	
	OPA_ENG	
Water (WAT)	En_En_RR_O09	$3^2 = 9$
	OPA_WAT	

Source: Own creation

The defined membership functions for the input and output variables are triangular membership functions because of their simplicity [36], because they can approximate most non-triangular functions [37] and because it is most popular in the performance measurement [38, 39].

The linguistic values assigned for the inputs are low (L) -parameters: (-0.5 0 0.5)-, medium (M) -parameters: (0 0.5 1)-, and high (H) -parameters:(0.5 1 1.5)-. Finally, the values of the Environmental Rating to Agri-food Industry (ERAI) output have been expressed as poor sustainability (PS), low sustainability (LS), medium sustainability (MS), high sustainability (HS), and top sustainability (TS).

The linguistic rules generation process has been guided by expert knowledge where the different indicators (SI, GM, E and OP) are equally weighted when included in the performance indicators range.

Once the inputs have been fuzzified, according to their own membership function and linguistic variables, the "if– then" rules for each group were generated. Subsequently, the individual fuzzy sets are related following the fuzzy rules to generate a final single membership function. Finally, a defuzzification method takes place taking into consideration the shape of that final membership function to solve a single crisp output value from the set. There are several defuzzification methods in the literature [40], and in this research it is used the centroid method due to it is the most frequently used [41]. The fuzzy logic toolbox of MATLAB was applied to entering the membership functions and fuzzy rules.

4. Results

Fuzzy Inference System decreases the offsetting effect that very high scores in one domain (strategic intent, governance and management, engagement or operational performance) may have on very low scores in another domain. The different domains range varies from 0 to 1, in a way that the values close to 1 have positive connotations, while values close to 0 have negative connotations.

The results reveal that 59.64% of the firms have a score above 50 and the other 40.36% are below 50. Of all firms with scores better than 50; 45.45% are European, 31.31% are North American and 23.23% are Australasian. Moreover, it is worth noting that among the top 20 more than half are European companies, 3 are American and only 6 are Australasian (Table 5). This seems to indicate that the environmental protection issues are more integrated in Europe than in the rest of the analysed world areas.

In order to analyse carefully these results and the accuracy of the methodology, we have focussed in the top 20 companies rated. We consider these companies as benchmark in environmental performance for the agri-food sector, taking into account the high level of non-available data in terms of operational performance indicators showed by the rest of the sample.

With the aim to analyse the offsetting effect related to adding aggregation method, Table 5 shows in eighth column how high levels in SI, GM and E domains could offset low levels in OP results.

Table 5. Top 20 Environmental Rating to Agri-food Industry (ERAI)

(1) Company/ Rank ERAI	(2) Region	(3) SI	(4) GM	(5) E	(6) OP	(7) ERAI	(8) Adding Aggregation Method	(9) Company/ Rank Adding Meth.
Comp_1	Europe	0.923	0.727	0.692	0.500	0.771	0.728	Comp_9
Comp_2	Europe	0.692	0.818	0.692	0.525	0.769	0.711	Comp_1
Comp_3	North America	0.769	0.909	0.654	0.500	0.765	0.708	Comp_3
Comp_4	Europe	0.692	0.727	0.654	0.500	0.764	0.705	Comp_5
Comp_5	Europe	0.846	0.818	0.654	0.500	0.763	0.695	Comp_8
Comp_6	Europe	0.692	0.636	0.808	0.500	0.761	0.682	Comp_2
Comp_7	Europe	0.692	0.636	0.808	0.500	0.761	0.681	Comp_10
Comp_8	North America	0.846	0.818	0.615	0.500	0.758	0.679	Comp_20
Comp_9	Europe	0.923	0.909	0.577	0.504	0.754	0.659	Comp_6
Comp_10	Asia	0.923	0.727	0.577	0.498	0.753	0.659	Comp_7
Comp_11	Europe	0.615	0.818	0.538	0.500	0.751	0.643	Comp_4
Comp_12	Europe	0.692	0.545	0.538	0.500	0.751	0.637	Comp_13
Comp_13	Oceania	0.692	0.818	0.538	0.500	0.751	0.630	Comp_17
Comp_14	Asia	0.615	0.636	0.538	0.500	0.751	0.618	Comp_11
Comp_15	Asia	0.538	0.636	0.538	0.500	0.751	0.572	Comp_14
Comp_16	Asia	0.615	0.545	0.538	0.499	0.750	0.569	Comp_12
Comp_17	Europe	0.769	0.727	0.500	0.525	0.750	0.560	Comp_19
Comp_18	Europe	0.615	0.545	0.462	0.500	0.723	0.553	Comp_15
Comp_19	Asia	0.692	0.545	0.538	0.464	0.723	0.549	Comp_16
Comp_20	North America	0.846	0.909	0.462	0.500	0.722	0.531	Comp_18

Source: Extraction to MATLAB

Observing the average score of each domain of the first 20 firms in the environmental agri-food rating, we notice that strategic intent domain and governance and management domain have the highest scores and operational performance domain the lowest score (Figure 2). This situation is common to the three studied regions -Europe, North America and Australasia- and reflects how the companies of this sector, despite having good results in aspects related to the definition of policies and the formalization of environmental management systems, have a lower environmental operational performance.

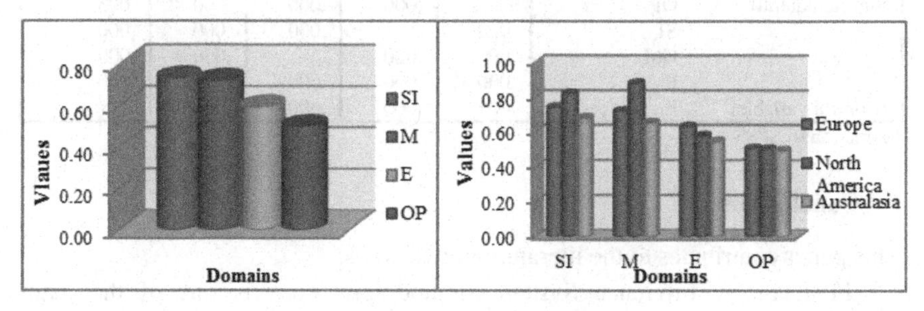

Figure 2. Top 20

Indeed, it is worth emphasizing that the top 50 and top 20 companies have a similar behavior. Thereby, the operational performance domain continues to have the lowest scores and Europe is the region with best the environmental performance in agri-food businesses (Figure 3). The results reveal a lack of integration of policies and environmental management systems in the agri-food sector. However, this situation is common to other sectors which have been evaluated by sustainably rating agencies [6].

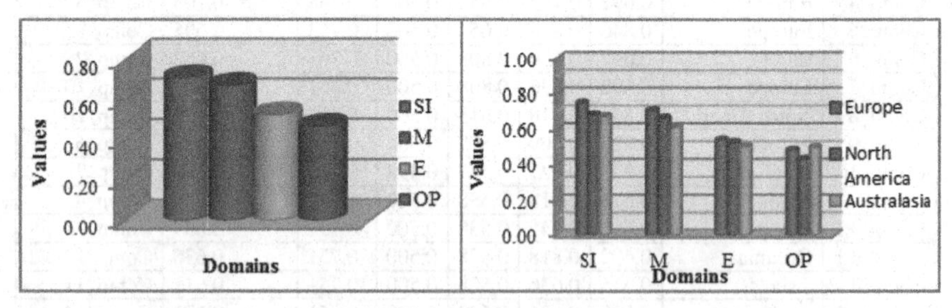

Figure 3: Top 50

On the other hand, in order to deep in the relationship among domains, the Factor Correlation Matrix obtained using linear regression has been analysed. The results show a high correlation between the three management and strategic policy domains SI-GM (0.857), GM-E (0,828) and E-SI (0.811) factors. However, the Operational Performance domain -which makes reference to environmental results measurement- shows the lower correlation with the other domains (Table 6). These results are consistent with previous research [6].

Table 6. Correlation Matrix

		OP	SI	GM	E	Employees
Pearson Correlation	OP	1,000	,537	,558	,578	,218
	SI	,537	1,00	,857	,811	,318
	GM	,558	,857	1,000	,828	,352
	E	,578	,811	,828	1,000	,462
(Control variable)	Employees	,218	,318	,352	,462	1,000
Sig. (unilateral)	OP	.	,000	,000	,000	,003
	SI	,000	.	,000	,000	,000
	GM	,000	,000	.	,000	,000
	E	,000	,000	,000	.	,000
(Control variable)	Employees	,003	,000	,000	,000	.

Extraction to SPSS

5. Conclusions

This paper contributes to the literature in two ways:

First, Fuzzy Inference System Methodology corrects one of the main weaknesses of methodologies based on the aggregation of scores, i.e. the possible offsetting of negative scores with good scores and introduces the role of the decision-maker in the assessment.

Stock markets –due to the activities of sustainability rating agencies and sustainability stock indices- have solved some problems related to the development of a synthetic sustainability index such as, selection of the indicators and techniques for aggregation of information. However, the problems of weighting and possible offsetting in the scorings remain unresolved.

Nevertheless, the flexibility of Fuzzy Inference Systems -where the definition of rules is a fundamental part of the system- allows to incorporate not only a technical approach but also other considerations according to the profile of the stakeholder through the rules' definition and the weighting given to different aspects.

Second, agri-food sector is highly dependent on natural resources and produces considerable and different impacts on the environment, in this sense it is necessary evaluate the environmental performance in agri-food industry by means on an Environmental Rating to Agri-food Industry (ERAI). The first results reveal a lack of integration of policies and environmental management systems in the agri-food sector.

Acknowledgments

This work is supported by P1.1B2010-04 and P1.1B2010-13 research projects and the Master in Sustainability and Corporate Social Responsibility offered by Universitat Jaume I of Castellon, Spain.

References

1. World Commission on Environment and Development (WCED). Our Common Future, Oxford University Press, Oxford (1987).
2. M.V. López, A. Garcia and L. Rodriguez, *J. Bus. Ethics* **75**, 285 (2007).
3. A. Mcwilliams, D.S. Siegel and P.M. Wright, *J. Manage. Stud.* **43**, 1 (2006).
4. EUROPEAN COMMISSION COM. Communication from the Commission Europe 2020. A strategy for smart, sustainable and inclusive growth. Brussels, (2010).
5. R. E. Freeman, J. S. Harrison, A. C. Wicks, B. L. Parmar and S. De Colle, 'Stakeholder Theory. The State of the Art.' Cambridge, UK: Cambridge University Press (2010).
6. E. Escrig, J.M. Rivera, M.J. Muñoz and M.A. Fernández. 'Integrating Sustainability through Fuzzy Logic: Fortune Global 100 Sustainability

Rating'. Computational Intelligence in Business and Economics Proceedings of the MS"10 International Conference (2010).
7. L.Z. Bakucs, I. Fertő and A. Havas, 'Future impact of new technologies upon food quality and health in Central Eastern European countries' in Studies on the Agricultural and Food Sector in Central and Eastern Europe, Vol. 46, Halle (Saale), IAMO, 82 (2008).
8. E.M. Dupuis, *Agric. Human Values* **17**, 285 (2000).
9. NOMISMA. - SOCIETÀ DI STUDI ECONOMICI 'European agriculture of the future the role plant protection products' BOLOGNA. Working paper (2008).
10. A. Awasthi, S.S. Chauhan and S.K. Goyal, *Int. J. Prod. Econ.* **126**, 370 (2010).
11. L. Fulponi, 'The globalization of private standards and the agri-food system' in Swinnen, J. (Ed): Global supply chains, standards, and the poor. Oxon, UK: CABI publications, 5 (2007).
12. P. Jones, D. Comfort, D. Hillier and I. Eastwood, *Br. Food J.* **107**, 423 (2005).
13. M. J. Maloni and M. E. Brown, *J. Bus. Ethics* **68**, 35 (2006).
14. M. Hartmann, *Eur. Rev. Agric. Econ.* **38**, 297 (2011).
15. OECD-FAO Agricultural Outlook 2010-2019. OECD Publishing and FAO (2011).
16. L. Salvati and M. Zitti, *Ecol. Econ.* **68**, 1093 (2009).
17. J.B. Pena, 'Problemas de la medición del bienestar y conceptos afines. Una aplicación al caso español', INE, Madrid (1977).
18. P. Zarzosa, *Spanish Journal of Economics and Finance* **24**, 139 (1996).
19. F. Martínez, M. Domínguez and P. Fernández, *Estudios de Economía Aplicada* **23**, 753 (2005).
20. L. Cherchye and T. Kuosmanen, 'Benchmarking Sustainable Development: A Synthetic Meta-index Approach'. Working Papers UNU-WIDER Research Paper, World Institute for Development Economic Research (UNU-WIDER) (2004).
21. K.F.R. Liu, *Environ. Manage.* **39**, 721 (2007).
22. B.M. Ruf, K. Muralidhar and K. Paul, *J. Manag.* **24**, 119 (1998).
23. G. Munda, P. Nijkamp and P. Rietveld, 'Fuzzy Multigroup Conflict Resolution for Environmental Management', in: J. Weiss (ed.) - The economics of project appraisal and the environment, Edward Elgar, Cheltenham, 161 (1994).
24. J.M. Rivera and M.J. Muñoz, *J. Bus. Ethics* **94**, 489 (2009).
25. L.A. Zadeh, *Information and Control* **8**, 338 (1965).

26. A.F. Shapiro, *Insur. Math. Econ.* **35**, 399 (2004).
27. D. Carrera and R. Mayorga, *J. Intell. Manuf.* **19**, 1 (2008).
28. J-S. R. Jang, *IEEE Trans. Syst. Man Cybern.* **23**, 665 (1993).
29. L. A. Andriantiatsaholiniaina, V. S. Kouikoglou and Y. A. Phillis, *Ecol. Econ.* **48**, 149 (2004).
30. M.J. Muñoz, J.M. Rivera and J.M. Moneva, *Ind. Manage. Data Syst.* **108**, 829 (2008).
31. GRI (Global Reporting Initiative). Sustainability Reporting Guidelines, G3 (2006).
32. G3 & FPSS. Sustainability Reporting Guidelines & Food Processing Sector Supplement (2011).
33. H. Schäfer, J. Beer, J. Zenker and P. Fernandes, 'Who is who in Corporate Social Responsibility Rating?' Bertelsman Foundation. University Stuttgart. Institute of Business Administration (2006).
34. N.S. Eccles, V. Pillay and D. De Jongh, *African Business Review* **13**, 21 (2009).
35. D.A. Krajnc and P. Glavič, *Resour. Conserv. Recycl.* **43**, 189 (2005).
36. H-Y. Lin, P-Y. Hsu and G-J. Sheen, *Expert Syst. Appl.* **32**, 939 (2007).
37. W. Pedrycz, *Fuzzy Sets Syst.* **64,** 21 (1994).
38. F.T.S. Chan and H.J. Qi, *Supply Chain Management: An international Journal* **8**, 209 (2003).
39. R. Ohdar and P.K. Ray, *Journal of Manufacturing Technology Management* **15**, 723 (2004).
40. C.C. Lee, *IEEE Trans. Syst. Man Cybern.* **20**, 419 (1990).
41. W-W. Wu and Y-T. Lee, *Expert Syst. Appl.* **32**, 499 (2007).

EVALUATION OF THE QUALITY OF A TOURIST SERVICE. APPLIED TO THE CASE OF STUDENT TOURISM*

LUISA L. LAZZARI

CIMBAGE, IADCOM, Facultad de Ciencias Económicas, Universidad de Buenos Aires Av. Córdoba 2122, Ciudad de Buenos Aires, C1120AAQ, Argentina

PATRICIA MOULIÁ

CIMBAGE, IADCOM, Facultad de Ciencias Económicas, Universidad de Buenos Aires Av. Córdoba 2122, Ciudad de Buenos Aires, C1120AAQ, Argentina

ANDREA PARMA

CIMBAGE, IADCOM, Facultad de Ciencias Económicas, Universidad de Buenos Aires Av. Córdoba 2122, Ciudad de Buenos Aires, C1120AAQ, Argentina

In the last decade, the evaluation of quality in the tourist sector has attracted the attention of many researchers. From the maketing perspective and its application to tourism, the evaluation of quality is considered a factor related to experiences derived from the use or consumption of a tourist product, and it is defined as a determinating factor of the customer´s subsequent behaviour, among which you have fidelity.

In this article a linguistic model of evaluation of the quality of a service is redefined by means of the usage of aggregation operators of linguistic information that operate directly with words and which are applied to the evaluation of a student´s trip.

1. Introduction

In the last decade, the evaluation of quality of the tourist sector has attracted the atention of many researchers, among other studies we can mention those carried out by Baker and Crompton [1]; Seddighi and Theocharous [2]; Ekinci *et al.* [3] y Yuksel [4].

From the marketing perspective and its application to the tourism sector, the evaluation of quality is considered a factor related to experiences derived from the use or consumption of a tourist product and this is defined as a determinating factor of the customer´s subsequent behaviour, among which we have fidelity [5].

* This work is supported by the Secretaría de Ciencia y Técnica of the Universidad de Buenos Aires, Proy. UBACYT 20020100100025.

Among the techniques to measure the perceived quality of a service is the SERVQUAL, created by Parasuraman *et al.* [6], which is the most widely accepted and extended way to measure the quality of service. It is based on considering quality as an attitude, and its measurement as the result of comparing customer´s expectations against their perception of the service received.

The SERVQUAL scale is the is the most applied in studies which evaluate the quality of different products or tourist offers [7], [8], [9], [10], [11]. However, some authors have concluded that the use of this methodology is insufficient to evaluate the quality of this sector [12], [13].

Brown *et al.* [14] consider that the most important limitations that the SERVQUAL has, arise primarily from conceptualizing the score given to the quality of service as an arithmetic difference between the valuation assigned to the expectations and its perceptions.

Their proposal consists in asking questions that allow individuals to express what their perceptions are as compared to their expectations for each of the items of the SERVQUAL measurement. They suggest formulating each item as a phrase starting with the word “how”, for example: How did you find the employees willingness to assist you? Each item of the survey is responded with a pre assigned scale value that has verbal descriptors for each position. The rank of the descriptors goes from *much worse than expected* up to *much better than expected*.

A review of the literature on quality management in tourism carried out by Serrano Bedía *et al.* [10]; reveals that there are many paths which are open for future research. In the case of hotel´s activity Santomá and Costa [11]; Akbaba [15]; and Ekinci [16] considerer that it is necessary to carry out an analysis of the quality management process, to improve its measuring instruments and to determine "universal" attributes to establish comparison standards.

Based on the proposal of Brown *et al.* [14], Lazzari [17] developed a linguistic model to evaluate the quality of a service. It is based on the dimensions or attributes of the evaluated service and it is sustained on the idea that consumers assess each one the attributes of the service received to form a global evaluation. It uses linguistic variables and overcomes the disadvantages caused by the difference in scores that the SERVQUAL uses.

In this paper this model is analysed and restated to evaluate the quality of the tourist sector. Aggregation operators of linguistic information are applied which compute directly with words developed by Xu [18], which also allow adding linguistic information that is linguistically weighted.

It is structured as follows: In section two the linguistic approach to be used in the design of the proposed model is discussed; in section three the linguistic model of evaluation of the quality of a tourist service is presented, in section four it is applied to the case of student tourism in Argentina and in section five some final comments are made.

2. Fuzzy Linguistic Approach

The fuzzy linguistic approach is an appropriate technique to deal with qualitative aspects of problems [19].

Following Xu [18], we consider a finite and totally ordered label set $S=\{s_i / i=0,\ldots,t\}$, which cardinality value is odd, and t is a positive integer. Each term s_i represents a possible value for a linguistic variable and it has the following characteristics:

i) $s_i > s_j$ iff $i > j$;

ii) There is the negation operator: neg $(s_i)=s_j$ such that $j=t-i$.

The mid linguistic label $s_{t/2}$ represents an assessment of "indifference" and the rest of labels are defined around it symmetrically.

For example, S can be defined as:

$$S=\{s_0=\text{very low},\ s_1=\text{low}, s_2=\text{medium}, s_3=\text{high}, s_4=\text{very high}\}$$

To preserve all the given information, Xu [20], [18], [21] extended the discrete linguistic label set S to a continuous linguistic label set $\bar{S}=\{s_\alpha / \alpha\in[-q,q]\}$, where q $(q>t)$ is a sufficiently large positive integer.

If $s_\alpha \in S$, then s_α is called an original linguistic label, otherwise, s_α is called a virtual linguistic label. Generally, the decision maker uses the original linguistic terms to evaluate attributes and alternatives, and the virtual linguistic labels can only appear in calculations [18].

Considering any two linguistic terms $s_\alpha, s_\beta \in \bar{S}$, and $\lambda\in[0,1]$, Xu [18] introduces operational laws of linguistic variables as follows:

$$s_\alpha \oplus s_\beta = s_{\alpha+\beta} \tag{1}$$

$$s_\alpha \oplus s_\beta = s_\beta \oplus s_\alpha \tag{2}$$

$$\lambda.s_\alpha = s_{\lambda\alpha} \tag{3}$$

Based on (1), (2) and (3) Xu [20], [18], [21] developed various linguistic aggregation operators, as mapping of $\bar{S}^n \rightarrow \bar{S}$, which compute with words directly.

In this section we present the *extended arithmetic averaging* (*EAA*) and the *extended weighted arithmetic averaging* (*EWAA*) due to the fact that they will be the linguistic operators used in our evaluation model.

Definition 1 [18]: Let *EAA*: $\overline{S}^n \rightarrow \overline{S}$. If

$$EAA(s_{\alpha_1}, s_{\alpha_2}, \ldots, s_{\alpha_n}) = \frac{1}{n}(s_{\alpha_1} \oplus s_{\alpha_2} \oplus \ldots \oplus s_{\alpha_n}) = s_{\overline{\alpha}} \tag{4}$$

where $\overline{\alpha} = \frac{1}{n}\sum_{j=1}^{n} \alpha_j$, then *EAA* is called the *extended arithmetic averaging operator.*

Definition 2 [18]: Let *EWAA*: $\overline{S}^n \rightarrow \overline{S}$. If

$$EWAA(s_{\alpha_1}, s_{\alpha_2}, \ldots, s_{\alpha_n}) = w_1\, s_{\alpha_1} \oplus w_2\, s_{\alpha_2} \oplus \ldots \oplus w_n\, s_{\alpha_n} = s_{\overline{\beta}} \tag{5}$$

where $\overline{\beta} = \sum_{j=1}^{n} w_j . \alpha_j$, $w = (w_1, w_2, \ldots, w_n)$ is the weight vector of the linguistic label s_{α_j}, $j = 1, \ldots, n$, $w_j \in [0,1]$ and $\sum_{j=1}^{n} w_j = 1$, then *EWAA* is called the *extended weighted arithmetic averaging* operator.

The fundamental aspect of the *EWAA* operator is that it computes the linguistic labels taking into account the importance of the information [18], [21]. If $w = (1/n, 1/n, \ldots, 1/n)$, then the operator *EWAA* = *EAA*.

To express the outcome of a linguistic information aggregation by means of a label of set *S* we approximate the subindex of the virtual label to an integer value by means of the usual round operation, i.e., *round* $(\overline{\beta})$.

3. Linguistic Model of Evaluation of the Quality of a Tourist Service

This model uses aggregation operators of linguistic information that operate directly with words and also it allows us to overcome the difficulties caused by the difference of the scores used by other approaches. The weighting of the attributes is done in the linguistic form, which leads to add linguistic information weighted linguistically.

The questionnaire is made for each service in particular and the number of questions depends on the attributes that are assessed in each case. Two additional items are also incorporated; one requests the overall perception of the quality of the service and the other questions the possibility of recommending the service to other individuals.

Each question is formulated in such a way that the reply requires a direct comparison between the expected and received service, similar to the one proposed by Brown *et al.* [14]. Each individual that carries out the survey expresses his opinion based on the service gap[†] of each attribute with any linguistic label of the set *S*.

$S = \{ s_4$ = much better; s_3 = better; s_2 = equal; s_1 = worse; s_0 = much worse$\}$

The importance assigned to each attribute of the service received is evaluated with a linguistic term of the set *L*.

$L = \{ l_4$ = very high; l_3 = high; l_2 = medium; l_1 = low; l_0 = very low$\}$

The global perception of the quality of services received is expressed with a label of the set *T*.

$T = \{ t_4$ = excellent; t_3 = very good; t_2 = good; t_1 = fair; t_0 = bad$\}$

If m is the quantity of attributes considered and n the cardinality of the sets *S*, *L* and *T* of linguistic terms, such that $j = 1,\dots,n$, the steps of the model are the following:

Step 1. *Aggregate opinion of the service gap of each attribute*

The aggregate opinion of the service gap (b_i) corresponding to each attribute a_i is obtained through the application of the linguistic information aggregation operator *EWAA*, as expressed in (6).

$$b_i = EWAA_{a_i}\left(s_{\alpha_1}, s_{\alpha_2}, \dots, s_{\alpha_n}\right) = s_{\overline{\beta}_i}, \; i = 1,\dots,m, \; j = 1,\dots,n \qquad (6)$$

where $\overline{\beta}_i = \sum_{j=1}^{n} w_j \alpha_j$ and the weighting vector of the linguistic label $s_{\alpha_j} \in S$ is $w = (w_1, w_2, \dots, w_n)$, with $w_j = \dfrac{F_j}{\sum_{j=1}^{n} F_j}$, $w_j \in [0,1]$ and $\sum_{j=1}^{n} w_j = 1$, F_j is the quantity of surveyed individuals which assigned the label s_{α_j} to the service gap of the attribute a_i.

[†] Service gap: is the difference that exists between the expectations of the client (expected service) with respect to a service and their perceptions (perceived service) when it has given.

Step 2. Aggregate importance of each attribute

The aggregate importance of each attribute (p_i) is obtained by applying (7).

$$p_i = EWAA_{a_i}\left(l_{\alpha_1}, l_{\alpha_2}, ..., l_{\alpha_n}\right) = l_{\bar{\lambda}_i}, \; i = 1, ..., m, \; j = 1, ..., n \tag{7}$$

where m is the quantity of attributes evaluated and $l_{\alpha_j} \in L$ $(j = 1, ..., n)$ is the linguistic label which indicates the importance assigned to the attribute a_i ($i = 1, ..., m$).

$\bar{\lambda}_i = \sum_{j=1}^{n} w_j \alpha_j$ and the weighting vector of the linguistic label l_{α_j} is $w = (w_1, w_2, ..., w_n)$, with $w_j = \frac{F_j}{\sum_{j=1}^{n} F_j}$, $w_j \in [0,1]$, $\sum_{j=1}^{n} w_j = 1$, where F_j is the number of individuals that assessed the importance of the attribute a_i with the label l_{α_j}.

Step 3. Aggregate opinion on global service gap

Once the aggregate service gap of each attribute is obtained with its respective importance, the collective global service gap is calculated through the use of the operator *EWAA*, defined in (5), as expressed in (8).

$$GSG = EWAA\left(s_{\bar{\beta}_1}, s_{\bar{\beta}_2}, ..., s_{\bar{\beta}_m}\right) = s_{\bar{\delta}}, \; i = 1, ..., m \tag{8}$$

where $\bar{\delta} = \sum_{i=1}^{m} w_i \bar{\beta}_i$, $i = 1, ..., m$, $w_i = \frac{\bar{\lambda}_i}{\sum_{i=1}^{m} \bar{\lambda}_i}$, such that $w_i \in [0,1]$ and $\sum_{i=1}^{m} w_i = 1$. $s_{\bar{\beta}_i}$ specifies the aggregate service gap of the attribute a_i and $l_{\bar{\lambda}_i}$ its collective importance.

To express the aggregated global service gap by means of a term of the set S, the subindex of the virtual label $s_{\bar{\delta}}$ is approximated to an integer value, through the usual rounding up operation (*round* $(\bar{\delta})$) and an original linguistic label is obtained.

Step 4. Aggregate global perception of the service

To obtain the aggregate global perception of the service, the *EWAA* operator is once again applied, as shown in (9).

$$g = EWAA\left(t_{\alpha_1}, t_{\alpha_2}, \ldots, t_{\alpha_n}\right) = t_{\bar{\gamma}}, \; j = 1, \ldots, n \tag{9}$$

$t_{\alpha_j} \in T$ ($j = 1, \ldots, n$) is the linguistic term which indicates the global quality of the services received. $\bar{\gamma} = \sum_{j=1}^{n} w_j \alpha_j$ and the weighting vector of the linguistic label t_{α_j} is $w = (w_1, w_2, \ldots, w_n)$, with $w_j = \frac{F_j}{\sum_{j=1}^{n} F_j}$, $w_j \in [0,1]$, $\sum_{j=1}^{n} w_j = 1$, where F_j is the quantity of individuals that assigned the label t_{α_j} to the global perception of the service received.

Step 5. Recommendation of services

The frequency of choice of each possibility considered in this item is calculated: absolutely recommend service; with restrictions and not recommended; and then the percentage of each one is obtained.

Step 6. Final evaluation

The results obtained in steps 3, 4 and 5 are compared.

4. Application to the Case of Student Tourism

In order to evaluate the satisfaction of the service offered by a student tourism company the linguistic model presented in the section 3 was applied.

Closed surveys were handed out to 102 passengers who were attending their last year of secondary school in a private institute incorporated into the official education programme of the city of Buenos Aires, Argentina.

Traditionally, secondary school students go on a graduation trip during the last year at school, which in most cases is to the city of San Carlos de Bariloche. The group under study visited this city for 10 days in October 2011.

Table 1 shows the characteristics of the population under study.

Table 1. Characteristics of the population under study

Age \ Sex	Women	Men	Total	%
17	42	28	70	68.63
18	19	12	31	30.39
19	0	1	1	0.98
Total	61	41	102	-
%	59.80	40.20	-	-

The service offered by the tourism company included transport, lodging, meals, excursions and nightlife.

Thirteen attributes were considered and each one was evaluated with a label of the set S. These attributes and the questions made in the handed out surveys are listed in Table 2. The questionnaire was tested initially with a small group of students, chosen at random.

Table 2. Evaluated attributes and questions asked

Attributes considered	Questions asked
a_1 : Transfer from the place of origin	How was the transfer from the place of origin as regards to your expectations?
a_2 : Hotel location	How did you find the hotel location as regards to your expectations?
a_3 : Hotel accommodation	How did you find the hotel accommodation as regards to your expectations?
a_4 : Hotel staff	How did the hotel staff assist you as regards to your expectations?
a_5 : Hotel cleanliness	How did you find the hotel´s cleanliness as regards to your expectations?
a_6 : Hotel services	How did you find the hotel services (TV, Internet, safe-deposit box, etc.) as regards to your expectations?
a_7 : Meals	How did you find the meals as regards to your expectations?
a_8 : Excursions	How did you find the excursions you went on as regards to your expectations?
a_9 : Group coordinators	How was the coordinator´s performance as regards to your expectations?
a_{10} : Clothes	How did you find the clothes which the company provided you as regards to your expectations?
a_{11} : Schedules	How did the company comply with the schedules as regards to your expectations?
a_{12} : Medical service	How did you find the medical service which the company offered as regards to your expectations?
a_{13} : Discos	How did you find the discos as regards to your expectations?

The importance assigned by the young people to each attribute was evaluated with a label of the set L and the global perception of the quality of the services received with a term of the set T

In order to evaluate the possibility of recommending the tourist company´s services to others, students were asked to complete Table 3.

Table 3. Recommendation of services

Would you recommend our services to people you know, friends and/or relatives?
Absolutely
With restrictions
Not recommended

4.1. *Results of the Evaluation*

After the survey was carried out we processed the obtained information.

Table 4 shows the observed frequencies and the aggregated service gap for each attribute, expressed by the virtual label and its approximation to the original label, which was calculated by the application of Step 1 of the model.

Table 4. Service gap for each attribute

	Observed frequencies					Service gap: aggregated evaluation	
Attribute	s_0	s_1	s_2	s_3	s_4	Virtual label	Original label
a_1	0	5	71	23	3	$s_{2.235}$	equal
a_2	0	2	33	55	12	$s_{2.755}$	better
a_3	0	8	40	36	18	$s_{2.627}$	better
a_4	2	6	54	33	7	$s_{2.363}$	equal
a_5	2	6	53	32	9	$s_{2.392}$	equal
a_6	0	5	42	40	15	$s_{2.637}$	better
a_7	0	6	9	34	53	$s_{3.314}$	better
a_8	0	5	23	36	38	$s_{3.049}$	better
a_9	1	2	29	40	30	$s_{2.941}$	better
a_{10}	1	12	32	40	17	$s_{2.588}$	better
a_{11}	6	42	37	14	3	$s_{1.667}$	equal
a_{12}	2	6	58	20	16	$s_{2.412}$	equal
a_{13}	0	0	7	18	77	$s_{3.686}$	much better

Of the thirteen attributes, one was evaluated in general as much better than expected (MB), seven better than expected (B) and five equal to expected (E).

Table 5 details the aggregate importance for each one, which was obtained by applying Step 2 of the model. Four attributes were considered of very high importance by the young people (30.77 %) and nine of high importance (69.33 %) as shown in Figure 1.

If the attributes are ordered according to the value of the virtual label from high to low the following order of importance is obtained: a_8 (Excursions), a_{13} (Discos), a_7 (Meals), a_{12} (Medical service), a_9 (Group coordinators), a_{10} (Clothes), a_5 (Hotel cleanliness), a_3 (Hotel accommodation), a_1 (Transfer from the place of origin), a_2 (Hotel location), a_4 (Hotel staff), a_{11} (Schedules) y a_6 (Hotel services).

Table 5. Aggregated importance of the attributes

	Observed frequencies					Aggregated importance	
Attribute	l_4	l_3	l_2	l_1	l_0	Virtual label	Original label
a_1	29	54	10	7	2	$l_{2.990}$	high
a_2	25	55	15	6	1	$l_{2.951}$	high
a_3	43	39	16	4	0	$l_{3.186}$	high
a_4	30	39	27	5	1	$l_{2.902}$	high
a_5	52	37	11	2	0	$l_{3.363}$	high
a_6	26	31	25	15	5	$l_{2.569}$	high
a_7	71	26	5	0	0	$l_{3.647}$	very high
a_8	83	17	2	0	0	$l_{3.794}$	very high
a_9	58	35	9	0	0	$l_{3.480}$	high
a_{10}	50	43	8	1	0	$l_{3.392}$	high
a_{11}	20	47	29	6	0	$l_{2.794}$	high
a_{12}	65	27	9	1	0	$l_{3.529}$	very high
a_{13}	77	20	3	2	0	$l_{3.686}$	very high

In order to calculate the global service gap regarding the received service the *Step* 3 of section 3 model is applied obtaining the label $s_{2.703}$ and its approximation to the original label s_3. In consequence the aggregate opinion over the global service gap is *better than expected.*

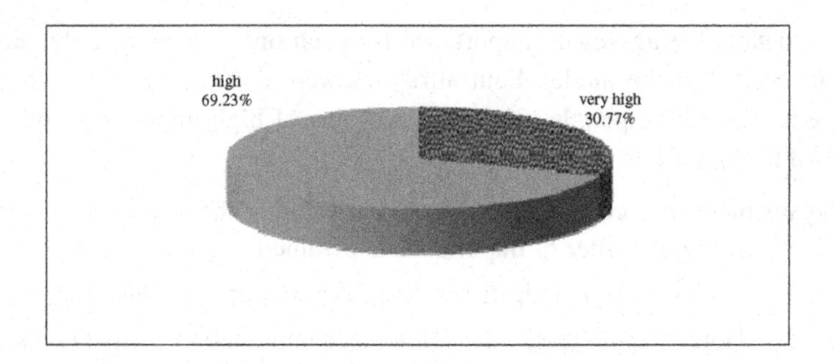

Figure 1. Percentage of evaluated attributes of high or very high importance.

The observed frequencies with respect to the global perception of the quality of the services received are shown in Table 6.

Their values indicate that for seventeen passengers the quality of the service received was excellent (16.67 %), sixty-four considered it very good (62.74 %) and twenty-one good (20.59 %). The vast majority of the population under study (79.41 %) stated that the service was very good or excellent which is consistent with the opinion added on the service gap previously obtained (better than expected).

Table 6. Global perception of the services received

Quality of service	Observed frequencies
Excellent	17
Very good	64
Good	21
Fair	0
Bad	0

If the information on Table 6 is added, which refers to the global perception of the services, in agreement with Step 4 of the section 3 model the label $t_{2.96}$ is obtained and its approximation to a term of the original set T indicates that the quality of the services was evaluated as very good. We can conclude that both the evaluation of the gap and the global perception of the service have been very satisfactory.

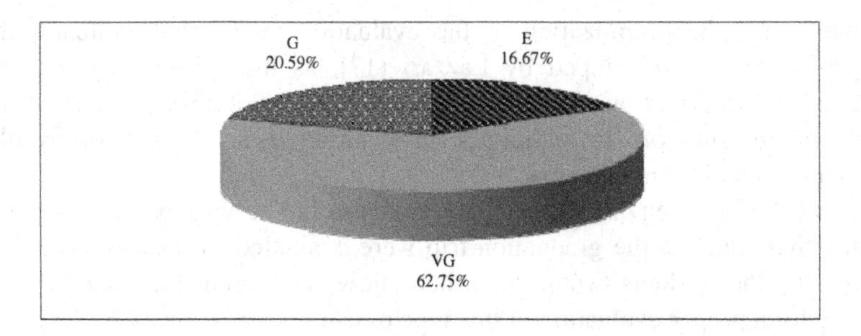

Figure 2. Percentage of young people who evaluated the services as excellent, very good or good.

All the young people who went on the trip would recommend the company´s services to people they know, friends or relatives. 67.67% would absolutely do it and 33.33%, with restrictions (Table 7 and Figure 3)

Table 7. Recommendation of the services

Would you recommend our services to people you know, friends and/or relatives?	
Absolutely	68
With restrictions	34
Not recommended	0

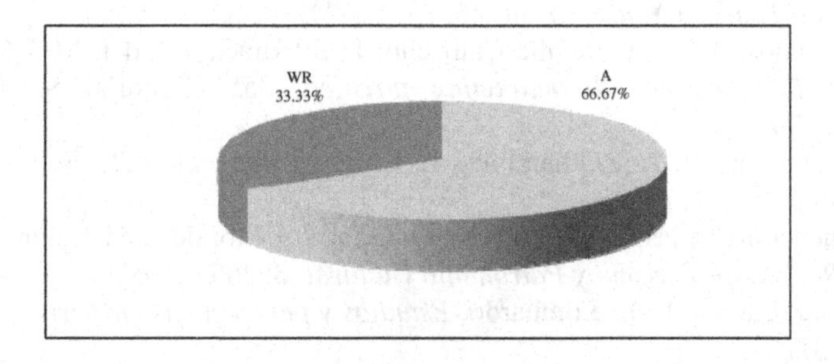

Figure 3. Percentage of students who recommended the services either absolutely or with restrictions

5. Final Comments

The aggregation operators of linguistic information that compute words directly defined by Xu [18] used in this case study allow a continuous representation of the linguistic information over their range. They represent a significant contribution for the optimization of the evaluation model that evaluates the quality of a service developed by Lazzari [17], as they allow to order and classify all the information obtained during an aggregation process without the loss of any information. In addition it also allows us to express the results through an original linguistic term.

The attributes taken into account to evaluate the service provided by the company that went on the graduation trip were evaluated as *important* or *very important* by the students (Table 5), which allows us to conclude that they are necessary for a proper evaluation of this type of trip.

It is necessary to agree on the cardinality of the set of linguistic terms used to express the information that should not necessarily be the one applied in this research. Miller [22], in his classic article, "The magical number seven, plus or minus two: some limits on our capacity for processing information", examines the limits of human capacity to process information, and considers between five and nine the amount of values that the human being can discriminate.

References

1. D. A. Baker and J. L. Crompton, *Annals of Tourism Research.* **27**, 785 (2000).
2. H. R. Seddighi and A. L. Theocharous, *Tourism Management.* **23**, 475 (2002).
3. Y. Ekinci, P. Prokopaki and C. Cobanoglu, *International Journal of Hospitality Management.* **22**, 47 (2003).
4. A. Yuksel, *Tourism Management.* **25**, 751 (2004).
5. M. Rey (coord.), M. A. Revilla Camacho, J. Gil Jiménez and J. M. López Bonilla, *Fundamentos de marketing turístico.* 355 (Editorial Síntesis, Madrid, 2004).
6. A. Parasuraman, V. A. Zeithaml and L. L. Berry, *Journal of Retailing.* **64**, 12 (1988).
7. M. Bethencourt Cejas, F. Díaz Pérez, O. González Morales and J. Sánchez Pérez, *Revista de Turismo y Patrimonio Cultural.* **3**, 265 (2005).
8. M. A. Gazzera and L. L. Lombardo, *Estudios y perspectivas en Turismo.* **6,** 361 (2007).
9. K. Hussain and E. H. Ekiz, *Estudios y perspectivas en Turismo.* **16**, 341 (2007).
10. A. M. Serrano Bedia, M. López Fernández and R. Gómez López, *Cuadernos de Turismo.* **20**, 251 (2007).
11. R. Santomá and G. Costa, *Revista de Análisis Turístico.* **3**, 27 (2007).
12. S. Luk and R. Layton, *Total Quality Management & Business Excellence.* **15**, 259 (2004).
13. M. Augustyn and A. Seakhoa-King, *Advances in Hospitality and Leisure.* **1**, 3 (2005).

14. T. J. Brown, G. A. Churchill and J. P. Peter, *Journal of Retailing*. **69**, 127 (1993).
15. A. Akbaba, *Hospitality Management*. **25**, 170 (2006).
16. Y. Ekinci, *Journal of Hospitality & Tourism Research*. **26**, 199 (2002).
17. L. L. Lazzari, *El comportamiento del consumidor desde una perspectiva fuzzy* (Tesis doctoral, Universidad de Valladolid, Valladolid, 2006).
18. Z. Xu, *International Journal of Information Technology & Decision Making*. **4**, 153 (2005).
19. L. A. Zadeh, Part I, *Information Sciences*. **8**, 199. Part II, *Information Sciences*. **8**, 301. Part III, *Information Sciences*. **9**, 43 (1975).
20. Z. Xu, *International Journal of Uncertainty Fuzziness and Knowledge-Based- Systems*. **12**, 791 (2004).
21. Z. Xu, in H. Bustince, F Herrera and J. Montero (eds.), *Fuzzy Sets and Their Extensions: Representation, Aggregation and Models*. 163 (Springer-Verlag, Berlin, 2008).
22. G. A. Miller, *Psychology Review*. **63**, 81 (1956).

FUZZY ANALYTIC HIERARCHY PROCESS APPROACH FOR E-COMMERCE WEBSITES EVALUATION

HUAN LIU

School of Software, Harbin University of Science and Technology, No.52 Xuefu Road, Harbin, 150080, China

Faculty of Applied Mathematics and Computer Science, Belarusian State University, No.4 Nezavisimosti avenue, Minsk, 220030, Belarus

VIKTOR V. KRASNOPROSHIN

Faculty of Applied Mathematics and Computer Science, Belarusian State University, No.4 Nezavisimosti avenue, Minsk, 220030, Belarus

SHUANG ZHANG

School of Information Science and Technology, Heilongjiang University, Harbin, 150080, China

College of Computer Science and Technology, Harbin Engineering University, Harbin, 150010, China

This paper presents a fuzzy multiple-criteria analysis approach for E-commerce website evaluation. After comparing with the current main methods, an E-commerce websites evaluation model has been constructed, and the design process has been presented. For E-commerce website evaluation, experts can just give linguistic comparing descriptions of evaluation criteria. The Fuzzy Analytic Hierarchy Process (FAHP) method is used to determine the weights of criteria among experts. It incorporated the attitudes of decision makers towards preference. A crisp overall performance value is obtained for each alternative based on the concept of Fuzzy Multiple-Criteria Decision Making (FMCDM). A case study consisting of five experts' interviews illustrates the proposed method.

1. Introduction

Nowadays, economic commerce (E-commerce) provides more convenient, faster and cheaper way of shopping, internet banking, employing etc. And E-commerce website has become a significant selling way of almost all enterprises.

As the result, it becomes necessary for both companies and customers to evaluate the e-commerce websites. However evaluation of an e-commerce website is not familiar with most of enterprises. It includes quite a lot of technical and professional knowledge.

In the evaluation process, there are many criteria and even sub-criteria. After comparison with current E-commerce websites evaluation methods, it was found that it is natural to bring in Analytic hierarchy process (AHP) [20], which is one of the most commonly used multiple-criteria decision making methods. To achieve the previous two aims, we decided to research an approach of evaluating e-commerce website based on Fuzzy Analytic Hierarchy Process (FAHP). Furthermore the construction of the proposed model and the whole designing process has been presented. Along with a case study is undertaken to determine the weights of criteria and sub-criteria for e-commerce website evaluation.

2. Analysis of E-commerce Websites Evaluation

2.1. *E-commerce*

Electronic commerce, commonly known as e-commerce, eCommerce or e-comm, refers to the buying and selling of products or services over electronic systems such as the Internet and other computer networks. However, the term may refer to more than just buying and selling products online. It also includes the entire online process of developing, marketing, selling, delivering, servicing and paying for products and services.

Originally, electronic commerce was identified as the facilitation of commercial transactions electronically, using technology such as Electronic Data Interchange (EDI) and Electronic Funds Transfer (EFT). These were both introduced in the late 1970s, allowing businesses to send commercial documents like purchase orders or invoices electronically [11]. By the end of 2000, many European and American business companies offered their services through the World Wide Web. Since then people began to associate a word "ecommerce" with the ability of purchasing various goods through the Internet using secure protocols and electronic payment services.

2.2. *E-commerce website*

E-commerce application is a complex system, for businesses, the E-commerce website plays different roles in the following aspects. So E-commerce websites take important positions in the whole E-commerce field.

1. E-commerce websites are the centers for E-commerce activities and information exchanges;
2. E-commerce websites are the gates of business enterprises to develop;
3. E-commerce websites are tools developing Internet marketing for enterprises;
4. E-commerce websites are platforms reflecting the personalized e-commerce services.

An E-commerce Website is typically comprised of three components: a front-end Web server, application server and back-end database. The front-end Web server usually handles the static component of the workload, such as images and infrequently-changing HTML pages. The application server provides an environment to invoke methods that implement the business and presentation logic of the application. Examples of these methods include PHP scripts, Active Server Pages (ASPs) and Java Servlets. The application logic issues a number of queries to the database, which stores the true dynamic state of the Web site (for example, the number of copies of a book in stock). The application server formats the returned database query results as an HTML page, which is passed back to the front-end Web server. Finally, the Web server returns the aggregated content as an HTTP response to the client. *Admission control* and coping with overload is used to prevent systems from being overwhelmed in the presence of persistent or transient overload. Research in this area can be roughly categorized under two broad approaches: reducing the amount of work required when faced with overload, and differentiating classes of customers so that response times of preferred clients do not suffer in the presence of overload. Multiple proposals have been offered for using QoS techniques on Web servers [1, 13, 21]. These have tended to include some form of classification in the form of client IP address, IP subnet, URL or cookie to identify requests as belonging to a particular differentiated level of service. To support these classes, these approaches also include admission control and request scheduling, in order to provide a particular server throughput, network bandwidth, or client response time.

2.3. *E-commerce website evaluation*

2.3.1. *The importance of evaluating E-commerce websites*

After observing a turbulent e-business environment with the burst of the dot.com bubble, companies realized that e-business is not a magic bullet and a license.

A key challenge for e-commerce organizations is to understand customer requirements and to develop their Web presence and back-office operations accordingly. An organization with a Web site that is difficult to use and interact with will project a poor image on the Internet and weaken the organizations position. It is therefore important that an organization be able to make an assessment of the quality of their e-commerce offering, as perceived by their customers and in the context of the industry. In doing so, organizations can improve their offerings over time and benchmark against competitors and best practice in any industry.

The importance of evaluating E-commerce websites success has long been recognized by both E-commerce websites researchers and practitioners. Evaluation is a challenging task because information systems are complex socio-technical entities, E-commerce website investment is related to intangible benefits and indirect costs, and financial data to measure impact of E-commerce websites typically are not accumulated.

Evaluation is the comparison of actual impacts against strategic plans. It looks at original objectives, at what was accomplished and how it was accomplished. It can be formative that is taking place during the life of a project or organization, with the intention of improving the strategy or way of functioning of the project or organization. It can also be summative, drawing lessons from a completed project or an organization that is no longer functioning. Evaluation is inherently a theoretically informed approach (whether explicitly or not), and consequently a definition of evaluation would have be tailored to the theory, approach, needs, purpose and methodology of the evaluation itself. Commonly the aim is to gain the weight over all criteria. Therefore, we constructed the evaluation process as the below, in which Z_E refers to the evaluation process, *A* refers to major evaluation algorithm, and *R* stands for the weighting result as in Eq. (1).

$$Z_E \xrightarrow{A} R \tag{1}$$

In general, two approaches are widely known: quantitative and qualitative. For quantitative methods, *R* as weights can be calculated through several mathematical *A* and Z_E can be described as Eq. (2), where *S* stands for structure of the evaluation method and *d* stands for data used in evaluation process; and for qualitative methods, *R* can be judged as “how good (bad) is it”.

$$Z_E = (S, d) \tag{2}$$

2.3.2. *Main methods evaluating e-commerce*

It has been found that several quantitative methods have been used in evaluating e-commerce websites. [18] and [19] have taken Quality Evaluation Method (QEM) to measure the functionality (global search, navigability and content relevancy), usability (site map, addresses directory), efficiency and site reliability of websites. The method was also used by [15] to evaluate product quality. Another method known as Analytic Hierarchy Process (AHP), developed first by Satty in 1971 was used to solve the scarce resources allocation and planning needs for the military. AHP later had become one of the most widely used tools for making decisions based on multiple-criteria. Grey analysis method (GA) was used to measure the distance between the set of every evaluation object's scores and the set of the best score of each criterion, and choose the object whose distance is the shortest to be the best website. It found that this method gave near value of evaluation [7].

Another important method was Data Envelopment Analysis (DEA). This method was used to evaluate multiple-criterion problems and improve the efficiencies. According to [8], DEA is a powerful quantitative, analytical method for measuring and evaluating performance.

In terms of qualitative methods several methods have been found. Zadeh initiated the fuzzy set theory and Bellman presented some applications of fuzzy theories to the various decision-making processes in a fuzzy environment [14]. Fuzzy theory is widely applicable in information gathering, modeling, analysis, optimization, control, decision making and supervision. Fuzzy is used in support of linguistic variables and there is uncertainness in the problem.

Barnes[2] designed a “WebQual” system to assess E-commerce quality, with no interests on quantity considering; Miranda[15] designed a quality evaluation method with criteria of functionality, usability, efficiency and reliability, but it can not combine experts opinions; Abd El-Aleem [8] constructed a mathematical model to compare website traffic, but had not covered the synthesizing the weights of several experts; Chu[6] presented the ranking of websites from best to worst using fuzzy logic, however could not know the absolute value of each website; and Hung[10] developed an evaluation instrument for E-commerce websites, which was only user’s satisfaction from the first-time buyer’s view and discussed less about quality analysis.

In terms of best evaluation method, it is difficult to pin point which is the best, quantitative or qualitative? This is because each has its advantages and disadvantages and researchers are experts in their own way and chose to evaluate based on their own expertise in analysis. In terms of measurements, which of the five categories is the best measurement? It is definitely an ideal if a comprehensive measurement is incorporated in an evaluation. (See Table 1)

Table 1. Comparing past five researches on E-commerce websites evaluation.

References of researches	Method	Characteristics studied	Remark
Barnes[2]	WebQual Index and factor analysis.	Web site usability, information quality, and service interaction quality	It's developed iteratively through application in various domains.
Miranda[15]	Quality Evaluation Method (QEM)	Functionality, usability, efficiency, reliability	Excessive number of attributes employed raises some subtle problems of computational nature
Abd El-Aleem [8]	Data envelopment analysis (DEA)	Design, usability and performance	Found that are four sites efficient and five inefficient
Chu[6]	Fuzzy logic	Usability, reliability, and cost	Presented the ranking of websites from best to worst. However could not know the absolute value of each website.
Hung[10]	satisfaction model	Reliability and validity	It's from the first-time buyer's viewpoint

2.3.3. *Proposed methods evaluating e-commerce*

Since the criteria of E-commerce websites evaluation have diverse significance and meanings, we cannot assume that each evaluation criteria is of equal importance. There are many methods that can be employed to determine weights such as the eigenvector method, weighted least square method, entropy method, AHP (Analytic Hierarchy Process), and LINMAP (linear programming techniques for Multidimensional of Analysis Preference). The selection of method depends on the nature of the problem. To evaluate E-commerce websites is a complex and wide-ranging problem, so this problem requires the most inclusive and flexible method. In (2), *d*'s domain has been define as *D*, which has been shown in (3) where *N* stands for numeral set, *P* stands for parameter set, and *L* stands for linguistic description set. However, in operation process of applying AHP method, it is more easy and humanistic for evaluators to assess "criterion A is much more important than criterion B" than to consider "the importance of principle A and principle B is seven to one". Hence, Buckley [3] extended Saaty's AHP to the case where the evaluators are allowed to employ fuzzy ratios in place of exact ratios to handle the difficulty for people to assign exact ratios when comparing two criteria and derive the fuzzy weights of criteria by geometric mean method. Therefore, in this study, we employ Buckley's method, FAHP, to fuzzify hierarchical analysis by allowing fuzzy numbers for the pairwise comparisons and find the fuzzy weights. In this section, we briefly review concepts for fuzzy hierarchical evaluation.

$$D = N \cup P \cup L, d \in D \tag{3}$$

3. Design of E-commerce Websites Evaluation Mode

The purpose of this section is to establish a hierarchical structure for solve the evaluation problem of E-commerce websites evaluation. The contents include two subsections: hierarchical structure of evaluation criteria and determining the weights of evaluation criteria.

3.1. *Hierarchical structure of evaluation criteria*

Design, reliability and usability are three criteria based on which the evaluation is performed. For each criterion, four sub-criteria have been considered [22]. In the last part of rules matching, there are four criteria for each standard and five assess characters for each criterion. Table 2 shows the hierarchical structure with criteria, sub-criteria and explanation [17].

3.2. *Determining weights of the evaluation criteria*

3.2.1. *General definitions and notifications*

- Fuzzy number

A fuzzy number is an extension of a regular number in the sense that it does not refer to one single value but rather to a connected set of possible values, where each possible value has its own weight between 0 and 1. This weight is called the membership function. A fuzzy number is thus a special case of a convex fuzzy set [9]. According to the definition of Laarhoven and Pedrycz [12], a triangular fuzzy number (TFN) should possess the following basic features.

Table 2. The hierarchical structure for E-commerce website evaluation

Criteria	Sub-criteria	Explanation
Usability (C_1)	*Accuracy* (C_{11})	Comparison features, for instance, availability of product reviews, documentation, and user's ability to verify the information from other sources.
	Authority (C_{12})	Company profile features like owner and contact details of the company, nature of products, company's official approval, copyright for the company's name.
	Current information (C_{13})	Information updating features, for example, indicating the dates when the site was first launched and last updated, mentioning company's annual report date.
	Efficiency (C_{14})	Speed and effectiveness of the page, for instance, necessary information should be visible within 10 seconds, thumbnail graphics or alternate texts are displayed when heavy graphics are being downloaded.
Reliability (C_2)	*Security* (C_{21})	Safety features like client authentication, secured payment system.
	Functionality (C_{22})	Functional features like presence of online help, information on product delivery method.
	Integrity (C_{23})	Features for robustness, fault tolerance, data consistency.
	Navigation (C_{24})	Navigation standards, for example, availability of shortcut or alternate paths, reaching destination within 3 mice clicks.
Design (C_3)	*Aesthetic features* (C_{31})	Visual characteristics features, for instance, use of colour, graphics, background, level of interactivity.
	Contents (C_{32})	Consistency features between the information and motive of the site.
	Layout (C_{33})	Formatting features like font face and size, page margin.
	Standard conformance (C_{34})	Regularity features, for instance, interface standard, programming.

A fuzzy number $\tilde{A}$ on R to be a TFN if its membership function $\mu_{\tilde{A}}(x): R \to [0,1]$ is equal to (4), where L and U stand for the lower and upper bounds of the fuzzy number $\tilde{A}$, respectively, and M for the modal value (see Figure 1). The TFN can be denoted by $\tilde{A} = (L, M, U)$ and the following is the operational laws of two TFNs $\tilde{A}_a = (L_a, M_a, U_a)$ and $\tilde{A}_b = (L_b, M_b, U_b)$, as shown [4].

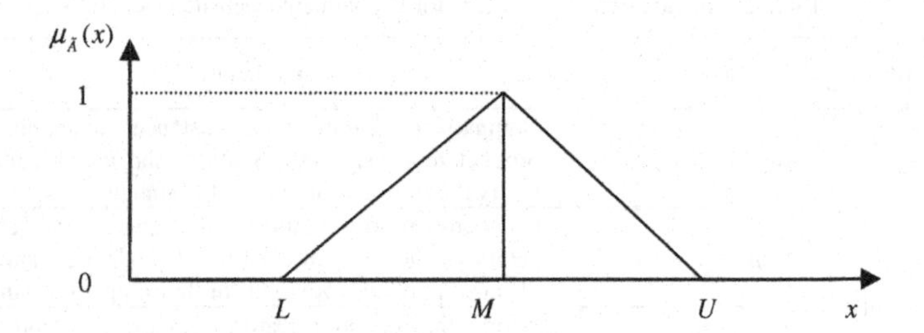

Figure 1. The membership function with the triangular fuzzy number

Addition of a fuzzy number $\oplus$

$$\tilde{A}_a \oplus \tilde{A}_b = (L_a, M_a, U_a) \oplus (L_b, M_b, U_b) = (L_a + L_b, M_a + M_b, U_a + U_b) \quad (4)$$

Multiplication of a fuzzy number

$$\tilde{A}_a \otimes \tilde{A}_b = (L_a, M_a, U_a) \otimes (L_b, M_b, U_b) = (L_a L_b, M_a M_b, U_a U_b) \\ for L_i > 0, M_i > 0, U_i > 0 \quad (5)$$

Multiplication of any real number k and a fuzzy number

$$k \bullet \tilde{A} = k \bullet (L, M, U) = (kL, kM, kU) \quad (6)$$

Subtraction of a fuzzy number

$$\tilde{A}_a \Theta \tilde{A}_b = (L_a, M_a, U_a) \Theta (L_b, M_b, U_b) = (L_a - L_b, M_a - M_b, U_a - U_b) \quad (7)$$

Division of a fuzzy number

$$\tilde{A}_a \Delta \tilde{A}_b = (L_a, M_a, U_a) \Delta (L_b, M_b, U_b) = (L_a / U_b, M_a / M_b, U_a / L_b) \\ for\ L_i > 0, M_i > 0, U_i > 0 \quad (8)$$

Reciprocal of a fuzzy number

$$\tilde{A}^{-1} = (L, M, U)^{-1} = (1/U, 1/M, 1/L) \quad for\ L > 0, M > 0, U > 0 \quad (9)$$

- Linguistic variables

According to Zadeh [23], it is very difficult for conventional quantification to express reasonably those situations that are overtly complex or hard to define; so the notion of a linguistic variable is necessary in such situation. A linguistic variable is a variable whose values are words or sentences in a natural or artificial language. Here, we use this kind of expression to compare two building E-commerce websites evaluation criteria by five basic linguistic terms, as "absolutely important," "very strongly important," "essentially important," "weakly important" and "equally important" with respect to a fuzzy five level scale (see Figure 2) [5]. In this paper, the computational technique is based on the following fuzzy numbers defined by Mon et al. [16] in Table 3. Here each membership function (scale of fuzzy number) is defined by three parameters of the symmetric triangular fuzzy number, the left point, middle point and right point of the range over which the function is defined. The use of linguistic variables is currently widespread and the linguistic effect values of E-commerce websites found in this study are primarily used to assess the linguistic ratings given by the evaluators.

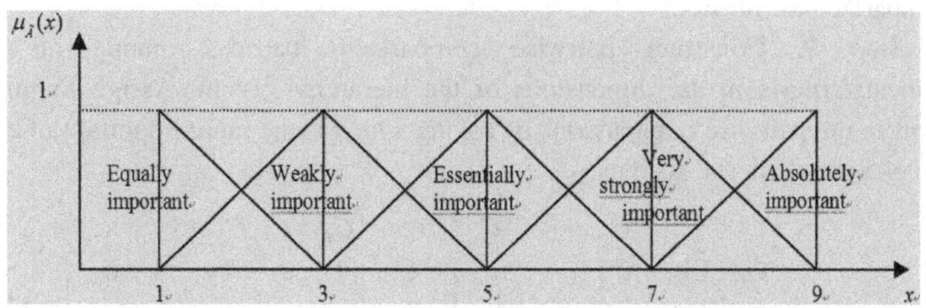

Figure 2. Membership function of linguistics variables for comparing two criteria.

Table 3. Fuzzy scale and linguistic expression of relative importance between two criteria and performance values

Intensity of importance	Fuzzy number	Definition of linguistic scale
1	$\tilde{1}$	Equal importance; *very poor*
3	$\tilde{3}$	Weak importance of one over another; *poor*
5	$\tilde{5}$	Essentially important; *normal*
7	$\tilde{7}$	Very strongly important; *good*
9	$\tilde{9}$	Absolutely important; *very good*
2, 4, 6, 8	$\tilde{2}$, $\tilde{4}$, $\tilde{6}$, $\tilde{8}$	Intermediate values between two adjacent judgments

- Ranking the fuzzy number

The result of the fuzzy synthetic decision reached by each alternative is a fuzzy number. Therefore, it is necessary that a nonfuzzy ranking method for fuzzy numbers be employed for comparison of each E-commerce websites. In other words, the procedure of defuzzification is to locate the Best Nonfuzzy Performance value (BNP). Methods of such defuzzified fuzzy ranking generally include mean of maximal (MOM), center of area (COA), and a-cut. To utilize the COA method to find out the BNP is a simple and practical method, and there is no need to bring in the preferences of any evaluators, so it is used in this study. The BNP value of the fuzzy number $\widetilde{R}_i$ can be found by the following equation:

$$BNP_i = [(UR_i - LR_i) + (MR_i - LR_i)]/3 + LR_i \qquad \forall i. \tag{10}$$

3.2.2. *Fuzzy analytic hierarchy process*

The procedure for determining the evaluation criteria weights by FAHP can be summarized as follows:

Step 1. Construct pairwise comparison matrices among all the elements/criteria in the dimensions of the hierarchy system. Assign linguistic terms to the pairwise comparisons by asking which is the more important of each two elements/criteria, such as

$$\tilde{A} = [\tilde{a}_{ij}] = \begin{matrix} & C_1 & C_2 & \cdots & C_n \\ C_1 & 1 & \tilde{a}_{12} & \cdots & \tilde{a}_{1n} \\ C_2 & \tilde{a}_{21} & 1 & \cdots & \tilde{a}_{2n} \\ \vdots & \vdots & \vdots & \vdots & \vdots \\ C_n & \tilde{a}_{n1} & \tilde{a}_{n2} & \cdots & 1 \end{matrix} = \begin{matrix} & C_1 & C_2 & \cdots & C_n \\ C_1 & 1 & \tilde{a}_{12} & \cdots & \tilde{a}_{1n} \\ C_2 & 1/\tilde{a}_{12} & 1 & \cdots & \tilde{a}_{2n} \\ \vdots & \vdots & \vdots & \vdots & \vdots \\ C_n & 1/\tilde{a}_{1n} & 1/\tilde{a}_{2n} & \cdots & 1 \end{matrix} \tag{11}$$

where

$$\tilde{a}_{ij} = \begin{cases} \tilde{1}, \tilde{3}, \tilde{5}, \tilde{7}, \tilde{9} & \text{criterion i is relative importance to criterion j;} \\ 1 & i = j; \\ \tilde{1}^{-1}, \tilde{3}^{-1}, \tilde{5}^{-1}, \tilde{7}^{-1}, \tilde{9}^{-1} & \text{criterion i is relative less importance to criterion j.} \end{cases}$$

Step 2. To use geometric mean technique to define the fuzzy geometric mean and fuzzy weights of each criterion by Buckley [3] as follows:

$$\widetilde{r}_i = (\widetilde{a}_{i1} \otimes \widetilde{a}_{i2} \otimes \cdots \otimes \widetilde{a}_{in})^{1/n}, \quad \widetilde{w}_i = \widetilde{r}_i \otimes (\widetilde{r}_1 \oplus \cdots \oplus \widetilde{r}_n)^{-1}, \tag{12}$$

where $\widetilde{a}_{in}$ is fuzzy comparison value of criterion i to criterion n, thus, $\widetilde{r}_i$ is geometric mean of fuzzy comparison value of criterion i to each criterion, $\widetilde{w}_i$ is the fuzzy weight of the ith criterion, can be indicated by a TFN, $\widetilde{w}_i = (Lw_i, Mw_i, Uw_i)$. Here Lw_i, Mw_i and Uw_i stand for the lower, middle and upper values of the fuzzy weight of the ith criterion.

4. Case of FAHP to E-commerce Websites Evaluation

In this section, an example of the application of FAHP to determine the weights of criteria and sub-criteria for E-commerce website evaluation is given to demonstrate this approach.

The overall goal has been stated as determining the weights of criteria and sub-criteria for E-commerce website evaluation. Based on Matlab, a general consensus among experts can be synthesized. To determine the relative importance of the evaluation criteria C_1 - C_3, they were pair-wise compared with respect to the goal by using the triangular fuzzy numbers.

4.1. *The weights calculation of the evaluation criteria*

According to the formulated structure of building E-commerce websites evaluation, the weights of the criteria hierarchy can be analyzed. The simulation process was followed by a series of interviews with decision-making group experts. Weights were obtained by using the FAHP method. The following example demonstrates the computational procedure of the weights of criteria for experts:

1. According to the interviews with five experts about the importance of evaluation dimensions, afterward the pairwise comparison matrices of dimensions(criteria) can be achieved as follows:

$$\begin{array}{c} \\ C_1 \\ C_2 \\ C_3 \end{array} \begin{array}{c} \begin{matrix} C_1 & C_2 & C_3 \end{matrix} \\ \begin{bmatrix} 1 & poor & good \\ & 1 & poor \\ & & 1 \end{bmatrix} \end{array} \qquad \begin{array}{c} \\ C_1 \\ C_2 \\ C_3 \end{array} \begin{array}{c} \begin{matrix} C_1 & C_2 & C_3 \end{matrix} \\ \begin{bmatrix} 1 & very\_poor & normal \\ & 1 & poor \\ & & 1 \end{bmatrix} \end{array}$$

experts_1 experts_2

$$\begin{array}{c} \\ C_1 \\ C_2 \\ C_3 \end{array} \begin{array}{c} \begin{matrix} C_1 & C_2 & C_3 \end{matrix} \\ \begin{bmatrix} 1 & less\_poor & good \\ & 1 & poor \\ & & 1 \end{bmatrix} \end{array} \qquad \begin{array}{c} \\ C_1 \\ C_2 \\ C_3 \end{array} \begin{array}{c} \begin{matrix} C_1 & C_2 & C_3 \end{matrix} \\ \begin{bmatrix} 1 & less\_poor & very\_good \\ & 1 & normal \\ & & 1 \end{bmatrix} \end{array}$$

experts_3 experts_4

$$\begin{array}{c} \\ C_1 \\ C_2 \\ C_3 \end{array} \begin{array}{c} \begin{matrix} C_1 & C_2 & C_3 \end{matrix} \\ \begin{bmatrix} 1 & less\_normal & very\_poor \\ & 1 & less\_very\_poor \\ & & 1 \end{bmatrix} \end{array}$$

experts_5

2. Applying the fuzzy numbers defined in Table 1, the linguistic scales can be transferred to the corresponding fuzzy numbers as below:

$$\begin{array}{c|ccc} & C_1 & C_2 & C_3 \\ C_1 & 1 & \tilde{3} & \tilde{7} \\ C_2 & \tilde{3}^{-1} & 1 & \tilde{3} \\ C_3 & \tilde{7}^{-1} & \tilde{3}^{-1} & 1 \end{array} \quad \begin{array}{c|ccc} & C_1 & C_2 & C_3 \\ C_1 & 1 & \tilde{1} & \tilde{5} \\ C_2 & \tilde{1}^{-1} & 1 & \tilde{3} \\ C_3 & \tilde{5}^{-1} & \tilde{3}^{-1} & 1 \end{array} \quad \begin{array}{c|ccc} & C_1 & C_2 & C_3 \\ C_1 & 1 & \tilde{3}^{-1} & \tilde{7} \\ C_2 & \tilde{3} & 1 & \tilde{3} \\ C_3 & \tilde{7}^{-1} & \tilde{3}^{-1} & 1 \end{array}$$

experts_1 experts_2 experts_3

$$\begin{array}{c|ccc} & C_1 & C_2 & C_3 \\ C_1 & 1 & \tilde{3}^{-1} & \tilde{9} \\ C_2 & \tilde{3} & 1 & \tilde{5} \\ C_3 & \tilde{9}^{-1} & \tilde{5}^{-1} & 1 \end{array} \quad \begin{array}{c|ccc} & C_1 & C_2 & C_3 \\ C_1 & 1 & \tilde{5}^{-1} & \tilde{1} \\ C_2 & \tilde{5} & 1 & \tilde{1}^{-1} \\ C_3 & \tilde{1}^{-1} & \tilde{1} & 1 \end{array}$$

experts_4 experts_5

3. Computing the elements of synthetic pairwise comparison matrix by using the geometric mean method suggested by Buckley [3]: that is $\tilde{a}_{ij} = (\tilde{a}_{ij}^1 \otimes \tilde{a}_{ij}^2 \otimes \tilde{a}_{ij}^3 \otimes \tilde{a}_{ij}^4 \otimes \tilde{a}_{ij}^5)^{1/5}$, for $\tilde{a}_{12}$ as an example:

$$\tilde{a}_{12} = (\tilde{3} \otimes \tilde{1} \otimes \tilde{3}^{-1} \otimes \tilde{3}^{-1} \otimes \tilde{5}^{-1})^{1/5} = ((1,3,5) \otimes (1,1,3) \otimes (\frac{1}{5},\frac{1}{3},1) \otimes (\frac{1}{5},\frac{1}{3},1) \otimes (\frac{1}{7},\frac{1}{5},\frac{1}{3}))^{1/5}$$

$$= ((1 \times 1 \times \frac{1}{5} \times \frac{1}{5} \times \frac{1}{7})^{1/5}, (3 \times 1 \times \frac{1}{3} \times \frac{1}{3} \times \frac{1}{5})^{1/5}, (5 \times 3 \times 1 \times 1 \times \frac{1}{3})^{1/5}) = (0.356, 0.582, 1.380)$$

It can be obtained the other matrix elements by the same computational procedure, therefore, the synthetic pairwise comparison matrices of the five representatives will be constructed as follows:

$$\begin{array}{c|ccc} & C_1 & C_2 & C_3 \\ C_1 & 1 & (0.356, 0.582, 1.380) & (0.181, 0.214, 0.336) \\ C_2 & (0.725, 1.718, 2.809) & 1 & (1, 2.667, 3.876) \\ C_3 & (2.976, 4.673, 5.525) & (0.258, 0.375, 1) & 1 \end{array}$$

4. To use Eq. (12) to obtain the fuzzy weights of dimensions for owners group, that is:

$$\tilde{r}_1 = (\tilde{a}_{11} \otimes \tilde{a}_{12} \otimes \tilde{a}_{13})^{1/3} = ((1,1,1) \otimes (0.356, 0.582, 1.380) \otimes (0.181, 0.214, 0.336))^{1/3}$$

$$= ((1 \times 0.356 \times 0.181)^{1/3}, (1 \times 0.582 \times 0.214)^{1/3}, (1 \times 1.380 \times 0.336)^{1/3}) = (0.401, 0.499, 0.774)$$

Likewise, we can obtain the remaining $\tilde{r}_2 = (0.898, 1.661, 2.237)$ and $\tilde{r}_3 = (0.916, 1.206, 1.768)$.

For the weight of each dimension, they can be done as follows:

$$\tilde{w}_1 = \tilde{r}_1 \otimes (\tilde{r}_1 \oplus \tilde{r}_2 \oplus \tilde{r}_3)^{-1}$$
$$= (0.401, 0.499, 0.774) \otimes ((0.401, 0.499, 0.774) \oplus (0.898, 1.661, 2.237) \oplus (0.916, 1.206, 1.768))^{-1}$$
$$= (0.401, 0.499, 0.774) \otimes (1/(0.774+2.237+1.768), 1/(0.499+1.661+1.206), 1/(0.401+0.898+0.916))$$
$$= (0.401, 0.499, 0.774) \otimes (0.209, 0.297, 0.451)$$
$$= (0.084, 0.148, 0.349)$$

Similarly, $\tilde{w}_2 = (0.188, 0.493, 1.009)$ and $\tilde{w}_3 = (0.191, 0.358, 0.797)$.

5. To employ the COA method to compute the BNP value of the fuzzy weights of each dimension:

To take the BNP value of the weight of usability (C_1) for experts as an example, the calculation process is as follows.

$$BNP_{w_1} = \left[(UR_1 - LR_1) + (MR_1 - LR_1)\right]/3 + LR_1$$
$$= \left[(0.349 - 0.084) + (0.148 - 0.084)\right]/3 + 0.084$$
$$= 0.194$$

Likewise $BNP_{w_2} = 0.563$, $BNP_{w_3} = 0.449$ and the weights for the remaining sub-criteria can be found as shown in Table 4.

Table 4. Weights of criteria and sub-criteria

Criteria	Weights of criteria	sub-criteria	Overall weights of sub-criteria
usability	0.194	C_{11}	0.053
		C_{12}	0.076
		C_{13}	0.033
		C_{14}	0.032
reliability	0.563	C_{21}	0.119
		C_{22}	0.065
		C_{23}	0.100
		C_{24}	0.279
design	0.449	C_{31}	0.153
		C_{32}	0.132
		C_{33}	0.089
		C_{34}	0.075

5. Conclusion

The reason of this study was to develop a scientific framework for the E-commerce websites evaluation. In commercial area, E-commerce website is a highly professional service, which involves significant information of company and clients, transaction functions and amount of specialized effort. Although judging the quality of the E-commerce websites may be subjective, evaluation of the E-commerce websites is even more so. In current methods of E-commerce websites evaluation, company agencies rely only on a panel of experts to perform the evaluation, neglecting the fuzziness of subjective judgment and other relative interest groups perception in this process. Thus, an effective evaluation procedure is essential to promote the decision quality. This work examines this group decision-making process and proposes a multiple- criteria framework for E-commerce websites evaluation. To deal with the qualitative attributes in subjective judgment, this work employs FAHP to determine the weights of decision criteria for each relative expert representative. This process enables decision makers to formalize and effectively solve the complicated, multiple-criteria and fuzzy perception problem of most appropriate E-commerce websites evaluation. A case study of proposed E-commerce websites evaluation is used to demonstrate the approach. The basic concepts applied were understandable to the decision making groups, and the computation required is straightforward and simple. It will also support the enterprises in making critical decisions during the selecting of E-commerce websites' alternatives.

References

1. J. Almeida, M. Dabu, A. Manikutty and P. Cao, in *Proc. Workshop on Internet Server Performance*, Madison, USA, June 23, 1998, eds. P. Cao and S. Sarukkai, pp. 1-16.
2. S. J. Barnes and R.T. Vidgen, *J. Electron. Commer. R.* **3**, 114 (2002).
3. J. J. Buckley, *Fuzzy Set. Syst.* **17**, 233 (1985).
4. S. J. Chen and C. L. Hwang, *Fuzzy multiple attribute decision making: methods and applications.* (Springer-Verlag New York, 1992).
5. H. K. Chiou and G. H. Tzeng, *Int. J. Fuzzy Syst.* **3**, 466 (2001).
6. F. Chu and Y. Li, in *Proc. Int. Conf. "Management Science and Engineering"*, Lille, France, October 5-7 2006, pp.111-115.
7. J. Deng, *Syst. Control. Lett.* **1**, 288 (1982)
8. A. El-Aleem, W. El-Wahed, N. Ismail and F. Torkey, *World Academy of Science, Engineering and Technology*, **4**, 20 (2005).
9. M. Hanss, *Applied Fuzzy Arithmetic: An Introduction with Engineering Applications.* (Springer, Netherlands, 2005)
10. W. Hung and R. J. McQueen, *Electron. J. Inform. Syst. Eval.* **7**, 31 (2004)
11. M. Y. Ivory and M. A. Hearst, *ACM. Comput. Surv.* **33**, 470 (2001).
12. P. J. M. V. Laarhoven and W. Pedrcyz, *Fuzzy Set. Syst.* **11**, 199 (1983).

13. K. Li and S. Jamin, in *Proc. "the Nineteenth Annual Joint Conference of the IEEE Computer and Communications Societies"*, Tel-Aviv, Israel, March 26-30, 2000, pp. 651-659.
14. D. Marincas, *J. Appl. Quant. Methods* **2**, 289 (2007)
15. F. Miranda, R. Corte's and C. Barriuso, *Electron. J. Inform. Syst. Eval.* **9**, 73 (2006).
16. D. Mon, C. Cheng and J. Lin, *Fuzzy Set. Syst*, **62**, 127 (1994).
17. L. Olsina, G. Lafuente and G. Rossi, in *Proc. "the First International Conference on Electronic Commerce and Web Technologies"*, September 4-6, 2000, eds. K. Bauknecht, S. K. Madria and G. Pernul, pp. 239–252
18. L. Olsina and G. Rossi, *IEEE Multimedia* **9**, 20 (2002)
19. L. Olsina and G. Rossi, *The Electon. J. Argentine Society Inform. Operations Res.* **3**, No. 1.
20. T. L. Saaty, *The Analytic Hierarchy Process*, (McGraw-Hill, New York, USA, 1980)
21. T. Voigt, R. Tewari, D. Freimuth and A. Mehra, in *Proc. of the USENIX Annual Technical Conf.*, Boston, USA, June 25-30, 2001, editor C. Cole, pp. 189-202.
22. L. Zadeh, *Inform. Control* **8**, 338 (1965)
23. L. Zadeh, *Inform. Sciences* **8**, 199 (1975)

ANALYSIS OF INDUSTRIAL CLUSTER AGENTS RELATIONS USING FUZZY SUBRELATIONS

ANTONI VIDAL-SUÑÉ
ALBERT FONTS-RIBAS

Department of Business Management, University Rovira i Virgili
Av. de la Universitat, 1; Reus, 43204, Spain

Industrial clusters try to exploit the effect of external economies and joint actions that come from the collaboration between their agents. But in order that these effects arise it is needed close cooperation partnerships between the agents in the industrial cluster, which could improve competitiveness. It's obvious, therefore, that analyzing which are the relationships between the agents in the industrial cluster is critical to make strategic decisions that promote and improve the competitiveness of the industrial cluster. This paper proposes a methodology based on obtaining a fuzzy relation from which, applying Moore's closure in an uncertain situation, we can identify subrelations that group industrial cluster agents depending on their degree of affinity based on the intensity of their relationships.

1. Introduction

The emergence of a flexible specialization production model has brought industrial dispersal or diffuse industrialization strategies, based on decentralized production models characterized by the concentration of companies in an industry in a environment geographically delimited, to acquire an increasing role, increasingly more intensely [1]. The different currents of thought that have analyzed this phenomenon have called it using different names (industrial districts, innovative environments, local production systems, *etc.*.), but, nowadays, Porter's proposal of industrial cluster has become the most used to refer to groups of companies in the same sector located in the same geographic area to share resources and capabilities and increase their competitiveness, both individually and globally [2].

Industrial clusters allow companies to improve their competitiveness because they take advantage of agglomeration economies, obtaining benefit from their proximity, from the existence of certain infrastructure and equipment in the territory, from diversified customer markets and labor markets, from a better access to information and knowledge, and from a social, cultural and institutional environment focused on the development of the main industrial cluster activity. Within the industrial cluster appear productive relations of cooperation of a certain intensity and consistency, based on the complementarity of the different production processes carried out by various companies in the same sector. When we analyze industrial clusters in a dynamic perspective we can see how their performance is a result of the integration of multiple different actions where many actors are involved, both individually and collectively [3]. The fact that this integration requires physical proximity relations, involves the configuration of unique spatial units in production, social, cultural, technological, political and institutional terms [4]. In that sense, Porter introduces the concept of industrial cluster, as the natural union of the companies in a particular sector, and with other related industries in a given territory [2]. These companies develop connections with a large number of support services to generate synergies, externalities, cooperation and dissemination of technology; characteristics that give the industry cluster competitive advantages.

An industrial cluster is a group of companies and institutions geographically close, and related to a particular field, linked by common and complementary features. In other words, the specialization of human capital, the flow of information, the innovation processes and the diffusion of technology, and the relations between suppliers and customers, provide the ideal framework for the emergence of external economies to the firm but internal to the territories. Geographic proximity facilitates communication, technological externalities, leads to efficient delivery of intermediate inputs at lower costs, and allows a greater market share of inputs and outputs, as well as a reserve of qualified local labor. These externalities produce effects on the territories, and affect the efficiency and the competitiveness of the companies in the industrial cluster.

In addition to that, the development of joint actions in a deliberated way by all companies in the industrial cluster allow to take greater advantage of the benefits of external economies offered by the territory and to generate, therefore, a greater collective efficiency [5]. The collective efficiency view emphasizes the strengthening of relations between actors in the industrial cluster (competitors, buyers, suppliers, institutions, *etc.*) to achieve more efficiency and to increase innovation. That is, he believes that companies in the industrial cluster set a structural situation where, in a relatively small geographic area with clearly defined limits, live a multitude of private and public economic agents involved in a high density network of contracts and formal and informal agreements for the coordination of production complementarities.

According to Porter [6], the existence of the industrial cluster facilitates the implementation of cooperation agreements that permits to exploit complementarities, economies of scale and scope as well as increase flexibility and the speed of reaction of firms to changes in the environment. Therefore, joint actions become a critical element for the correct work of industrial clusters, as they are closely related to the notion of inter-company cooperation as a result of trust and social capital [7, 8, 9]. In short, the industrial cluster and inter-organizational networks that are established in a territory with several players from the same production chain contribute to enhance the competitiveness of the companies that make up and, therefore, attach great importance to the network of relationships between them in order to improve their individual and collective performance [6].

Thus, the essence of any industrial cluster is based on a close network of agreements, formal and informal, between all agents which are part of it, and that are maintained continuously over time. That is, we can define an industrial cluster as a compact network of relationships developed between actors within a specific geographical area. Consequently, the identification of key relationships between industrial cluster agents, who make a difference in terms of competitiveness, can become a basic part for the development of public and private policies, focused at enhancing competitiveness of companies in the industrial cluster. The argument is that both the quantity and quality of the network of structural relationships between the actors of a territory determine the competitiveness of companies located on it. If the quality of relational contracts between the agents in the industrial cluster is based on the generation of added value for the whole industrial cluster, the analysis of the structural relations network that exists is the basis for formulating management actions which permit to improve the performance of companies in the industrial cluster.

Consequently, it would be highly interesting to know the relationships between the various agents in the industrial cluster, and the degree of intensity. The problem lies in the difficulty to capture and measure the intensity of relations between agents and, therefore, to analyze how it affects the competitiveness of companies in the industrial cluster. In order to cover this analysis, and given the lack of tools for it, it has recently been developed a methodology based on the identification of strong subrelations within an industrial cluster, which shows the structural network of relationships between their agents [10, 11, 12].

This is an analytical tool used to study the relationships within the industrial cluster among their main agents, for a number of critical issues (technology, innovation, training, *etc.*) that determine his more or less synergistic performance, and that facilitates the development of a strategy that can improve the competitive conditions of the industrial cluster [10]. This tool, called Matrix Structural Relations, allows to establish relationships between agents in a particular industry cluster, analyzing the relationships and links between its elements, so that you can see the set of relationships between the agents in an industrial cluster, and consequently determine the type and the quality of these relationships. However, the methodology used by this matrix consists of the subjective allocation, by researchers, of a fixed previously values depending on how we estimate the relationship between agents (based on information obtained through questionnaires and interviews).

This procedure tries to approximate to the density of the network of relationships within the industrial cluster. For this reason we consider that, because the evaluation of relations between agents is based on highly subjective perceptions of the actors involved, their analysis would be more relevant using the tools they have developed the Theory of Fuzzy sub-Sets.

Therefore, this paper presents a methodology for analyzing the relationships between industrial cluster agents based on obtaining a fuzzy relation from which, applying Moore's closure in a uncertainly situation, to identify subrelations that join industrial cluster agents depending on their degree of affinity based on the intensity of their relationships. As Capó *et al.* Pointed [12], any industrial cluster can have internal cores within the relations between agents are more intense, that is, where the links are stronger related to other subsets of relations. The aim is to identify these strong cores or maximum subrelations between industrial cluster agents.

Before describing, in the third section, the proposed methodology through an example, the second section presents the axiomatic that allows his application. The work concludes with the presentation of the conclusions.

2. Obtaining subrelations: Moore's closure

Topology studies the properties of topological spaces, being interested in the comparison of objects and their classification. In general, topology refers to a family of subsets of a given set, which meet certain rules. This supposes that for a structure induced by a binary relationship, these rules are equivalent to the transitivity of the ratio. Given the case, as it occurs with the relations between the agents of an industrial cluster, that relations were not transitive, then we must use poorer mathematical structures, but more adaptable to economic reality, as they are pretopologies. Specifically, given a set E, the obtained the set of parts or power set P(E). Given a functional application Γ from P(E) to P(E), we will say that Γ is a pretopology of E, if and only if [13, 14]:

1. $\emptyset \in P(E)$
2. $E \in P(E)$
3. $\Gamma \emptyset = \emptyset$
4. $\forall A_j \in P(E)$: $A_j \subset \Gamma A_j$; also here, the fourth axiom forces to:
5. $\Gamma E = E$

In its application to a management phenomenon, it must be interpreted the application functional Γ in the sense that you can include the notion of relationship. Then, it is said that the pretopology requires, according to the fourth axiom, that a grouping of elements of the set E is related to another which comprises at least the same elements [15].

As in ordinary pretopology, the functional application Γ takes the name "adherent application" or simply "adherence". Also, now we can associate Γ to the "interior application" or simply "interior", δ, that we obtain in the following way [16]:

$$\forall A_j \in P(E) : \delta A_j = \overline{\Gamma \overline{A}_j}$$

where $\overline{A}_j$ is the complement of A_j.

It is straightforward, then defining the "closed" and the "opened" [17]. In fact, an element of the power set A_j is a closed when:

$$A_j = \Gamma A_j$$

And element of the power set is an opened if:

$$A_j = \delta A_j$$

Since:

$$(A_j = \Gamma A_j) \Rightarrow (\overline{A}_j = \Gamma \overline{A}_j)$$

$$(A_j = \delta A_j) \Rightarrow (\overline{A}_j = \delta \overline{A}_j)$$

it necessary follows:

$$A_j \in P(E) \Rightarrow \overline{A}_j \in P(E)$$

Then, we conclude that, if the set of closed and opened contains A_j, it also must contain $\overline{A}_j$.

Given a pretopology, it will be said to be isotonous if:

$$\forall A_j, A_k \in P(E) : (A_j \subset A_k) \Rightarrow (\Gamma A_j \subset \Gamma A_k)$$

or in another way:

$$\forall A_j, A_k \in P(E) : (A_j \subset A_k) \Rightarrow (\delta A_j \subset \delta A_k)$$

This implies, in our case, that, when a grouping is formed by some people and another group with the same people plus others, the grouping related to the second will be made up of the same people of the relate done to first and possibly to others.

One of the concepts more used for the treatment of the groupings is the Moore's closure, base of the theory of the affinities. So it exists a closure of Moore if the functional application Γ of a set of parts P(E) on P(E), has the properties of extension, idempotency and isotony [18]. Then, since all isotonous pretopology fulfils the conditions of extension and isotony, if it also had the one of idempotency, we would be in presence of a Moore's closure. Axiomatic of Moore's closure is [13, 14]:

1. $\emptyset \in P(E)$
2. $E \in P(E)$
3. $\forall Aj \in P(E): Aj \subset \Gamma Aj$, extension
4. $\forall Aj \in P(E): \Gamma(\Gamma Aj) \subset \Gamma Aj$, idempotency
5. $\forall Aj, Ak \in P(E): (Aj \subset Ak) \Rightarrow (\Gamma Aj \subset \Gamma Ak)$, isotony

In the Moore's closure $\Gamma E = E$, as a result of the extension. Nevertheless it is not necessary condition that $\Gamma \emptyset = \emptyset$, as it happens in the pretopologies. Thus, not all Moore's closures are pretopologies. But, when a Moore's closure satisfy:

$$\emptyset \in P(E): \Gamma \emptyset = \emptyset$$

then, this Moore's closure is a isotonous pretopology with idempotency.

Moore's closure occupies an important place in the process of developing the algorithm for the treatment of maximum grouping problems, which forces to establish a way that allows to find Moore's closures from a concept affordable enough [15, 19]. To this end, the graph theory is particularly useful for developing schemes in which the relationship between elements play an important role. A graph can be represented in matrix form as well as sagittately, limiting ourselves here to the first of these forms.

From a fuzzy relation $[R_\alpha]$ between the elements of a reference E, with $E = \{E_i / i = 1 \ldots n\}$, we have that $[R_\alpha] = E \times E$, constituting a regular graph of level α, where [18, 20][a]:

$$[R_\alpha] = \{(E_i, E_i) \in E \times E / \mu_R(E_i, E_i) \geq \alpha\}, \text{ with } \alpha \in [0,1]$$

[aa] The fuzzy relation $[R_\alpha]$ can also be configured between two different benchmarks, ie $[R_\alpha] = E \times D$, with $E = \{E_i / i = 1 \ldots n\}$ and $D = \{D_j / j = 1 \ldots m\}$. Although this is not the case of the problem we address in this paper.

The matrix corresponding to this graph, at the level α, shows by the valuations in the interval [0, 1], the degree of intensity in the relationship between each pair of elements of the set of reference E. In this regard, the predecessors and successors of an element E_i can be defined as:

E_j it's a successor of E_i at level α if $(E_i, E_j) \in [R_\alpha]$
E_i it's a predecesor of E_i at level α if $(E_i, E_j) \in [R_\alpha]$

According to Gil Aluja, and Kaufmann and Gil Aluja [21, 18], these definitions allow us to find, for a given level α, the connection to the right R_α^+, that is, the functional application R_α^+ of P(E) in P(E) such that, for all $A_j \in$ P(E), R_α^+ is the subset of elements of E that are successors to the α level of any element belonging to A_j. Stated another way, for each element A_j of P(E) we have all groups of elements with which it has affinity. This is usually expressed as:

$$R_\alpha^+ A_j = \{ E_i \in E / (E_i, E_j) \in [R_\alpha], \forall E_i \in A_j \}, \text{ with } R_\alpha^+ \varnothing = E$$

Similarly, there is the connection on the left R_α^- at a certain level α, as the functional application of R_α^- of P(E) to P(E) such that, for all $A_j \in$ P (E), R_α^- is the subset of elements of E which are predecessors of any element α level belonging to A_j. Thus, each group of elements A_j of P(E) is related to all group elements with which has affinity. This is usually expressed as:

$$R_\alpha^- A_j = \{ E_i \in E / (E_i, E_j) \in [R_\alpha], \forall E_i \in A_j \}, \text{ with } R_\alpha^- \varnothing = E$$

The connection on the right ($R_\alpha^+ A_j$) and the connection on the left ($R_\alpha^- A_j$) can be found directly by simply reading at the fuzzy relation $[R_\alpha]$ as follows:

$$\forall E_i \subset A_j \in P(E): \qquad R_\alpha^+ A_j = \bigcap R_\alpha^+ \{ E_i \}, \text{ with } E_i \subset A_j$$
$$R_\alpha^- A_j = \bigcap R_\alpha^- \{ E_i \}, \text{ with } E_i \subset A_j$$

This shows that it suffices to observe for each group of rows (columns) in the fuzzy relation $[R_\alpha]$ those columns (rows) where valuations are at or above the α-cut considered in all rows (columns) form the affinity group.

Finally, the max-min convolutions of R_α^- with R_α^+ and R_α^+ with R_α^- provide, at level α, the two Moore's closures (M) of P(E) corresponding to the fuzzy relation $[R_\alpha]$.Which is expressed as[b]:

[b] It uses the letter M (Moore) to denote respectively the adherent application (Γ) and the interior application (δ) within of pretopology.

$$M_\alpha^{(1)} = R_\alpha^- A_j \circ R_\alpha^+ A_j$$
$$M_\alpha^{(2)} = R_\alpha^+ A_j \circ R_\alpha^- A_j$$

Bringing the set of Moore's closures consist of those elements $A_j \in P(E)$ that, as a pretopology, meet that $A_j = \Gamma A_j$ and $A_j = \delta A_j$, and for which the properties of extension, idempotency and isotonic are verified [18].

Following Gil Aluja [21], we denote by $C(E, M^{(2)})$ the closed subset of P(E) corresponding to Moore's closure $M^{(2)}$. Since $R_\alpha^- A_j$ is a closed of P(E) to $M^{(2)}$, we can write:

$$C(E, M^{(2)}) = \bigcup R_\alpha^- A_j, \text{ with } A_j \in P(E)$$

and, similarly, to be $R_\alpha^+ A_j$ a closed for $M^{(1)}$, and designating by $C(E, M^{(1)})$ the closed subset of P(E) for Moore's closure $M^{(1)}$, we have:

$$C(E, M^{(1)}) = \bigcup R_\alpha^+ A_j, \text{ with } A_j \in P(E)$$

The two families of closures C(E, M(1)) and C(E, M(2)) are isomorphic to each other and dual relative one to another, antitone nature. This is expressed as:

$$A \in C(E, M^{(1)}) \Rightarrow (B = R_\alpha^- A \in C(E, M^{(2)}) \text{ and } R_\alpha^+ B = A$$
$$B \in C(E, M^{(2)}) \Rightarrow (A = R_\alpha^+ B \in C(E, M^{(1)}) \text{ and } R_\alpha^- A = B$$

These families of closed can be associated with each other and are, each, a finite lattice. Furthermore, as pointed out, by the max-min convolution, both one and the other of these families of closed provide the groups with the greatest possible number of elements of the reference E. Thus, in all the vertices of each lattice place we put in one of them a group of elements of a family of closed and the other clusters of the other family of closed.

Is easy to verify that, when the two lattices are superimposed, one is obtained, which contains in each of the vertices the relation of the maximum groups of elements of the E set. When this happens it is said that there is an affinity. This lattice provides structured and ordered relations between maximum groups. When to this lattice are added, at its top and bottom, the edges (Ø, E) and (E, Ø), we are facing a Galois lattice, which sets the two sets of Moore's closures which have as upper and lower ends these relationships.

3. Application to the analysis of industrial cluster relations

For a better understanding of the procedure to follow in its application to relations between agents within an industrial cluster, we will follow a simplified example. Obviously, in an industrial cluster a lot of agents are involved, so that the number of potentially existing relationships grows exponentially, which is the reason why it would be enormously complex and repetitive to use a "real" example, since our aim is simply narrative and descriptive of the used method.[c] For this reason, as indicated by Capó *et al.* [12], although the true potential of the method is obtained when applied individually considering each and every one of the agents that form an industrial cluster, usually with reasons of simplification, grouping the agents in large types is presented because, if it is made at a displeasure level, the great number of combinations that arise often render impractical the analysis.

First we should identify, in general terms, the agents involved in an industrial cluster by major types, which constitute the reference set E. In this respect, we synthesized, for example, as follows:

E_1 : Public organizations
E_2 : University and Technological and Scientific Centers
E_3 : Companies within the main activity sector of the industrial sector
E_4 : Supplier companies
E_5 : Customer companies

That means, $E = \{ E_1 , E_2 , E_3 , E_4 , E_5 \}$, so that all parts of E or its power set P(E), composed of 32 elements (E being composed of 5 elements, we have 2^5 combinations), is:

$$P(E) = \{ \{\emptyset\} , \{E_1\} , \{E_2\} , \{E_3\} , \{E_4\} , \{E_5\} , \{E_1 , E_2\}, \{E_1 , E_3\}, \{E_1 , E_4\} , \{E_1 , E_5\} , \{E_2 , E_3\} , \{E_2 , E_4\} , \{E_2 , E_5\} , \{E_3 , E_4\} , \{E_3 , E_5\} , \{E_4 , E_5\} , \{E_1 , E_2 , E_3\} , \{E_1 , E_2 , E_4\} , \{E_1 , E_2 , E_5\} , \{E_1 , E_3 , E_4\} , \{E_1 , E_3 , E_5\} , \{E_1 , E_4 , E_5\} , \{E_2 , E_3 , E_4\} , \{E_2 , E_3 , E_5\} , \{E_2 , E_4 , E_5\} , \{E_3 , E_4 , E_5\} , \{E_1 , E_2 , E_3 , E_4\} , \{E_1 , E_2 , E_3 , E_5\} , \{E_1 , E_2 , E_4 , E_5\} , \{E_1 , E_3 , E_4 , E_5\} , \{E_2 , E_3 , E_4 , E_5\} , \{E_1 , E_2 , E_3 , E_4 , E_5\} \}$$

[c] In fact, in the application to the analysis of relationships in a given industrial cluster, given the large number of potential relationships that may exist, it should apply the method described by some computer program. Consider that the number of elements of the set P(E) or power set of the benchmark set is 2^n, where n is the number of items contained in the reference set E.

First, it analyzes the positive relationships between agents in the industrial cluster. That is, those where the relationship is "I win-you win", and create value for the industrial cluster. The choice of positive collaboration is present when companies or institutions of the industrial cluster make a formal or informal attitude to help the parties to the relationship to achieve their goals. This attitude creates value to businesses and reduces both research and process development costs, *etc.*, becoming a key element in an industrial cluster.

To obtain the fuzzy relation [Rα] it can be consulted, using questionnaires, a representative from each agent in the industrial cluster directly involved in the relationships with other agents, with the intention that each one of them express a valuation in the range [0, 1] about their relationships with each and every one of the other agents of the industrial cluster[d], where the maximum value 1 indicates a fully satisfactory and positive relationship with the other agent, that is, that it permits to achieve the objectives of the relationship (development of new technology, to conquer new markets, *etc.*) in an effectively and efficiently way, and in a climate of confidence and profit from the consulted agent point of view, whereas the minimum value 0 indicates no positive relationship with the corresponding agent. Thus, intermediate valuations in the interval [0, 1] indicate the degree of intensity in the satisfaction and performance obtained (depending on the objectives), from the consulted agent point of view, in the relationship. Given the nature of the problem addressed, based on the analysis of relationships between agents, the relationship of an agent with himself is ruled out. Let's suppose that the fuzzy relation arising from this consultation is the one shown in Table 1:

---

[d] Obviously, several representatives are also available for one participant in the industrial cluster. Under these circumstances, it would get half the valuation of all for every possibility of relationship with other agents. Furthermore, instead of using simple valuations may also be used fuzzy subsets (confidence intervals and triplets, triangular fuzzy numbers, *etc.*), see thereon Gil Aluja (2003b).

Table 1. Fuzzy relation of positive relationships between industrial cluster agents.

		E_1	E_2	E_3	E_4	E_5
	E_1	—	.72	.82	.34	.48
	E_2	.94	—	.78	.81	.33
$[R_\alpha]$ =	E_3	.82	.78	—	.95	.76
	E_4	.58	.73	.74	—	.22
	E_5	.45	.52	.86	.18	—

Then, it comes to obtain the connection to the right and the connection to the left of this fuzzy relation to the desired level α to perform the analysis of the relationships. In our example, for simplicity, we follow the procedure only for α = .7, in this way, we rewrite the above fuzzy relation with a 1 in the boxes that have a value α ≥ .7, and with a 0 otherwise (the fuzzy matrix or relation $[R_{0.7}]$ becomes the following boolean matrix):

Table 2. Boolean matrix of positive relationships (α = .7).

		E_1	E_2	E_3	E_4	E_5
	E_1	—	1	1	0	0
	E_2	1	—	1	1	0
$[R_{0.7}]$ =	E_3	1	1	—	1	1
	E_4	0	1	1	—	0
	E_5	0	0	1	0	—

Now we are able to obtain the right connection, assigning each element of P(E) elements of the same P(E) in which there is a 1 at the corresponding rows:

$R^+_{0.7}\,\emptyset = E$, $R^+_{0.7}\{E_1\} = \{E_2, E_3\}$, $R^+_{0.7}\{E_2\} = \{E_1, E_3, E_4\}$,
$R^+_{0.7}\{E_3\} = \{E_1, E_2, E_4, E_5\}$, $R^+_{0.7}\{E_4\} = \{E_2, E_3\}$, $R^+_{0.7}\{E_5\} = \{E_3\}$,
$R^+_{0.7}\{E_1, E_2\} = \{E_3\}$, $R^+_{0.7}\{E_1, E_3\} = \{E_2\}$, $R^+_{0.7}\{E_1, E_4\} = \{E_2, E_3\}$,
$R^+_{0.7}\{E_1, E_5\} = \{E_3\}$, $R^+_{0.7}\{E_2, E_3\} = \{E_1, E_4\}$, $R^+_{0.7}\{E_2, E_4\} = \{E_3\}$,
$R^+_{0.7}\{E_2, E_5\} = \{E_3\}$, $R^+_{0.7}\{E_3, E_4\} = \{E_2\}$, $R^+_{0.7}\{E_3, E_5\} = \emptyset$,
$R^+_{0.7}\{E_4, E_5\} = \{E_3\}$, $R^+_{0.7}\{E_1, E_2, E_3\} = \emptyset$, $R^+_{0.7}\{E_1, E_2, E_4\} = \{E_3\}$, $R^+_{0.7}\{E_1, E_2, E_5\} = \{E_3\}$, $R^+_{0.7}\{E_1, E_3, E_4\} = \{E_2\}$, $R^+_{0.7}\{E_1, E_3, E_5\} = \emptyset$, $R^+_{0.7}\{E_1, E_4, E_5\} = \{E_3\}$, $R^+_{0.7}\{E_2, E_3, E_4\} = \emptyset$, $R^+_{0.7}\{E_2, E_3, E_5\} = \emptyset$, $R^+_{0.7}\{E_2, E_4, E_5\} = \{E_2\}$, $R^+_{0.7}\{E_3, E_4, E_5\} = \emptyset$, $R^+_{0.7}\{E_1, E_2, E_3, E_4\} = \emptyset$,
$R^+_{0.7}\{E_1, E_2, E_3, E_5\} = \emptyset$, $R^+_{0.7}\{E_1, E_2, E_4, E_5\} = \{E_3\}$,
$R^+_{0.7}\{E_1, E_3, E_4, E_5\} = \emptyset$, $R^+_{0.7}\{E_2, E_3, E_4, E_5\} = \emptyset$,
$R^+_{0.7}\{E_1, E_2, E_3, E_4, E_5\} = R^+_{0.7}\,E = \emptyset$

Also, the connection is obtained to the left, assigning to each element of P(E) the same elements of P(E) in which a value exists in the corresponding columns:

$R^-_{0.7}\,\emptyset = E$, $R^-_{0.7}\{E_1\} = \{E_2, E_3\}$, $R^-_{0.7}\{E_2\} = \{E_1, E_3, E_4\}$,
$R^-_{0.7}\{E_3\} = \{E_1, E_2, E_4, E_5\}$, $R^-_{0.7}\{E_4\} = \{E_2, E_3\}$, $R^-_{0.7}\{E_5\} = \{E_3\}$,
$R^-_{0.7}\{E_1, E_2\} = \{E_3\}$, $R^-_{0.7}\{E_1, E_3\} = \{E_2\}$, $R^-_{0.7}\{E_1, E_4\} = \{E_2, E_3\}$,
$R^-_{0.7}\{E_1, E_5\} = \{E_3\}$, $R^-_{0.7}\{E_2, E_3\} = \{E_1, E_4\}$, $R^-_{0.7}\{E_2, E_4\} = \{E_3\}$,
$R^-_{0.7}\{E_2, E_5\} = \{E_3\}$, $R^-_{0.7}\{E_3, E_4\} = \{E_2\}$, $R^-_{0.7}\{E_3, E_5\} = \emptyset$,
$R^-_{0.7}\{E_4, E_5\} = \{E_3\}$, $R^-_{0.7}\{E_1, E_2, E_3\} = \emptyset$, $R^-_{0.7}\{E_1, E_2, E_4\} = \{E_3\}$,
$R^-_{0.7}\{E_1, E_2, E_5\} = \{E_3\}$, $R^-_{0.7}\{E_1, E_3, E_4\} = \{E_2\}$, $R^-_{0.7}\{E_1, E_3, E_5\} = \emptyset$,
$R^-_{0.7}\{E_1, E_4, E_5\} = \{E_3\}$, $R^-_{0.7}\{E_2, E_3, E_4\} = \emptyset$, $R^-_{0.7}\{E_2, E_3, E_5\} = \emptyset$,
$R^-_{0.7}\{E_2, E_4, E_5\} = \{E_3\}$, $R^-_{0.7}\{E_3, E_4, E_5\} = \emptyset$, $R^-_{0.7}\{E_1, E_2, E_3, E_4\} = \emptyset$,
$R^-_{0.7}\{E_1, E_2, E_3, E_5\} = \emptyset$, $R^-_{0.7}\{E_1, E_2, E_4, E_5\} = \{E_3\}$,
$R^-_{0.7}\{E_1, E_3, E_4, E_5\} = \emptyset$, $R^-_{0.7}\{E_2, E_3, E_4, E_5\} = \emptyset$,
$R^-_{0.7}\{E_1, E_2, E_3, E_4, E_5\} = R^-_{0.7}\,E = \emptyset$

Applying the max-min convolution $R^-_{0.7}\,A_j \circ R^+_{0.7}\,A_j$, closed are obtained (for which it holds that $A_j = \Gamma A_j$, which are indicated by *), representing the first Moore's closure $M_{0.7}^{(2)}$ (adherent application Γ)[e]:

$\emptyset \rightarrow E \rightarrow \emptyset$ *
$E_1 \rightarrow E_2, E_3 \rightarrow E_1, E_4$
$E_2 \rightarrow E_1, E_3, E_4 \rightarrow E_2$ *
$E_3 \rightarrow E_1, E_2, E_4, E_5 \rightarrow E_3$ *
$E_4 \rightarrow E_2, E_3 \rightarrow E_1, E_4$
$E_5 \rightarrow E_3 \rightarrow E_1, E_2, E_4, E_5$
$E_1, E_2 \rightarrow E_3 \rightarrow E_1, E_2, E_4, E_5$
$E_1, E_3 \rightarrow E_2 \rightarrow E_1, E_3, E_4$
$E_1, E_4 \rightarrow E_2, E_3 \rightarrow E_1, E_4$ *
$E_1, E_5 \rightarrow E_3 \rightarrow E_1, E_2, E_4, E_5$
$E_2, E_3 \rightarrow E_1, E_4 \rightarrow E_2, E_3$ *
$E_2, E_4 \rightarrow E_3 \rightarrow E_1, E_2, E_4, E_5$
$E_2, E_5 \rightarrow E_3 \rightarrow E_1, E_2, E_4, E_5$
$E_3, E_4 \rightarrow E_2 \rightarrow E_1, E_3, E_4$
$E_4, E_5 \rightarrow E_3 \rightarrow E_1, E_2, E_4, E_5$
$E_1, E_2, E_4 \rightarrow E_3 \rightarrow E_1, E_2, E_4, E_5$

---

[e] Only we present no empty arches and elements.

$E_1 , E_2 , E_5 \rightarrow E_3 \rightarrow E_1 , E_2 , E_4 , E_5$
$E_1 , E_3 , E_4 \rightarrow E_2 \rightarrow E_1 , E_3 , E_4$ *
$E_1 , E_4 , E_5 \rightarrow E_3 \rightarrow E_1 , E_2 , E_4 , E_5$
$E_2 , E_4 , E_5 \rightarrow E_3 \rightarrow E_1 , E_2 , E_4 , E_5$
$E_1 , E_2 , E_4 , E_5 \rightarrow E_3 \rightarrow E_1 , E_2 , E_4 , E_5$ *
$E_1 , E_2 , E_3 , E_4 , E_5 = E \rightarrow \emptyset \rightarrow E$ *

Accordingly, the family of closed corresponding to $C(E, M^{(2)})$, for $\alpha = .7$, is:

$$C(E, M^{(2)}) = \{ \{\emptyset\} , \{E_2\} , \{E_3\} , \{E_1 , E_4\} , \{E_2 , E_3\} , \{E_1 , E_3 , E_4\} , \{E_1 , E_2 , E_4 , E_5\} , \{E\} \}$$

Similarly, applying the max-min convolution $R^+_{0.7} A_j \circ R^-_{0.7} A_j$ are obtained closed (for which it holds that $A_j = \delta A_j$, which are indicated by *), representing the second Moore's closure $M_{0.7}^{(1)}$ (interior application δ):

$\emptyset \rightarrow E \rightarrow \emptyset$ *
$E_1 \rightarrow E_2 , E_3 \rightarrow E_1 , E_4$
$E_2 \rightarrow E_1 , E_3 , E_4 \rightarrow E_2$ *
$E_3 \rightarrow E_1 , E_2 , E_4 , E_5 \rightarrow E_3$ *
$E_4 \rightarrow E_2 , E_3 \rightarrow E_1 , E_4$
$E_5 \rightarrow E_3 \rightarrow E_1 , E_2 , E_4 , E_5$
$E_1 , E_2 \rightarrow E_3 \rightarrow E_1 , E_2 , E_4 , E_5$
$E_1 , E_3 \rightarrow E_2 \rightarrow E_1 , E_3 , E_4$
$E_1 , E_4 \rightarrow E_2 , E_3 \rightarrow E_1 , E_4$ *
$E_1 , E_5 \rightarrow E_3 \rightarrow E_1 , E_2 , E_4 , E_5$
$E_2 , E_3 \rightarrow E_1 , E_4 \rightarrow E_2 , E_3$ *
$E_2 , E_4 \rightarrow E_3 \rightarrow E_1 , E_2 , E_4 , E_5$
$E_2 , E_5 \rightarrow E_3 \rightarrow E_1 , E_2 , E_4 , E_5$
$E_3 , E_4 \rightarrow E_2 \rightarrow E_1 , E_3 , E_4$
$E_4 , E_5 \rightarrow E_3 \rightarrow E_1 , E_2 , E_4 , E_5$
$E_1 , E_2 , E_4 \rightarrow E_3 \rightarrow E_1 , E_2 , E_4 , E_5$
$E_1 , E_2 , E_5 \rightarrow E_3 \rightarrow E_1 , E_2 , E_4 , E_5$
$E_1 , E_3 , E_4 \rightarrow E_2 \rightarrow E_1 , E_3 , E_4$ *
$E_1 , E_4 , E_5 \rightarrow E_3 \rightarrow E_1 , E_2 , E_4 , E_5$
$E_2 , E_4 , E_5 \rightarrow E_2 \rightarrow E_1 , E_3 , E_4$
$E_1 , E_2 , E_4 , E_5 \rightarrow E_3 \rightarrow E_1 , E_2 , E_4 , E_5$ *
$E_1 , E_2 , E_3 , E_4 , E_5 = E \rightarrow \emptyset \rightarrow E$ *

Thus the family of closed $C(E, M^{(1)})$, for $\alpha = .7$, is:

$$C(E, M^{(1)}) = \{ \{\emptyset\} , \{E_2\} , \{E_3\} , \{E_1 , E_4\} , \{E_2 , E_3\} , \{E_1 , E_3 , E_4\} , \{E_1 , E_2 , E_4 , E_5\} , \{E\} \}$$

Both families of closed have the same cardinal, that means, they have the same number of elements (in particular, for our example, 8), and are dual in antitone nature. Furthermore, as shown in Figure 1, the lattices of both Moore's closures are isomorphic.

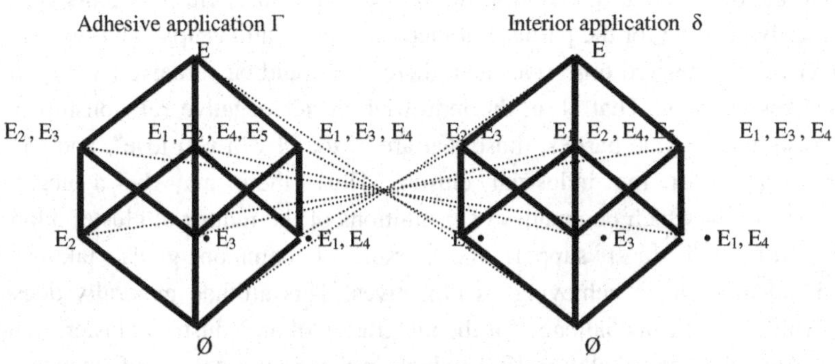

Figure 1. Moore's closures lattices for R ($\alpha = .7$).

If one of the lattices is rotated 180º and then superimposed, we can verify the isomorphism and we can observe the affinities between agents of industrial cluster that they possess in common. This lattice then is a Galois lattice, which presents the affinities or maximum subrelations between the elements of reference E in an structured and ordered way, in our example for level $\alpha = .7$, as it is showed in Figure 2.

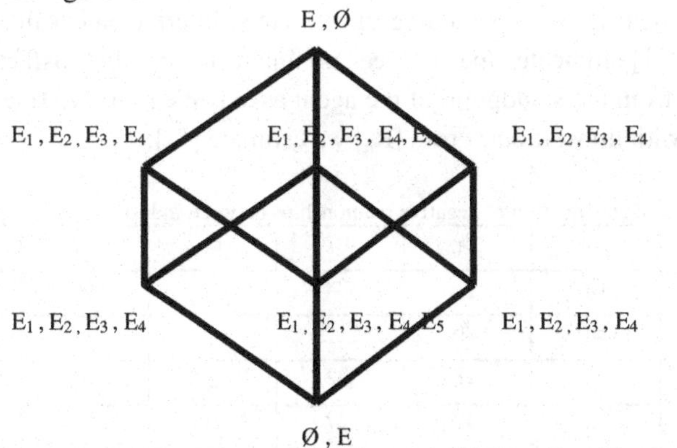

Figure 2. Positive affinities Galois' lattice for R ($\alpha = .7$).

The isomorphism between Moore's lattices, for level $\alpha = .7$, is specified into the following affinities:

$$E_2 \rightarrow E_1, E_3, E_4 \quad : \quad E_1, E_2, E_3, E_4$$
$$E_3 \rightarrow E_1, E_2, E_4, E_5 \quad : \quad E_1, E_2, E_3, E_4, E_5$$
$$E_1, E_4 \rightarrow E_2, E_3 \quad : \quad E_1, E_2, E_3, E_4$$

On the other hand, the relationship between industrial cluster agents are not necessarily positive for the parties but there may be relationships that don't allow to achieved the desired objectives and, therefore, could be perceived as negative for the asked agent. That is, in the industrial cluster negative relationships can also arise between the parties, those that are of the "I win-you lose", and which destroy value for the industrial cluster. Thus, there may be a negative collaboration in which companies or institutions of the industrial cluster adopt a selfish role and don't support the pursuit of common goals, taking an individualistic role in achieving its objectives. This attitude generally doesn't favor value and it is a challenge for the integration of an industrial cluster. In this sense, from the fuzzy relation $[R_\alpha]$, which indicates the degree of intensity of positive relationships between the agents of industrial cluster, its complement can be constructed, which we will call $[S_\alpha]$, where $[S_\alpha] = [\overline{R}_\alpha] = 1 - [R_\alpha]$, indicating, therefore, the intensity of negative relationships between agents in the industrial cluster. In the fuzzy relation $[S_\alpha]$, the maximum value of 1 indicates a totally unsatisfactory and negative relationship with the other agent, that is, it doesn't allow to achieve the objectives set out in the relationship or is counterproductive or, if applicable (when R has the value 1), no negative relationship with the corresponding agent. Thus, intermediate valuations in the interval [0, 1] indicate the degree of intensity of dissatisfaction in the relationship from the standpoint of the agent asked. We return to rule the relation of an agent with himself out. From $[R_\alpha]$ we estimate $[S_\alpha]$:

Table 3. Fuzzy relation of negative relationships between industrial cluster agents.

$[S_\alpha] =$	E_1	E_2	E_3	E_4	E_5
E_1	—	.28	.18	.66	.52
E_2	.06	—	.22	.19	.67
E_3	.18	.22	—	.05	.24
E_4	.42	.27	.26	—	.78
E_5	.55	.48	.14	.82	—

We follow the procedure also only for $\alpha = .7$, and rewrite $[S_\alpha]$ with a 1 in the boxes that have a value $\alpha \geq .7$, and a 0 otherwise (the fuzzy relation matrix or becomes the following boolean matrix):

Table 4. Boolean matrix of negative relationships ($\alpha = .7$).

$[S_{0.7}] =$

	E_1	E_2	E_3	E_4	E_5
E_1	___	0	0	0	0
E_2	0	___	0	0	0
E_3	0	0	___	0	0
E_4	0	0	0	___	1
E_5	0	0	0	1	___

Thus the connection on the right is:

$S^{+}_{0.7}\,\emptyset = E$, $S^{+}_{0.7}\{E_1\} = \emptyset$, $S^{+}_{0.7}\{E_2\} = \emptyset$, $S^{+}_{0.7}\{E_3\} = \emptyset$, $S^{+}_{0.7}\{E_4\} = \{E_5\}$,
$S^{+}_{0.7}\{E_5\} = \{E_4\}$, $S^{+}_{0.7}\{E_1, E_2\} = \emptyset$, $S^{+}_{0.7}\{E_1, E_3\} = \emptyset$, $S^{+}_{0.7}\{E_1, E_4\} = \emptyset$,
$S^{+}_{0.7}\{E_1, E_5\} = \emptyset$, $S^{+}_{0.7}\{E_2, E_3\} = \emptyset$, $S^{+}_{0.7}\{E_2, E_4\} = \emptyset$, $S^{+}_{0.7}\{E_2, E_5\} = \emptyset$,
$S^{+}_{0.7}\{E_3, E_4\} = \emptyset$, $S^{+}_{0.7}\{E_3, E_5\} = \emptyset$, $S^{+}_{0.7}\{E_4, E_5\} = \emptyset$,
$S^{+}_{0.7}\{E_1, E_2, E_3\} = \emptyset$, $S^{+}_{0.7}\{E_1, E_2, E_4\} = \emptyset$, $S^{+}_{0.7}\{E_1, E_2, E_5\} = \emptyset$,
$S^{+}_{0.7}\{E_1, E_3, E_4\} = \emptyset$, $S^{+}_{0.7}\{E_1, E_3, E_5\} = \emptyset$, $S^{+}_{0.7}\{E_1, E_4, E_5\} = \emptyset$,
$S^{+}_{0.7}\{E_2, E_3, E_4\} = \emptyset$, $S^{+}_{0.7}\{E_2, E_3, E_5\} = \emptyset$, $S^{+}_{0.7}\{E_2, E_4, E_5\} = \emptyset$,
$S^{+}_{0.7}\{E_3, E_4, E_5\} = \emptyset$, $S^{+}_{0.7}\{E_1, E_2, E_3, E_4\} = \emptyset$, $S^{+}_{0.7}\{E_1, E_2, E_3, E_5\} = \emptyset$,
$S^{+}_{0.7}\{E_1, E_2, E_4, E_5\} = \emptyset$, $S^{+}_{0.7}\{E_1, E_3, E_4, E_5\} = \emptyset$,
$S^{+}_{0.7}\{E_2, E_3, E_4, E_5\} = \emptyset$, $S^{+}_{0.7}\{E_1, E_2, E_3, E_4, E_5\} = \emptyset$

And the connection on the left is:

$S^{-}_{0.7}\,\emptyset = E$, $S^{-}_{0.7}\{E_1\} = \emptyset$, $S^{-}_{0.7}\{E_2\} = \emptyset$, $S^{-}_{0.7}\{E_3\} = \emptyset$, $S^{-}_{0.7}\{E_4\} = \{E_5\}$,
$S^{-}_{0.7}\{E_5\} = \{E_4\}$, $S^{-}_{0.7}\{E_1, E_2\} = \emptyset$, $S^{-}_{0.7}\{E_1, E_3\} = \emptyset$, $S^{-}_{0.7}\{E_1, E_4\} = \emptyset$,
$S^{-}_{0.7}\{E_1, E_5\} = \emptyset$, $S^{-}_{0.7}\{E_2, E_3\} = \emptyset$, $S^{-}_{0.7}\{E_2, E_4\} = \emptyset$, $S^{-}_{0.7}\{E_2, E_5\} = \emptyset$,
$S^{-}_{0.7}\{E_3, E_4\} = \emptyset$, $S^{-}_{0.7}\{E_3, E_5\} = \emptyset$, $S^{-}_{0.7}\{E_4, E_5\} = \emptyset$,
$S^{-}_{0.7}\{E_1, E_2, E_3\} = \emptyset$, $S^{-}_{0.7}\{E_1, E_2, E_4\} = \emptyset$, $S^{-}_{0.7}\{E_1, E_2, E_5\} = \emptyset$,
$S^{-}_{0.7}\{E_1, E_3, E_4\} = \emptyset$, $S^{-}_{0.7}\{E_1, E_3, E_5\} = \emptyset$, $S^{-}_{0.7}\{E_1, E_4, E_5\} = \emptyset$,
$S^{-}_{0.7}\{E_2, E_3, E_4\} = \emptyset$, $S^{-}_{0.7}\{E_2, E_3, E_5\} = \emptyset$, $S^{-}_{0.7}\{E_2, E_4, E_5\} = \emptyset$,
$S^{-}_{0.7}\{E_3, E_4, E_5\} = \emptyset$, $S^{-}_{0.7}\{E_1, E_2, E_3, E_4\} = \emptyset$, $S^{-}_{0.7}\{E_1, E_2, E_3, E_5\} = \emptyset$,
$S^{-}_{0.7}\{E_1, E_2, E_4, E_5\} = \emptyset$, $S^{-}_{0.7}\{E_1, E_3, E_4, E_5\} = \emptyset$,
$S^{-}_{0.7}\{E_2, E_3, E_4, E_5\} = \emptyset$, $S^{-}_{0.7}\{E_1, E_2, E_3, E_4, E_5\} = \emptyset$

Applying the max-min convolution $S^{-}_{0.7}\ A_j \circ S^{+}_{0.7}\ A_j$ the closed which represent the first Moore's closure $M_{0.7}^{(2)}$ (Γ adherent application) are obtained, for $\alpha = .7$:

$$E_4 \rightarrow E_5 \rightarrow E_4$$
$$E_5 \rightarrow E_4 \rightarrow E_5$$

Accordingly, the family of closed corresponding to $C(E, M^{(2)})$, for $\alpha = .7$, is:

$$C(E, M^{(2)}) = \{\ \{\emptyset\}\ ,\ \{E_4\}\ ,\ \{E_5\}\ ,\ \{E\}\ \}$$

In the same way, applying $S^{+}_{0.7}\ A_j \circ S^{-}_{0.7}\ A_j$ the closed which represent the second Moore's closure $M_{0.7}^{(1)}$ (δ interior application) are obtained, for $\alpha = .7$:

$$E_4 \rightarrow E_5 \rightarrow E_4$$
$$E_5 \rightarrow E_4 \rightarrow E_5$$

Accordingly, the family of closed corresponding to $C(E, M^{(1)})$, for $\alpha = .7$, is:

$$C(E, M^{(1)}) = \{\ \{\emptyset\}\ ,\ \{E_4\}\ ,\ \{E_5\}\ ,\ \{E\}\ \}$$

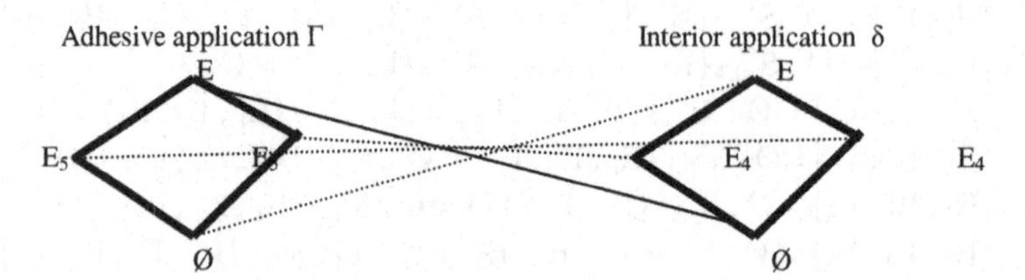

Figure 3. Moore's closures lattices for S (α = .7).

So we have the Galois' lattice shown in Figure 4, with a single negative affinity between agents in the industrial cluster:

$$E_4 \rightarrow E_5 \ :\ E_4, E_5$$
$$E_5 \rightarrow E_4 \ :\ E_4, E_5$$

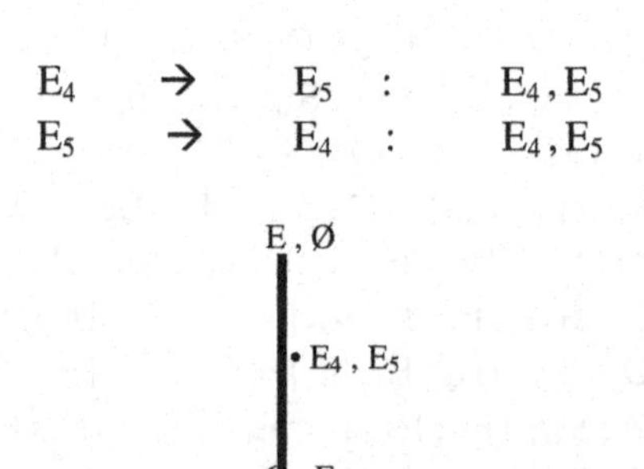

Figure 4. Negative affinities Galois' lattice for S (α = .7).

Finally, connecting the two lattices of Galois obtained, one for positive relationships (E^{+}) and the other for negative relationships (E^{-}), for the vertex (Ø,

E), that is, by rotating the lattice which represents the negative relationship , we obtain a map of relations between actors in the industrial cluster, to the level α = .7 (see Figure 5).

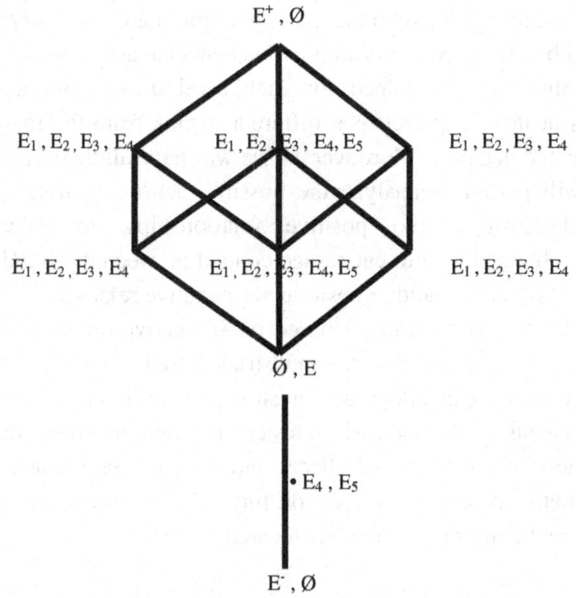

Figure 5. Positive and negative relations map (α = .7).

4. Conclusions

The scheme we have proposed is aimed at an eminently practical point of view, for immediate use in the most diverse realities that normally crop up in the daily events of industrial clusters and business management.

The fact of being able to present the affinity groups using a Galois' lattice provides a non-negligible benefit. Through the lattice, they are provided in a visual, clear and simultaneous way, absolutely all the optimal groupings among industrial cluster agents. Thus, a simple look at the lattice provides all possibilities of relationship, both positive and negative, for a given level α of the fuzzy relation. Obviously, when the value of the level α required is increased, in the analysis we would expect a lower number of relations identified, as between elements of the referential subrelations affinities that are evaluated a greater force is required. Conversely, when the value of the level α required is decreased, the number of identified relationships tends to be higher, since the subrelations between elements of the referential or affinities are evaluated require less force. Consequently, although in the present work we have focused on providing our expository and descriptive example of the methodology to follow for a single level α, for the entire analysis of the relations between the agents of industrial cluster subrelations or maximum groups that arise for every α levels should be identified, according to this hendecadary system.

The relations map obtained for each level α, will provide all relevant relationships at this level, between different agents from the industrial cluster, both positive and negative. Moreover, as we will have all these relations for each α level, it will permit to analyze the possible actions to transform identified negative relationships into positive relationships, to enhance positive relationships obtained, and to encourage contact between those industrial cluster agents where we haven't neither positive nor negative relations.

It is, therefore, an instrument based on subjective opinions (valuations) of representatives of each agent in the industrial cluster, which, from its treatment by the fuzzy logic, can adopt action strategies to improve mutual relations between all agents of the industrial cluster, and thus try to increase the global competitiveness of the industrial cluster and each of the companies and agents that make them up, also in search of further economic development of the territory where the industrial cluster is located.

References

1. M. Castells, *The information age: Economy, society and culture. Volume I: The rise of the network society*. New York: Blackwell (1996).
2. M. E. Porter, *The competitive advantage of nations*. New York: Free Press (1990).
3. G. Becattini and E. Rullani, "Sistemas productivos locales y mercado global". *Información Comercial Española*, No. 754, pp. 11-24 (1996).
4. B. Lecop, "Proximité et rationalité économique". *Revue d'Economie Regionale et Urbaine*, No. 3-4, pp. 321-342 (1993).
5. H. Schmitz, "Collective efficiency: Growth path for small-scale industry". *Journal of Development Studies*, Vol. 31, No. 4, pp. 529-566 (1995).
6. M. E. Porter, *On competition*. Cambridge (MA): Harvard Business School Publishing (1998).
7. J. Humphrey and H. Schmitz, *Principles for promoting clusters and networks of SMEs*. Viena: UNIDO (1996).
8. K. Nadvi, "The cutting edge: Collective efficiency and international competitiveness in Pakistan". *Oxford Agrarian Studies*, Vol. 27, No. 1, pp. 81-107 (1999).

9. K. Nadvi, "Facing the new competition: Business associations in developing country industrial cluster". *Discussion Papers*, No. DP/103. International Labour Organization, Geneva (1999).
10. E. Masiá, J. Albors, E. Golf, E. and L. Pérez, "La matriz estructural de relaciones: Propuesta de un modelo de análisis de cluster". *V Congreso de Ingeniería de Organización*. Valladolid – Burgos, september 4-5(2003).
11. E. Masiá, J. Albors, E. Golf and J. Capó, "Identifying key technology success factors in an industry by the application of an analysis model to the links of the productive value chain among the main economic agents of a microcluster". *Proceedings of the International Conference of International Association for Management of Technology*, IAMOT. Washington (DC), april 3-7 (2004).
12. J. Capó, M. Expósito and E. Masiá, "Análisis estratégico de clusters a través del estudio de las relaciones entre sus agentes". *Economía Industrial*, No. 370, pp. 209-216 (2008).
13. J. Gil Aluja, "Clans, affinities and Moore's fuzzy pretopology". *Fuzzy Economic Review*, Vol. VIII, No. 2, pp. 3-24 (2003).
14. J. Gil Aluja, "Elementos pretopológicos básicos para la modelización de la incertidumbre", in: RACEF (ed.), *De computis et scripturis* [pp. 199-224]. Barcelona: Real Academia de Ciencias Económicas y Financieras (2003).
15. J. Gil Lafuente, "Automatismos y racionalidad en la toma de decisiones para sustituir a un deportista en momentos decisivos". *Cuadernos de Gestión*, Vol. 8, No. 1, pp. 39-58 (2008).
16. J. Gil Aluja and A.M. Gil Lafuente, *Algoritmos para el tratamiento de fenómenos económicos complejos. Bases, desarrollos y aplicaciones.* Madrid: Ramón Areces (2007).
17. U. Höhle and A. Sostek, "Axiomatic foundations of fixed-basis fuzzy topology". En: Höhle, U.; Rodabaugh, S. E. (eds.), *Mathematics of fuzzy sets logic, topology, and measure theory* [pp. 123-272]. Boston: Kluwer Academic Publishers (1999).
18. A. Kaufmann and J. Gil Aluja, *Técnicas de gestión de empresa. Previsiones, decisiones y estrategias*. Madrid: Pirámide (1992).
19. J. Gil Lafuente, "Formation of groups of mutually interchangeable players". *Proceedings of the International Conference on Modeling, Simulation and Neural Networks*, AMSE. Mérida (Venezuela), october 22-24 (2000).
20. J.M. Lafosse-Marin, *Moore closure and fuzzy graph.* Department of Mathematics. University of Alger (no date).
21. J. Gil Aluja, *Elements for a theory of decision in uncertainty*. Dordrecht: Kluwer Academic Publishers (1999).

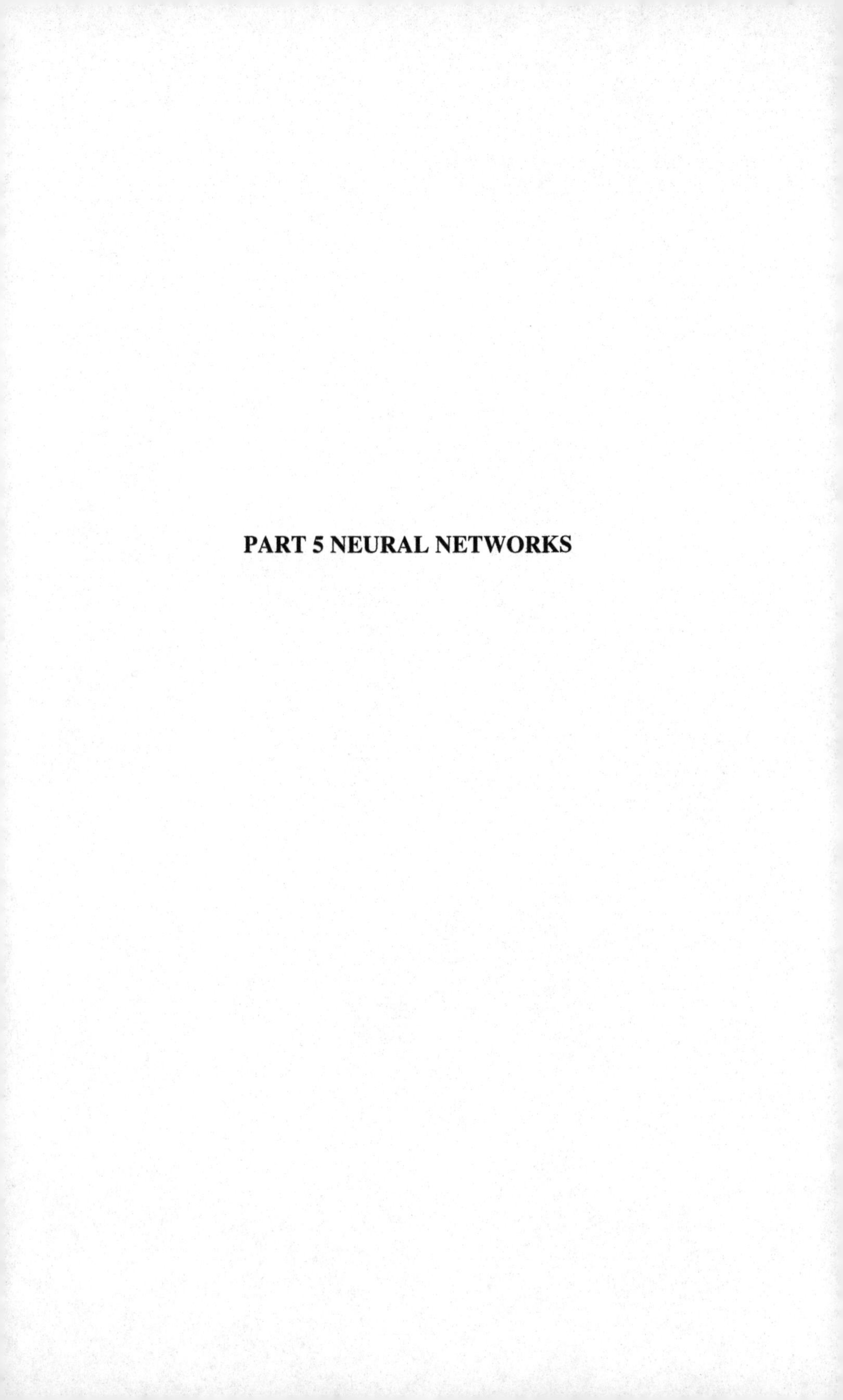

PART 5 NEURAL NETWORKS

EVOLUTIONARY NEURAL NETWORK CLASSIFIERS FOR MONITORING RESEARCH, DEVELOPMENT AND INNOVATION PERFORMANCE IN EUROPEAN UNION MEMBER STATES *

MÓNICA DE LA PAZ-MARÍN

Department of Management and Quantitative Methods, ETEA, University of córdoba, C/ Escritor Castilla Aguayo 4, Córdoba, 14005, Spain

PILAR CAMPOY-MUÑOZ

Department of Economics, University of Córdoba, C/ Escritor Castilla Aguayo 4 Córdoba, 14005, Spain

CÉSAR HERVÁS-MARTÍNEZ

Department of Computing and Numerical Analysis, University of Córdoba, Campus of Rabanales, Edificio Einstein, 3th floor, Córdoba, 14071, Spain

The present work deals with the classification of the Research, Development (R&D) and innovation performance in 25 European Union (EU) Member States that follows the linear R&D model. As proxy indicators, expenditure in R&D, the personnel involved in these activities (inputs or enablers), patents as well as scientific publications (outputs), are taken into account, together with variables related to education and economy in order to classify R&D performance in 25 European Union (EU) Member States. This study classify these countries from 2005 to 2008 employing a set of variables that characterize them and finding the most relevant ones for this classification. The Multilayer Perceptron Model (MLP) trained by Evolutionary Algorithms (also called ESUNN) and the Product-Unit Neural Network models trained by Evolutionary Algorithms (EPUNN) classified yearly country patterns in clusters, which had been

* This work was partially subsidized by the Spanish Inter-Ministerial Commission of Science and Technology under Project TIN2011-22794, the European Regional Development fund, and the "Junta de Andalucía", Spain, under Project P08-TIC-3745.

previously obtained employing unsupervised algorithm k-means clustering that detected behavioural patterns among countries in the same cluster. Four different classes of national R&D performance are found through this algorithm: Low, Moderate, High and Innovation-driven countries. Finally, in order to analyse the appropriateness of our methodology, it is compared to other classification methods normally used in machine learning. The results show that while various methods of classification exist (like the one presented in this paper), our methodology obtains models with a significantly lower number of coefficients, without decreasing their accuracy and could be employed as a complementary tool to monitor R&D performance in the EU.

1. Introduction

Research, Development (R&D) and innovation have become, especially in these days of economic downturn and budget constraint, the keys for economic and smart growth in a knowledge-based society and the driving forces for national competitive advantage. Europe's competitiveness, our future standard of living, depends on our ability to incorporate the outputs of the innovation process in products, services, business and social processes and models. This is why R&D and innovation have been at the heart of, first, the Lisbon Strategy (2000), re-launched in Barcelona (2008) and, today, in the Europe 2020 Strategy and the European Research Area.

The R&D effort is a very complex structure with multiple factors to resource allocation strategies and to convert them into innovations. In response to competitive international pressure, firms' survival and competitive advantage rely upon R&D ability, and hence, upon innovation. The underlying argument for R&D public and private expenditure, is that the more resources a country invests in innovation, the higher its expected productivity [8]; it will be more competitive, leading to a more inclusive, knowledge-based and sustainable economy.

Two important underlying assumptions must be considered in this paper. The first is the technical change, which is found in Romer´s model of economic growth [24], his most important work. This model is based on the underlying assumptions that: technical change lies at the heart of economic growth, that this change arises because of intentional actions taken by people who respond to market incentives and that instructions for working with raw materials are different from other economic goods.

Regarding the second premise, the linear innovation model, one of the first important step towards the understanding of the innovation process was taken by Kline and Rosenberg in 1986 [13]. But although one of the key elements of that model of the innovation process is the understanding that research and innovation are linked in a non-linear and interactive manner, we assume the linear-model because, as Godin remarks, this model functions as a social fact. Rival and optional models can do little because of the lack of statistics [7].

All these factors result in an increasing demand for and interest in finding overall measures of efficiency and productivity in R&D investment and innovation. Scholars and experts started investigating the topic from different albeit complementary perspectives. Prior studies generally tested and evaluated the efficiency of R&D investments using parametric and non-parametric techniques (mainly Data Envelopment Analysis and Stochastic Frontier Analysis) at macro [15, 20] and micro level (country) and micro level (firms and R&D programs and projects) and at different moments in the innovation process (largely divided in the literature in ex-post and ex-ante types). Although many researchers have studied the subject of competitiveness through innovation, most of the studies have been focused at firm level and seek to explain patterns of international competition, emphasizing the importance of the home country's characteristics in determining the competitive position of its firms in international markets.

At the macro-level, the European Innovation Scoreboard examines differences in R&D and innovation policies' efficiency by assuming that efficiency to be the ratio of outputs over inputs. Here it is measured by comparing the ratio between a composite indicator score for one or more input dimensions and one or more output dimensions. A wide range of evaluation methodologies and indicators for evaluating the socio-economic impact of R&D have been also presented as a toolbox document by the European Commission [6] but, to date, few works have been based on Artificial Neural Networks. Data Mining and Cluster Analysis techniques have been used on regional innovation systems [10] and for the competitiveness of nations [30].

The most popular neural network model could be the Multilayer Perceptron (MLP) due to its simple architecture yet powerful problem-solving ability, where neurons are grouped in layers and only forward connections exist [26].

However, alternatives to MLP have appeared in the last few years: Product Unit Neural Network (PUNN) models are an alternative to MLPs and are based on multiplicative neurons instead of additive ones. They correspond to a special class of feed-forward neural network introduced by Durbin and Rumelhart [5].

In many cases, neural networks that use sigmoid-unit basis functions[†] (SUNN) and networks that use product-unit basis functions (PUNN) are trained by using evolutionary algorithms (EA), obtaining significant advantages with this method compared to traditional training approaches [29]. One of the most important aspects of using of Evolutionary Programming (EP) algorithms as a modelling methodology is their ability to make the complexity of the network more flexible during training through the use of structural mutation operators that add and delete nodes and add and delete connections.

The aim of this work focuses on the prediction of the classification of the R&D performance in European countries thanks to their assignment into clusters, which will help to monitor European Strategies for R&D and innovation. First, k-means clustering (unsupervised algorithm) is applied to detect behavioural patterns among 25 EU Member States between 2005 and 2008. As a result of clustering, a number of classes are set to define the characteristics of each one. Then a multiclass classifier is built to assign each country-year observation to its corresponding cluster according to a set of specific features that characterize that country. To build that classifier, we develop neural network models using Sigmoid Unit Neural Networks (SUNN) and Product Unit Neural Networks (PUNN) trained with an EA. Thus, Evolutionary Algorithms for Artificial Neural Networks (EANN) are used to classify 25 European countries according to their R&D performance in one of the classes obtained thanks to the clustering procedure. These EANN use structural operation mutations that allow us to build models with a reduced number of basis functions and connections, which determine a lower number of coefficients in the model.

The study has the following structure: first, the methodology section is devoted to clustering methodology and class descriptions, neural networks, multiclass classification and evolutionary algorithm methodologies; second, the experimental study is carried out with the description of the database, the results and the analysis of the best model. Finally, conclusions are drawn about experimental results.

---

[1] Called MLP or SUNN in this paper.

2. Methodology

2.1. *K-means clustering and classes description*

A simple K-means clustering algorithm [12] was used, implemented in WEKA software [10], due to its ease in implementation and low computational cost. Given that there was a significant decrease in the cluster sum of the squared errors when we increase k, a value of k=4 was chosen.

Using the economic analysis of those patterns and cluster centroids, the profile of each group was drawn up and labeled by classes as follows (for descriptions of variables, see Table I).

- Moderate innovation countries (cluster 1): countries in which R&D plays a less than central role. R&D intensity is not well developed either in the public and private sectors or, on average, in the number of researchers and human resources in Science and Technology (S&T). So, these countries have lagged behind in performance with very low patenting intensity and numbers of scientific publications. These countries are not economically strong (in terms of employment rates, GDP and real labor productivity growth) and give little emphasis to PhD graduates and life-long learning, although they present good performance in community trademarks and license and patent revenues.

- Innovation-driven countries (cluster 2): this class involves the most developed countries. They are economically prosperous, and they present the largest proportion of investment in R&D, researchers, human resources in S&T and doctoral graduates. We also find emphasis on tertiary and life-long education, which is representative of their education systems. This has provided the workforce with the skills needed for a changing environment and has laid the groundwork for high levels of technological adoption and innovation. They present their best performances in scientific publications and patent revenues as well.

- Low innovation countries (cluster 3): mainly represented by the transition economies of the New Member States (except Greece and Portugal). As new economies, they involve considerable growth in GDP and in Real Labour Productivity growth-per-hour-worked (RLPGH) due to a high domestic demand following a period of socialism, among other reasons.

Nonetheless, their economies do not seem to be based either on education or on R&D investment and could be an obstacle for future growth.

- High innovation countries or followers (cluster 4): countries in this cluster fit well into the model of technological competitiveness with high average values in most variables and are very close to cluster 2 in the number of PhD graduates, the employment rate, number of patents by residents, and medium and high-technology exports (these two latter cases hold the highest position). However, they present lower average values in terms of the profitability of their trademarks and license and patent revenues as well as in the number of persons enrolled in tertiary education. Lifelong learning is not as good as one might suppose in this group of countries. Thus, their performance economically and in education is worse than in the innovation-driven countries cluster, although they fall close behind.

Mapping these clusters (see figures 1-3), it can be observed that only two country-year patterns change cluster throughout the time span: Malta and Estonia. Both change from low to a moderate innovation cluster, but while the former moves in 2006, the latter moves in 2008.

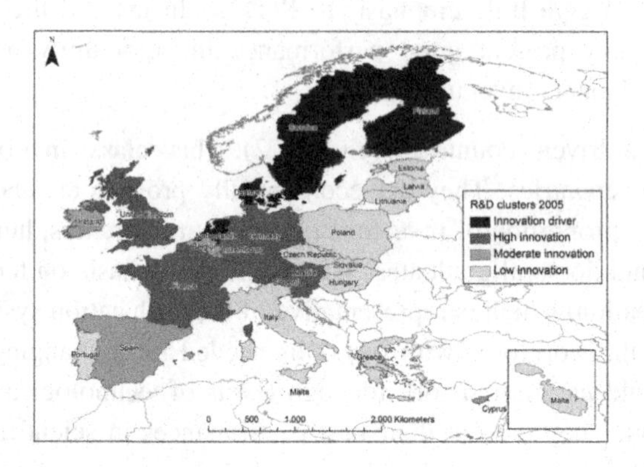

Figure 1. Clusters with country-year patterns 2005.

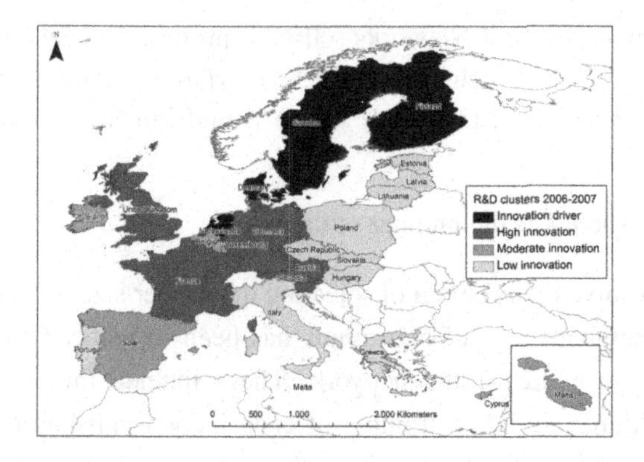

Figure 2. Clusters with country-year patterns 2006-2007

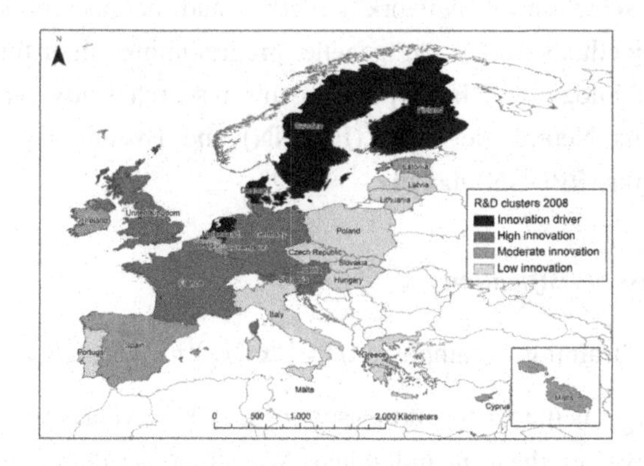

Figure 3. Clusters with country-year patterns 2008.

2.2. *Neural Networks*

Neural Networks (NNs) have become an important tool for classification since recent research activities have identified them as a promising alternative to conventional classification methods, such as the linear discriminant analysis or decision trees. Different types of NNs are now being used for classification purposes [16]: multilayer perceptron neural networks (MLP), where the transfer functions are Sigmoidal-Unit basis functions, SU; Radial Basis Functions (RBF), kernel functions where the transfer function are usually Gaussian [3]; the

General Regression Neural Networks (GRNN) proposed by Specht [28]; a class of multiplicative NNs which comprises such types as sigma-pi networks; and Product-Unit networks, PU [5,19], where a multiplicative node is given as $y_i = \prod_{i=1}^{k} x_i^{w_{ji}}$, where k is the number of inputs.

In order to solve the problem of selecting the proper size for the hidden layer of the net, a new category of algorithms has been introduced to automatically determine the structure of the network. These include the orthogonal least-squares algorithm; individual training of each hidden unit based on functional analysis; constructive methods, where the structure of the network is built incrementally; pruning methods that start with an initial selection of a large number of hidden units which is reduced as the algorithm proceeds; and the simultaneous selection of network structure and parameters by employing optimization methods based on genetic programming algorithms, EP. This training methodology will be applied in this research study on Evolutionary Sigmoidal-Units Neural Networks (ESUNN) and Evolutionary Product-Unit Neural Networks (EPUNN) models.

2.3. *Multiclass classification*

Let a training sample $D = \{(\mathbf{x}_n, \mathbf{y}_n); n = 1,2,...,N\}$ be where $\mathbf{x}_n = (x_{1n},...,x_{kn})$ is the vector of measurements taking values in $\Omega \subset \mathbb{R}^k$ and y_n is the class level of the *n-th* individual. We adopt the common technique of representing the class levels using a "1-of-Q" encoding vector $\mathbf{y} = \left(y^{(1)}, y^{(2)},..., y^{(Q)}\right)$ such as $y^{(l)} = 1$ if $\mathbf{x}$ corresponds to an example belonging to class l and $y^{(l)} = 0$ otherwise. Based on the training sample we wish to find a *ANN* $(\hat{\boldsymbol{\theta}})$ that can result in a good classification of the patterns in the generalization set. This would be the same as obtaining a decision function $C:(\Omega,\theta) \rightarrow \{1,2,...,Q\}$ to classify the individuals. A misclassification occurs when C assigns an individual (based on measurements vector) to class j when it is actually coming from a class $l \neq j$.

For a g *ANN* $(\hat{\boldsymbol{\theta}})$ classifier, a classification problem with Q classes and N training or testing patterns is considered, obtaining a $Q \times Q$ contingency or confusion matrix $M(g)$:

$$M(g) = \left\{ n_{ij}; \sum_{i,j=1}^{Q} n_{ij} = N \right\} \tag{1}$$

where n_{ij} represents the number of times the patterns are predicted by classifier g to be in class j when they really belong to class i. Let us denote the number of patterns associated with class i by

$$f_i = \sum_{j=1}^{Q} n_{ij}, i = 1, \ldots, Q \tag{2}$$

To evaluate the performance of the classifiers three scalar measures are defined that take the elements of the confusion matrix into consideration from different points of view. Let $S_i = n_{ii}/f_i$ be the number of patterns correctly predicted to be in class i with respect to the total number of patterns in i (sensitivity for class i). Therefore the sensitivity for class i estimates the probability of correctly predicting a class i example. From the above quantities the first comparison measure of a multiclass classifier define the sensitivity S of the classifier as the minimum value of sensitivities for each class $S = mín\ \{S_i;\ i = 1, \ldots, Q\}$. The second measure is the correct classification rate or accuracy,

$$CCR = (1/N) \sum_{i=1}^{Q} n_{ii} \tag{3}$$

that is the rate of all the correct predictions. The third measure is Cohen's Kappa coefficient, as an association measure between the class that *a priori* belongs to a pattern and the assignation that *a posteriori* assigns the classifier to that class.

Thus, we consider the three-dimensional measure (*CCR, MS, K*) associated with classifier g. The measure tries to evaluate three features of a classifier throughout the generalization set: global performance in the whole dataset, the performance in each class and the degree of association between pattern distributions in classes before and after classifier application.

The output layer of the *ANN* ($\hat{\theta}$) classifier is interpreted from the point of view of probability, which considers the soft-max activation function:

$$g_l(\mathbf{x},\theta_l) = \frac{\exp f_l(\mathbf{x},\theta_l)}{\sum_{l=1}^{Q} \exp f_l(\mathbf{x},\theta_l)} \quad \text{for } l = 1,\ldots,Q \tag{4}$$

where $g_l(\mathbf{x},\theta_l)$ is the probability a pattern **x** has of belonging to class *l*, $\theta_l = (\beta_l, \mathbf{w}_1,\ldots,\mathbf{w}_M)$, $\beta_l = (\beta_1^l,\ldots,\beta_M^l)$ is the *l-th* vector of weights of the output node, M is the number of hidden nodes, $\mathbf{w}_j = (w_0^j,\ldots,w_K^j)$ for $j = 1,\ldots,M$, is the vector of input weights of the hidden node j, and $f_l(\mathbf{x},\theta_l)$ is the output of the *l-th* output node for pattern **x** given by:

$$f_l(\mathbf{x},\theta_l) = \beta_0^l + \sum_{j=1}^{M} \beta_j^l \sigma_j \left(w_0^j + \sum_{i=1}^{k} w_i^j x_i \right) \quad \text{for } l = 1,\ldots Q\text{-}1$$

$$f_Q(\mathbf{x},\theta_Q) = 0 \tag{5}$$

where $\sigma(\bullet)$ is the sigmoidal activation function of the nodes in the hidden layer.

The classification rule coincides with the optimal Bayes rule. Thus the classification rule makes an individual be assigned to that class which has the maximum probability, given vector measurement **x**

$$C(\mathbf{x}) = \hat{l}\text{, where } \hat{l} = \arg\max_l g_l(\mathbf{x},\hat{\theta}_l)\text{, for } l=1,\ldots,4 \tag{6}$$

2.4. *Evolutionary Algorithm*

The evolutionary algorithm for SUNN (ESSUN) is detailed in Figure 4, where p^B is the best-optimized ESUNN returned by the algorithm. The main characteristics of the algorithm are the following:

1. Representation of the individuals. The algorithm evolves architectures and connection weights simultaneously, each individual being a fully specified ESUNN. ESUNNs are represented using an object-oriented approach and the algorithm deals directly with the ESUNN phenotype. Each connection is specified by a binary value indicating if the connection exists along with a real value representing its weights.

2. Error and Fitness Functions. Our fitness function is a decreasing transformation of cross-entropy error because the Entropy function is continuous and helps the algorithm to enhance the classifiers more gradually than with the use of CCR. However, the relationship between CCR and Entropy error strongly depends on the dataset structure. Hence, regarding experimental results, using Entropy elitism is more suitable for some datasets to get higher test accuracy, but maintaining the best CCR individual can be more appropriate for some other datasets [9]. In general, the relationship between CCR and cross-entropy error strongly depends on the data base structure. Hence, regarding experimental results, in general, using cross-entropy elitism is more suitable to obtain higher generalization accuracy. For this reason, the EP algorithm returns the best cross-entropy individual as solutions. Then, the error function given by cross-entropy error for N observations associated with the ESUNN model, is:

$$L^*(\theta) = \frac{1}{N}\sum_{n=1}^{N}\left[-\sum_{l=1}^{Q-1} y_n^{(l)} f_l(\mathbf{x}_n, \theta_l) + \log \sum_{l=1}^{Q-1} \exp f_l(\mathbf{x}_n, \theta_l)\right] \tag{7}$$

where $y_n^{(l)}$ is equal to 1 if the pattern $\mathbf{X}_n$ belongs to the *l-th* class and equal to 0 otherwise. The fitness measure needed for evaluating the individuals (Figure 4, steps 2, 7 and 16) is a strictly decreasing transformation of the error function $L^*(\theta)$ given by $A(f) = \frac{1}{1+L^*(\theta)}$ where $0 < A(f) \le 1$.

3. Initialization of the Population. The initial population is generated trying to obtain ESUNNs with the maximum possible fitness. First, 5,000 random ESUNNs are generated (Figure 4, step 1), where the number of SUNNs M is a random value in the interval [Mmin, Mmax].

The number of connections between all SUNNs of an individual and the input layer is a random value in the interval [1, k] and all of them are connected with the same randomly chosen input variables. In this way, all the SUNNs of each individual are initialized in the same random subspace of the input variables. A random value in the [-I, I] interval is assigned for the weights between the input layer and the hidden layer and in the [-O,O] interval for those between the hidden layer and the output layer. The individuals obtained are evaluated using the fitness function and the initial population is finally obtained by selecting the best 500 SUNNs (Figure 4, steps 2-4).

4. Parametric Mutation. This operator is accomplished for each coefficient of the model with Gaussian noise and applying a standard simulated annealing process for accepting or rejecting modifications (Figure 4, step 10) alters the value of the coefficients of the model. The connections are modified by adding Gaussian noise, $w(t+1) = w(t) + \xi(t)$, where $\xi(t) \in N(0,T(g))$ and $N(0,T(g))$ represent a one-dimensional normally distributed random variable with mean 0 and with variance in the network temperature ($T(g) = 1 - A(g)$) [18].

5. Structural Mutation. It implies a modification in the structure of the ESUNNs (Figure 4, step 11) and allows the exploration of different regions in the search space, helping to maintain the diversity of the population. There are four different structural mutations similar to the mutations in the GNARL model [1]: hidden node addition, hidden node deletion, connection addition and connection deletion, which are applied sequentially to each network. The number of nodes added or deleted in hidden node addition and hidden node deletion is calculated as $\Delta_{min} + uT(g)[\Delta_{max} - \Delta_{min}]$, u being a random uniform variable in the interval [0, 1], Δ_{min} and Δ_{max} a minimum and maximum number of nodes specified as parameters. The severity of mutations depends on the temperature $T(g)$ of the neural network model, defined by $T(g) = 1-A(g)$ $0 < T(g) < 1$. Structural connection mutations are performed as follows:

- Connection addition. Connection addition mutations are first performed in the hidden layer and then in the output layer. When adding a connection from the input layer to the hidden layer, a node from each layer is selected randomly, and then the connection is added with a random weight. A similar procedure is performed from the hidden layer to the output layer.
- Connection deletion. In the same way, connection deletion mutation is first performed in the hidden layer and then in the output layer, choosing randomly the origin node randomly from the previous layer and the target node from the mutated layer.

We apply connection mutations sequentially for each mutated neural net, first, adding (or deleting) $1+u_0\Delta_0$ connections from the hidden layer to the output layer and then, adding (or deleting) $1+u_h\Delta_h$ connections from the input layer to the hidden layer, u being a random uniform variable in the interval [0, 1], Δ_0 and Δ_h previously defined ratios of the number of connections in the hidden and the output layer, and n0 and nh the current number of connections in the output and the hidden layers. Parsimony is also encouraged evolving networks by attempting the four structural mutations sequentially, where node 1 or connection deletion is always attempted before addition. Moreover, the deletion operations are made with higher probability. If a deletion operation is successful, no other mutation will be made. If the probability does not select any mutation, one of the mutations is chosen at random and applied.

ESUNN Algorithm:

Input: Training dataset (D)

Output: Best optimized SUNN (p^B)

1: $P^I \leftarrow \{p_1^I, \ldots, p_{5000}^I\}$ p^I is a randomly generated SUNN

2: $\forall p_i^I \in P^I \; f_i^I \leftarrow A(p_i^I)$ {Evaluate fitness}

3: $P \leftarrow \{p_{(1)},\ldots,p_{(5000)}\}$, $(p_{(i)} \prec p_{(j)}) \Leftrightarrow (f_i^I > f_j^I)$ {Sort individuals in P^I by increasing f_i^I }

4: $P \leftarrow \{p_{(1)},\ldots,p_{(500)}\}$ {Retain the best 500 SUNNs}

6: **while not** Stop Condition **do**

7: $\forall p_i \in P \quad f_i \leftarrow A(p_i)$ {Evaluate fitness}

8: $P \leftarrow \{p_{(1)},\ldots,p_{(500)}\}$ $(p_{(i)} \prec p_{(j)}) \Leftrightarrow (f_i > f_j)$ {Sort individuals in P by increasing f_i }

9: $p^B \leftarrow p_{(1)}$ {Store Best Individual}

10: $P^P \leftarrow \{p_{(1)},\ldots,p_{(50)}\}$ {Parametric mutation parents (best 10% of individuals)}

11: $P^S \leftarrow \{p_{(1)},\ldots,p_{(449)}\}$ {Structural mutation parents (best 90% of individuals minus one)}

12: $\forall p_i^P \in P^P$, $p_i^P \leftarrow$ parametric Mutation (p_i^P) {Apply parametric mutation}

13: $\forall p_i^S \in P^S$, $p_i^S \leftarrow$ structural Mutation (p_i^S) {Apply structural mutation}

14: $P \leftarrow P^P \cup P^S \cup \{p^B\}$ {Offspring including the elite}

15: **end while**

16: $\forall p_i \in P$, $f_i \leftarrow A(p_i)$ {Evaluate fitness}

17: $P \leftarrow \{p_{(1)},...,p_{(500)}\} (p_{(i)} \prec p_{(j)}) \Leftrightarrow (f_i > f_j)$ {Sort individuals in P by increasing f_i }

18: $p^B \leftarrow p_{(1)}$

19: **return** p^B

Fig. 4. ESUNN training algorithm framework.

Although this section focuses on the ESUNN algorithm, for the EPUNN model we employ the same training algorithm framework but in the third step (initialization of the population) the random value in the [-I, I] interval assigned for the weights between the input layer and the hidden layer is much lower, usually [-1,1]. More details about the EP algorithm can be consulted in [17] and [18].

3. Experimental study: predicting a country's R&D performance

3.1. *Dataset description*

The insights gained from the use of the EANN's algorithms were applied to a dataset of 25 EU Members for R&D performance classification. Due to data availability (until 2008 in most official databases), 100 country-year observations have been considered since no changes between clusters of country-year items are expected, similar way to some other studies [27]. The incorporations of Bulgaria and Romania are dated in 2007, thus scientific and technological European policy and strategy were not directly applicable and so their inclusion has not been considered appropriate for this classification.

The difficulty in finding data about R&D and innovation [2] as well as the missing data for a number of countries forces us to select proxy variables in most cases. Thus, fifteen main variables were selected, as shown in table 1, for characterizing R&D performance at country level following the input/output orientation in their interpretation. We ascribe to the idea that the production of knowledge requires specific investments in R&D and that the role of human capital is of great importance, thus the amount of funds and the number of researchers were selected as a proxy for labor input and capital input of R&D intensity, respectively. The R&D expenditure was broken down into public and business sectors.

Data were obtained from various sources (Eurostat´s official website, OECD Main Science and Technology Indicators, World Bank Database and SCImago Journal & Country Rank in the case of scientific publications per country), adjusting when necessary to 1000 per population.

Despite this, an imputation has been carried out for missing data when necessary (it occurs in up to 1.3% of the cases); this imputation was made by linear regression [4]. Six models were fit for the tasks at hand, one for each variable with missing data, (PHD06, GERDGO, GERDBU, TPATRE, PATREV and RDPERS). The dependent variable is the year for which there is no data. The covariates are the remaining years without missing data. All models were fitted to a=0.05 and a determination coefficient $R^2 > 0.90$.

Among the resulting set of variables of R&D activity [22], scientific publications have been considered as the major output of research and are widely used to evaluate the performance of researchers. Patents were also selected since they have often been used as the direct output of innovation process because technical advance and technological innovation are difficult to measure.

Table 1. List of variables

Code	Variables	Source
	R&D enablers	
HUMLF	Human Resources in Science and Technology as a share of the labour force	Eurostat/ OECD
RDPERS	R&D personnel, as a share of the labour force.	Eurostat
GERDBU	Gross Domestic Expenditure on R&D, Business Sector as % of GDP	Eurostat
GERDGO	Gross Domestic Expenditure on R&D, Government Sector as % of GDP	Eurostat
	R&D outputs	
SPUBLI	Number of scientific publications per 1000 population	SCImago JCR
TPATRE	Worldwide patent applications filed through the Patent Cooperation Treaty procedure or with a national patent office (residents) per 1000 population	World Bank Database
	Education	
PHD06	Number of PhD graduates (ISCED 6) per 1000 population	Eurostat
TERTIT	Number of persons who are enrolled in tertiary education (including university and non-university studies) in the regular educational system in each country per 1000 population	Eurostat
LLEARN	Lifelong learning (% of persons aged 18 to 64)	Eurostat
	Economy	
GDPGRO	Growth rate of GDP volume - percentage change with respect to previous year	Eurostat
RLPGH	Real labour productivity growth per hour worked (previous year)	Eurostat
EMPLO	Total employment rate	Eurostat
PATREV	License and patent revenues from abroad as % of GDP	Eurostat
TRADEM	Community trademarks per billion GDP (in PPS€)	Innometrics/Eurostat
MHTEXP	Medium and High-technology exports (% of manufactured exports)	Innometrics/Eurostat

R&D performance includes the perspective of education with two variables, PhD graduates and tertiary education students, which is one of the main objectives of government R&D policies because human resources, with their managerial and organizational skills, play an ever-increasing role in the performance of R&D activities. Finally, economic variables like Gross Domestic Product (GDP) growth, per-hour-growth of real labour productivity and medium and high technology exports, are taken into account to locate patterns among countries.

3.2. *Results*

We have compared Evolutionary Sigmoidal-Unit Neural Networks (ESUNNs) and Evolutionary Product Unit Neural Networks (EPUNNs) with nine state-of-the-art methods that are well-known in the literature. Eight of them have been configured and run in WEKA [11] and the Simple Linear Discriminant Analysis (SLDA) method is available in SPSS [21]. The methods used for comparison are [14]: MLP: a neural network classifier that uses back propagation to calculate weights. SLDA: a multivariate statistical procedure that derives equations to classify instances [25]. C4.5: a classifier tree for generating a pruned or unpruned decision tree. AdaBoost100: a classifier tree based on the AdaBoost.M1 algorithm with a maximum of 100 iterations. LMT: a classifier for building logistic model trees, which are classification trees with logistic regression functions at the leaves. NaiveBayes: a classifier whose numeric estimator precision values are chosen based on the analysis of the training data. SLogistic: a classifier for building linear logistic regression models. MLogistic: a classifier for building a multinomial logistic regression model with a ridge estimator. SVM: a classifier for building a linear model (maximum-margin-hyperplane) over a kernel space resulting in a nonlinear classifier. A Gaussian kernel is used with the selection of the SVM hyperparameters (regularization parameter C, and width of the Gaussian functions γ); a grid search algorithm a 10- fold cross validation, using the following ranges: $C \in \left\{2^{-5}, 2^{-3}, \ldots 2^{15}\right\}$ and $\gamma \in \left\{2^{-15}, 2^{-13}, \ldots 2^{3}\right\}$

A comparison of the accuracy of eleven methods in predicting the R&D performance of each country is shown in Table 2. From a descriptive point of view, Best ESUNN, Best EPUNN, Best MLP, LMT, SLogistic, Mlogistic and SVM models obtain equal results in CCR_G (100), MS_G (100) and K_G (1) for the generalization set. Nevertheless, concerning the number of connections of each model (see last column of Table II), the Best ESUNN model presents the lowest number of coefficients (20); thus this is the model selected, which will be further explained.

With respect to the results obtained in the 30 runs for the three stochastic algorithms (see Table 3), it is clear that the best results come from the MLP neural network, although the ESUNN methodology provides the second best results with a high mean (98% for CCR_G) and a low standard deviation, SD, (2.73% for CCR_G). The principal difference between these methodologies is the number of connections or model coefficients, because for MLP the mean is 44 and for ESUNN the mean is 26.57 with a SD= 3.47.

In this manner, considering accuracy and the lower number of connections, we recommend ESUNN methodology for country-year classification.

Table 2. Statistical results of the CCR_G, MS_G, K_G and number of connections (#conn.)

Method[a]	CCR_G(%)	MS_G(%)	K_G	#conn.
Best ESUNN	**100**	**100**	1	20
Best EPUNN	**100**	**100**	1	26
Best MLP	**100**	**100**	1	44
SLDA	96	80	0.94	24
C4.5	84	77	0.78	**13**
AdaBoost100	52	0	0.31	24
LMT	**100**	**100**	1	27
NaiveBayes	92	80	0.89	124
SLogistic	**100**	**100**	1	27
MLogistic	**100**	**100**	1	48
SVM	**100**	**100**	1	96

Table 3. Mean and Standard Deviation (SD) for stochastic methods

Method[a]	CCR_G(%) Mean±SD	MS_G(%) Mean±SD	K_G Mean±SD	# conn. Mean±SD
ESUNN	98.00±2.73	92.33±9.60	0.97±0.05	**26.57±3.47**
EPUNN	94.00±4.79	84.55±11.13	0.92±0.07	29.93±4.66
MLP	**100.00±0.00**	**100.00±0.00**	**1.00±0.00**	44.00±0.00

a. The best quantitative result method is represented in bold face.

In the case of the stochastic algorithms shown in table 3, the experimental design was conducted using a holdout procedure with 30 runs. Approximately 75% of the patterns were randomly selected for the training set and the remaining 25% for the test set [23].

3.3. *Best model*

Once the algorithm has been run 30 times, the 30 best models are obtained, both for ESUNN and EPUNN. Then, the following ESSUN model is chosen: this model consists of nine variables in the input layer, two hidden nodes with sigmoid transfer function units and three nodes in the output layer which return the probability a pattern has of belonging to each class. From them, the probability of membership in the fourth class is calculated. The selected input variables were TERTIT, LLEARN, GERDGO, TRADEM, RLPGH, GPGROW, TPATRE, PATREV and HUMLF.

Interest in the proposed best ESUNN model is due to the fact that it improves the results of other approaches (see Table 3) and because it provides a (non-linear) interpretable model. Table 4 shows the expression of the probability of this best ESUNN model as well as its performance:

Table 4. Probability expression and performance of the best ESUNN model.

Best ESUNN model
$f_1(\mathrm{x}, \theta_1) = 4.69 - 18.69 * SU_1$
$f_2(\mathrm{x}, \theta_2) = 9.3 - 13.62 * SU_2$
$f_3(\mathrm{x}, \theta_3) = 0.49 + 13.49 * SU_1 - 23.59 * SU_2$
$f_4(\mathrm{x}, \theta_4) = 0$
$SU_1 = \dfrac{1}{(1 + EXP - (-9.32 + 8.07 * TERTIT + 9.31 * TRADEM - 4.08 * RLPGH + 5.03 * PATREV + 3.68 * HUMLF))}$
$SU_2 = \dfrac{1}{(1 + EXP - (-12.44 + 3.42 * TERTIT - 9.61 * LLEARN - 9.04 * GERDGO - 3.07 * GDPGRO + 7.32 * TPATRE + 4.47 * HUMLF))}$
$CCR_G = 100\%$; $MS_G = 100\%$; $K_G = 1$

Table 4 also shows the construction of sigmoid unit SU_1 as a function of variables TERTIT, HUMLF (labour force skills), PATREV, TRADEM (the profitability of innovation through patents and trademarks) and RLPGH (real labour productivity growth per-hour-worked). The same table shows the construction of SU_2 as a function of variables TERTIT, HUMLF (as well as SU_1) and LLEARN (which denotes the importance of education for labour force skills), GERDGO (public policy support for R&D investment that stimulates the innovation process in the private sector), TPATRE (main proxy indicator for measuring a country's innovation capability) and GDPGRO (the most common indicator of an economy's well-being).

On the other hand, if one looks at the coefficients of the sums of the exponents that belong to the sigmoidal units, along with the importance of variables according to the probability each one has of belonging to class (g_l) in Table 5, the variables which have the strongest effects for measuring R&D performance at country level are those that present (++) and (--). Variables with (+) or (-) have a lower effect and those with (=) have no significant effects. This means that an increase in variable value implies mainly an increase (+), a decrease (-) or non-significant changes (=) in the probability of belonging to the corresponding cluster.

Table 5. Influence of each variable on a higher or lower probability of appearing in a given cluster

Variable	Probability Cluster 1	Probability Cluster 2	Probability Cluster 3	Probability Cluster 4
TERTIT	(--)	(--)	(+)	(++)
LLEARN	(--)	(++)	(+)	(--)
GERDGO	(-)	(++)	(-)	(--)
TRADEM	(--)	(--)	(++)	(++)
RLPGH	(+)	(=)	(=)	(--)
GDPGRO	(=)	(=)	(=)	(=)
TPATRE	(--)	(++)	(+)	(--)
PATREV	(--)	(--)	(++)	(++)
HUMLF	(-)	(=)	(-)	(=)

Thus, the variables that exert a major influence on the probability of belonging to cluster 2 (Innovation driven economies) are LLEARN, GERDGO and TPATRE. While these variables increase the probability of being included in cluster 2, TERTIT, TRADEM and PATREV tend to reduce it. The variables that have no effects on such a probability are GDPGRO, RLPGH and HUMLF.

Interestingly, the number of tertiary students (TERTIT) tends to strongly increase a country's R&D performance in cluster 4 (high innovation). Along with variable lifelong learning, the EU strategy could therefore continue to support education, the key to employment, as it is the most important base to increase necessary skills in knowledge-based economies.

4. Conclusions

A classification of European countries according to their R&D and innovation performance (based on the traditional R&D linear model) can be useful to assess their position compared to other countries with respect to reaching competitiveness and long-term sustainability objectives. In this study, after the use of unsupervised algorithm k-means clustering with four resulting clusters, we examined nine machine learning and two evolutionary algorithms as well as neural networks classifiers to predict the R&D performance classification in 25 EU Member States, to identify the best model and major variables out of 15 that can influence the probability of belonging to each class.

Our analyses pinpointed the variables that exert a major influence on the R&D performance of a country belonging to "innovation-driven countries" (cluster 2), which are TERTIT, TRADEM and PATREV. While these variables improve R&D performance classification, LLEARN, GERDGO and TPATRE tend to reduce it. Interestingly, the number of tertiary students seems to tend to increase a country's R&D performance since education is the base for increasing necessary skills in a knowledge-based economy. Nations will also need to consider investing in education in addition to R&D since these higher skills are basic in the application of new industry and service technologies.

This technique has to be considered a complementary tool to manage the extensive information provided by the number of official report indicators and methodologies. Our aim is to help experts to classify countries or predict their R&D performance in future years with innovation scores and publicly available country data, and then using the best model obtained, to identify the major contributing factors that could estimate the above-mentioned R&D and innovation performance with the fewest variables possible.

The present research demonstrates that nine out of fifteen variables like those in our dataset could be used to predict the R&D performance of a country reasonably well. Although our set of 15 variables resulted in very reasonable proxies, overlooked variables must be considered in future studies. If we have the appropriate numbers are available, the implications of our model would appear to be worthwhile in future comparative research performance on the cross-country performance, using nine out of a number of variables used in similar studies.

References

1. P.J. Angeline, G.M. Saunders and J.P. Pollackm, *IEEE Trans. Neural Netw.* **5**, 54 (1994).
2. B.C. Rao, *Int. J. Innov. Manage.* **14**, 823 (2010).
3. C.M. Bishop, *Neural Comput.* 3, 579 (1991).
4. S.F. Buck, *J. R. Stat. Soc.* **B22**, 302 (1960).

5. R. Durbin and D. Rumelhart, *Neural Comput.* **1**, 133 (1989).
6. G. Fahrenkrog, W. Polt, J. Rojo, A. Tübke and K. Zinöcker, *Technical Report EUR20382EN.* (2002).
7. B. Godin, *Technol. Hum. Values* **31**, 639 (2006).
8. Z. Griliches, *R&D and Productivity: The Econometric Evidence*. University of Chicago Press (1998).
9. P.A. Gutiérrez, C. Hervás-Martínez and M. Lozano, *Soft Comput.* **14**, 599 (2009).
10. V. Hájková and P. Hájek, Proceedings of Communication and Management in Technological Innovation and Academic Globalization (COMATIA´10), 46 (2010).
11. M. Hall, E. Frank, G. Holmes, B. Pfahringer, P. Reutemann and I. Witten, *ACM SIGKDD Explorations Newsl.* **11**, 10 (2009).
12. J.A Hartigan and M.A. Wong, *J. R. Stat. Soc.* **C28**, 100 (1979).
13. S.J. Kline and N. Rosenberg, The Positive Sum Strategy: Harnessing Technology for Economic Growth. National Academy Press, 275 (1986).
14. N. Landwehr, M. Hall and E. Frank, *Mach. Learn.* **59**,161 (2005).
15. M. Kim, H. Lee, S. R. Yee and K. Choe, *Int. J. Innov. Technol. Manage.* **8**, 295 (2011).
16. R.P. Lippmann, *IEEE Commun. Mag.* **27**, 47 (1989).
17. A.C. Martínez-Estudillo, C. Hervás-Martínez, F.J. Martínez-Estudillo and N. García-Pedrajas, *IEEE Trans. Syst. Man Cybern.* **B36**, 534 (2006).
18. A.C. Martínez-Estudillo, C. Hervás-Martínez, F.J. Martínez-Estudillo and N. García-Pedrajas, *Neural Netw.* **19**, 447 (2006).
19. F.J. Martínez-Estudillo, C. Hervás-Martínez, P.A. Gutiérrez and A.C. Martínez-Estudillo, *Neurocomputing* **72**, 548 (2008).
20. W. Nasierowski, *Int. J. Innov Technol. Manage.* **7**, 389 (2010).
21. M. Norusis, SPSS 15.0 Advanced Statistical Procedures Companion. Prentice Hall Press (2007).
22. OECD. Main Science and Technology Indicators. OCDE (2010).
23. L. Prechelt, Tech. Rep. Karlsruhe University **21/94**, (1994).
24. P.M. Romer, *J. Polit. Econ.* **98**, S71 (1990).

25. D.J. Sheskin, Handbook of parametric and nonparametric statical procedures. Chapman and Hall/CRC (2011).
26. K.A. Smith and J.N.D. Gupta, *Comput. Oper. Res.* **27**, 1023 (2000).
27. F. Solt, *Social Sci.* **90**, 231 (2009).
28. D.F. Specht, *IEEE Trans. Neural Netw.* **2**, 568 (1989).
29. X. Yao and Y. Liu, *IEEE Trans. Neural Netw.* **8**, 694 (1997).
30. S. H. Zanak and I. Becerra-Fernandez, *Eur. J. Oper. Res.* **166**, 185(2005).

MEMORY IN FINANCIAL TIME SERIES: FROM INVESTOR BEHAVIOR TO ARTIFICIAL NEURAL NETWORKS

M. TERESA SORROSAL-FORRADELLAS
M. GLÒRIA BARBERÀ-MARINÉ
LISANA B. MARTINEZ
MARÍA-JOSÉ GARBAJOSA-CABELLO

Department of Business, Universitat Rovira i Virgili, Avda. Universitat 1
Reus, 43204, Spain

Related to the concept of memory, the value of an asset in the past and the learning experience are key elements which influence investor behavior and, consequently, the future evolution of financial prices. In this study we focus on memory of time series, that is to say, in the way that past observations affect the future values of a financial variable. We use artificial neural networks because of its flexibility to adjust to any type of functional relationship, without the need to define it previously. As a specific case, we apply a backpropagation network to predict the price of the IBEX-35 index. Our results suggest that future prices depend on past prices, but this influence is not permanent.

1. Introduction

The existence of memory in financial markets is an interesting debate in the literature. There are different meanings of memory and each one requires a specific analysis and employs different methodologies to establish the existence or not of past influences over prices of financial assets.

Even, if we restrict the concept of memory to the dependence on time series, it is very difficult to assure that a particular financial market has memory. It is necessary to establish the period of analysis and the frequency of data, and results will depend on these time factors. Also, the methodology used will influence the results about the existence or inexistence of memory, but there are not concluding studies to decide which methodology is better than others.

Our study assumes that past information influences future prices of financial assets. This assumption is based on the observation of certain phenomena (the so-called calendar effects, the existence of bear and bull markets, among others) which show that occasionally the Efficient Market Hypothesis (EMH) is not satisfied. Moreover, the investor rationality, a necessary condition for the EMH, is refuted by many studies related to risk aversion, overreaction and other behavioral patterns.

In this context, our work aims to distinguish between different types of memory that can be found in financial markets, focusing our attention on a particular type of memory (which explains the influence of past values in the training of future financial prices). We will apply backpropagation neural networks over the IBEX-35 values, from 1987 to 2010.

The paper is organized as follows. Section II presents the Efficient Market Hypothesis definition and Section III explains some arguments against it, with special emphasis on those related to past effects over financial prices and with the rationality of investors. Section IV distinguishes the different types of memory in financial markets. Section V presents an analysis of the so-called memory-dependence, which is typical of financial time series. Section VI focuses on the methodology of artificial neural networks and particularly on multilayer perceptron networks with algorithm of backward propagation of the error. Section VII shows the empirical study over the IBEX-35 time series and finally, section VIII presents the main conclusions of the analysis.

2. The Efficient Market Hypothesis

The Efficient Market Hypothesis was introduced by Fama (1970) and predicts that the price of an asset includes all past available information. Consequently, the price at each moment is statistically the best estimator of the intrinsic value of the asset.

According to the information included in the asset price, the EMH can be divided into three categories:

- Weak efficiency: the available information is limited to the time series of historical prices or returns of the asset.
- Semi-strong efficiency: to the information of weak efficiency is added all the public available information.
- Strong efficiency: the set of information includes all the public as well as private information.

In the context of time series analysis, the EMH has been interpreted as the independence hypothesis between the values of a series. Conceptually, this independence implies that a variable X_t has not influence over other variable Y_t. Mathematically, this relationship should be analyzed by using the correlation function between X_t and Y_t. In our work, the assumption of independence implies that there is not relationship between successive increases in the price of an asset or, in other words, there is no relationship between the value of the asset today (X_t) and the price of the same asset delayed k periods (X_{t-k}).

Additionally, it is accepted that successive changes in asset prices have identical probability distribution. Combining both factors we obtain that the random walk is the optimal model to analyze identically and independent distributed financial time series.

To consider the random walk model means that changes in future prices are independent of past changes, that is to say, future changes do not depend on previous changes in sequential or chronological way. Consequently, it is not possible to find repeated patterns. Thus, the best strategy, in absence of new information, is to consider that the price in $t+1$ will be the same that the price in t. The prediction error using other methodologies will be always, in the long term, bigger than using this approximation.

Following Fama (1965), there are not enough arguments to support the idea that information arrives to the market in a systematic form and not randomly, then, there is not argument to defend a non-random nature of price changes.

A necessary condition for the EMH is that investors should be able to interpret correctly and immediately the news which arrive at the market and act rationally, adjusting asset prices and avoiding arbitrage situations.

There are some critics with respect to the rationality of economic agents, such as Peters (1999) and McFadden (1999), who point out the existence of time delays between the arrival of new information and agents reaction, the undervaluation and subjective valuation of this information, the heterogeneity in the agent behavior respect to the risk or the influence to be part of a collective in the decision making.

In the next section, we refer to anomalies detected in financial markets which are contrary to the EMH and some of the theories that explain the inexistence of rational investor behavior.

3. Investor Behavior and Market Anomalies

The validity of EMH has been discussed since Fama (1965) defined the efficient markets. Arguments against the EMH are based both in theoretical and empirical explanations. Beja (1977) and Grossman and Stiglitz (1980) argue that in a real market asset prices cannot reflect all relevant information and therefore, there are not really efficient markets. According to LeRoy and Porter (1981), asset prices are more volatile than expected if the EMH was satisfied. De Bondt and Thaler (1985) and Chopra *et al.* (1992) refer to the overreaction of investors to explain markets inefficiency and the existence of anomalies such as the January effect.

Lehman (1990) presents the predictability of some asset prices as another element contrary to efficient markets. Laffont and Maskin (1990) argue that the existence of imperfect competition markets is incompatible with the EMH. Shiller (2000) and Shleifer (2000) focus their criticisms on the investor rationality. From an empirical point of view, some recent studies analyze the behavior of prices for several markets. In this sense, Narayan (2008) concludes that in the G7 countries all analyzed processes are stationary and therefore contrary to the EMH. Lee *et al.* (2010) find that for 32 developed and for 26 emergent countries the EMH does not hold, with the only exception of India and Malaysia where this theory can not be refused.

Although other studies support the EMH, there is no doubt that at certain times and in certain markets, there are anomalies due to investor behavior which allow us to find a relationship between asset prices evolution and what happened in the past. These facts are object of study in this section and in the rest of the work.

Anomalies in financial markets would not exist if economic agents were rational. In this context, a rational investor is able to process correctly all relevant information in order to establish the price of an asset and to act accordingly to maximize the expected utility. In financial terms, rationality implies the maximization of expected returns at a given level of risk. But a first element to consider is the cost of information. In the market there are small and large investors and not all of them have the same access to market information, at the same time and of the same quality. So, the cost of obtaining and processing this information is a factor that can delay the price adjustment.

Moreover, even assuming that investors have all the information, their decisions follow patterns that cannot be explained only by economic theories. Human beings are influenced by different phenomena with origin in psychological, sociological and anthropological theories. In Shiller (1999) there is an interesting review of these theories and their relationships with financial situations that contradict models based on the EMH.

Probably, the prospect theory (Kahneman and Tversky, 1979) is the behavioral theory which has more influence in the economic context. It is an alternative to the expected utility maximization theory, where the utility is replaced by a value function, and the function to maximize is adjusted by weights that do not match the probability that the event happens. According with this theory, agents behave as if events with very little probability to happen were impossible and those with a high probability to happen were certain. This theory has been used by Siegel and Thaler (1997) to explain the phenomena that Mehra and Prescott (1985) called "equity premium puzzle", that designates the fact that the difference between returns on equity assets and fixed income assets returns is much greater than it can be explained using standard models that incorporate the hypothesis of rational investors.

In addition to the prospect theory, there are different theories that have their origins in the psychological and sociological study of human behavior and have been used to explain anomalies in financial markets. Shiller (1999) mentions some of them: regret theory, cognitive dissonance, the anchor, the theory of mental compartments, overconfidence, over and under reaction, the disjunction effect, cultural and social contagion and global structure, among others. These theories break the assumption of rationality and allow us to understand anomalies that cannot be explained by classical financial theory but that appear in financial markets.

From all possible anomalies, we focus on those that have their origins in the influence of past information. The most important are calendar effects, among which we stress the January and the weekend effect (Boudreaux (1995); Hansen *et al.* (2005)). Lo (1991), Cheung (1995) and Henry (2002) present several examples about dependence detection in financial time series. Murphy (1999) analyzes pattern recognition in the graph of financial asset prices and Galbraith (1991) highlights the memory and forgetfulness effects in financial markets.

The different nature of past events behind these anomalies leads us to distinguish different types of memories in financial markets.

4. Memory in Financial Markets

We can find many definitions of "memory" in financial markets. The traditional interpretation considers the functional relationship between the values of a variable (price or return of the financial asset) over time. We will call it memory-dependence. The discussion about the existence or not of memory in financial markets and the study on how to model financial series have been focused on this type of memory. As mentioned before, anomalies due to the lack of investor rationality refute the EMH and the hypothesis of independence between observations. Consequently, it is necessary to search for alternative models to random walk in order to model time series with memory-dependence. The first of them was developed by Hurst (1951) although the most used has been the ARFIMA model (Hosking, 1981). In the next section, we explain these models as well as some examples of applications to financial markets.

The use of models that consider long-term memory pursues to improve predictions obtained with models based on the random walk. The assumption behind it is that the same functional relationship found between past data will continue in the future.

Related to this idea is the second memory type that we have called pattern-memory. It is interpreted as a repetition of the same patterns or figures in the chart which shows the evolution of asset prices. This fact also relates the concept of memory with the constant behavior of investors who always repeat the same action patterns in similar situations. In this way, their actions will be reflected in repetitive graphic guidelines. In practice, guidelines are not identical but similar. However, note the difference between the two meanings of memory. In memory-dependence the mathematical relationship between past and future values of a series is invariable. In pattern-memory, investor behavior remains unchanged so it is possible to detect patterns of evolution of asset prices over time.

Pattern-memory introduces investor behavior as an explanation for prices evolution in financial markets. Including personal elements increases the complexity of the research, bringing us a social perspective to the knowledge of the financial system. Despite the arguments about the existence of this type of memory are based on the behavior of economic agents, it is assumed that they do not change their behavior because of past experiences. Thus, some authors suggest that this happens because there is no memory in financial markets, and then the same mistakes are repeated over and over again (like speculative bubbles generated throughout history). But some other facts highlight that sometimes investors use information from the past to modify their behavior.

The learning ability and the effects of the past that modify the investor behavior constitute the called collective memory. This memory can explain in large part the anti-inflationary behavior of the Bundesbank as a reaction to the historic German hyperinflation, the efforts in accounting due to scandals such as Enron, and a different behavior in financial markets during the second conflict between US and Iraq as a result of the experience of stock markets reactions in 1991 (Schneider and Troeger, 2006).

In each of the three types of memory described above the investor behavior appears as an explanatory factor of past effects. In memory-dependence, it is the delay between the arrival of information and its reflect in the asset price what explains the existence of this phenomenon. The delay may be due to the market inefficiency in processing and spreading information, because investors are waiting for trends, for the existence of transaction costs, etc. In pattern-memory, the investors behavioral patterns which associate present and past (resonance with respect to the past) explains the regular-graphic figures in a chart. Finally, collective memory includes collectively produced effects in financial markets due to forgetfulness or to memory of events from the past that can produce changes in investor behavior and decisions.

Although these relationships between the three types of memory in financial markets, we will focus only on memory-dependence. Basically, there are two reasons for this choice:

- This type of memory has been the most analyzed in financial literature, both from a theoretical and empirical perspective. Therefore, there is an extensive collection of works that serves as starting point for our study.
- By its own definition, this type of memory is easily captured by a mathematical model in quantitative terms.

Consequently and as a first approach to the study of memory in financial markets, we analyze some models for the treatment of memory-dependence. Hereinafter, referred as only memory.

5. Financial Time Series with Long-Term Memory

The meaning of 'memory' in a time series is not unanimous. In an intuitive way, we can understand memory of a set of chronological ordered observations of a variable as the fact that future values depend on past values. The duration of this effect allows us to distinguish between *permanent* and *temporal* memory. In the former, a past observation has effect over the value of all subsequent observations. In the temporal memory this effect attenuates over time producing a long-term memory or a short-term memory depending on the maximum distance in which the effect lasts. If the value of a variable at a given time has not effect over the future values of the same variable, we can say that the time series which fits the data has not memory.

In financial context, the long term memory is the most relevant in terms of prediction, since permanent memory is difficult to exist (it implies a perfect stationary or a permanent trend that avoid the possibility to obtain a profit from the asset) and short term memory is not enough to take benefits of the time series modeling. Consequently, it is necessary to look for models that capture the time series behavior with long term memory. Therefore, the first step is to determine the criteria that define this kind of series.

Even in the simplest case that we restrict the measure of the memory in a time series to the correlation structure, we find several criteria (*e.g.* see Pons (1998) for a review). For example, a time series presents long term memory if $\lim_{T\to\infty} A \neq 0$, being $A = \frac{1}{T}\sum_{k=1}^{T}\rho^2(k)$ and $\rho(k)$ the autocorrelation function for k periods. In a similar way, a time series also has memory when $\sum_{k=1}^{\infty}\left|\rho(k)\right|$ is no convergent. These are only two examples of criteria in order to detect log term memory in time series. Nevertheless, models to study the behavior of these series rely on the value of certain parameters that account for the nature of the memory. For its relevance in the modeling of financial time series we only mention the R/S, the modified R/S and ARFIMA models.

The rescaled range or range over deviation (R/S) analysis, introduced by Hurst (1951), measures the degree of the influence between observations of a time series. It is defined as the range of the partial sums of the deviations of the series with respect to its mean, rescaled by the standard deviation. Although Hurst applied it for studying natural phenomena, Mandelbrot (1972), Lo (1991) and Peters (1991 and 1992), among others, have used it to detect long term memory in economics. Formally, it is defined as the following procedure. Firstly, from observed data, Z_t, we obtain the series $X_t = \ln Z_{t+1}/Z_t$, which is divided in A consecutive periods of length N without overlapping. For each one of these A periods we calculate the range defined as $R_{i,N} = \max_{1\le k\le N}(x_{i,N,k}) - \min_{1\le k\le N}(x_{i,N,k})$ with $i = 1,\ldots,A$; being $x_{i,N,k} = \sum_{j=1}^{k}(x_{i,j} - \mu_{i,N})$ and $\mu_{i,N}$ the mean of all the X_t which belongs to the i-period of length N. The *R/S* statistic for a particular N is defined as $(R/S)_N = 1/A\sum_{i=1}^{A}(R_{i,N}/S_{i,N})$, with $R_{i,N}$ as defined before and $S_{i,N} = [1/N\sum_{j=1}^{N}(x_{i,j} - \mu_{i,N})^2]^{1/2}$. The relationship between the statistic and the period length is determined by $(R/S)_N = \alpha \cdot N^H$, being α a constant value and H is called the Hurst coefficient. By taking logarithms, we obtain $\log(R/S)_N = \log(\alpha) + H\cdot\log(N)$. From this expression we can estimate H as the slope of a linear relation. For our study, the most relevant fact is the value of the Hurst coefficient. If $H = 0.5$, the time series has no memory. For $0 < H < 0.5$, the series is not persistent (it exhibits mean reversion). Finally, for $0.5 < H < 1$, the series is persistent. Nevertheless, from the original work of Hurst, there have been other approaches to estimate the value of H. One of the most used is the DFA (Detrented Fluctuation Analysis) method at Peng, *et al.* (1994).

The modified R/S analysis, introduced by Lo (1991), is an extension of the original *R/S* analysis in order to eliminate the short term memory influence and stress only the effects of long term memory. The modified R/S statistic Q_N is the arithmetic mean of the A statistics $Q_{i,N}$ obtained from:

$$Q_{i,N} = \frac{1}{\sigma_{i,N}^2 + 2\sum_{j=1}^{q}\omega_j(q)\gamma_{i,j}}\left[\max_{1\le k\le N}(x_{i,N,k}) - \min_{1\le k\le N}(x_{i,N,k})\right] \quad (1)$$

where $x_{i,N,k}$ is defined in the same way that in the *R/S* analysis, σ^2 is the variance of the interval, γ is the autocovariance function and the weighting factor $\omega_j(q)$ is given by $\omega_j(q)=1-j/(q+1)$ with $q < N$. Usually, $q=[k_n]=\left[(3n/2)^{1/2}(2\hat{\rho}/1-\hat{\rho})^{2/3}\right]$, where [] is used to symbolize the biggest integer that is minor or equal to k_n and $\hat{\rho}$ is the estimator of first order autocorrelation coefficient of the data. Analogously as we have mentioned before, if $Q_N = 0.5$ the time series has no memory, but differently to the previous analysis, Q_N only measures the long term memory so it is possible to obtain values close to *0.5* in series that present a Hurst coefficient quite different from this value.

Finally, we mention the ARFIMA (AutoRegressive Fractally Integrated Moving Average) process as an example of econometric model that is used for modeling financial time series with long term memory. They are a generalization of ARIMA models, developed by Granger and Joyeaux (1980) and Hosking (1981), with the difference that ARFIMA models allows non integer differencing powers. Formally, given an autoregressive process $AR(p):\Phi(L)\,y_t=a+\varepsilon_t$, with $\Phi(L)=1-\varphi_1L-\varphi_2L^2-\ldots-\varphi_pL^p$, and given a moving average process $MA(q):y_t=a+\Theta(L)\varepsilon_t$, with $\Theta(L)=1-\theta_1L-\theta_2L^2-\ldots-\theta_qL^q$, then a process X_t follows an ARFIMA(p,d,q) structure if X_t is a solution of the stochastic differential equation $\Phi(L)(1-L)^d X_t=\Theta(L)\varepsilon_t$, where ε_t is a white noise variable, p and q are integer values and $d\in(-0.5,0.5)$ in order to obtain a stationary and invertible process. If $d\in(-0.5,0)$ the time series is not persistent, if $d=0$ the process has no memory or the memory is very short and if $d\in(0,0.5)$ the time series has persistent long term memory. The calculation of the parameter 'd' is one of the main difficulties of these models. One possibility is to use the relationship $d = H - 0.5$ (where H is the Hurst coefficient) or the estimated method introduced by Geweke and Porter-Hudak (1983).

This review is very restrictive considering the huge literature in order to model time series with long term memory. Other models such as GARCH, FIGARCH or SARFIMA models can be used when the series present stationary components or the variance are not constant. Moreover we can find another methods to estimate the H coefficient, for example, DFA analysis, wavelets, etc. However, the aim of this section is just to show some procedures in order to study the dependence between past and future observations widely used in the financial literature.

There are a lot of empirical applications of these methodologies in financial market series (assets or indexes prices) in order to find evidence of memory. Obviously, results will depend on three factors: (i) the used methodology; (ii) the particular features of the market under study; (iii) the time period used as a reference for the analysis and the frequency of the data.

One of the early works in this context is Greene and Fielitz (1977). The authors apply the R/S analysis to 200 daily stock return series listed on the New York Stock Exchange, founding that in most of them exist long term memory (with a H coefficient higher than *0.5*). As mentioned before, Lo (1991) introduces the modified R/S analysis. In his work, with daily and monthly return indexes from the Center for Research in Security Prices, he does not obtain evidence of long term memory in the American market. Later works combine the application of the R/S analysis with the modified R/S analysis (or only the last one) to detect the effects of long term memory while omitting short term effects.

There are some works focusing on the study of an isolated market. In this way, Barkoulas and Baum (1996) apply the Geweke and Porter-Hudak test over composite and sectoral stock indexes and firms' returns series of the American market and only find memory in 5 of the 30 studied firms. Blanco and Santamaría (1996) analyze the Spanish market with data from the Madrid Stock Exchange General Index and some sectoral indexes. Their results depend on the methodology used (modified R/S analysis and estimation of the parameter in ARFIMA models) but the existence of long term memory seems clear, except for the electrical sector. Applying the same methodology, Mills (1993) obtains no evidence for English stocks returns. From 13 assets of the Athens stocks market, Panas (2001) finds in all the cases a Hurst coefficient higher than 0.5 for the period 1993-98. A wider period is analyzed by McKenzie (2001) in the Australian market. He uses the modified R/S analysis and finds a high level of persistence with monthly data from 1876 to 1996.

We also find other studies which analyze the indices behavior of developed and emerging markets. In this line, Cheung (1995) use monthly data from Morgan Stanley Capital International index for eighteen countries. Applying the modified R/S analysis he does not find evidence of long term memory. Nevertheless, using the Geweke and Porter-Hudak test to estimate the d parameter of the ARFIMA models, he finds dependence for Austria, Belgium, Italy, Japan and Spain. Gil-Alana (2006) uses other estimation methods for this parameter working with daily data from 1986 to 1997, in order to detect long term memory in Singapore and Hong Kong but to refuse the presence of memory in United States. Contrary to these results, Henry (2002), by using ARFIMA models and monthly data from 1982 to 1998 concludes that exists long term memory in Germany, Japan, South Korea and Taiwan, while there is no evidence of memory in United States, United Kingdom, Hong Kong, Singapore and Australia. Kasman *et al.* (2009) conclude that it is more usual to find long term dependence in emerging countries than in developed ones. Thus, they apply ARFIMA models to eight emerging Central and Eastern European countries, obtaining memory existence for Hungary, Czech Republic, Slovenia and Estonia. Assaf (2006) performs a similar work in emerging countries, adding the modified R/S analysis, and finds long term memory in Egypt and Morocco, and negative persistence in Jordan and Turkey.

Berg and Lihagen (1998) use the Geweke and Porter Hudak method and the modified R/S analysis in order to analyze the long term memory in the Swedish market. They use different data frequencies (monthly, weekly and daily) of the Stockholm stock market and they obtain that there is evidence of long term dependence only during the first half of the past century. Moreover, Dajcman (2012), considers long term memory as a dynamic concept. He does not find long term memory in the eight analyzed countries (Austria, Hungary, France, Germany, United Kingdom, Spain, Ireland and Czech Republic) although in his analysis obtains that the d parameter from the ARFIMA models increased after the World Trade Center attack, specially in the most developed countries, with a lower increase in Hungary and Czech Republic. Also the current sovereign debt crisis in Euro Area has led to an increase of this parameter in Spain and Ireland.

We have seen that the analysis of the dependence of past returns in future returns for a particular asset depends on the methodology used, on the typology of the market and on the data considered. In this sense, we believe that, in order to achieve a useful concept of memory in financial markets it is necessary to consider the memory such as a dynamic concept in relation to a specific market, data and particular time. Artificial neural networks offer a more flexible framework for modeling time series. For this reason, this instrument can be an appropriate methodology to analyze long term memory.

6. Artificial Neural Networks and Financial Memory

Following Kohonen (1989), we define an artificial neural network as a set of parallel massively interconnected elements, with hierarchical structures that pretend to interact with the real world in the same way that the neural biological system does. Its implementation is carried out by a computer program that incorporates a mathematical algorithm that acts as a learning function.

Neurons are the basic units of the artificial neural network and they are grouped in different levels, named layers. We can distinguish between neurons from the input layer (they receive the information from the outside), from the output layer (they give the answer of the system), and from the hidden layers (they connect the input layer with the output layer). Each neuron has a value or state of activation that can be inhibition or excitation (in an absolute way or in some degree). The actualization of this value depend on the function of activation and on one threshold θ. Additionally, the transfer function converts the state of activation of a neuron in an output signal that is transmitted to the other neurons connected with it. The signal is modified by the weight corresponding to each connection. The modification of the weights is known as the learning process. The particular structure of each network (number of neurons, layers, transfer function, kind of learning, etc.) depends on the problem that is being solved.

Zhang *et al.* (1998) point out some advantages of using artificial neural networks for prediction. Neural networks do not need to set, a priori, a subjacent model to fit the data. Networks can generalize and, consequently, can infer future values not known from the knowledge obtained from the data introduced into the network, even if there is noise in the data. Because of its flexible structure, networks can fit any kind of function or time series. Moreover, they have the advantage to work with non linear functions, more similar to the real models that they try to forecast.

From the variety of artificial neural networks, we will use the multilayer perceptron with backward error propagation learning (or backpropagation networks), developed by Rumelhart, Hinton and Williams (1986).

The design of these networks allows them to fit functions and, consequently, they are very useful to predict values of a time series. Backpropagation networks associate an input vector $X_p = (x_{1p}, x_{2p}, \ldots, x_{Np})$ with an output vector $Y_p=(y_{1p}, y_{2p}, \ldots, y_{Mp})$, being P the number of observations of the system. This type of network has a structure composed by an input layer of N neurons, one output layer with M neurons and can have one or more hidden layers. The number of hidden layers and the number of neurons in them will depend on the particular problem, being this design an election of the researcher. Backpropagation networks are characterized for supervised learning, that is to say, it is needed to have a set of data to train the network where the desired output vector $Dp= (d_{1p}, d_{2p}, \ldots, d_{Mp})$ is known. The learning process is off line. It implies that in a first step the weights of the network are modified and after this process, the weights remain constant. The modification of the weights w_{ji} from the connections between the neurons i and j is done according to the learning algorithm known as generalized delta rule or Widrow-Hoff rule, minimizing the error or difference between the output vector and the desired vector for the set of data used to train the network. To do this, the algorithm modifies the value of the weights starting from the output layer to the input layer through proportional changes to the vector gradient of the error function.

Graphically, a backpropagation network with a hidden layer of j neurons is shown in Figure 1.

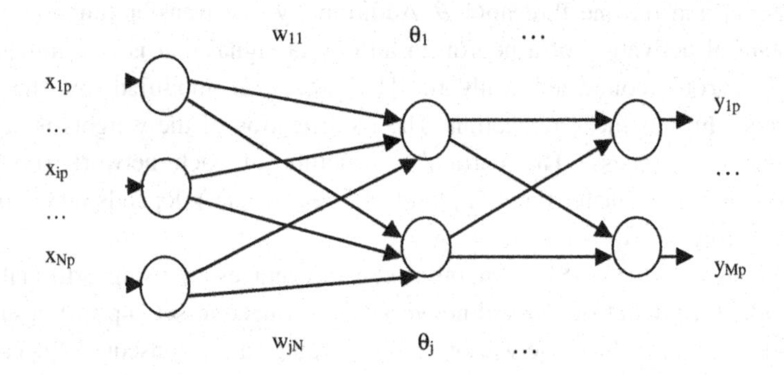

Figure 1. Backpropagation network structure

The implementation of a backpropagation neural network requires eight steps: (1) To introduce the input patterns $X_p = (x_{1p}, x_{2p}, ..., x_{Np})$ to the system, associating each component to one neuron of the N units from the input layer. (2) To propagate the information to the hidden neurons. Each hidden neuron j receives the signal $Net_{jp} = \sum_{i=1}^{N} w_{ji} \cdot x_{ip} + \theta_j$. (3) To transform the input information from the hidden neuron in output information, using a transfer function f that has to be continuous and derivable, $y_{jp} = f_j\left(net_{jp}\right)$. (4) To propagate the information following the same procedure until the output of the system is achieved, $y_{kp} = f_k(net_{kp}) = f_k(\sum_{j=1}^{L} w_{kj} \cdot y_{jp} + \theta_k)$. (5) To calculate the error committed by the network, using the expression $E_p = 1/2 \sum_{k=1}^{M} \delta_{kp}^2$, where $\delta_{kp} = \left(d_{kp} - y_{kp}\right) \cdot f_k^{'}\left(net_{kp}\right)$ and $f_k^{'}$ is the derivate of the transfer function associated to the neuron k of the output layer. (6) To propagate backwards the error to the hidden layers, using $\delta_{jp} = f'(net_{jp}) \cdot \sum_k w_{jk} \cdot \delta_{kp}$. (7) To modify the weights of the network. The weights from the connections that arrive to the output layer are modified $wkj\ (t+1) = wkj\ (t) + \alpha\ \delta kp\ yjp$, as well as the weights from the connections in the hidden neurons $wji\ (t+1) = wji\ (t) + \alpha\ \delta jp\ xip$. In both cases, α is a parameter that represents the learning coefficient. (8) To repeat the process with the next pattern until the global error committed by the network has an acceptable level.

The use of this particular kind of artificial neural network in the financial context has been common. Together with other types of networks, we can find examples of its application in Refenes (1995) and Trippi and Turban (1996). In these works there are applications of the backpropagation networks to stock market prediction, bankruptcy prediction, thrift institution failures, bond rating and credit scoring.

In a recent work, Atsalakis and Valavanis (2009) analyze more than a hundred papers that apply artificial neural networks and neuro-fuzzy techniques to predict financial variables. Although in their study are listed other methodologies, the number of papers that use backpropagation networks are enough to stress the importance of this instrument to predict financial time series. In most of the cases, results with neural networks improve the results from alternative models, using a lower number of data. Nevertheless, it is necessary to point out that the election of the best architecture of the neural network for a particular problem is a non solved trouble. Currently, the decision is taken through a trial and error procedure in order to minimize the committed error by the network.

7. An application to the Spanish index IBEX-35

In our work, we propose the use of artificial neural networks to fit the time series that captures the price evolution of the IBEX-35. Nevertheless, the aim of the study is not prediction per se. Our objective is to analyze the effects of past values of the index over future values, taking into account a double time perspective: the starting point of the period to train the network and the number of lagged data that are considered to form a new price.

We work with closing prices of the index from the 5th of January, 1987 until 31st of December 2010 considering a total number of 6.260 observations. Initially with all these data, we train a backpropagation network with an input layer of 20 neurons, one hidden layer of 5 neurons and an output layer with a unique neuron. Each neuron of the input layer captures one price of the IBEX-35 (previously normalized[*] between the range *[-1, 1])* in order to fit the price of the index in the following day. We have to normalize the data because we use the sigmoid tangent function as the transfer function between input and hidden layers. The transfer function between hidden and output layers is linear. Once the training process has finished, we introduce the data to obtain the price of the 3rd of January, 2011. With this value, the result of the network, and the real prices from the 19 days before we look for the result of the network to the next day, the 4th of January 2011. This procedure is repeated until to obtain the 5 next prices. The aim we pursue is to examine the predictive power of the network in relation to the strategy of considering that the best prediction is the price of the day before.

---

[*] x (normalized) $= 2\cdot(x - x_{min})/(x_{max} - x_{min}) - 1$

The obtained results in this first approximation are shown in Table 1:

Table 1. Results of a backpropagation network 20x5x1, training data set 1987-2010.

Date	Real value	Network value	Last known value
03/01/2011	9888.3	9878.9	9859.1
04/01/2011	9888.4	9907.0	9859.1
05/01/2011	9801.4	9903.1	9859.1
06/01/2011	9702.7	9910.2	9859.1
07/01/2011	9560.7	9931.1	9859.1

The aim is to obtain the best prediction for one week. For this reason, we consider that the real prices of the IBEX-35 are not known and we take as a forecast for the 5 days latter the last known price. We measure the quality of the fit through the mean squared error[†].

The mean squared error committed by the network is 195.5, while if we take into consideration that the price for the 5 next days will be the same that the last known price, the error of the forecast is 154.0. We can observe that the network offers worse results than the situation where we consider that the efficient market hypothesis is true.

A possible explanation for this fact is that we have considered a long period of time to train the network. That is to say, as the time distance increases, the influence of past values is less relevant, being possible that these large past values disturb the training process of the network. This fact can be easily seen if we graphically represent the evolution of IBEX-35 prices from January 1987 from December 2010. This evolution is shown in Figure 2.

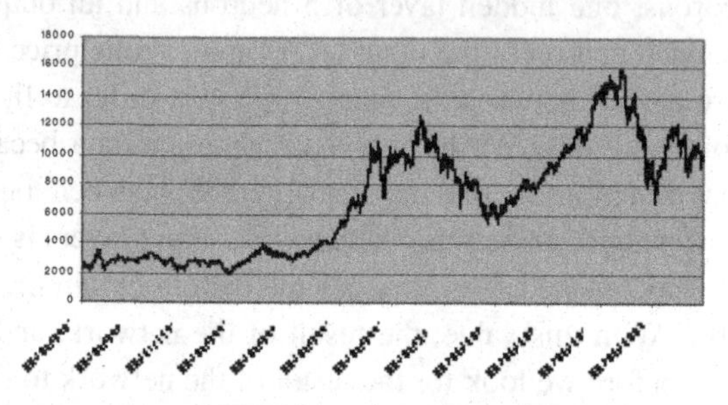

Figure 2. IBEX-35 evolution from 1987 to 2010.

[†] Mean Squared Error: MSE= $\sqrt{\frac{\sum_{i=1}^{n}\left(x_i - x_i\left(real\right)\right)^2}{n}}$

As we can see in the graph, the evolution of the IBEX-35 prices has been very variable depending on the considered period. Initially, there was a relatively constant trend that was maintained in time. Because we have trained the network with all the available data, the first years of the index evolution also have influenced the formation of the weight matrix. This matrix has been used to predict a period in which the market had a different behavior with respect to the behavior in the 80's from the past century. In order to prove if the market, in terms of functional dependence with respect to the previous prices, has forgotten the data from long time ago, we will repeat the analysis considering a lower number of years.

We repeat again the training of a backpropagation network with 20 input neurons, 5 neurons in the hidden layer and one neuron in the output layer, but in this case we only train the network with the prices starting at the 3rd of January of 2000 (2.870 observations). The 5 predicted prices compared with real data and with those obtained considering the inexistence of memory are shown in Table 2.

Table 2. Results of a backpropagation network 20x5x1, training data set 2000-2010.

Date	Real value	Network value	Last known value
03/01/2011	9888.3	9883.7	9859.1
04/01/2011	9888.4	9890.3	9859.1
05/01/2011	9801.4	9883.8	9859.1
06/01/2011	9702.7	9886.5	9859.1
07/01/2011	9560.7	9864.3	9859.1
	MSE	163.0	154.0

From Table 2 we can see that the committed error by the network is still higher than that obtained when considering the last known value as prediction. However, this error has decreased with respect to the committed error in the previous network (the one we trained with all the data). The mean squared error has decreased from 195.5 to 163.0, a reduction of 17%.

As we mentioned before, with this example we examine the memory effects in two ways: studying the optimal starting point of the time series (past information from long time ago can be not relevant) and analyzing the number of lags taken into account as input variables (the number of past prices that form the new ones). Consequently, we will increase the number of input variables.

From the results that we have obtained by training the network with data starting at year 2000, we extend the number of inputs to 30, 60 and 120 variables. The results are summarized in Table 3.

Table 3. Results of backpropagation networks with 20, 30, 60 and 120 input units, 5 hidden units in one layer and one output neuron. Training data set 2000-2010.

Date	Real value	Network value 20 var	Network value 30 var	Network value 60 var	Network value 120 var	Last known value r
03/01/2011	9888.3	9883.7	9849.1	9855.3	9871.6	9859.1
04/01/2011	9888.4	9890.3	9871.7	9822.9	9822.9	9859.1
05/01/2011	9801.4	9883.8	9879.2	9787.4	9767.4	9859.1
06/01/2011	9702.7	9886.5	9844.6	9816.7	9809.0	9859.1
07/01/2011	9560.7	9864.3	9813.8	9803.2	9778.2	9859.1
	MSE	163.0	135.7	124.4	113.4	154.0

From Table 3 we can observe that when more inputs are used in the network (historical prices of the index delayed *1, 2, ...n* periods), the error of the prediction is reduced. Note that the obtained error using 30 variables is lower than the error associated with the prediction when we use the last known value. According to these results, we can conclude that the time series of the IBEX-35 prices has memory, and that the goodness of the prediction improves if we consider a bigger number of past information.

8. Conclusions

Two factors lead us to analyze the concept of memory in financial markets; the evidence that investors are not always rational and the existence of phenomena that demonstrate that the past influences the behavior of future prices. In this work, we have distinguished three main types of memory: first, the associated with time series of financial prices which explains the functional relationship between past and future observations of a variable. Second, and related to the first one, as a repetition of patterns in charts that describe the evolution of asset prices. The third type of memory highlighted all past events and prior information that modifies the investors behavior and therefore affects future prices.

Focusing our attention on the first meaning of memory, we have used backpropagation networks to analyze the effect of past data in a time series. While the most common application of this type of network is the prediction through the functional relationship underlying the series, we have used them to analyze the goodness of fit by modifying two key elements of the memory in a times series: the starting point of the series and the number of observations that most directly affect the price formation of an asset. In the case of the IBEX-35 index, we found that the inclusion of data from 1987 do not benefit the fit of the series. Nevertheless, if we consider a smaller number of data on time (since 2000) this fit improves. Moreover, the inclusion of a great number of past prices as input variables in the network also improve the results.

We are aware that our conclusions are very specific to the time period analyzed. As has been mentioned at the beginning of this study, the results obtained should be contextualized to the specific market, the time period and the methodology that has been used.

For future research, we should contrast this analysis at different time periods (for example, adding the data for the 2011 and predicting values of early 2012) to prove if results are consistent with the previous ones. Another interesting research line could be the use of other backpropagation network structures, either increasing the number if hidden layers or modifying the number of neurons in the hidden layer.

Despite this fact, our work wants to open a new approach to analyze the memory in financial time series, collecting the importance of the starting point in the time series studied, as well as the effects of the number of delays considered to obtain the best fit.

Additionally, artificial neural networks can be applied to the other types of memory also introduced in this work, being it possible to give an overview of past effects with the same methodology.

References

1. A. Assaf, "Dependence and mean reversion in stock prices: The case of the MENA region" in *Research in International Business and Finance*, 20, p. 286 – 304 (2006)
2. G.S. Atsalakis and K.P.Valavanis, "Surveying stock market forecasting techniques – Part II: Soft computing methods" in *Expert Systems with Applications*, 36, p. 5932 – 5941 (2009)
3. J.T. Barkoulas and C.F. Baum, "Long-term dependence in stock returns" in *Economics Letters*, 53, p. 253 – 25, (1996)

4. A. Beja, *The Limits of Price Information in Market Processes*, Working Paper nº 61 Research Program in Finance. University of California, Berkeley (1977)
5. L. Berg and J. Lyhagen, "Short and Long Run Dependence in Swedish Stock Returns" in *Applied Financial Economics*, 8 (4), p. 435 – 443 (1998)
6. N. Blasco and R. Santamaría, "Testing memory patterns in the Spanish stock market" in *Applied Financial Economics*, 6 (5), p. 401 – 411 (1996)
7. D.O. Boudreaux, "The Monthly Effect in International Stock Markets: Evidence and Implications" in *Journal of Financial and Strategic Decisions*, 8 (1) , p. 15 – 20 (1995)
8. Y.W. Cheung, "A search for long memory in international stock market returns" in *Journal of International Money and Finance*, 14 (4), p. 597 – 615 (1995)
9. N. Chopra, J. Lakonishok and J.R. Ritter, "Measuring abnormal performance" en *Journal of Financial Economics*, 31 (2), p. 235 - 268 (1992)
10. S. Dajcman, "Time-varying long-range dependence in stock market returns and financial market disruptions – a case of eight European countries" in *Applied Economics Letters*. (forthcoming) (2012)
11. W.F.M. De Bondt and R.Thaler, "Does the Stock Market Overreact?" in *The Journal of Finance*, 40 (3), p. 793 – 805 (1985)
12. E.F. Fama, "The Behavior of Stock-Market Prices" in *The Journal of Business*, 1, p. 34-105 (1965)
13. E.F. Fama, "Efficient Capital Markets: A Review of Theory and Empirical Work" in *Journal of Finance*, 25 (2), p. 383 – 417 (1970)
14. E.F. Fama, "Market efficiency, long-term returns, and behavioral finance", in *Journal of Financial Economics*, 49 (3), p. 283 – 306 (1998)
15. J.K. Galbraith, *A Short History of Financial Euphoria*. New York: Penguin Books (1991)
16. J. Geweke and S. Porter-Hudak, "The estimation and application of long memory time series models" in *Journal of Time Series Analysis*, 4, p. 221-238 (1983)
17. L.A. Gil-Alana, "Fractional integration in daily stock market indexes" in *Review of Financial Economics*, 15, p. 28 – 48 (2006)
18. C.W.J. Granger, R. Joyeux, "An introduction to long-memory models and fractional differencing" in *Journal of Time Series Analysis*, 1, p. 15-29 (1980)
19. M.T. Greene, B.D. Fielitz, "Long-term dependence in common stock returns" in *Journal of Financial Economics*, 4 (3), p. 339 – 349 (1977)
20. S.J. Grossman, J.E. Stiglitz, "On the impossibility of Informationally Efficient Markets" in *The American Economic Review*, 70 (3), p. 393 – 408 (1980)

21. P.R. Hansen, A. Lunde and J.M. Nason, "Testing the Significance of Calendar Effects", working paper Federal Reserve Bank of Atlanta (2005)
22. O.T. Henry, "Long Memory in Stock Returns: Some International Evidence" in *Applied Financial Economics*, 12 (10), p. 725 – 729 (2002)
23. J.R.M. Hosking, "Fractional differencing", in *Biometrika*, 68 (1), p. 165 – 176 (1981)
24. H.E. Hurst, "Long-term storage of reservoirs", in *Transactions of the American Society of Civil Engineers*, 116, p. 770 – 808 (1951)
25. D. Kahneman and A. Tversky, "Prospect Theory: An Analysis of Decision under Risk" in *Econometrica*, 47(2), p. 263 – 292 (1979)
26. A. Kasman, S. Kasman, and E. Torun, "Dual long memory property in returns and volatility: Evidence from the CEE countries' stock markets" in *Emerging Markets Review*, 10, p. 122 – 139 (2009)
27. T. Kohonen, *Self-Organization and Associative Memory*. Berlin: Springer-Verlag (1989)
28. J.-J. Laffont and E.S. Maskin, "The Efficient Market Hypothesis and Insider Trading on the Stock Market" in *Journal of Political Economy*, 98 (1), p. 70 – 93 (1990)
29. C.-C. Lee, J.-D. Lee and C.-C.Lee, "Stock prices and the efficient market hypothesis: Evidence from a panel stationary test with structural breaks" in *Japan and the World Economy*, 22 (1), p. 49 – 58 (2010)
30. B.N. Lehmann, "Fads, Martingales and Market Efficiency" in *The Quarterly Journal of Economics*, 105 (1), p. 1 – 28 (1990)
31. S.F. LeRoy, R.D. Porter, "The Present-Value Relation: Test Based on Implied Variance Bounds" in *Econometrica*, 49 (3), p. 555 – 574 (1981)
32. A.W. Lo, "Long-Term Memory in Stock Market Prices" in *Econometrica*, 59 (5), p. 1279 – 1313 (1991)
33. B.B. Mandelbrot, "Statistical methodology for nonperiodic cycles: from covariance to R/S analysis" in *Annals of Economic and Social Measurement*, 1, p. 259 – 290 (1972)
34. D. McFadden, "Rationality for Economists?" in *Journal of Risk and Uncertainty*, 19, p. 73 – 105 (1999)
35. M. D. McKenzie, "Non-periodic Australian Stock Market Cycles: Evidence from Rescaled Range Analysis" in *The Economic Record*, 77, p. 393 – 406 (2001)
36. R. Mehra and E.C. Prescott, "The Equity Premium: A Puzzle", in *Journal of Monetary Economics*, 15, p. 145 – 162 (1985)
37. T.C. Mills, "Is there long-term memory in UK stock returns?" in *Applied Financial Economics*, 3, (4), p. 303 – 306 (1993)
38. J.J. Murphy, *Technical Analysis of the Financial Markets*. New York, Institute of Finance (1999)

39. P.K. Narayan, "Do shocks to G7 stock prices have a permanent effect? Evidence from panel unit root tests with structural change" in *Mathematics and Computers in Simulation*, 77 (4), p. 369 – 373 (2008)
40. E. Panas, "Estimating fractal dimension using stable distributions and exploring long memory through ARFIMA models in Athens Stock Exchange" in *Applied Financial Economics*, 11 (4), p. 395 – 402 (2001)
41. C.-K. Peng *et al.*, Mosaic organization of DNA nucleotides" in *Physical Review E*, 49 (2), p. 1685 – 1689 (1994)
42. E.E. Peters, *Chaos and Order in the Capital Markets. A New View of Cycles, Prices, and Market Volatility*. New York: John Wiley&Sons, Inc. (1991)
43. E.E. Peters, "R/S Analysis Using Logarithmic Returns" in *Financial Analysts Journal*, p. 81-82 (1992)
44. E.E. Peters, *Complexity, Risk, and Financial Markets*. New York: John Wiley & Sons, Inc. (1999)
45. E. Pons Fanals, *Conseqüències economètriques del grau de memòria en dades temporals*. Doctoral Thesis. Universitat de Barcelona (1998)
46. A.-P. Refenes, (ed.): *Neural Networks in the Capital Markets*. Chichester: Wiley. (1995)
47. D.E. Rumelhart, G.H. Hinton and R.J. Williams, "Learning representations by back-propagating errors" in *Nature*, 323, p. 533–536 (1986)
48. G. Schneider and V.E.Troeger, "War and the World Economy: Stock Market Reactions to International Conflicts" in *The Journal of Conflict Resolution*, 50 (5), p. 623 – 645 (2006)
49. M. Sewell, "History of the Efficient Market Hypothesis", Research Note RN/11/04, UCL Department of Computer Science (2011)
50. H. Shefrin,; Statman, M., "The Disposition to Sell Winners Too Early and Ride Losers Too Long", in *Journal of Finance*, 40, p. 777 – 790 (1985)
51. A. Hleifer, *Inefficient Markets: An Introduction to Behavioral Finance*. Oxford University Press, New York (2000)
52. R.J. Hiller, "Human Behavior and the Efficiency of the Financial System", in Taylor, J.B. (ed.), *Handbook of Macroeconomics*, Vol. 1, Elsevier Science, p. 1305 – 1340 (1999)
53. R.J. Shiller, *Irrational Exuberance*, Princeton University Press, Princeton, New Jersey, (2000)
54. J.J. Siegel and R.H. Thaler, "Anomalies: The Equity Premium Puzzle" in *The Journal of Economic Perspectives*, 11 (1), p. 191 – 200 (1997)
55. A. Subrahmanyam, "Behavioural Finance: A Review and Synthesis" in *European Financial Management*, 14 (1), p. 12 – 29 (2007)
56. R.R. Trippi and E. Turban, *Neural Networks in Finance and Investing*, Chicago, Irwin (1996)

57. G. Zhang, B.E. Patuwo and M.Y. Hu., "Forecasting with artificial neural networks: The state of the art" in *International Journal of Forecasting*, 14, p. 35 – 62 (1998)

CAPITAL STRUCTURE IN THE SPANISH CHEMICAL INDUSTRY. HOW DOES THE FINANCIAL CRISIS AFFECT?

CÀMARA-TURULL, X.
Departament de Gestió d'Empreses, Universitat Rovira I Virgili
Avda. Universitat, 1, Reus E-43204, Spain

BORRÀS BALSELLS, X.
Departament de Gestió d'Empreses, Universitat Rovira I Virgili
Avda. Universitat, 1, Reus E-43204, Spain

SORROSAL-FORRADELLAS, M.T..
Departament de Gestió d'Empreses, Universitat Rovira I Virgili
Avda. Universitat, 1, Reus E-43204, Spain

FERNÁNDEZ IZQUIERDO, M.A.
Departamento de Finanzas y Contabilidad, Universidad Jaume I
Avda. Sos Baynat, s/n, Castellón de la Plana E-12071, Spain

The financial crisis that began in 2008 has revived interest in the significance of the capital structure of corporations. This paper analyses the Pecking Order Theory using a sample of Spanish chemical companies. We pose the same hypotheses first presented by Fama and French in 2002, but employ a different methodology: self-organizing maps, specifically Kohonen maps. Our research reaches similar conclusions to those of Fama and French (2002): More profitable companies present lower leverage and companies with higher growth rates also have higher leverage.

1. Introduction

There has been ongoing theoretical and empirical research into the capital structure of corporations since Modigliani and Miller presented their seminal article in 1958 about the irrelevance of capital structure in terms of a firm's value in perfect markets.

Since then, many theories have been developed that, building upon this research, have tried to adapt it to market imperfections. The first of these was the Trade-Off Theory which incorporates the tax benefits of debt (Modigliani and Miller, 1963) and the bankruptcy costs that it might generate (Kraus and

Litzemberger, 1973). Another line of research is derived from the Agency Theory (Jensen and Meckling, 1976), which deals with the conflict between shareholders and debt-holders. Finally, a third approach is based on the costs that asymmetric information generates, which leads to another two theories: signalling theory (Ross, 1977; Leland and Pyle, 1977) and the Pecking Order Theory (Myer and Majluf, 1984). Despite numerous empirical studies, there is still no general consensus among researchers on the decisive factors in determining a company's optimal capital structure. As Myers (1984) says, the theories are not designed to be general, but to explain the behaviour of a subsample of firms. So, if the sample is big enough, more than one theory can be validated.

The current global financial crisis has revived the interest on this topic. Primarily, the influence that the low interest rates for the period 2002-2006 have had on the crisis. Secondly, the lack of liquidity in the financial sector and its consequence on companies debt since 2008.

Therefore, the main purpose of our research is to examine financing capital decision-making in the Spanish chemical sector through the Pecking Order Theory, using the method proposed by Kohonen based on an unsupervised neuronal net (self-organizing maps, SOMs).

Neuronal nets have frequently been applied in the field of finance because they present clear advantages over other methods. They allow non-linear processes to be used which involve the net's increasing capacity to approximate functions, classify patterns, increase its immunity to noise, and improve interconnectivity.

The main advantage of an unsupervised training rules net is that the net learns to adapt through experiences collected during previous training patterns without being influenced by the subjective decisions of experts.

In a previous paper, Camara-Turull et al (2009) analyze the period 1999-2006 and observe the incidence of low interest rates in the capital structure. In this paper we extend the study for the period 2007-2010 for the same sample of companies[a].

In the following section we describe the main contributions of the Pecking Order Theory and define the working hypotheses used by Fama and French (2002). Next, we present the sample of companies and the variables used in the study and the methodology applied. We then present our results and finish with the primary conclusions that can be drawn from this work.

---

[a] Due to missing data, the original sample has been reduced from 158 to 146 companies.

2. The Pecking Order Theory

The Pecking Order Theory proposed by Myers and Majluf in 1984 is widely accepted in the world of finance. The theory is based on the costs of the asymmetric distribution of information that exists between companies and capital markets. Company managers have access to and use internal information about the expected returns of future investments. This asymmetrical information leads investors to think that company managers will only issue new shares to finance investments when these are overvalued. Investors react to this extension with a down-correction of the share price. To prevent this from happening, managers will first use financial sources not affected by the costs of the asymmetric information, such as internal funds, and only if these are not sufficient will they resort to other capital sources less affected by those costs: first debt, then hybrid securities like convertible bonds, and finally equity issues.

Several empirical studies that have attempted to validate the Pecking Order Theory have reached differing conclusions. Fama and French confirmed the Pecking Order Theory in their research of 2002 only to then reject it in their research of 2005.

This research aims to provide a new empirical contribution to the existing literature by attempting to validate the Pecking Order Theory in the chemical industry sector. In keeping with Fama and French (2002), we present four hypotheses about the relation between debt and different financial-economic variables: return, growth, volatility and non-debt tax shelter:

Hypothesis 1. According to the Pecking Order Theory, the relationship between a firm's leverage and its return should be negative, because the higher the return a company has, the greater the volume of internally generated funds it should have, and therefore the lower its debt.

Hypothesis 2. The relationship between a firm's leverage and its potential growth is positive. The more the company grows, the bigger its need for debt should be. It can also be interpreted as the greater future potential a firm has, the smaller its leverage should be in order to maintain a low level of risk and undertake future investments without needing to issue risky assets (Myers and Majluf, 1984)

Hypothesis 3. The greater the volatility of a company, the smaller its leverage should be because the reliability of future cash flows should be smaller as well.

Hypothesis 4. Finally, a bigger tax shelter increases internally generated company funds (unless the EBITDA is not enough to cover amortizations).

3. Methodology

3.1. *Sample Design*

The information used in this research comes from the SABI database. We considered the companies with the code CNAE 24, Chemical Industry, during the period between the 2007 and 2010 financial years, both of them included.

From the original sample all the firms that did not have all the information needed or whose information was illogical were removed. In the end, the sample consisted of 146 companies for the 2007-2010 period, equalling a total of 584 observations per variable.

3.2. *Variables*

The proxy variable for company leverage is the debt to equity ratio. The proxy variables for company returns are return on assets (ROA) and return on equity (ROE). Growth opportunities were measured by means of increases in sales and assets from one period to next. The proxy variable for volatility is the real assets log (Fama and French, 2002) and the proxy variable for tax shelter (not generated from debt) is the amortization ratio measured as amortization over total assets.

3.3. *Self-Organizing Maps (SOM)*

Self-Organizing Maps (SOMs) are a specific type of artificial neural network developed by T. Kohonen. These networks distribute the input information (data or patterns in n-vectors components) in a bi-dimensional space, according to the similarity among patterns.

SOMs are hetero-associated networks (input patterns are associated with different nature outputs), with off-line learning (training and function phases are clearly differentiated), unsupervised (there is no prior information about the groups that the network may create so self-organized) and competitive (when a new pattern is presented there is only one active unit on the map).

The network structure features an input and an output layer. The input layer has n neurons that collect one pattern component. The output layer is made up of m x p neurons of the map of characteristics.

There are three connections between the neurons: i) Feed-forward connections between every neuron of the input layer and output layer. ii) Lateral connections between the neurons of the input layer and those of the output layer defined in their neighbouring area. iii) Recurrent connections in which every unit connects to itself in the output layer.

The SOM function is carried out in four stages: first, the data is entered and it flows throughout the connections between the input and output layers. In the second stage, the m x p output layer units collect the information received and create lateral connections (increasing the influence to those nearby) and recurrent connections that emit an exit signal modified by a continuous transfer function.

In the third stage, a competition is set up in the output layer in order to achieve a winner neuron that minimizes the distance between the weights associated with its connections and the components of the input patterns. In the last step, the weights of the winner neuron and its neighbours are modified according to the distance by a learning coefficient that decreases as the network learns to ensure the convergence to equilibrium. The process is repeated with the rest of input patterns and new iterations are conducted until the final map of characteristics is defined.

The SOM can be applied to solve multiple problems in many different fields, including those that require pattern recognition, data codification, optimization or data grouping. In our research we have applied the SOM to analyze the relationship between some relevant indicators of the performance of chemical companies and their capital structure. The SOM allows companies to be grouped according to their relevant performance indicators and the relationship between the firms and their leverage to be evaluated.

4. Results

This construction work was performed using a toolbox for Matlab designed by professor Kohonen's research group at Helsinki University. After the training process we achieved the map shown in Figure 1.

We identified the clusters from the U-matrix for the variables described above and for the four-year period ending in 2010. The resulting map was built by a double optimisation: i) maximum homogeneity within each group and ii) a minimum number of groups.

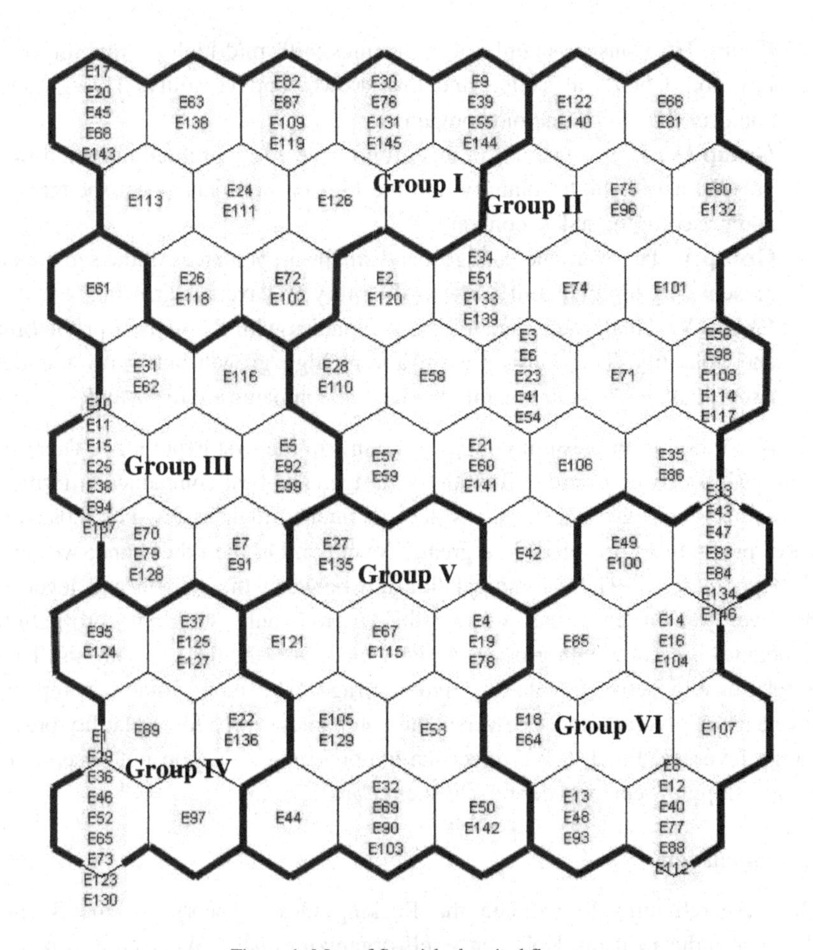

Figure 1. Map of Spanish chemical firms.

Our interpretation of the defined groups based on the weight maps is as follows:

Group I. This group consists mainly of low profitability, low growth, low volatility and high non-debt fiscal shelter companies. These are also the smallest[b] companies in the sample.

Group II. These are the companies with high profitability and the highest growth, mid-low volatility and the lowest non-debt fiscal shelter. They are younger companies.

---

[b] Company size is defined according to the number of workers.

Group III. Consists mainly of companies with mid-high profitability mid-low non-debt fiscal shelter and low growth and volatility. This group is comprised of small and old companies.

Group IV. The companies in this group have a low profitability, the lowest growth, a very high volatility and the highest non-debt fiscal shelter. It is comprised of the oldest companies.

Group V. These are the youngest and smallest companies of the sample and present very high volatility, low profitability and average growth.

Group VI. This group contains the companies with the highest profitability and volatility. These also present a very high growth but a low non-debt fiscal shelter. These are mainly the largest companies of the sample.

According to the resulting maps, we confirm the first hypothesis: There is a relationship between profitability and leverage. The best companies in terms of profitability are those that use less debt to finance their assets. For those with lower profitability we observe a greater leverage. On the other hand, we reject the Hypothesis 2: There is no relationship between the growth and leverage. However we observe that during this period only the high profitability companies present a high growth. Again we confirm the third hypothesis: There is relationship between volatility and leverage. The more volatile companies have a small leverage and vice versa, the companies with a low volatility present a high leverage. Finally, We reject the hypothesis 4 as we do not observe any relationship between non-debt fiscal shelter and leverage.

5. Conclusions

This research aims to validate the Pecking Order Theory for the Spanish chemical industry using Kohonen's self-organizing maps. We used a sample of 146 companies for the period 2007-2010.

After analysing the results of our study, we can conclude that there is a relationship between profitability and leverage and between volatility and leverage, which validate the first and third hypotheses described in section 2. This is more evident on the extreme groups. Group I presents the lowest profitability and volatility and also the highest leverage while the group VI presents the highest profitability and volatility with the lowest leverage.

This cannot be extended to growth and non-debt fiscal shelter, which do not have this relationship with leverage. Therefore the second and fourth hypotheses cannot be validated.

These results differ from those obtained for the 1999-2006 period. Despite of volatility (risk) was not a relevant variable before the crisis, during the crisis is having an important influence on the capital structure of the companies.

On the other hand, during the precrisis period, the companies with lower growth have lower leverage, but higher growth only corresponds to higher leverage in the case of mid-low profitability. However, during the current crisis period, only the high profitability companies can afford high growth levels

In future research, we try to extend the time period of the analysis in order to analyze the post crisis situation. We also want to differentiate among mid-low size companies and the large ones. We also will complement this research by repeating the analysis using other methodologies such as factor analysis, analysis of panel data and neural backpropagation.

References

1. B. Back, K. Sere and H. Vanharanta, *Account Manag. Inform. Tech.* Vol. 8, 191 (1998).
2. X. Camara-Turull, F.X. Borràs, M.T. Sorrosal and M.A. Fernández, *Proc. of the MS'10 International Conference, Barcelona, 221* (2009)
3. E.F. Fama and K. French, *Rev. Financ. Stud.* Vol. 15, 1 (2002).
4. E.F. Fama and K. French, *J. Financ. Stud.* Vol. 76, 549 (2005).
5. M. Jensen and W. Meckling, *J. Financ. Econ.* Vol. 5, 305 (1976).
6. T. Kohonen, *Self-Organization and Associative Memory*. Berlin: Springer-Verlag (1989).
7. T. Kohonen, *Self-Organizing Maps.* Berlin: Springer-Verlag (1997).
8. A. Kraus and R. Litzenberger, *J. Financ.* Vol. 28, 911 (1973).
9. H.Y. Leland and D. Pyle, *J. Financ.* Vol. 32, 371 (1977)..
10. F. Modigliani and M.H. Miller, *Am. Econ. Rev.* Vol. 48, 297 (1958).
11. F. Modigliani and M.H. Miller, *Am. Econ. Rev.* Vol. 53, 433 (1963).
12. S.C. Myers, *J. Financ.* No. 39, 575 (1984).
13. S.C. Myers and N. Maljuf, *J. Financ. Econ.* Vol. 13, 187 (1984).
14. S. Ross, *Bell J Econ.* Vol. 8, 24 (1977).

USING NEURAL NETWORKS TO MODEL SOVEREIGN CREDIT RATINGS: APPLICATION TO THE EUROPEAN UNION*

RAÚL LEÓN, MARÍA JESÚS MUÑOZ
Dept. Finance and Accounting, Universitat Jaume I
Campus Riu Sec s/n 12071 Castellón de la Plana, Spain

Credit rating agencies are being widely criticized because the lack of transparency in their rating procedures and the huge impact of the ratings they disclose, mainly their sovereign credit ratings. However the rationale seems to be that although credit ratings have performed worse than their aim, they are still the best available solution to provide financial markets with the information that their participants base their decisions on. This research work proposes a neural network system that simulates the sovereign credit ratings provided by two of the most important international agencies. Results indicate that the proposed system, based on a three layers structure of feed-forward neural networks, can model the agencies' sovereign credit ratings with a high accuracy rate, using a reduced set of publicly available economic data. The proposed model can be further developed in order to extent the use of neural networks to model other ratings, create new ratings with specific purposes, or forecast future ratings of credit rating agencies.

Keywords: Neural networks, Sovereign credit rating, European Union, Credit rating modelling.

JEL Codes: C45, D8, N24

1. Introduction

During the very last years, credit ratings have become the most important tool for bankruptcy prediction of firms and countries. Credit ratings can be defined as evaluations of a potential borrower's ability to repay debt, prepared by a credit bureau at the request of the lender. For the specific purpose of this research work, credit ratings are defined as the alphabetical indicators of credit risk provided by international rating agencies.

In spite of their increasing importance in financial markets, credit rating agencies do not disclose the precise factors and weights used in their ratings generation. Rating agencies claim to use complex processes considering non-

---

* A preliminary version of this paper was presented at the 2012 ASME International Conference on Modeling and Simulation, New York (USA), May-June 13–23, 2012.

linear interactions between different variables, which include quantitative and qualitative data on financial and non financial information (Bennell et. al, 2006). As a result, modelling credit rating by means of quantitative or ruled based techniques is a challenging process.

Literature provides many research works aimed at modelling credit ratings by means of different statistical methods. Those include multiple discriminant analysis (Altman, 1968; Carleton and Lerner, 1969; Raman, 1981; Taffler, 1983), regression analysis (Horton, 1970; Rubinfield 1973), ordered probit (Linden et. al, 1998; Trevino and Thomas, 2000 a,b, 2001) and options-based approaches (e.g. KMV Corporation, see Bessis, 2002), among others. However, the use of those econometric methods involves introducing assumptions with respect to the underlying properties and relationships within the data. Those assumptions are particularly difficult to hypothesize in the context of credit rating because of the lack of transparency of credit rating agencies.

The use of neural networks for credit rating modelling is particularly appropriate because they do not require prior specification of theoretical models (Trigueiros and Taffler, 1996) and they are able to deal with incomplete information or noisy data (Vellido et al., 1999; Malhotra and Malhotra, 2003). They are usually used in economics and finance in researches where variables are in non-linear relations (Granger, 1991).

The aim of this work is to advance in the use of neural networks in credit ratings. To this end, a neural networks based structure is proposed to simulate sovereign credit ratings of the European Union countries. The model uses publicly available data on economic and financial issues of European countries, as well the ratings published by some of the most important agencies.

The rest of this work is structured as follows. Section 2 provides theoretical background on neural networks and their use in credit ratings modelling. In Section 3, it is presented a brief review on credit ratings, credit rating agencies and sovereign credit ratings. Section 4 presents the data and models employed to evaluate the feasibility of using neural networks for sovereign credit rating modelling. Main results are then presented in Section 5. Finally, Section 6 discusses on results and future research.

2. Neural networks

Neural networks are powerful technique inspired by the way biological nervous systems process information. This technique consists on a large number of interconnected elements (neurons) working at the same time through a set of algorithms. Thus, neural networks can solve real problems if these can be mathematically represented.

Neural networks have the ability to learn from experience, adapting their behaviour according a specific environment in order to improve their performance. To that end, neural networks need to be trained to approximate an unknown function or process, based on available input and output data. In this regard, one of the most common procedure to train neural network classifiers is the back-propagation (Rumelhart et al., 1986), which is based on a optimization problem that look for a set of network parameters, specifically weights, with the end of obtaining the best classification performance (Mazurowski et al., 2008).

Neural networks have been utilized in a variety of applications, which can be grouped in four fundamental categories: clustering, classification, function approximation and prediction. A neural network can get into groups objects/individuals that are similar to each other. Moreover, it can be used to assign each object/individual to a specific class, which is particularly useful for credit rating modelling. In respect to function approximation, neural networks, from input vectors, construct a function that generates approximately the outputs of the unknown process that is expected to model. If the time factor is considered, the function approximation can be used to forecast, in which the function values are represented using time series.

A significant group of researchers (Vellido et al., 1999; Malhotra and Malhotra, 2003) argue that neural networks can be a more appropriate tool than traditional statistical tools, because: (a) the underlying functions controlling business data are generally unknown and neural networks do not require a prior specification function, only a sample of input-output data to learn and train the process; (b) neural networks are flexible – the brain adapts to new circumstances and can identify nonlinear trends by learning from the data; (c) neural networks can work with fuzzy data (very common in economics); and (d) they are able to deal with incomplete information or noisy data and can be very effective especially in situations where it is not possible to define the rules or steps that lead to the solution of a problem.

In this regard, numerous empirical research has compared neural network methodology with econometric techniques for modelling ratings, and consistent with theoretical arguments, the results clearly demonstrate that neural networks represent a superior methodology for calibrating and predicting ratings relative to linear regression analysis, multivariate discriminant analysis and logistic regression (e.g. Bennell et al., 2006; Surkan and Singleton, 1990; Kim et al., 1993; Daniels and Kamp's, 1999). Leshno and Spector (1996) even point out that the methods traditionally used in credit risk analysis, which include regression analysis, multivariate discriminant analysis, and logistic regression among others, represent special cases of neural networks, and therefore it is not surprising that they are appropriate for credit rating modelling.

Increasingly, academics are exploring neural networks methodology as a new tool for modelling decision process and predict in the area of finance, such us corporate financial distress and bankruptcy (Ahn et al., 2000; Lee et al., 1996), loan evaluation and credit scoring (Malhotra and Malhotra, 2003; Baesens et al., 2003), and bond rating, both from private corporations and sovereign issuers (Chaveesuk et al., 1999; Bennell et al., 2006).

Therefore, given that neural networks have been used for replicating unknown processes with complex relationships among variables and imperfect data, we consider neural networks as an appropriate methodology to model the behaviour of sustainability rating agencies.

3. Credit ratings

Ratings are an invaluable instrument in globalized financial markets. Lenders and investors have nowadays a huge number of possible credits, but only a passing knowledge of most of borrowers. Furthermore, during the last few years, global securities markets have become an increasingly important source of external funding for many emerging economies, including countries and corporations. Within this context, credit rating agencies play a useful role in financial decision-making by providing market participants with information about the credit risk associated with different financial investments (Kräussl, 2005), and more precisely, about the probability that borrowers will default in its financial commitments.

A wide range of participants, including issuers, investors and regulators use the information provided by rating agencies in their decision-making (Cantor and Packer, 1997; Duff and Einig, 2009; Stolper, 2009). The information generated by credit rating agencies is mainly delivered in the form of credit ratings, which are alphabetical indicators of the probability that borrowers will not fulfil the obligations in their debt issues. Typically, a credit rating has been used by investors to assess the probability of the subject being able to pay back a loan. However, in recent years, participants have started to give new uses to credit ratings, which include among others to adjust insurance premiums, to determine employment eligibility, and establish the amount of a utility or leasing deposit (Falavigna, 2012).

According to debtors, credit ratings may be classified in four main categories:

1. **Corporate** credit ratings are related public and private ratings on companies and their debt instruments, including bank loans, senior and subordinated debt, commercial paper and preferred stock.
2. **Sub national** credit ratings evaluate the repayment capability of entities in the tiers of government lower than the federal or central government. Sub national entities include states/provinces, counties, cities, towns, public utility companies, school districts and other special purpose governments which have the capacity to incur debt
3. **Sovereign** credit ratings include ratings on foreign and local debt issuance of countries.
4. **Supranational** credit ratings are addressed to institutions established and controlled by their sovereign government shareholders. Those include some of largest issuers in international capital markets, such as the European Investment Bank and the International Bank for Reconstruction and Development.

As far as credit ratings agencies declare, credit ratings are not based on mathematical formulas. Instead, credit rating agencies use their experience and judgment, based on both objective and subjective criteria, in determining what public and private information –quantitative as well as qualitative- should be considered and how it has to be weighted in giving a rating to a particular company or government.

Rating agencies emphasize that the credit rating process involves the use of a wide range of variables considering financial and non-financial information about the object being assessed, and also variables related to industry and market-level factors. (Hájek, 2011). However, rating agencies do not specify neither what determines their ratings nor their rating procedure (Mora, 2006). The precise factors they use in their ratings, and the aggregations processes and the related weights of these factors used in determining a credit rating, are not publicly disclosed by the rating agencies. Furthermore, the credit rating agencies underline that they do not employ a specific formula to combine their assessments of political and economic factors to derive the overall rating (Kräussl, 2005). As a result, credit ratings issued by different rating agencies on a specific object do not have necessarily to be the same, what originates a lack of security in the decision making of financial markets participants.

3.1. *Sovereign credit ratings*

During the last few decades, sovereign credit ratings have gained importance as more governments with greater default risk have borrowed in international bond markets. Sovereign credit ratings have important implications for international capital flows and for the linkages between company ratings and sovereign ratings (Mora, 2006). They have a strong influence on the cost borrowers must face, and they can enhance the capability of countries' governments and private sectors to access global capital markets, attract foreign direct investment, encourage domestic financial sector development, and support governments' efforts on financial and economic improvements and transparency (Alsakka and ap Gwilym, 2010). It is generally believed that improving a country's transparency, information control, financing costs and sovereign risk levels is expected to increase international capital inflows and improve the general level of development in financial markets and their financial integration with world capital markets (Kim and Wu, 2008).

There is also evidence that sovereign ratings strongly determine the pricing of sovereign bonds and that sovereign spreads incorporate market participants' views of expected credit rating changes (Erb et al., 2000). A good country rating is a key success factor of the availability of international financing since it directly influences the interest rate at which countries can borrow on the international financial market, and it may also impact the rating of its banks and companies, and is reported to be correlated with national stock returns. (Van Gestel et al., 2006). By opposite, as a direct consequence of being lowly rated, firms and countries may face higher interest rates, or even to the refusal of a loan by creditors (Falavigna, 2012).

While the ratings have proved useful to governments seeking market access, the difficulty of assessing sovereign risk has led to agency disagreements and public controversy over specific rating assignments (Cantor and Packer, 1995). Furthermore, during the last few years, and as a consequence closely linked to global crisis, sovereign credit ratings have become widely criticized for exacerbating the crisis when they downgraded the countries in the midst of the financial turmoil. As a result, the financial markets have shown some scepticism toward sovereign ratings when pricing issues. However, they are still considered as the best measure of a country's credit risk available nowadays as internal default data is missing (BCBS, 2004; Cantor and Packer, 2006)

In addition to the above mentioned problems, which are related to the four categories of credit ratings, sovereign credit ratings present one additional problem. Countries, unlike firms, rarely default because of the availability of international emergency credit (most of their problems being liquidity and not solvency related) and the high cost of future credit should they default. As a consequence, the rating agencies' objective of providing estimations of the probability that borrowers will not fulfil the obligations in their debt issues can be considered plausible at the level of corporations, but it is problematic at the sovereign level (Mora, 2006)

This paper focuses on sovereign ratings for several reasons. From a usefulness perspective, investors are increasingly focused on international diversification, and hence an understanding of sovereign credit risk is very important. Furthermore sovereign ratings have historically represented a ceiling for the ratings assigned to financial institutions, corporate and provincial governments, although the ceiling is no longer applied in an absolute sense by the largest three agencies (Alsakka and ap Gwilym, 2009). Therefore, contributing on the understanding of sovereign credit rating agencies, and the factors and weights they use in their ratings is essential for the transparency of the markets. From a practical perspective, the amount of public available historic data on sovereign credit ratings is considerably higher than data on the other categories, which makes it easier to have at disposal enough data for training and testing the proposed models.

4. Models and data

The development of a neural network system for facing classification problems, as well as others, starts with de definition of a sample. This study uses sovereign credit rating of countries in the European Union between years 1980 and 2011.

Once the sample is defined, it is necessary to define the neural networks input and output variables, a neural network model suitable for the problem being addresses and the selected input and output variables, and two datasets containing the necessary data to accomplish the training process of the neural network, which are a dataset of input data and a dataset with the corresponding target values. Those datasets are essential for the accuracy of the trained neural network, since they are the examples where the networks learn from.

4.1. *Input variables and training input dataset*

Literature has largely examined the variables that mainly determine the sovereign credit ratings, and findings may indicate that sovereign ratings are generally consistent with economic fundamental. Cantor and Packer (1996) show that per capita income, inflation, external debt, an indicator of economic development and an indicator of default history all explain 90% of the variation in the ratings of 49 countries observed in 1995. The conclude that high ratings are assigned to countries with high per capita income, low inflation, more rapid growth, low ratio of foreign currency external debt to exports, absence of a history of default on foreign currency debt since 1970, and a high level of economic development, which means to be classified as an industrial country by the International Monetary Fund. Those variables have been used by many authors in sovereign credit rating modeling (Afonso, 2003; Mora, 2006; Trevino and Thomas 2000a, 2001; Bennel, 2006) and it has to be noted that they are also consistent with those that the rating agencies claim being using in assessing sovereign credit worthiness (Beers and Cavanaugh, 1999; IBCA, 1997; Truglia, 1999).

In line with literature, following variables have been chosen as the inputs for our neural network model. All data used to populate the training input dataset have been sourced from the World Economic Outlook Database (IMF, 2011) offered by the International Monetary Fund in its website, and the AMECO database of the European Commission's Directorate General for Economic and Financial Affairs (EC, 2011).

- **External Balance**: Annual current account balance relative to GDP. Current account is all transactions other than those in financial and capital items.
- **Fiscal Balance**: Annual general government deficit (-) or surplus (+) relative to GDP, calculated as general government revenue less general government expenditures.
- **Gross Debt / Exports of goods and saves**: total liabilities that require payment or payments of interest and/or principal at a date or dates in the future in relative to exports
- **Gross domestic product (GDP) per capita**: GDP of previous year expressed in current U.S. dollars per person
- **Inflation**: Annual consumer price rate consumer prices
- **Unemployment rate**: according to OECD harmonized definition, number of unemployed persons as a percentage of the labor force.

4.2. *Output variables and training target dataset*

There are a large number of credit rating agencies that publish their ratings, but only a few have risen to international prominence (Cantor and Packer, 1994). The rest are national or at best continental organizations. The most popular credit rating agencies are Moody's Investor Service (http://www.moodys.com), Standard & Poor's (http://www.standardpoor.com), and Fitch (http://www.fitchratings.com) (Cantor and Packer, 1996).

Those agencies use a rating based on alphabetical indicators to inform about the quality of the different financial assets issued by borrowers. Those indicators range from default to highest quality. While a evaluation of default is used to indicate that in the agencies' opinion opinions the issuer has entered into bankruptcy filings, administration, receivership, liquidation or other formal winding-up procedure, the highest quality denotes the lowest expectation of default risk, and it is assigned only in cases of exceptionally strong capacity for payment of financial commitments, capacity that is also highly unlikely to be adversely affected by foreseeable events. Table 1 shows he measurement scales used by the tree most important rating agencies.

Table 1. Standard and Poor's, Moody's and Fitch rating systems

Characterization of debt and issuer (source: Moody's)		**Moody's**	**Standard and Poor's**	**Fitch**
Highest quality	Investment grade	Aaa	AAA	AAA
High quality		Aal	AA+	AA+
		Aa2	AA	AA
		Aa3	AA-	AA-
Strong payment capacity		A1	A+	A+
		A2	A	A
		A3	A-	A-
Adequate payment capacity		Baal	BBB+	BBB+
		Baa2	BBB	BBB
		Baa3	BBB-	BBB-
Likely to fulfil obligations, ongoing uncertainty	Speculative grade	Bal	BB+	BB+
		Ba2	BB	BB
		Ba3	BB-	BB-
High credit risk		B1	B+	B+
		B2	B	B
		B3	B-	B-
Very high credit risk		Caal	CCC+	CCC+
		Caa2	CCC	CCC
		Caa3	CCC-	CCC-
Near default with possibility of recovery		Ca	CC	CC
			C	C
Default		C	SD	RD
			D	D

Fitch offers in its website a file containing all historic data of sovereign credit ratings while Moody's offers and interactive web application by means of which all historic data of their sovereign credit ratings can be easily downloaded. By opposite, Standard and Poor's offers limited access to historic credit ratings, and only provide historic information of sovereign credit ratings initially determined on or after June 26, 2007, according to the Securities Exchange Act of 1934. Since we are using publicly available information and the available data from Standard and Poor's is very scarce for being used in neural networks training, our data for the credit rating modelling are from Moody's and Fitch. More concretely, we use foreign their currency sovereign credit ratings for countries in the European Union.

Both agencies provide sovereign credit ratings history in a timeline format. Starting on the assessment each country got the first time it was rated, Moody's and Fitch provide a sequence of temporal marks were changes on the rating happened –in the case of Moody's, it is also detailed the periods of time during witch the sovereign credit were on watch. Those time lines were used to create a dataset for each agency containing the distribution of foreign currency sovereign ratings at the end of year. Figures 1 and 2 show foreign currency sovereign credit rating distributions for Moody's and Fitch. Note that the distribution of ratings provided by Fitch start on 1994 instead of 1980, since it was the year the agency began assessing sovereign bonds.

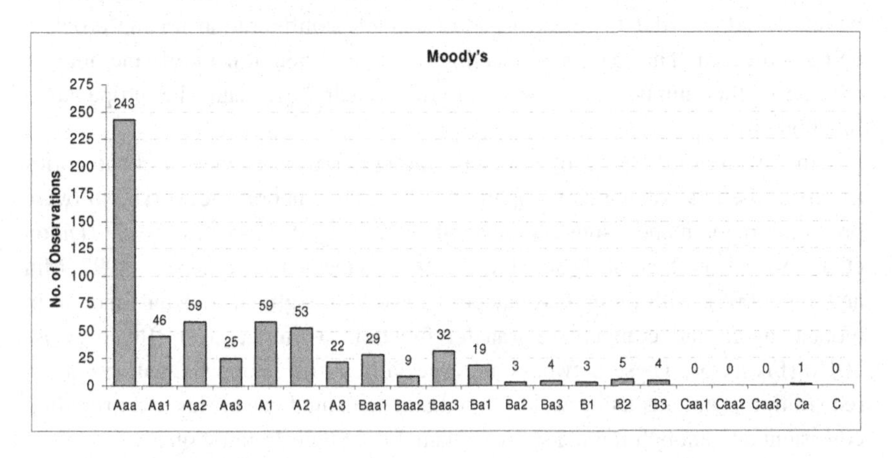

Figure 1. Foreign currency sovereign ratings distribution 1980–2011 provided by Moody's.

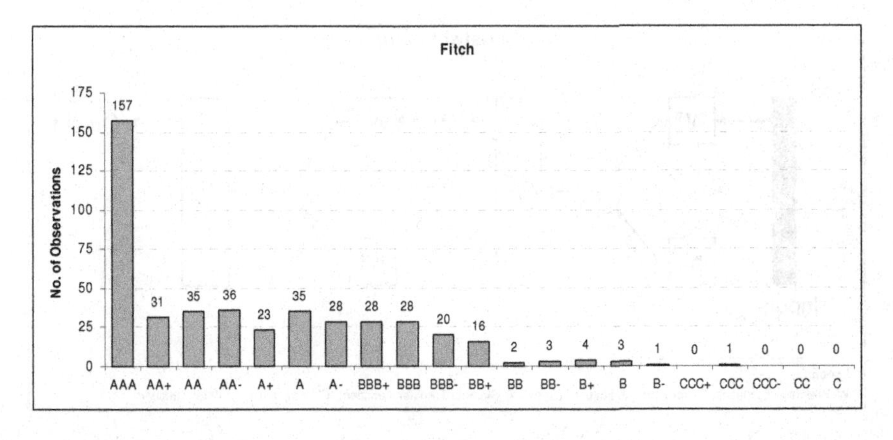

Figure 2. Foreign currency sovereign ratings distribution 1994–2011 provided by Fitch

4.3. *Neural networks model*

From a low level perspective, a neural network is a network made of several simple processors. Each unit has its own memory, and they are interconnected by communication channels that allow processor units to receive and send information to other processors. Furthermore, those channels have specific weighs which are adjusted by a training algorithm on the basis of some training patterns. Once a network is designed and trained, it is expected to learn from examples and exhibit some structural capability for generalization (Falavigna, 2012).

Regarding the neural networks employed, there are some aspects that should be addressed in order to select the most suitable configuration for the problem being addressed. That includes selecting the type of neural network, the number of layers, the number of neurons used at each layer and the propagation functions.

In the case of the modelling a credit rating that uses a close set of categories to asses issuers repayment capability, literature neural networks software providers recommend using a N-layered feed-forward network ($N>=2$) (Dillon et. al, 1979; Hornik et. al, 1989; Hornik, 1993; Olmeda and Fernandez, 1997; Min and Lee, 2005), with outputs as categories and with sigmoid transfer function in hidden layers and competitive transfer function at output layer (Beale et al., 2010) (Figure 3). These networks are especially useful in approximating pattern recognition problems using well defined and separated categories and providing consistent and enough input and target data during their training phase.

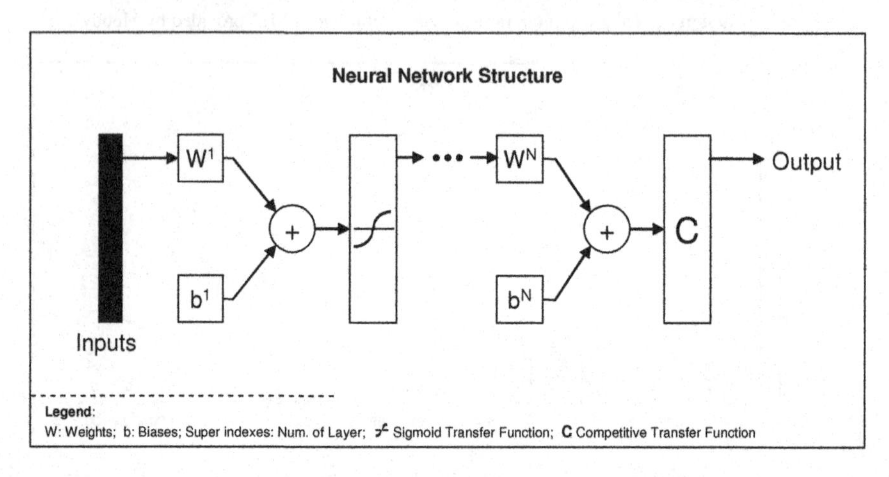

Figure 3. Neural Network for sovereign credit ratings modeling

Literature provides indications on how determine an approximation of the optimal number of neurons of hidden layer, and formulas such as *2i+1* or *0.75i*, where *i* represents the number of input variables, have widely used in many researches (Salchenberger et. al, 1992; Patuwo et. al, 1993; Olmeda and Fernandez, 1997; Chauhan et. al, 2009). However, the optimal number of neurons must be found empirically because feed-forward networks use gradient method in learning, and it is therefore possible that the learning algorithm gets stuck in local minimum within the error function. That problem can be solved by adding additional neurons or changing other network parameters.

One single neural network can solve quite complex problems. However, neural networks can also be combined in complex structures specially designed to maximize the accuracy by exploiting the specific properties of different neural networks. In this paper it is used a structure similar to the one employed by Falavigna (2012), which is expected to minimize the potential error in classifications using neural networks with non dichotomous outputs.

Table 2. Three layer structure for sovereign credit rating using dichotomous neural networks

Group	Moody's	S&P	Fitch	Net						
				1	1.1	1.0	1.1.1	1.1.0	1.0.1	1.0.0
G1	Aaa	AAA	AAA	1	1	-	1	-	-	-
G2	Aa1	AA+	AA+	1	1	-	0	-	-	-
	Aa2	AA	AA	1	1	-	0	-	-	-
	Aa3	AA-	AA-	1	1	-	0	-	-	-
G3	A1	A+	A+	1	0	-	-	1	-	-
	A2	A	A	1	0	-	-	1	-	-
	A3	A-	A-	1	0	-	-	1	-	-
G4	Baa1	BBB+	BBB+	1	0	-	-	0	-	-
	Baa2	BBB	BBB	1	0	-	-	0	-	-
	Baa3	BBB-	BBB-	1	0	-	-	0	-	-
G5	Ba1	BB+	BB+	0	-	1	-	-	1	-
	Ba2	BB	BB	0	-	1	-	-	1	-
	Ba3	BB-	BB-	0	-	1	-	-	1	-
G6	B1	B+	B+	0	-	1	-	-	0	-
	B2	B	B	0	-	1	-	-	0	-
	B3	B-	B-	0	-	1	-	-	0	-
G7	Caa1	CCC+	CCC+	0	-	0	-	-	-	1
	Caa2	CCC	CCC	0	-	0	-	-	-	1
	Caa3	CCC-	CCC-	0	-	0	-	-	-	1
	Ca	CC	CC	0	-	0	-	-	-	1
		C	C	0	-	0	-	-	-	1
G8	C	SD	RD	0	-	0	-	-	-	0
		D	D	0	-	0	-	-	-	0

That structure consists of n levels and 2n dichotomous neural networks, being 2n-1 the number of networks in the level l. Each input data is processed by one single neural network at every level, and the output it generates determine which net will be used in the next level. The combination of the outputs of the three neural networks that process each specific case determines its rating

As the above described structure allows classifying data in 2n categories, the ratings being modelled have been reorganized in 8 categories. While it could be possible to use finer categories, the smaller and closer categories are, the lower accuracy would have the neural network structure. Table 2 shows the employed structure of neural networks. Note that Groups G7 and G8 have a very limited representation in the sample, and therefore, training the Net 1-0-0 is not possible. Those categories are not considered in this research.

5. Results

The experiment was conducted separately for each one of the rating agencies – using in both cases the same training input dataset, and two scripts were codified. The first script generated the necessary training sub datasets for each of the 6 neural networks according to groups previously defined. It is necessary to clarify that during the training process, the training target dataset is used to determine what neural network will be trained at each level with a specific case, without considering the output this case would have generated in a trained system. Table 3 shows the number of inputs for all networks and the number of targets for each possible network output Note that Net1.0.0 was not implemented, since only one case is available for both rating agencies and it is not enough for training a network.

The second script trained the networks and reorganized their outputs in a dataset containing, for each input case, a set with the outputs of the corresponding nets at each of the three levels.

Table 3. Training subsets for networks in the system

Net	Fitch			Moody's		
	No. Inputs	Nº. Targets		No. Inputs	Nº. Targets	
		Output 1	Output 0		Output 1	Output 0
Net1	450	421	29	615	577	38
Net 1.1	421	259	162	577	373	204
Net 1.0	29	29	0	38	38	0
Net 1.1.1	259	157 (G1)	102 (G2)	373	243 (G1)	130 (G2)
Net 1.1.0	162	86 (G3)	76 (G4)	204	134 (G3)	70 (G4)
Net 1.0.1	29	21 (G5)	8 (G6)	38	26 (G5)	12 (G6)

For the training of each neural network, the training dataset was randomly classified in two sets as follows. The first set, containing a 80% of the cases, was used to train the networks with the Levenberg-Marquardt. The second set, including a 20% of the cases, was used to validate that the networks generalized and to stop training before over fitting.

Finally, a confusion matrix was generated to determine the accuracy of each system. Table 4 shows confusion matrix for Fitch, while Table 5 shows the confusion matrix for Moddy's.

Table 4. Confusion matrix for Fitch model

Fitch

Outputs							
G1	**144** 32.0%	**38** 8.4%	**0** 0.0%	**0** 0.0%	**0** 0.0%	**0** 0.0%	**79.1%** 20.9%
G2	**13** 2.9%	**56** 12.4%	**7** 1.6%	**4** 0.9%	**1** 0.2%	**0** 0.0%	**69.1%** 30.9%
G3	**0** 0.0%	**8** 1.8%	**66** 14.7%	**18** 4.0%	**2** 0.4%	**0** 0.0%	**70.2%** 29.8%
G4	**0** 0.0%	**0** 0.0%	**13** 2.9%	**52** 11.6%	**11** 2.4%	3 0.7%	**65.8%** 34.2%
G5	**0** 0.0%	**0** 0.0%	**0** 0.0%	**1** 0.2%	**7** 1.6%	**0** 0.0%	**87.5%** 12.5%
G6	**0** 0.0%	**0** 0.0%	**0** 0.0%	**1** 0.2%	**0** 0.0%	**5** 1.1%	**83.3%** 16.7%
	91.7% 8.3%	**54.9%** 45.1%	**76.7%** 23.3%	**68.4%** 31.6%	**33.3%** 66.7%	**62.5%** 37.5%	**73.3%** 26.7%
	G1	**G2**	**G3**	**G4**	**G5**	**G6**	

Targets

As it can be observed, both systems reach a quite high level of accuracy, and most misclassifications are one-group error. However, a higher sample and a more accurate selection on input variables and neural network parameters would be expected to increase the accuracy of the system. Furthermore, it has to be noted that errors are mainly related to cases which have bee better classified by the neural network systems than they were classified by rating agencies. This tendency may arise as a result of the training datasets, which present an unbalanced distribution where the highest classification is much more frequent than any other, and where negative ratings –those referred to speculative categories- are very infrequent.

Table 5. Confusion matrix for Moody's model

Moody's

Outputs	G1	G2	G3	G4	G5	G6	
G1	**223** 36.3%	**58** 9.4%	**13** 2.1%	**6** 1.0%	**2** 0.3%	**0** 0.0%	**73.8%** 26.2%
G2	**10** 1.6%	**50** 8.1%	**2** 0.3%	**2** 0.3%	**6** 1.0%	**0** 0.0%	**71.4%** 28.6%
G3	**10** 1.6%	**22** 3.6%	**118** 19.2%	**36** 5.9%	**9** 1.5%	**4** 0.7%	**59.3%** 40.7%
G4	**0** 0.0%	**0** 0.0%	**1** 0.2%	**24** 3.9%	**5** 0.8%	**3** 0.5%	**72.7%** 27.3%
G5	**0** 0.0%	**0** 0.0%	**0** 0.0%	**0** 0.0%	**4** 0.7%	**0** 0.0%	**100%** 0%
G6	**0** 0.0%	**0** 0.0%	**0** 0.0%	**2** 0.3%	**0** 0.0%	**5** 0.8%	**71.4%** 28.6%
	91.8% 8.2%	**38.5%** 61.5%	**88.1%** 11.9%	**34.3%** 65.7%	**15.4%** 84.6%	**41.7%** 58.3%	**68.9%** 31.1%

Targets

6. Discussion and final remarks

The obtained results, whereas not surprising, confirm that, due to their usefulness for generalization and classification, neural networks can be used for credit ratings modelling. Using a comprehensive dataset comprising sovereign credit ratings of rating agencies and public information on countries over the period 1980–2011, this paper shows that neural networks can provide accurate classifications of sovereign credit ratings. Obviously, the problem of modelling credit rating agencies scores is very close to the variables introduced in the model, and a more accurate selection of input variables could significantly enhance results. Furthermore, it is also possible that using averages or tendencies of some variables during some previous years, the accuracy of the systems could increase.

It should be noted that although rating agencies claim that the experience and subjective judgment of their analysts are essential in determining the ratings, results seem indicate that a neural networks system based on a small set of input variables based on publicly available financial and no financial information could provide accurate classifications of credit ratings. This result is in line with other researches where neural networks are successfully used to model different credit ratings (Benell et.al, 2006; Falaviga, 2012; Hájek 2011). From those remarks it seems possible to generalize the use of neural networks systems for the development of credit rating tools addressed to different types of products.

Furthermore, by means of neural networks and having access to expert's knowledge, it could be possible to create rating tools for other proposes such as the internal rating systems of banks. In this regard, and starting from Basel II proposals, it could worth a try to research on the suitability of banks using their own credit rating systems based on neural networks in determining the amount of capital they need to put aside for different types of loans.

Neural networks systems may also be used to predict future credit ratings, at it is possible to use predicted variables as inputs for trained neural networks systems. In this regard, credit rating forecasting may be really useful for issuers and investors, since it could be used by analysts as an informing and supporting tool for their decision making processes, in order to reduce the costs or risks of their financial operations.

However, it is still necessary further research in order to better understand the main variables that determine credit ratings provided by agencies, and to test different neural networks configurations and structures until better results are obtained. Furthermore, the same research should also be conducted using different credit ratings at corporations, sub national and supranational levels.

Acknowledgements

This work is supported by P1.1B2010-04 and P1.1B2010-13 research projects and the Master in Sustainability and Corporate Social Responsibility offered by Universitat Jaume I of Castellón, Spain.

References

1. Afonso, A. (2003). "Understanding the determinants of sovereign debt ratings: evident for the two leading agencies". Journal of Economics and Finance, Vol. 27, No. 1, p. 56–74.
2. Ahn, B.S.; Cho, S.S.; Kim, C.Y. (2000). "The integrated methodology of rough set theory and artificial neural network for business failure prediction". Expert Systems with Applications, Vol. 18, No. 2, 65–74.
3. Alsakka, R.; ap Gwilym, O. (2009). "Heterogeneity of sovereign rating migrations in emerging countries, Emerging Markets Review, Vol. 10, p. 151–165.
4. Alsakka, R.; ap Gwilym, O., (2010). "Leads and lags in sovereign credit ratings". Journal of Banking & Finance, Vol. 34, p. 2614–2626.

5. Altman, E.L. (1968). "Financial ratios, discriminant analysis and the prediction of corporate bankruptcy". Journal of Finance, Vol. 23, No. 3, p. 589–609.
6. Baesens, B.; Setiono, R.; Mues, C.; J. Vanthienen, (2003). "Using Neural Network Rule Extraction and Decision Tables for Credit-Risk Evaluation". Management Science, Vol. 49, No. 3, p.312–329.
7. Basel Committee on Banking Supervision (2004). International convergence of capital measurement and capital standards.
8. Beale, M.H.; Hagan M.T and Demuth, H.B (2010). "Neural Network Toolbox™ User's Guide". The MathWorks, Inc. Natick M.A.
9. Beers, D. T.; and Cavanaugh, M. (1999). "Sovereign credit ratings: A primer, Standard & Poor's Counterparty Ratings Guides", 1st Quarter
10. Bennell J.A, Crabbe, D.; Thomas, S, and ap Gwilym, O. (2006). "Modelling sovereign credit ratings: Neural networks versus ordered probit". Expert Systems with Applications, Vol. 30, p. 415–425.
11. Bessis, J. (2002). Risk management in banking (2nd ed.). West Sussex: Wiley.
12. Cantor R.; Packer F. (1994). "The credit rating industry". Quarterly Review (Summer–Fall). Federal Reserve Bank of New York, New York
13. Cantor, R.; Packer, F. (1995). "Sovereign Credit Ratings". Current Issues in Economics and Finance, Vol. 1, No. 3.
14. Cantor, R.; Packer, F. (1996). "Determinants and inputs of sovereign credit ratings". FRBNY Economic Policy Review, Vol. 2, No. 2, p. 37–53.
15. Cantor, R.; Packer, F. (1997). "Differences in opinion and selection bias in the credit rating industry". Journal of Banking and Finance, Vol. 21, p. 1395–1417.
16. Carleton, W.T.; Lerner, E.M. (1969). "Statistical credit scoring of municipal bonds". Journal of Money, Credit and Banking, Vol. 1, No. 4, p. 750–764.
17. Chauhan, N.; Ravi, V.; Chandra, D.K. (2009). "Differential evolution trained wavelet neural networks: Application to bankruptcy prediction in banks". Expert Systems with Applications, Vol. 36, p. 7659–7665.
18. Chaveesuk, R.; Srivaree-Ratana C.; Smith A.E. (1999). "Alternative neural network approaches to corporate bond rating". Journal of Engineering Valuation and Cost Analysis, Vol. 2, No. 2, p. 117–131.
19. Daniels, H.; Kamp, B. (1999). "Application of MLP networks to bond rating and house pricing". Neural Computing and Applications, Vol. 8, p. 226–234.
20. Dillon, W.R.; Calantone, R.J.; Worthing, P. (1979). "The new product problem: An approach for investigating product failures". Management Science, Vol. 25, p. 1184–1196.
21. Duff, A.; Einig, S. (2009). "Understanding credit ratings quality: evidence from UK debt market participants". The British Accounting Review, Vol. 41, p.107–119.

22. Erb, C.; Harvey, C.R.; Viskanta, T. (2000). "Understanding Emerging Market Bonds". Emerging Markets Quarterly. Spring 2000, p. 7–23.
23. European Commision (2011). AMECO database of the European Commission's Directorate General for Economic and Financial Affairs. Accessed at http://ec.europa.eu/economy_finance/) on 1st Dec, 2011.
24. Falavigna, G. (2012). "Financial ratings with scarce information: A neural network approach". Expert Systems with Applications, Vol. 39, p. 1784–1792.
25. Granger, C.W.J. (1991). "Developments in the nonlinear analysis of economic series". The Scandinavian Journal of Economics, Vol. 93, No. 2, p. 263–276.
26. Hájek, P. (2011). "Municipal credit rating modelling by neural networks". Decision Support Systems, Vol. 51, p.108–118.
27. Hornik, K. (1993). "Some new results on neural network approximation". Neural Networks, Vol. 6, p. 1069–1072.
28. Hornik, K.; Stinchcombe, M.; White, H. (1989). "Multilayer feedforward networks are universal approximators". Neural Networks, Vol. 2, p. 359–366.
29. Horton, J.J. (1970). "Statistical classification of municipal bonds". Journal of Bank Research, Vol. 3, No. 1, p. 29–40.
30. IBCA. (1997). Sovereign rating methodology.
31. IMF (2011) World Economic Outlook Database: September 2011. International Monetary Fund. Accessed at http://www.imf.org/external/index.htm on 1st Dec, 2011.
32. Kim, J. W.; Weistroffer, H. R.; and Redmond, R. T. (1993). "Expert systems for bond rating: A comparative analysis of statistical, rule-based and neural network systems". Expert Systems, Vol. 10, p. 167–188.
33. Kim, S.-J.; Wu, E. (2008). "Sovereign credit ratings, capital flows and financial sector development in emerging markets", Emerging Markets Review, Vol. 9, p. 17–39.
34. Kräussl, R. (2005). "Do credit rating agencies add to the dynamics of emerging market crises?". Journal of Financial Stability, Vol. 1, p. 355–385.
35. Lee, K.C.; Han, L., and Kwon, Y. (1996). "Hybrid neural network models for bankruptcyprediction". Decision Support Systems, Vol. 18, 63–72.
36. Leshno, M.; and Spector, Y. (1996). "Neural network prediction analysis: The bankruptcy case". Neurocomputing, Vol. 10, p. 125–147.
37. Linden, F.; McNamara, G.; Vaaler, P. (1998). "Idiosyncratic region and rather effects on sovereign credit ratings". Proceedings of the Academy of Management annual meeting in San Diego, California, USA.
38. Malhotra, R.; Malhotra D. K. (2003). "Evaluating consumer loans using neural networks". Omega, Vol. 31, No. 2, p. 83-96.
39. Mazurowski, M.A.; Habas, P.A.; Zurada, J.M.; Lo, J.Y.; Baker, J.A.; Tourassi, G.D. (2008). "Training neural network classifiers for medical

decision making: The effects of imbalanced datasets on classification performance". Neural Networks, Vol. 2, p. 427-436.
40. Min, J. H.; and Lee, Y.-C. (2005). "Bankruptcy prediction using support vector machine with optimal choice of kernel function parameters". Expert Systems with Applications, Vol. 28, p. 603–614.
41. Mora, N. (2006). "Sovereign credit ratings: guilty beyond reasonable doubt?". Journal of Banking and Finance, Vol. 30, No. 7, p. 2041–2062.
42. Olmeda, I.; Fernandez, E. (1997). "Hybrid classifier for financial multicriteria decision making: The case of bankruptcy prediction". Computational Economics, Vol. 10, p. 317–335.
43. Patuwo, E.; Hu, M. Y.; Hung, M. S. (1993). "Two-group classification using neural networks". Decision Sciences, Vol. 24, No. 4, p. 825–845.
44. Raman, K.K. (1981). "Financial reporting and municipal bond rating changes". The Accounting Review, Vol. 56, No. 4, p. 910–926.
45. Rubinfield, D. (1973). "Credit ratings and the market for general obligation municipal bonds". National Tax Journal, Vol. 26, No. 1, p. 17–27.
46. Rumelhart, D.E.; Hinton, G.E.; Williams, R.J. (1986). Learning Internal Representations by Error Propagation. In Rumelhart, D. E.; McClelland, J.; Eds.
47. Salchenberger, L.M.; Cinar, M.E.; Lash, N.A. (1992). "A neural networks: A new tool for predicting thrift failures". Decision Sciences, Vol. 23, p. 899–916.
48. Stolper, A. (2009). "Regulation of credit rating agencies": Journal of Banking and Finance, Vol. 33, p. 1266–1273.
49. Surkan, A.J.; Singleton, J.C. (1990). "Neural networks for bond rating improved by multiple hidden layers". Proceedings of IEEE International Conference on Neural Networks, Vol. 2, p. 163–168.
50. Van Gestel, T.; Baesens,B.; Van Dijcke, P.; Garcia J.; Suykens J.A.K.; Vanthienen, J. (2006). "A process model to develop an internal rating system: Sovereign credit ratings". Decision Support Systems, Vol 42, p. 1131–1151.
51. Taffler, R. (1983). "The assessment of company solvency and performance using a statistical model". Accounting and Business Research, Vol. 13, p. 295–307.
52. Trevino, L.; and Thomas S. (2000a). "Systematic differences in the determinants of foreign currency sovereign ratings by rating agency". Discussion papers in accounting and management science 00-153, School of Management, University of Southampton, UK.
53. Trevino, L.; and Thomas S. (2000b). "The statistical determinants of local currency sovereign ratings". Discussion papers in accounting and management science 00-158, School of Management, University of Southampton, UK.

54. Trevino, L.; and Thomas, S. (2001). "Local versus foreign currency ratings: What determines sovereign transfer risk?". Journal of Fixed Income, Vol. 11, No. 1, p. 65–76.
55. Trigueiros, D.; Taffler, R. (1996). "Neural networks and empirical research in accounting". Accounting and Business Research, Vol. 26, p. 347–355.
56. Truglia, V. J. (1999). "Moody's sovereign ratings: A ratings guide". Moody's Iinvestors Service Global Credit Research, special comment, March.
57. Vellido, A.; Lisboa, P.J.G.; Vaughan, J.; (1999). "Neural networks in business: a survey of applications (1992 – 1998)". Expert Systems with Applications, Vol. 17, p. 51-70.

THE EFFECT OF CHANGES OF THE HURST EXPONENT IN RETURN PREDICTABILITY: THE CASE OF THE DUTCH MARKET

LAURA LANZARINI

Instituto de Investigación en Informática LIDI,
Universidad Nacional de la Plata,
50 y 120 La Plata, Buenos Aires, Argentina

AURELIO FERNÁNDEZ BARIVIERA

Departament of Business, Universitat Rovira i Virgili,
Avenida de la Universitat,1 Reus, Spain

M. BELÉN GUERCIO

Departament of Business, Universitat Rovira i Virgili,
Avenida de la Universitat,1 Reus, Spain
Consejo Nacional de Investigaciones Científicas y Técnicas (CONICET), Argentina

CRISTINA TOMÁS-MONTERDE

Departament of Business, Universitat Rovira i Virgili,
Avenida de la Universitat,1 Reus, Spain

The Efficient Market Hypothesis, in its weakest form, tells that security prices reflect all the information contained in the series of past prices and precludes the possibility of forecasts based on them. This paper explores if changes in the Hurst exponent affect the forecasts provided by an Artificial Neural Network. We use a Multilayer Perceptron network to forecast the daily return of the indices of stock and corporate bonds in the Dutch market. The network is trained using a back propagation algorithm. Our main findings are: (i) the Artificial Neural Network reaches better returns than a simple buy-and-hold strategy and (ii) the change in the Hurst exponent, that supposedly reflects a change in the long-range memory in the time series, does not increase the goodness of the forecast. This implies that the Efficient Market Hypothesis in its weak form is cast into doubt but the change in the memory endowment is not detected by the ANN.

1. Introduction

Informational efficiency is a classic topic in financial economics. The role of capital markets in economics is very important. Since capital markets helps to allocate resources, it is on the best interest of the population that these resources are allocated in the most efficient way. One necessary condition for this allocation is that the prices in the stock and bond markets reflect properly the investment quality. In other words, prices must convey all relevant information to the public. This is exactly what the Efficient Market Hypothesis (EMH) says. A market is informational efficient if prices reflect all available information. In fact, Eiteman *et al.*[1], affirms that, in an efficient market, prices are "fair and equitable". The discussion in economics is focused on the information set against which the EMH should be tested. Fama [2], classifies informational efficiency in three categories: (i) weak efficiency, if stock prices reflect all the information contained in the history of past prices, (ii) semi-strong efficiency, if prices reflect all public known information, in addition to past prices, and (iii) strong efficiency, if prices reflect all kind of information, public and private. As a corollary, we cannot forecast prices based on the same information of the market because this information is immediately incorporated into prices.

According to the EMH, prices must follow a stochastic process without memory. One of the most common models is the random walk model. However, there are several examples of informational inefficiency. Especially beginning in the 1970s, researchers begun to report what was called at that moment "anomalies". One of the departures from the random walk model that is most difficult to rationalize within the standard financial theory is the presence of long memory. If time series exhibits long-range memory, then prediction can be based on past prices. Predictions in finance have been based upon standard statistical forecasting methods for many decades. Some decades ago, price forecasting did not receive much attention because of the limited computing capacity. With the advent of more powerful computers and more complex statistical methods, empirical research became a growing area of financial economics. Empirical research in financial economics and in econophysics detected the presence of nonlinear dynamics in financial markets. Nonlinearity implies that past price change can have a wide effect in future prices.

In this aspect, Artificial Neural Networks (ANNs) constitute mathematical constructs that helps to deal with nonlinear structures. ANNs are a class of biological inspired nonlinear models aimed to mimic neural systems.

Wong and Selvi [3], affirm that ANN are used in different disciplines, and "offer a significant support in terms of organizing, classifying and summarizing data", constituting a promising alternative tool for pattern recognition.

The use of ANN in economics and finance is broad and accepted. The use of neural networks to predict future movements in stock prices and returns is based on the idea that investors are rational and learn from past experience.

Supervised ANNs are characterized by their ability to learn, without assuming any explicit econometric model or relations in the time series.

Nakamura [4], finds that ANN gives better inflation forecasts than autorregresive models. Atsalakis and Valavanis [5] applies a neuro-fuzzy model to predict returns one day ahead and their results pose into question the EMH. [6] uses a modular neural network to predict call options, concluding that this modeling enhances the traditional Black & Scholes model. Wang [7], uses a combination of ANN and GARCH model and shows that this combination gives better results than the single use of ANN. Khashei and Bijari [8], proposes a model based on the Box and Jenkings [9] model and an ANN, obtaining better results than with the use of solely an ANN. Lanzarini *et al.* [10], uses an ANN, during different market situations (bear, stable and bull markets) in order to assess changes in predictability according to market situations.

The aim of this paper is to test if the change in the Hurst exponent can be used as an element to increase the predictability of stock and bond indices changes, which, in turn, will allow to test the weak form of market efficiency. We develop an Artificial Neural Network, that follows a trading rule and we compare the result with a buy-and-hold strategy. If the market is efficient the technical trading rule cannot outperform the market.

2. Long-range dependence

The seminal study of long range dependence of time series is Hurst [11]. In his paper, Hurst detected the presence of long memory in a variety of hydrological and biological time series. For many years, the R/S method constituted the most classical one to study the behavior of time series. However this method presents some drawbacks, specially in nonstationary time series [12]. For a survey on de different methods for estimating the Hurst exponent see Tacqu *et al.* [13], Montanari *et al.* [14] and Serinaldi [15].

One of the methods that is currently used and avoids the detection of spurious autocorrelation is the Detrended Fluctuation Analysis (DFA) developed by Peng *et al.* [16]. The algorithm for its calculation is described in detail in Peng *et al.* [17]. This method is considered better suited for dealing with financial time series as described in Bariviera [18]

3. Model

The prediction was solved by means of an ANN. For introductory texts on ANN see [19] and [20]. These kinds of constructs tend to simulate the way human beings learn, by examples and experience. Basically we can think of a neural network as a directed graph whose nodes are called neurons and the arcs that connect them have an associated weight. This value in some sense represents the "knowledge" acquired. Neurons are organized into layers according to their function: the input layer provides information to the network, the output layer provides the answer and the hidden layers are responsible for carrying out the mapping between input and output [19]. In this paper we use a multiperceptron neural network. It is a feedforward network, totally connected, organized in three layers: 9 input neurons, four neurons in a single hidden layer and one output neuron. This architecture coincides with the one used in [21] and [22]. The training of the multiperceptron is supervised and uses a backpropagation algorithm based in the gradient technique, adding the moments terms in order to speed convergence. The network was designed to forecast the market return.

Let $P = (p_1, p_2, ..., p_L)$ be the sequence of indices of figure 1, then the return at the moment $t + \rho$ is computed as indicated in (1):

$$r_{t+\rho} = \ln\left(\frac{p_{t+\rho}}{p_t}\right) \tag{1}$$

where $p_{t+\rho}$ and p_t are two price indices, ρ is the holding period, and $r_{t+\rho}$ is the continuous compound return. The fact that the training is supervised, implies knowing the expected value for each of the examples that will be used in the training.

Thus, it is required a set of ordered pairs $\{(X_1, Y_1), (X_2, Y_2), \ldots, (X_j, Y_j), \ldots, (X_M, Y_M)\}$ being $X_j = (x_{j,1}, x_{j,2}, \ldots, x_{j,N})$ the input vector and Y_j the answer value that it is expected that the network learns for that vector. In this case:

$$x_{j,k} = r_{j+\rho+k-1} = \ln\left(\frac{p_{j+\rho+k-1}}{p_{j+k-1}}\right) \qquad k = 1, \ldots N \tag{2}$$

$$Y_j = r_{j+2\rho+N-1} = \ln\left(\frac{p_{j+2\rho+N-1}}{p_{j+\rho+N-1}}\right) \tag{3}$$

The maximum number of pairs (X_j, Y_j) that can be formed with L indices is $M = L - N - \rho + 1$. The first half of them were used to train the network and the second half to verify its performance. Once the network is trained, its answer for vector X_j is computed as indicated in equation (4).

$$Y_j' = G\left(a_0 + \sum_{i=1}^{4} a_i F\left(b_{0,i} + \sum_{k=1}^{9} x_{j,k} b_{k,i}\right)\right) \tag{4}$$

where $x_{j,k}$ is the value corresponding to the k – th input defined in (2), $b_{k,i}$ is the weight of the arch that links the k – th neuron of the input with the i – th hidden neuron and a_i is the weight of the arch that links the i–th hidden neuron with the single output neuron of the network. We should note that each hidden neuron has an additional arch, whose value is indicated in $b_{0,i}$. This value is known as bias or trend term. A similar thing happens to the output neuron with the weight a_0. Finally, the obtained expected sign Y'_j will be used to do the corresponding forecast: +1 corresponds to an upward movement in the index -1 corresponds to a downward movement in the index.

4. Data and methodology

We use daily data of one index of corporate bonds (Barclays) and of the stock index (AEX) of Netherlands. The period under study goes from 31/07/1998 until 04/11/2011, with 3460 datapoints.

The profitability measures used on pairs (X_j , Y_j) of the training set are the following:

- ANN Buy&Hold Train: is the return obtained by a simple buy & hold strategy and is computed by adding all the expected returns of the training set as indicated in (5)

$$bhTrain = \sum_{j=1}^{M/2} Y_j \tag{5}$$

- ANN Buy&Hold Test: is equivalent to the previous measure but applied to the testing set.

$$bhTest = \sum_{j=1+M/2}^{M} Y_j \tag{6}$$

- Sign prediction ratio: We consider only the values 1 and –1 that were correctly predicted by the network.

$$SPR = \frac{\sum_{j=1+M/2}^{M} matches\left(Y_j, Y_j'\right)}{M/2} \tag{7}$$

$$Matches(Y_j, Y_j') = \begin{cases} 1 & if\ sign(Yj) = sign(Y_j') \\ 0 & otherwise \end{cases} \wedge \tag{8}$$

where sign is the sign function that maps +1 when the argument is positive and –1 when the argument is negative.

- The maximum return is obtained by adding all the expected values in absolute value

$$MaxReturn = \sum_{j=1+M/2}^{M} abs\left(Y_j\right) \tag{9}$$

and represents the maximum achievable return, assuming perfect forecast.

- The total return is computed in the following way

$$TotalReturn = \sum_{j=1+M/2}^{M} sign\left(Y_j^{'}\right) Y_j \tag{10}$$

where sign is the sign function. Notice that the better the network prediction the larger the total return.

- Ideal Profit Ratio is the ratio between the total return (10) and the maximum return (9).

$$IPR = \frac{TotalReturn}{MaxReturn} \tag{11}$$

- Sharpe Ratio is the ratio between the total return and its standard deviation. The different values of the total return arise from the several independent runs in the training of the network. This will give different networks that will generate different total returns.

$$SR = \frac{\mu_{TotalReturn}}{\sigma_{TotalReturn}} \tag{12}$$

5. Empirical results

Fernández Bariviera *et al.* (2012) detected a change in the behavior of the Hurst exponent due to the subprime crisis in seven European countries. Taking this into account, we compute the Hurst exponent using the DFA method for the two indices. The data used to separate the two periods is 15/09/2008, the day of the fall of Lehman Brothers. Grammatikos and Vermeulen [24] find that the effects of the subprime crisis became more evident in European markets, in particular in bond yields, after this date. According to our results show two distinct dynamics. On the one hand, the corporate bond index exhibits long-range dependence after the crisis but not before. On the other hand, the stock market index does not exhibit long memory in none of the two subperiods under examination.

Table 1. Estimation of the Hurst exponent

	Before crisis	After crisis
BARCLAYS	0.5187 (0.5653)	0.5797 (2.5372)
AEX	0.4840 (-0.5349)	0.5336 (1.033)

Taking this information into account we explore the profitability of the ANN in the two subperiods and for the whole period.

We did 20 independent runs for each of the subperiods. The maximum number of iterations was 3000. The initial weights for the network were distributed uniformly between −2.5 and 2.5. The learning speed was 0.05.

The functions F and G used by the neural network are:

$$F(n) = \frac{2}{1+e^{-2n}} - 1 \tag{13}$$

$$G(n) = n \tag{14}$$

Function (13) is a sigmoidal function bounded between −1 and 1. Function (4) is a linear function. In this way F allows hidden neurons to produce small values (either negative or positive), and G permits the net to produce continuous unbounded outputs.

We show the results obtained, by averaging the 20 runs and the performance of the ANN is compared with a buy-and-hold strategy. We also compute the performance metrics detailed in equations (7), (10), (11) and (12).

Our results are somewhat mixed. According to them, we detect that the ANN outperform the buy-and-hold strategy in the corporate bond index. In the case of the period 1998-2008 the ANN obtained a total return of 0.4693, whereas the passive strategy obtained -0.5824. For the period 2008-2011, the ANN total return was -0.0738, while the buy-and-hold strategy losses -0.1810. Regarding the stock index, the results are similar. In the first subperiod buy-and-hold return and ANN reach the same return, but in the second subperiod the ANN is better

If we look at the Ideal Profit Ratio (IPR), we observe that the prediction performance, *vis-à-vis* the perfect forecast is better in the first subperiod rather than in the second. This result is contradictory to our finding that the Hurst exponent in the second subperiod is greater than 0.5. It means that, either the ANN could not detect a change in the long-range dependence or that the Hurst exponent is an inadequate measure of long memory.

In order to analyze in detail the results of the ANN, we inform in Table 3 and Table 4 about the prediction ratios. It is very interesting that, regarding stock returns, the ANN predicts positive returns better than negative returns. Nevertheless, predictions of corporate bond returns behave differently. In the first subperiod the ANN predicts 52.56% of the negative returns and only 1.5% of the positive returns. In the second subperiod the ANN predicts only 12.59% of the negative returns but guess correctly 34.97% of the positive returns. This distinct behavior in stock and bonds markets could indicate that the stochastic dynamics in both markets are different.

Table 2. ANN Results

Period	B&H train	B&H test	SPR	TR	IPR	SR	MR
BARCLAYS_1998_2011	-0.0337	-0.1755	0.4676	-0.7145	-0.0986	-3.7338	7.2420
BARCLAYS_1998_2008	-0.1364	-0.5824	0.5406	0.4693	0.1045	7.7894	4.4905
BARCLAYS_2008_2011	0.9538	-0.1810	0.4756	-0.0738	-0.0422	-0.5599	1.7469
AEX_1998_2011	-2.2441	-1.3500	0.4780	-2.8456	-0.0621	-3.5645	45.8052
AEX_1998_2008	-2.9202	1.1302	0.5893	1.1302	0.0422		26.7222
AEX_2008_2011	1.5983	-1.0065	0.4899	-0.9860	-0.0977	-4.1416	10.0919

Table 3. Prediction ratio of corporate bond returns

		BARCLAYS_1998_2011		BARCLAYS_1998_2008		BARCLAYS_2008_2011	
		Prediction					
		−1	+1	−1	+1	−1	+1
True change	−1	33.54%	17.36%	52.56%	2.47%	12.59%	40.93%
	+1	35.87%	13.23%	43.47%	1.50%	11.51%	34.97%

Table 4. Prediction ratio of stock returns

		AEX_1998_2011		AEX_1998_2008		AEX_2008_2011	
		Prediction					
		−1	+1	−1	+1	−1	+1
True change	−1	24.26%	19.71%	0.03%	41.05%	3.39%	45.85%
	+1	32.48%	23.54%	0.02%	58.90%	5.15%	45.60%

6. Conclusions

We compare the performance of an ANN with a naïve buy-and-hold strategy for the stock index and the corporate bond index of The Netherlands during the period 1998-2011. We split the time series into two non-overlapping subperiods: 1998-2008 and 2008-2011. The division line was 15/09/2008, the day of the fall of Lehman Brothers. Both subperiods exhibits different Hurst exponents. According to our results, the ANN outperforms the buy-and-hold strategy in both subperiods. However, the change in the Hurst exponent is not detected by the ANN, since the Ideal Profit Ratio of the second subperiod is worse than the first subperiod. We detect a distinct behavior of stock and bond markets in both periods, which could indicate the asymmetric impact of the crisis in them. In particular we detect that the stock market is more efficient than the corporate bond market, since the prediction in the latter is worse than in the former market. Consequently the EMH for the corporate bond index is cast into doubt. We believe that more research on this topic could be of interest for practitioners and policy makers. In future works, we would like to explore the possibility to include the Hurst exponent as an input of the ANN.

References

[1] W.J. Eiteman, C.A. Dice and D.K. Eiteman, McGraw-Hill, New York, 4th edition (1966).
[2] E.F. Fama, *J. Financ.* **25**, 383 (1970).
[3] B.K. Wong and Y. Selvi, *Inform. Manage.* **34**, 129 (1998).
[4] E. Nakamura, *Econ. Lett.* **86**, 373 (2005).
[5] G.S. Atsalakis and K.P. Valavanis, *Expert Syst. Appl.* **36**, 10696 (2009).
[6] N. Gradojevic, R. Gençay and D. Kukolj, *IEEE T Neural Networ.* **20**, 626 (2009)
[7] Y.H. Wang, *Qual Quant.* **43**, 833 (2009).
[8] M. Khashei and M. Bijari, *Expert Syst. Appl.* **37**, 479 (2010).
[9] G.E.P. Box, G.M. Jenkins and G.C. Reinsel, *Prentice Hall*, Englewood Cliffs (1994).
[10] L. Lanzarini, J.M. Iglesias and A. Fernández Bariviera, World Congress IFSA (2011).
[11] H.E. Hurst, *Trans. Amer. Soc. Civil Eng.* **116**, 770 (1951).
[12] P. Grau-Carles, *Physica A.* **287**, 396 (2000).
[13] M.S. Taqqu, V. Teverovsky and W. Willinger, *Fractals.* **3**, 785 (1995).
[14] A. Montanari, M.S. Taqqu and V. Teverovsky, *Math. Comput. Model.* **29**, 217 (1999).
[15] F. Serinaldi, *Physica A.* **389**, 2770 (2010).

[16] C.K. Peng, S.V. Buldyrev, S. Havlin, M. Simons, H.E. Stanley and A.L. Goldberger, *Phys. Rev.* E. **49**, 1685 (1994).
[17] C.K. Peng, S. Havlin, H.E. Stanley and A.L. Goldberger, *Chaos*. **5**, 82 (1995).
[18] Bariviera, A.F., *Physica A.*,**390**, 4426 (2011).
[19] J.A.Freeman and D.M. Skapura, *Addison-Wesley Publishing Company*, (1991).
[20] P. Isasi and I.M. Galván, *Pearson - Pentice Hall*, (2004).
[21] R. Gençay, *J. Int. Econ.* **47**, 91 (1999).
[22] F. Fernández-Rodríguez, C. González-Martel and S. Sosvilla-Rivero, Econ. Lett. **69**, 89 (2000).
[23] A. Fernández Bariviera, M.B. Guercio and L.B. Martinez, *Econ. Lett.* http://dx.doi.org/10.1016/j.econlet.2012.04.047 (2012).
[24] T. Grammatikos and R. Vermeulen, *J. Int. Money Financ.* **31,** 517 (2012).

PART 6: KNOWLEDGE MANAGEMENT AND INNOVATION

ORGANIZATIONAL LEARNING IN COMPLEX ENVIRONMENTS: EXPLORATION AND EXPLOITATION IN A NK LANDSCAPE

BOCANET ANCA
University of Naples Federico II, Engineering School, Dept. of Business and Managerial Engineering, Piazzale Tecchio 80, 80125, Naples, Italy

IANDOLI LUCA
University of Naples Federico II, Engineering School, Dept. of Business and Managerial Engineering, Piazzale Tecchio 80, 80125, Naples, Italy

PONSIGLIONE CRISTINA
University of Naples Federico II, Engineering School, Dept. of Business and Managerial Engineering, Piazzale Tecchio 80, 80125, Naples, Italy

ZOLLO GIUSEPPE
University of Naples Federico II, Engineering School, Dept. of Business and Managerial Engineering, Piazzale Tecchio 80, 80125, Naples, Italy

In today's complex and dynamic business environment, organizational learning is a key factor for success (Nonaka, 1991). Within the organizational learning research, finding a trade-off between exploration and exploitation has been proposed as a way to survive in a complex, competitive environment. March's (1991) seminal paper is a go-to citation for anybody talking about exploration and exploitation. Many attempts to replicate and extend the original model have been proposed, but none considered the complexity of the external environment. This work aims at filling this gap and at extending March's exploration-exploitation model (1991) by modelling the external environment as an NK Landscape (Kauffman, 1993).

1. Introduction

This paper is based on the assumption that organizational learning is a purposive quest to retain and to improve competitiveness, productivity and innovativeness in uncertain technological, market and environmental circumstances (Dharmadasa, 2009). Within the organizational learning research, finding a trade-off between exploration and exploitation has been proposed as a way to survive in a complex, competitive environment.

March's (1991) seminal paper, "Exploration and Exploitation in Organizational Learning" is a go-to citation for anybody talking about exploration and exploitation. Many attempts to replicate and extend the original model have been proposed, but none considered the complexity of the external environment. This study aims at extending March's exploration-exploitation model (1991) by modeling the external environment as an NK Landscape (Kauffman, 1993).

One key element to be considered when analyzing the exploration-exploitation dynamics within the organizations is their connection with the complexity of the external environment. Environmental dynamism and competitive intensity may moderate the performance effects of balancing exploration and exploitation, so that the effectiveness of exploratory innovation improves in turbulent environments, whereas exploitative innovation becomes more beneficial in competitive environments (Jansen et al., 2006). Understanding the influence of complexity on the performance of human organizations can lead to major gains in the conduct of human affairs.

We start from a model of mutual learning in organizations (March, 1991) and analyze how the environmental complexity influences the intra-organizational balance between exploration and exploitation strategies. The aspect of how the external complexity influences the balance between exploration and exploitation remains to be analysed as the existing literature does not provide specific models to deal this issue.

This outline raises the following research question:

What effect has the environmental complexity on the emerging balance between exploration and exploitation within organizations?

This research question can be articulated into the following sub-questions:

How can we model the concept of reality complexity in which organizations evolve?

What is the effect of the internal and external complexity on the balance between exploration and exploitation processes?

In studying the complexity of organizational behavior as an interaction of multiple interdependent processes, a systematic methodology for theory development and analysis is needed. Specifically, computational modeling has unique advantages in this respect (Axelrod 1997; Taber and Timpone, 1996). Well suited for the study of complex behavioral systems, computer simulations show greatest utility for gaining theoretical insights through developing theories and exploring their consequences (Cohen and Cyert, 1965). While a number of typologies of simulation models have been proposed (e.g., Burton 2003, Cohen and Cyert, 1965, Macy and Willer, 2002), the agent-based modeling is the approach used to model the learning behavior of individual and organizational agents and to examine the effects of exploration and exploitation on organizational knowledge.

2. Background

This section is articulated in two parts; in the first one we introduce the concepts of exploration and exploitation, in the second one we describe the March's model of exploration and exploitation and discuss some of its main extensions.

2.1 *Exploration and exploration in organizational learning*

The concepts of exploration and exploitation have been used in various contexts such as technology and product innovation (e.g., Danneels, 2002; Greve, 2007; He and Wong, 2004; Tushman, 2003), strategic alliances (e.g., Beckman, Haunschild and Phillips, 2004; Koza and Lewin, 1998; Lavie and Rosenkopf, 2006; Rothaermel, 2001; Rothaermel and Deeds, 2004), and senior-management teams (e.g., Beckman, 2006; McGrath, 2001). Furthermore, the notions of exploration and exploitation have been investigated at different levels of analysis, generating research at the individual (e.g., Mom, Van den Bosch and Volberda, 2007), group (e.g., Beckman, 2006; McGrath, 2001), organizational (e.g., Benner and Tushman, 2002; Greve, 2007; Harreld, O'Reilly and Tushman, 2007; Jansen, Van Den Bosch and Volberda, 2006), inter-organizational (e.g., Lavie and Rosenkopf, 2006; Lin, Yang and Demirkan, 2007; Rothaermel, 2001; Vassolo, Anand, ad Folta, 2004), and industry levels (e.g., Gilsing and Nooteboom, 2006).

Most of the organizational learning scholars investigated exploration and exploitation concepts as learning types: double loop vs. single loop learning (Argyris and Schon, 1978); generative vs. adaptive learning (Senge, 1990); acquisitive vs. experimental learning (Dess et al., 2003); product innovation-oriented vs. production-oriented learning (McKee, 1992); second-order vs. first-order learning (Levinthal and March, 1981; Rosenkopf and Nerkar, 2001; Nooteboom, 2000) and learning in chaotic conditions vs. learning in stable conditions (Cheng and Van de Ven, 1996).

Scholars have classified exploration and exploitation also as knowledge creation and knowledge reutilization processes. Knowledge exploration and exploitation are based on knowledge flow that is, and will be, repeated continuously throughout an organization's history: knowledge flow generates knowledge outcomes that can be reused later (Maki, 2008). Mainstream studies presented exploitation as the process of gaining competence by adopting, synthesizing, and applying current or existing knowledge, whereas exploration represents the ability to acquire new knowledge (Levinthal and March, 1993; Liu, 2006; McNamara and Baden-Fuller, 1999). Van den Bosch et al. (1999) considered exploitation as knowledge absorption efficiency and exploration as knowledge scope and flexibility, while Sheremata (2000) considered them as collective vs. creative action.

Last but not least, exploration/exploitation concepts have been characterized as search processes (Katila and Ahuja, 2002; Levinthal, 1997; Rivkin and Siggelkow, 2003). Vermeulen and Barkema (2001: 459) defined exploration as the "search for new knowledge" and exploitation as the "ongoing use of a firm's knowledge base." Exploration was operationalized as search scope (i.e., the propensity to cite different patents), whereas exploitation was operationalized as search depth (i.e., the propensity to cite certain patents repeatedly) (Katila and Ahuja, 2002).

Coming back to organizational learning literature, March (1991) defines exploration as 'things captured by terms such as search, variation, risk taking, experimentation, play, flexibility, discovery, innovation', and exploitation as 'such things as refinement, choice, production, efficiency, selection, implementation, execution' (March: 71). This definition allows for various interpretations. As Sinkula (1994), Slater and Narver (1995) later affirmed, exploration is a manifestation of organizational learning characterized by activities such as search, variation, risk-taking, discovery, innovation, and research and development. March (1991) continues stating that the distinction between exploration and exploitation captures a number of fundamental differences in firm behavior that have significant consequences on a firm's performance. Exploration is associated with organic structures, loosely coupled systems, path breaking, improvisation, autonomy and chaos, and emerging markets and technologies. March (1991, p. 85) posits that the outcome of exploration can be difficult to measure in the short-term. He argues that the organizational return from exploration can be uncertain, distant, and often negative: the distance in time and space between the locus of learning and the locus for the realization of returns is usually greater in the case of exploration than in the case of exploitation, as is the uncertainty. In short, exploration might be effective but due to its long-term nature, it might lack a high degree of efficiency. Exploitation on the other side has been related to efficiency, centralization, convergence, and tight cultures, whereas exploration has been associated with flexibility, decentralization, divergence, and loose cultures (Benner and Tushman, 2003; Jansen et al. 2006).

Previous research on organizational learning and innovation has consistently argued that exploration and exploitation draw on different structures, processes, and resources (He and Wong, 2004), and they differ significantly in their performance outcomes over time. By reducing variety, increasing efficiency and improving adaptation to current environments, exploitation activities can produce positive performance effects in the short run. However, these short-term performance improvements might come at the expense of long term performance, since the reduced variety and the adaptation to an existing environment become liabilities as environments change over time. Firms emphasizing exploitation in their activities might lack the capability to adapt to significant environment changes. The recipe that makes these firms successful in the short run might endanger their success in the long run. Exploration-oriented activities help the firm to develop new knowledge and create those capabilities necessary to survive and prosper in the long run. However, exploration activities are uncertain in their pay-offs and their performance effects occur in the long run. Without a balancing orientation towards exploitation, exploration can be similarly detrimental for the firm locking it into a cycle in which "failure leads to search and change which leads to failure which leads to more search, and so on" (Levinthal and March, 1993: 105).

2.2. *March's model of exploration and exploitation*

Central to March's 1991 paper is a simulation model representing the formation and the evolution of the learning process of an organization from its members and vice versa. The original model is based on an external reality, an individual knowledge about the external reality, and an organizational code representing an approximation of the external reality derived from individuals' knowledge. There are four key features of the model:

- The organization's environment, called *external reality,* is independent of organization's members' beliefs. The reality is modeled as an m-dimensional vector, each of dimensions taking a value of 1 or -1 with equal probability.

- *N individuals* holding beliefs about each of the m dimensions of the organization's environment. The individuals' beliefs can take the values of -1, 0, or 1, where 0 represents the absence of a belief about a particular dimension of the reality. We will refer to beliefs with the value "0" as the "I don't know" beliefs.

- There is an *organizational code*, or the storage of all the knowledge that the organization has accumulated over time in its process of learning from its members. Organization's members change their beliefs through the process of learning from this code as a consequence of socialization and education. In each period, if the code differs on a particular dimension from the beliefs of an individual, the later will change his belief according to that of the code with the probability of p1. This is the probability that reveals how successful is the learning from the *code (*socialization process*)*

- The organization's code adjusts its beliefs to the ones of those individuals whose beliefs better match the ones of reality, with the probability of p_2. How? First, it is allocated a *score* to each individual and to the code. The score is given by the number of dimensions whose beliefs agree with those of the reality. The individuals with a lower score than the one of the code will be ignored. The individuals left are grouped and called *superior group,* they are the ones with dominant beliefs. Within the superior group, the *majority belief* on each dimension is selected. For every dimension, if the code has the same belief like the majority belief from the superior group, it will remain unchanged. But if the code differs from the majority belief of the superior group, it will change according to the later with the probability $1\text{-}(1\text{-}p_2)^k$, where k is the number of individuals within the superior group that share the majority belief minus the number of individuals who do not.

The initial conditions of the model consist of a fixed reality, m dimensional, with each dimension taking with equal probability values of 1 and -1; an organizational code initialized with neutral beliefs on all dimensions; n individuals, m dimensional, each dimension taking with equal probabilities the values of 0, 1, -1. The state of knowledge is measured at any particular time as the proportion of reality correctly represented in the organizational code and on average in individuals' beliefs for every period. Thus, knowledge depends on the extent to which beliefs match the external reality. But neither the individuals, nor the organization contain any information of reality. The organizational code knows just which individuals are closer to reality than it is, but not on which dimensions. In this context, both organization and the members can reproduce false beliefs in their processes of exploration and exploitation. Changes in beliefs help in eliminating the differences between the code and the individuals. Consequently, the beliefs of individuals and the code converge over time. As individuals in the organization become more knowledgeable, they also become more homogeneous with respect to knowledge. Equilibrium is reached when all individuals and the code share the same (not necessarily accurate) belief with respect to each dimension (March, 1991, p.75). From this point, nothing can change in the system.

Most of the studies that extended March's original model analyzed what impact has different types of organizational structures on exploration-exploitation activities (Bray and Prietula, 2007; Fang et al., 2007, 2010; Kane and Prietula, 2006; Miller et al., 2006). The rest of the papers examined the role of the environmental dynamism on the exploration-exploitation learning processes within organizations (Bray and Prietula, 2007; Fang et al., 2010; Kim and Rhee, 2009). Table 1 summarizes the characteristics of main extensions of March's original model.

Table 1: March's model extensions

Title	References	Extensions
Influence and Structure: Extending a model of organizational learning	Kane. and Prietula (2006)	- the influence of others (individuals learning from each other); - the influence of groups (thee population is divided into functional groups and the learning at group level is introduced); - consequence of structure (team-based and hierarchical structures)
Adding interpersonal learning and tacit knowledge to march's exploration-exploitation model	Miller et al. (2006)	(1) direct interpersonal learning, (2) locating individuals in a space, which makes the distinction between local and distant search relevant, (3) recognizing that knowledge has a tacit dimension that cannot be transmitted through codification.
'Exploration and exploitation revisited: extending March's model of mutual learning'	Rodan (2005)	Introduced a number of real-world organizational features.
Extending March's Exploration and Exploitation: Managing Knowledge in Turbulent Environments	Bray and Prietula (2007)	A reporting structure allows for multi-tier organizational hierarchies The effects of a knowledge management system that collects knowledge from a set ratio of experts.
Information Technology and Organizational Learning: An Investigation of Exploration and Exploitation Processes	Kane and Alavi (2005)	Introduce IT-enabled learning mechanisms: communication technology (e-mail), knowledge repositories of best practices, and groupware.

'Exploration and Exploitation: The Influence of Organizational Structure on Organizational Learning'	Fang (2007)	They argue that an organization divided into semi-isolated subgroups may help strike this balance. They simulated an organization, systematically varying the interaction pattern between individuals to explore how the degree of subgroup isolation and inter-group connectivity influences organizational learning.
'Exploration and exploitation: internal variety and environmental dynamism'	Tohyun and Mooweon (2009)	(1) conceptualization and variation on two dimensions – amplitude and frequency – of environmental dynamism (2) articulating the notion of internal variety in an organization.

Miller et al. (2006) paper is maybe the first work that extended most of March's model's components. They extended the model by considering learning between individuals, by locating them in a problem space which make the distinction between local and distant search and by recognizing a tacit dimension of the organizational learning which cannot be transmitted through the organizational code. Tacit knowledge can only be transferred directly from person to person, not via an organizational code. The individuals are placed in a grid in which each has four neighbours (north, east, south, and west). Individuals learn through engaging in local and distant search. Local search means finding the best performer among one's four neighbours and then updating each belief according to that of the superior neighbour with probability p3. If two or more neighbours have equally good performance, one of them is chosen randomly as the superior. If the best-per- forming neighbour has a knowledge level lower than the searcher, then the individual engages in distant search. Distant search means randomly drawing four individuals from the population and choosing the best performer among them. If the knowledge of this best performer is superior to that of the searcher, then the searcher adopts each of the source's beliefs with probability p4.

The main findings of Miller et al. (2006) work are: first, in the presence of turnover, high rates of local learning are advantageous because rapid local learning allows for some retention of tacit knowledge. Second, the turnover does not influence the accumulation of codified knowledge. Third, except when turnover is extremely low and the rate of local learning is high, turnover is detrimental to the accumulation of tacit knowledge (Miller et al., 2006: 719).

Also Fang et al. (2007) extend the original model of March by considering the influence of organization's structure on organizational learning. In this context, exploitation occurs from learning across subgroups, which facilitates rapid diffusion and assimilation of currently superior knowledge, while reducing heterogeneity of knowledge within the firm. Exploration arises from the parallel, isolated learning within each subgroup, which preserves the variety of knowledge in an organization. A productive balance between exploration and exploitation can thus be achieved when an organization is broken down into semi-autonomous subunits with a small fraction of cross-group links.

3. The proposed March-NK model

The methodological section of this paper aims at extending March's exploration-exploitation model (1991) by modeling the external environment as an NK Landscape (Kauffman, 1993) and understanding, in this way, the influence of increasing complexity of the background in which organizations perform. The March-NK model represents the core of this paper, incorporates the logic of March (1991) on the dynamics between exploration and exploitation learning modes, and the NK model as a method to represent complexity of the environment. By representing the complexity of the external environment as a fitness landscape, we manage to create a more realistic organizational context. Complexity increases with the degree of interdependencies between agents' beliefs, and, in this way, we can "tune" the landscape just by modifying one parameter, K.

Although NK model was originally developed for biological evolution means, the model can appeal also to organizational researchers. This appeal is due to the NK model's explicit representation of interactions among the components of combinatorial systems and of how these interactions affect each component's performance, and therefore systemic performance as a whole.

The elements of the proposed model are summarized in the following list.

- Individuals

Individuals represent the members of an organization, or of any kind of institution. They have their own opinions and beliefs and they continuously learn and change their knowledge map, by socialization and learning from the memory of the organization. In the March-NK model, the performance implication of each knowledge belief is assumed to be unknown to the agents. They have to search the landscape of possibilities and actively engage in undertaking configurations of beliefs. This search is not comprehensive since the total possible combinations overcome by far the number of attempts. A new configuration is only adopted when the performance improves.

- Organizational Code (OC)

OC represents the storage of all the knowledge, ideas and experience that the organization has accumulated over time in its process of learning from its members. We assume here that organizational knowledge is not only incorporated into the heads of organizational members but also into a set of routines, shared representations, artifacts which shape individual behaviors, and so on. All these features form the organizational memory; here all the capabilities/competencies accumulated are stored.

- Organizational learning

Strictly speaking, "organizational learning" is only a metaphor since "all learning take place inside human heads", thus, as Simon (1991) says, "an organization learns in only two ways, by the learning of its members, or by injecting new members who have knowledge the organization did not previously have". The organization adapts to the beliefs of those members with higher fitness than the organization. This process represents the upward causal influence of the members on the organization. The probability that the organization will conform to the dominant viewpoint of its superior members is represented by the parameter p2.

- Organizational members' learning

Members constantly alter their beliefs according to an organizational socialization process. This process represents the downward causal influence of the organization on its members. If the fitness of the organizational code is higher than that of an individual, this individual will update its beliefs to those of the organizational code with probability p1.

- The search space

Central in our model is the representation of the search space. This space is obtained by using the NK model, in which:

- N reflects the number of dimensions, the number of significant components or attributes characterizing an adaptive entity.
- "b" is the number of levels each N component can assume and it is typically binary.
- K represents the number of epistatic links, the number of other n components that are interdependent with a given component. Therefore, b^N reflects the size of the design space, which increases exponentially with increasing N. The interdependence parameter, K, ranges from 0 to N-1 while it "tunes" the landscape (Kauffman, 1993). When K=0, the landscape is highly correlated (i.e. the fitness of nearest neighbour is highly correlated) with a single local, therefore global, optimum. As K increases to N-1, the landscape becomes highly *rugged*, with many local optima and steep slopes.

In March's model (1991) the organization is modeled as a number of individuals and an organizational code, both holding beliefs about a fixed external reality. The effects of the environment are indirect, neither the individuals nor the organization experience reality.

Our model integrates March's simulation model with Kauffman's NK search algorithm (1993). The idea is to replace the 'reality' from March's model with a rugged landscape formed by individuals and organizational code in their attempt to search the environment. The scores of the individuals and of the organizational code represent the payoffs calculated according to the NK model. The generation of the NK Landscape is the most challenging step within the entire development process. The NK space is generated at the beginning of each simulation run. It is conceptualized as a matrix of all possible positions in the N-dimensional binary space and their corresponding fitness. The overall landscape is created by randomly generating $2^{(k+1)}$ *N fitness values. The mapping for a belief x is given by:

$$f(x,N,K)=\frac{\sum_{i=1}^{N} f_i(x_i;x_{j(i)}^{1}....x_{j(i)}^{K})}{N}, \quad i\notin j(i)$$

For any i we obtain a vector of indexes j(i) mapping from N to Nk and where $x_{j(i)}^{K}$ means that the index of x is the kth element of the vector j(i).

The fitness landscape is generated at the beginning of each simulation run. We have first created a matrix of all possible positions in the landscape (the N-dimension binary space) and their corresponding fitness. The global fitness (the 'score' from March's model) is calculated by selecting the maximum fitness and placing the appropriate entry in the corresponding position.

3.1 *Simulation of the model*

The simulation of the model starts by defining the parameters and the probabilities; the following step is the score calculation for the organizational code and the individuals. The fitness landscape is created every cycle of the process. There are 2m possible values to define the fitness landscape. Each belief can take 2(k+1) values (as each belief is interdependent of other K beliefs). The model is based upon the fact that both code and individuals are trying to learn mutually, and in this process they are trying to obtain overall better score. A group of superior individuals is formed, representing the organizational members with the highest fitness/ score/ performances. The Organizational Code (OC) adapts to the main belief of this group with probability p2, and also inferior individuals adopt the OC's beliefs, and the cycle is repeating until both the OC and the individuals reach the equilibrium knowledge.

The results of this model are sensitive to the sequencing of steps presented in figure 1. The NK landscape is generated at the beginning of each simulation run followed by the initialization of the code and individuals with equal probabilities, score calculation, updating individuals and code, calculating the score for the updated values until we obtain the same equilibrium value for the score of the organizational code and the average score of the members of the organization.

Figure 1: Steps of the March-NK model

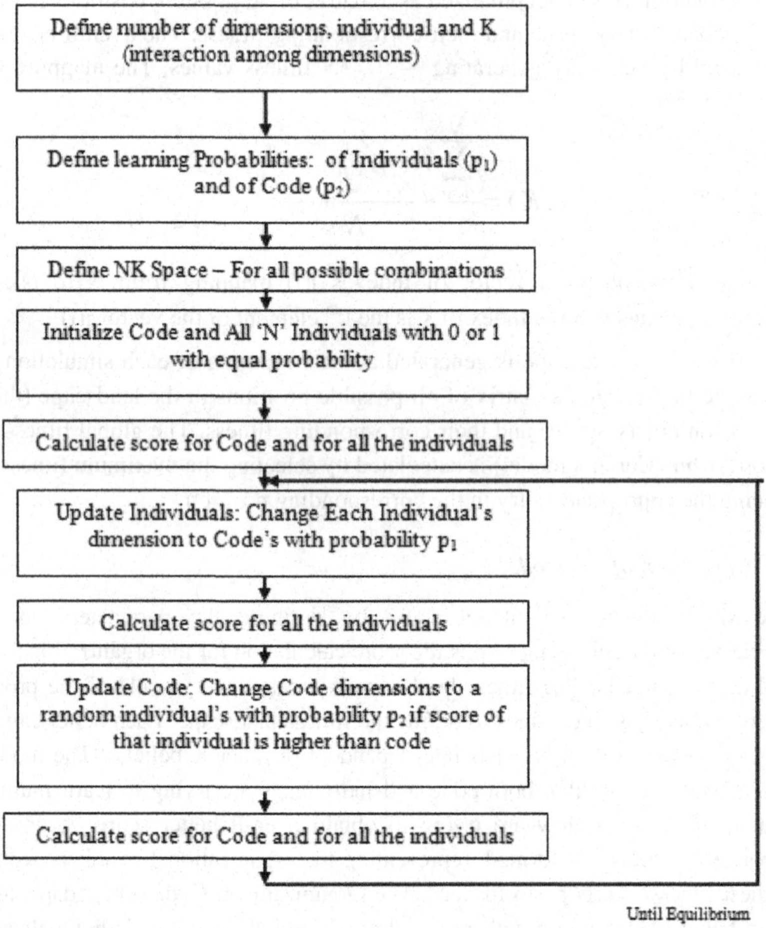

Define number of dimensions, individual and K (interaction among dimensions)

Define learning Probabilities: of Individuals (p_1) and of Code (p_2)

Define NK Space – For all possible combinations

Initialize Code and All 'N' Individuals with 0 or 1 with equal probability

Calculate score for Code and for all the individuals

Update Individuals: Change Each Individual's dimension to Code's with probability p_1

Calculate score for all the individuals

Update Code: Change Code dimensions to a random individual's with probability p_2 if score of that individual is higher than code

Calculate score for Code and for all the individuals

Until Equilibrium

4. Experimental settings

Based on the assumption that "the equilibrium level of knowledge attained by an organization depends interactively on the two learning parameters" (March, 1991:75), for this model we explored three main situations. This section is devoted to a brief presentation of performed simulation experiments. Table 2 presents the description of the three experiments developed for the March-NK model.

Table 2: Experiments for March-NK model

Experiment 1 **Effects of Learning Rates on Equilibrium Knowledge**	This experiment analyzes the effect of complexity on learning performances of an organization represented as a closed system. In particular, the aim of this experiment is to understand the impact of the rugged problem space on the dynamics of the learning rates p_1 and p_2.
Experiment 2 **Effects of Heterogeneous Socialization Rates on Equilibrium Knowledge**	This experiment initializes an organization composed of both slow learners (p_1=0.1) and fast learners (p_1=0.9) to investigate the effect of heterogeneous socialization rates in different complex environments.
Experiment 3 **Effect of Turnover and Socialization Rates on Period-20 Knowledge**	An alternative method to generate diversity in organizations is by considering the turnover rate. In this experiment, for each time period, each member has probability p_3 of leaving the firm. If one member leaves the organization, it is replaced with a new individual. The new member will have an initial randomly assigned knowledge.

For the experiments reported here, the number of dimensions is fixed at 30, the number of organizational members is fixed at 50, and the degree of interdependency between dimensions (complexity parameter) is fixed at 1, 3, 5, 10, and 15. The value of p1 (the socialization rate) is varied over nine levels (0.1:0.9) and p2 (organizational learning) over three levels (0.1, 0.5, and 0.9) to consider slow, medium and fast learning. For each set of parametric combinations we performed 80 runs and reported the average score of the organizational code at the equilibrium.

These experiments reproduce exactly the experiments performed by March in 1991 in order to allow us to both analyze the effects of increasing complexity on exploration-exploitation trade-off and the differences in the behavior of March and of our model.

Table 3 illustrates the experimental settings more in depth.

Table 3: Experimental Settings for March-NK model

Experiment	p1 (members learning from the organizational code)	p2 (organization learning from the superior members)	p3 (turnover rate)	K (complexity parameter)
1	0.1, 0.2,…….,0.9	0.1, 0.5, and 0.9		1, 3, 5, 10, 15
2	0,1, 0.2,….,0.9	0.5	-	1, 3, 5, 10, 15
3	0.1 and 0.9	0.5	0.1, 0.2,.,0.9	1, 3, 5, 10, 15

We used MatLab 2009 package. Each simulation was repeated 80 times in order to obtain accurate results. After the first round each simulation used the learned episodes from the previous round, but randomized the agents' positions and identity.

5. Results

Figure 2: Effects of learning rates on Average Equilibrium Knowledge (K=1)

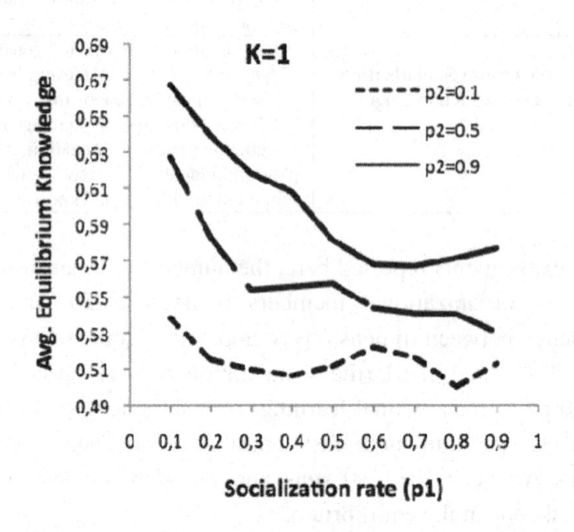

Figure 2 reports the effect of the learning rates on the equilibrium knowledge. The aim of this experiment is to understand the impact of the rugged problem space (determined by the parameter K) on the dynamics of learning rates p1 and p2. On the x-axis it is represented the socialization rate of the members of an organization, the probability regulating individuals' learning from the organizational code. The y-axis represents the average equilibrium knowledge, the points where the individuals' learning and the organizational learning converge to equilibrium.

In the case of figure 2 the problem space is characterized by a low value of complexity, meaning that each belief is related to one other belief. It preserves March's findings (1991) that maximized equilibrium knowledge is reached when organizational code adapts quickly and there is a diversity of beliefs maintained thanks to a slow socialization rate. We also notice from figure 3 that as K increases the average equilibrium knowledge for each value of p1 and p2 tends to converge to 0.5, which means that the complexity infuses a randomness effect on the overall system performance. Because of this entropy observed, it is very difficult to establish a rule in order to cope with the constant increasing complexity.

Figure 3: Effects of learning rates on Average Equilibrium Knowledge

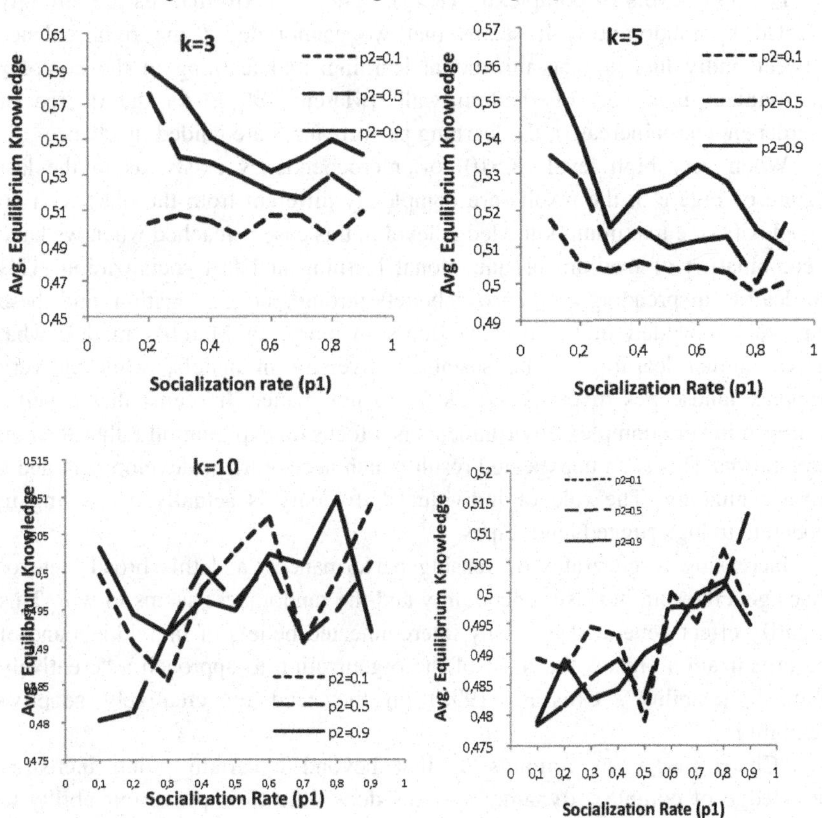

Another result is that for low and moderate values of complexity ($0<K\leq 5$) it is possible to find qualitatively the results of March (1991) and also of Miller et al. (2006) in terms of the right balance between exploration and exploitation. This result is best illustrated in figure 3. Best performances are achieved when the organizational memory adapts very fast to the best practices in organization and individuals are able to preserve some of their initial diversity. So, for low and moderate levels of complexity, a balance between exploration and exploitation is possible to be determined. Different from March's and Miller's findings, there is not a big difference between performances for low level of socialization (p1) and for high levels of p1 (for different values of K). This can imply that the role of diversity in influencing the equilibrium knowledge decreases as K increases due to a strong effect of randomness. In other words, the role of the exploration learning rate to inject diversity is not fundamental for the overall learning in the presence of rugged landscape.

For high levels of complexity ($K>5$), system's performances are strongly affected by randomness. It seems that we cannot detect the right balance between individual and organizational learning, and learning in the complex environment is a sort of random walk (March, 1991). As the degree of interdependences increases, the learning performances are guided by chance.

When very high level ($K>10$) of interdependency exists, as in the last picture of Figure 3, the results are completely different from the ones with no complexity; the maximum knowledge level in this case is reached when we have a combination of medium organizational learning and fast socialization. This can lead to a spreading of incorrect beliefs throughout organization, and these may get embedded in the organization's memory. In March's model, what drives mutual learning is the sustained diversity in beliefs, while in very complex landscapes diversity seems to do not matter. It seems that a better approach in very complex environments is a focus on exploitation rather than on exploration. This is an unexpected result which needs further development and a close evaluation. The role of individuals' diversity is actually decreasing in moderate to high rugged landscapes.

Increasing K generates decreasing performances, and this broad state of chaos generates an intrinsic uncertainty and the randomness seems to win. This butterfly effect generated by many interconnected beliefs of individuals and of the organization creates the need of the organization to approach a "creatively adapted flexibility". Crossan (1998) on the need for creatively adaptive flexibility:

"Chaos theory … reminds us that beyond a certain point, increased knowledge of complex, dynamic systems does little to improve our ability to extend the horizon of predictability of those systems. We can know, but we cannot predict. Hence, having the capacity to respond in a spontaneous fashion is critical.... Interpreting the environment, seeing it in its full richness and complexity is one of the critical challenges facing organizations. Organizations are often plagued by the inability of their members to break out of familiar patterns of interpreting customer needs, or competitive responses.... Expanding individual and organizational ability to perceive opportunities and threats to the environment is only valuable, however, if that new understanding is reflected in the pattern of actions of the organization: its strategy (p. 595).... "

Even Kauffman in one of his studies (1994: 154) suggests that systems tend to evolve into the edge of chaos on their own, whether they begin in an ordered or a chaotic state. Complex problems with a high degree of interdependency create rugged landscapes with multiple local peaks, and as a result, organization may become easily stuck (Levinthal, 1997; Rivkin, 2001).

Also, the more rugged a landscape, the higher the possible swings in performance. The K parameter influences the extent to which two configurations differ in performance. The maximum performance difference between two neighbouring configurations is given by (K+1)/N. It also implies that the expected performance difference between two configurations increases in K and in the number of changed attributes. Those properties of the NK model tend to make agents of the model more hesitant in more complex landscapes.

5.1. *Experiment 2: Effects of heterogeneous socialization rates*

An additional aspect of search performance is how the heterogeneity of adopted configurations evolves over time (Levinthal, 1997). As previous work relates, heterogeneity among searchers is a persistent feature in more complex landscapes, because searchers tend to get stuck on local peaks. Homogeneous groups were composed of similarly framed individuals while the heterogeneous ones were composed of differently framed individuals. For this model, heterogeneous groups were composed of members with different levels of socialization rates (different levels of p1).

The results obtained in the experiments on heterogeneous socialization rates are surprising comparing with the ones derived from March's paper (Figure 4). In complex environments, homogeneous population is desirable, whereas in stable worlds heterogeneity is a valuable property, as it injects knowledge diversity in organization. What can be the reason of such a controversial outcome?

In general, personnel heterogeneity as a strategic resource has received little theoretical and empirical attention even though the human element has been argued to affect organizational action (Thompson, 1967) and strategic choice (Finkelstein and Hambrick, 1996) and has grown in importance to firm performance along with the critical role of knowledge (Grant, 1996; Zahra and George, 2002). Empirical research produces two conflicting hypotheses: value in diversity (Cox and Blake, 1991) and ineffective workgroup functioning (Williams and O'Reilly, 1998). Research supports both the view that workforce heterogeneity enhances performance through the use of higher overall group problem solving abilities (Hoffman and Maier, 1961; McLeod, Lobel, and Cox, 1996) and the view that these aggregate differences inhibit performance by reducing social integration (Jackson, Stone, and Alvarez, 1993) and informal communication (Smith et al., 1994). These inconsistencies have led to the conclusion that workforce heterogeneity will not be found to improve firm performance until researchers gain an understanding of relevant contextual factors (Williams and O'Reilly, 1998). In fact, the wild dynamism between agents' opinions represents in its nature an environment productive for diversity, as beliefs continuously change and adapt. Previous research has shown that interaction in homogeneous groups is conducive to polarization of opinions. Specifically, groups composed of like-minded individuals tend to make judgments that are more extreme than the average of the individual members' judgments (Isenberg, 1986). Heterogeneity in adopted configurations is a persistent outcome when performance landscapes are rugged (positive K). According to Levinthal (1997: 942), "after a brief period of considerable experimentation with radically different forms, there is a steady convergence to a small set of forms that correspond to the local peaks in the landscape."

Finally, the first set of results from these first two experiments produces important consequences with respect to a central challenge for firms – the conflicting demands of survival and performance. In the model without external complexity (K=0), the optimal search strategy from the perspective of survival is that of pure exploitation, even though this is sub-optimal from a performance perspective. Under these conditions, pure exploitation firms will come to dominate the population of survivors under selection even though their performance will be not the best. The introduction of complexity significantly alters the survival and performance implications for an optimal search strategy. Indeed, at higher levels of complexity the strategy that optimizes survival requires more exploration than does the strategy that optimizes performance.

Figure 4: Experiment 2: March model vs. March-NK model

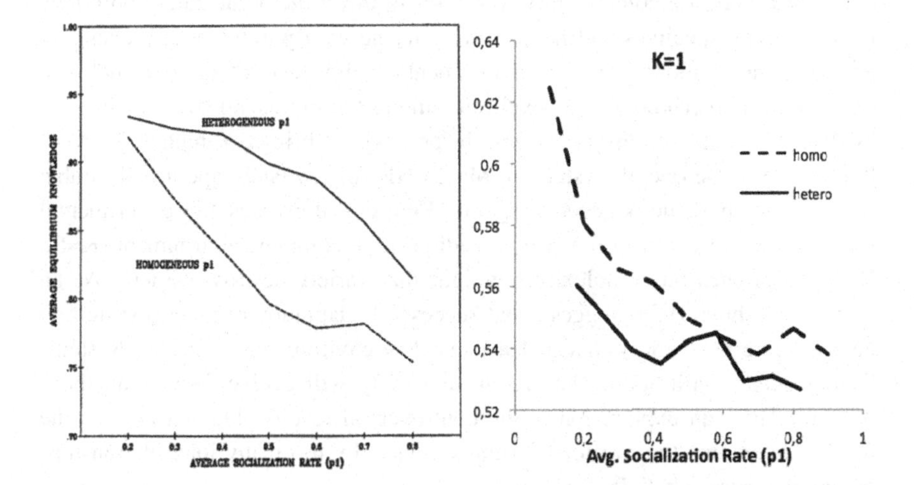

5.2. *Experiment 3: Effect of turnover on period-20 knowledge*

An alternative method to generate diversity in organizations is by considering the turnover rate. In this experiment, for each time period each member has a probability p3 of leaving the firm. If one member leaves the organization it is replaced with a new individual. The new member will have an initial randomly assigned knowledge.

Best performances are obtained for high levels of turnover and high socialization rate indifferent of how complex the landscape is. In March's (1991) model a strong negative correlation exists between turnover rate and average member knowledge, while a positive correlation exists between length of service in the organization and average member knowledge. Therefore, as the turnover rate increases, length of service and subsequently average member knowledge decrease. However, the effects of turnover on organizational learning do not adhere to a similar linear relationship. The effect of turnover on organizational learning reflects a nonlinear trade-off. "The combination of slow learning and rapid turnover leads to inadequate exploitation, ...[But] a modest level of turnover, by introducing less socialized people, increases exploration, and thereby improves aggregate knowledge" (March, 1991, p. 78-79). In practice, this result means that a typical "new hire" is naive compared with the member he is replacing, so the gains in organizational learning do not stem from the superior knowledge of the new hires but from their diversity. If in the static contexts a modest amount of turnover helps to inject the organization with new beliefs and perspectives and fill lost diversity necessary to adapt to a changing environment, in more complex environments a high level of turnover helps in obtaining a higher knowledge level rate among the organizational members. If in March's static environment the heterogeneity brings a higher level of knowledge to the overall system, in March-NK rugged landscape it is desirable to maintain more homogeneous agents. Figure 5 illustrates the experimental results on the effect of turnover in a medium-high complex environment (K=5). Different studies on complexity highlight that variety destroys variety. As an example, Ashby (1958) suggests that successful adaptation requires a system to have an internal variety that at least matches environmental variety. Systems having agents with appropriate requisite variety will evolve faster than those without. Thus, an explanation to the controversial results obtained may be the need to overcome the overload diversity caused by too many interrelationships among the agent's beliefs.

Figure 5: Effects of turnover in the presence of moderate complexity

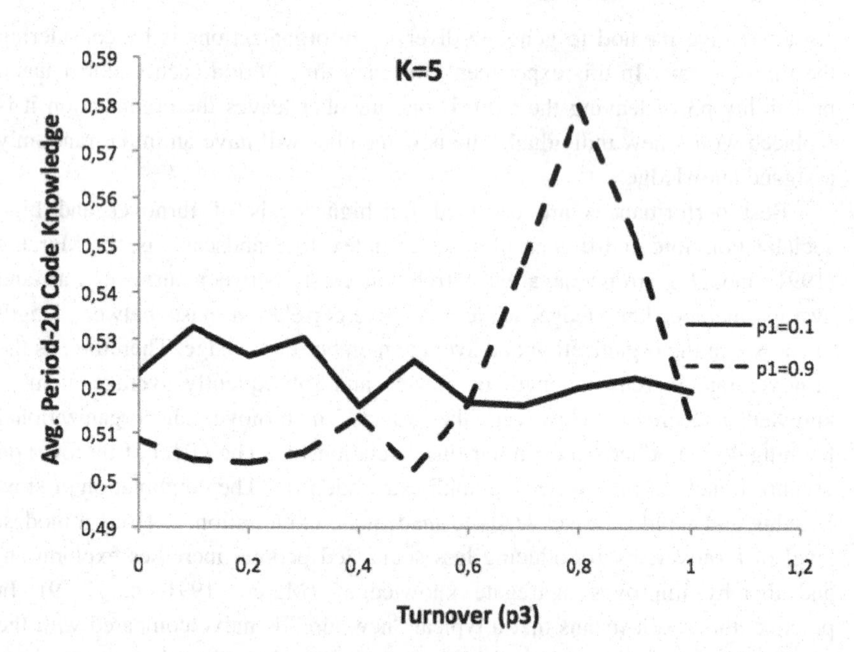

6. Conclusions

From the theoretical point of view this study intends to deepen the understanding of exploration-exploitation dynamics in a continuously changing external context. It aims towards a theory building perspective where the mixture of exploration and exploitation activities can be manipulated with the environmental dynamism. Computer programs offer the possibility of creating 'artificial' societies in which individuals and collective actors such as organizations could be directly represented and the effect of their interactions observed. The model resulted can be used as a platform to support managers' decisions and scholars to better understand and to explore the effects of combining different earning strategies according to the increasing external complexity. This work also contributes to the existing research on modeling learning modes in organizations in a complex problem space. Specifically, this study models the "space of possibilities" in which organizational learning takes place as a fitness landscape where organizational and individual opinions are interrelated and depend on the ones of an external reality. The omniscience external environment from March's (1991) model is now represented more realistically and can be manipulated by varying a parameter of complexity.

One of the main results obtained is that complexity (high level of interaction among dimensions) brings a constant negative impact on the performance of overall system analysed. Complexity has a downward effect on an organization's knowledge level. As K increases, the learning performances tend to converge to an average knowledge equilibrium value (approx. 0.5), which means that the complexity infuses a randomness effect on the overall system performance. Because of this entropy observed, it is very difficult to establish a rule in order to cope with the constant increasing complexity. For low and moderate levels of complexity, a balance between exploration and exploitation is possible to be determined. In these cases, best performances are achieved when the organizational memory adapts very fast to the best practices in organization and individuals are able to preserve some of their initial diversity. For high levels of complexity ($K>5$), system's performances are strongly affected by randomness. It seems that we cannot detect the right balance between individual and organizational learning rates, between exploration ad exploration: learning in the complex environment is a sort of random walk (March, 1991).

If in March's model what drives mutual learning is sustained diversity in beliefs, in complex landscapes diversity seems to do not matter. The role of individuals' diversity is actually decreasing in moderate to high rugged landscapes.

References

Argyris C., Schon, D. A. (1978). *Organizational learning: a theory of action perspective*. Addison-Wesley.

Ashby W.R. (1958). "Requisite variety and its implications for the control of complex systems", *Cybernetica* 1:2, p. 83-99.

Axelrod R. (1997), *The complexity of cooperation: Agent-based models of competition and collaboration*, Princeton, NJ: Princeton University Press.

Beckman C.M, Haunschild P.R., Phillips D.J. (2004). Friends or strangers? Firm-specific uncertainty, market uncertainty, and network partner selection. *Organization Science*, 15: 259-275.

Beckman C.M. (2006), "The influence of founding team company affiliations on firm behavior", *Academy of Management Journal*, 49(4), 741–758.

Benner, M.J., Tushman M.L. (2002). "Process management and technological innovation: A longitudinal study of the photography and paint industries", *Administrative Science Quarterly*, 47: 676-706.

Benner, M.J., Tushman M.L. (2003). "Exploitation, exploration, and process management: The productivity dilemma revisited", *Academy of Management Review*, 28: 238-256.

Bray D., Prietula M, (2007). Extending March's Exploration and Exploitation: Managing Knowledge in Turbulent Environments. 28th International Conference on Information Systems (ICIS) - Awarded Best Paper in KM Track. http://ssrn.com/abstract=962535

Burton, R. M. (2003). Computational laboratories for organization science: Questions, validity and docking. *Computational and Mathematical Organization Theory*, 9: 91–108.

Cheng, Y.T., and Van De Ven, A.H. (1996). "Learning the innovation journey: Order out of chaos?", *Organization Science*, 7: 593-614.

Cohen K. J., Cyert R. M. (1965). Simulation of Organizational Behavior. In James G. March (Ed.), *Handbook of Organizations*: 305-334. Chicago, IL: Rand McNally.

Cox T.H., Blake S. (1991). Managing cultural diversity: Implications for organizational competitiveness, *Academy of Management Executive, Vol. 5, No 3.*

Cyert, R. M., March, J. G. (1992). *The behavioral theory of the firm (2nd ed.).* Oxford, U.K.: Blackwell

Danneels, E. (2002). "The dynamics of product innovation and firm competences", *Strategic Management Journal*, 23(12), 1095–1121.

Dess G. G., Ireland R. D., Zahra S. A., Floyd S. W., Janney J. J., Lane P. J. (2003). Emerging issues in Corporate entrepreneurship. *Journal of Management*, 29(3): 351-378.

Dharmadasa, P. (2009), Organisational Learning, Innovation and Performance in Family-Controlled Manufacturing Small and Medium-Sized Enterprises

(SMEs) in Australia, PhD Thesis, Faculty of Business, Technology and Sustainable Development, Bond University, Queensland, Australia.

Eve R.A., Horsfall S., Lee M.E. (Eds.) (1997). *Chaos, Complexity and Sociology. Myths models and theories*. Sage Publications. USA.

Fang, C. et al. (2007), "Exploration and Exploitation: The Influence of Organizational Structure on Organizational Learning? *International Journal of Manpower*, Volume: 32, Issue: 5/6, Ieee, Pages: 537-566.

Finkelstein, S., Hambrick D. C. (1996). *Strategic leadership: Top executives and their effects on organization*. New York: West Publishing Company.

Gilsing, Victor A. Nooteboom B. (2006). Exploration and exploitation in biotechnology, *Research Policy*, forthcoming.

Grant R.M., (1996). Toward a knowledge-based theory of the firm, *Strategic Management Journal*, Vol. 17.

Greve, H.R. (2003). Organizational learning from performance feedback: A behavioral perspective on innovation and change. New York, NY: Cambridge University Press.

Harreld J., O'Reilly B., Charles A., Tushman Michael L. (2007). Dynamic capabilities at IBM: Driving strategy into action. Stanford GSB Working Paper.

He, Z. Wong, P. (2004), Exploration vs. Exploitation: An Empirical Test of the Ambidexterity Hypothesis, *Organization Science*, 15, 481-494.

Hoffman L. R., Maier N. R. F. (1961), Sex differences, sex composition, and group problem solving", *Journal of Abnormal and Social Psychology*, 63, 453-456.

Isenberg, D. J. (1986). Group polarization: A critical review and meta analysis. *Journal of Personality and Social Psych*ology, 50, 1141–1151.

Jackso, S. E., Stone V. K., Alvarez E. B. (1992). Socialization amidst diversity: Impact of demographics on work team oldtimers and newcomers. In L. L. Cummings & B. M. Staw (Eds.), *Research in organizational behavior* (Vol. 15, pp. 45-110). Greenwich, CT JAI Press.

Jansen J. J. P., van den Bosch F. A. J., Volberda H. W. (2006), Exploratory Innovation, Exploitative Innovation, and Performance: Effects of Organizational Antecedents and Environmental Moderators, *Management Science*, 52: 1661–74.

Kane G. C., Alavi M. (2005). "Information Technology and Organizational Learning: An Investigation of Exploitation and Exploration Processes," *Proceedings of the 26th International Conference on Information Systems*, Las Vegas, NV, December 2005.

Kane G., Prietula M. (2006). Influence & Structure: Extending a Model of Organizational Learning, Extended abstract prepared for the Twelfth Annual Organizational Winter Science Conference, Steamboat Springs CO, February 2-6.

Katila R., Ahuja G. (2002). Something old, something new: A longitudinal study of search behavior and new product introduction, *Academy of*

Management Journal, 45: 1183-94.

Kauffman Stuart A, (1993), *The Origins of Order, Self-Organization and Selection in Evolution*, New York Oxford University Press.

Kim, T. and Rhee, M. (2009), Exploration and exploitation: Internal variety and environmental dynamism, *Strategic Organ*ization, 7/1: 11-41.

Koza M. P., Lewin A. Y. (1998). The co-evolution of strategic alliances. *Organization Science*, 9: 255–264.

Lavie D., Rosenkopf L., (2006). Balancing exploration and exploitation in alliance Formation, *Academy of Management Journal*, 49, 797–818.

Levinthal D. A., March J. G. (1981). A model of adaptive organizational search. *Journal of Economic Behavior and Organization*, 2: 307-333.

Levinthal D.A., March J.G. (1993). The myopia of learning, *Strategic Management Journal*, 14: 95-112.

Levinthal D.A, (1997). Adaptation on Rugged Landscapes, *Management Sciente,* Vol 43., No 7.

Lin, Z., Yang H., and Demirkan I., (2007), "The performance consequences of ambidexterity in strategic alliance formations: Empirical investigation and computational theorizing", *Management Science*, 53 1645–1658.

Liu W. (2006). Knowledge exploitation, knowledge exploration, and competency trap. *Knowledge & Process Management*, 13(2), 144-161.

Louis MR, (1980). Surprise and sense making: What newcomers experience in entering unfamiliar organizational settings, *Administrative Science Quarterly*, Vol 25, No. 2.

Macy M. W., Willer R. (2002). From factors to actors: Computational sociology and agent-based modeling. *Annual Review of Sociology*, 28: 143–166.

McGrath R.G. (2001), "Exploratory learning, innovative capacity, and managerial over- sight", Academy of Management Journal, 44(1), 118–131.

McKee, D. 1992. An organizational learning approach to product innovation. Journal of Production Innovation Management, 3: 232-245.

McLeod, P. L., Lobel, S. A., & Cox, T. H., Jr. (1996). Ethnic diversity and creativity in small groups. Small Group Research, 27: 246-264.

McNamara, P., and Baden-Fuller, C. (1999), "Lessons from the Celltech case: Balancing knowledge exploration and exploitation in organizational renewal", *British Journal of Management*, 10: 291-307.

March, J. G. 1991. "Exploration and exploitation in organizational learning". *Organization Science*, 2: 71–87.

Miller, K. D., Zhao, M., & Calantone, R. (2006). Adding interpersonal learning and tacit knowledge to

March's exploration-exploitation model". *Academy of Management Journal*, Vol. 49, No. 4, 693–706.

Mom, T.J.M., Van den Bosch, F.A.J., and Volberda, H.W. (2007), "Investigating managers' exploration and exploitation activities: The influence of top-down, bottom- up, and horizontal knowledge inflows", *Journal of Management Studies*, 44(6), 910–931.

Nooteboom, B. (2000), *Learning and innovation in organizations and economies*, Oxford University Press: Oxford.

Rivkin, J. 2001. Reproducing knowledge: replication without imitation at moderate complexity. Org. Sci, 12 274-293.

Rivkin, J. W., and Siggelkow, N. (2003), "Balancing search and stability: Interdependencies among elements of organizational design", Management Science, 49: 290-311.

Rodan S. (2005), Exploration and Exploitation Revisited: Extending March?s Model of Mutual Learning, *Scandinavian Journal of Management*, vol. 22: 407-28.

Rosenkopf L., Nerkar, A. (2001), Beyond local search: Boundary spanning, exploration, and impact in the optical disk industry, *Strategic Management Journal*, 22: 287-306.

Rothaermel, F. T. (2001). Incumbent's advantage through exploiting complementary assets via interfirm cooperation. *Strategic Management Journal*, 22: 687–699.

Rothaermel F. T., Deeds, D. L. 2004. Exploration and exploitation alliances in biotechnology: A system of new product development. *Strategic Management Journal*, 25: 201–222.

Senge P. M. 1990. *The fifth disc*ipline. New York: Doubleday.

Sheremata W.A. (2000), "Centrifugal and centripetal forces in radical new product development under time pressure", *Academy of Management Review*, 25: 389-408.

Simon H. A. (1991). Organizations and markets. *Journal of Economic Perspectives*, 5(2): 25-45.

Sinkul, J.M. (1994). Market information processing and organizational learning, *Journal of Marketing*, 58 (January), 35-45.

Slater S. F., Narver J. C. (1995). Market orientation and the learning organization. Journal of Marketing, 59(July), 63–74.

Smith K.G., Smith K.A., Olian J.D., Sims H.P., O'Bannon D.P., Scully J.A., (1994), "Top management team demography and process: The role of social integration and communication", *Administrative Science Quarterly*, Vol. 39, No. 3

Taber Charles S., Timpone Richard J. (1996). *Computational Modeling* (Sage University Paper Series on Quantitative Applications in the Social Sciences, 07-113). Newbury Park, CA: Sage.

Thompson James D. (1967). *Organizations in Action*. New York: McGraw-Hill.

Tushman M.L. (2003), "Innovation streams and ambidextrous organizational designs: On building dynamic capabilities", working paper, Harvard University.

Van Den Bosch F.A.J., Van Wijk R. A. (1999). Transition processes towards the N-form corporation: Strategic implications for knowledge flows, in M.A. Hitt, P.G. Clifford, R.D. Nixon, & K.P. Coyne (eds.), *Dynamic strategic resources: Development, diffusion and integration*, Chichester: John Wiley & Sons Ltd.

Vassolo R., Anand J., Folta, T. , (2004). Portfolio effect in real options: The case of equity alliances in biotechnology. *Strategic Management Journal*, 25: 1045-1061.

Vermeulen, F., Barkema, H.G. 2001. Learning through acquisitions. *Academy of Management Journal*, 44: 457-476

Williams K.Y., O'Reilly C.A. (1998), “Demography and diversity in organizations: A review of 40 years of research”, *Research In Organizational Behavior*, Volume: 20, Issue: 20.

Zahra S.A., Gorge G., (2002). “Absorptive capacity: A review, reconceptualization, and extension”, *Academy of Management Review,* vol 27, No 2.

VARIABLES FOSTERING KNOWLEDGE MANAGEMENT CLASSICAL THEORY VS. UNCERTAINTY THEORY

GERARDO GABRIEL ALFARO CALDERÓN'
Novena # 474 Col Guadalupe C.P. 58140 Morelia
Michoacán, Méx. Tel (443) 326-63-96

FEDERICO GONZÁLEZ SANTOYO, JUAN J. FLORES
Rincón de Barranquillas 555, Fracc. Arboledas, C.P. 58000
Morelia, Michoacán, México, Tel (443) 299-20-71

VÍCTOR GERARDO ALFARO GARCÍA
Novena # 474 Col Guadalupe C.P. 58140 Morelia
Michoacán, Méx. Tel (443) 326-63-96

JEL Code: M13, M14, M15

Abstract:

There is a number of variables considered as fostering knowledge management. This set of variables includes organizational culture, leadership of the owner manager, relational assets, and structural assets. This article presents a comparison of the variables considered as fostering knowledge management using classical theory vs. Uncertainty theory, using the linguistic label approach.

Keywords: Knowledge Management, Culture, Structural Assets, Relational Assets, Leadership, Linguistic Labels

Objective:

The goal of this paper is to compare classic theory vs. uncertainty theory though linguistic lables on the variables organizational culture, leadership of the owner manager, relational assets, and structural assets from the knowledge management model for small and medium enterprises.

Introduction

Nowadays, companies need to posses a competitive advantage and survive. Furthermore, they need to position themselves in global markets as world-class companies. This is no different for companies in Michoacan. Nonetheless, given their structural characterization, 97% of them fall within the classification of micro, small, and medium companies; only 3% of them are large companies.

Most importantly, most of the companies in Michoacan are undercapitalized, with intermitent processes, obsolete technology, and low quality levels. For these companies to become world-class companies and compete in gobal markets, they require a structural conversion in their components, but even more so in its enterpreneural culture of their intelectual assets.

Therefore, it is very important to include knowledge management and transfer. This can be supported by the use of the virtuous circle (R & D). This allows the transfer and appropriation of knowledge in an efficient and effective way. Knowledge management seeks to transfer knowledge and accumulated and documented experience, such as optimal enterpreneural practices in all its areas. Knowledge is documented based on quality management processes, and obtains value by being a basis for enterpreneural practices. Once this knowledge has been registered and documented, it becomes an intelectual asset of high value for the companies.

It is essential to support the knowledge transfer process and management of information technology and system design for the process to be managed in a more comprehensive and optimal manner. If that happens, it allows timely and appropriate decision making, such that it reduces the performance risk in human resources that conceptualize, design, and operate companies.

The process of knowledge management, can guide efforts towards the identification, collection, and organization of knowledge that we have today, facilitates the processes to generate new knowledge. It strengthens and promotes innovation to create a competitive advantage.

So it is necessary for companies to have a basis on which they should have the knowledge base at the professional level. In order to yield an optimal work performance, it is necessary to have sufficient and consistent reference material, accurate documentation of the processes that characterize all functional areas, tools and methodologies for optimal development of the work. The company must optimally design its organizational structure (it can be vertical, horizontal, circular, matricial and intelligent). It is necessary to strengthen the skills, technical knowledge, optimal design of activities; we must have a clear project a precise definition, activities, stories and results.

1. Knowledge Management Model for Pymes

This model has been generated from an exhaustive review of the literature in representative knowledge management models, modified to the characteristics of manufacturing PyMES[1] in Morelia.

- Conceptualization of knowledge management – most representative models:
  - Kogut and Zander (1992). The company's knowledge resides in coordinated human resources; companies are social communities where individual actions are linked to a set of organizational principles.
  - Knowledge creation and transfer translates to innovation and learning from failures and successes in the organization - Von Krogh, Nonaka y Aben (2001).
  - The main knowledge source lies in people and relationships among them - Tejedor y Aguirre (1998).
  - The knowledge creation process (Nonaka y Takeuchi (1999)) amplifies organizationally. Knowledge is created by individuals and makes them a part of the organization's knowledge network.
  - Systemic process that allows the interaction of all management elements that affect directly the organization's personality: culture, leadership style, strategy, structure, and information systems - Tejedor y Aguirre (1998), Andersen A. (1999).
  - The commitment by the administration to strengthen policies on culture and knowledge management - Tejedor y Aguirre (1999).
  - Dynamic process where knowledge goes from people to organization and back to people - Andersen A. (1999).

- With respect to the PyMES characteristics
  - The high motivation of the owner manager, his degree of influence in the organization, and the relationship with suppliers and customers.
  - Ability to change and adjust to innovation.
  - Flexibility.

- The success factors of this kind of companies:

  - Personal skills of the owner manager.
    - Ability towards management and effective leadership.

[1] from Spanish "Pequeñas y Medianas Empresas – Small and Medium Enterprises

- Ability to establish an adequate organizational culture, ability to obtain and use resources and take the opportunities.
- Commitment towards the company's success.
- Experience, capability, and knowledge to perform his duties.
- To know what he wants.
- Believe in himself.
- Leadership and motivational skills.
- Effective communication and relation with emplyees, suppliers, and customers.
- Ability to solve technical problems and innovate.
- Binding strength among the founder members of the company. This strength must be based on respect and mutual trust.
- Facilitate the accumulation of knowledge, originating from the interaction of skills and attitudes from the organization members and the opportunities that arise in the environment.

- Employees' skills.
  - Ability to solve technical problems.
  - Abilities and attitudes that determine the quality of products and possibility of innovation.
  - Experience, ability, and knowledge to develop work activities.
  - Commitment towards the company's success.
  - Effective communication and relation with the owner manager, employee-employee, employee-client, and employee-supplier.

1.1 Variables included in the Knowledge Management Model for manufacturing Pymes

The model has a systemic approach, where each and every variable are related and their influence is explained below:

1.1.1. Existing culture in organization

In order to develop knowledge management in the company, it is necessary for the owner manager to believe and align the culture towards continuous learning and manage the learned concepts. Culture promotes:

- Transmition of identity to the members of the organization.
- Facilitate the commitment with something bigger than myself.
- Reinforce stability of the social system.
- Provide premises recognized and accepted for decision making.

A culture compatible with knowledge is one of the most important conditions that drive a project to success. O'Dell y Grayson (1998) state that companies with an open culture, that motivate knowledge will have more success in their transfer. Ruggles (1997) mentions that one of the main barriers for knowledge transfer is the lack of an open culture that supports its members. An intensive communication and a culture that accepts new ideas and be prepared to support exploration of its processes and activites, favors knowledge management.

Andersen A. (1999), Tejedor and Aguirre (1998), mention culture as a facilitating element for knowledge management, since it favors learning and innovation, including actions that reinforce an attitude open to change.

The main manager must take advantage of the flexibility, and capability to innovate that characterize his company. Based on his leadership skills, the manager must create a culture that moves human resources in problem identification, search for creative solutions, improve individual and group work, redesign learning processes according to moral values. He must as well support the company's vision, work in participation, create a trust environment, and commit towards the company's success, so that this culture nurtures knowledge management.

1.1.2. Leadership Style

Castells (1999) states that the knowledge management process requires full participation of all organization members, such that individuals share what they know with everyone else.

Ruggles (1998) mentions that the lack of support from the high management is a significative barrier for knowledge management.

Andersen (1999) states that to reinforce the company's critical abilities it is necessary to have a leadership that defines a strategy to define the objective and knowledge use.

Tejedor y Aguirre (1998) mention that the organization conditions can act as an obstacle to organizational learning, blocking all possibilities of personal development, communication, relation with its environment, creation, etc.

Knowledge lies in and is generate by people that work at the company. Acknowledgement by high management is vital; they must use methods and procedures to lead the company towards knowledge management - Davenport y Prusak (2001). A company's greatest asset is knowledge – if it cannot generate new knowledge, it is doomed to cease existing.

Thus, leadership style is a facilitating element in the process of knowledge management and must be included in the proposed model.

1.1.3. Structural Assets

Structural assets represent structured knowledge collected by information and communication systems. These systems are used to store and transmit information, generally composed by intellectual property assets. I.e., registered trade marks, patents, knowledge stocks, author rights, available technology, work processes, management systems, etc.

Stewart (1997) points out these assets are twofold: gather knowledge stocks to sustain work clients appreciate and speed up the flow of information in the company. The main goal is to use these assets to create value.

Thus, these assets must be perfectly integrated to allow an optimal knowledge management.

1.1.4. Relational Assets

This element is an important knowledge management support; it values the organization's capacity to maintain and promote relations with its surroundings. There are a number of factors that can be evaluated, and brought up to clients and suppliers; these factors are client's loyalty, satisfaction, novelty of the brand, and strategic alliances, among others.

The product's feedback the company gets from customers allows the increase its knowledge base to innovate the same product. That is a reason for the inclusion of this element in the proposed knowledge management model.

1.1.5. Elements that generate knowledge

Organizations, as non-human entities, learn as people that compose them are capable of learning and willing to do it. Only people learn (Tejedor y Aguirre 1998). People, involved in every aspect and every step, make knowledge management possible. People manage knowledge; this is a cyclic spiral process that starts at the individual level and moves towards organization, towards inter-organization, and back to individuals, where it starts over again. The process starts at a higher level (see Figure 1.1).

The model includes a person as an individual, the organization as an enterprise, and inter-organization as the structure of relations outside the company. The inter-relation of these elements is fostered in the model, given the characteristics of PyMEs.

The model considers human assets as useful knowledge for the organization. This knowledge includes learning capabilities, labor satisfaction, skills, group work abilities, leadership, etc.

Human assets are important to knowledge management through an effective organization of structural assets. This allows the company to develop productive relational assets Barceló y Cols (2001). Every organization, regardless of its size, owns intellectual assets (in the form of implicit or explicit knowledge). The proposed model of knowledge management in PyMEs integrates intellectual assets to the best features of knowledge management. See Figure 1.2.

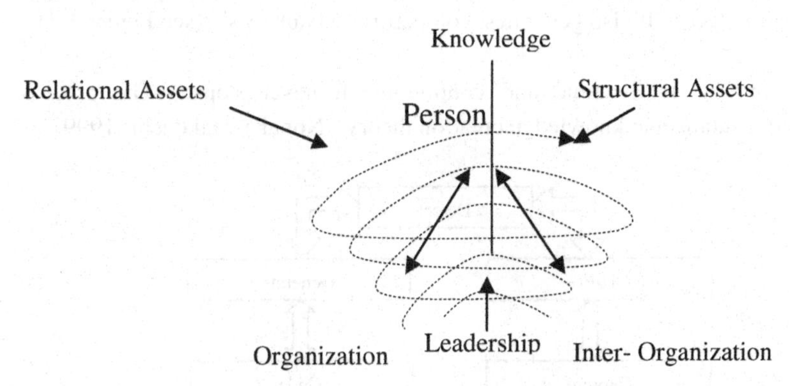

Figure 1.1. Growing effect of knowledge in actors of knowledge management

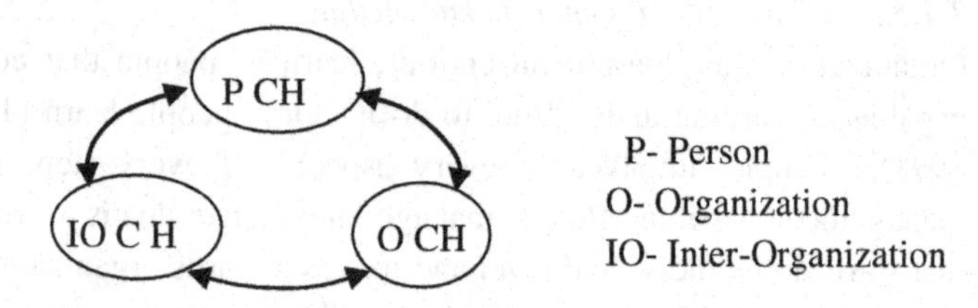

Figure 1.2. Elements that generate knowledge management

Persons' relations, organizational culture, and the knowledge management process allow knowledge to be generated by human assets. Knowledge is organized through structural assets, making it available to organizational assets. Now, since the model is dynamic and continuous, the company's knowledge increases continuously.

1.1.6. Knowledge Management Process

During the development of this model, we obtained our own definition of knowledge management. This definition works as the mechanism that allows the knowledge management process' main actors to generate an use knowledge. This definition reads as follows:

"Dynamic and interactive process seeking to detect, generate, code, transfer, capture, and use knowledge to achieve goals and solve the problems the organization faces. It also generates, competitive advantages", (see Figure 1.3).

The process is dynamic and continuous; it never stops. The process implicitly contains the knowledge creation theory - Nonaka y takeuchi (1999).

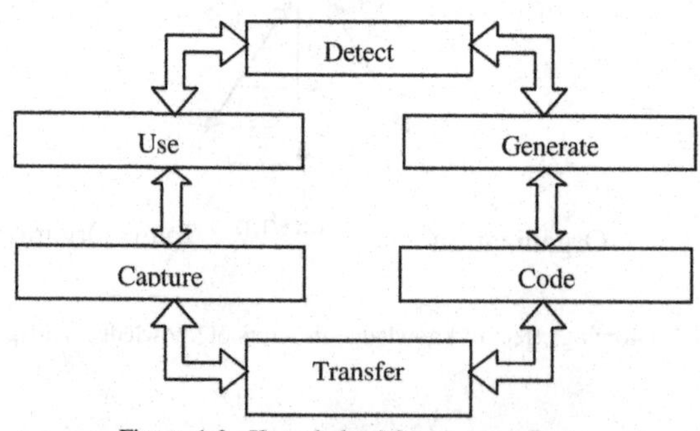

Figure 1.3. Knowledge Management Process

PyMEs have a simple and sometimes informal structure. This fact turns into an advantage when it comes to implement a knowledge management process. When we integrate the previously mentioned elements: culture, leadership style, structural assets, relational assets, generating elements, and the knowledge management process, we obtain the knowledge management model for manufacturing PyMEs. Figure 1.4. shows this proposal.

This model has a systemic approach ; it allows the interaction of the knowledge management process – they are not independent, but are connected among them.

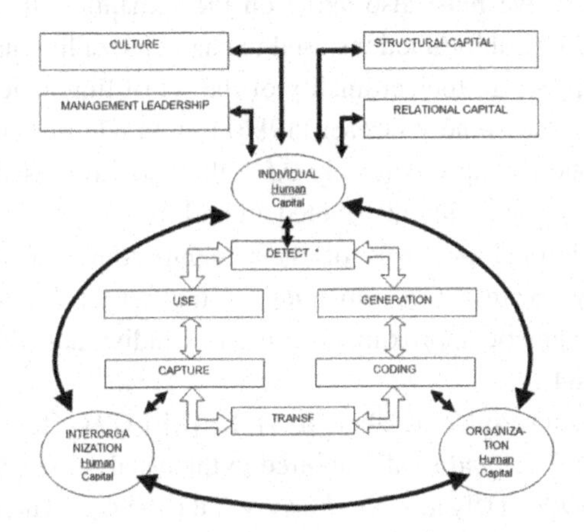

Figure. 1.4. Knowledge Management Model for manufacturing PyMEs

2. Analysis using Linguistic Labels

Decision-making classical models do not have much in common with what happens in the real world. In many real-world decision-making processes, the objectives, constraints, and actions are not known with precision (Lazzari 2005). The individuals that participate in the problem simply cannot provide exact numerical values for preference degrees from one alternative to another. Under these circumstances, a more realistic approach is to use linguistic labels, instead of exact numeric values, assuming the domains of the involved variables is a set of linguistic terms.

This approach to tackle the decision making problem is based on fuzzy set theory – it is known as the linguistic approach. The approach is applicable when the involved variables are qualitative in nature (Zadeh, 1975; Tong y Bonissone, 1980; Delgado, Verdegay y Vila 1993; Herrera y Herrera-Viedna, 2000). That way we can model more adequately a greater number of real situations. This approach represents information about individuals more adequately. The fuzzy approach has been successfully applied to many problems that involve qualitative aspects, evaluated through linguistic terms.

A linguistic variable, as opposed to a numeric variable, can take on values that are not numbers, but words or natural language sentences (Zadeh, 1975).

A decision making linguistic model assumes the existence of an appropriate set of terms or labels (which depends on the problem domain); individuals use this set of terms to express their preferences.

We must agree about the granularity level that will be used to express the label set (Zadeh, 1975); we must also agree on the semantics of those labels. That is, the kind of membership functions used to characterize linguistic terms.

Granularity corresponds to the cardinality of the set of linguistic terms used to express information. Bossione y Decaer (1986) use an odd number of labels, defining the middle one as "approximately 0.5"; this label represents a neutral state and the rest are symmetrically distributed around it.

Fuzzy numbers, defined in terms of their membership functions in the interval [0,1], usually express the semantics of the set of linguistic terms. Linguistic terms are linguistic approximations used by individuals (Zadeh, 1979; Tong y Bonissone, 1984).

In this proposal, we use interval labels [0,1], $L=\{l_i\}, i \in H=\{0,\ldots,t\}$, with an odd arity; intervals are finite and totally ordered in the usual sense (Zadeh, 1979, Bonissone y decaer, 1986; Delgado, Verdegay y Vila, 1993). The center label represents an uncertainty of approximately 0.5 and the rest is distributed semantically on both sides. A label li represents a possible value of a linguistic variable or fuzzy property defined in [0,1].

3. Evaluation of Knowledge Management variables through Classic Theory

In order to verify the contribution of the knowledge management variables in manufacturing PyMEs, we applied a survey. The the resulting information will be analyzed as follows:

Variable Culture.

Resident culture in manufacturing PyMEs was analyzed, concluding it is a fostering element for knowledge management.

Variable Structural Assets.

Surveying this variable was directed to get information about the investment done by this kind of companies towards acquisition, ownership, and knowledge transfer with the following results:

From the previous analysis, manufacturing PyMES, there is fostering in structural assets investment for storage media and knowledge flow. They invest 29% of their sales in this factor.

Table 3.1 Descriptive Satistics Parameters for Variable Culture

Statistical Parameter	Value	Incidence in the interval
Mean	54,54	Almost always
Median	56,5	Almost always
Mode	67	Always
Std. Dev.	14,086	Sometimes/Almost always ($\mu \pm \sigma = 68\%$)
Skewness	-0,553	

Table 3.2 Statistical Parameters of Structural Assets

Statistical Parameter	Value	Incidence in the interval
Mean	29.19	21-40 %
Median	29	
Mode	29	
Std. Dev.	10.92	0 – 20% / 21 – 40%($\mu \pm \sigma = 68\%$)
Skewness	-0,39	

Variable Relational Assets:

The analysis of this variable was directed to obtain information about: Knowing the relation of the enterprise with its suppliers, clients, competitors, industrial associations, and educational institutions. The obtained results were the following:

Table 3.3 Statistical Parameters of Relational Assets of PyMEs

Statistical Parameter	Value	Incidence in the interval
Mean	18.44	Almost always
Median	19	
Mode	22	Always
Std. Dev.	4.38	Almost always / Always ($\mu \pm \sigma$ =68%)
Skewness	-1.88	

From this analysis, we can conclude that the relations of the PyMES almost always occur.

Variable Leadership Style

Leadership Style from PyMES occasionally fosters knowledge management. This is observed once we processed the items related to this variable. The results are shown in Table 3.4.

Table 3.4 Statistical Parameters of Leadership Style

Statistical Parameter	Value	Incidence in the interval
Mean	22.8	Sometimes
Median	22	
Mode	18	
Std. Dev.	6.1	Almost never / Sometimes / Almost always ($\mu \pm \sigma$ =68%)
Skewness	0.3	

4. Evaluation of the Knowledge Management Process using fuzzy theory and linguistic labels

To evaluate the importance of an attribute, we use a set of 5 linguistic labels $L=\{l_0,l_1,l_2,l_3,l_4\}$. The semantics of those labels is given by the TFN in intervals [0,1], given in Table 4.1. Linguistic labels contain four real numbers.

	Linguistic label	TFN
l_4	Always	(0.8,0.9,1.0,1.0)
L_3	Almost Always	(0.5,0.7,0.8,0.9)
L_2	Sometimes	(0.3,0.45,0.55,0.7)
L_1	Almost Never	(0.1,0.2,0.3,0.45)
L_0	Never	(0.0,0.0,0.1,0.2)

The aggregated opinion resulting from the survey with respect to each variable as a generator of knowledge management is expressed as a mean fuzzy number. We compute the mean of each the set of TFN, corresponding to the linguistic terms.

The process performed to each knowledge management variable is shown in the following table.

Variable Culture:

FRECUENCY	INTERVALS					=	RESULTS				
5	(0	0	0.1	0.2	)	=	(0	0	0.5	1	)
14	(0.1	0.2	0.3	0.45	)	=	(1.4	2.8	4.2	6.3	)
14	(0.3	0.45	0.55	0.7	)	=	(4.2	6.3	7.7	9.8	)
22	(0.5	0.7	0.8	0.9	)	=	(11	15	17.6	19.8	)
31	(0.8	0.9	1	1	)	=	(25	28	31	31	)
				SUM			(40	41	52	61	)
				MEAN			(0.5	0.6	0.71	0.79	)

The result is the following TFN:

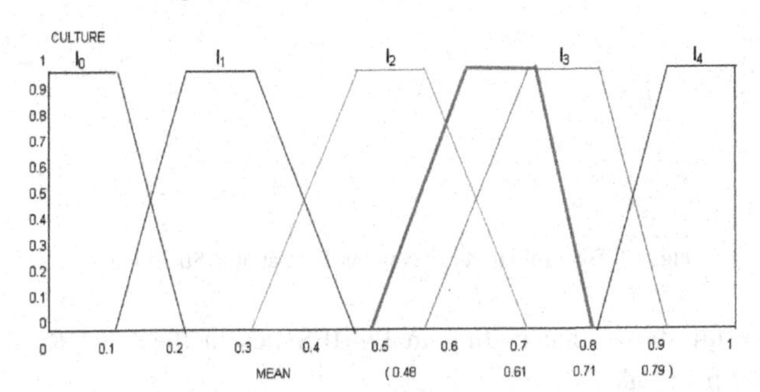

Fig. 4.1 Trapezoidal Fuzzy Number for Variable Culture

Fig. 4.1. shows that Resident culture in this kind of companies oscillates between linguistic labels Sometimes and Almost Always. Knowledge management is fostered Almost Always, matching classic theory.

Variable Structural Assets:

For this variable, labels are substituted as indicated in the following tables.

Scale

Never ------------------ Unknown

Almost Never --------- 0 - 20%

Sometimes ------------- 21 - 40%

Almost Always ------- 41 - 60 %

Always --------------- 61 % +

FRECUENCY	INTERVALS						RESULTS				
18	(0	0	0.1	0.2	)	=	(0	0	1.8	3.6	)
40	(0.1	0.2	0.3	0.45	)	=	(4	8	12	18	)
24	(0.3	0.45	0.55	0.7	)	=	(7.2	11	13.2	16.8	)
2	(0.5	0.7	0.8	0.9	)	=	(1	1.4	1.6	1.8	)
2	(0.8	0.9	1	1	)	=	(1.6	1.8	2	2	)
				SUM			(14	22	30.6	42.2	)
				MEAN			(0.2	0.3	0.36	0.49	)

The result is the following TFN:

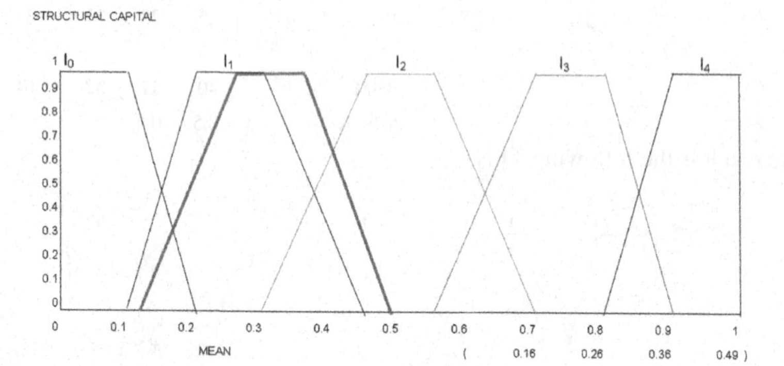

Fig. 4.1 Trapezoidal Fuzzy Number for Variable Structural Assets

The result shows that coding in PyMES lies in the label for 0 a 20% of investment from sales.

Variable Relacional Assets:

FRECUENCY	INTERVALS						RESULTS				
3	(0	0	0.1	0.2	)	=	(0	0	0.3	0.6	)
5	(0.1	0.2	0.3	0.45	)	=	(0.5	1	1.5	2.25	)
18	(0.3	0.45	0.55	0.7	)	=	(5.4	8.1	9.9	12.6	)
40	(0.5	0.7	0.8	0.9	)	=	(20	28	32	36	)
20	(0.8	0.9	1	1	)	=	(16	18	20	20	)
				SUM			(42	55	63.7	71.5	)
				MEAN			(0.5	0.6	0.74	0.83	)

The result is the following TFN:

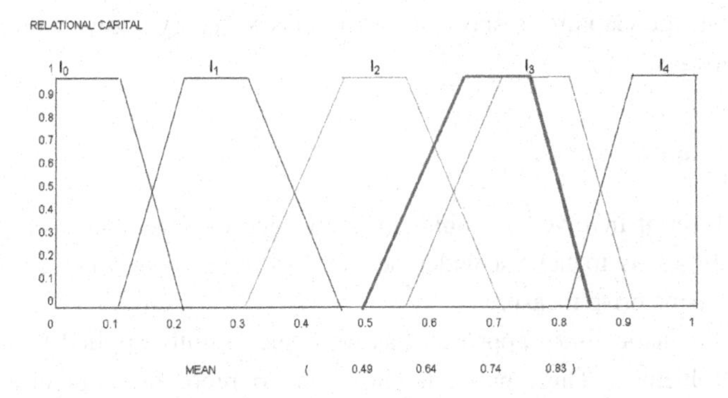

Fig. 4.3 Trapezoidal Fuzzy Number for Variable Relational Assets

The TFN indicates that knowledge transfer occurs almost always, matching classic theory.

Variable Leadership Style

FRECUENCy	INTERVALS						RESULTS				
6	(0	0	0.1	0.2	)	=	(0	0	0.6	1.2	)
28	(0.1	0.2	0.3	0.45	)	=	(2.8	5.6	8.4	12.6	)
34	(0.3	0.45	0.55	0.7	)	=	(10	15	18.7	23.8	)
12	(0.5	0.7	0.8	0.9	)	=	(6	8.4	9.6	10.8	)
6	(0.8	0.9	1	1	)	=	(4.8	5.4	6	6	)
				SUM			(24	35	43.3	54.4	)
				MEAN			(0.3	0.4	0.5	0.63	)

The result is the following TFN:

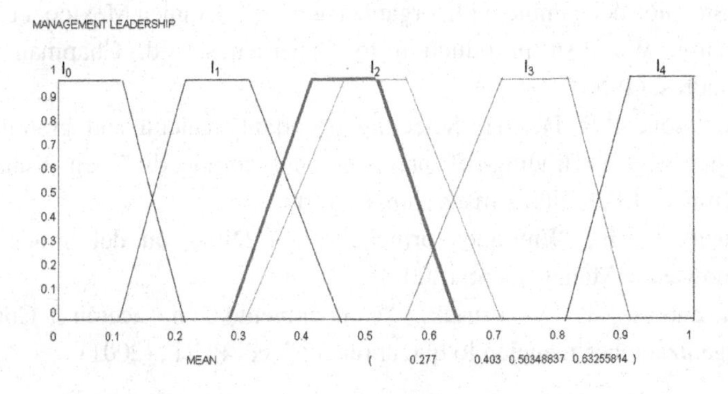

Fig. 4.4 Trapezoidal Fuzzy Number for Variable Leadership Style

Knowledge Capture is sporadic, while classic theory shows a slight bias to almost always.

5. Conclusions

The analysis of involved variables in knowledge management, using linguistic labels, allows us to have a wider decision spectrum than what classic theory provides using crisp measures.

The linguistic fuzzy approach has been successfully applied to many real-world problems. This approach allows us to represent imprecise available information in a more appropriate way. The decider can be expressed in natural language, using linguistic variables. The linguistic approach also facilitates convergence of the language to shared meanings.

6. References:

1. Alfaro C. G., González S.F. "Modelo de Gestión del Conocimiento en Pequeñas y Medianas Empresas", Ed. Ilustre Academia Iberoamericana de Doctores Méx. (2011)
2. A.Kaufmann, J. Gil Aluja. *Las matemáticas del azar y de la incertidumbre (elementos básicos para su aplicación en economía).* Editorial Centro de Estudios Ramón Areces. España. (1990)
3. Andersen A., "El Mangement en el siglo XXI" ED.Granica Buenos Aires, (1999)
4. Andersen A., "KMAT (Knowledge Management Assessment Tool) Andersen A. Study London, (1999)
5. Argyris C., "Conocimiento para la acción: Una guía para superar obstáculos del cambio en la organización", ed. Granica México, (1999)
6. Ashby, W., "An introduction to Cybernetics" Ed. Chapman & Hall Londres, (1956)
7. Bonissone P.P. Decker, Selecting uncertanty calculi and granulary: An experiment in trading-off precision and complexity", en Kanal, L.H. Lemmer, J.F. (edits) Amsterdam, (1986)
8. Bueno C. E., "Enfoques principales en Dirección del conocimiento" Knowledge Management, (2002)
9. Davenport, T. y Prusak, "Conocimiento en acción: Cómo las organizaciones manejan lo que aprenden", ed. PHH., (2001)

10. Delgado M., Verdegay J.L.;Vila,M.A. "Linguistc decision making models". Intenational Journal of Intelligent Systems vol. 7, (1993)
11. Drucker P.F., "The new productivity Challenge" Harvard Business Review, (1991)
12. Gil Lafuente A.M. *El análisis de las inmovilizaciones en la incertidumbre.* Ariel. España. (2004)
13. González S.F, Flores R. B, Gil Lafuente A.M. *Procesos para la toma de decisiones en un entorno globalizado.* Editorial Universitaria Ramón Areces. España. (2011)
14. Hall Richard, "The strategic analysis of intangible resource", Strategic Management Journal, (1992)
15. Lazzari Luisa L. et. Al. "Métodos de agregación de variables lingüísticas",- Facultad de Ciencias Económicas - Universidad de Buenos Aires

MULTI-OBJECTIVE FUZZY MODELS IN THE SELECTION OF INNOVATIONS IN THE AGRICULTURAL AREA*

LUIS M. RIVERA VILAS
Universitat Politécnica de Valencia
Dpto. Economía y Ciencias Sociales
Campus de Vera s.n. 46022 Valencia, Spain

NATALIA LÓPEZ-MOSQUERA GARCÍA
MERCEDES SÁNCHEZ GARCÍA
Universidad Pública de Navarra
Dpto. Gestión de Empresas
Campus Arrosadía, 31006 Pamplona, Spain

There are currently two multi-objective fuzzy models widely used in the area of business decision making, the Weighted Max-Min model and the Weight-Added Model. In this paper we compare the results obtained from using these two models in the case of the selection of an agricultural innovation, both in the case of their being weighting between the different objectives and in the case of there not being. The results obtained allow us to recommend the first model rather than the second. A system is also provided which makes it easy to determine the maximum and minimum values for each objective, fundamental data required to calculate the tolerances of the various models.

This is where the abstract should be placed. It should consist of one paragraph giving a concise summary of the material in the article below. Replace the title, authors, and addresses with your own title, authors, and addresses.

1.1. *Introduction*

Decisions on the adoption of new technologies in agriculture are usually multi-objective given that although new technology tends to produce more income per unit, this is usually at the cost of greater investment. In this context, the agri-food sector, innovativeness is considered to be one of the most important factors allowing a firm to challenge major competitors both in national and international markets [1,2,3,4,5]. However, at the productive level, although new agricultural technology usually produces a higher yield per unit, it can also be of lower

---

* This work is supported by the Project number AGL2009-13303-C02-01 of the Spanish Ministry of Science and Innovation.

quality, that is to say, less of what is produced may be of commercial quality. There thus arises the difficulty in maintaining continuous innovation in the agricultural sector [6], regardless of the strategies employed by firms [7]. It is the situation of information asymmetry in this market which can significantly condition the success of the adoption of innovation in his sector [8,9,10]. Thus the agricultural decision maker is commonly confronted with technology adoption situations which involve both quantitative and qualitative objectives, for example both income and quality, and furthermore, these maybe assigned different levels of importance. The meaning of this information asymmetry makes its presence felt for the decision makers in a lack of information about objectives and restrictions and they find themselves expressing their objectives in vague or imprecise terms such as, "I'd like to obtain high quality with sufficient income."

In all these cases fuzzy theory is a good tool to use in real situations to help in making decisions when multiple objectives, both quantitative and qualitative, with different levels of importance, as well as imprecise statements regarding objectives and constraints, are in play [11,12].

Consistent with the above, the purpose of this paper is threefold: firstly to examine the multi-objective fuzzy models present in the literature, secondly, to carry out an application of these in a real situation of new technology application in the agricultural sector, which would allow for comparisons to be made between the results obtained and for the offering of a series of recommendations regarding their practical application and thirdly and finally, to provide a methodology which would allow for the simplifying and objectifying of maximum and minimum values for each objective, fundamental values for calculating the tolerances of the different models analyzed.

The structure of the sections of this study follows the steps set out above. Accordingly, the following section is devoted to the analysis and presentation of the existing multi-objective fuzzy models. In the third section these models are applied to a realistic technology application situation in the greenhouses of Almería (Spain), the results found examined and a series of recommendations made for their implementation. We believe that this is the first application of these models in the field of agricultural innovation and that this provides the novel contribution of this study.

1.2. *Methodology. Examination of the Multi-objective Fuzzy Models.*

A multi-objective, fuzzy approach with a set of goals G, B being the sub-set of objectives to be maximized and C the sub-set of objectives to be minimized (G = B C) [13] can be expressed in the following way:

Find x (1)

Subject to

$$g_k(x) \leq \sim a_k \quad \text{for all } g_k \in B$$

$$g_k(x) \geq \sim a_k \quad \text{for all } g_k \in C$$

$$Ax \leq b$$

$$x \geq 0$$

where a_k represents the aspiration level of the fuzzy goal g_k, $g_k(x) \leq \sim a_k$ means that "$g_k(x)$ *is essentially greater than or equal to* a_k", and $g_k(x) \geq \sim a_k$ means that "$g_k(x)$ *is essentially smaller than or equal to* a_k". A is an m x n matrix of coefficients and b, is an m x1 vector of constants of Crips system constraints, where x is an mxn vector of the decision variables.

In the agricultural area an example of a fuzzy model with three objective functions to plan crops, could be as follows: minimize water consumption, minimize waste production and maximize revenue from a farm, subject to the feasibility set.

The multi-objective fuzzy approach is something we owe to [11], who in 1978 proposed expressing each of the objective functions in a lineal membership thus obtained for each of the equivalent fuzzy numbers through the definition of the functions of membership or achievement. For an objective Z_k, the achievement function $\mu_{Zk}(x) \in [0,1]$ that converts it into a fuzzy number is based on obtaining a relative relationship for each objective as is shown in the following:

In the case of the objective being to minimize the achievement or membership function ($\mu g_k(x)$) is defined as,

In the case of the objective being to minimize the achievement or membership function ($\mu g_k(x)$) is defined as,

$$\mu g_k(x) = \begin{cases} 1 & \text{if } g_K \leq a_K \\ \dfrac{U_k - g_k(x)}{U_k - a_k} & \text{if } a_K \leq g(x) \leq U_K \quad \text{for } g_k(x) \leq \sim a_k \\ 0 & \text{if } g_K \geq U_K \end{cases} \quad (2)$$

The membership function in the case that minimize is the objective is defined as ($\mu_{Zl}(x)$) is,

$$\mu g_k(x) = \begin{cases} 1 & \text{if } g_k \geq a_k \\ \dfrac{g_k(x) - L_k}{a_k - L_k} & \text{if } L_K \leq g_k(x) \leq a_k \quad \text{for } g_k(x) \geq \sim a_k \\ 0 & \text{if } g_k \leq L_k \end{cases} \quad (3)$$

Where L_k and U_k are, respectively, lower and upper limits for the *k*th goal. Specifically, the membership functions in the case of the objective being to maximize and the objective being to minimize are given in Figure 1.

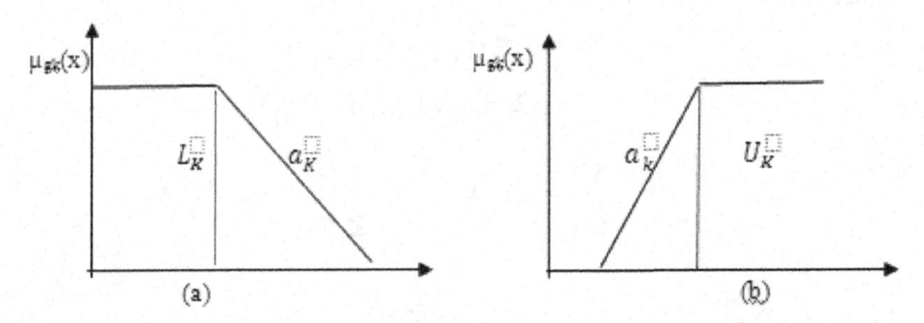

Figure 1. Objective functions as fuzzy numbers (a) in the case of minimization of the Zk function and (b) in the case of maximization of the Zl function.

Finally, the approach to the lineal multi-objective fuzzy model, based on [11] is the following:

Maximize λ (3)

Subject to:

$\lambda \leq \mu_{Zj}(x) \quad j=1,2,\ldots,q$ for all the objective functions

$g_r(x) \leq b_r \quad r=1,2,\ldots,m$ for all the restrictions

$x_i \geq 0 \quad i=1,2,\ldots,n$ for all the decision making variables

$$\lambda \in [0,1]$$

The first approach, known as Max-Min, takes no account of the different relative importance that the objectives considered might have for the decision makers, that is to say, all of the objective functions are considered to be equally important.

The second model analyzed, that of [13] can be expressed in the following way:

Maximize $\sum_{j=1}^{q} w_j \, \mu Zj(x)$ (4)

Subject to:

$$g_r(x) \leq b_r \,,\ r=1,\ldots,m$$

$$x_i \geq 0 \,,\ i=1,\ldots,n$$

$$\sum_{j=1}^{q} w_j = 1 \,,\quad w_j \geq 0$$

The previous is usually expressed in the following way [12]

Maximize $\sum_{j=1}^{q} w_j \lambda_i$ (5)

Subject to:

$\lambda_i \leq \mu_{Zj}(x)$ j=1,2, . . . , q for all the objective functions

$g_r(x) \leq b_r$, r=1,..., m

$x_i \geq 0$, i=1,..., n for all the decision making variables

$$\sum_{j=1}^{q} w_j = 1 \quad , \quad w_j \geq 0 \; ,$$

$$\lambda_j \in [0,1]$$

Although this model allows the relative importance of different objectives to be considered, some authors believe that the solutions found are not coherent with the importance given to the objectives of the model.

Finally [14] also known as the Weighted Max-Min model, allows the different levels of importance of the objectives to be considered.

The model can be expressed as follows:

Maximize λ (6)

Subject to:

$w_j \lambda_i \leq \mu_{Zj}(x)$ j=1,2, . . . , q for all the objective functions

$g_r(x) \leq b_r$, r=1,..., m

$x_i \geq 0$, i=1,..., n for all the decision making variables

$$\sum_{j=1}^{q} w_j = 1 \quad , \quad w_j \geq 0 \; ,$$

$$\lambda_j \in [0,1]$$

According to its author, this model provides an optimum solution in which the levels of achievement of the different objectives are as close as possible to the weights given to them, although optimum results in which the level of achievement of some objective would be superior to the unit cannot be achieved. There are different positions with regard to the use of these models with objective weightings. Thus, [15] holds that the use of weighting is unrealistic for two fundamental reasons, the first is due precisely to the context of uncertainty in which the decision is made and the second has to do with the impossibility of considering the infinite trade-offs derived from the possible weightings.

If it is decided to use objective weightings, as is normally the case in the literature reviews, there exist different possibilities including the use of the lexicographic method which consists of solving the model sequentially, first considering the first level of priority and after obtaining the solution, considering in sequence the following priority levels [16]. Another weighting possibility comes from [17], consisting of establishing verbal priorities like "very important" and "moderately important" and combining these with the desirable achievement degree at each level. A variation of this proposal is that of [18], which included linguistically defined weights in a scalarized objective function with fuzzy arithmetic operations. [19] proposed a novel fuzzy goal programming method where the hierarchical levels of the goals are imprecisely defined. It is based on an additive achievement function structure.

A possibility that is currently widely used to establish the weights of the different objectives is based on [20] AHP (Analytic Hierarchy Process) which consists of decision makers expressing their preferences "paired" among the objectives on a scale from 1 to 9. Examples of the use of this system can be found in [21,22,23]. Other studies have used the system of eliciting the weights of the objectives, this being a previously used system known as ANP (Analytic

Network Process), [24]. Examples can be found in the work of [25,26]. One interesting line to pursue in future research would be to carry out empirical work on the level of prediction of the different types of weighting in a multi-objective fuzzy model

1.3. *Selection of Innovations in the Agricultural Sector by Multi-objective fuzzy models.*

This section will examine the potential of multi-objective fuzzy models for the selection of innovations in the agricultural sector. In order to do this and in line with the objectives set out, two technologies currently used in greenhouse tomato production, "Traditional with 1.33stems/m2" and "Traditional with 2 stems/m2" will be compared with a new technology that is being experimentally trialed and which is known as "Hangers with 2 stems/m2", which contrasts with the traditional system in which the tomato plant climbs up until it reaches the wire and then falls to the ground. This new technology consists of maintaining the plant moving ever upwards, which allows for the optimization of the capture of solar radiation and an increase in planting density, though this system produces a slight decline in the quality of the tomato obtained, by comparison with the traditional system. For more information about these production systems see [27].

The three objectives used in the multi-objective fuzz model to make a decision on this new technology are, firstly, the maximization of commercial production measured in kg/m2, which is an objective of the Production type, secondly, the minimization of production costs measured in Euros/m2, this is an objective of the Financial type, and finally, the maximization of the Percentage of Prime Quality Stems. Each objective is valid for the three possible technologies, which represent an objective of the Commercial type.

The empirical elements used in this numerical example are shown in Table 1, [27]. Note that this approach corresponds with a multi-objective assumption as there are various objectives and the optimum selection of each objective clashes with the selection of the others. Thus, on the basis of the previous data the optimum choice when production costs are considered will focus on hangar technology, which produces the greatest production costs and thus clashes with the second objective (the minimization of costs) and the third objective, (the maximization of the Percentage of Prime Quality Stems), as it leads to a Percentage of Prime Quality Stems lower than the highest possible.

Table 1. Data for each of the criteria for each of the three production alternatives analyzed. Source: Cajamar, 2.011.

Type of Production	Commercial Production kg/m^2	Production Costs €/ m^2	Percentage of Prime Quality Stems	Income €/ m^2
Traditional with 1.33stems/m^2	18.8	5.9	68	10.2
Traditional with 2 stems/m^2	21.1	7.1	75	11.0
Hangars 2 stems/m^2	28.8	8.1	70	15.4

The multi-objective proposal has held it to be possible that, on the one holding there might exist three types of production and also has established as a restriction an income of greater than 13 Euros/m^2, which represents the expectations of the decision maker for the upcoming period.

To avoid the construction of membership functions, having to know the desired value for each objective as well as its maximum tolerance, use has been made of the method devised by [28,29] who do so by independently calculating for each Z_K the maximum value Z_k^+ and the minimum value Z_k^- , that is to say by independently resolving the following two models for each objective:

Z_k^+ = Max Z_k, $x \in X_d$ and Z_k^- = Min Z_k, $x \in X_d$

Where X_d is the of feasible solutions ($x/Ax \leq b$)

This immediately produces the desired value and tolerance for each objective considered. So if the objective is to maximize the desired fuzzy value a_k for all $g_k \in B$ would be Z_i^+ and if the objective is to minimize the desired fuzzy value a_k for all $g_k \in C$ would be Z_i^-. The tolerance for each of the objectives would always be $Z_i^+ - Z_i^-$.

The specific proposals for the three objective functions and their corresponding restrictions for each of three models in which x1, x2 y x3 represent the decision variables, specifically the area given over to each of the three production systems, are given as follows:

max= 18.8*x1 + 21.1*x2 + 28.8*x3; (8)

min=5.9*x1 + 7.1*x2 + 8.1*x3;

max= 68*x1 +75*x2 +70*x3;

subject to:

x1+x2+x3=1;

10.2* x1 + 11.0*x2 + 15.4*x3 >= 13;

x1, x2 y x3 >=0;

The two optimum results, Z_i^+ y Z_i^-, obtained for each of the three objectives are those shown in Table 2, which also shows the calculated tolerance, given for the difference $Z_i^+ - Z_i^-$

Table 2. z_i^+ and z_i^- for the three objectives considered.

Objetive	z_i^+ Maximum	z_i^- Minimum	Tolerance $z_i^+ - z_i^-$
Z_1 Maximize Production Value kg/m^2	28.8	24.18	4.62
Z_2 Minimize Production Costs €/m^2	8.1	7.09	1.01
Z_3 Maximize Prime Category Stems	72.73	69.08	3.65

Thus the two fuzzy models compared (Weighted Max-Min and Weight-Added) can be set out as follows. The transformation functions of the objectives in fuzzy numbers are those given in the Appendix. The software used is Lingo Version 11. With regard to the weightings for the three objectives, which can be easily obtained from [24] AHP method, the following values are considered: w1= 0.608, w2= 0.10 y w3= 0.272, which are supposed to come from Saaty's preference matrix. Specifically, the original matrix for these values is the following $\begin{bmatrix} 1 & 4 & 3 \\ 0,25 & 1 & 0,33 \\ 0,33 & 3 & 1 \end{bmatrix}$ and it has a consistency ratio of (RC) of 0.0639, less than 0.10 and therefore good enough to use.

Furthermore and as has already been indicated, in the case of both models the assumption that the objectives have the same importance is also considered, that is to say, w1=w2=w3=0,333. Table 3 shows the proposal of the four models analyzed. The first is the Weighted Max-Min multi-objective fuzzy model first in its weighted version (9) and then it its equally weighted version (10). There then appears the Max-Min multi-objective model in its two versions, weighted (11) and equally weighted (12)

Table 3. The Weighted Max-Min and Weight-Added Models.

$$\max = \lambda \tag{9}$$

$$\begin{gathered} 0.608 * \lambda <= ((18.8 * x1 + 21.1 * x2 + 28.8 * x3) - 24.18)/4.62; \\ 0.120 * \lambda <= (8.1 - (5.9 * x1 + 7.1 * x2 + 8.1 * x3))/ 1.01 ; \\ 0.272 * \lambda <= ((68 * x1 + 75 * x2 + 70 * x3) - 69.08)/3.65; \\ 10.2 * x1 + 11 * x2 + 15.4 * x3 >= 13; \\ x1 + x2 + x3 = 1; \end{gathered}$$

$$\max = \lambda; \tag{10}$$

$$\begin{gathered} 0.333 * \lambda <= ((18.8 * x1 + 21.1 * x2 + 28.8 * x3) - 24.18)/4.62; \\ 0.333 * \lambda <= (8.1 - (5.9 * x1 + 7.1 * x2 + 8.1 * x3))/ 1.01 ; \\ 0.333 * \lambda <= ((68 * x1 + 75 * x2 + 70 * x3) - 69.08)/3.65; \\ x1 + x2 + x3 = 1; \\ 10.2 * x1 + 11 * x2 + 15.4 * x3 >= 13; \end{gathered}$$

$$\max = 0.608 * \lambda 1 + 0.120 * \lambda 2 + 0.272 * \lambda 3; \tag{11}$$

$$\begin{gathered} \lambda 1 <= ((18.8 * x1 + 21.1 * x2 + 28.8 * x3) - 24.18)/4.62; \\ \lambda 2 <= (8.1 - (5.9 * x1 + 7.1 * x2 + 8.1 * x3))/ 1.01 ; \\ \lambda 3 <= ((68 * x1 + 75 * x2 + 70 * x3) - 69.08)/3.65; \\ x1 + x2 + x3 = 1; \\ 10.2 * x1 + 11 * x2 + 15.4 * x3 >= 13; \end{gathered}$$

$$\max = 0.333 * \lambda 1 + 0.333 * \lambda 2 + 0.333 * \lambda 3; \tag{12}$$

$$\begin{gathered} \lambda 1 <= ((18.8 * x1 + 21.1 * x2 + 28.8 * x3) - 24.18)/4.62; \\ \lambda 2 <= (8.1 - (5.9 * x1 + 7.1 * x2 + 8.1 * x3))/ 1.01 ; \\ \lambda 3 <= ((68 * x1 + 75 * x2 + 70 * x3) - 69.08)/3.65; \\ x1 + x2 + x3 = 1; \\ 10.2 * x1 + 11 * x2 + 15.4 * x3 >= 13; \end{gathered}$$

There follows Table 4 which shows the four solutions obtained for each of the two models analyzed both for the case of the weightings used (w1= 0.608, w2= 0.10 y w3= 0.272) and for the case of the equally weighted, which uses the same weight for each objective. Figure 4 shows in columns, on one side the values for Zi (i=1,2 y3), which represent the value obtained for each optimum solution (x1, x2, x3) for each of the three objectives considered and in the other, the level of the achievement value μ_i for each objective (w1=w2=w3=0.333). In view of the results obtained the Weighted Max-Min model should be considered preferable to the Weight-Added Model as the solutions obtained by it are coherent with the importance given in the weights to the objectives. It thus can be seen for example that in the case of equal weighting the Weight-Added Model (final column of Figure 3) has achievement functions ($\mu_{1)}$ in which the values obtained are not similar for each of the objectives with the solution ($\mu_{3=}$ 0,99) clearly leaning towards the first objective, the achievement level of the first objective ($\mu_{1=}$0,09). Exactly the contrary occurs in the case of the Mi Weighted Max-Min model in which the solutions obtained are coherent with the importance of the objectives for the decision maker, thus in this model the levels of achievement of the objectives ($\mu_{1=}$0.787, $\mu_{2=}$0.155, $\mu_{3=}$0.352) are coherent with the weights given to them (w1= 0.608, w2= 0.10 and w3= 0.272).

Table 4. Comparison of the solution of the two models

	Weighted Max-Min model		Weight-Added Model	
	Weighting	Same Weights	Weigthing	Same Weights
Z1	27.81	26.21	28.8	24.6
Z2	7.94	7.66	8.1	7.6
Z3	70.36	70.68	60.0	68.18
X1	0.032	0.118	0.0	0.0
X2	0.086	0.184	0.0	0.545
X3	0.882	0.698	1.0	0.454
μ_1	0.787	0.439	1.0	0.09
μ_2	0.155	0.439	0.0	0.54
μ_3	0.352	0.439	0.25	0.999

If the objective were to make a multi-objective fuzzy proposal that would find a single solution, all that would be necessary would be to add the condition that the decision variables which represent the utilization of different technologies be binary (one or zero)[†] .

In this case the solution obtained for the Weighted Max-Min model would be:
x1=x2=0, x3=1, Z1= 28.8 , Z2=8.1 , Z3= 70.0 μ_1= 1,0 μ_2= 0.0 y μ_3= 0.252
In the case of the Weight-Added Models the new solutions would be:

[†] In the Lingo language each of the three previous proposals would include three new restrictions of the @bin (xi), i=1,2,3 type.

$x1=x2=0$, $x3=1$, $Z1= 28.8$, $Z2=8,1$, $Z3= 60.0$ $\mu_1= 0.176$ $\mu_2= 0.0$ y $\mu_3= 0.150$

Once again the solutions produced by the first model exceed in terms of achievement and coherence values the importance placed on each of the objectives of the second and so it should be the preferred choice.

1.4. *Conclusions*

The approach set out is entirely appropriate for multi-objective situations where the way the objectives are stated is not precise. It also leads to lineal optimization models which can be easily resolved with existing software. Furthermore, decision makers do not have to be able to make very precise statements of their objectives, they only have to identify the objectives and their respective weights and importance, with the desired values and tolerances for each one objective being indirectly deduced from the initial proposal of each model, calculating the maximum and minimum values for each $[(Z]_i^+ \text{ y } Z_i^-)$, as has been previously shown. This involves a simplified system of calculation for each of these values.

With regard to the models analyzed it is evident that the solutions provided by the Weighted Max-Min model are better suited to the weightings given to each objective and so it should be the preferred choice ahead of the Weight-Added Model. Note therefore how important it is that the levels of the achievement models for the objectives obtained in the solution be coherent with the weightings given to each objective by the decision maker.

Naturally the possibility remains open that the objective function or the restrictions may not be lineal but this does not currently lead to any problems. It is also possible to utilize other membership functions to establish the objectives in fuzzy terms, for example, relations of the triangular or trapezoidal type with it being the analyst, on the basis of his or her experience and the data available, being the one to take the decision in this regard.

Appendix

The $\mu_{Z1}(x)$ function for the first objective, to maximize production measured in kg/m^{2}, is shown as follows where, $Z_1(x)$=18,8*x1+21,1*x2+18,8*x3

$$\text{(a)}\ \mu Z_1(x) = \begin{cases} 1 & \text{for } Z_1 \geq 24{,}18 \\ (Z_1 1^{\uparrow}(x) - 24{,}18)/4{,}62 & \text{for } 24{,}18 \leq Z_1(x) \leq 28{,}8 \\ 0 & \text{for } Z_1 \leq 28{,}8 \end{cases} \quad \text{(A.1)}$$

The $\mu_{Z2}(x)$ function for the second objective, minimize production costs measured in Euros/m^2, is shown as follows where $Z_2(x)$=5,9*x1+7,1*x2+8,1*x3

$$\text{(A.2)}\ \text{(b)} \quad \begin{cases} 1 & \text{for } Z_k \leq 7{,}09 \\ \mu Z_2(x) = (8{,}1 - Z_2)/1{,}01 & \text{for } 7{,}09 \leq Z_2(x) \leq 8{,}1 \\ 0 & \text{for } Z_k \geq 8{,}1 \end{cases}$$

Finally the $\mu_{Z3}(x)$ function in the case of the third objective, maximize the percentage of prime quality stalks, is shown as follows where $Z_3(x)$= 68*x1 + 75*x2 + 60*x3;

$$\text{(A.3)}\ \text{(c)} \quad \begin{cases} 1 & \text{for } Z_1 \geq 72{,}73 \\ \mu Z_3(x) = (Z_{\downarrow}3^{\uparrow}(x) - 69{,}08/3{,}65) & \text{for } 69{,}08 \leq Z_1(x) \leq 72{,}73 \\ 0 & \text{for } Z_k \leq 69{,}08 \end{cases}$$

The objective functions in fuzzy terms are shown in the following graph for each of the three objectives,

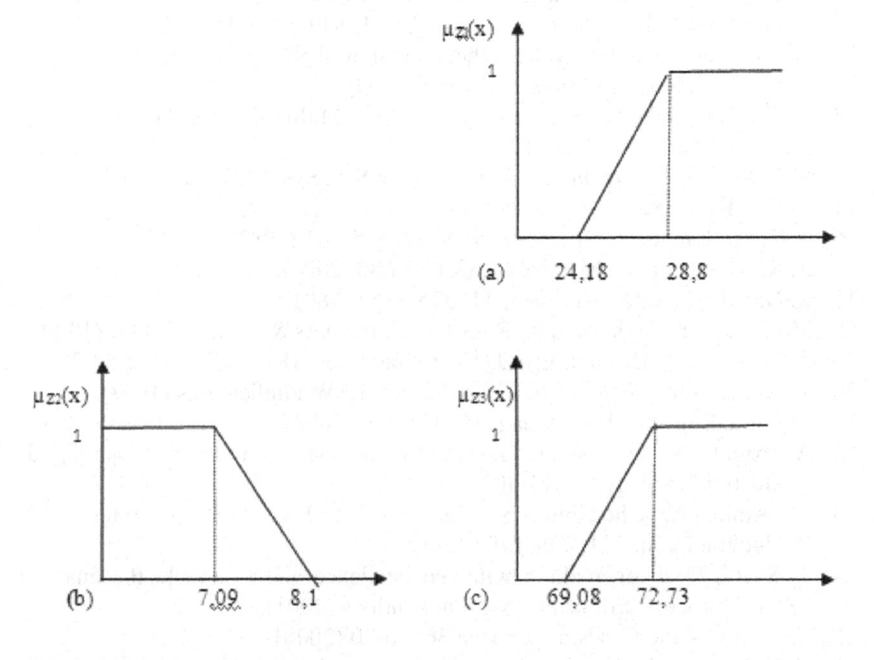

Figure 2. The Objective functions in fuzzy terms: (a) Z_1 Commercial Production, (b) Z_2 Production Costs and (c) Z_3 Percentage of Prime Category Stalks.

References

1. R. Rama, Agribus.12, 123-134 (1996).
2. R. Rama, Handbook of innovation in the food and drink industry. New York. Haworth Press, 12, 123-134 (2008).
3. K. Grunert , H. Harmser, M. Meulenberg, E. Kuiper, T. Ottowitz, F. Declerck, B. Traill and G. Göransson, A framework for analysing innovation in the food sector. Product and process innovation in the food industry. Blackie Academic and Professional. London. UK (1997)
4. B. Traill and M. Meulenberg, Agribusiness, 18, 1-21 (2002).
5. F. Capitanio, A. Coppola and S. Pascucci, British Food J. 111, 820-838 (2009).
6. O. Alfranca, R. Rama and N. Von Tunzelmann, Technovation, 24, 599-614 (2004).
7. O. Brazei and I. Verstinsky, J. Bus. Vent, 21, 75-105 (2006).
8. C. Beckford, D. Barker and S. Bailey ECKFORD, Singapore J. Tropical Geogr. 28, 273-286 (2007).

9. B. Bigliardi and A. Dormio, Eur. J. Innov. Manag. 12, 223-242 (2009).
10. T. Fortuin and S. Omta, British Food J. 111, 839-851 (2007).
11. H. Zimmermann, Fuzzy Set Theory and is Applications". Forth Edition. Kluwer Academic Publishers, Boston (1993).
12. M. Sawaka, Fuzzy Sets and Interactive Multiobjective Optimization". Plenum Press. New York (1993).
13. R. Tiwari, S. Dharmahr and J. Rao, Fuzzy Sets Sys. 24, 27-34 (1987).
14. C. Lin, Fuzzy Sets Sys.142, 407-420 (2004).
15. S. Gass, Computers Operations Res. 12, 525-541 (1987).
16. C. Romero, Eur. J. Oper. Res. 153, 675-686 (2004).
17. R. Naradimhan, Decision Sci. 11, 325-336 (1980).
18. Mohandas, T. Phelps and K. Ragsdell, Computers & Struc. 37, 1–8, (1990).
19. A. Onur and P. Drobila, Eur. J. Operational Res. 181, 1427-1433 (2007).
20. T. Saaty, Toma de decisiones para líderes. RSW Publications (1997).
21. S. Barla, Logistics Inf. Manag. 16, 451-459 (2003).
22. A. Amid, A. Ghodsmid, S. Ghodspour and C. O`Brien, Internat. J. Production Econ. 104, 394-407 (2006).
23. A. Amid, A. Ghodsmid, S. Ghodspour and C. O`Brien, Internat. J. Production Econ. 131, 139-148 (2011).
24. T. Saaty, Decision making with independence and feedback: the analytic network process. Editorial RSW Publications (2001).
25. E. Demirtas and O. Ustün, Omega 36, 76-90 (2008).
26. C. Kahraman, U. Cebeci and Z. Ulukan, Logistics Infor. Manag. 16, 583-394 (2003).
27. Fundaci6n Cajamar, Informes y Monografías 28. Available at: www.Cajamar.es (2011).
28. Y. Lai and C. Hawng, Fuzzy Multiple Objective Decision Making. Methods and Applications. Springer-Verlag. Berlin (1994).
29. C. Hawng and K. Yoo, Multiple Attribute Decision Making: Methods and Applications. Springer-Verlag. Heidelberg (1981).